COMPLETE WATERFOWL STUDIES

VOLUME III
GEESE & SWANS

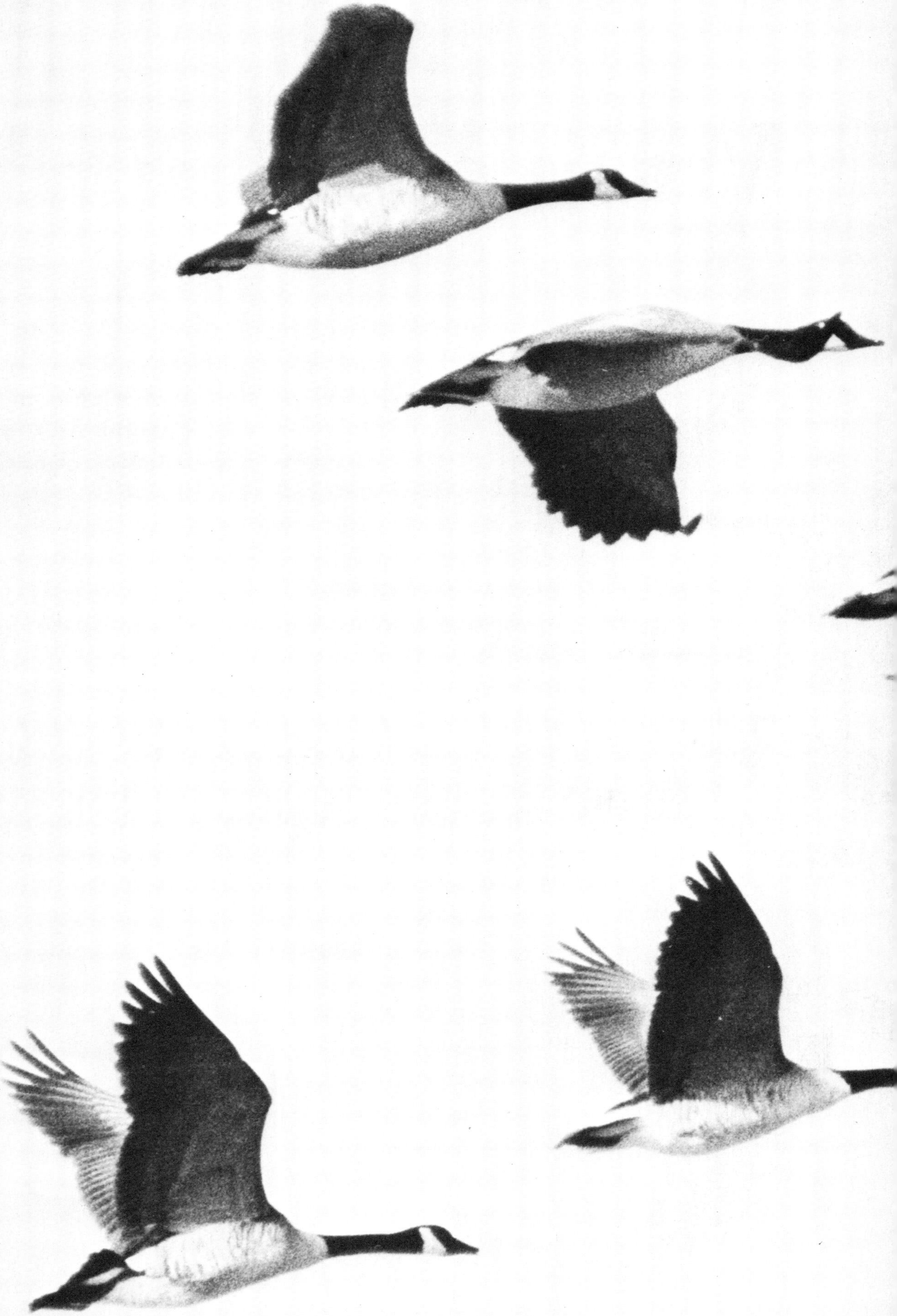

COMPLETE WATERFOWL STUDIES

BRUCE BURK

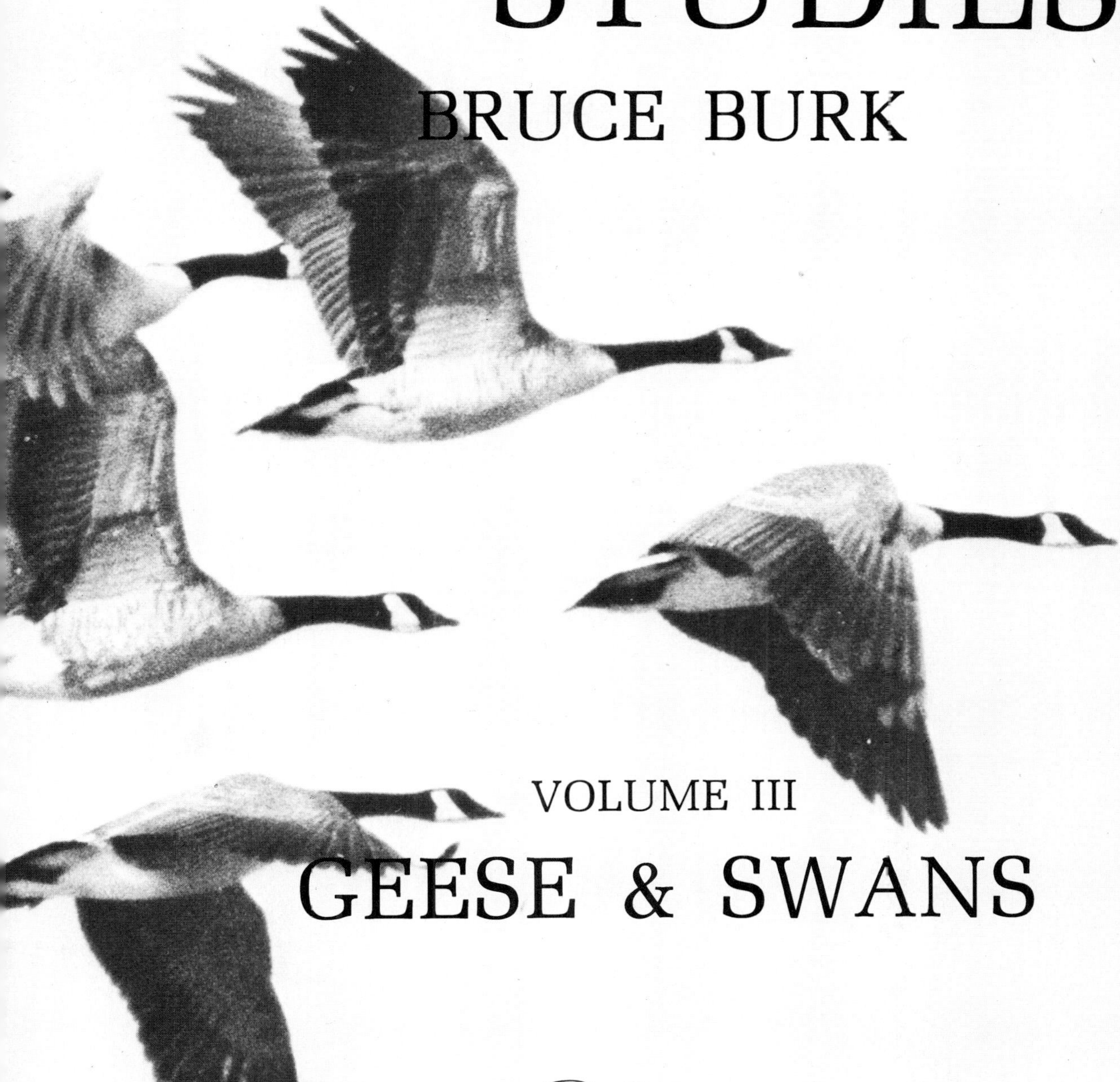

VOLUME III

GEESE & SWANS

Schiffer Publishing Ltd

All photographs and drawings by author.
Waterfowl classified after Delacour,
WATERFOWL OF THE WORLD, Dover

Library of Congress Catalog Number: 84—51260.

Printed in the United States of America.
ISBN: 0-88740-027-2
Published by Schiffer Publishing Limited, Box E, Exton, Pennsylvania 19341

This book may be purchased from the publisher.
Please include $1.50 postage.
Try your bookstore first.

Dedicated to my wife,

Dorothy

In appreciation of her help, encouragement,
patience, and understanding.

ACKNOWLEDGEMENTS

My many artist, taxidermist, and other bird loving friends, who encouraged me to proceed with my earlier pictorial waterfowl studies, have now inspired me to undertake new camera studies of waterfowl encompassing a much greater scope of a higher quality.

Although I have been helped by many, I would especially like to convey my most sincere appreciation and thanks to the following: Mr. and Mrs. Charles Pilling, Seattle, Washington; Mr. and Mrs. David Jackson, Vancouver, British Columbia; Mr. and Mrs. Chester Andrews, Reno, Nevada; Mr. and Mrs. Gordon Ekberg, Herman, Minnesota; Mr. Clayton Derby, Norcross, Minnesota; Mr. and Mrs. Ronald Escher, Dumont, Minnesota; Dr. Paul Johnsgard, Lincoln, Nebraska, Mr. Joel Miller, Willows, California; and Mr. Leonard Lee Rue, Blairstown, New Jersey.

VOLUME III
GEESE AND SWANS

CONTENTS

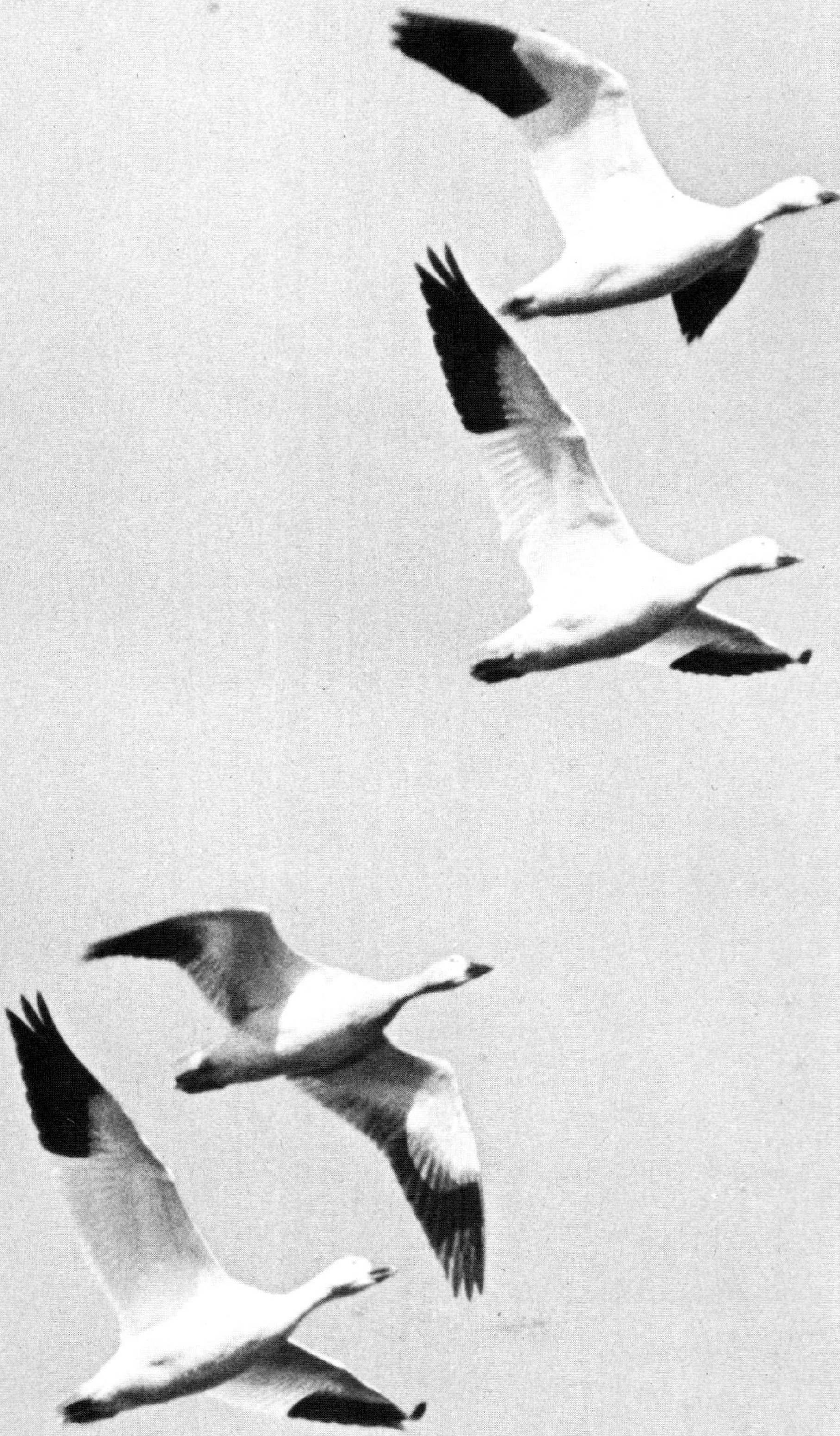

VOLUME III
GEESE AND SWANS

The best-known and most admirable characteristics of geese and swans are fidelity and intelligence. These birds mate for life, and it is believed that only the widowed, or those who have been inadvertently separated, take new mates. While the male does not actually help incubate the eggs, he constantly guards the female and the nest and is prepared to give his life, if necessary, for their safety. Later, when the eggs are hatched, he does his full share in the rearing and protecting of the young. The family migrates and winters as a unit and remains together for almost a full year—until nature again arouses the reproductive urge in the parents.

During the breeding season, geese and swans are generally antisocial, and aggressively and jealously guard their own particular nesting territory—areas which vary greatly in size. They are, however, completely tolerant of ducks and other marsh birds. The nests of most geese and swans usually are piles of vegetation. Muskrat houses, located in the water, are in great demand as nesting sites. Barnacle geese and red-breasted geese prefer to nest on ledges of cliffs, and Canada geese on occasion have been known to nest in trees and on some man-made structures.

Both geese and swans have been ruthlessly slaughtered in the past and as a result have become very wary and distrusting in the wild, although they are the most easily tamed of all waterfowl. Geese and swans are considered to possess more intelligence than any other waterfowl.

In most cases, the size of the body and neck length of geese are intermediate between ducks and swans. The fore-and-aft leg position and general posture of geese, both on land and water, is quite similar to dabbling ducks. These features, plus proportionately smaller feet and longer legs, located closer together, permit geese to walk and run easily without the typical waddle of ducks. Geese, with the exception of brant and emperor geese, are more at home on land than any of the other waterfowl, and obtain most of their food by grazing like sheep and cattle on grasses and young grain sprouts. Also like grazing animals, they are very gregarious, except during the nesting season. Although geese swim well and dive adeptly when the necessity arises, most geese feed in water only occasionally. Brant are much more aquatic and feed almost exclusively on marine vegetation, except during the breeding season. Emperor geese obtain a great deal of their food along the seashore, much of which is shellfish and other marine organisms. All geese are strong flyers and for their size possess almost as much maneuverability as ducks. They can, and often do, perform spectacular aerobatics, especially when it is necessary to lose altitude rapidly. Their endurance during the long, migratory flights is legendary; they are capable of flying at great altitudes, and their flight speeds are very nearly as fast as ducks.

Swans are larger and heavier than geese—the trumpeter swan is the heaviest of all flying birds—and their necks are longer in proportion to their bodies. Because of their short legs and large feet, they walk with more effort than geese and are much more comfortable in the water than on land. They feed mainly on aquatic vegetation, which they reach with their long necks, upending like dabbling ducks when necessary. Due to their great weight, swans experience more difficulty in taking off than geese but, once in the air, they are powerful flyers. These pure white, majestic birds, with their long, outstretched necks and slow wing beat, are gracefulness personified.

The voices of geese and swans are loud and far-carrying. The large goose species and the trumpeter swan have deeper, more resonant calls as compared to the smaller geese and to whistling swans, whose voices are higher pitched. In addition to these loud calls, they all have a variety of softer, conversational calls.

Comparative bills of swans and Canada geese.

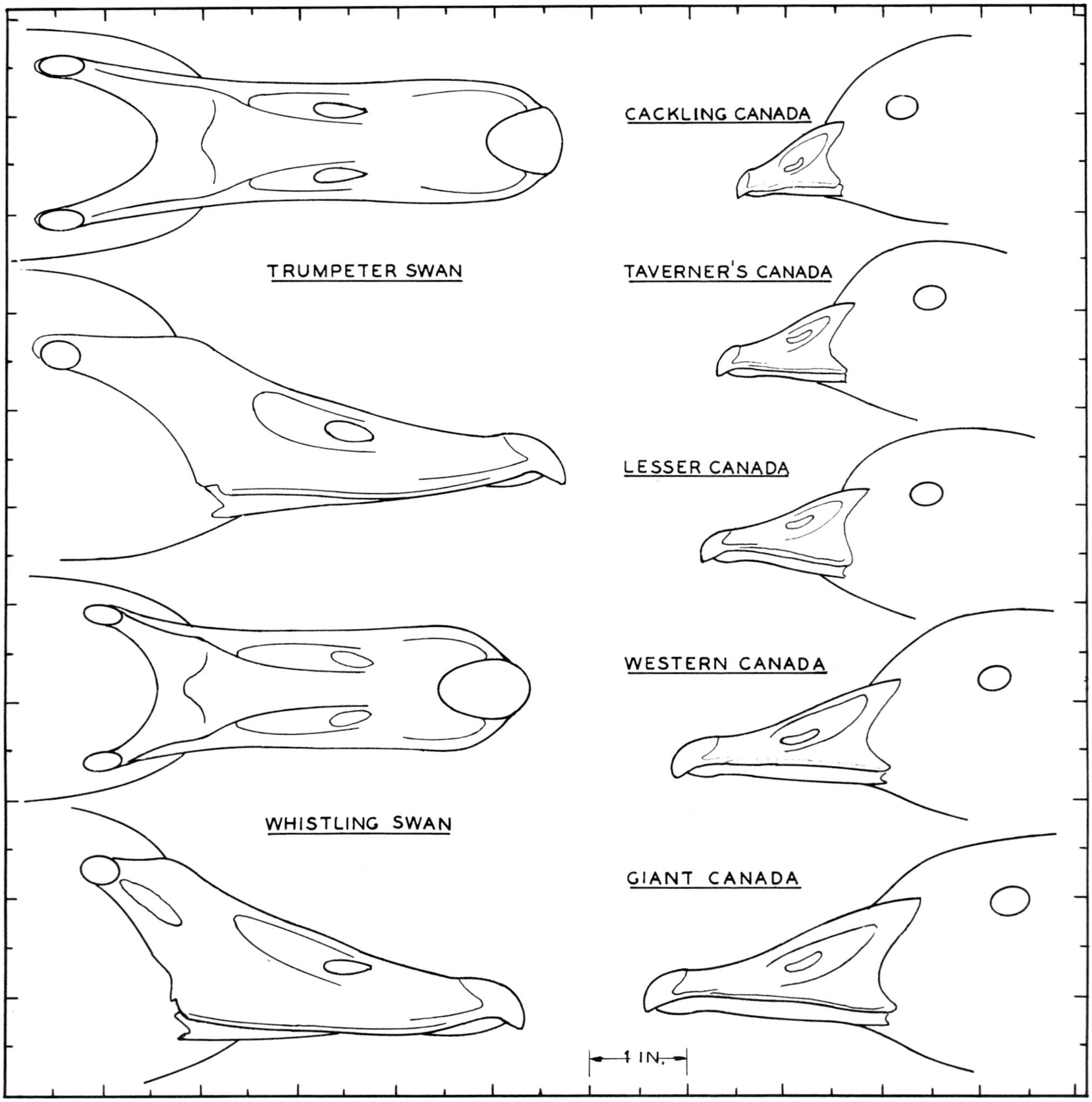

CHAPTER 33

Canada Geese

Branta canadensis
(Color Photos—pages 41, 42, & 43)

The Canada goose, king of the waterfowl, is the most widely distributed and best known of all North American birds. Honkers, as birds of the larger subspecies are fondly called, are more American than the bald eagle and, in the opinion of many, should have been made our national emblem.

Many works have been written about these most remarkable birds, and they have often been eulogized in song and poetry. However, nothing does them more justice than Kortright's thumbnail character sketch: "Sagacity, wariness, strength, and fidelity are characteristics of the Canada goose, which, collectively, are possessed in the same degree by no other bird. The Canada in many respects may serve as a model for man."

The Canada goose subspecies include our largest and smallest geese; but all of these birds, regardless of size or general coloration, have in common one very conspicious physical characteristic—a black head and neck and a white throat patch. While there is considerable intergrading among the races, eleven subspecies of the Canada goose are recognized by Delacour. The differences in overall size, coloration, length of neck, and bill size are of primary interest to the carver-artist; the feather markings of the Canada subspecies are very similar.

The giant Canada goose (*Branta canadensis maxima*), as the name implies, is the largest subspecies. For many years this goose was believed to have become extinct during the early 1900s. However, later reports, seldom authenticated, were made by hunters taking Canadas whose weights were in the 12- to 18-pound range. In 1960, Harold C. Hanson. (*The Giant Canada Goose*) identified members of this group wintering in Minnesota. Further investigation revealed other free-flying flocks. Also, several captive groups had been perpetuated for years by Carl Strutz, Jamestown, North Dakota, and by other game breeders. The *maxima* is a large, long-necked, light-colored, relatively long-bodied bird averaging in weight from 10 to 18 pounds, with some captive birds exceeding 20 pounds. The upper part of the throat patch on many giant Canadas has a rearward hook. White on the forehead and an incomplete white ring at the base of the black neck appear to be fairly common markings. The feet and tarsi of this race are dark olive rather than black, as on other Canadas, and are larger in proportion to their bodies.

The western Canada goose (B. *c. moffitti*) is second in size to the giant Canada. A bird weighing 12 to 13 pounds is considered very large. The *moffitti* is a large, long-necked, light-colored goose. They breed and winter in the Great Plains area and the western states.

The Todd's or interior Canada goose (B. *c. interior*), the most numerous of the Canadas, is slightly smaller on the average than the western Canadas (males weigh from 6 to 11 pounds) and are quite similar in appearance, except for coloration. The color of the sides, chest, and breast of the interior Canada is intermediate between the western Canada and the dark subspecies (*B. c. occidentalis* and *fulva*). This race is found primarily in the central states.

The Atlantic Canada goose (*B. c. canadensis*) is similar in size to the interior Canada, but its coloration (sides, chest, and breast) is more nearly like that of the western Canada. These geese winter along the Atlantic Coast from Nova Scotia to the Chesapeake Bay.

There are two races of medium-to-large size, dark-colored Canada geese: the Vancouver Canada goose (*B. c. fulva*) and the dusky Canada Goose (*B. c. occidentalis*). The Vancouver Canadas are of about the same weight as the western Canadas but are somewhat stockier. The coloration of their sides, chests, and breasts are the same as of their backs, scapulars, and wing coverts. The smaller dusky Canada is even darker in coloration, approaching the color of chocolate. These two subspecies breed along the British Columbia coast. The Vancouver Canadas breed and winter along the Pacific Coast from southern Alaska south to Oregon. The dusky Canadas winter mainly in the Willamette Valley of Oregon.

The small Canadas, according to Delacour, are composed of five subspecies: cackling Canada (*B. c. minima*), Richardson's Canada (*B. c. hutchinsi*), Aleutian Canada (*B. c. leucopareia*), Taverner's Canada (*B. c. taverneri*), and the lesser Canada (*B. c. parvipes*). These Canadas have shorter necks and longer wings relative to their overall body lengths as compared to the larger subspecies. Their bills are correspondingly shorter.

The cackling Canada goose is the smallest of the subspecies and is often not much larger than a mallard duck. Its coloration is dark but not quite as dark as the dusky Canada. An occasional cackler will have a narrow, incomplete white band at the base of its black neck and usually the white throat patch will be incomplete along the center line of the throat. Also, some adult cacklers have a beautiful reddish-gold tinge to their chest feathers. This subspecies has the shortest neck and the greatest wing span relative to its overall body length. In addition, cacklers have the shortest bills. They are easily distinguished from the honkers by their short necks and more rapid wing beat.

The average size of the Richardson's Canadas is slightly larger than the cacklers and they are light in coloration, similar to the Atlantic Canadas. These geese winter along the coasts of the Gulf States. Differences in size and coloration between this subspecies and the lesser and Taverner's Canadas are small. Some ornithologists believe these races should be considered a single subspecies.

The Aleutian Canada is about the same size as the Richardson's Canada and its coloration is intermediate between the cackler and the Richardson's. A fairly wide white band at the base of the black neck is a common marking of this subspecies. The population of this race is very small and was on the verge of extinction due to a number of factors—the most important of which was the introduction by fur farmers of the blue phase arctic fox and the red fox to most of their nesting grounds in the Aleutians Islands. Because of its poor accessibility and harbor facilities, foxes were not released on Buldir Island. Some Aleutian Canadas continue to breed on this island, and their number appears to be increasing. Certain areas in the Sacramento Valley of California, where the Aleutians have historically wintered, have been closed to the hunting of all dark colored geese. This action seems to be a contributing factor to the apparent increase in numbers of Aleutian Canada geese.

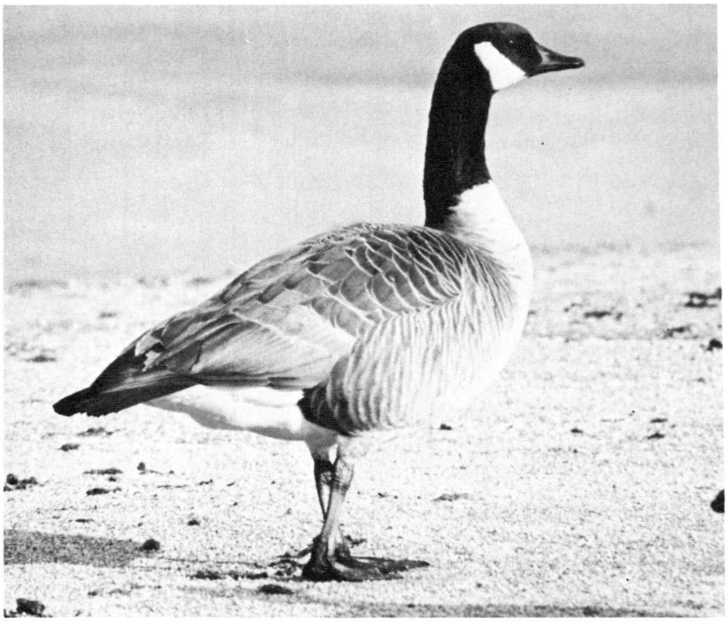

CANADA GEESE (Branta canadensis)

Subspecies	Page No.	Coloration	Wintering Area	Approvimate Weight	Average Overall Length	Average Wing Span	Ratio Span to Length	Ratio Neck Length to Overall Length
			LARGE (Commonly called "honkers")					
Giant Canada *(B. c. maxima)*	6-9	light	Northern Central States	10-18 pounds	48.0*	75.0*	156%	34-35%
Western Canada *(B. c. moffitti)*	9-26	light	Great Plains & Western States					
Todd's or Interior *(B. c. interior)*	11	medium	Central States& Atlantic Coast	7-13 pounds	37.2	68.8	185%	32-33%
Atlantic Canada *(B. c. canadensis)*	27-28	medium to light (lighter under-parts)	Atlantic Coast					
Vancouver Canada *(B. c. fulva)*	29	dark	Pacific Northwest	7-13 pounds	34.3	64.3	187%	31.5%
			MEDIUM					
Dusky Canada *(B. c. occidentalis)*	30-31	very dark	Williamette Valley of Oregon	4-8 pounds	28.6	57.9	200%	30%
Lesser Canada *(B. c. parvipes)*	32	light	Great Plains States					
			SMALL					
Taverner's Canada *(B. c. taverneri)*	35	medium to dark	California					
Aleutian Canada *(B. c. leucopareia)*	33-34	medium	Washington, Oregon, and California	3½-5½ pounds	26.5	52.0	196%	28-29%
Richardson's Canada *(B. c. hutchinsi)*		light	Texas and Mexico					
Cackling Canada *(B. c. minima)*	36-40	dark	So. British Columbia to California	2½-4 pounds	24.4	52.0	213%	24-25%

Note Due to great variations in the size of individual subspecies, the above information, at best, should be considered an approximate average.
*From *The Giant Canada Goose* (Harold C. Hanson) -one specimen-

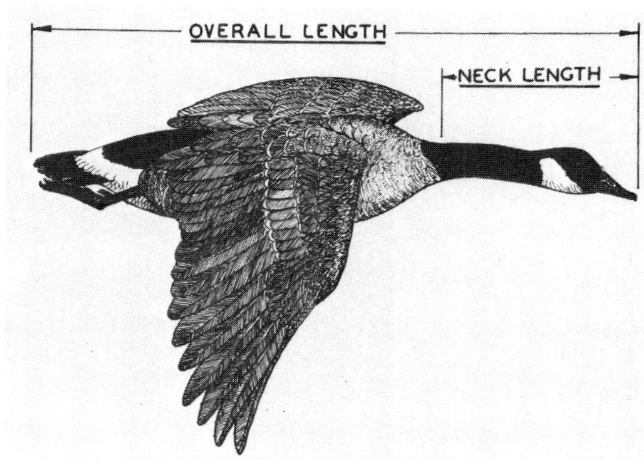

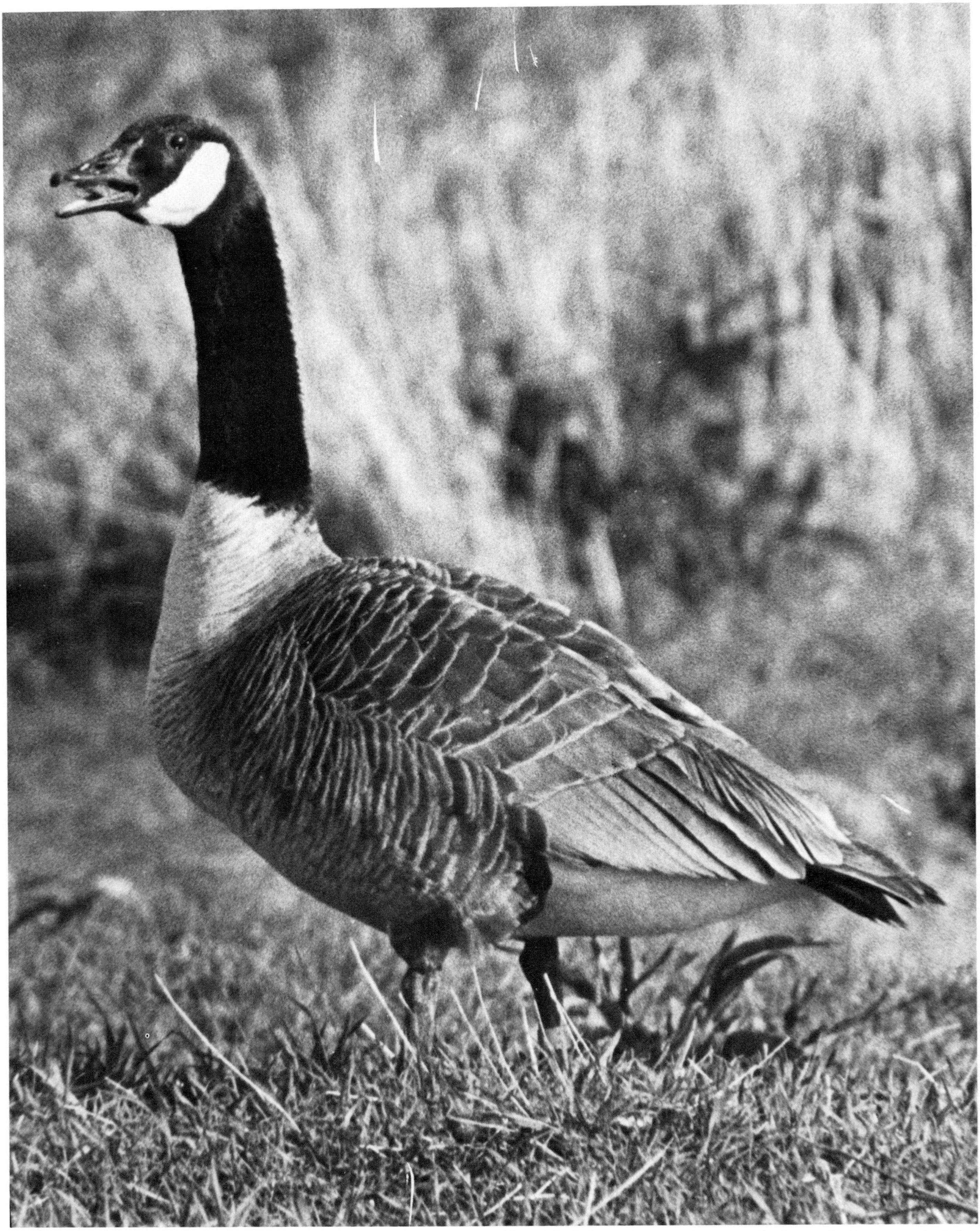

33-1 King of the waterfowl—the giant Canada goose gander. Weights of over 20 pounds have been recorded for this subspecies. His general coloration is quite light. Giant Canada geese are found in the Northern Central States.

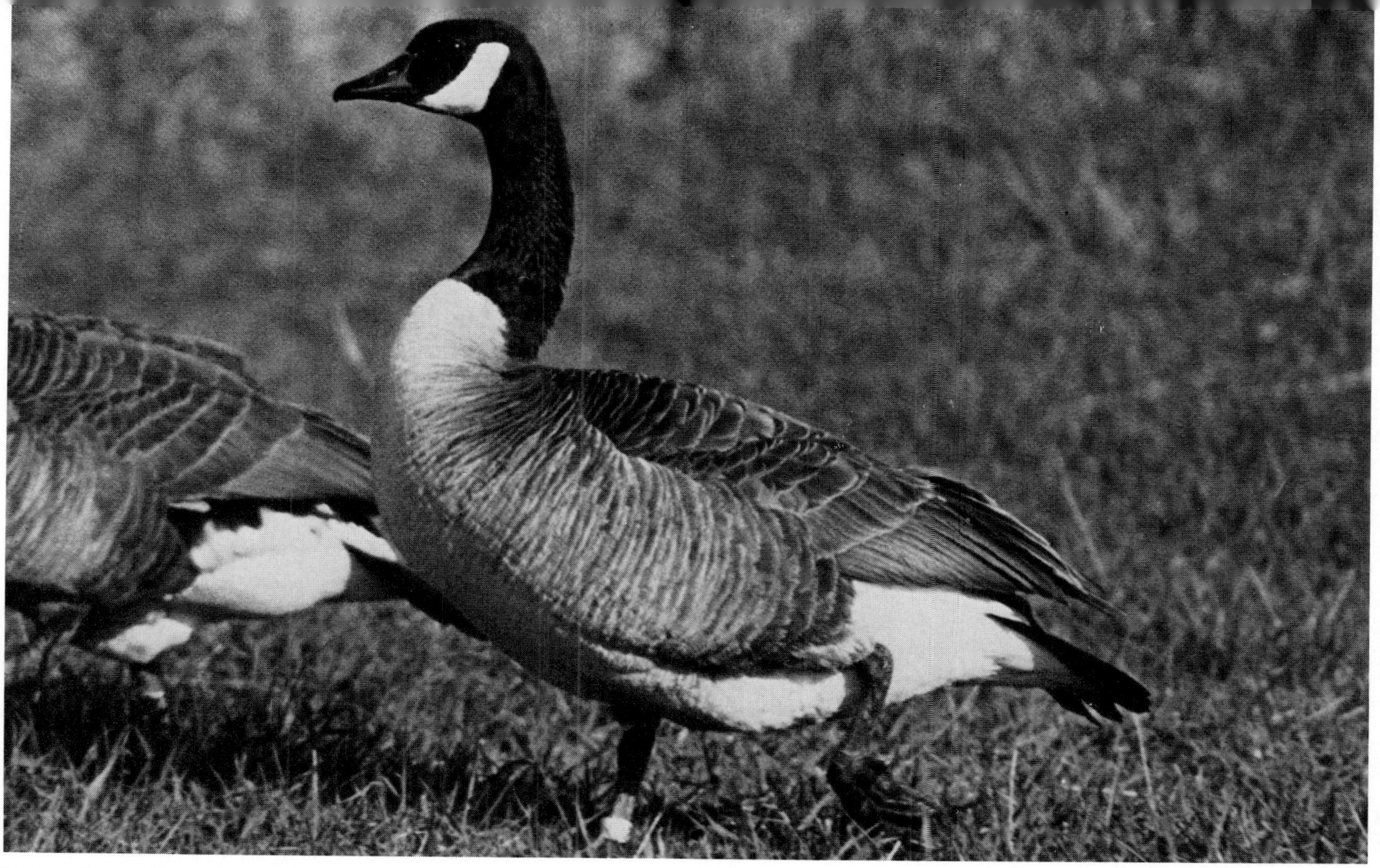

33-2 Giant Canada gander takes a stroll. His feet are larger in proportion to his body than other Canada subspecies and are a dark olive color.

33-3 Good profile of the giant Canada. Note rearward hook on the upper part of his white throat patch—a common feature of many giant Canadas.

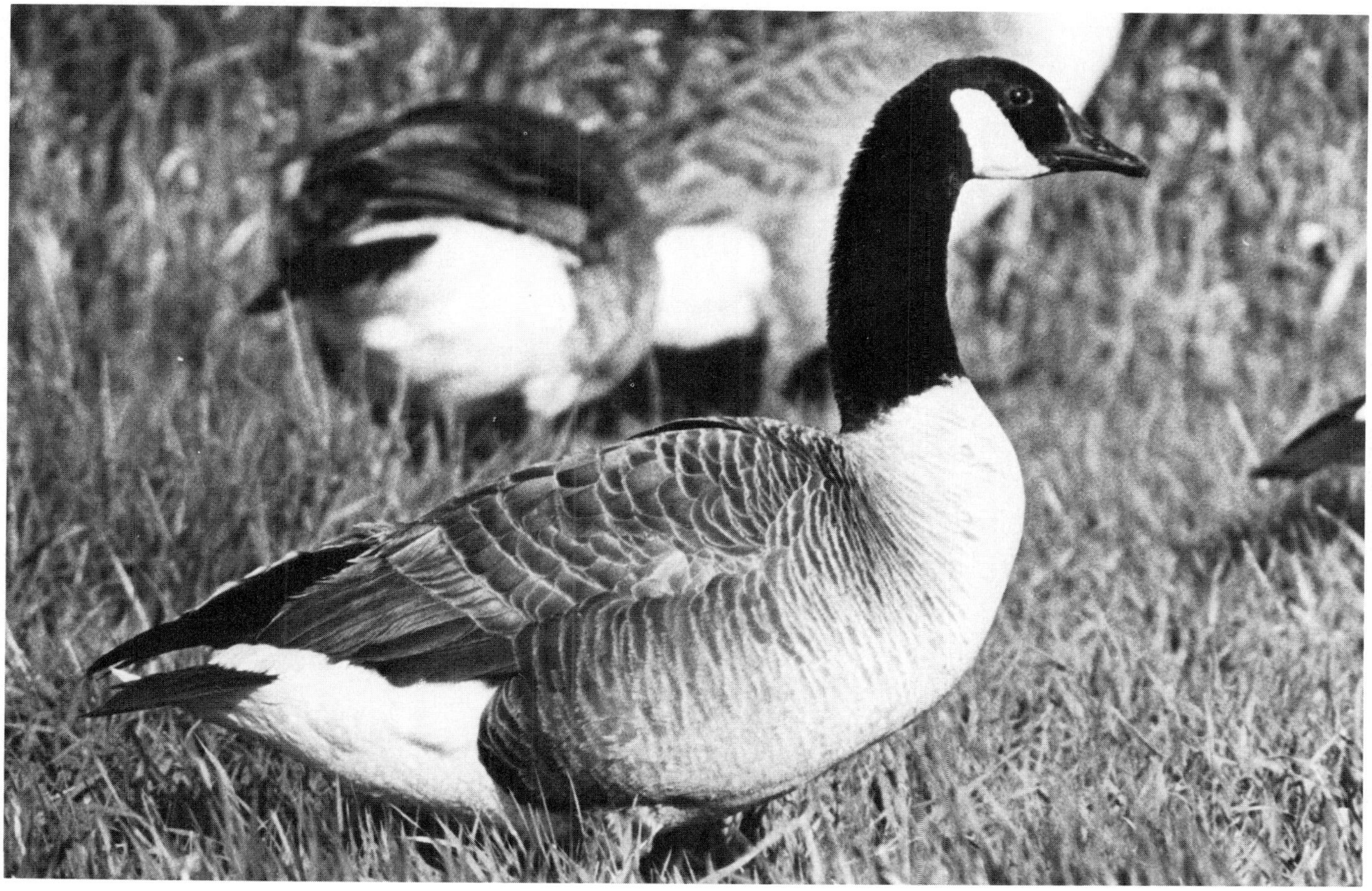

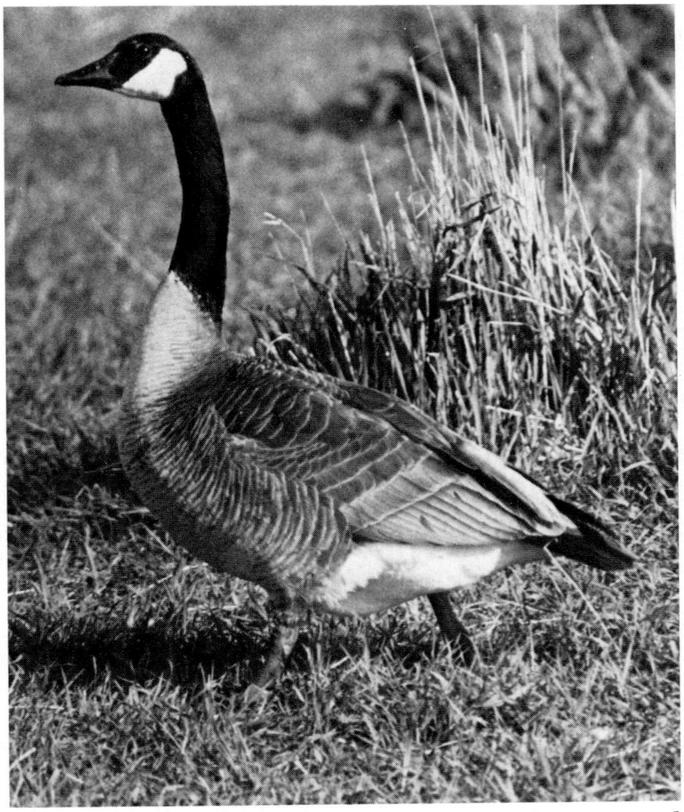

33-4 This giant Canada is very alert. The rearward hook of this goose's white throat patch is quite evident. Notice his long bill.

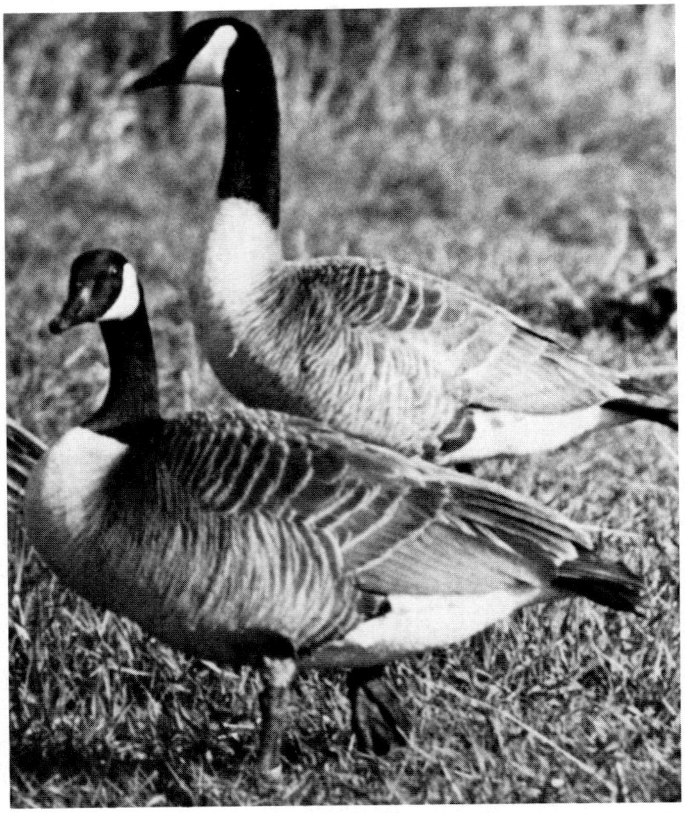

33-5 Pair of giant Canadas. Bird in the foreground is a female.

33-6 Another pair of giants. The male in the foreground is in a pleasing, alert pose.

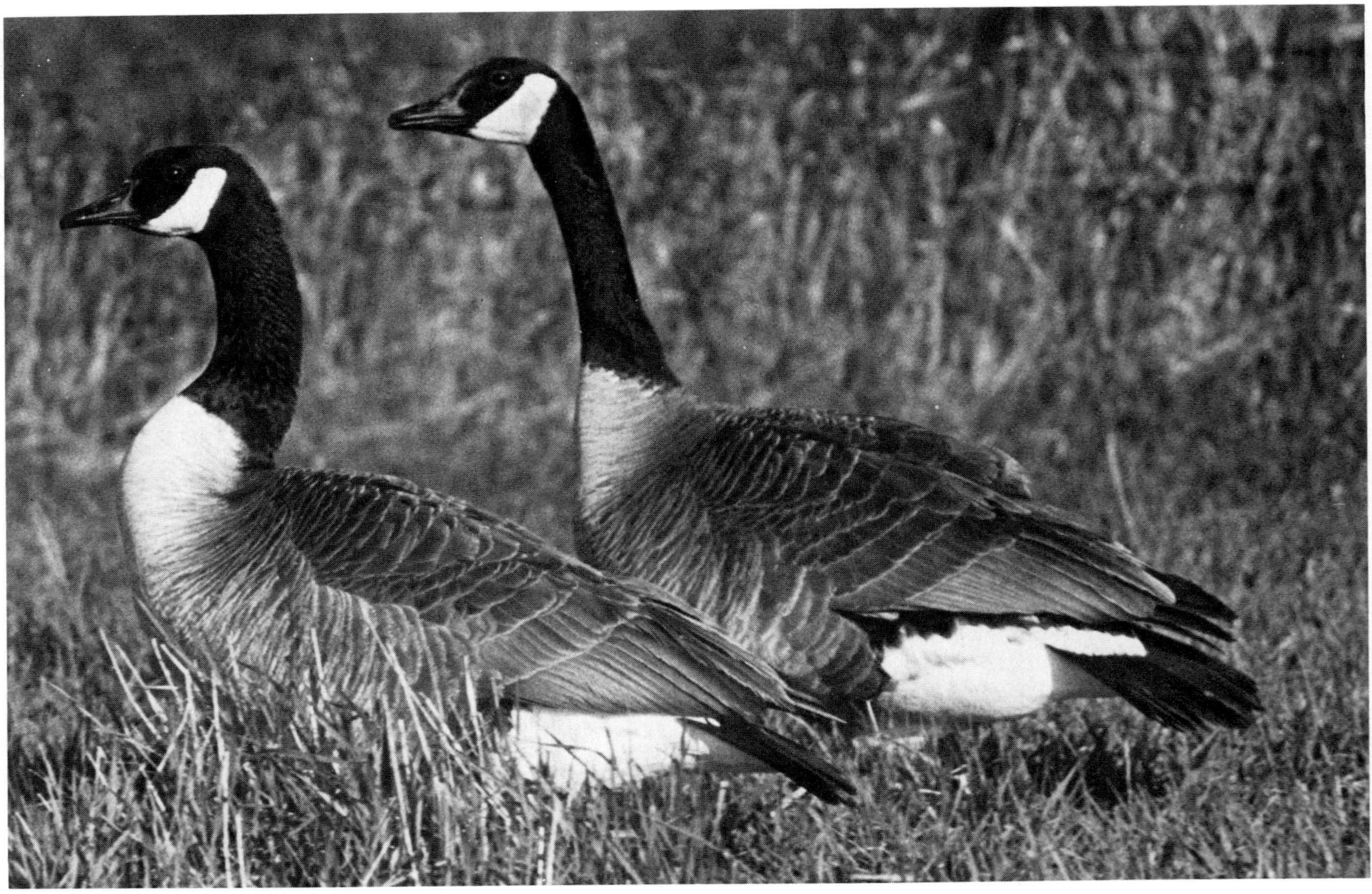

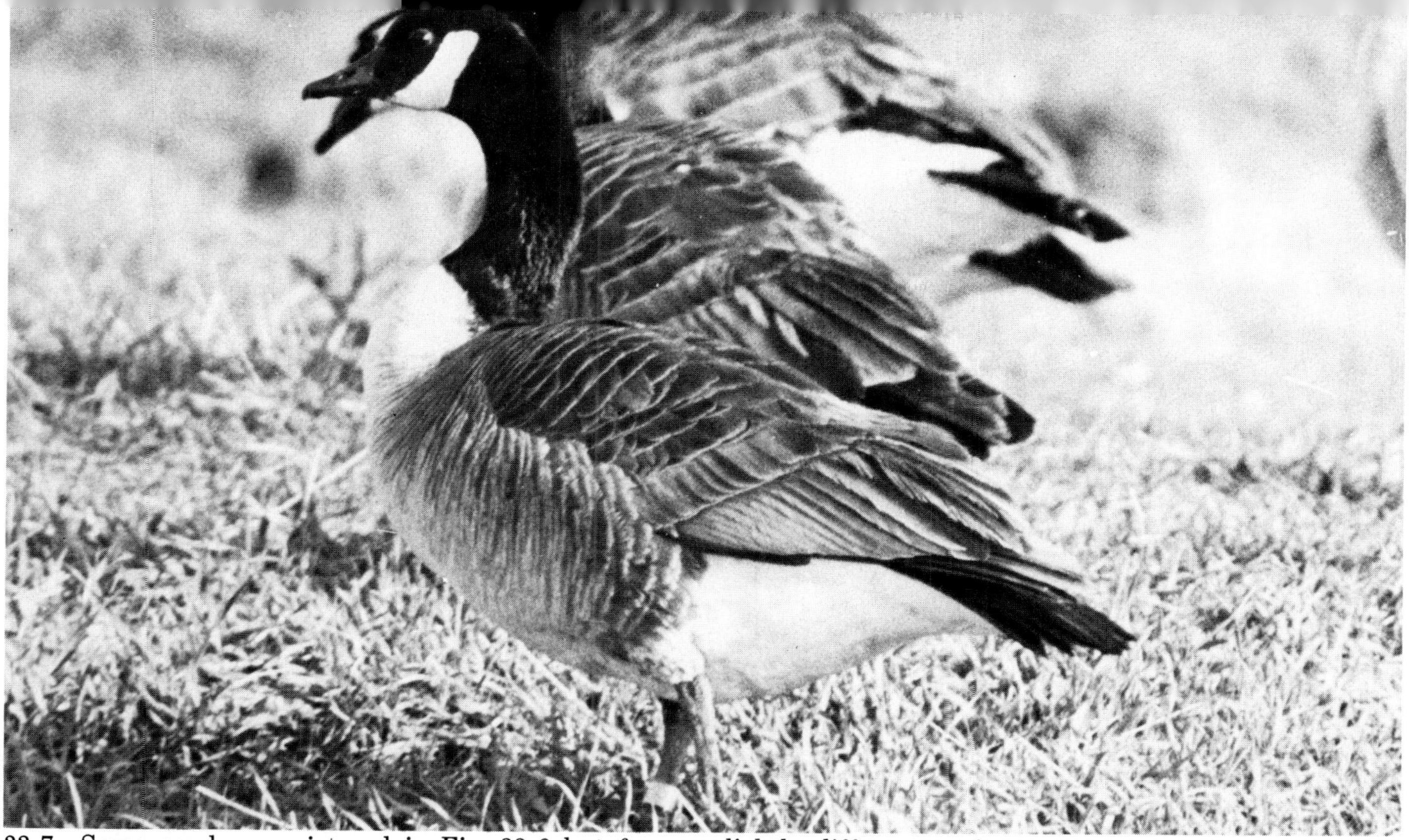

33-7 Same gander as pictured in Fig. 33-6 but from a slightly different angle.

33-8 A pair of giant Canadas proudly show off their family.

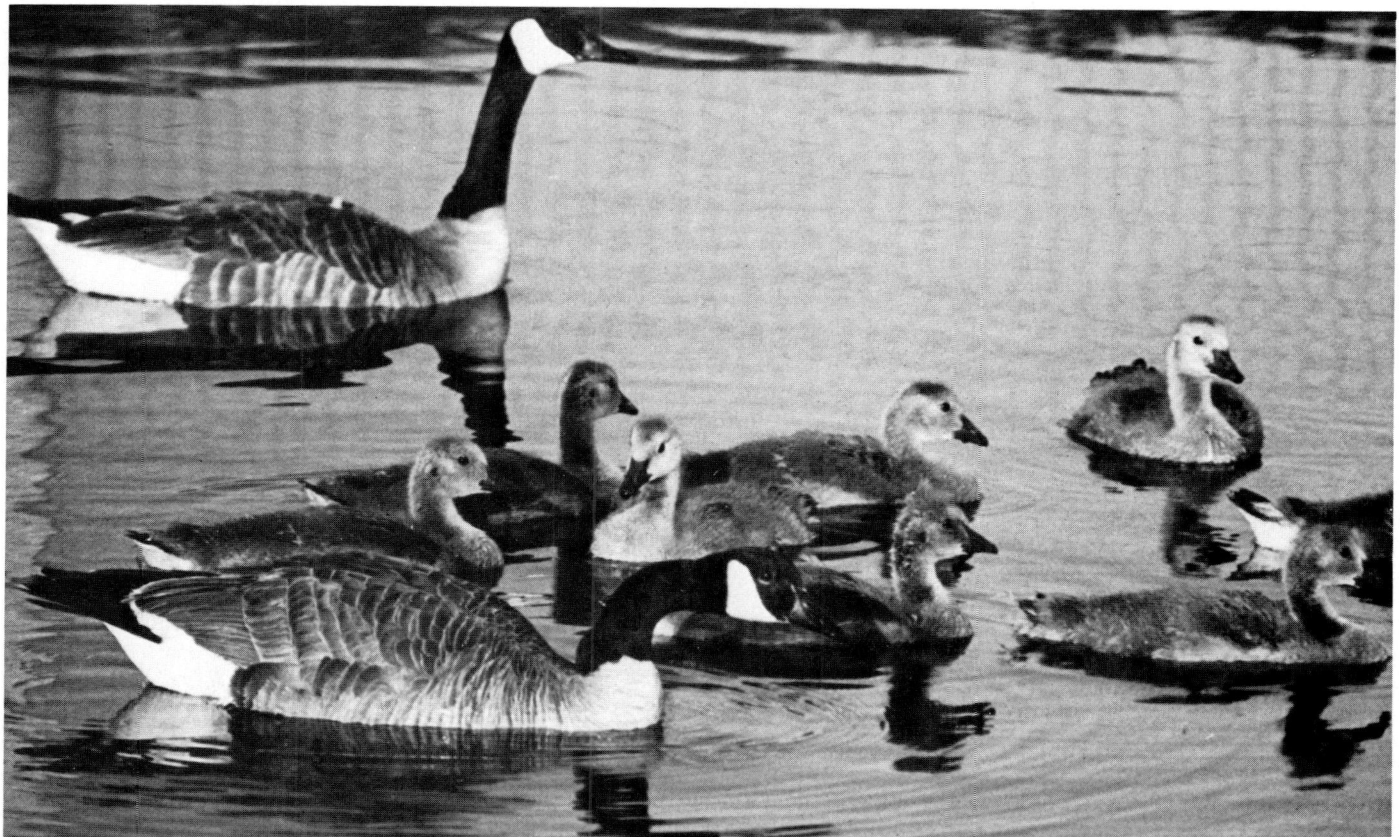

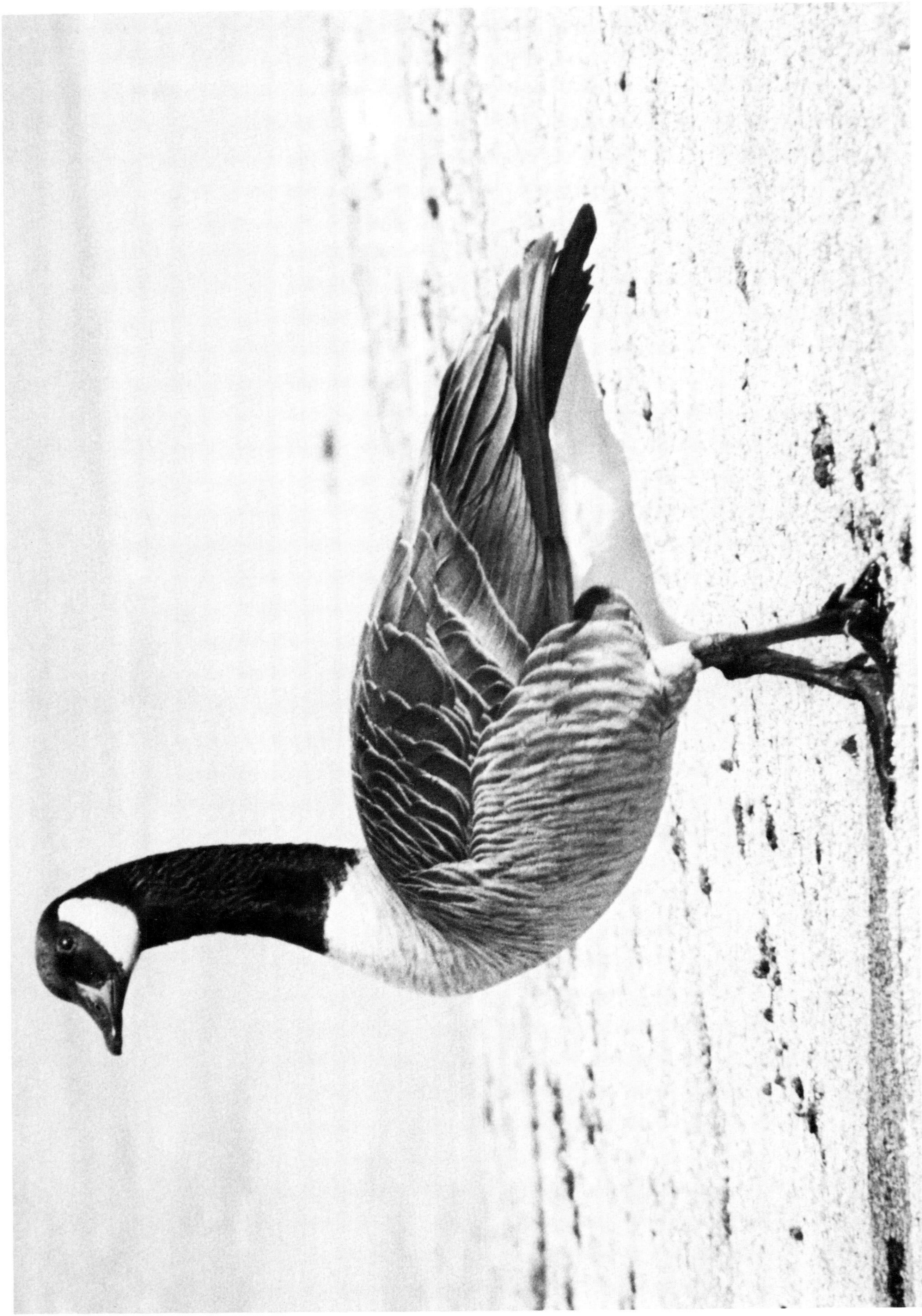

33-9 The Western Canada male. He is a beautiful gander in an exceptionally fine pose.

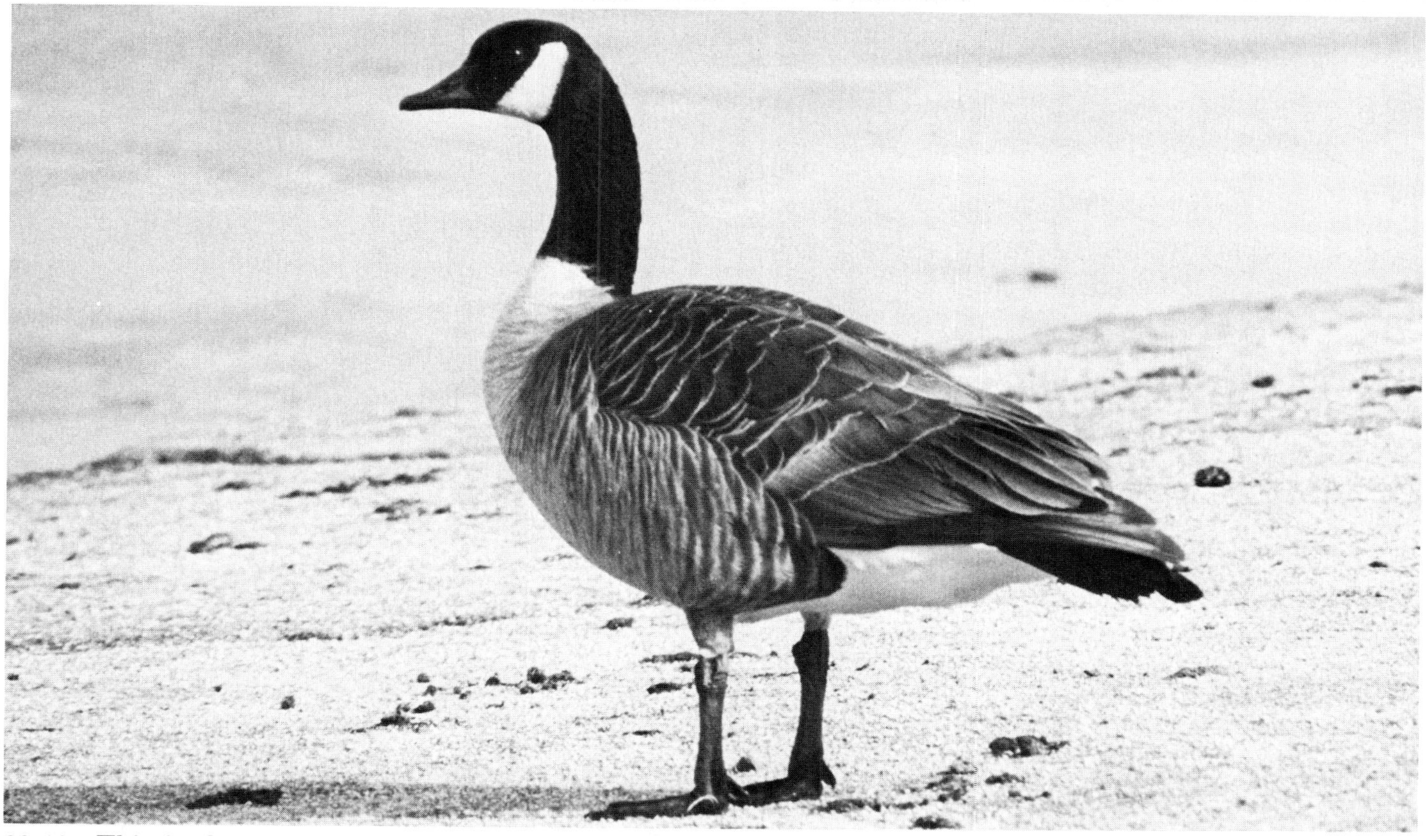

33-10 This is the same bird as shown in Fig. 33-9. He has changed his pose slightly.

33-11 Rear view of a Todd's, or Interior, Canada goose. This very similar subspecies is usually slightly darker than the Western Canada goose.

33-12 Rear view of a Western Canada goose. Body shape and lateral leg placement show up well in this photograph.

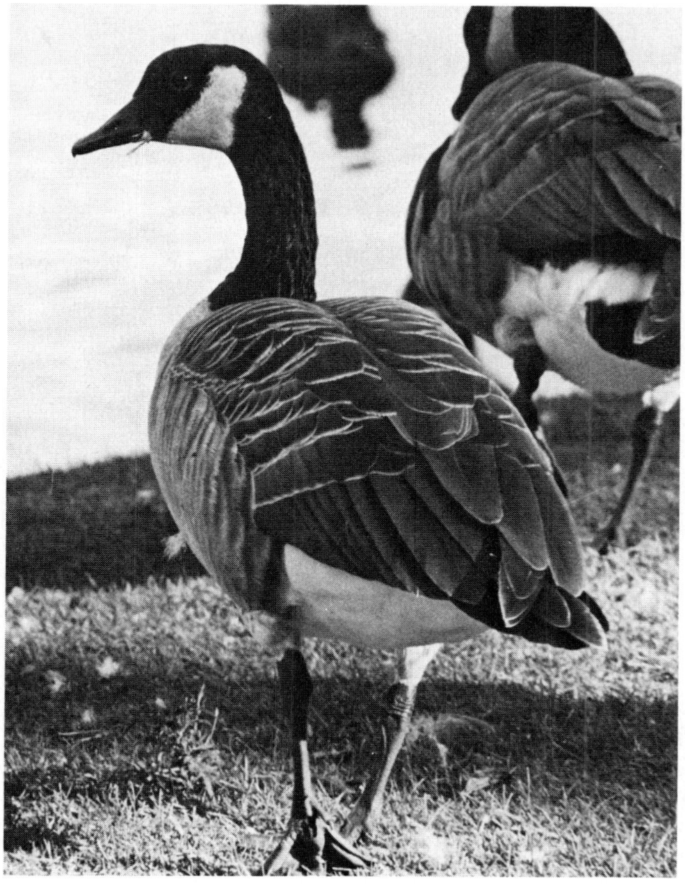

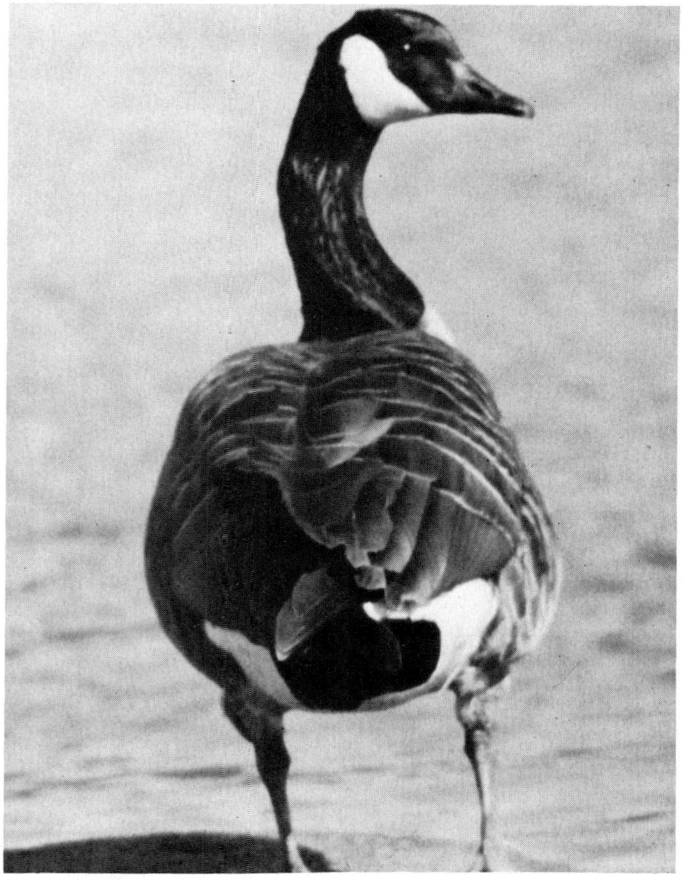

33-13

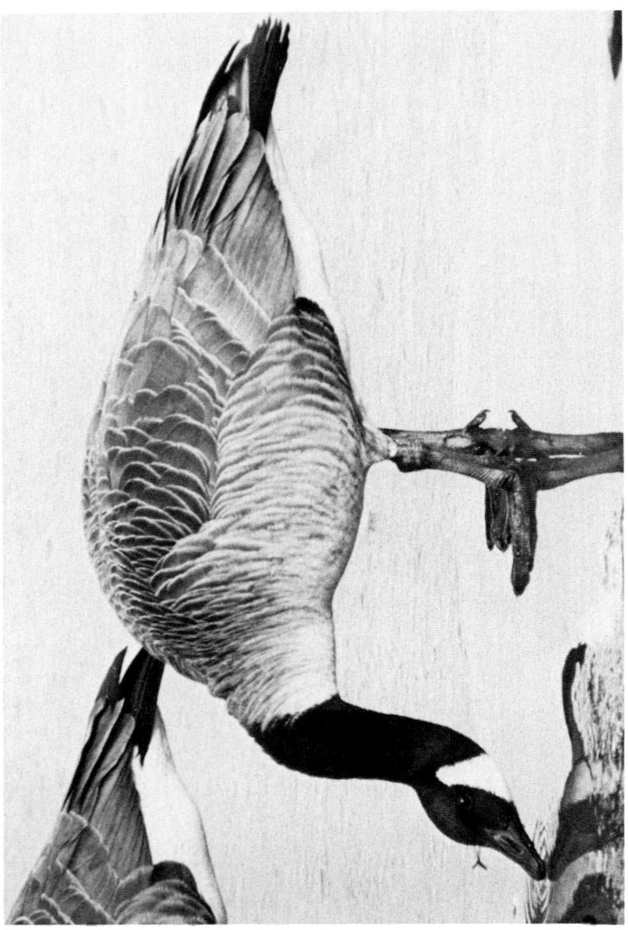

33-14

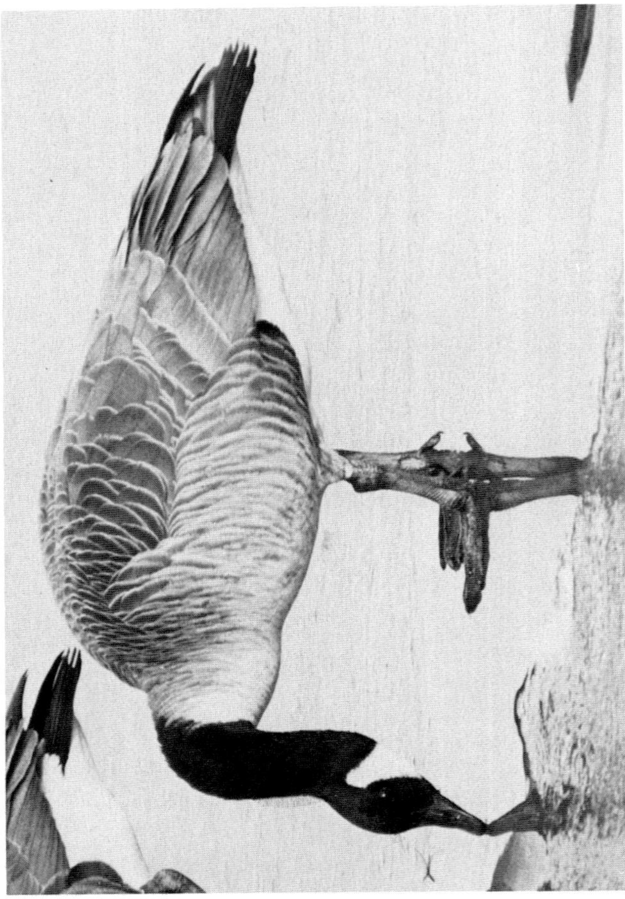

33-15

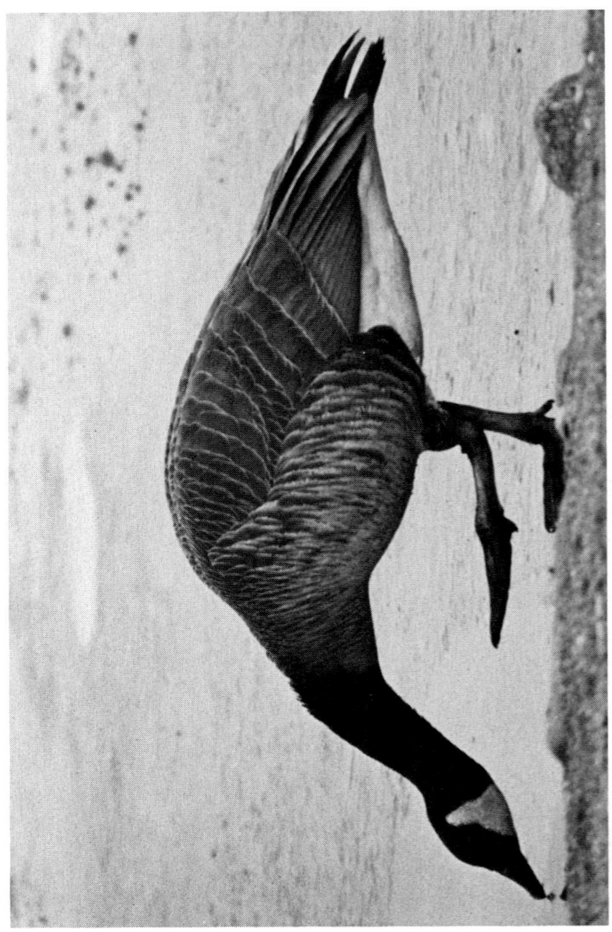

33-16

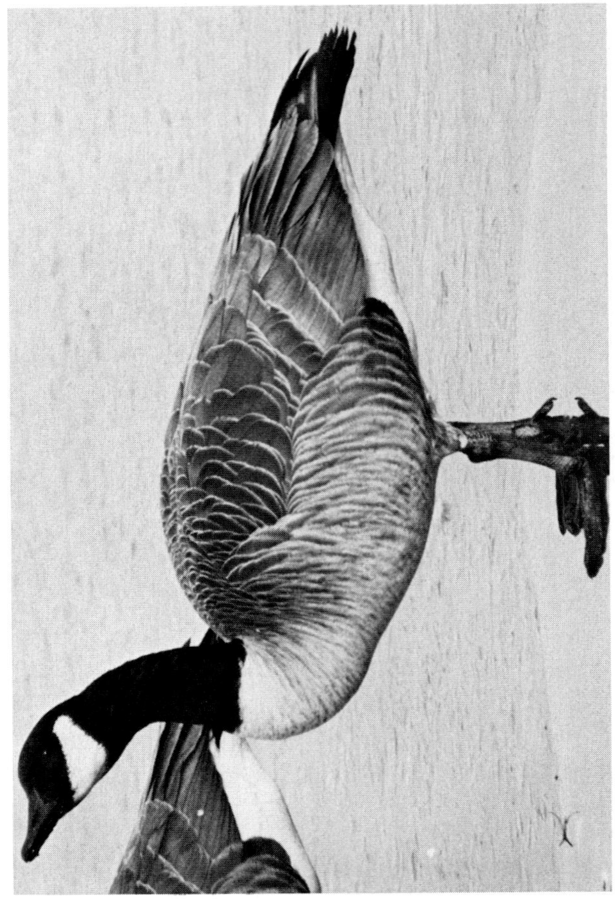

Four studies of drinking Western Canada Geese. Note their graceful, flowing neck lines.

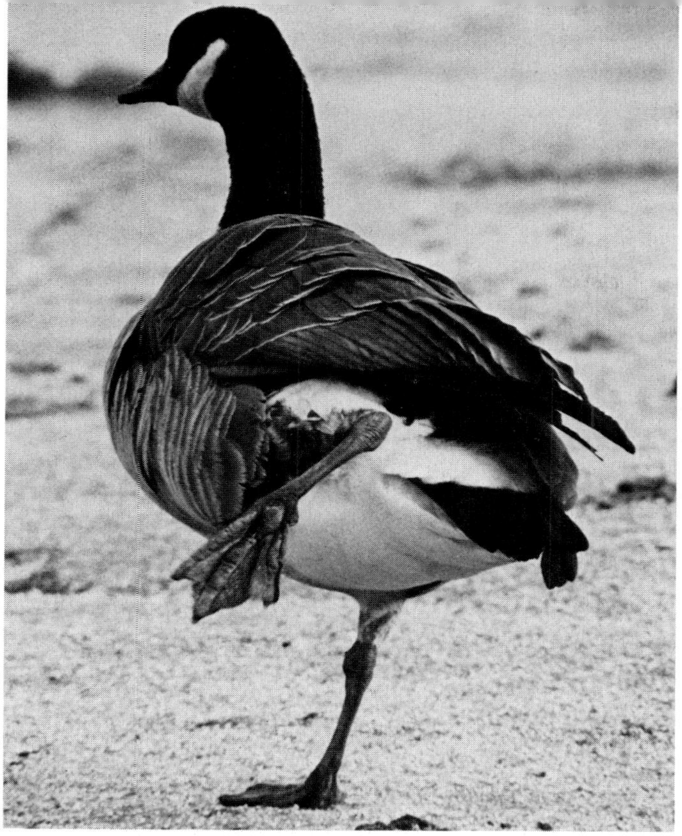

33-17 This Western Canada goose is about to tuck his left foot under his side feathers.

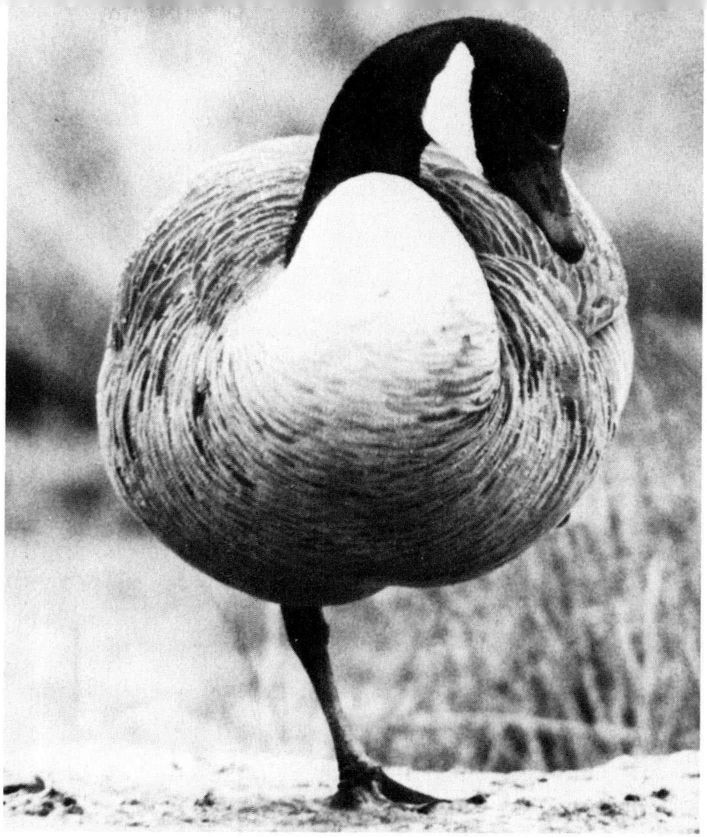

33-18 Good front view of a Western Canada resting on one leg. Especially notice his cross-sectional body shape and the placement of his leg and foot.

33-19 Profile view of a Western Canada. He was preening his partially expanded wing but stopped to keep an eye on the author. Notice how his upper chest bulges.

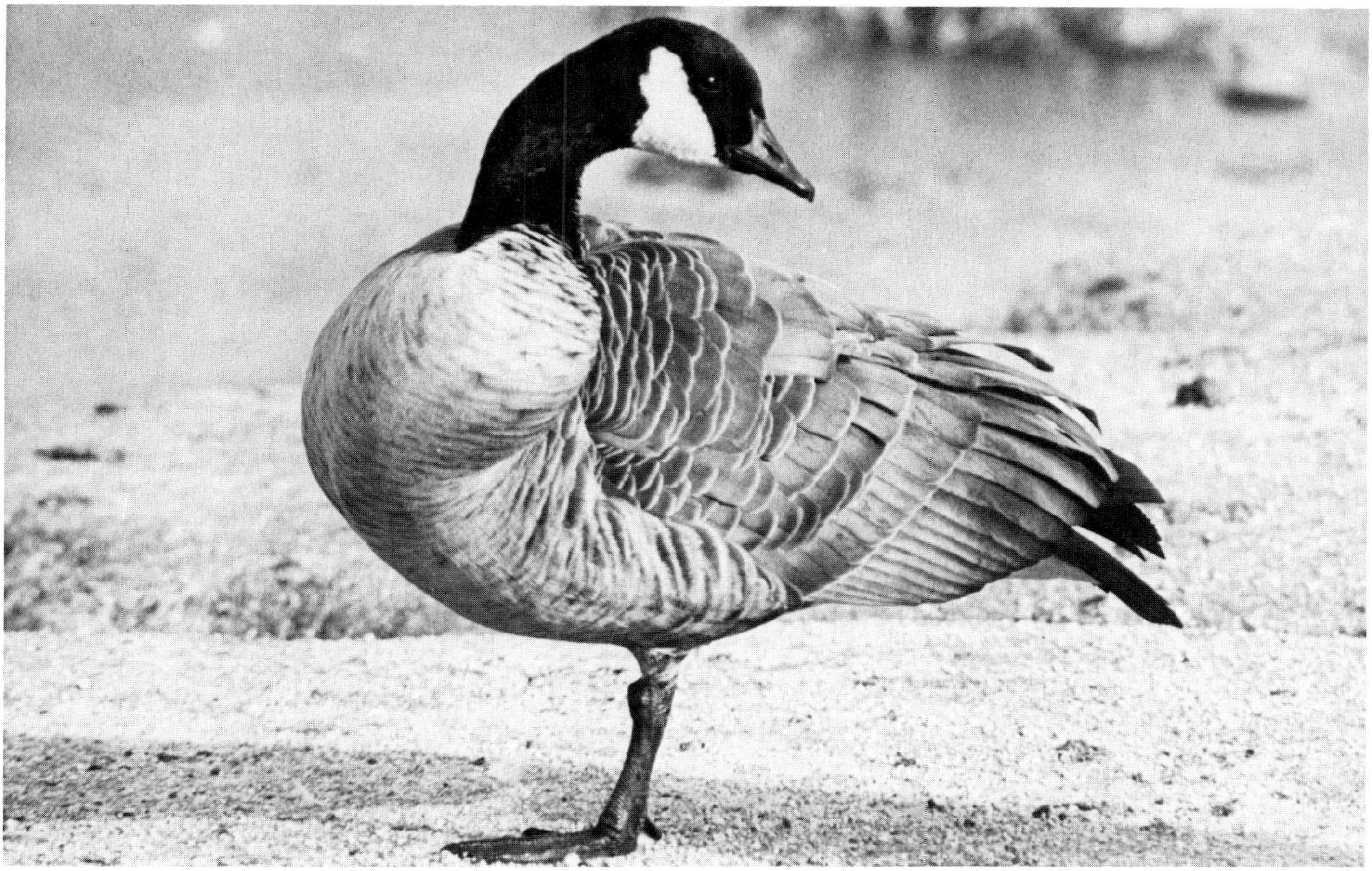

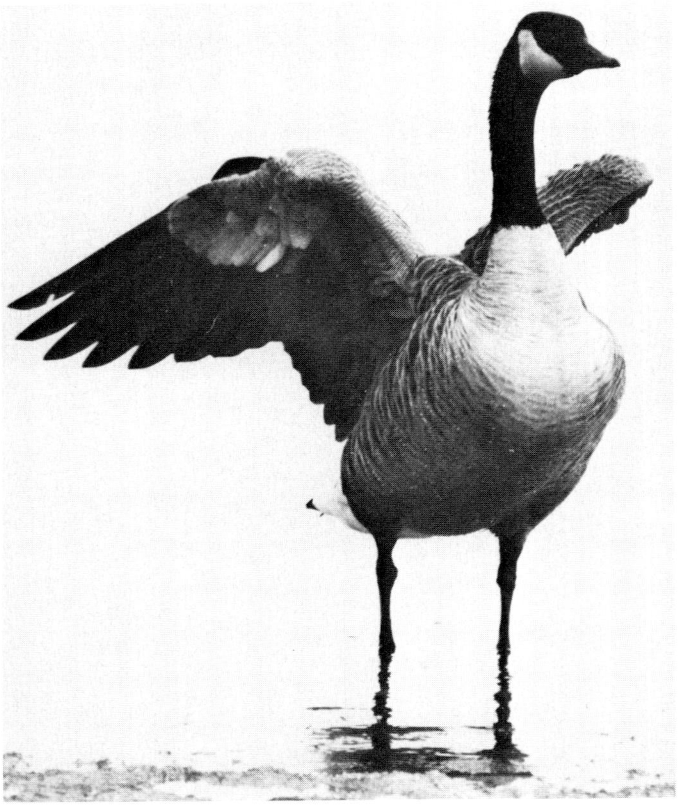

33-20 A Western Canada stretches his wings.

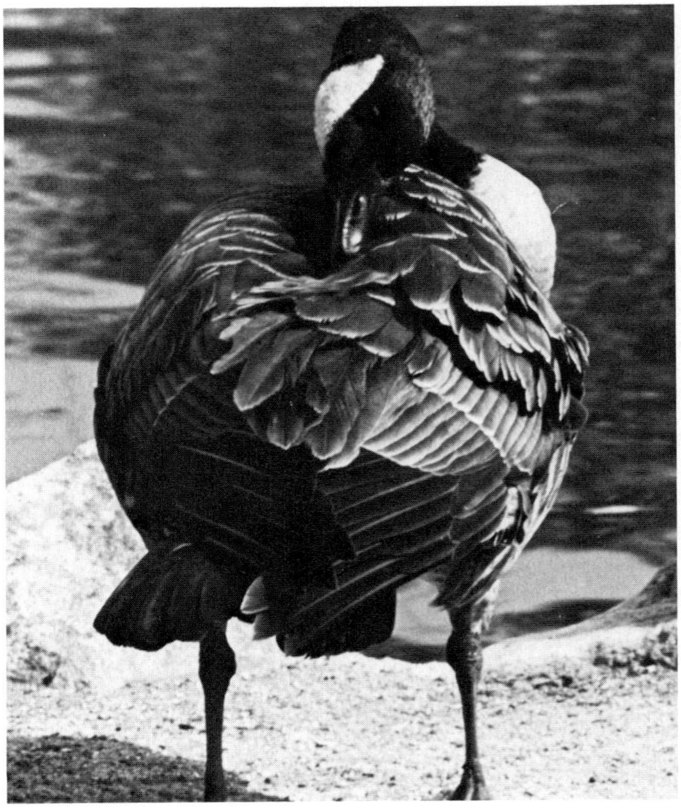

33-21 Preening Western Canada. Note head and neck position.

33-22 Another view of a Western Canada stretching his wings. A considerable amount of wing detail can be seen in this photograph.

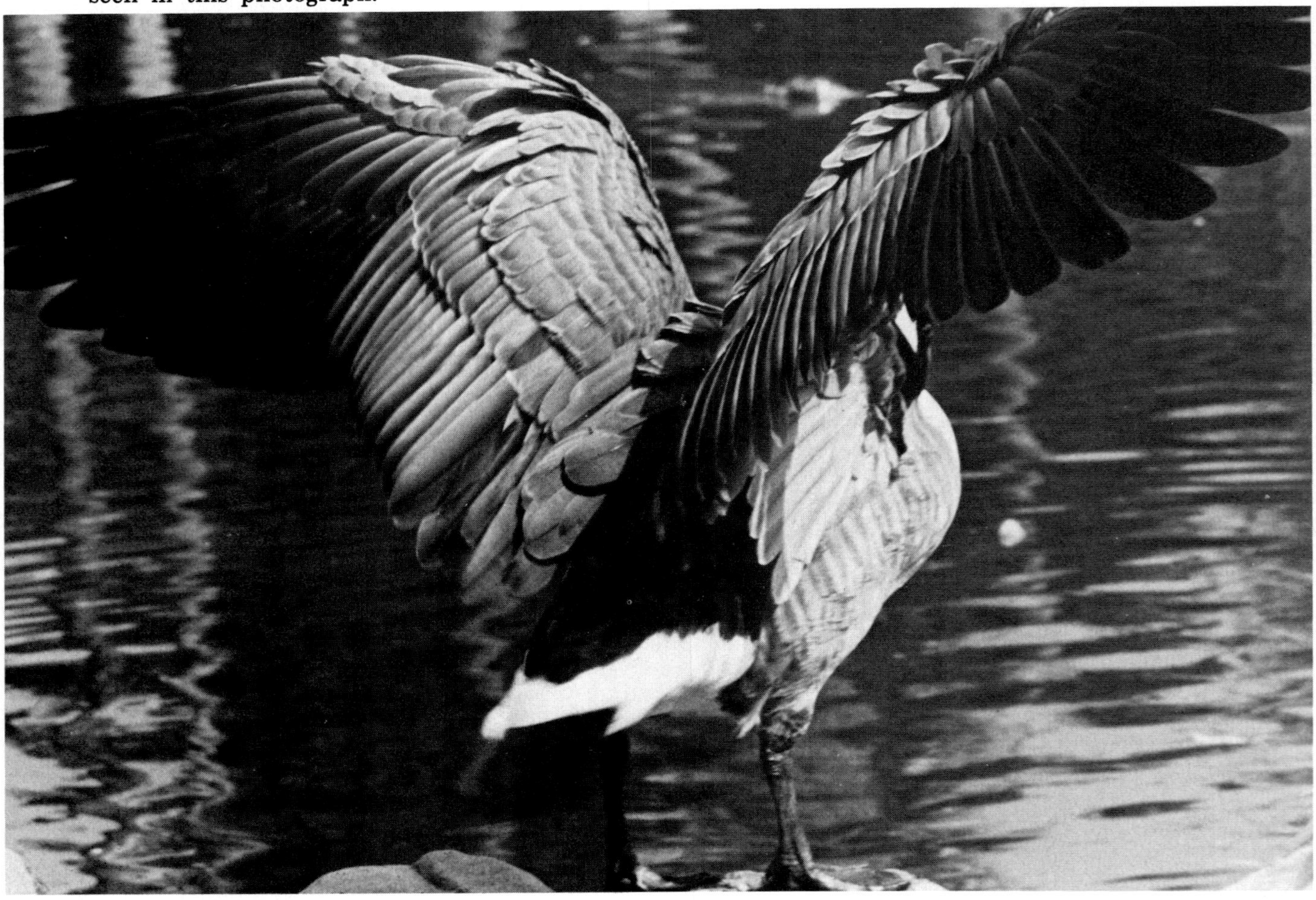

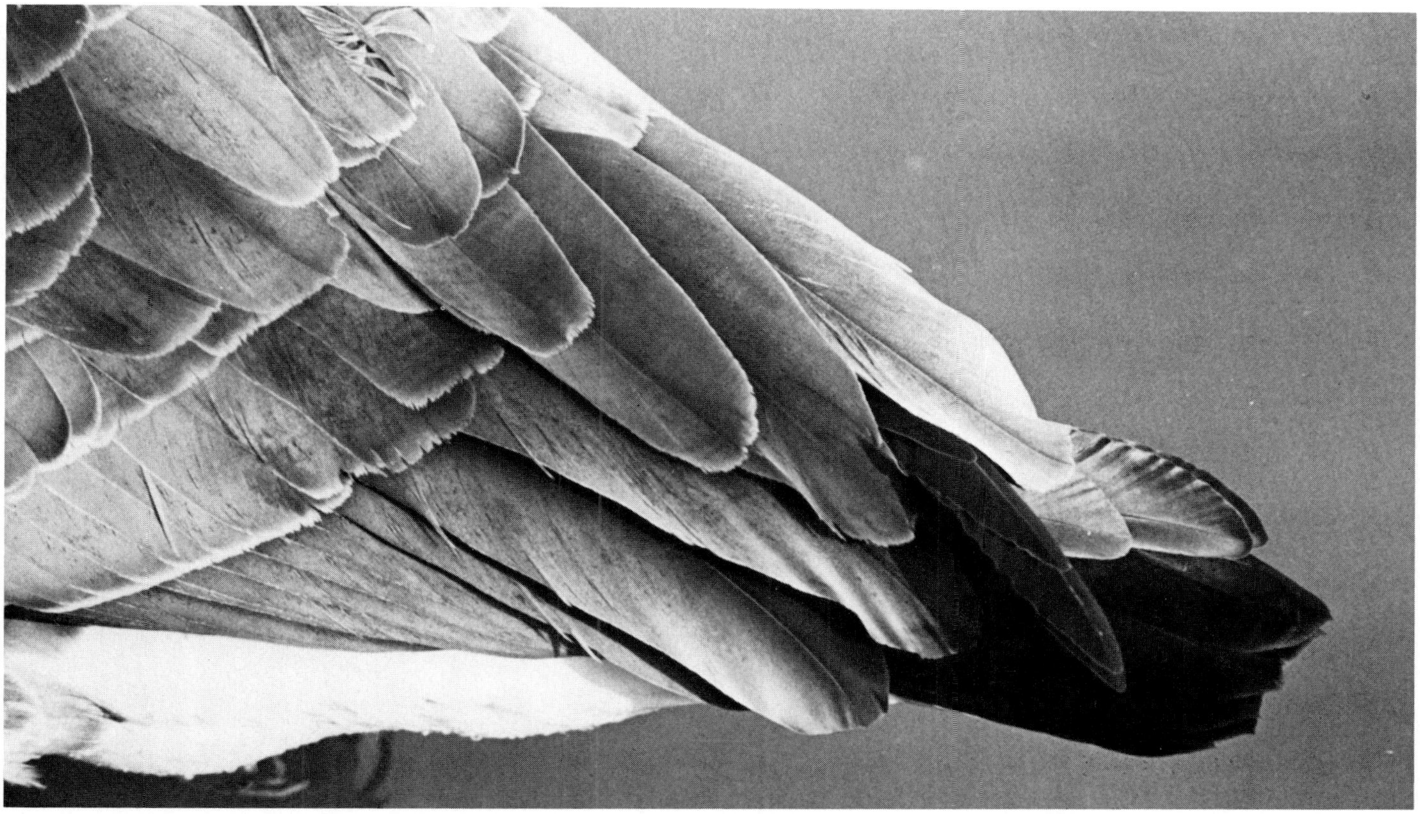

33-23 Close-up showing the crossed primaries, tertials, and tail feathers. The large tertial feathers are normally wavy as pictured here.

33-24 The crossed and folded primaries are slightly expanded in this photo. The shape of the tail is also clearly shown here.

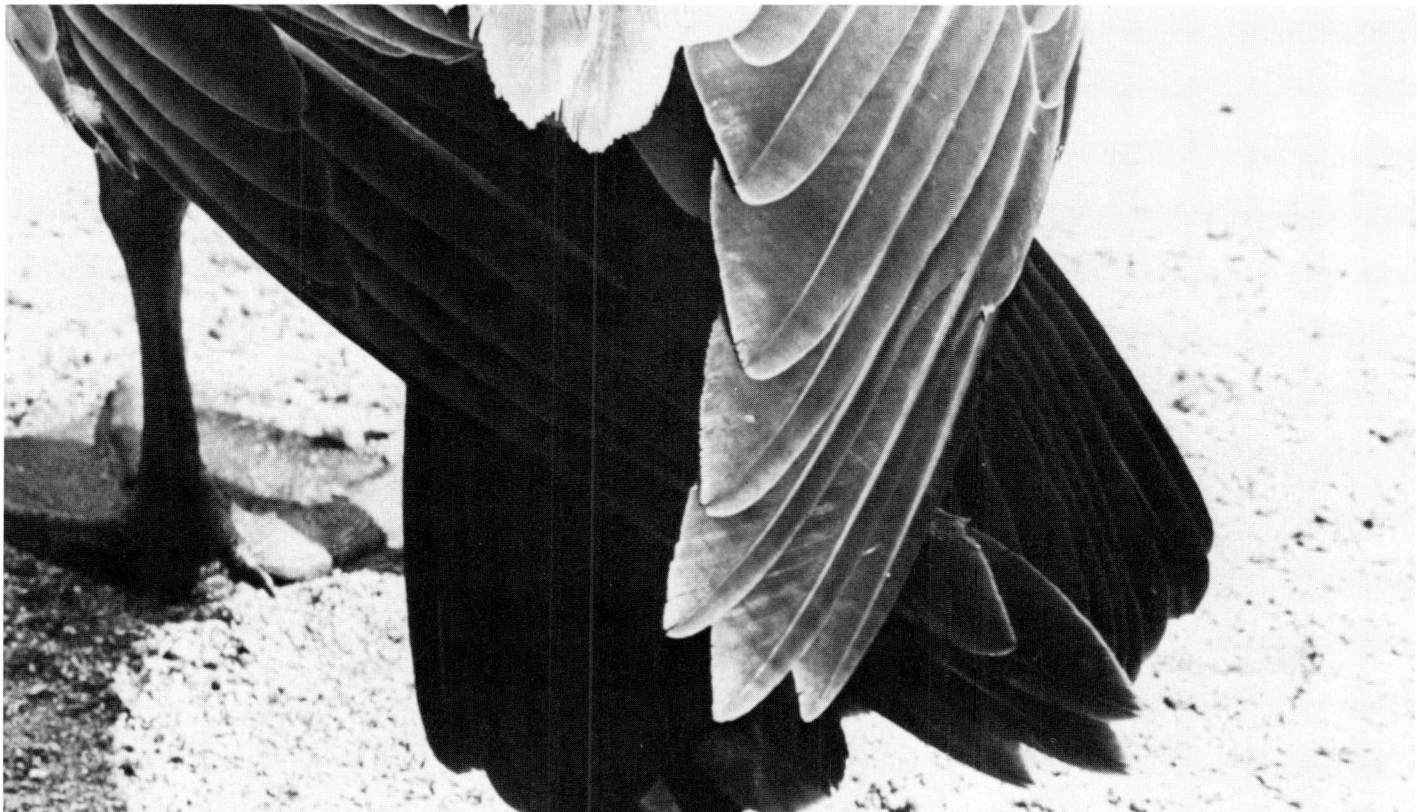

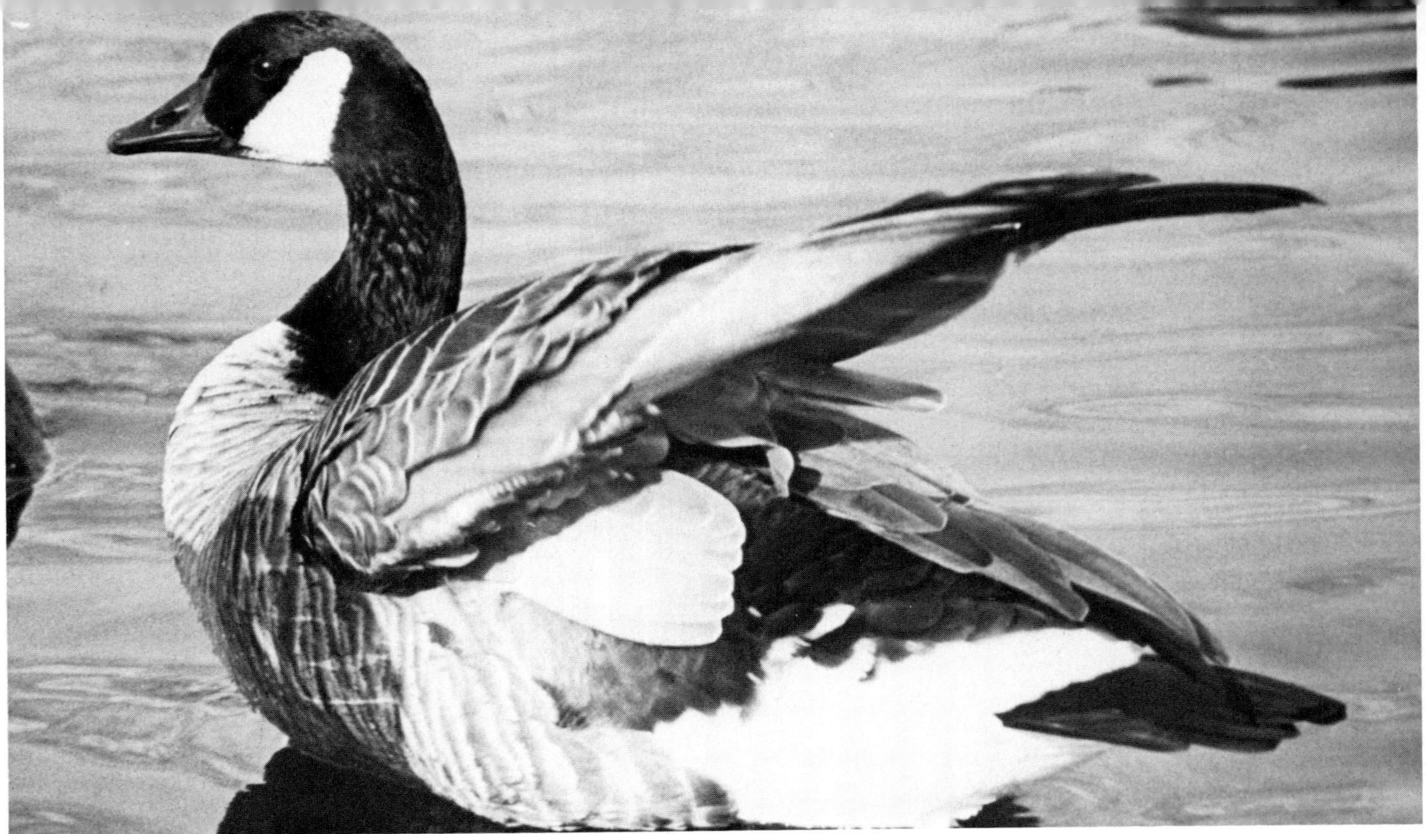

33-25 A Western Canada goose raises one wing. Especially note the fan-shaped axillar feather group.

33-26 This Western Canada honker preens his back feathers.

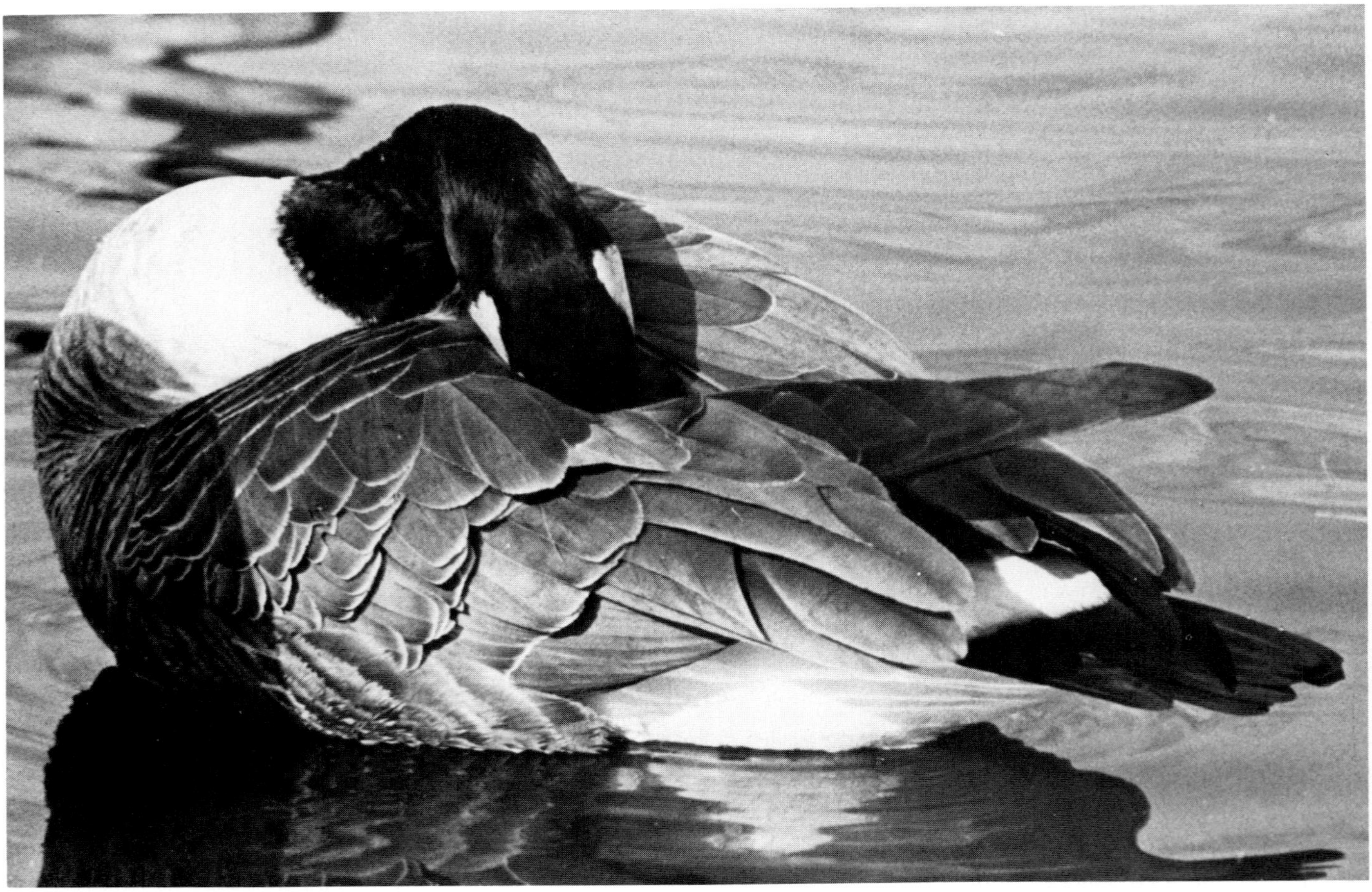

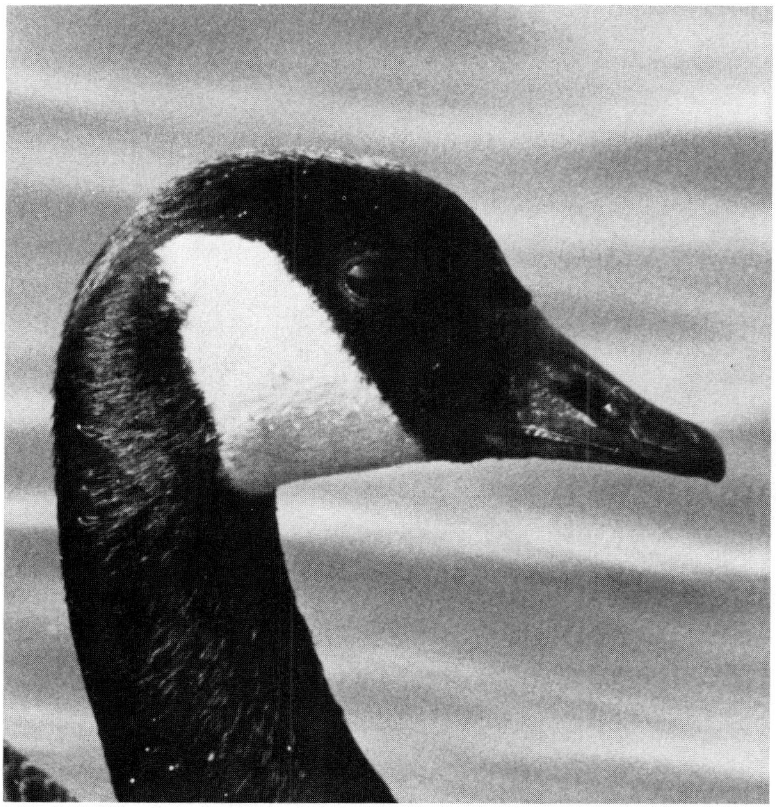

33-27

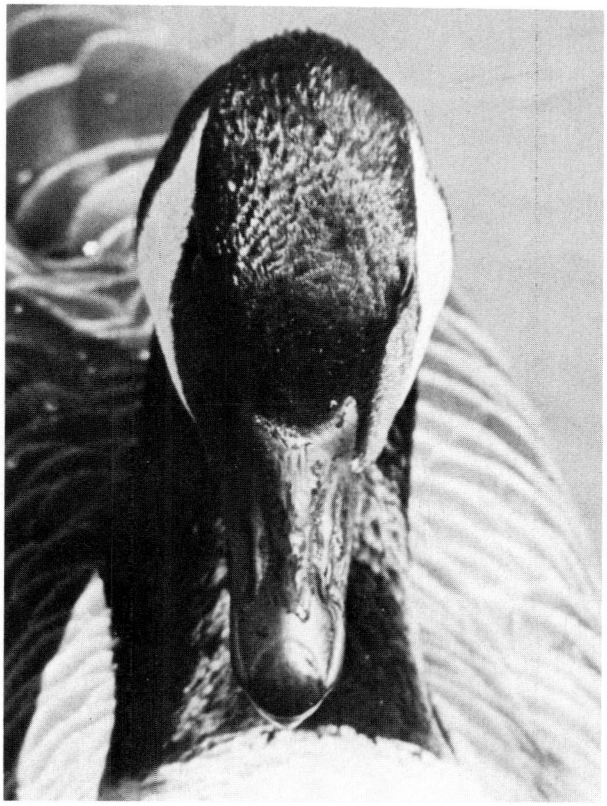

33-28

Profile, front, and rear views of the Western Canada goose's head and bill.

33-29

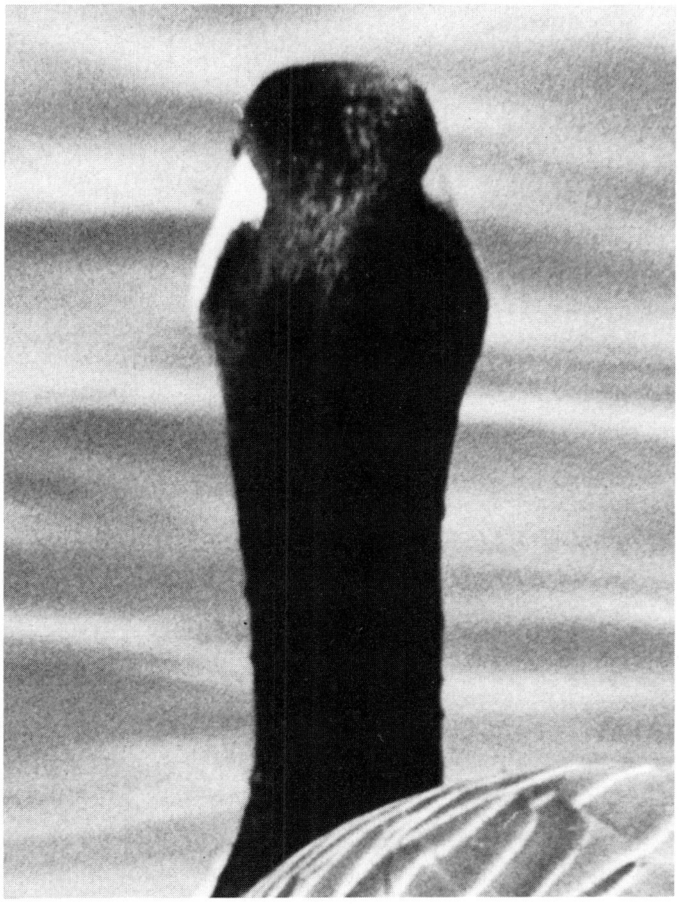

33-30

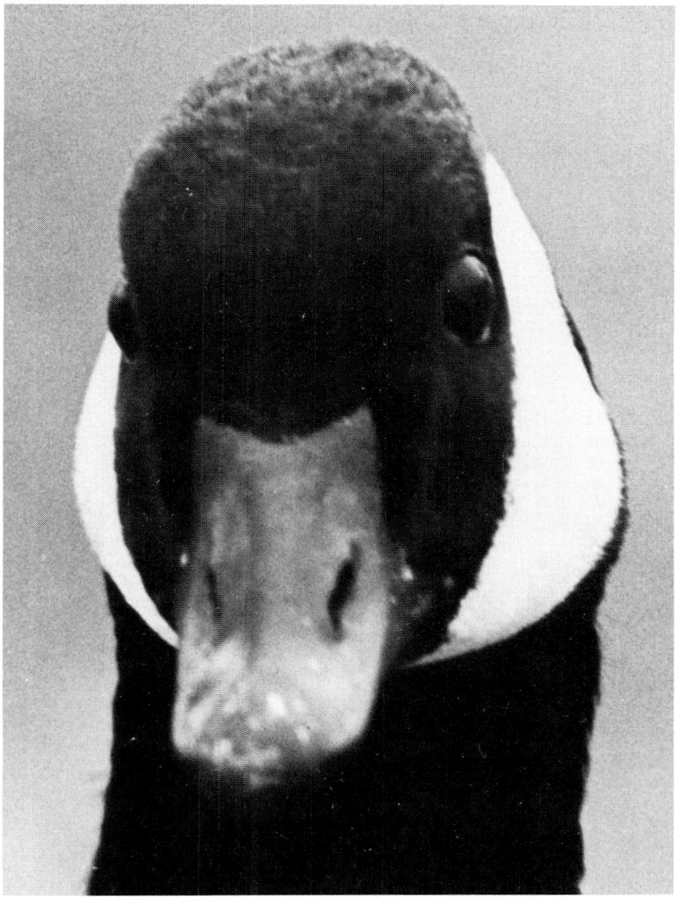

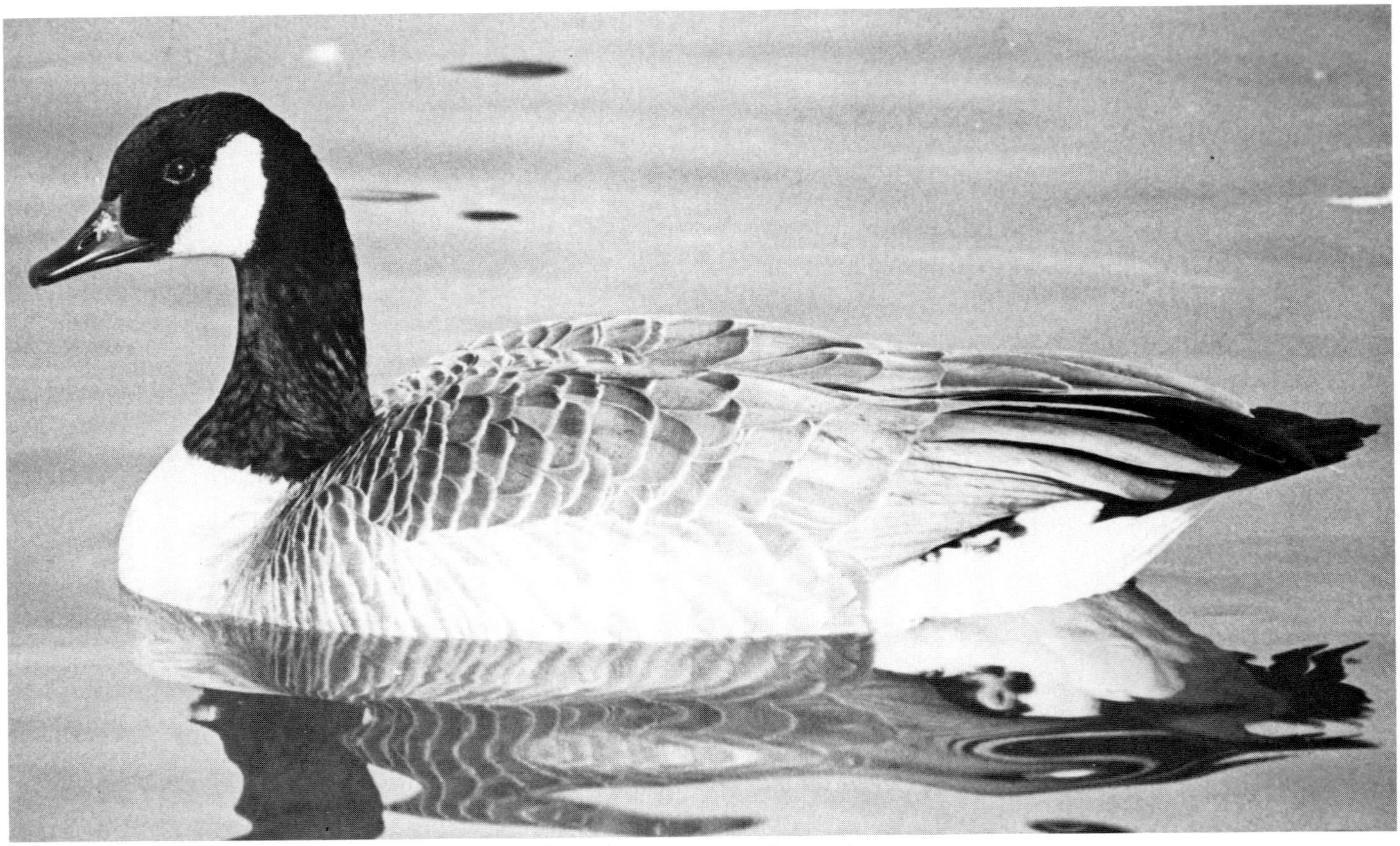

33-31 Good profile of a relaxed Western Canada goose on the water.

33-32 Goose raises his head to permit a drink of water to run down his throat.

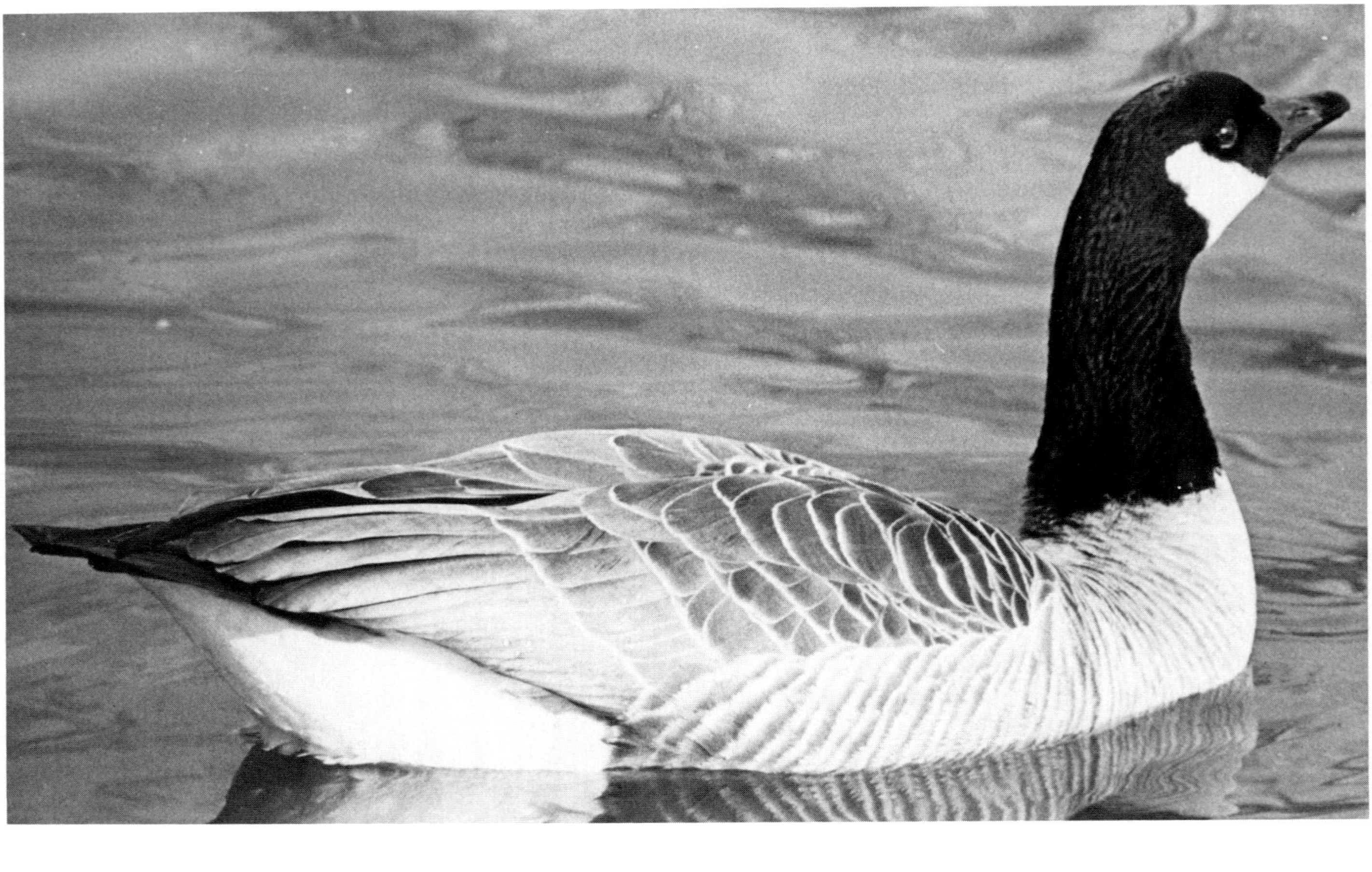

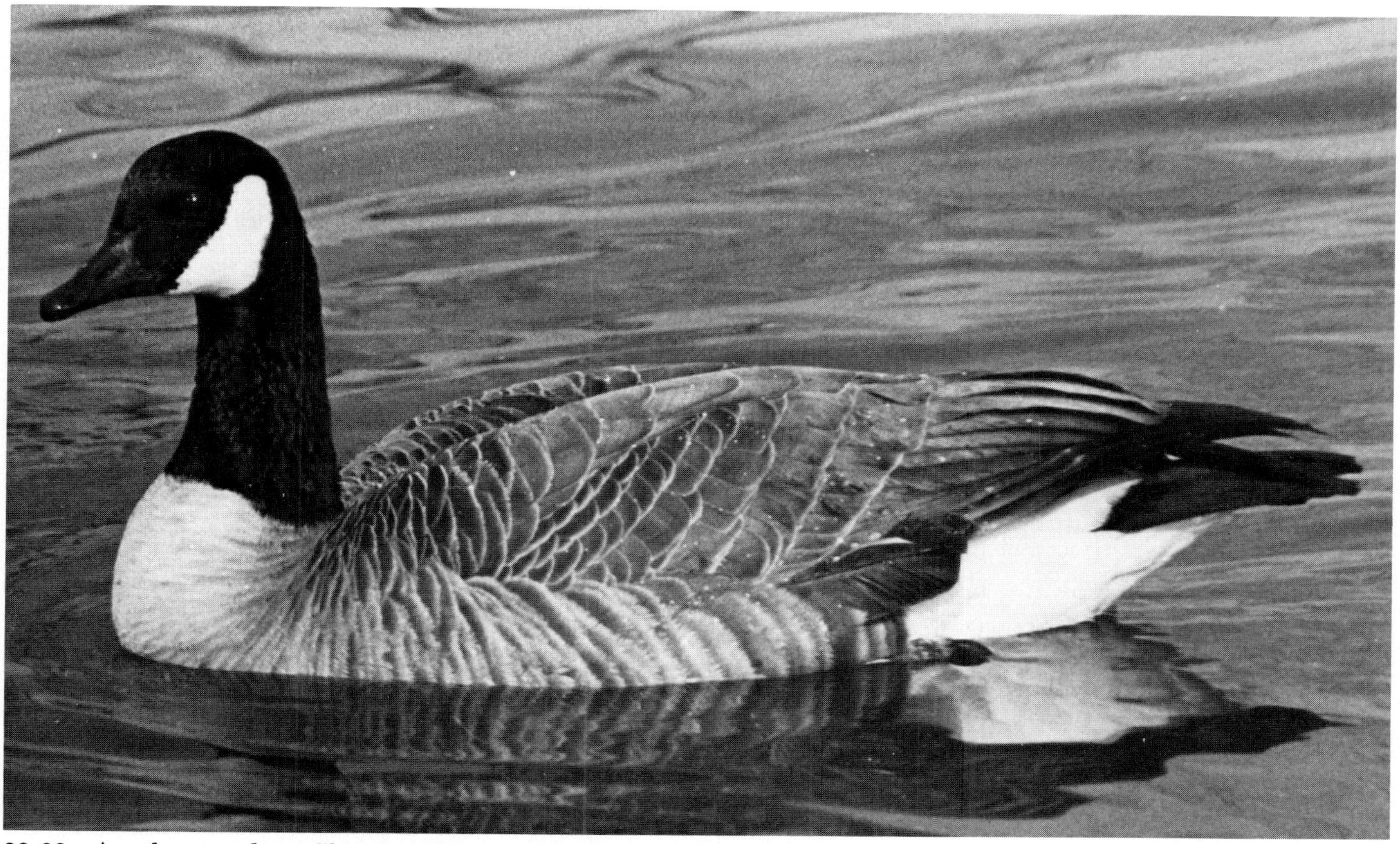

33-33 Another good profile of a floating Western Canada goose.

33-34 Rear views of Western Canada geese show body shape and feather patterns. 33-35

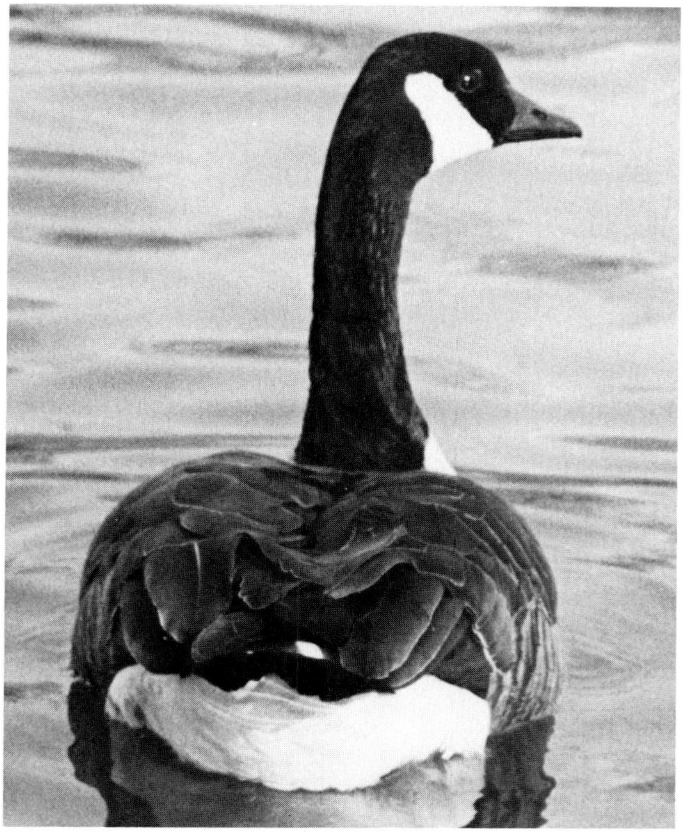

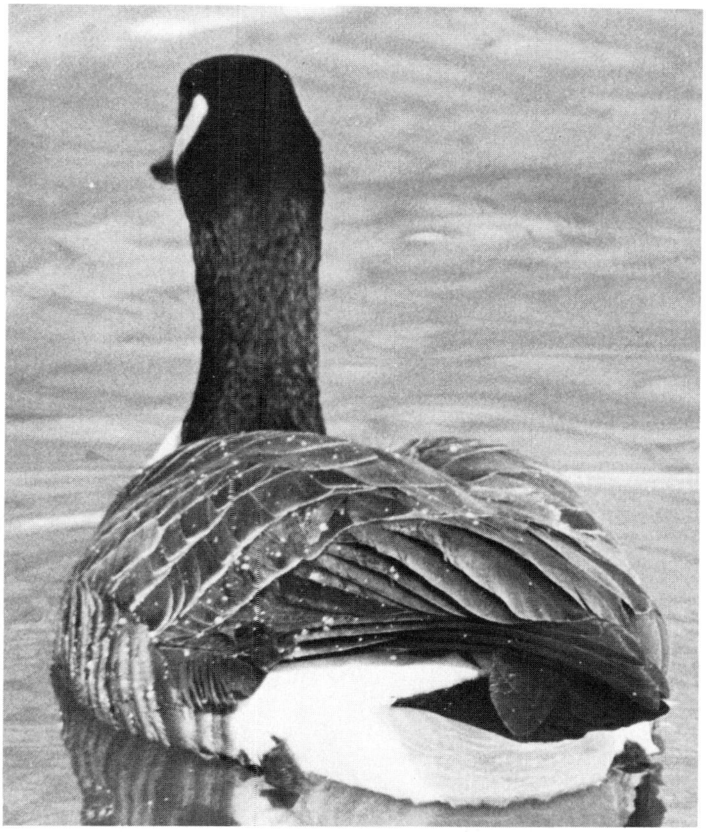

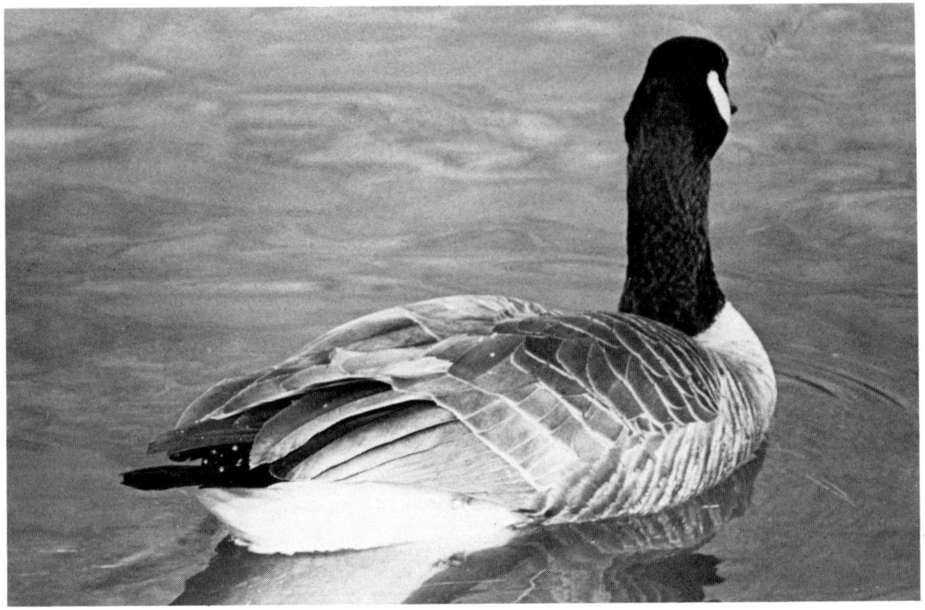

33-36

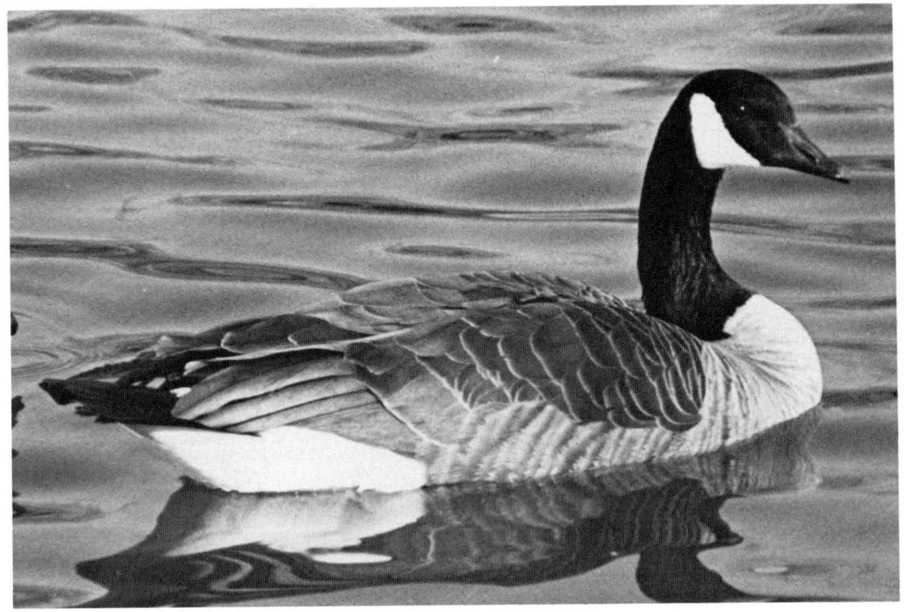

33-37

Four more studies of floating Western Canada geese.

33-38

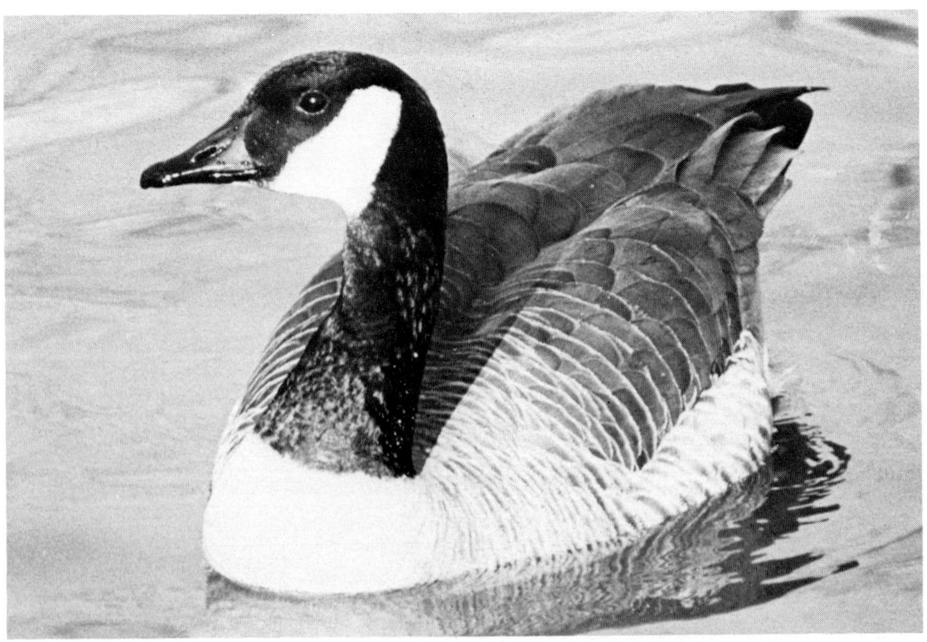

33-39

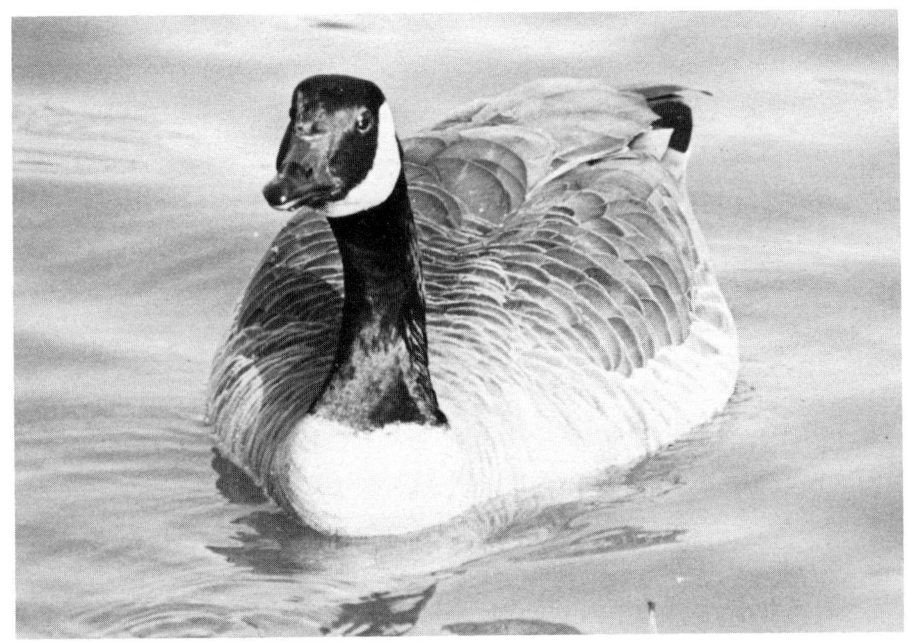

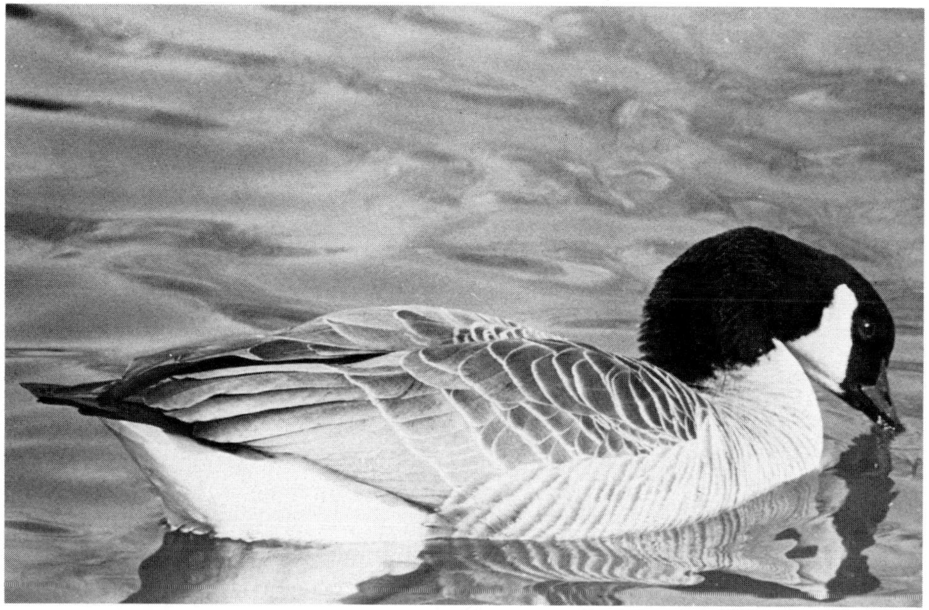

33-40

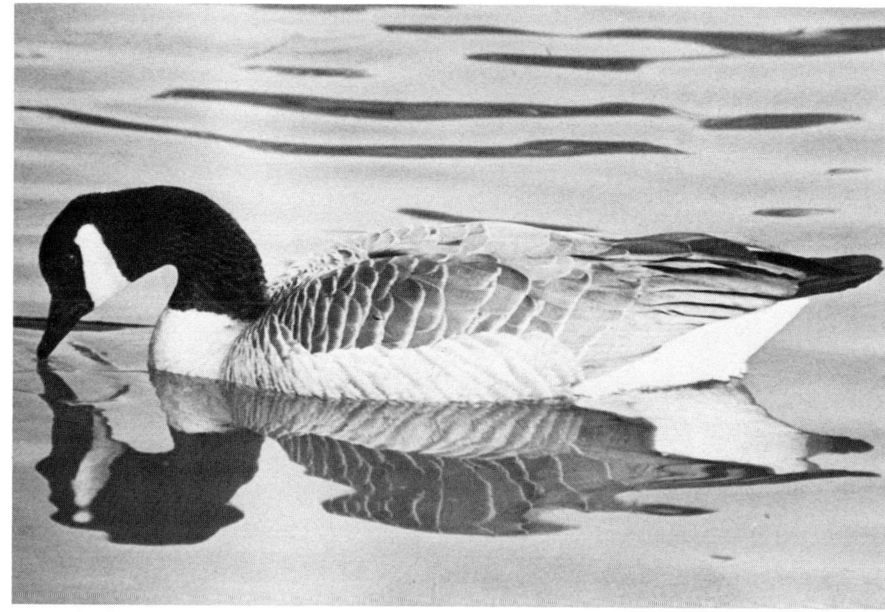

33-41

Western Canada geese dabble in the water.

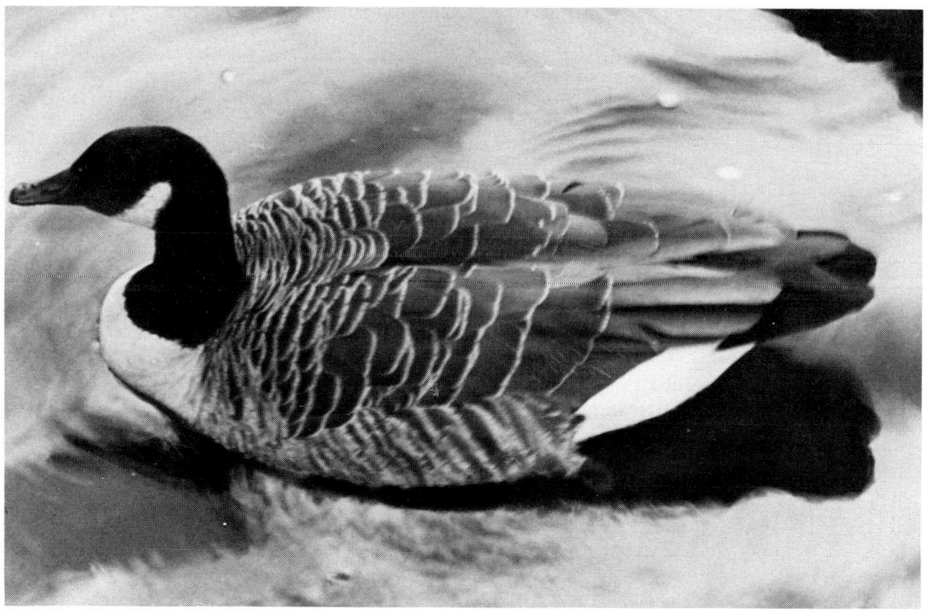

33-42

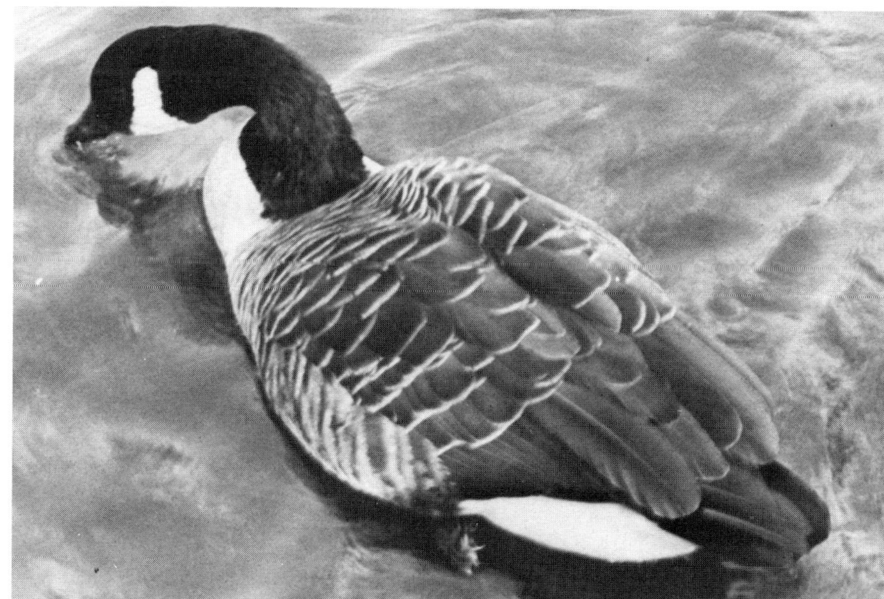

33-43

Higher camera angle shows body planform and feather patterns.

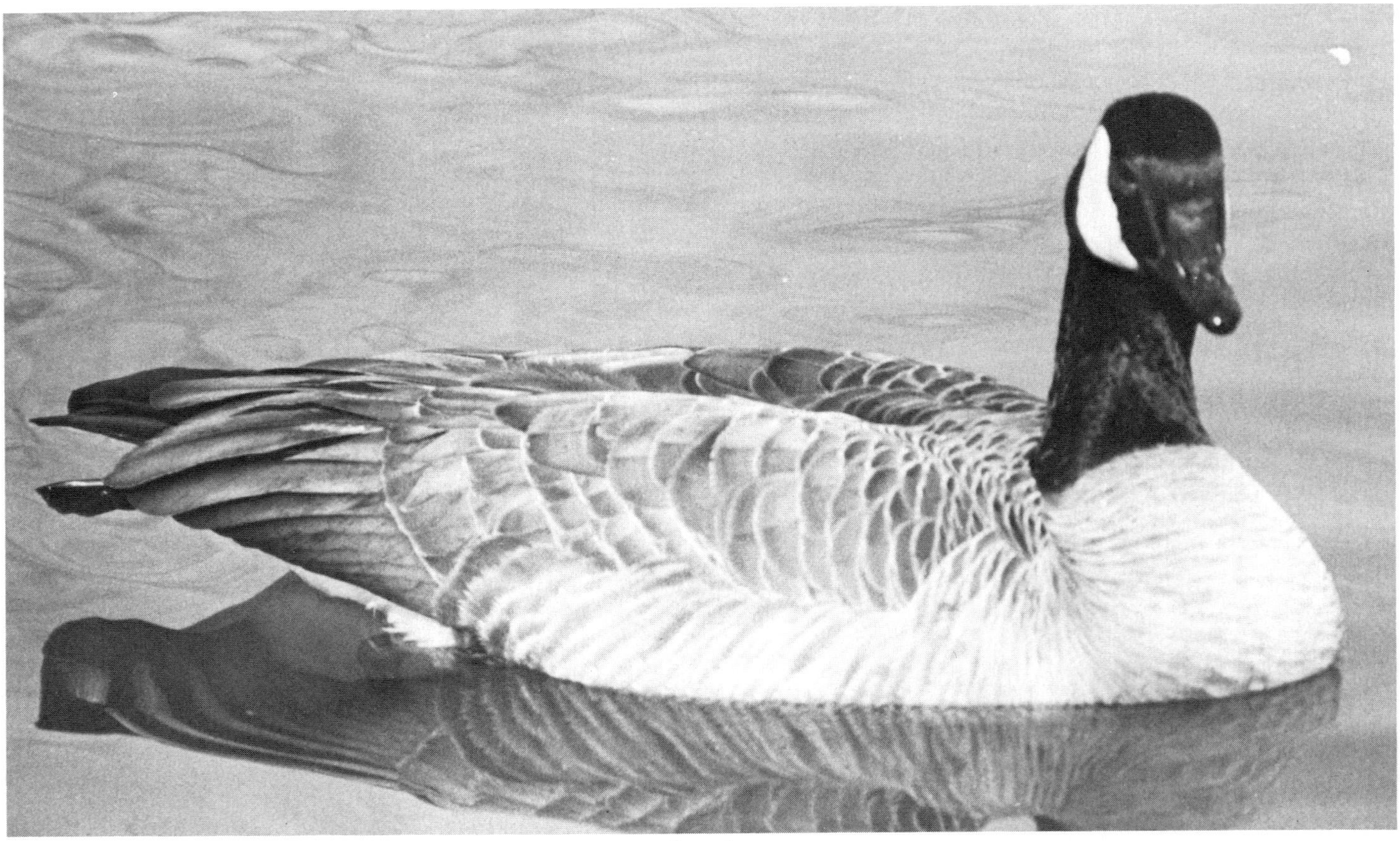

33-44 Western Canada goose relaxes as she floats idly along.

33-45 Floating Western Canada goose—nice head position.

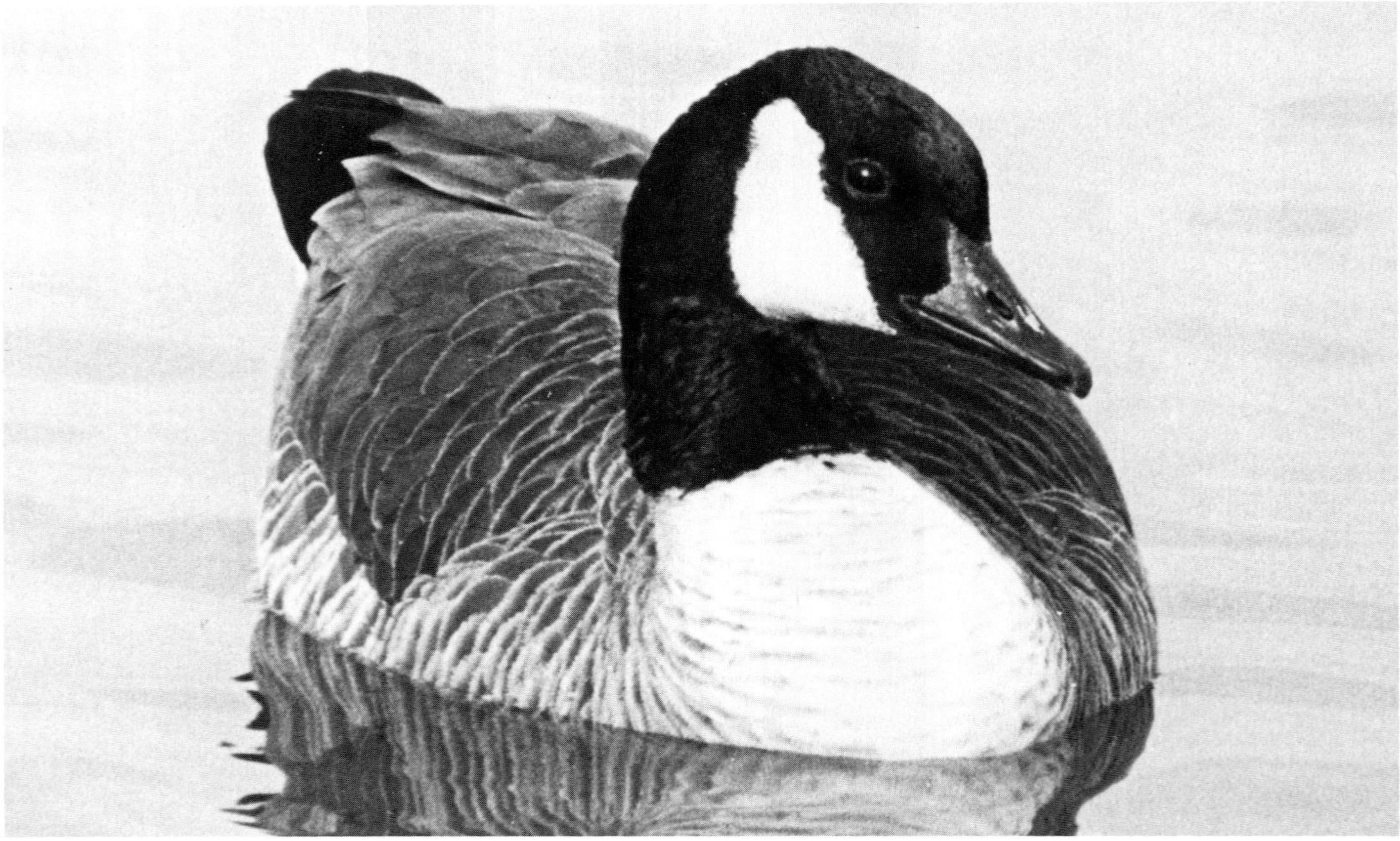

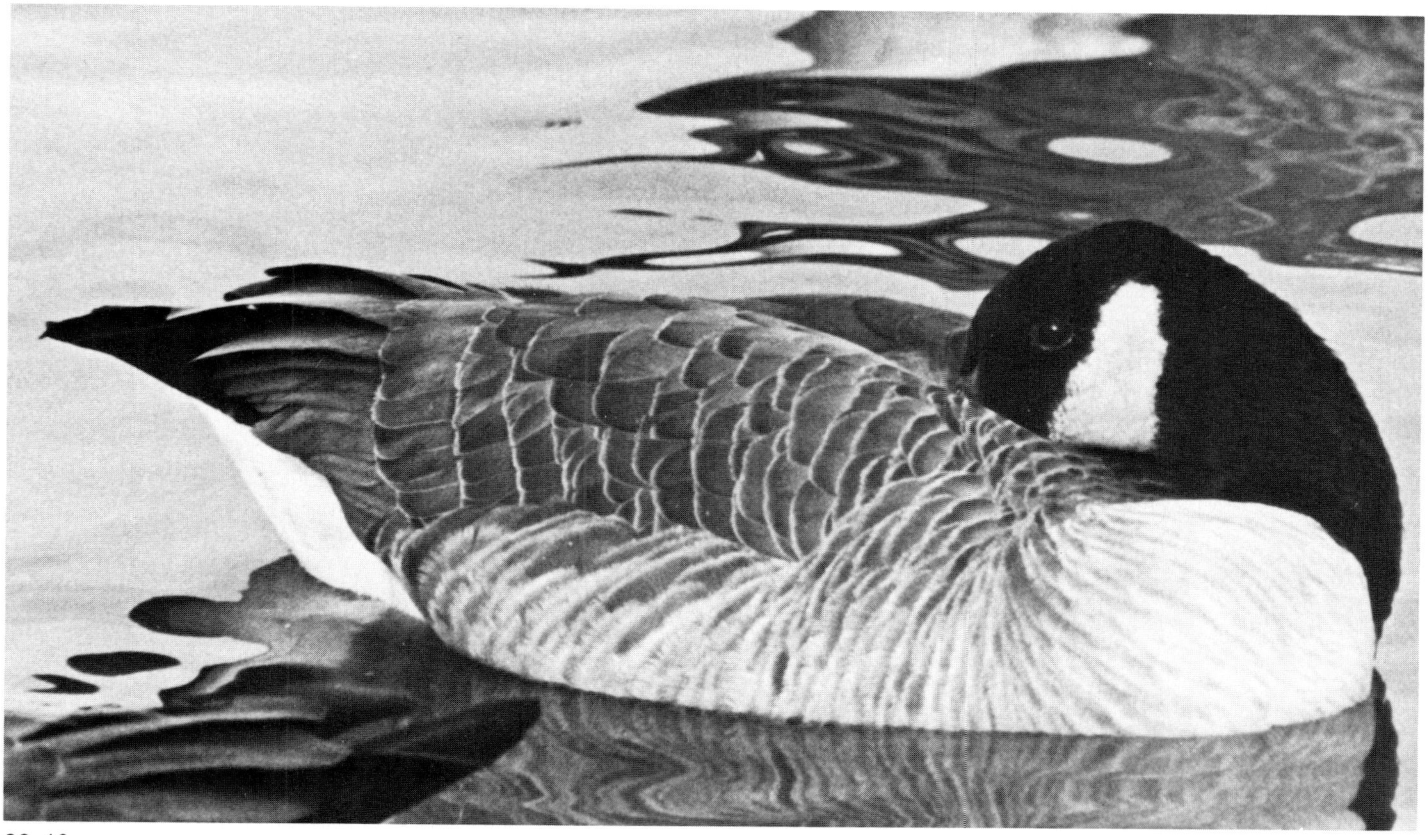

33-46

Two views of a Western honker in the sleeping position.

33-47

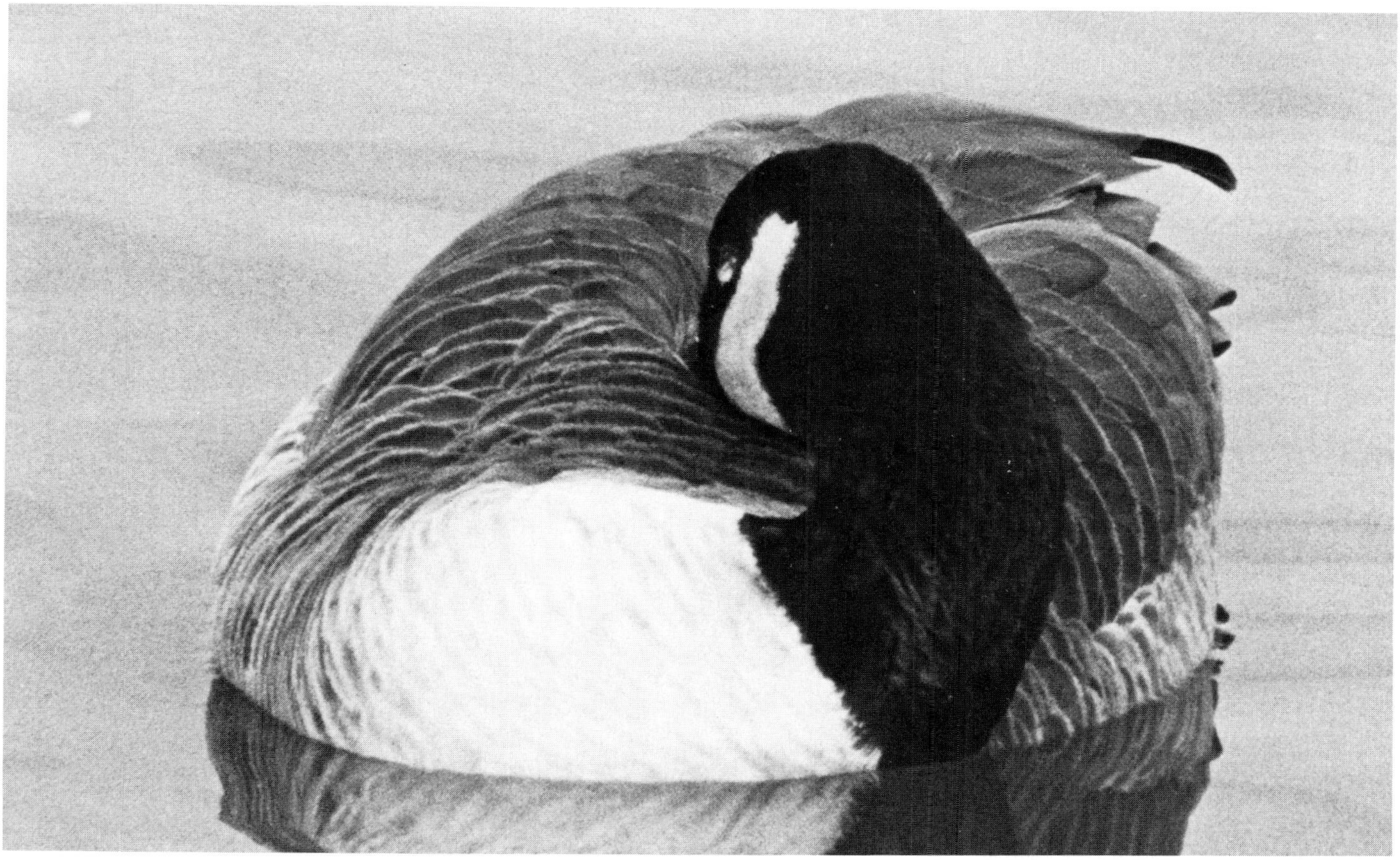

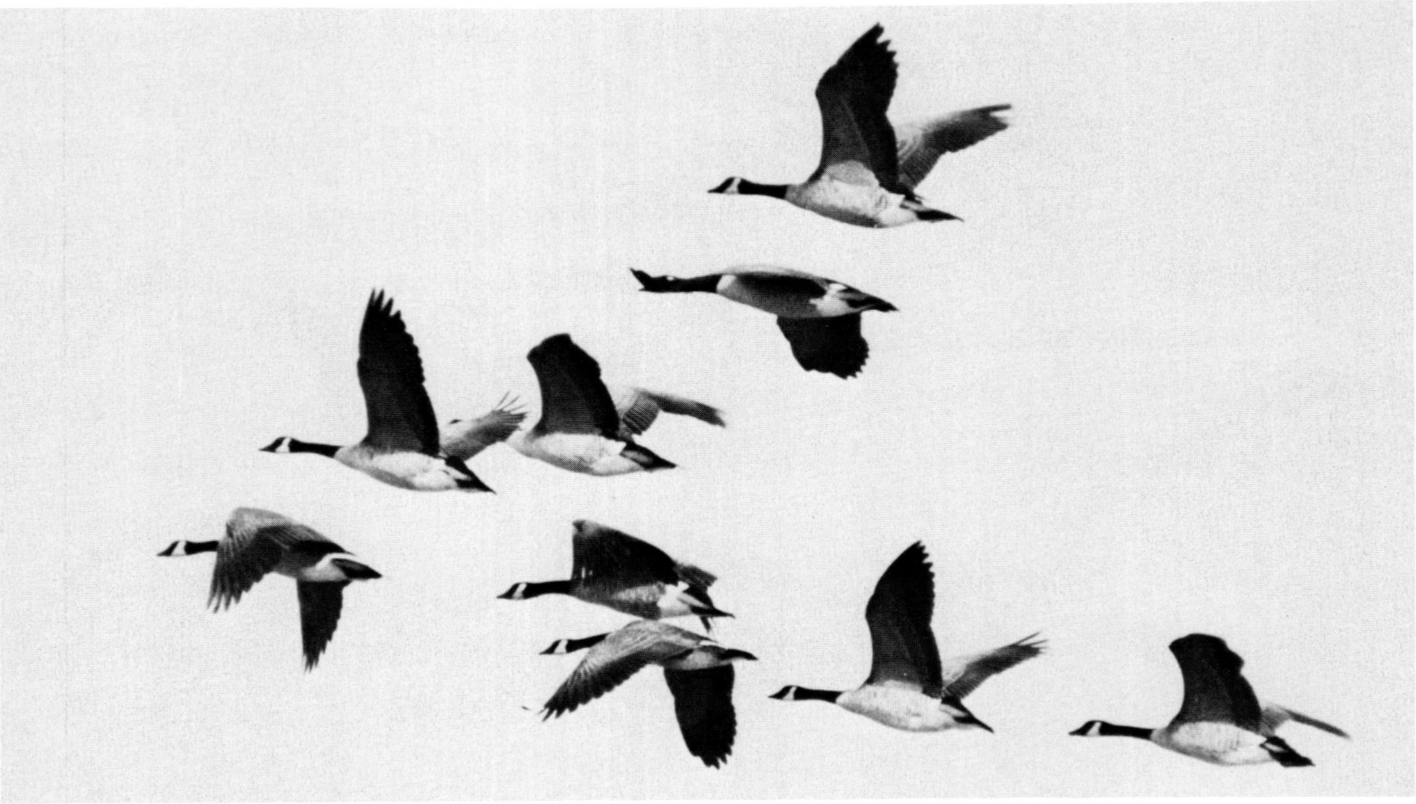

33-48 A group of Western honkers move into an echelon formation as they climb out.

33-49 Four Western Canadas with wings fixed glide in to look over the landing site.

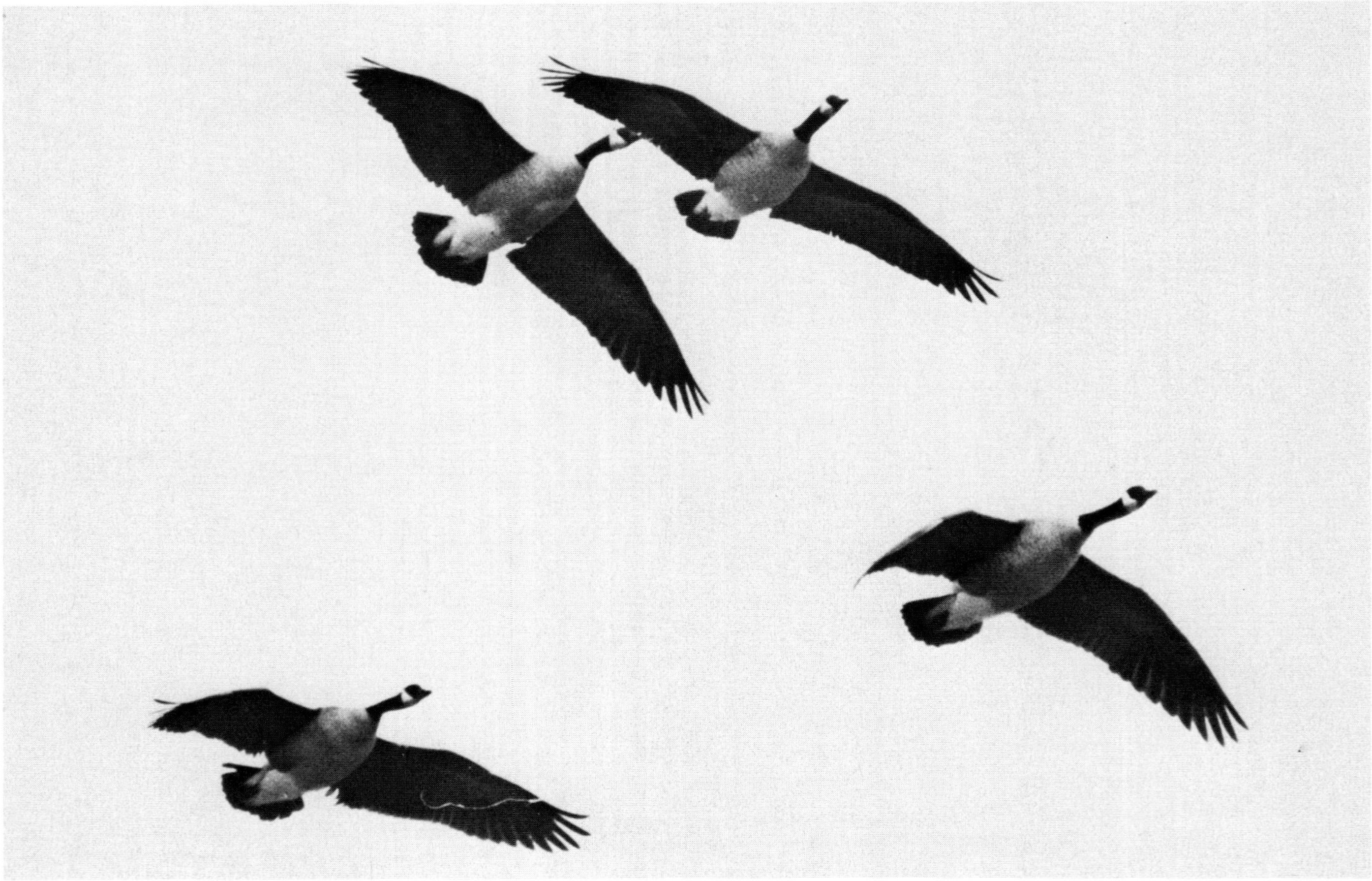

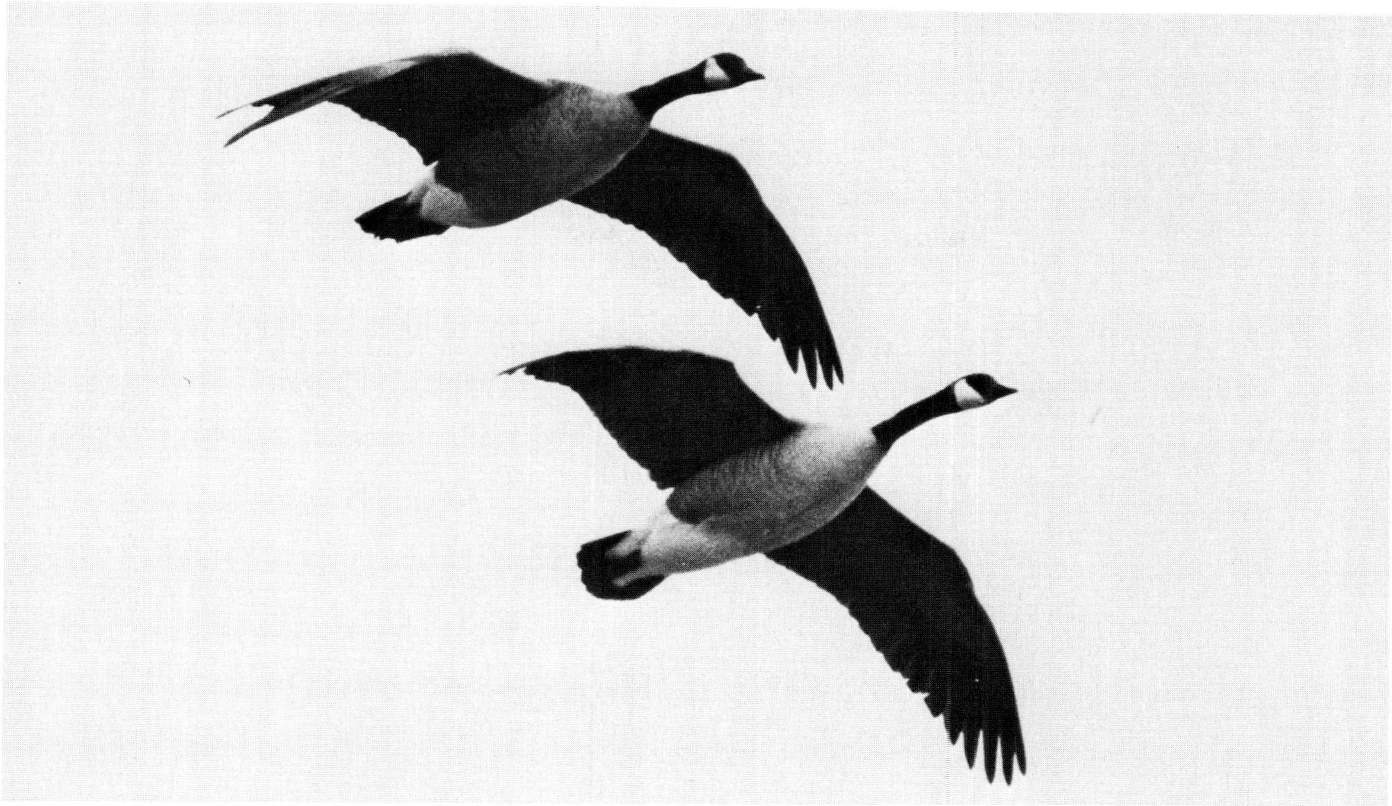

33-50

Two pairs of Western Canadas on the "final approach".

33-51

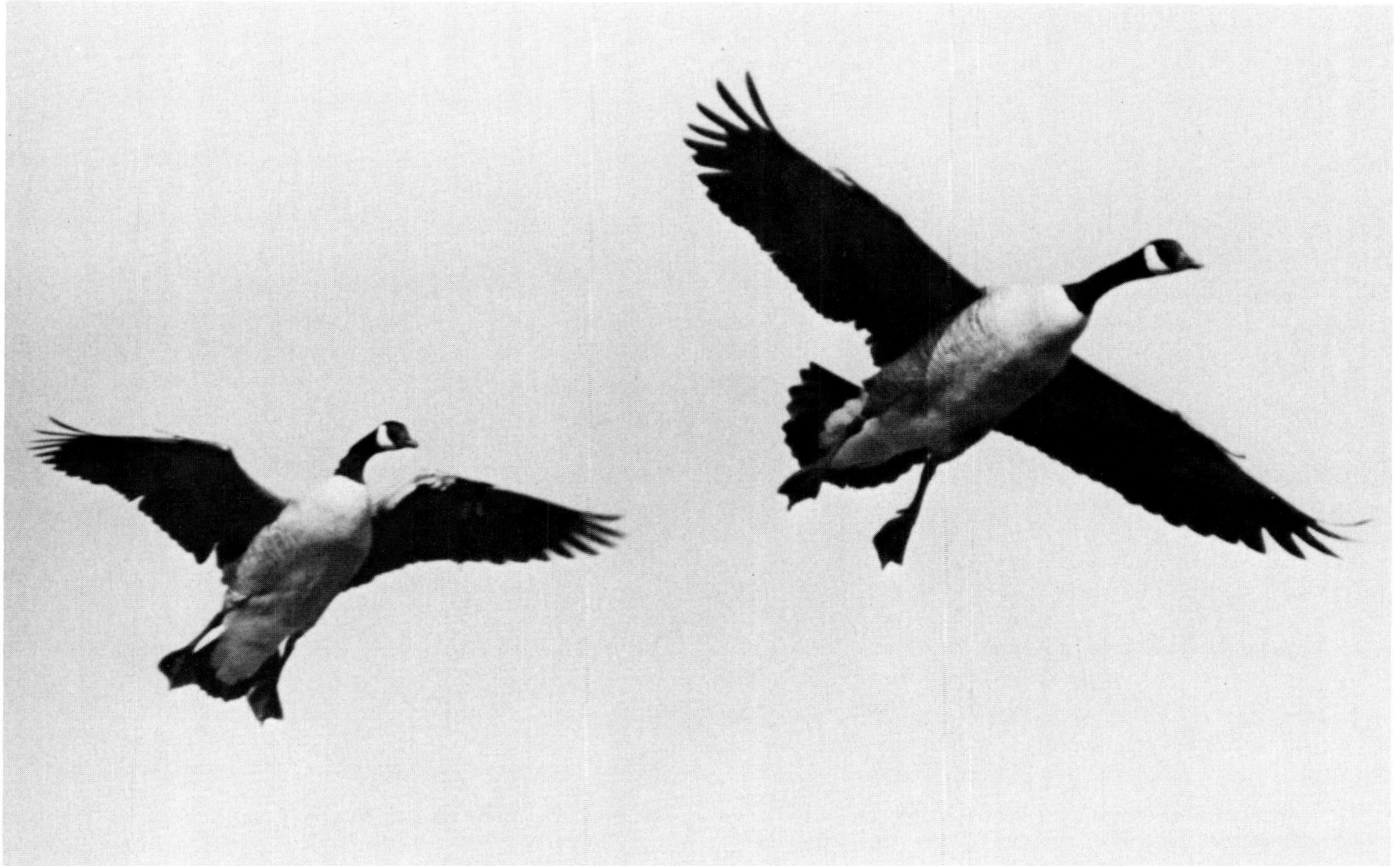

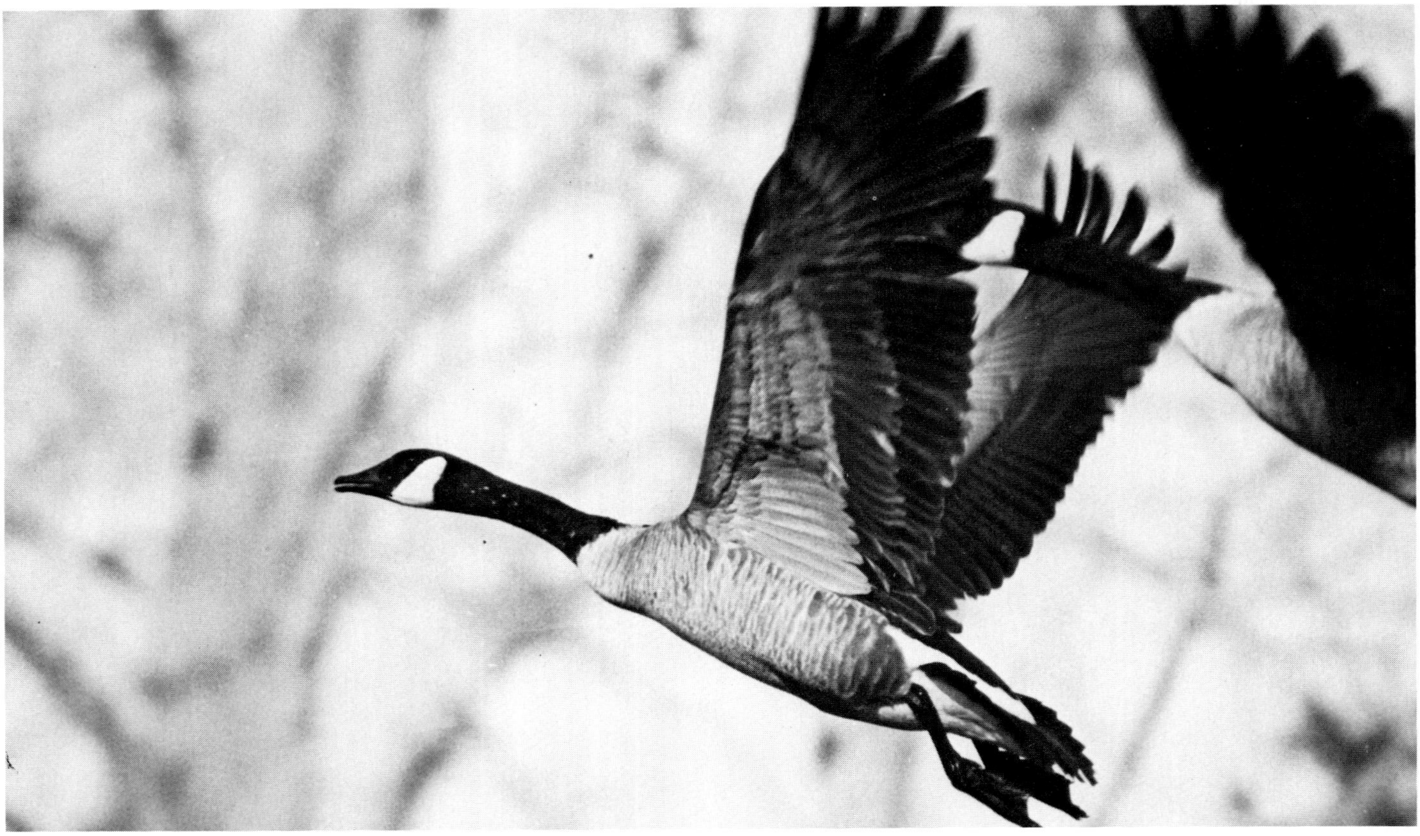

33-52 A pair of honkers climbing shortly after takeoff. Note flattened body, wing detail, and leg and feet position.

33-53 Three Western Canadas take off for their feeding grounds.

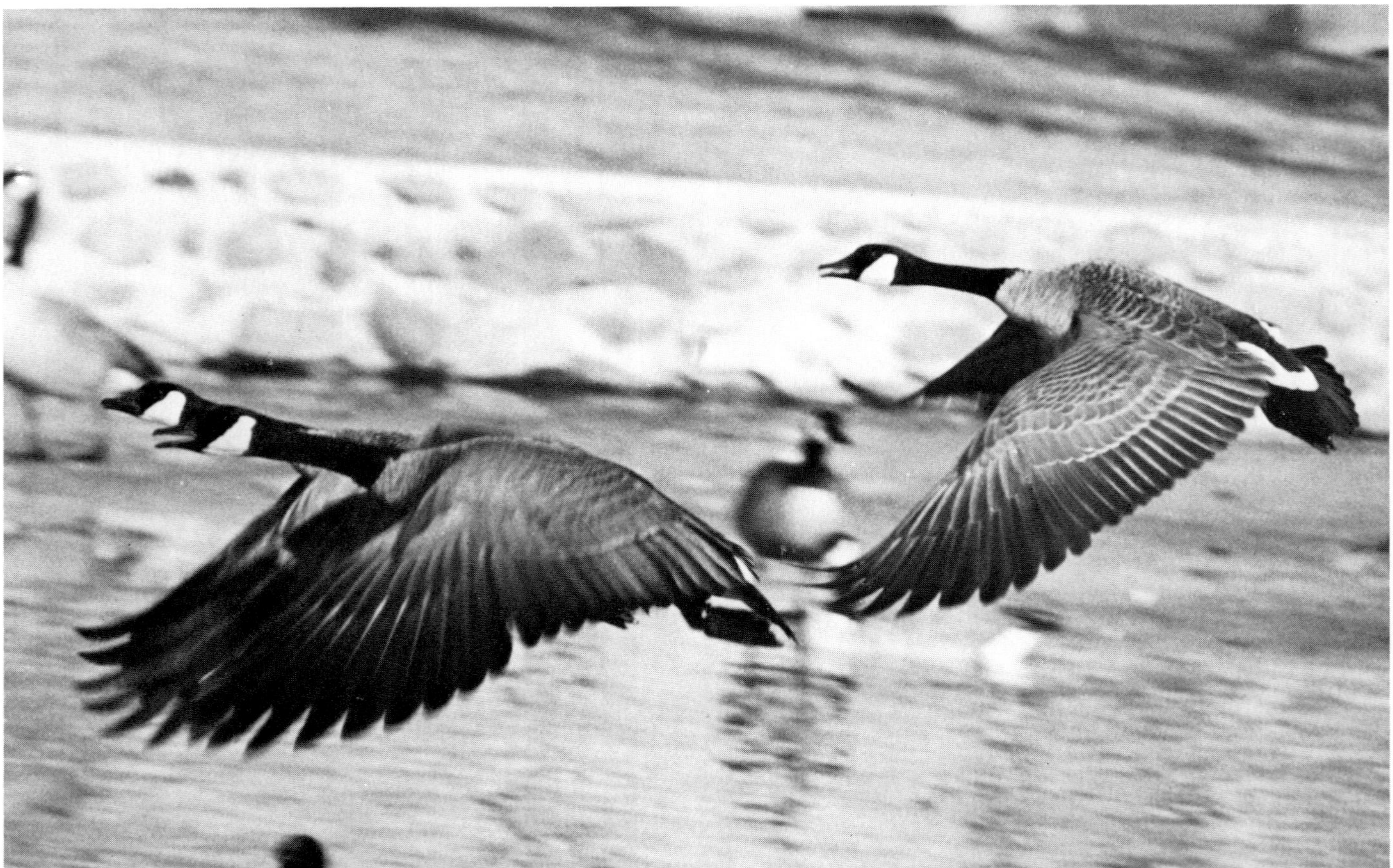

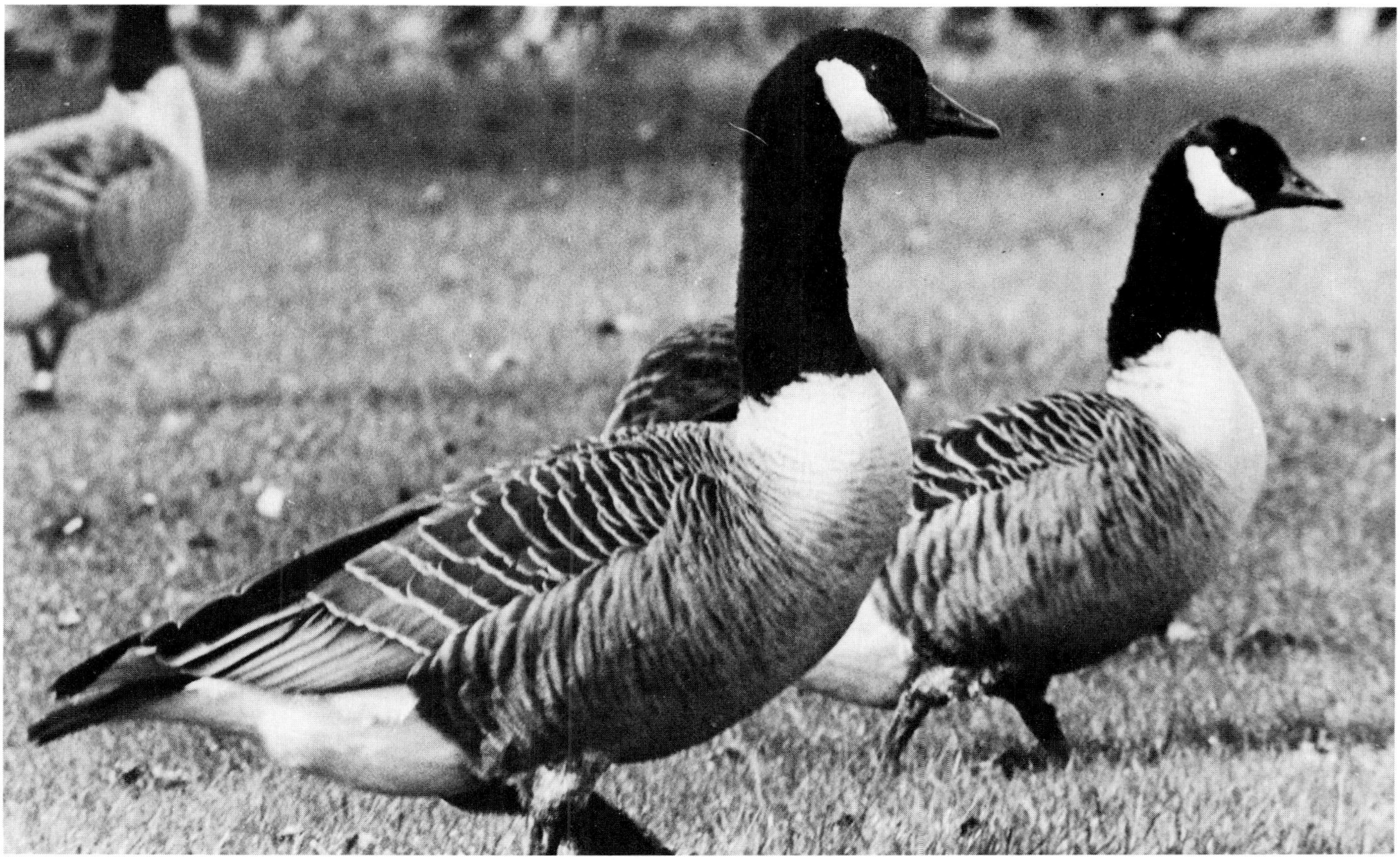

33-54 Pair of Atlantic Canada geese. They are about the same size as the Western Canada but are somewhat darker in coloration.

33-55 Nice profile of an Atlantic Canada gander.

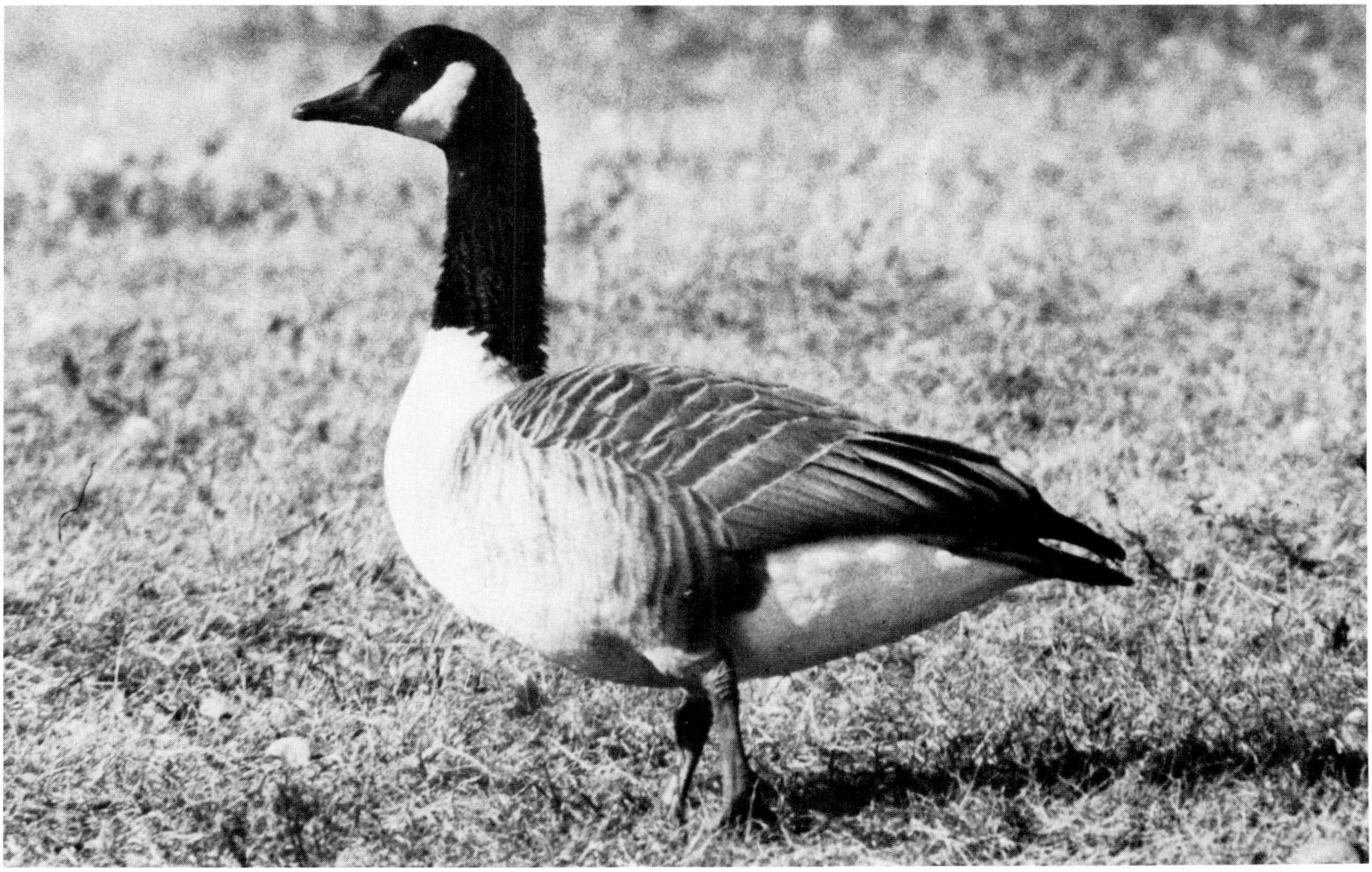

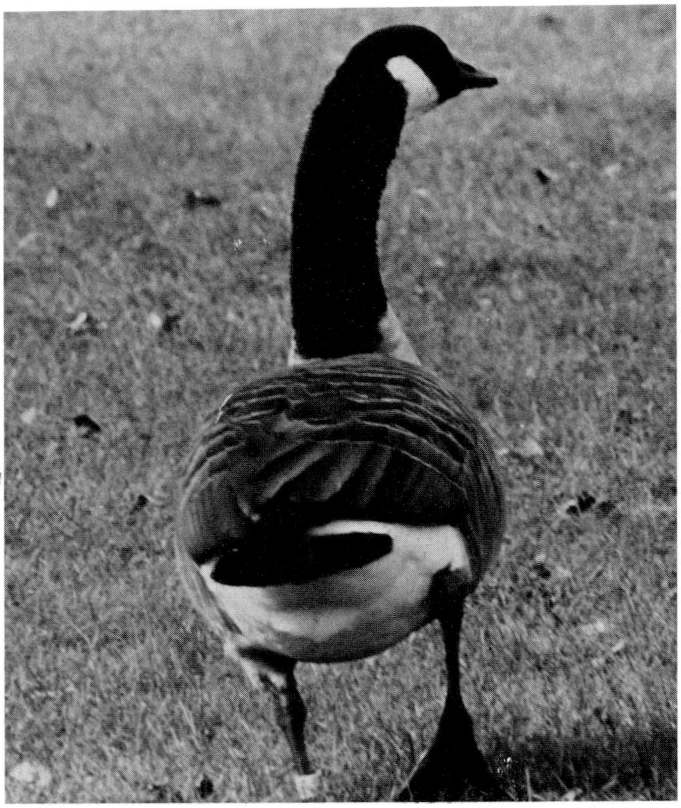

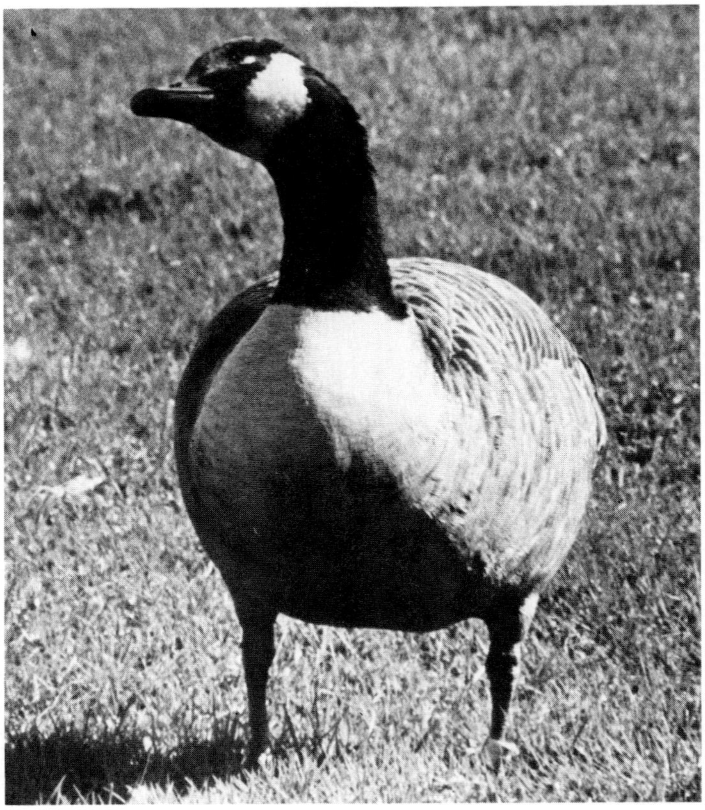

33-56 Rear and front views of Atlantic Canada geese. The bird on the left has turned his head so that he can look upward. 33-57

33-58 This Atlantic honker is very much alert.

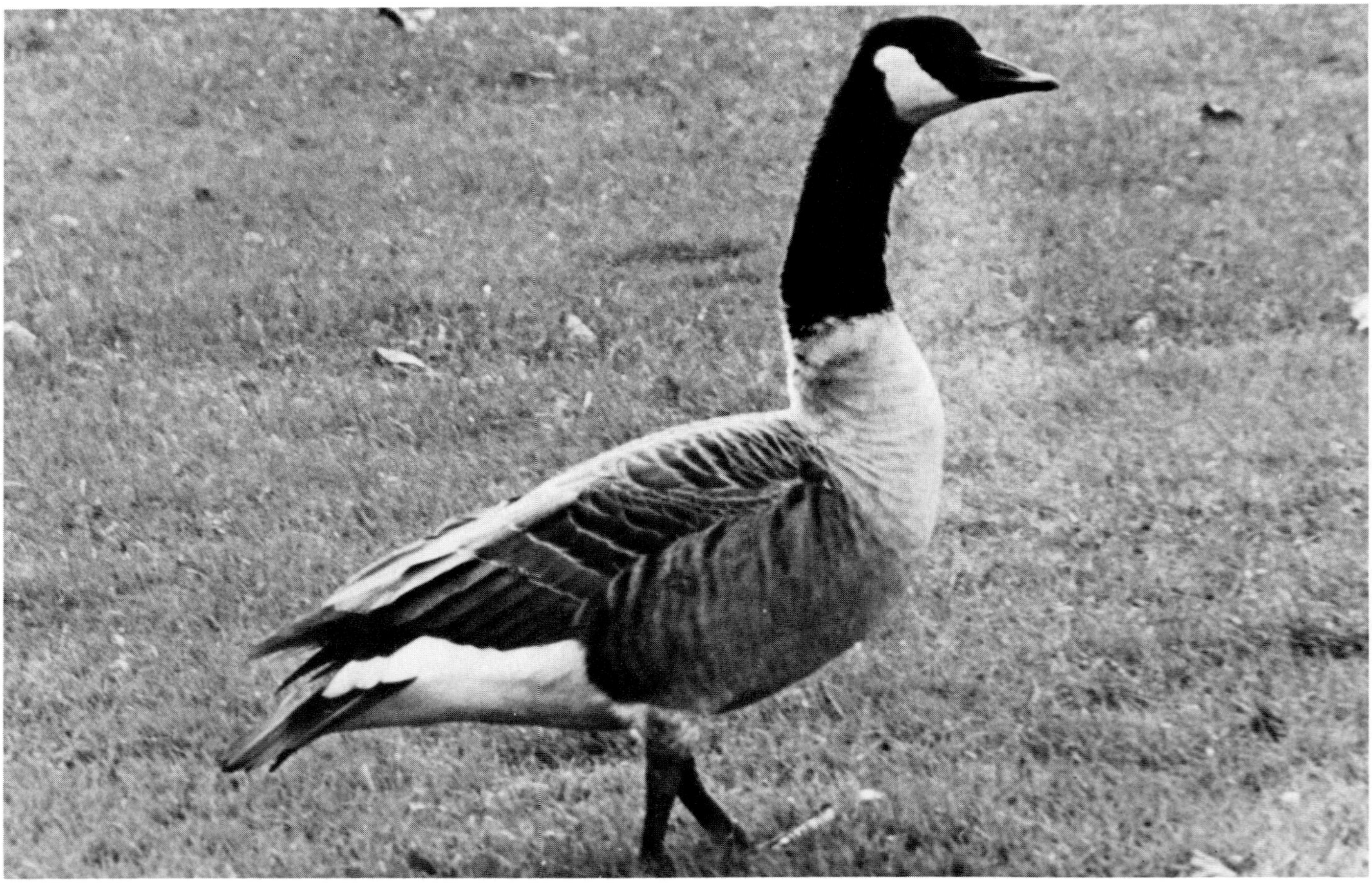

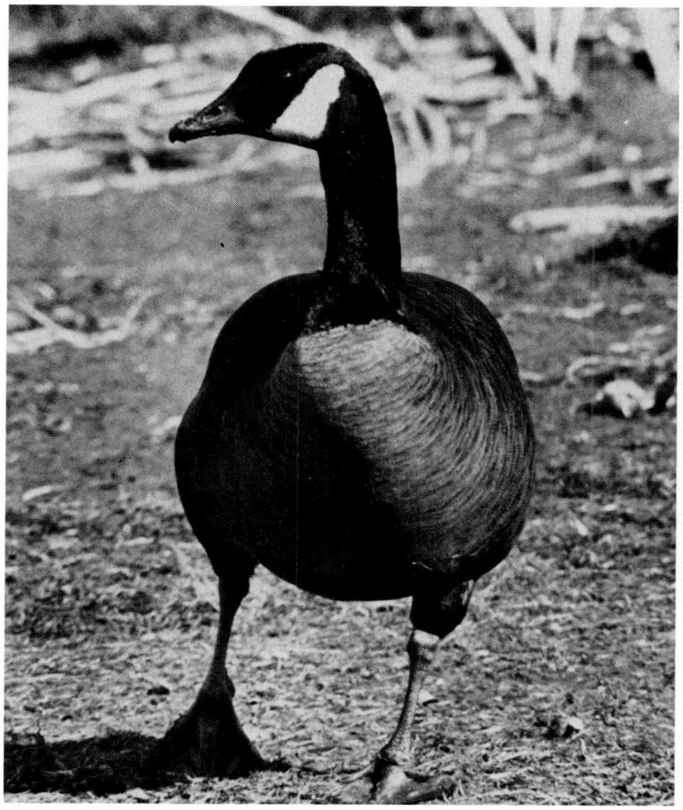

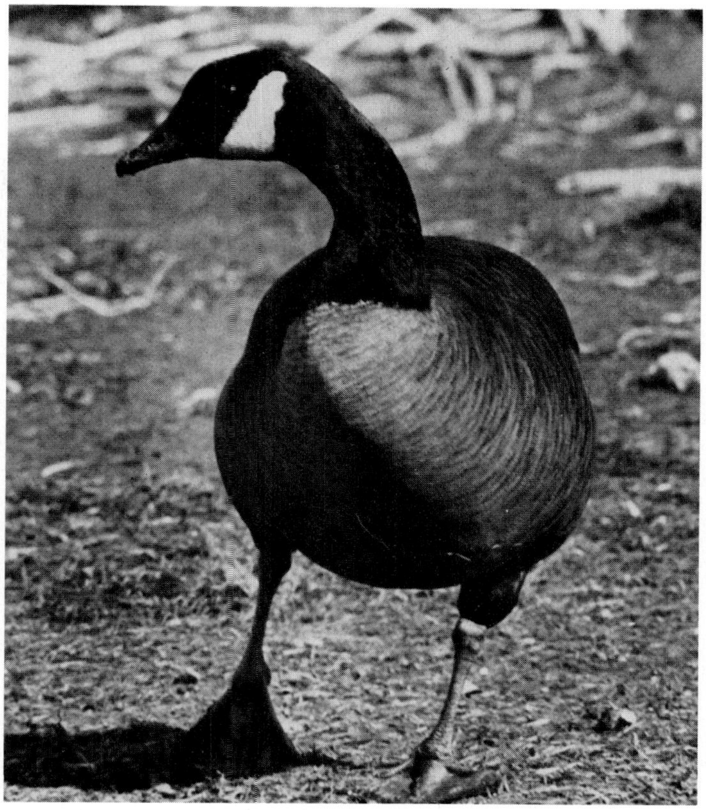

33-59 Front views of Vancouver Canada geese. Their general coloration is much darker than the Western and Atlantic Canadas but they are similar in size. 33-60

33-61 A striding Vancouver Canada goose.

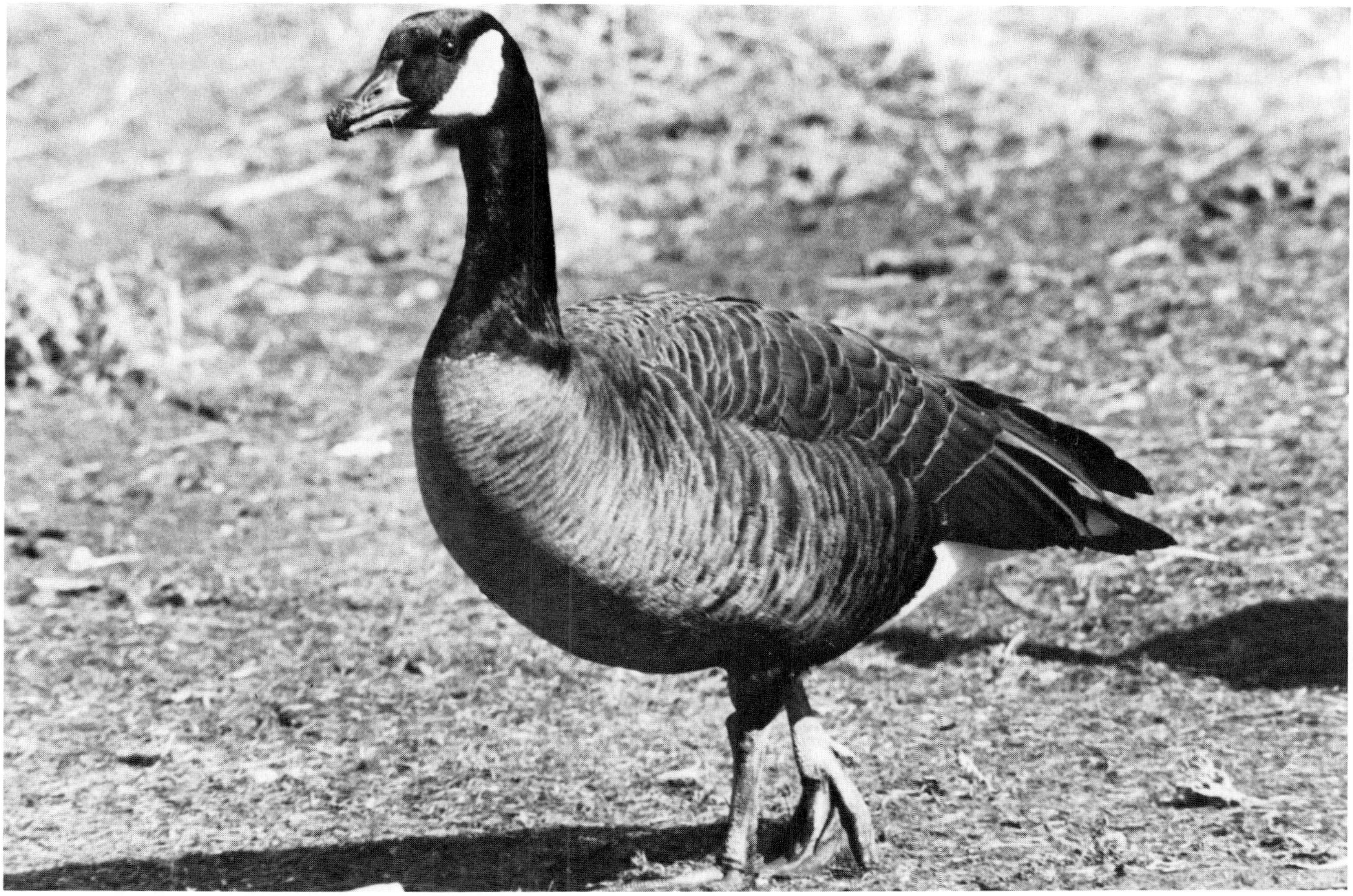

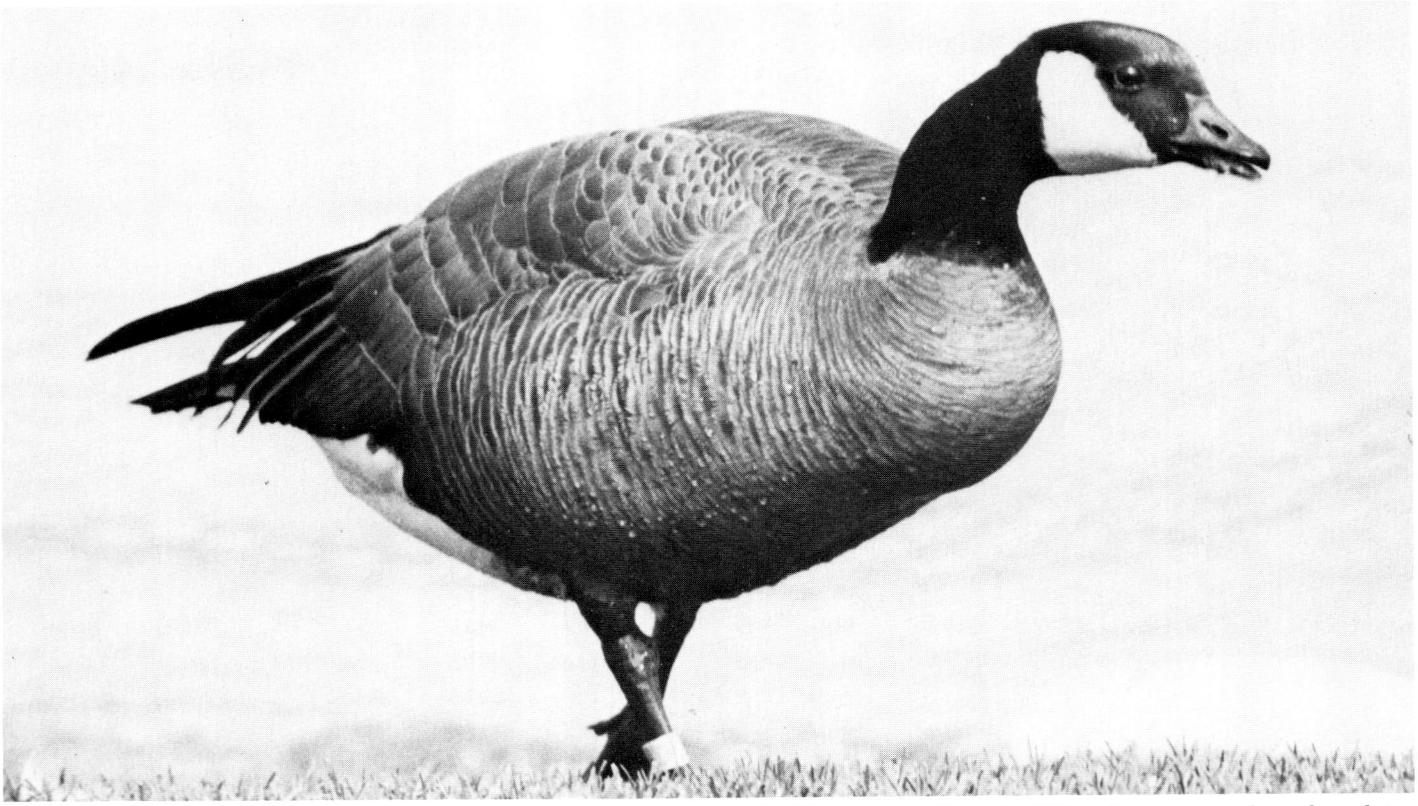

33-62 The smaller Dusky Canada goose is even darker than the Vancouver Canada. His color approaches chocolate.

33-63 Front view of the Dusky Canada goose.

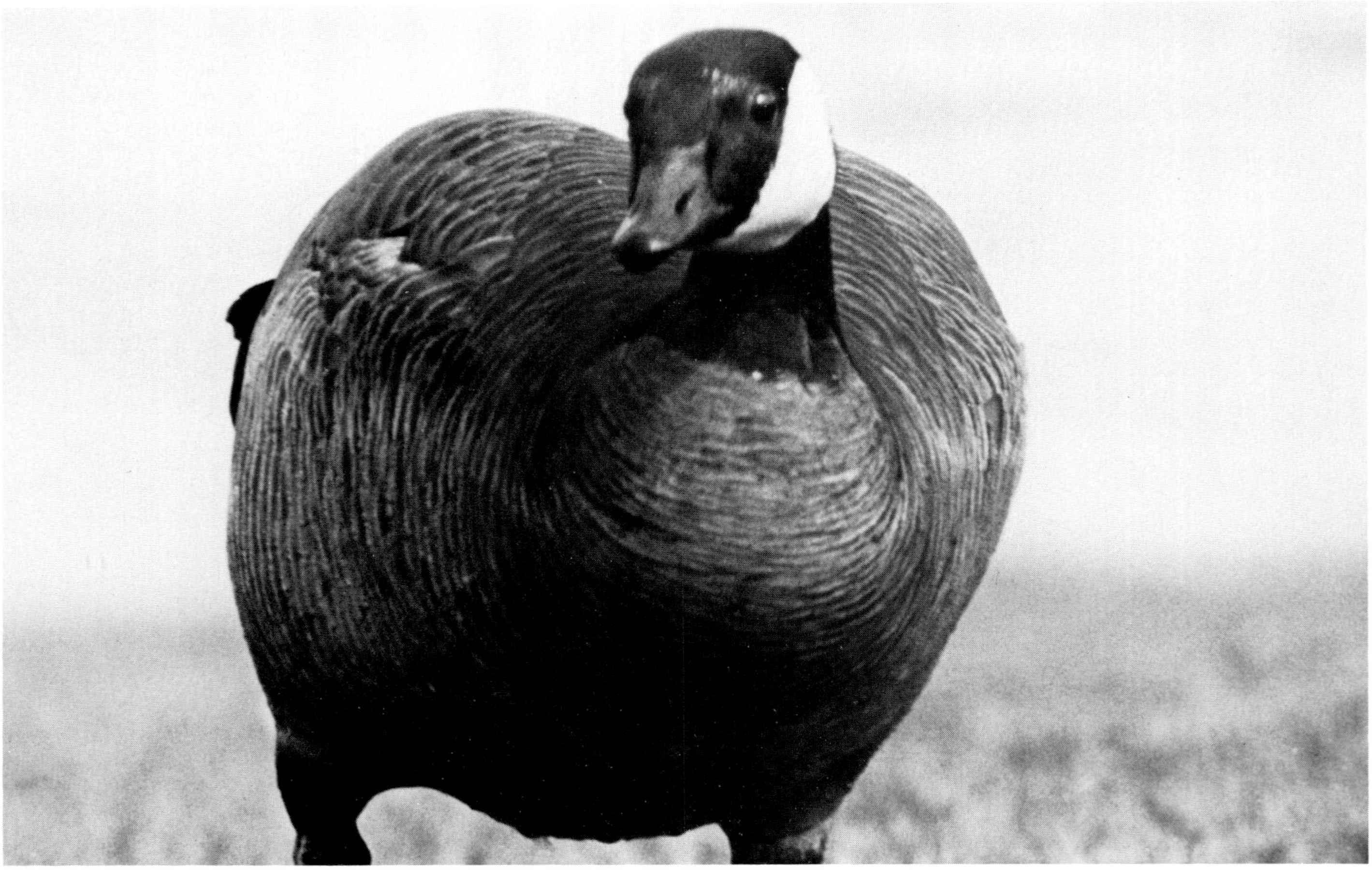

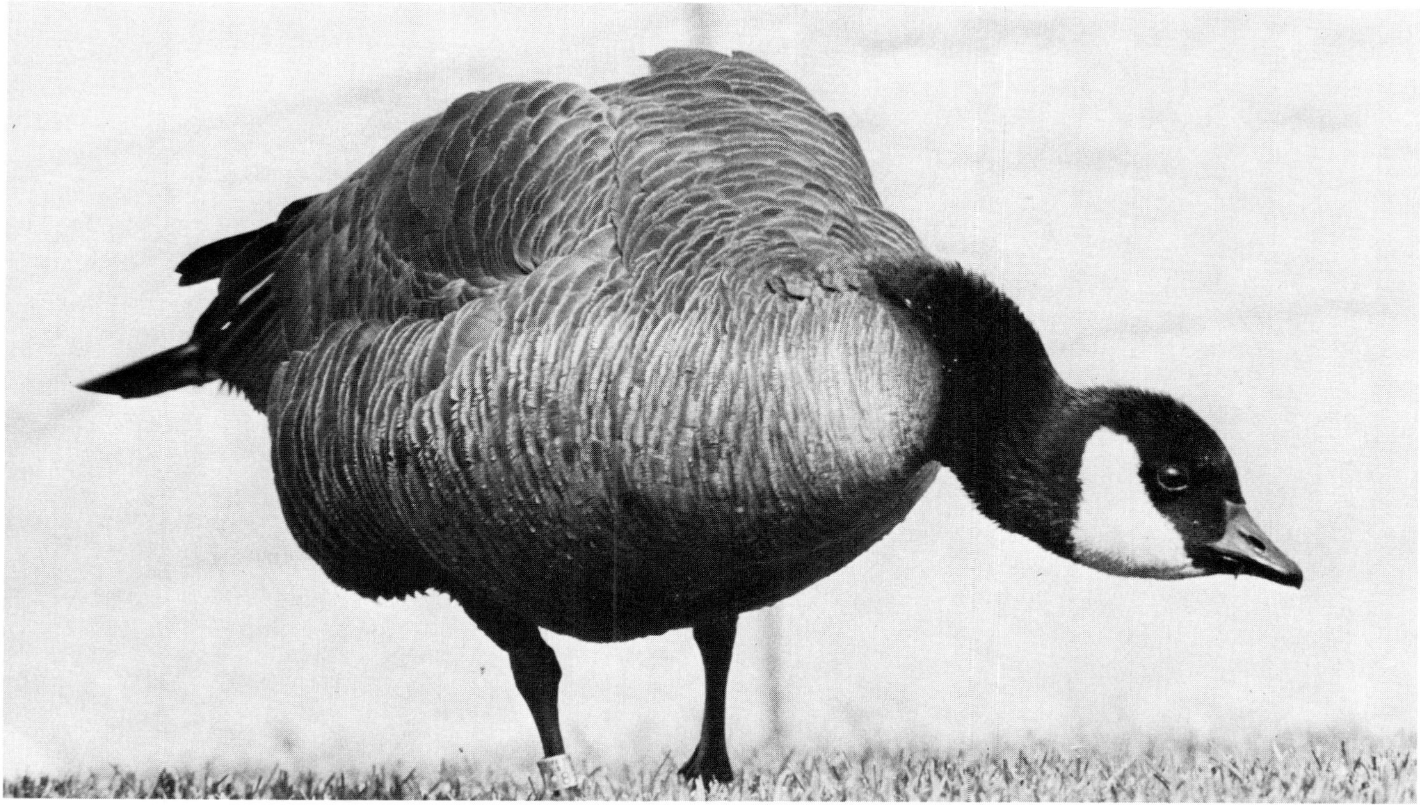

33-64 A Dusky Canada ruffles his feathers and assumes a threatening pose.

33-65 Good head, neck, and bill study of the medium size Dusky.

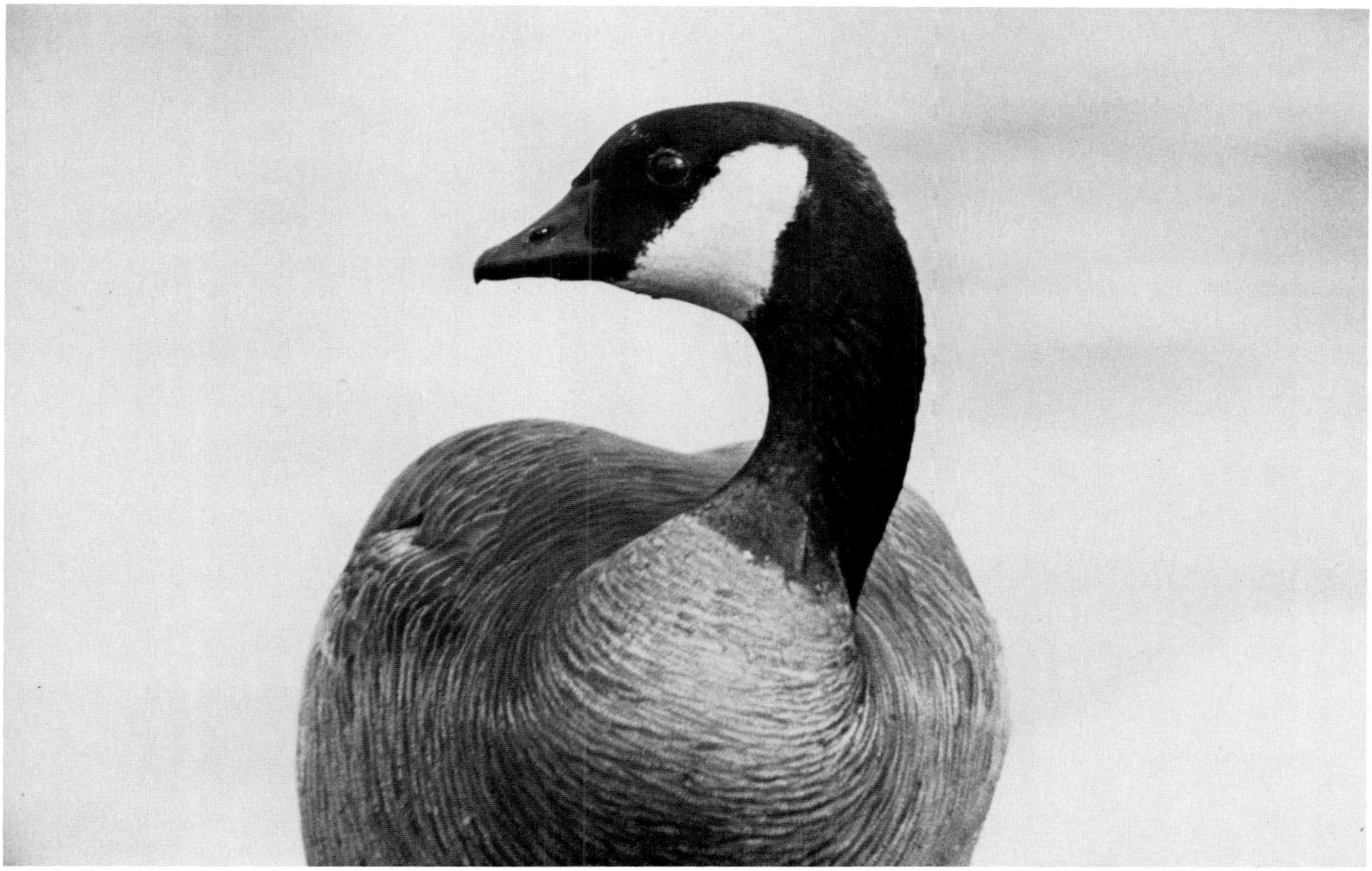

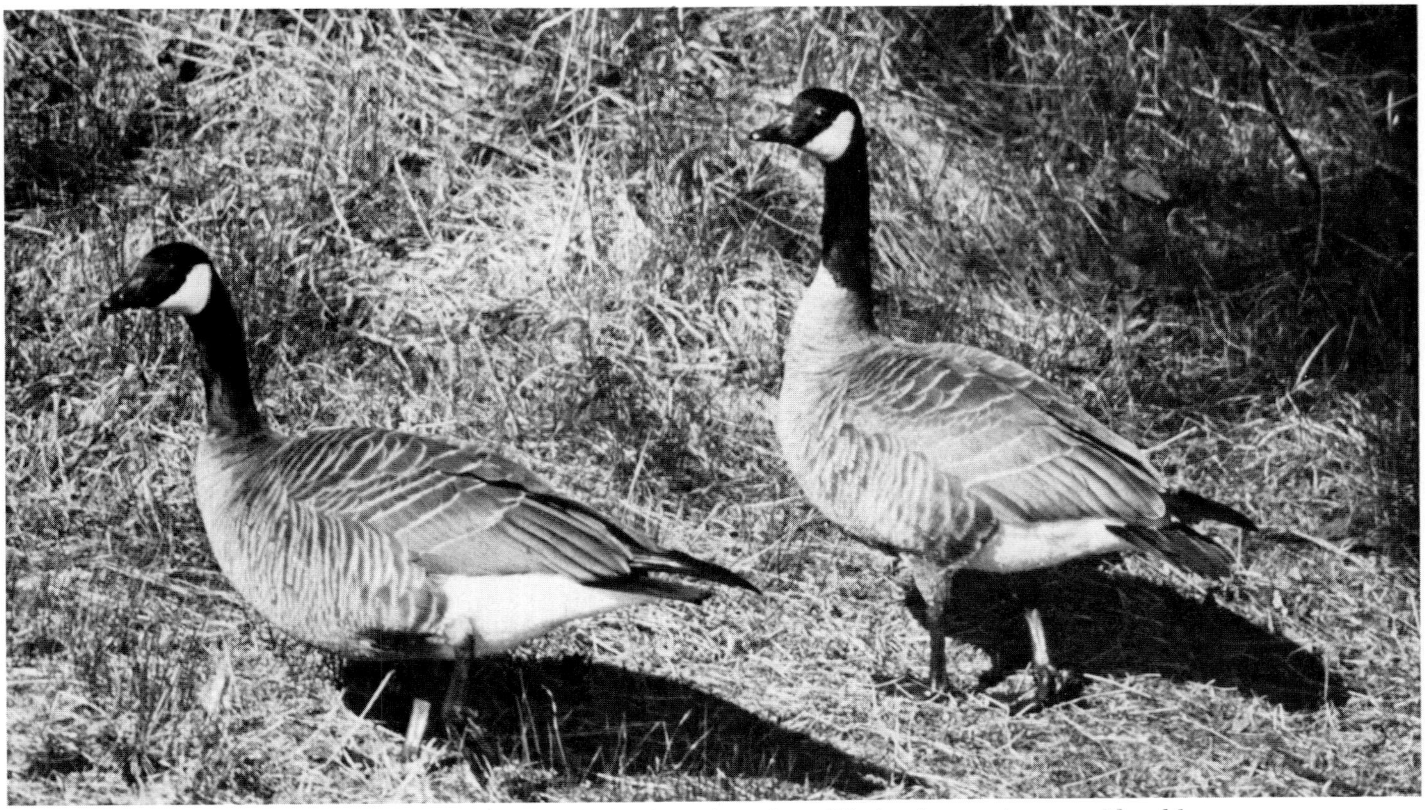

33-66 Lesser Canada geese. They are quite light in coloration. Their size varies considerably.

33-67 Lesser Canada goose, male.

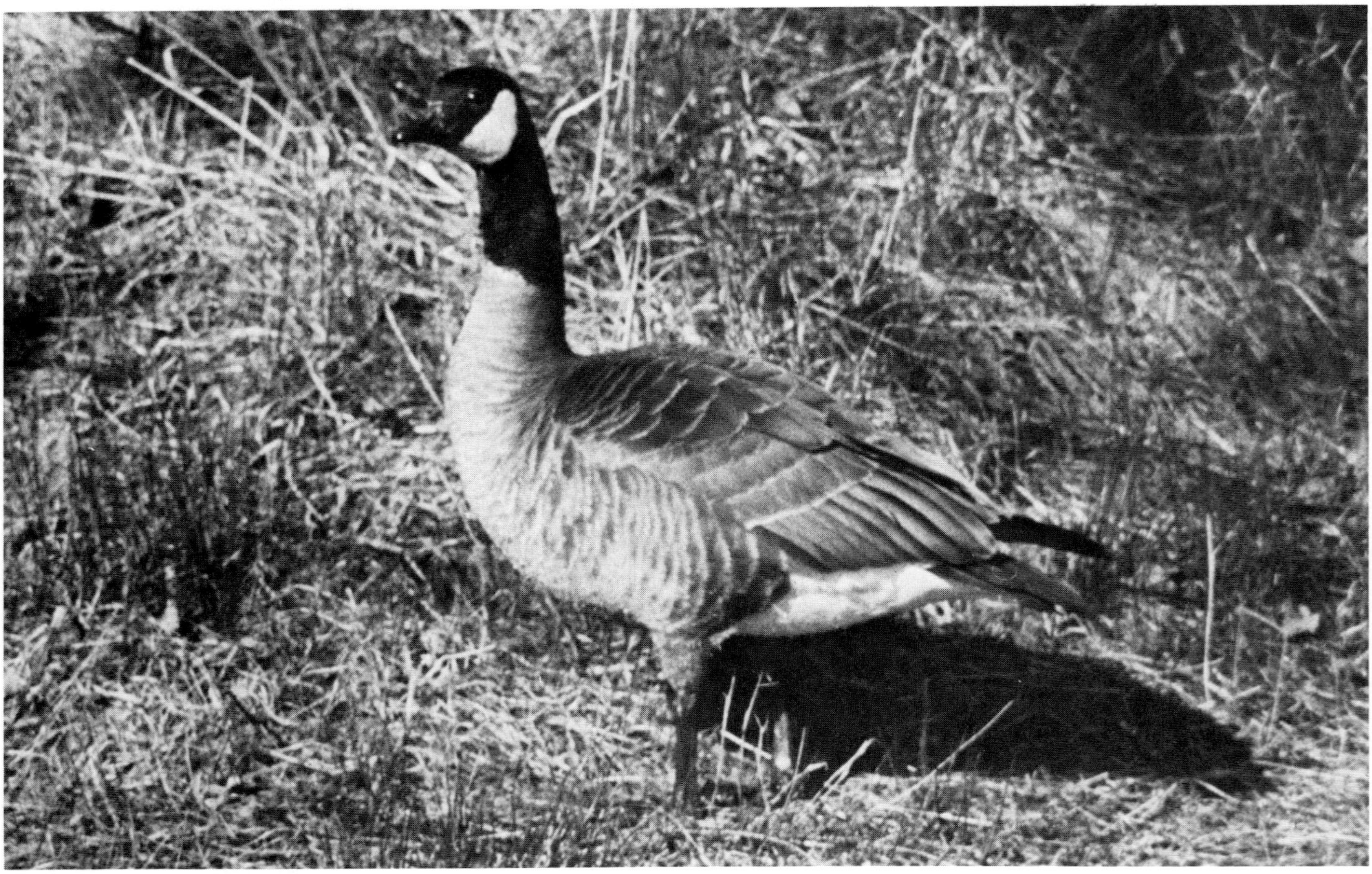

33-68

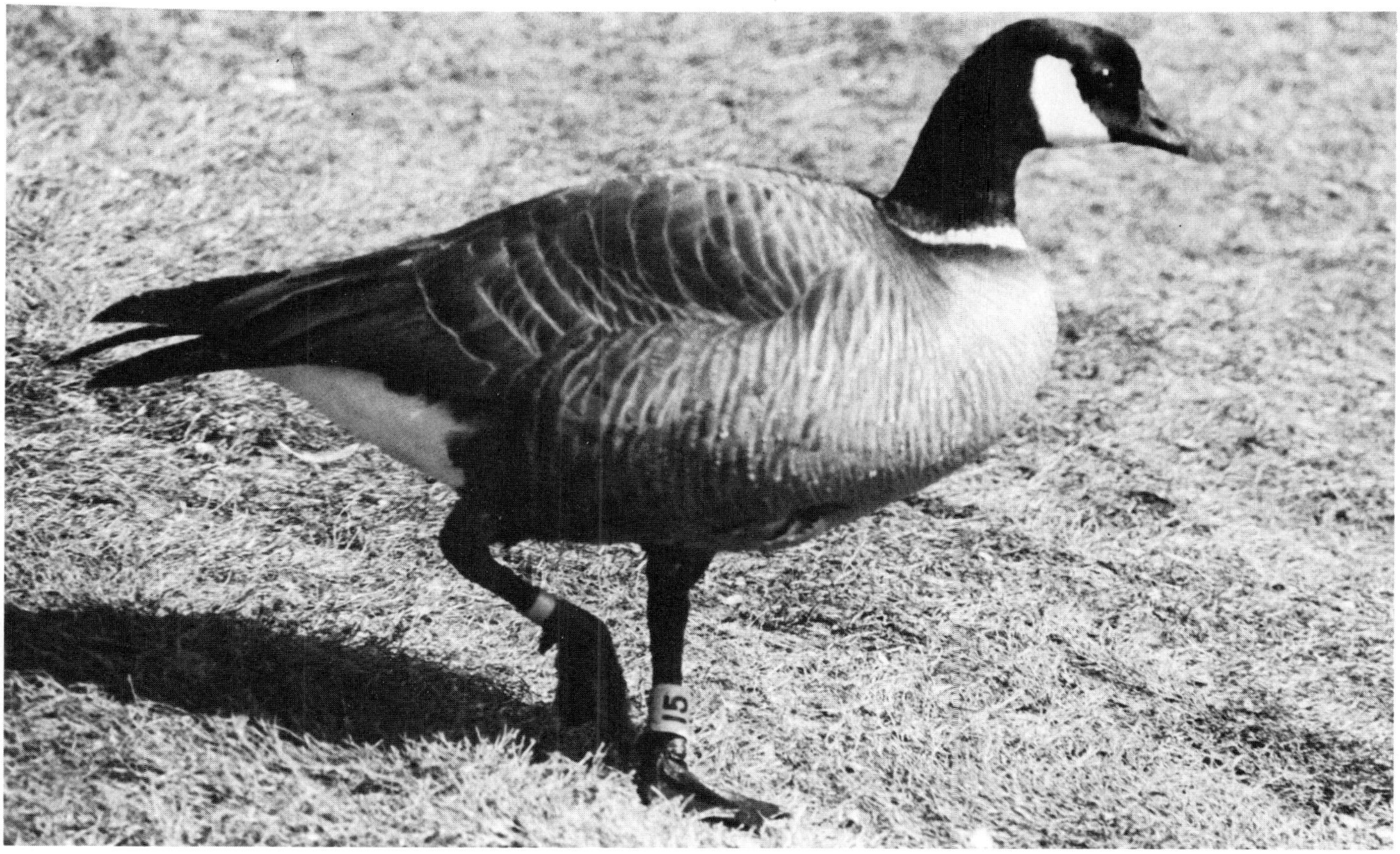

Striding Aleutian Canada goose. The fairly wide white band at the base of the black stocking is a common marking of this subspecies.

33-69

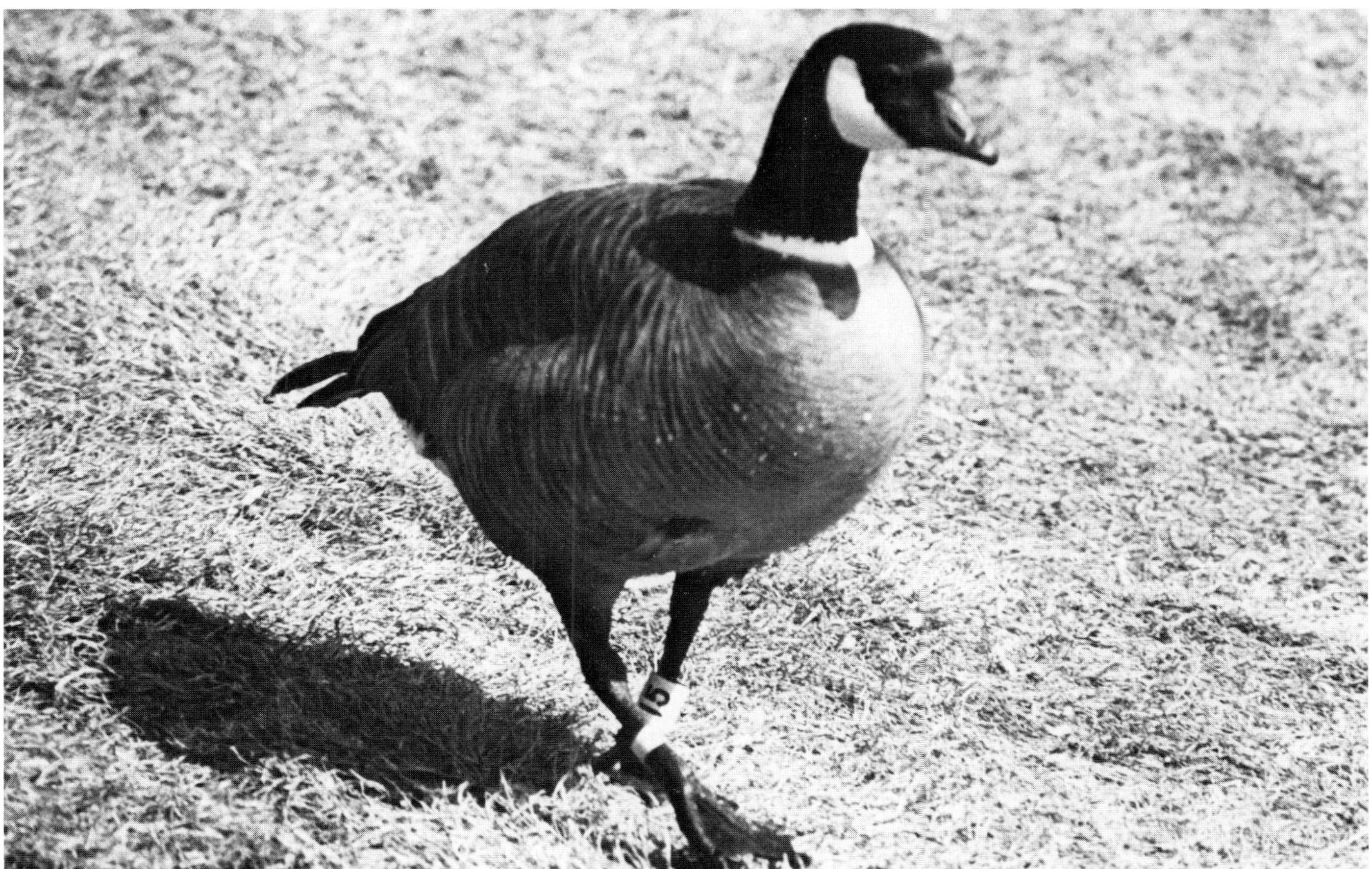

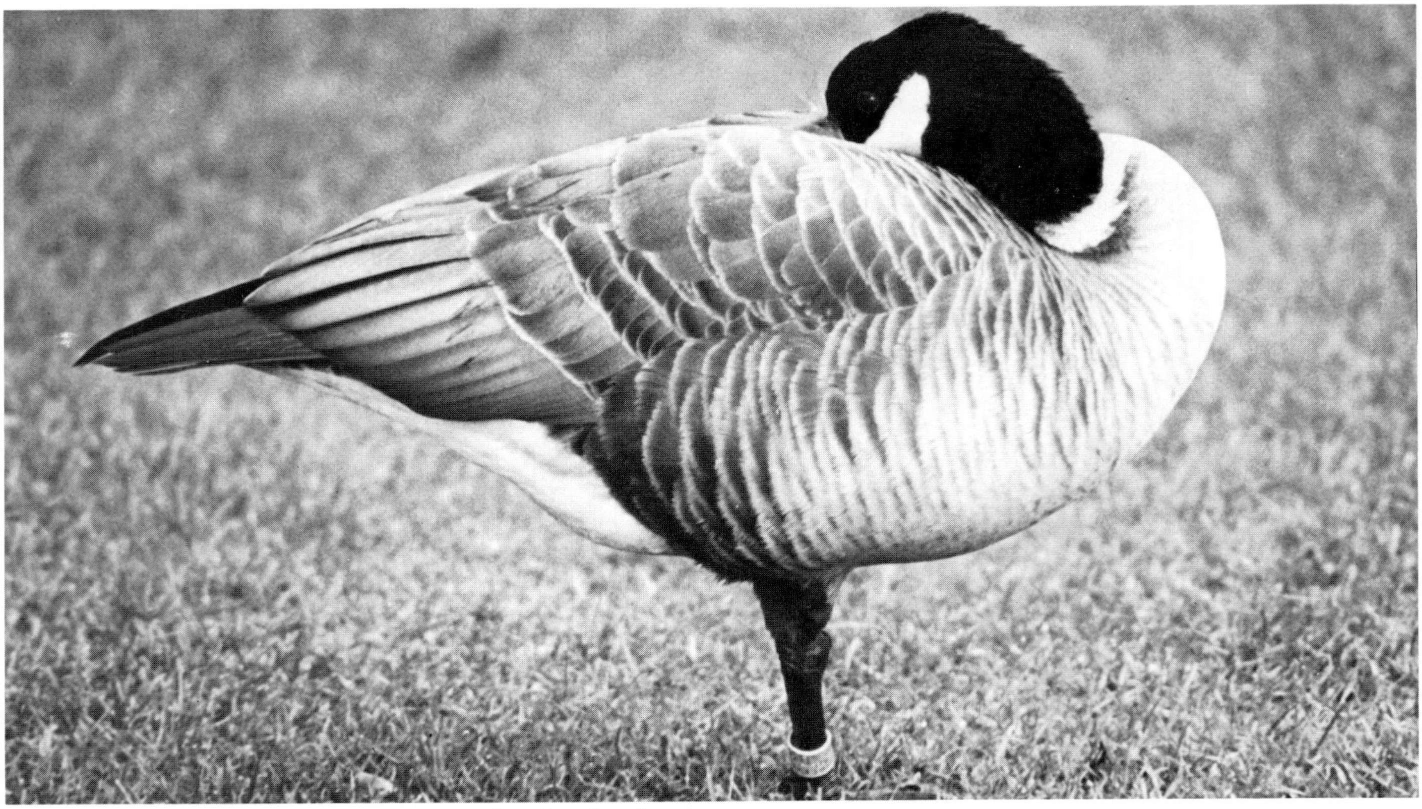

33-70 An Aleutian Canada goose in the classic sleeping pose.

33-71 The Aleutian Canada is somewhat larger in size and lighter in coloration than the Cackling Canada goose.

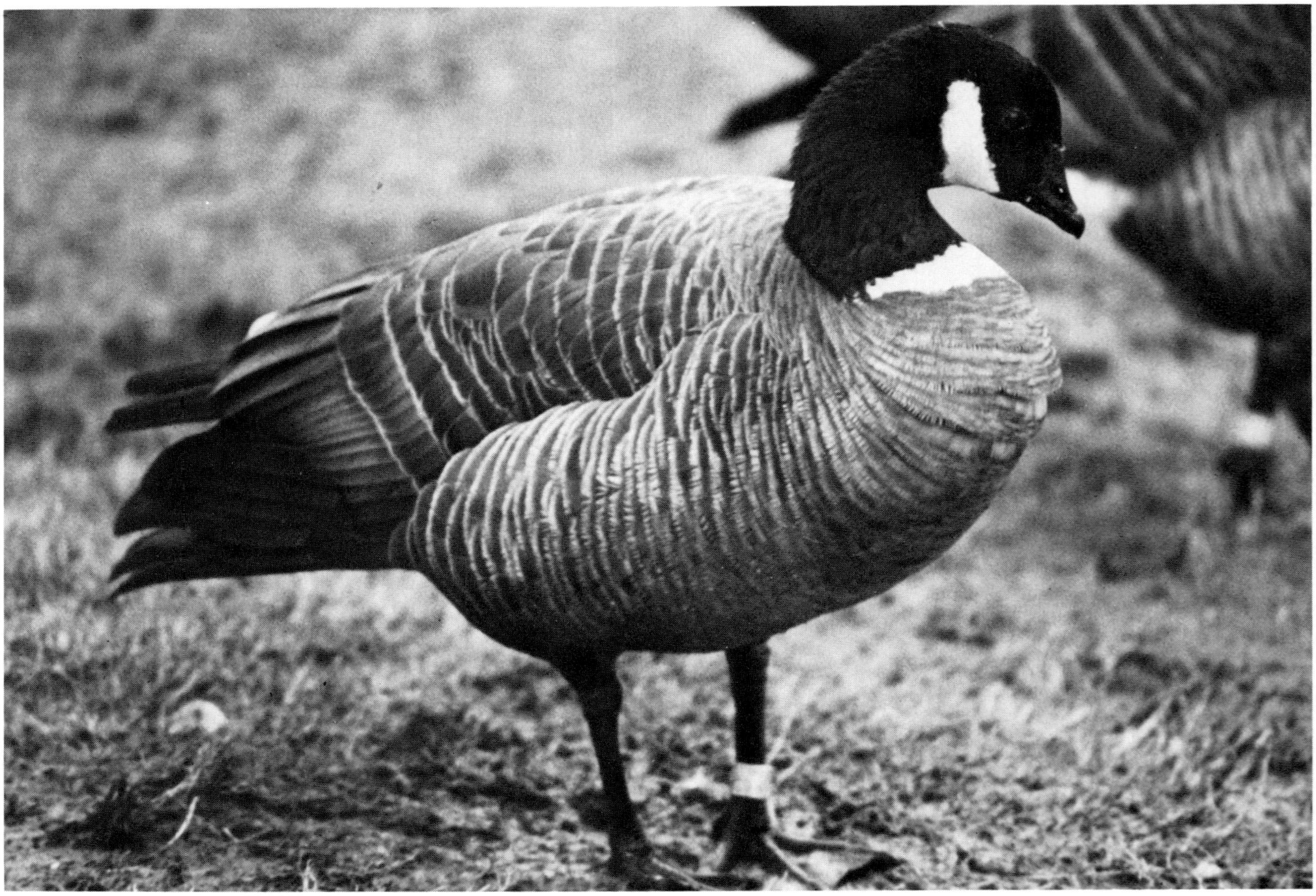

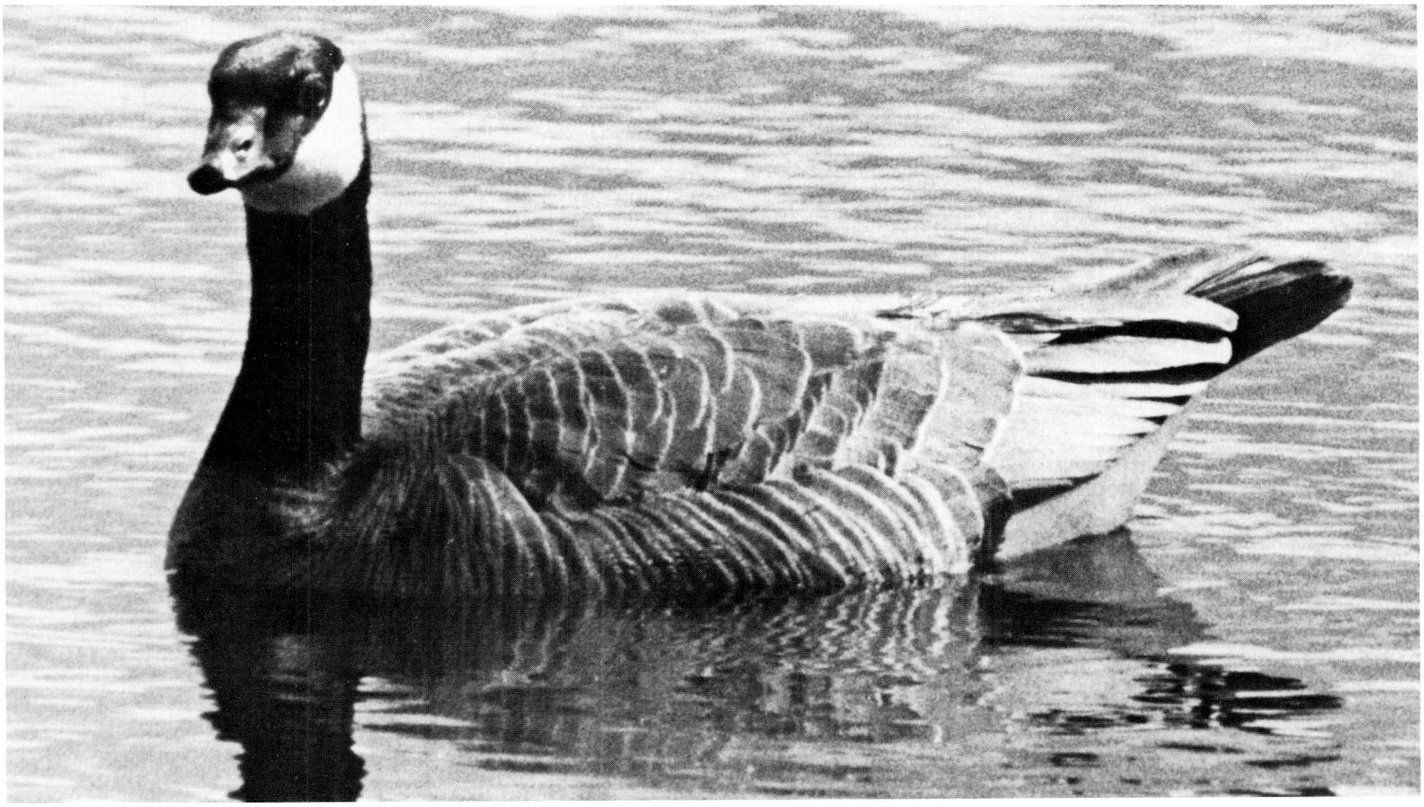

33-72

Tavener's Canada geese, sometimes called Western Lessers. The bird in the lower photograph is being aggressive—nice profile pose.

33-73

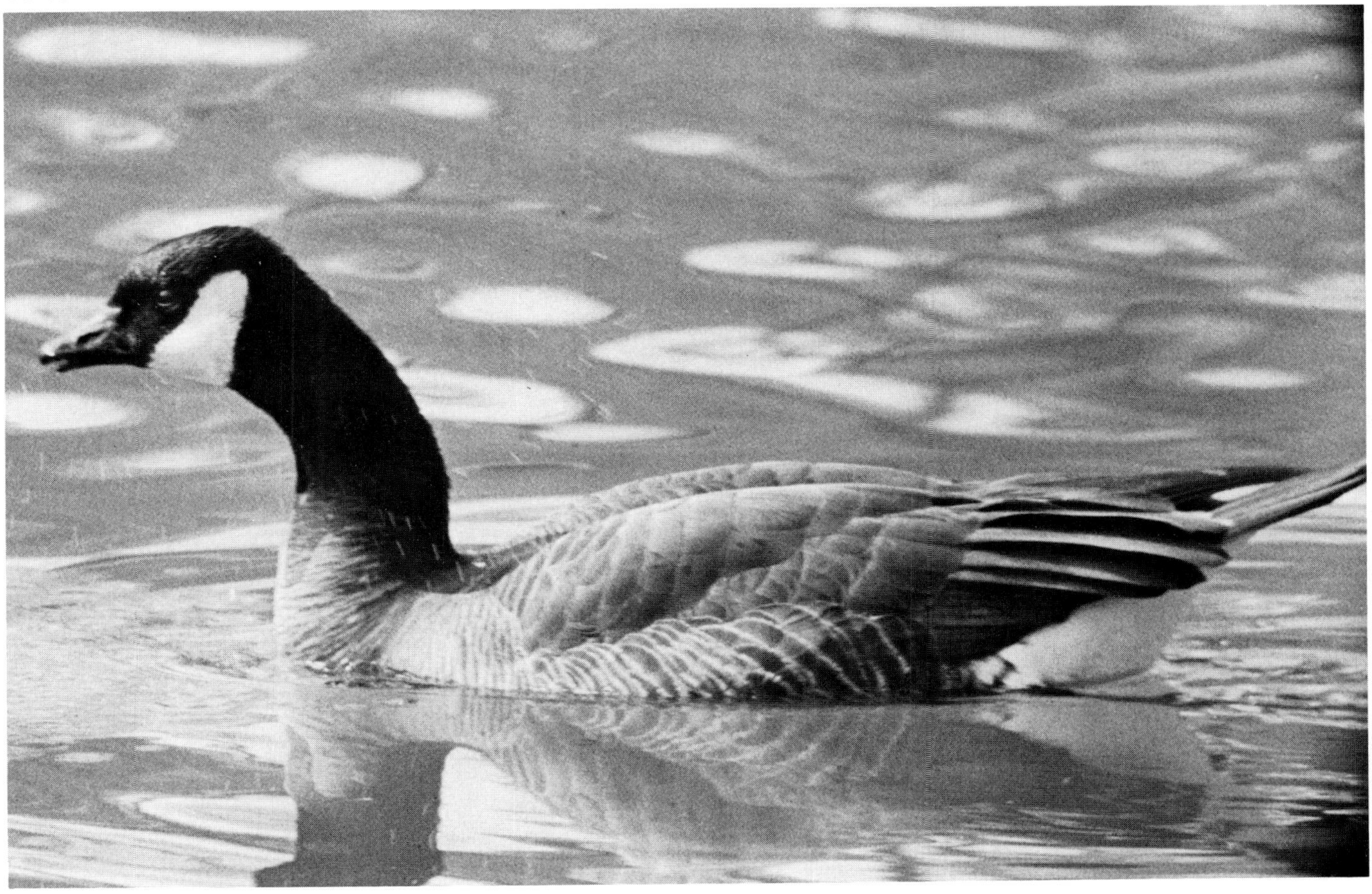

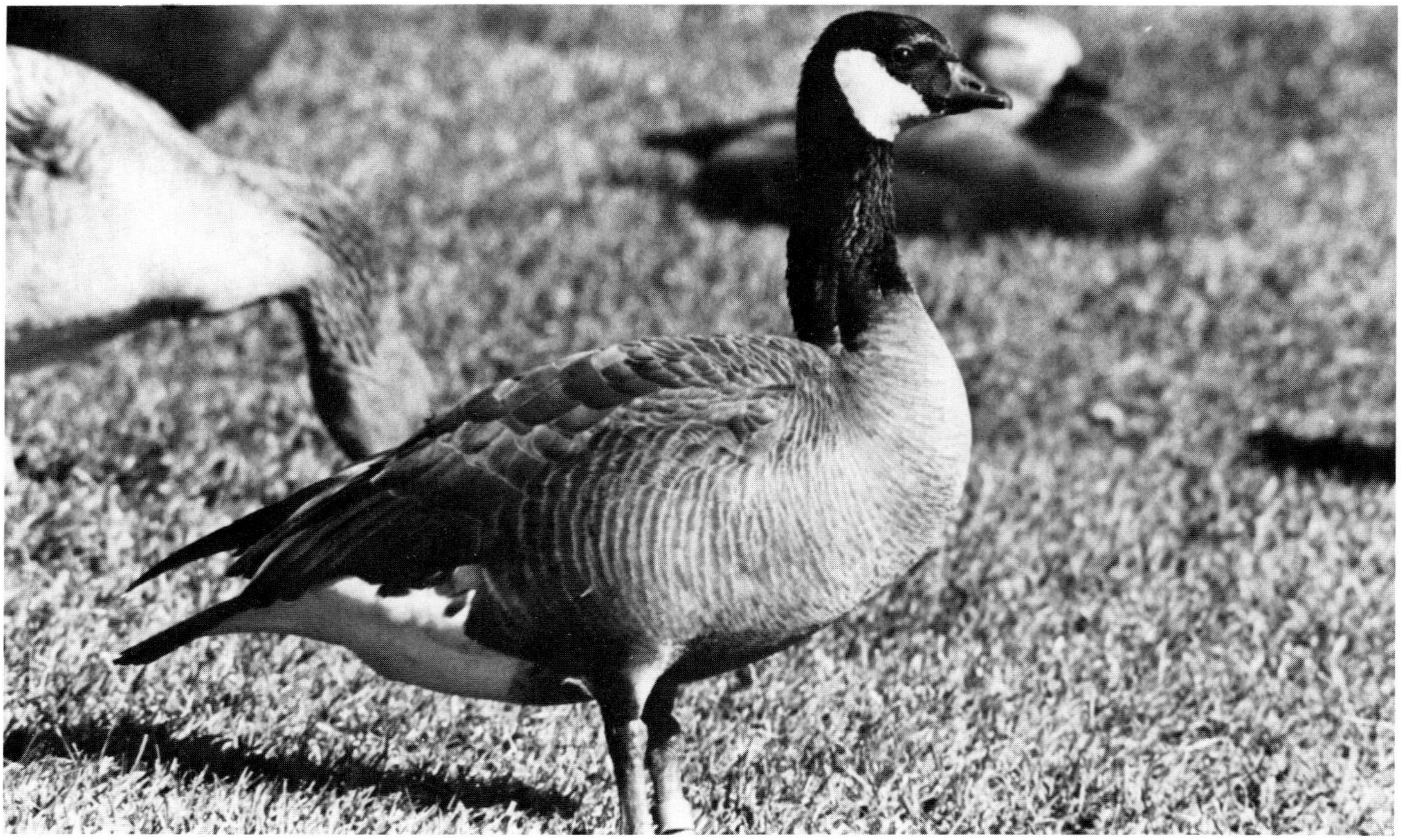

33-74

Two studies of the Cackling Canada goose. He is the smallest of our geese—about the size of a mallard duck. His general coloration is dark.

33-75

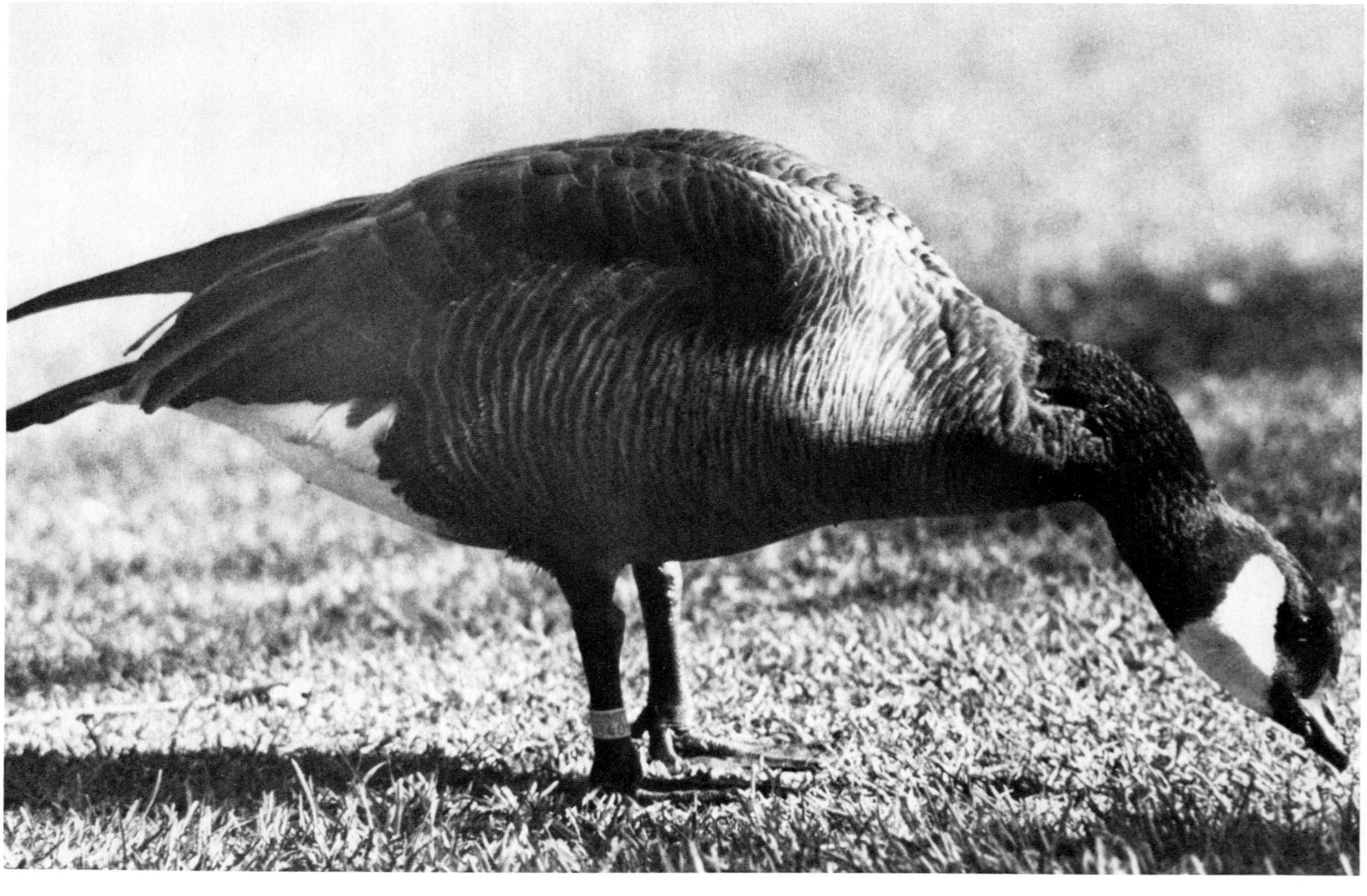

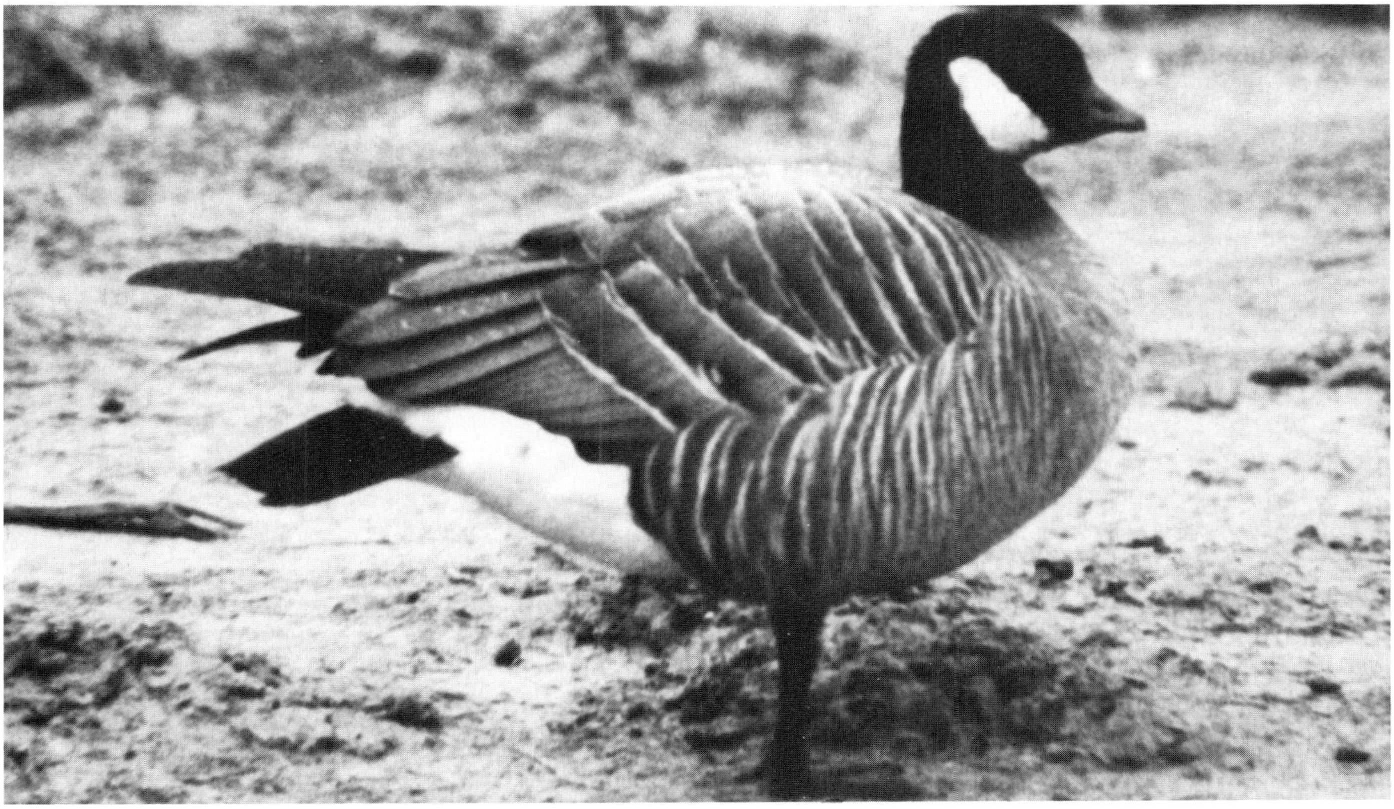

33-76

Two more studies of little Cacklers.

33-77

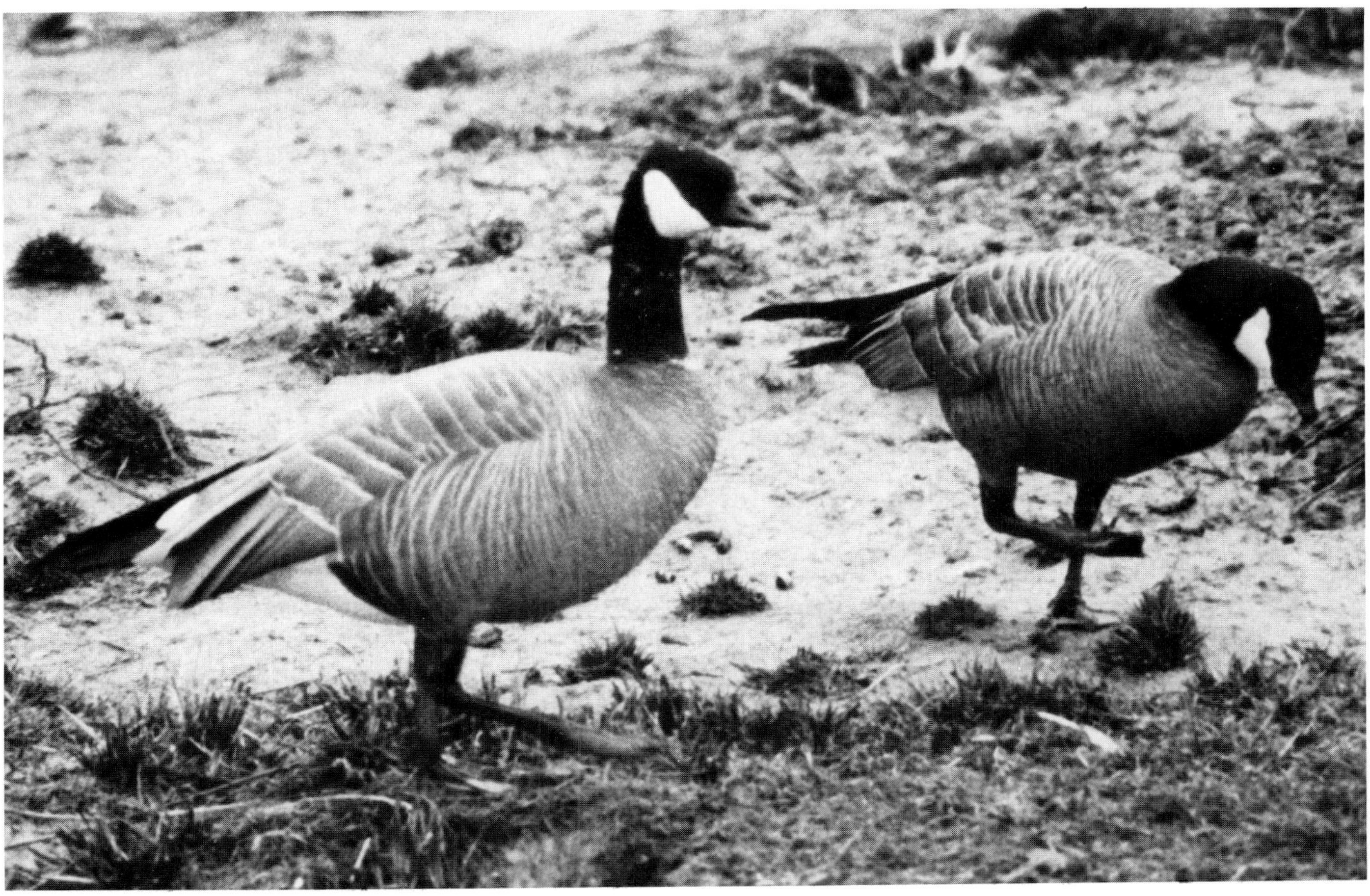

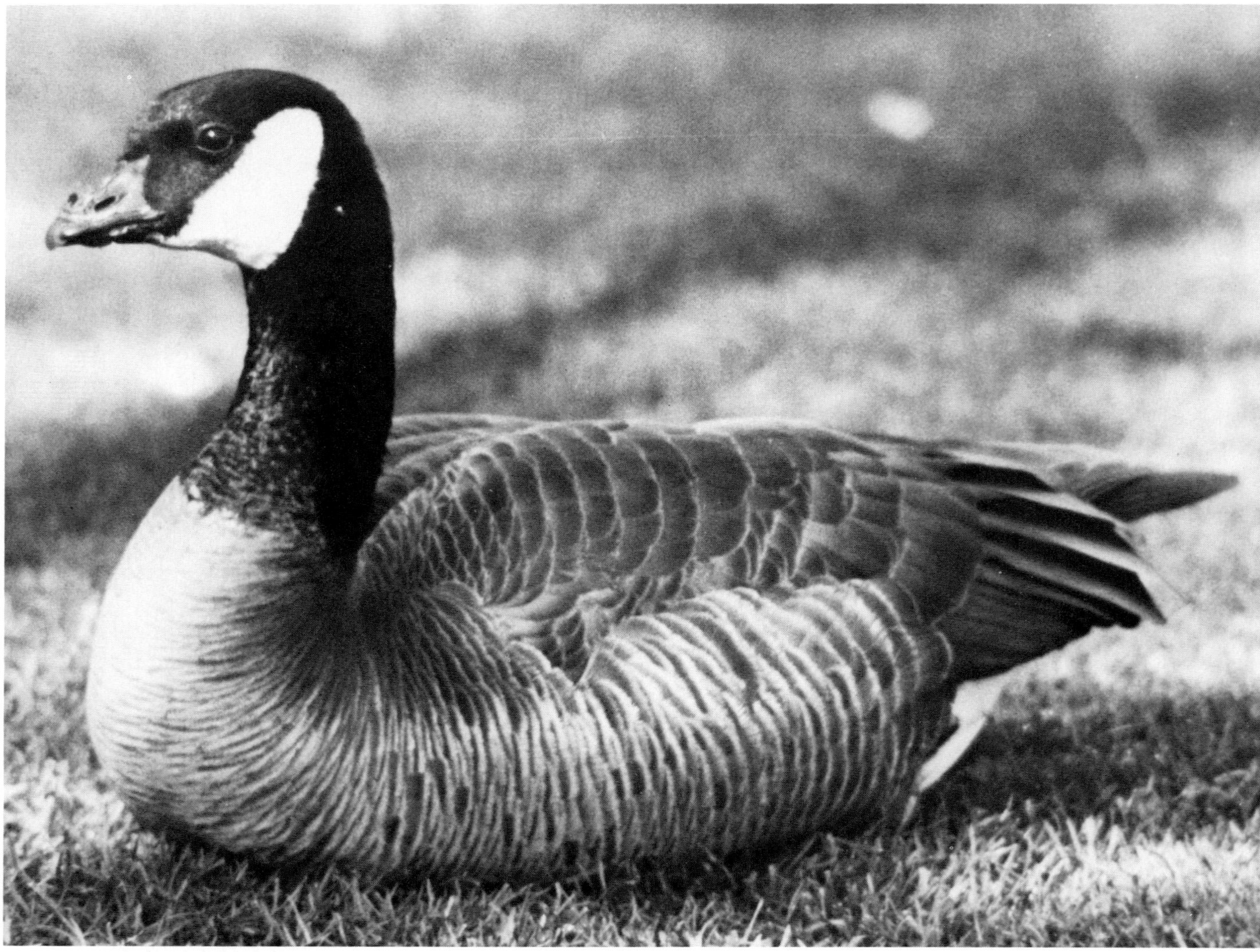

33-78 A tiny Cackler gander rests on the grass.

33-79 Two studies of floating Cackling Canadas. 33-80

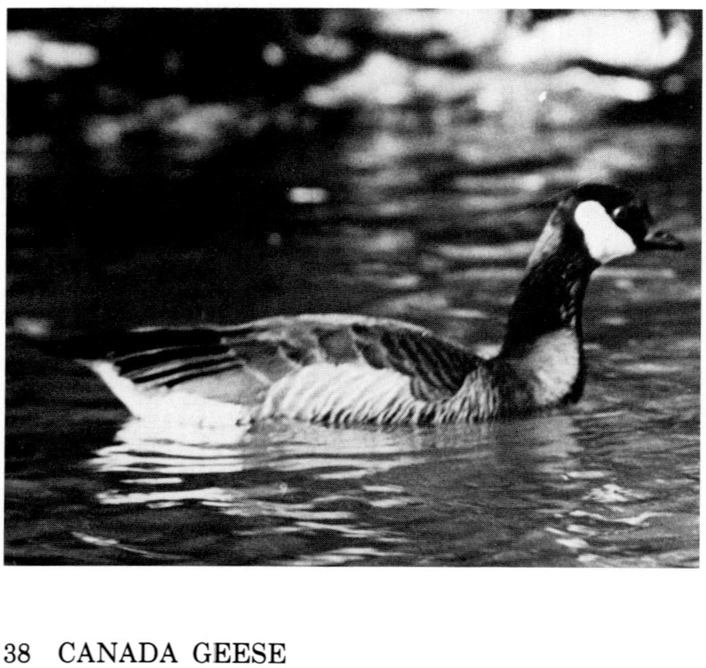

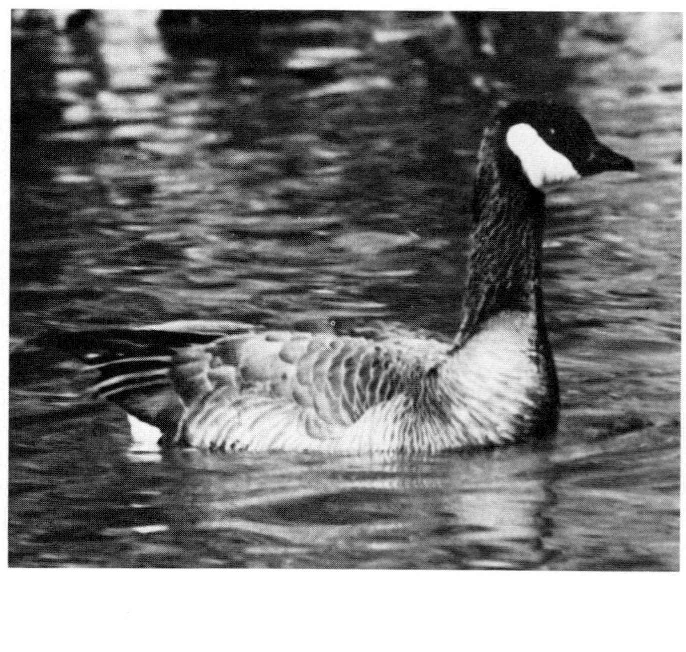

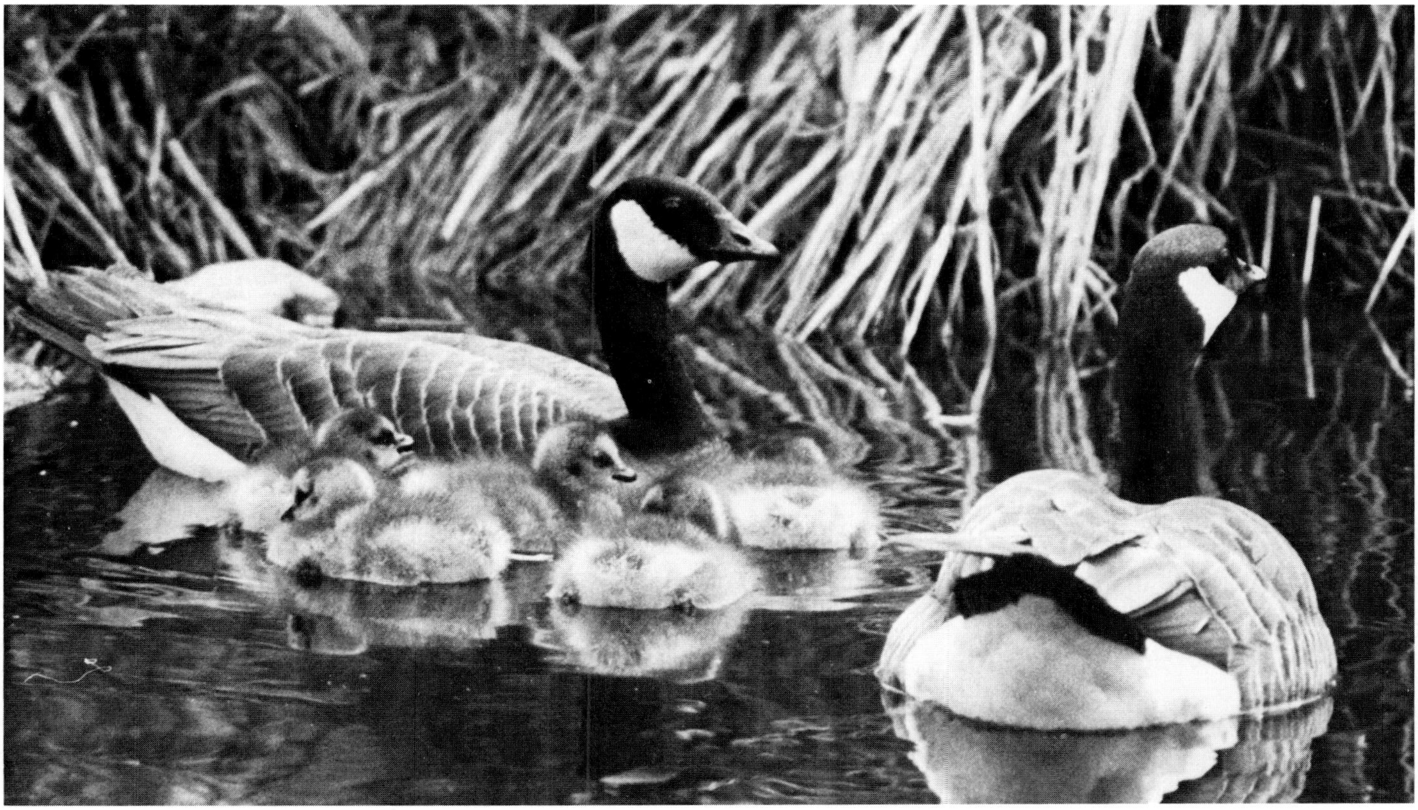

33-81

A pair of Cacklers are very protective of their little brood.

33-82

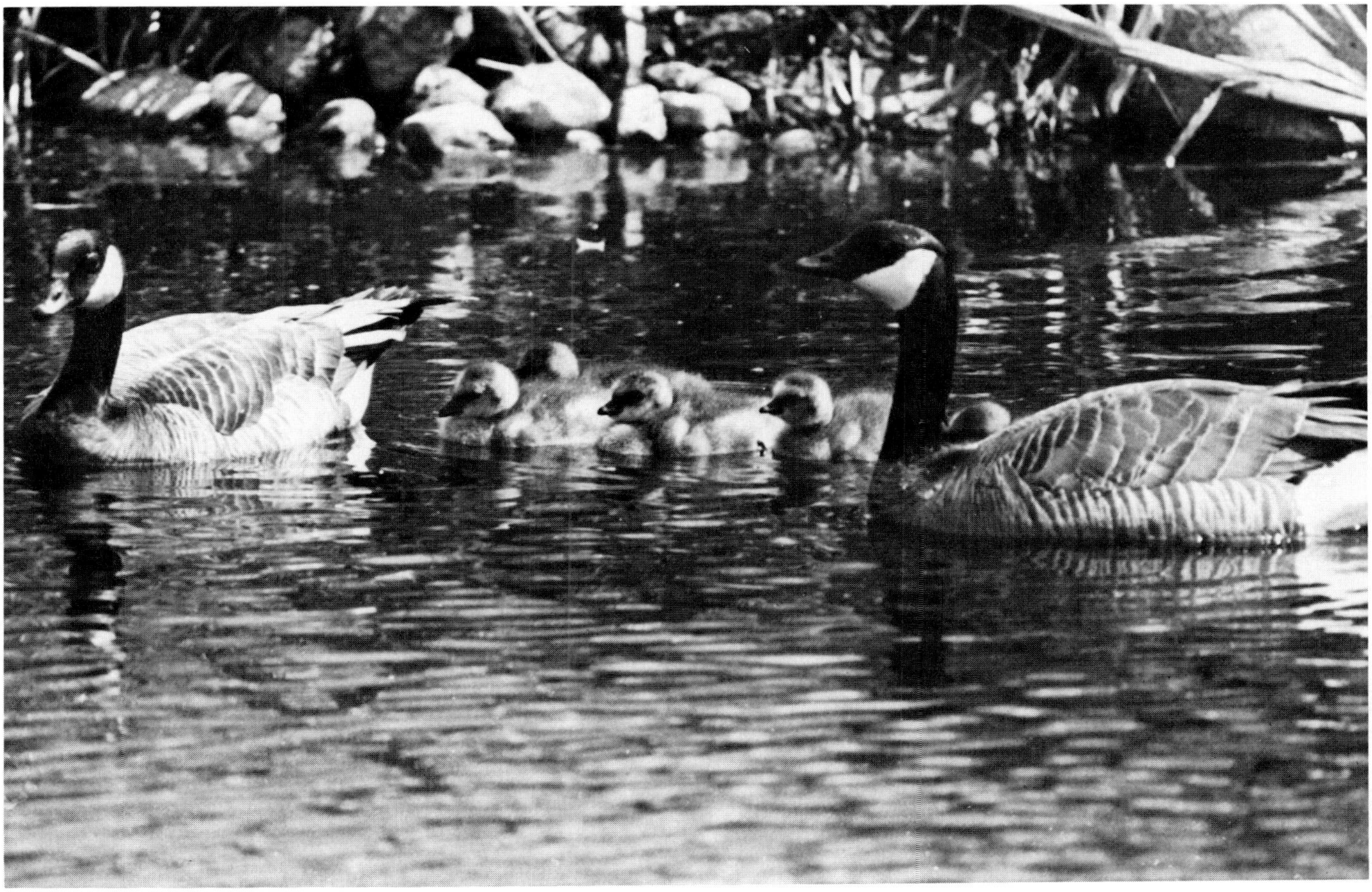

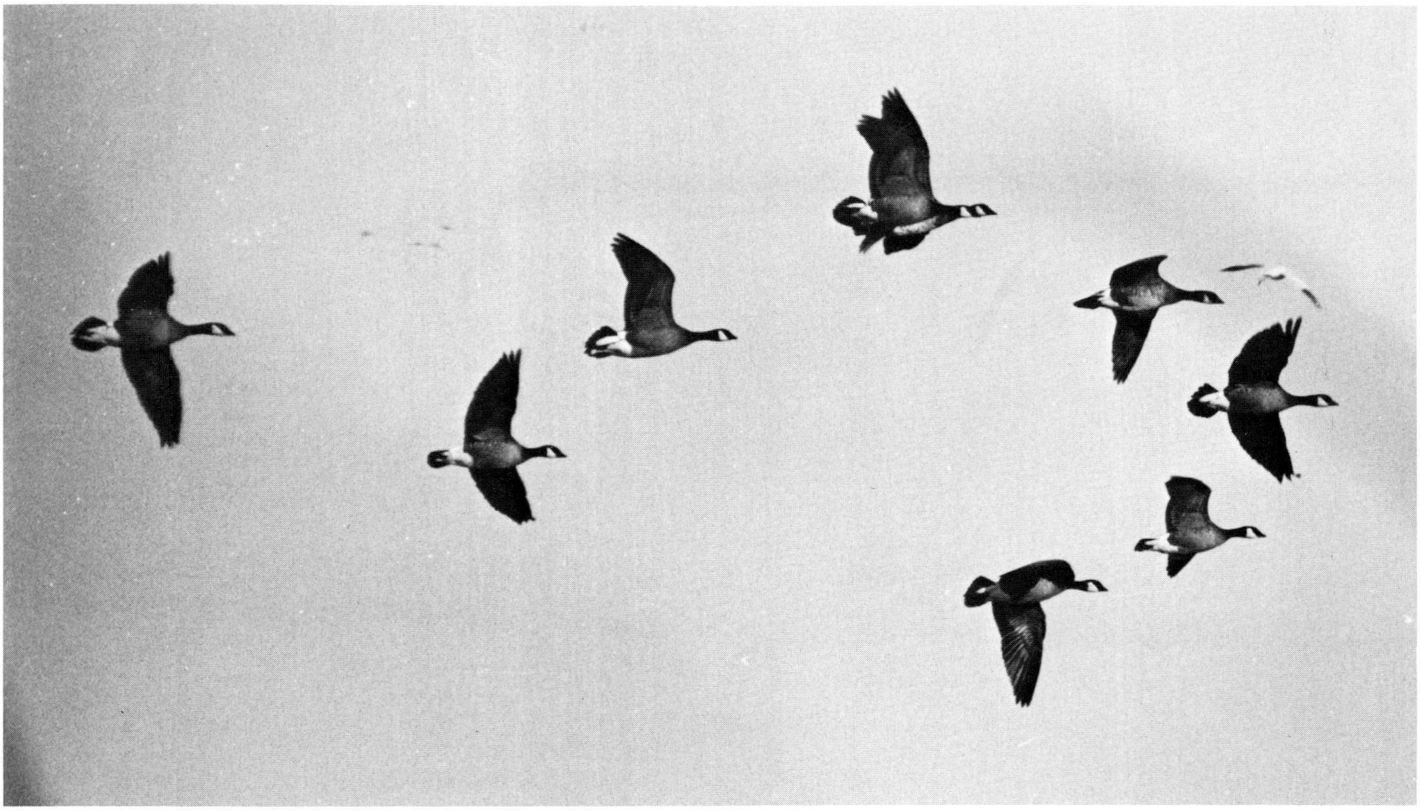

33-83

Cackling Canadas are quite easily identified in flight by their short necks and more rapid wing beat.

33-84

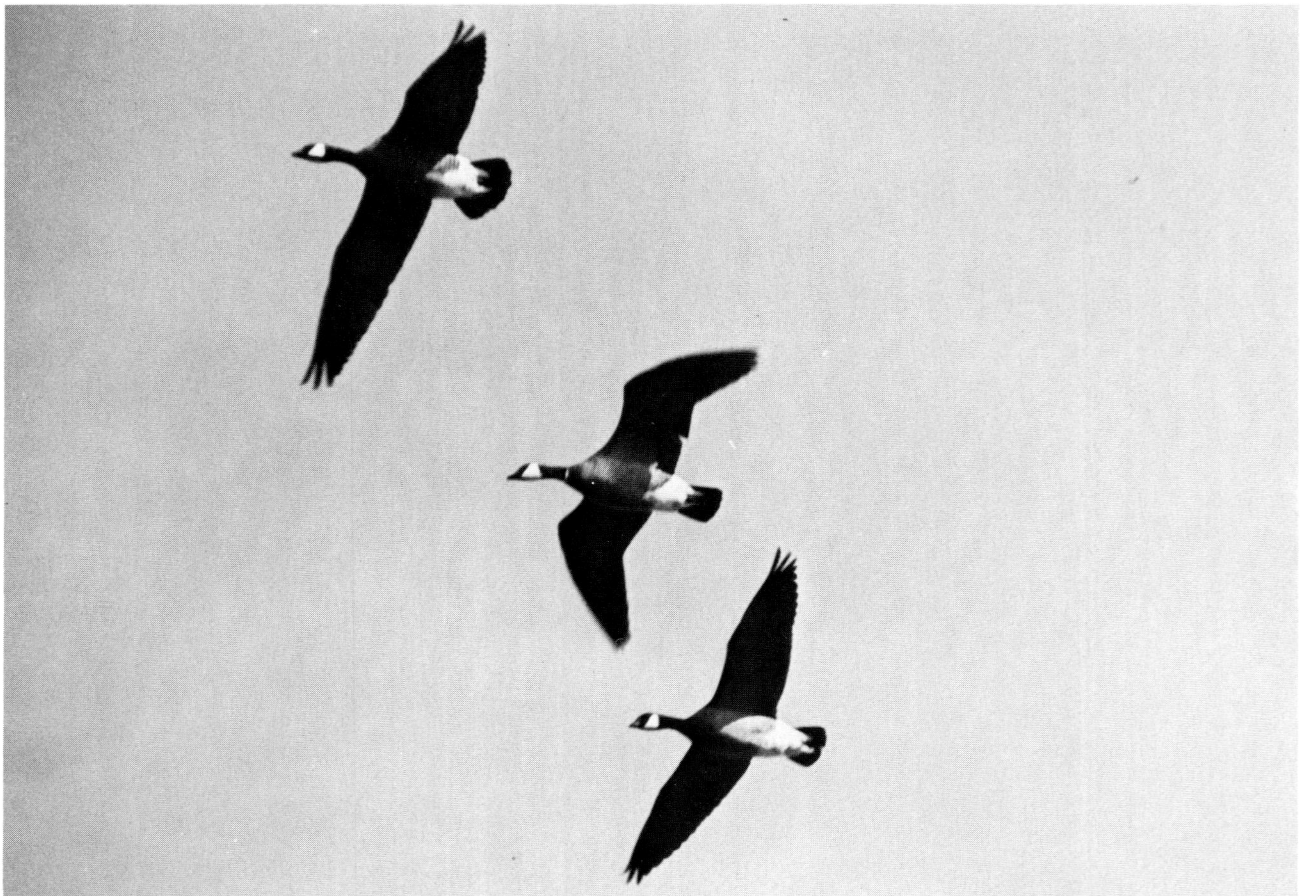

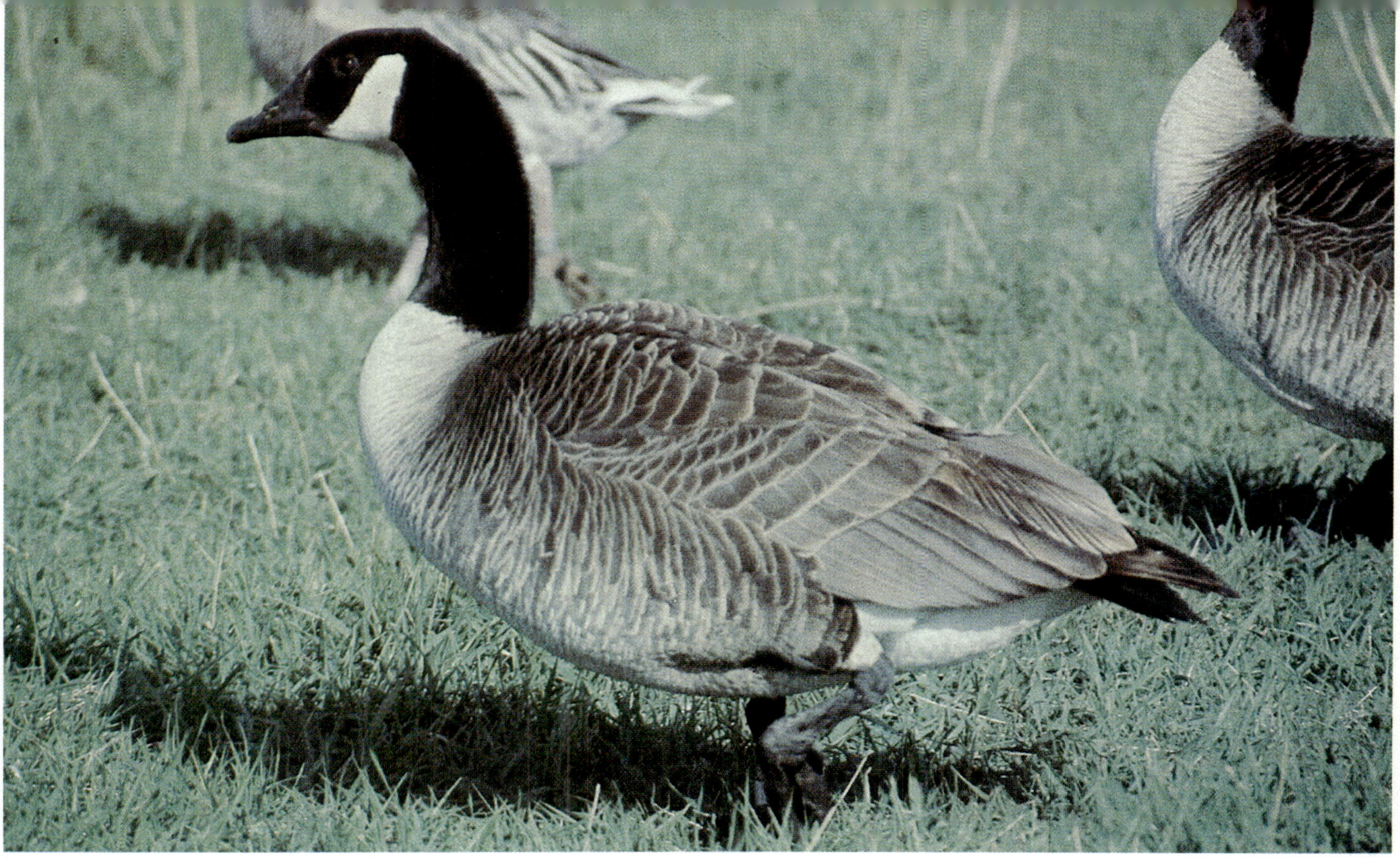

III-1 Giant Canada Goose—male. (Chapter 33)

III-2 Giant Canada Geese—pair with brood. (Chapter 33)

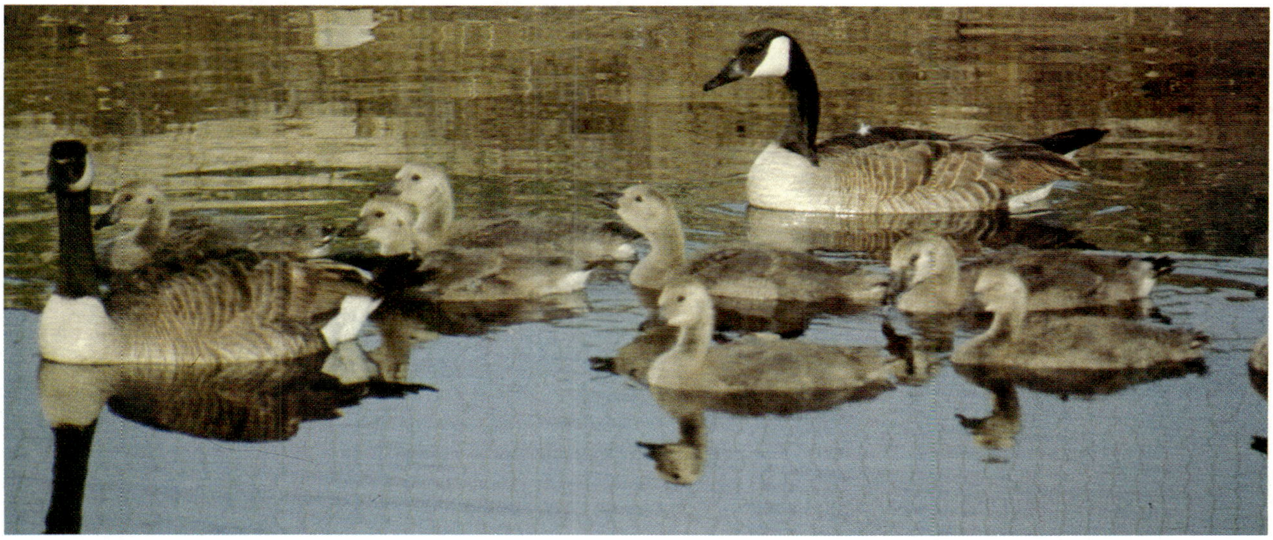

III-3 Cackling Canada Geese—pair with brood. (Chapter 33)

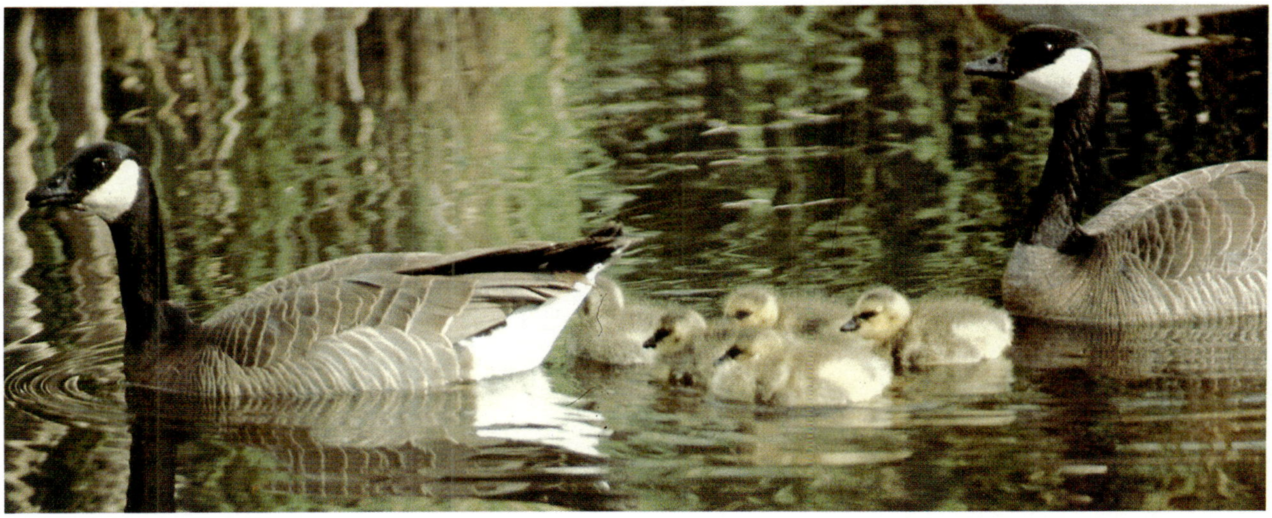

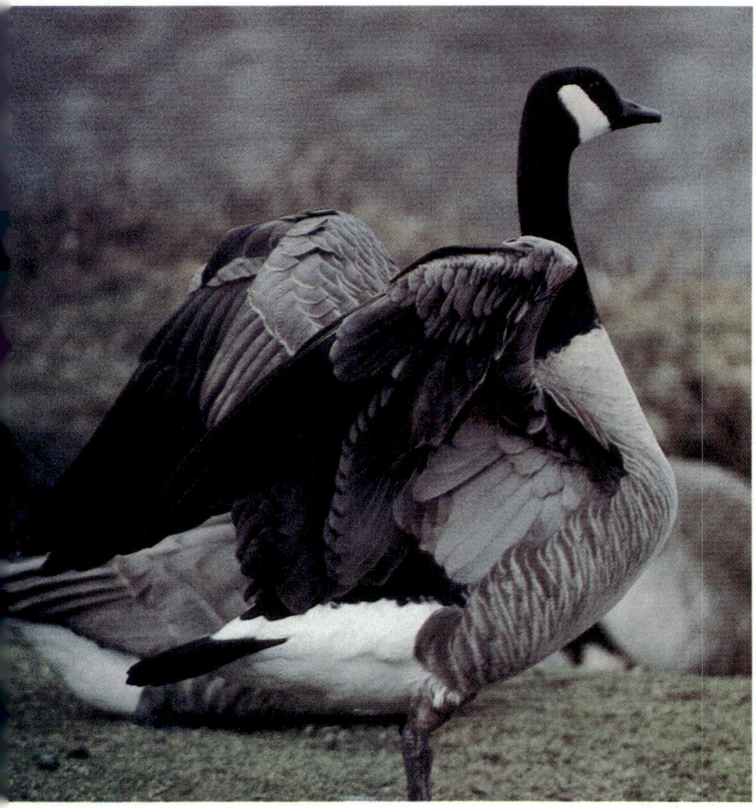

III-4

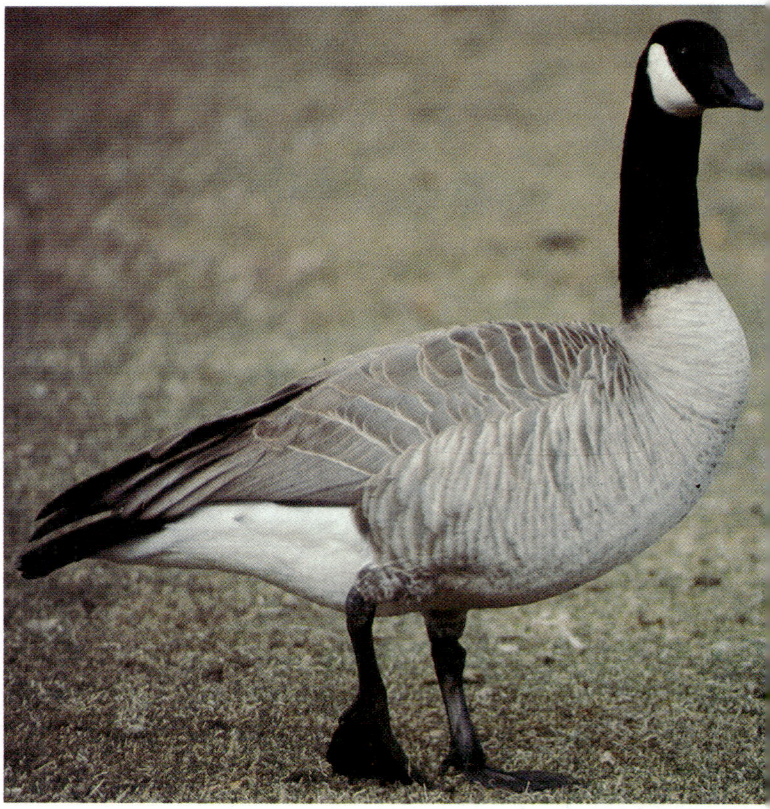

III-5

Western Canada Geese. (Chapter 33)

III-6

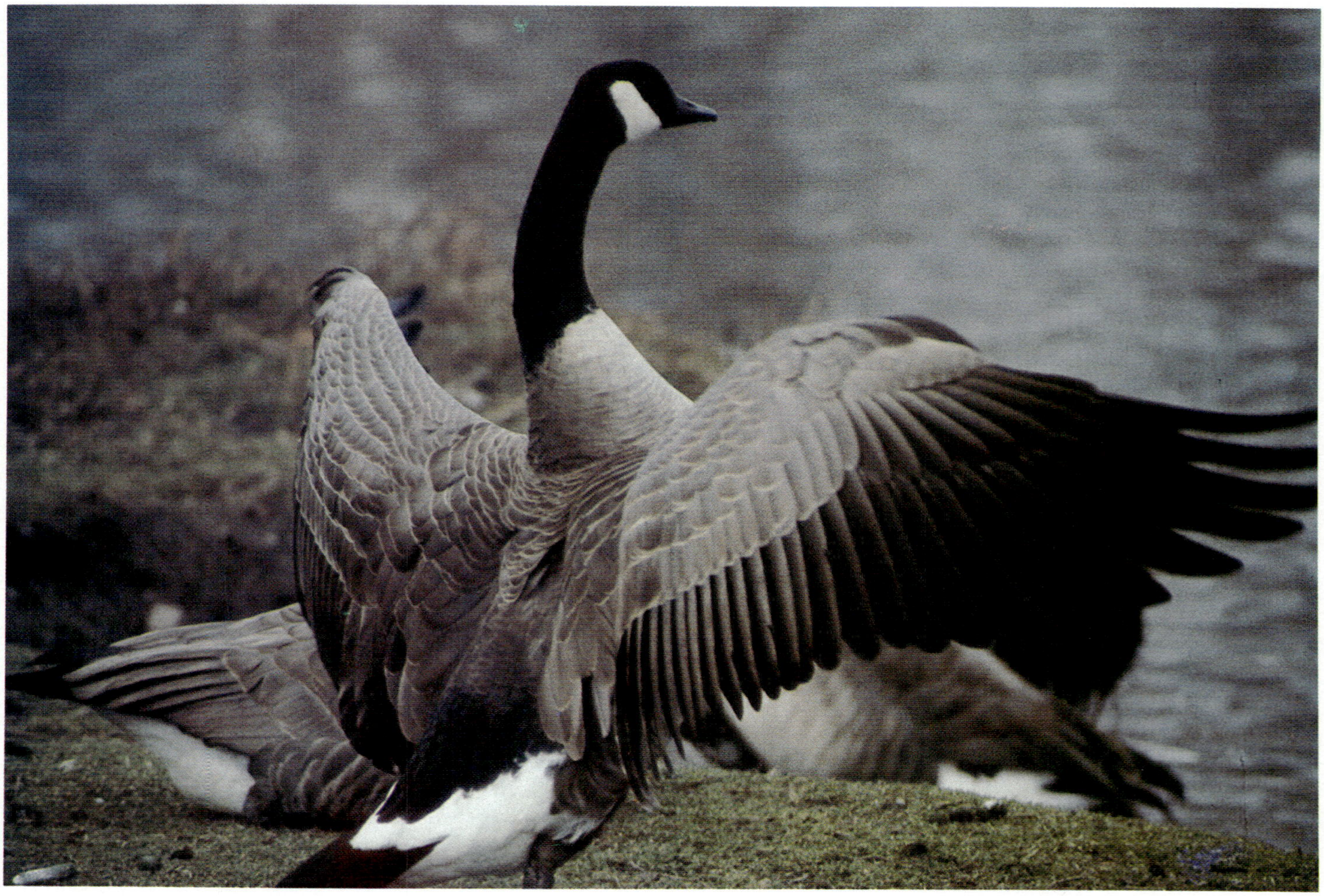

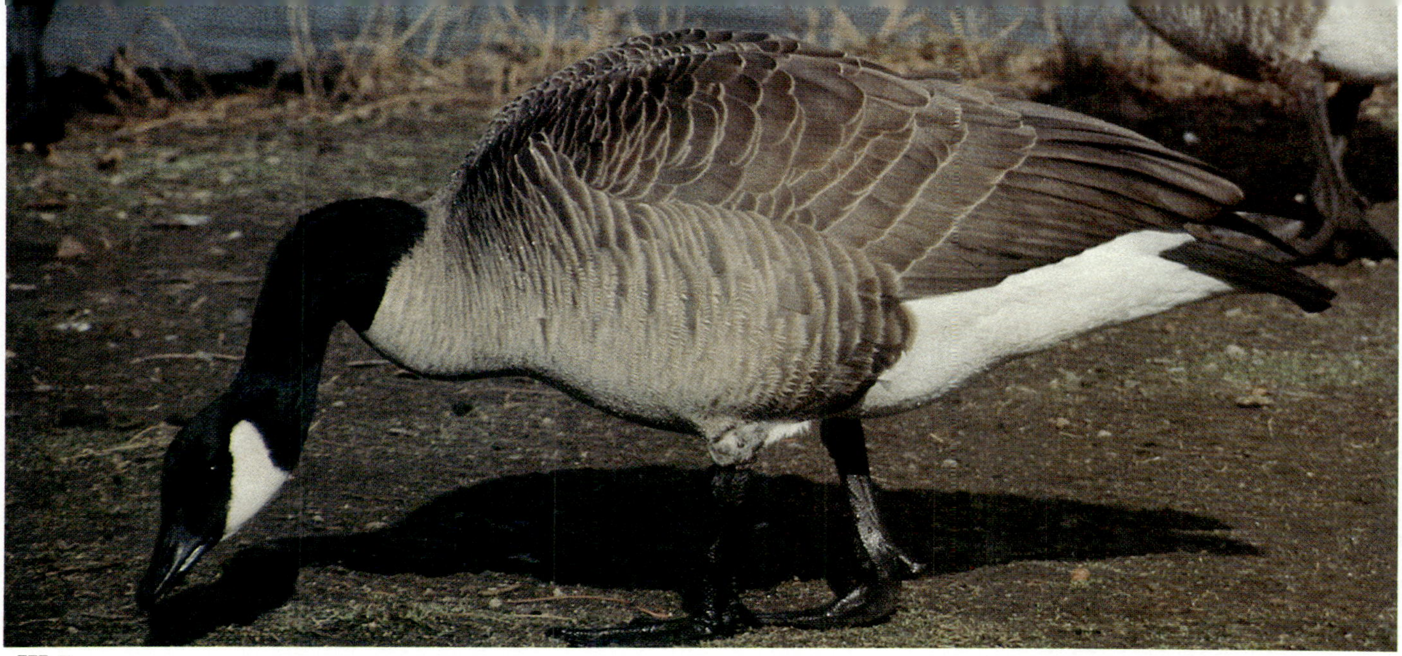

III-7
III-8

Western Canada Geese. (Chapter 33)

III-9

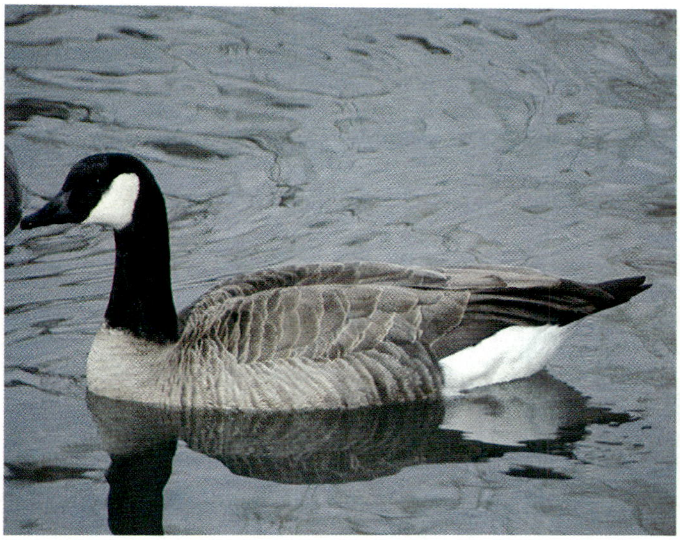

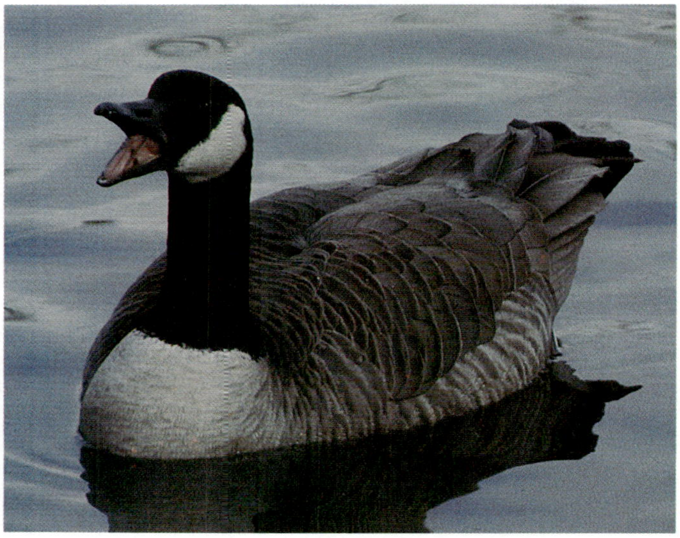

III-10 Cackling Canada Goose. (Chapter 33)

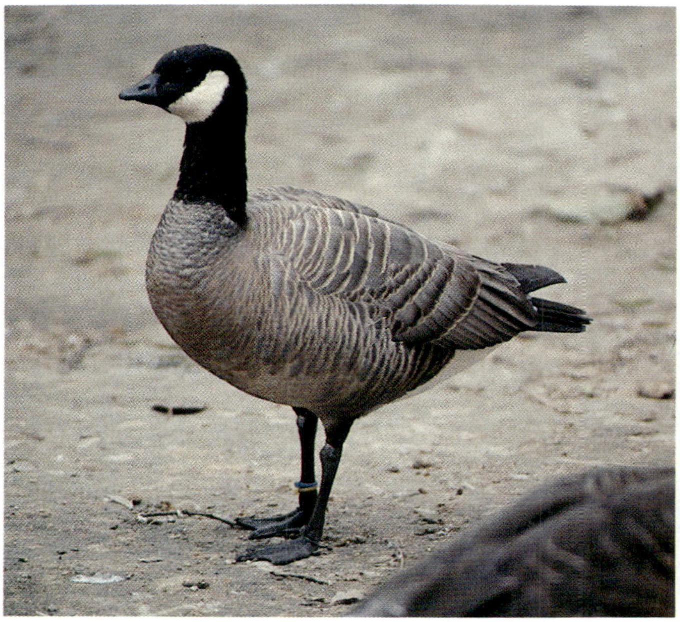

III-11 Aleutian Canada Goose. (Chapter 33)

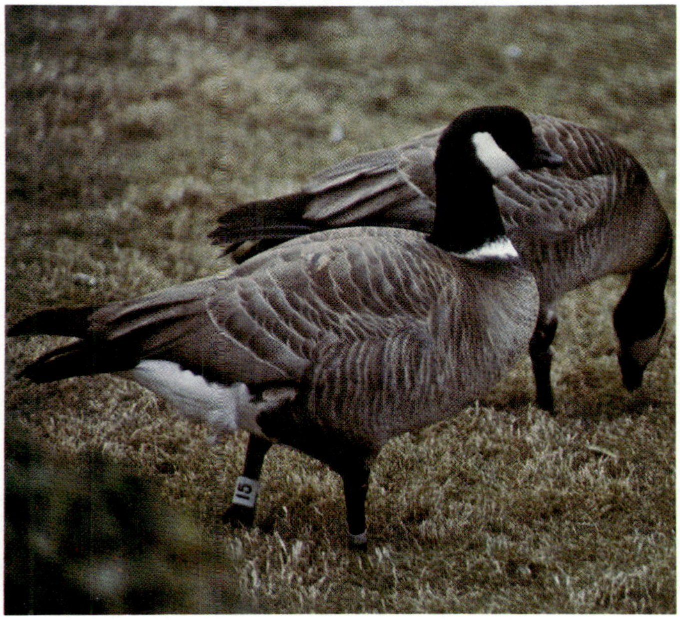

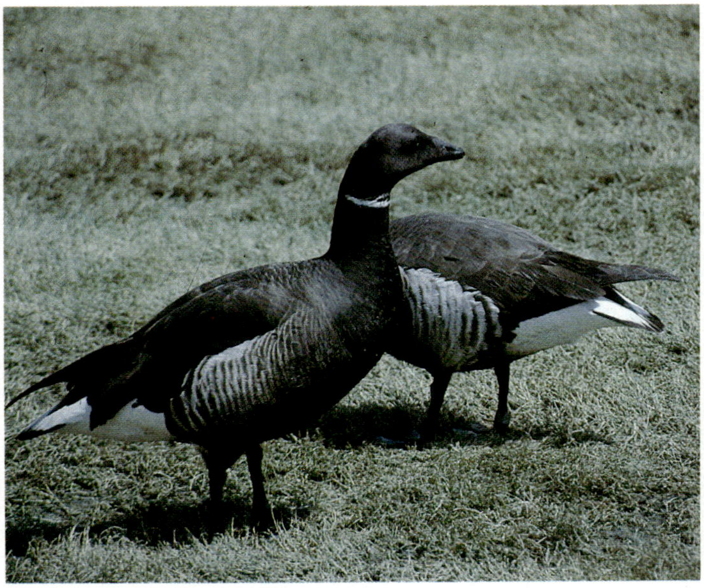

III-12

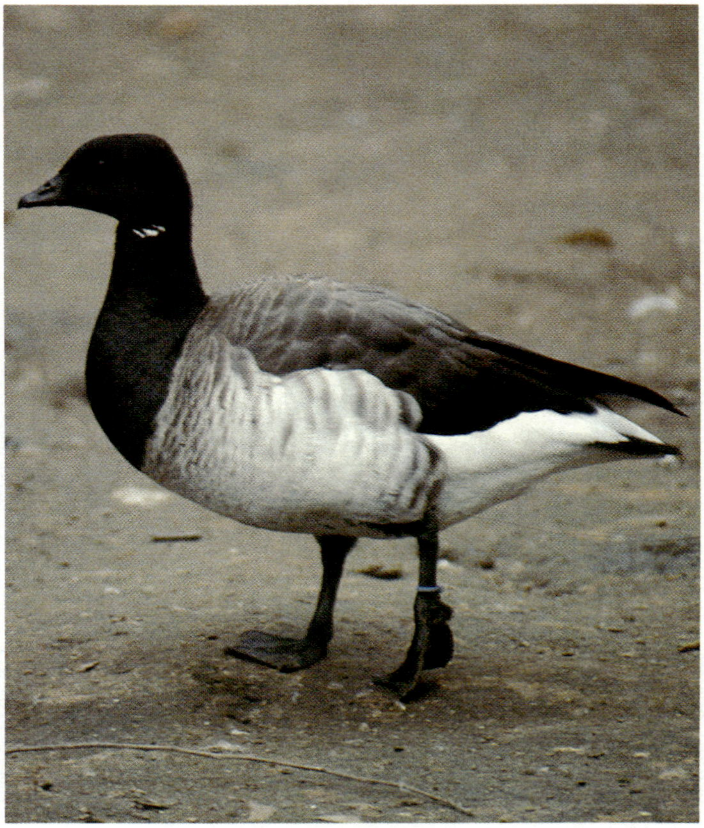

III-13 Atlantic Brant. (Chapter 34)

Pacific Brant. (Chapter 34)

III-14

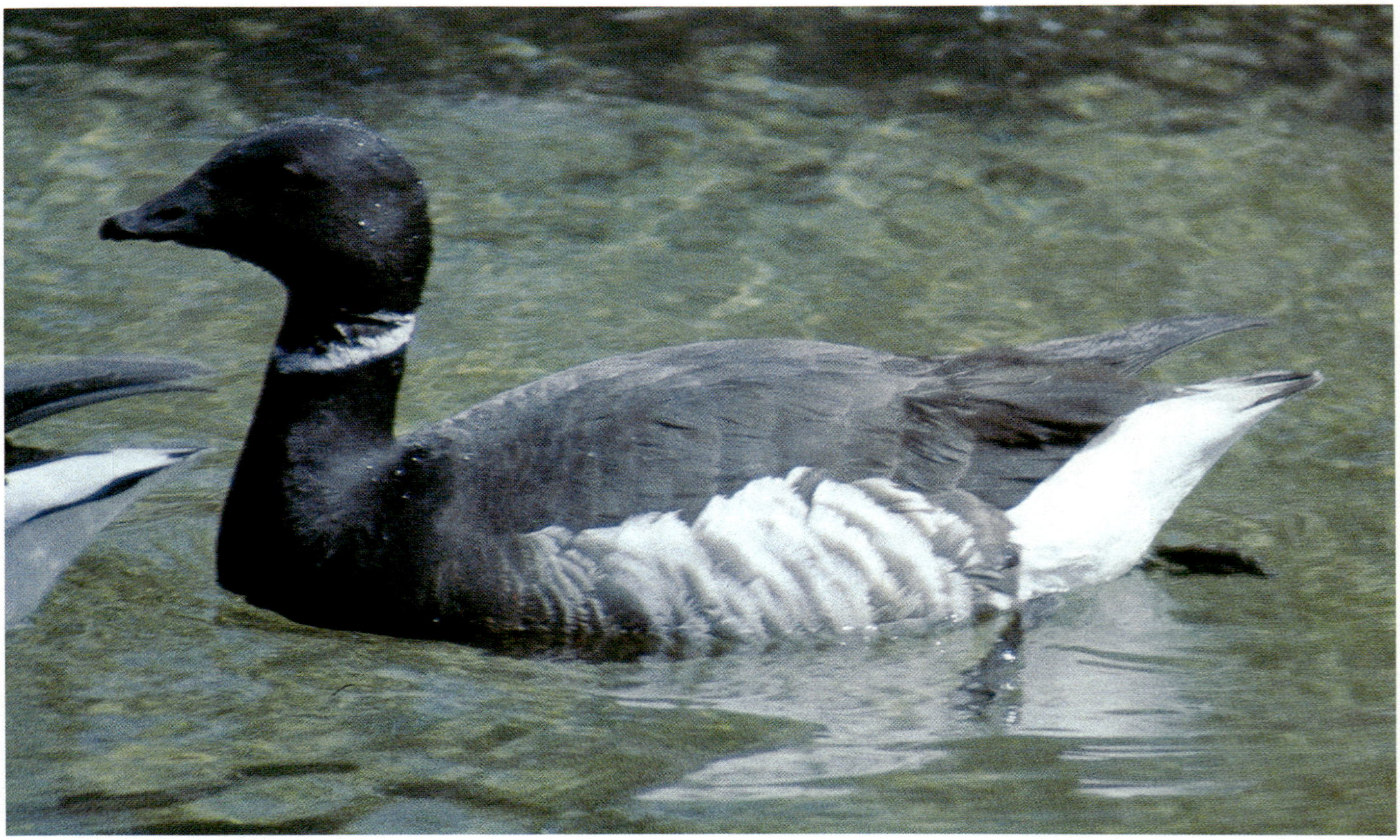

CHAPTER 34

Brant-
Pacific and Atlantic

Pacific-*Branta bernicla orientalis* Atlantic-*Branta bernicla hrota*

(Color Photos—page 44)

Two brant species are indigenous to North America: Pacific, or black brant, of the Pacific Coast and Atlantic, or American brant, of the Atlantic Coast. These plump, short-necked, long-winged birds, slightly larger than a mallard duck, are true sea geese. Except during their nesting season, they are seldom away from the coastal waters. Well-developed salt glands enable them to subsist entirely on salt water and coastal vegetation.

Brant are graceful little geese. They sit buoyantly on the water with tails—almost completely covered by snow-white coverts—held high. Their well-shaped heads and small bills move daintily on smoothly flowing necks. The flight of the brant is swift, strong, and unusually low—just above the waves. Their flight formation differs, too, from that of other geese, as they typically fly in long, undulating lines formed at right angles to the direction of flight.

Although difficult to distinguish in flight, the two species have some differences in coloration and markings. The chest, neck, and breast of the black brant is dullish black; the coloration of the American brant in these areas is slightly grayer. The black brant has a chokerlike collar approximately 1 inch wide and incomplete at the back of the neck; the throat collar on the American brant is incomplete at both the front and back of the neck. The black chest of the black brant blends into the breast with no pronounced demarcation and shades into lighter and lighter slaty-brown, finally merging into the white underside about 5 inches forward of the tail. The black chest of the American brant is sharply defined against the light-gray breast that blends into the white underside approximately 7 inches from the tail. The American brant's side feathers are considerably lighter in coloration than the black brant's.

The back feathers, scapulars, and most wing coverts on juveniles of both species are edged with buffy-white. The throat collars of juveniles may be indistinct or missing.

The black brant breeds along the Arctic coast of Alaska and Canada, the islands to the north, and on the Arctic tundra of northwestern Siberia, east to the Khatanga River. The wintering population on this continent is distributed from southern British Columbia to Baja California. The American brant breed even farther north in eastern Arctic Canada, the islands to the north, northern Greenland, and Spitsbergen. The wintering population in North America is found along the Atlantic Coast from New Jersey to North Carolina. There may be some overlapping of nesting grounds but, apparently, very little crossbreeding occurs between these two brant species, although a few specimens of intermediate colorations have been recorded. The small amount of crossbreeding can probably be accounted for by the fact that most, if not all, breeding brant are mated prior to reaching the nesting area.

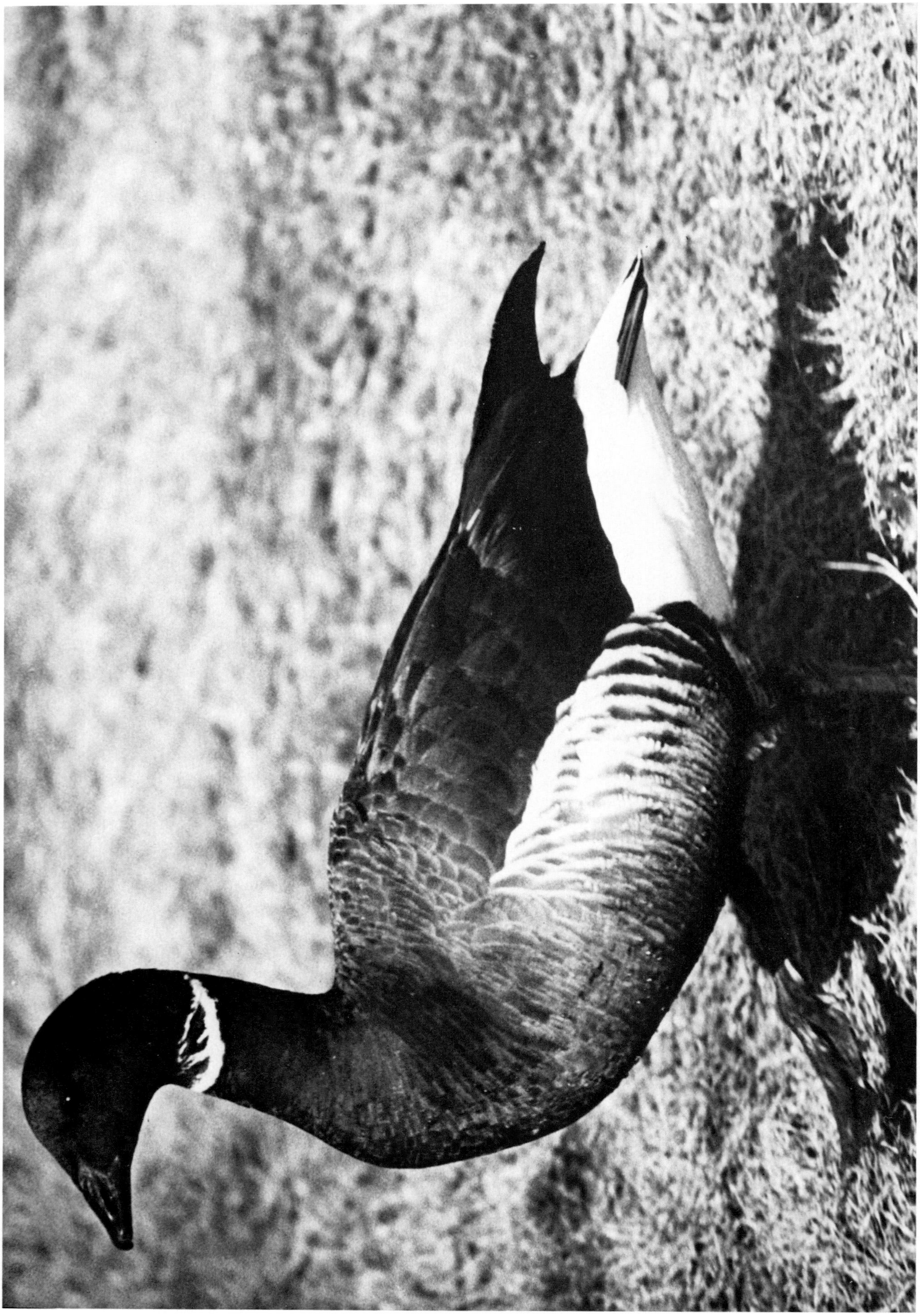

34-1 The Pacific, or black, brant is a beautiful and graceful little sea goose, not much larger than a mallard duck.

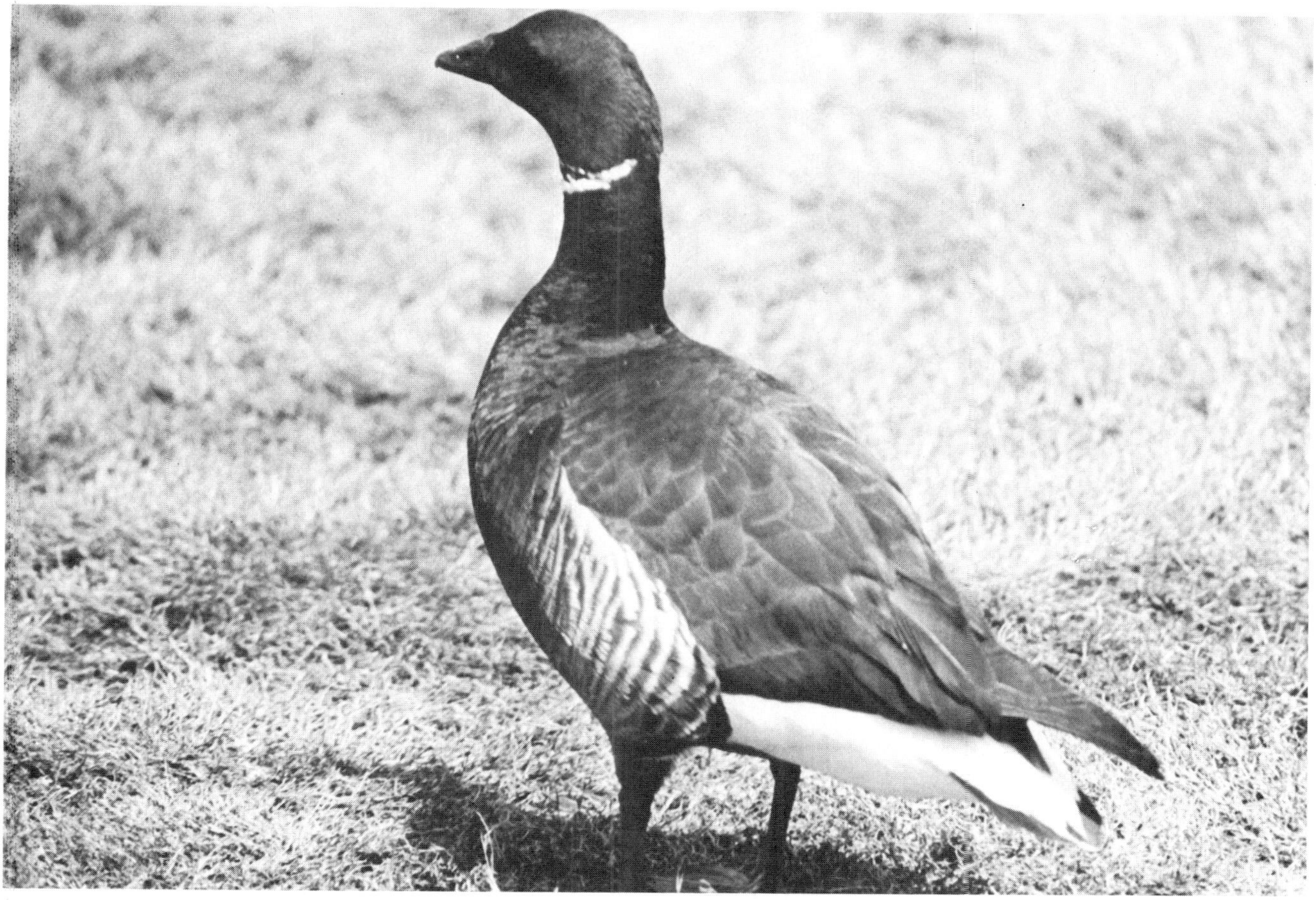

34-2 Three-quarter rear view of the Pacific brant. His white upper tail coverts almost hide his tail.

34-3 Pacific brant show off their smooth body contours and lateral leg positions. 34-4

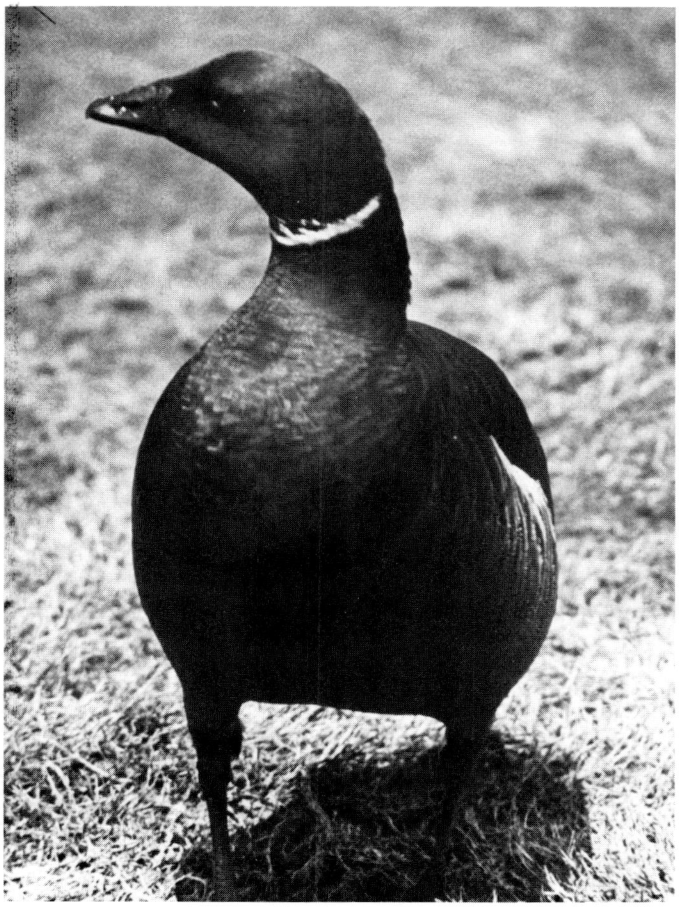

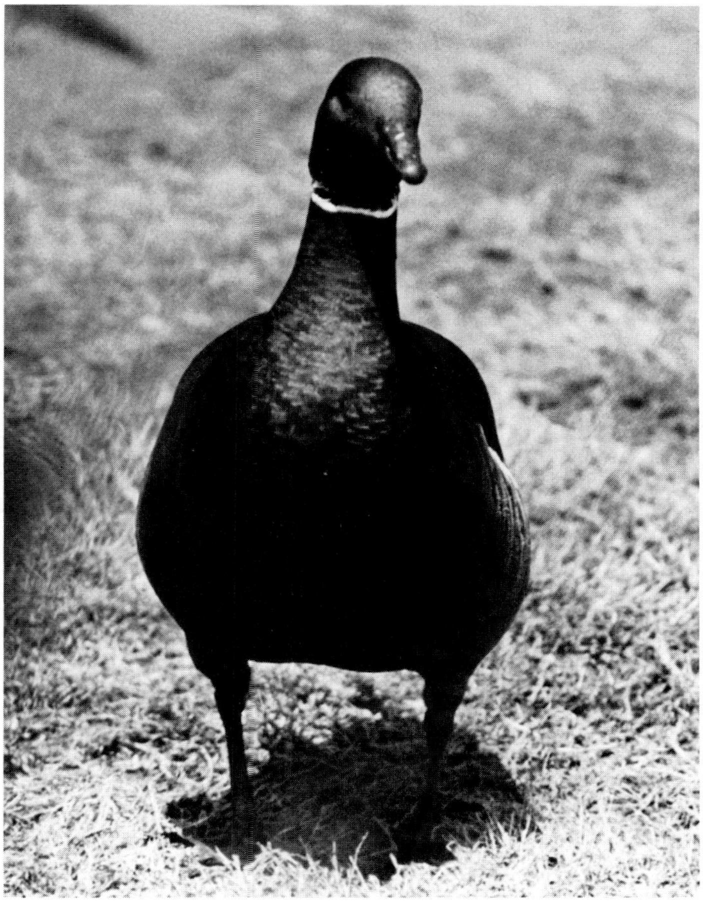

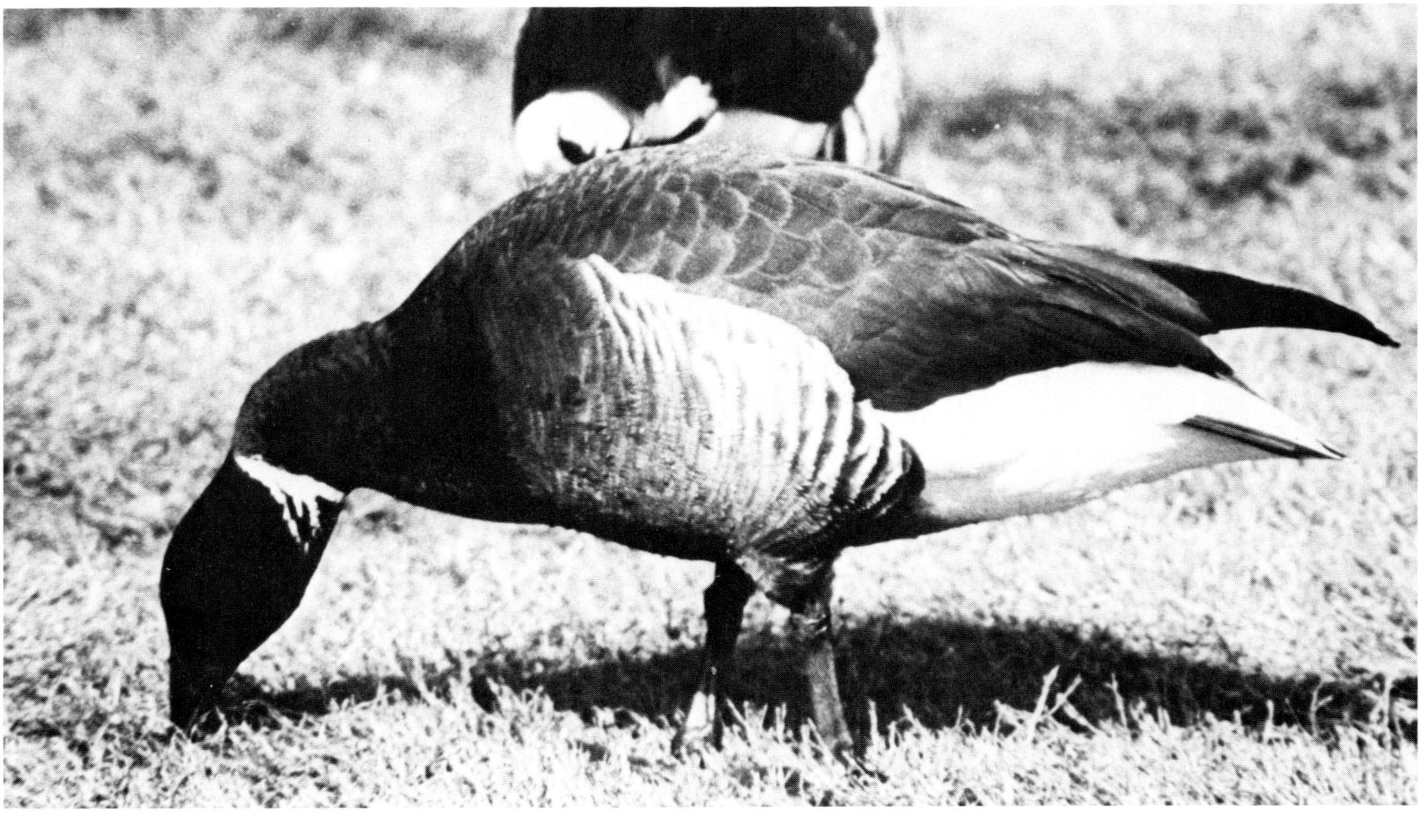

34-5

Black brant in the feeding position. Note the graceful neck lines.

34-6

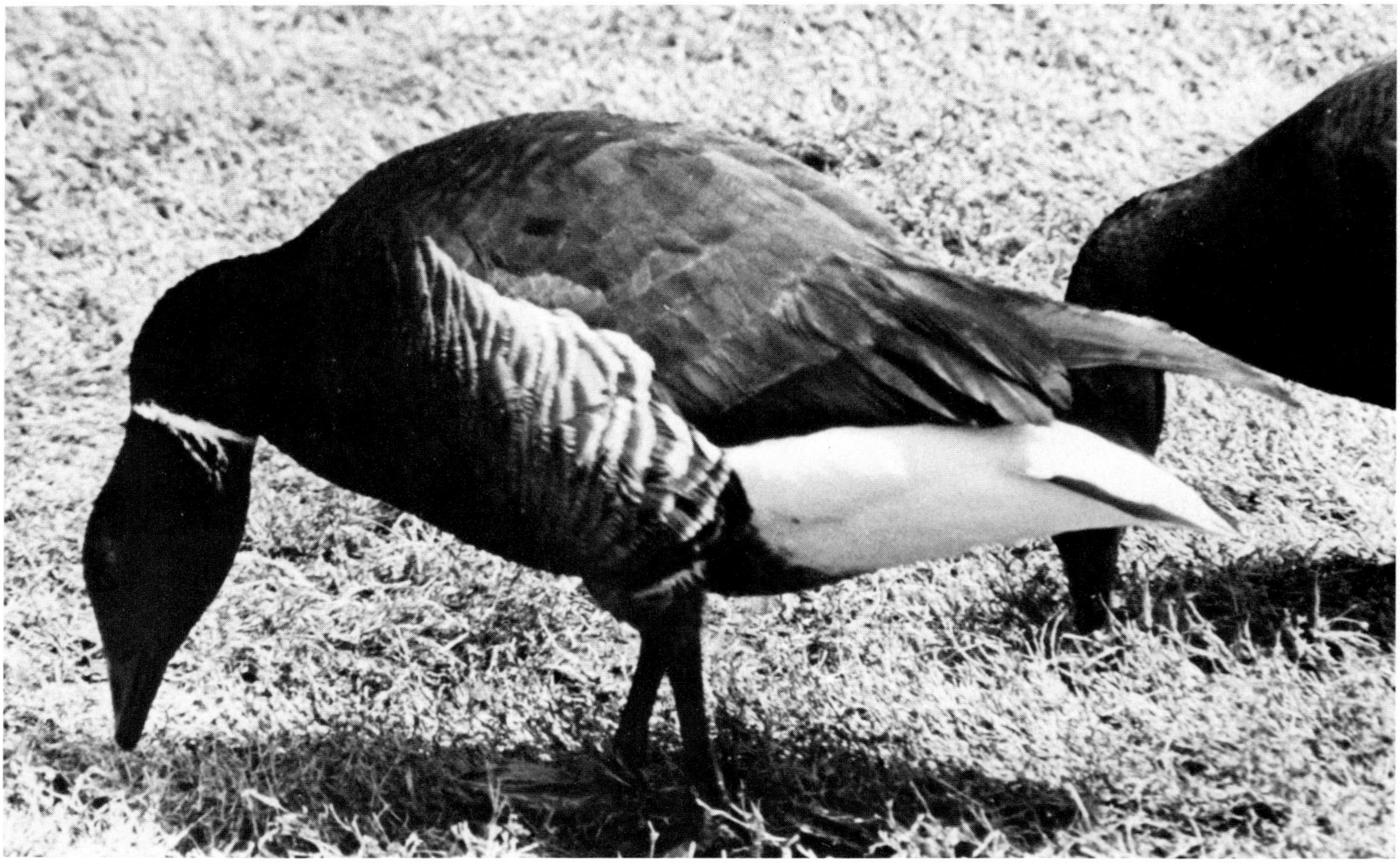

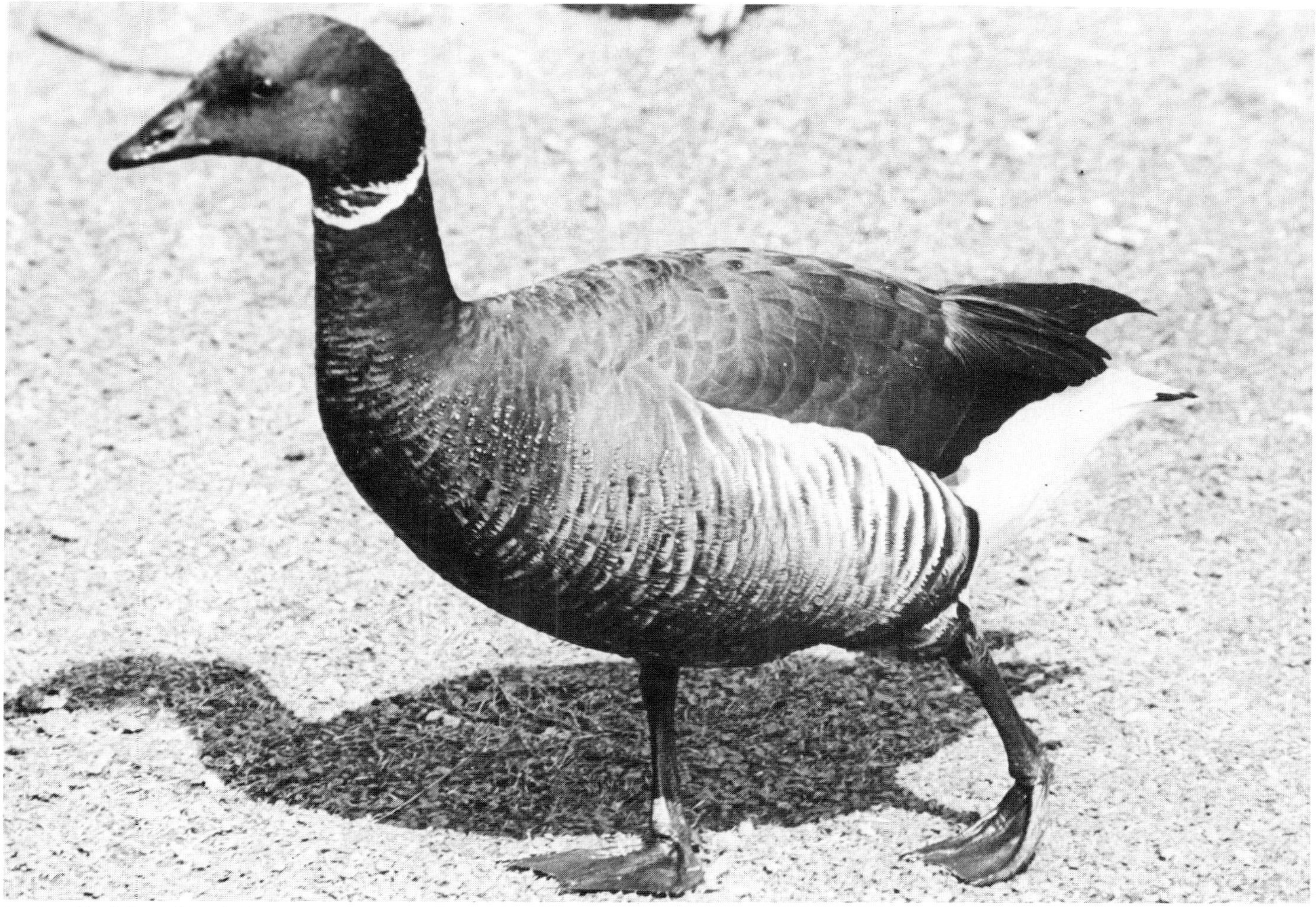

34-7 Striding black brant. Except during the breeding and nesting season, these little geese spend all their time in the ocean, usually in bays.

34-8 Little Pacific brant rests on the grass. Nice pose.

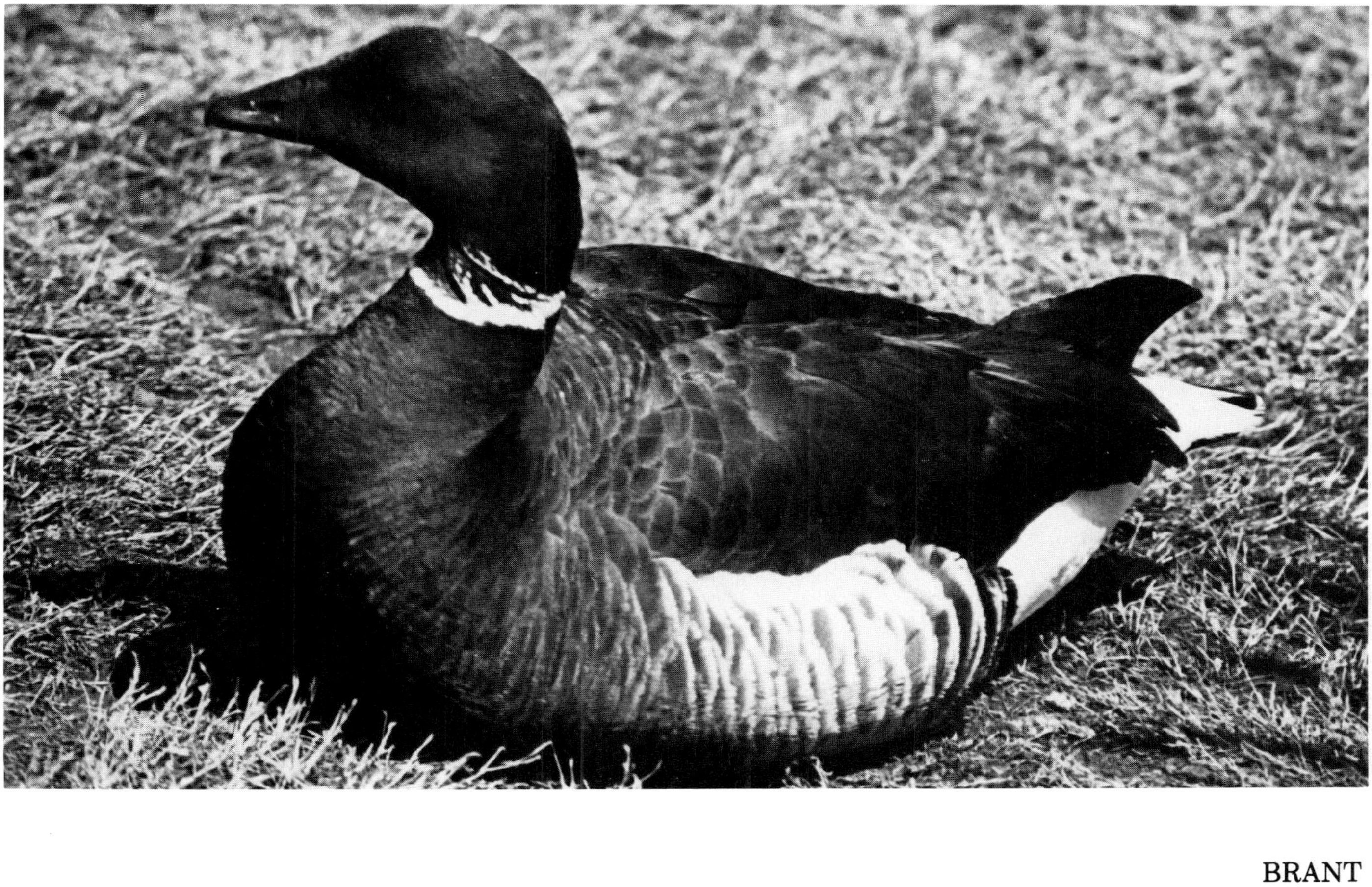

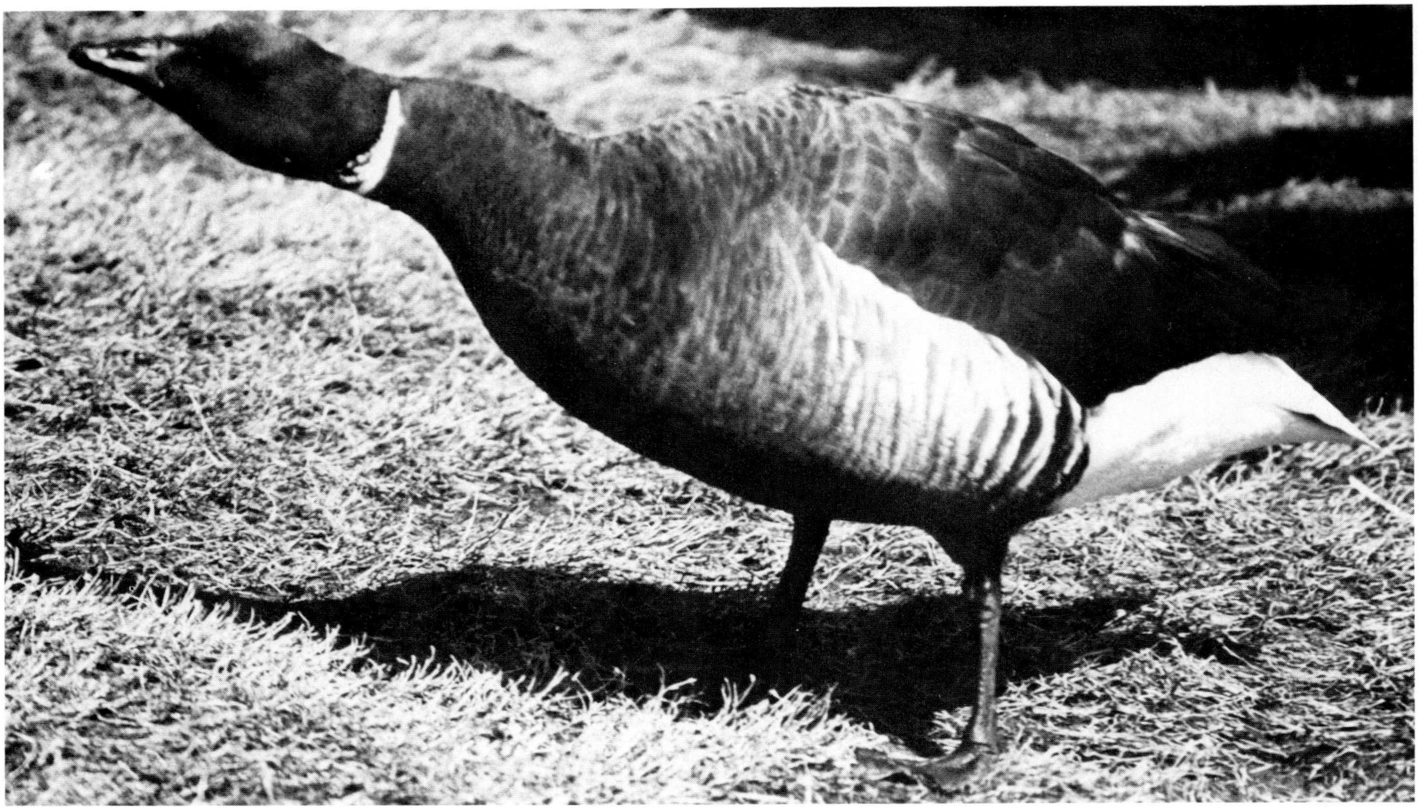

34-9

Pacific brant in aggressive poses. These photographs were taken during the mating season when brant are quite quarrelsome.

34-10

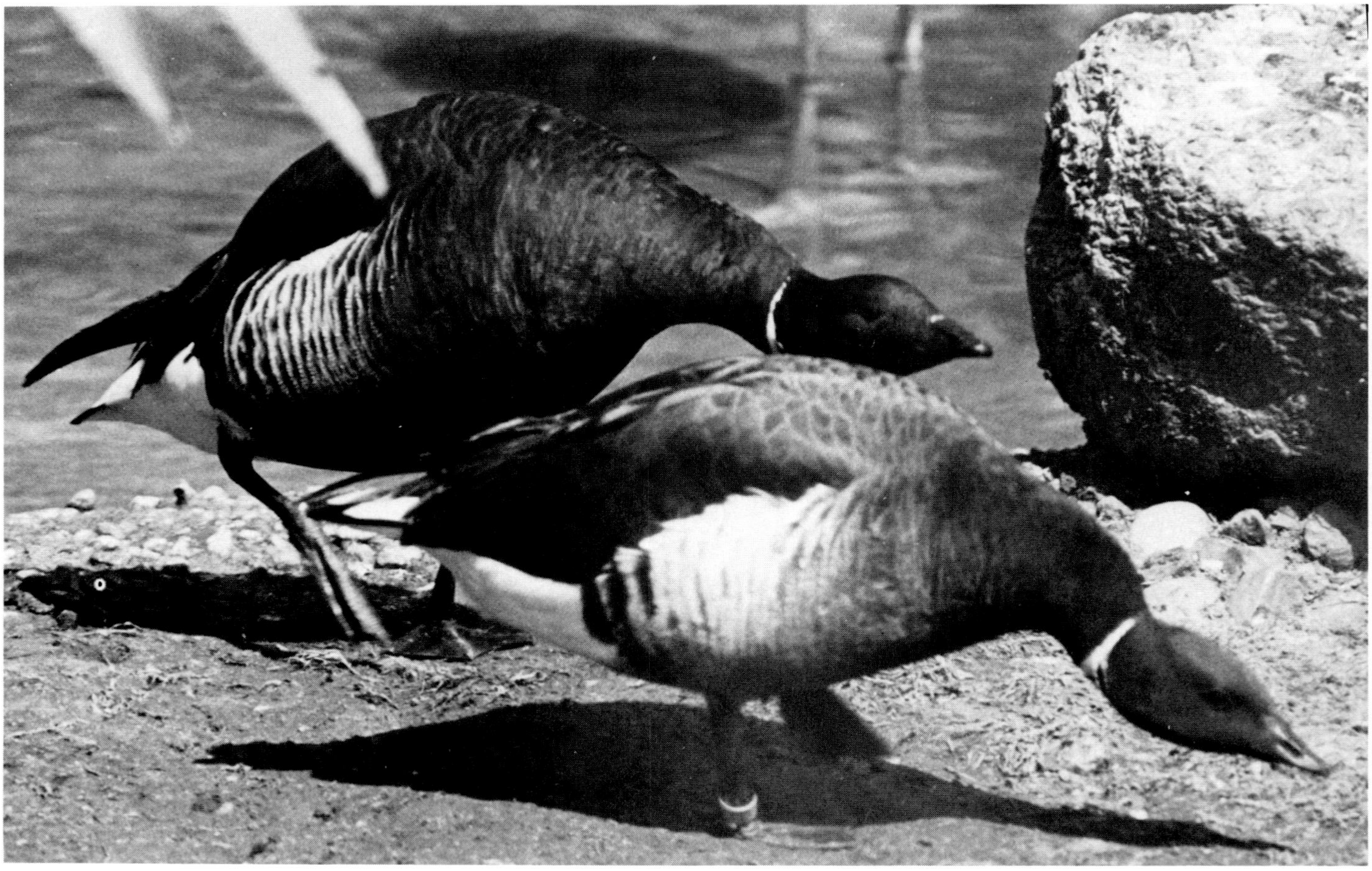

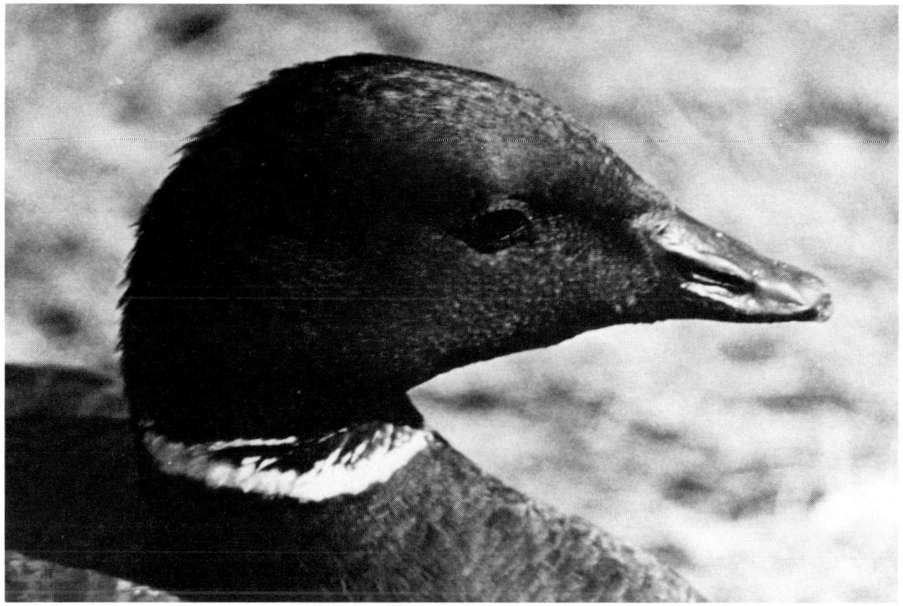

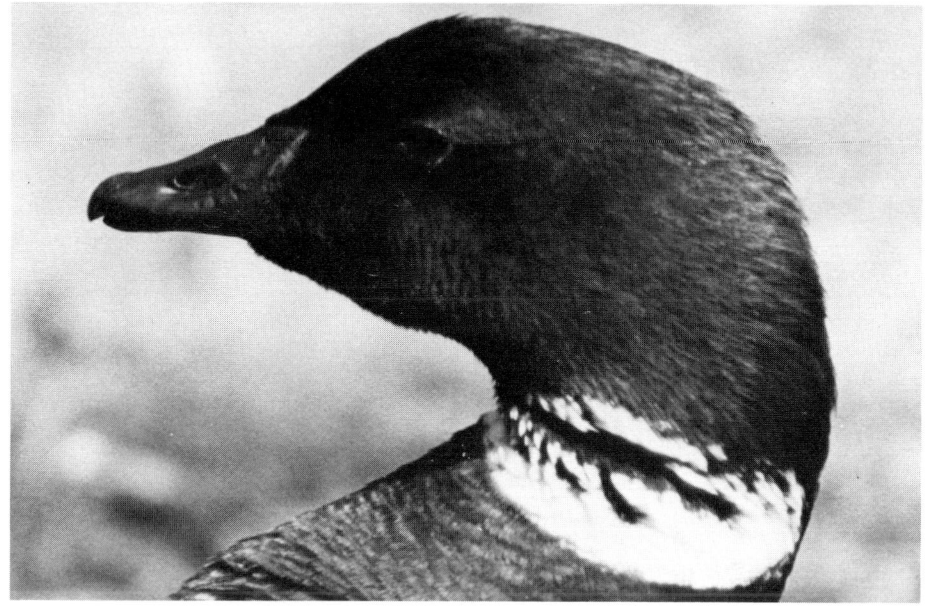

34-11 Profile views of the black brant's head and bill. 34-12

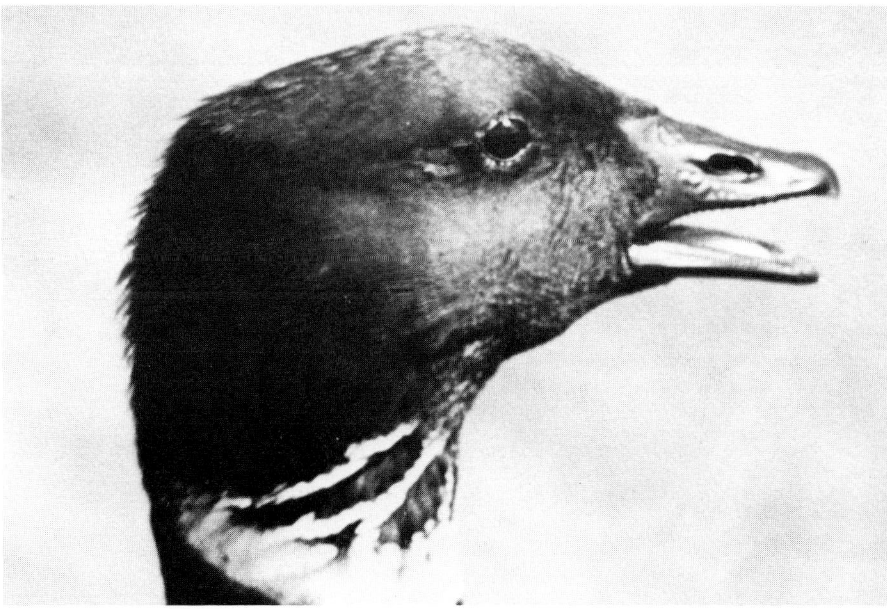

34-13 Pacific brant calling. Especially notice the details of his chokerlike collar.

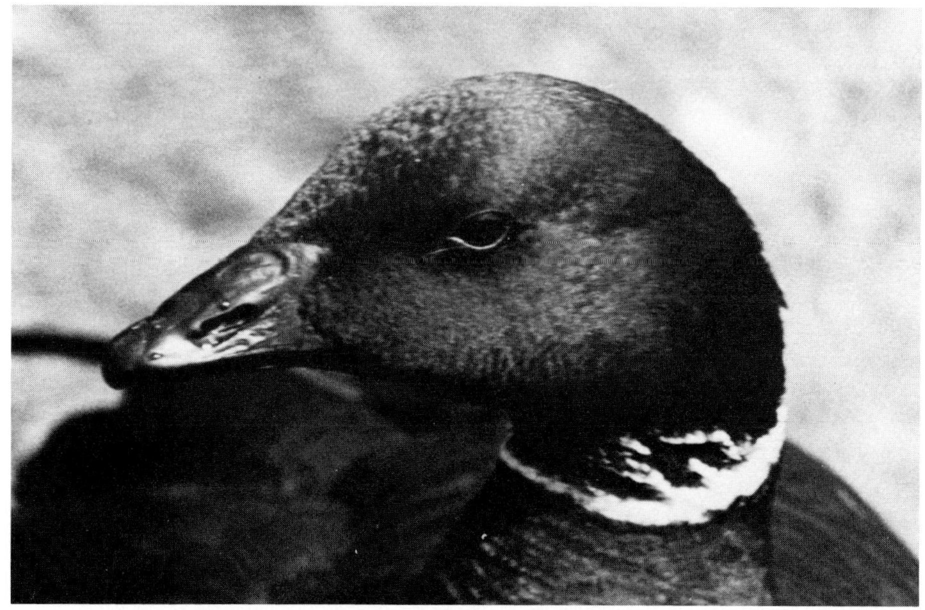

34-14 Another view of his head, bill, and collar.

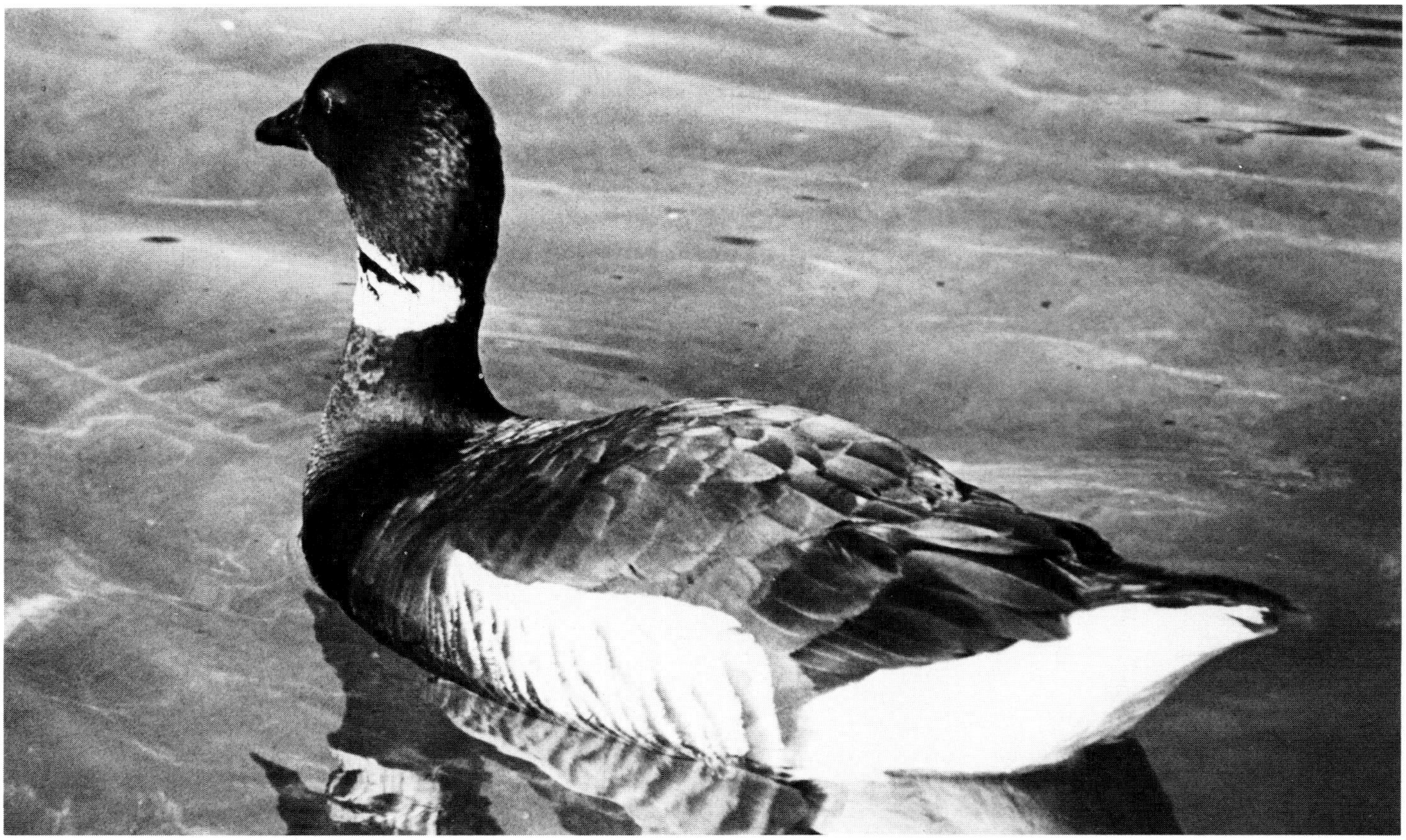

34-15

Pacific brant float buoyantly and daintily on the water.

34-16

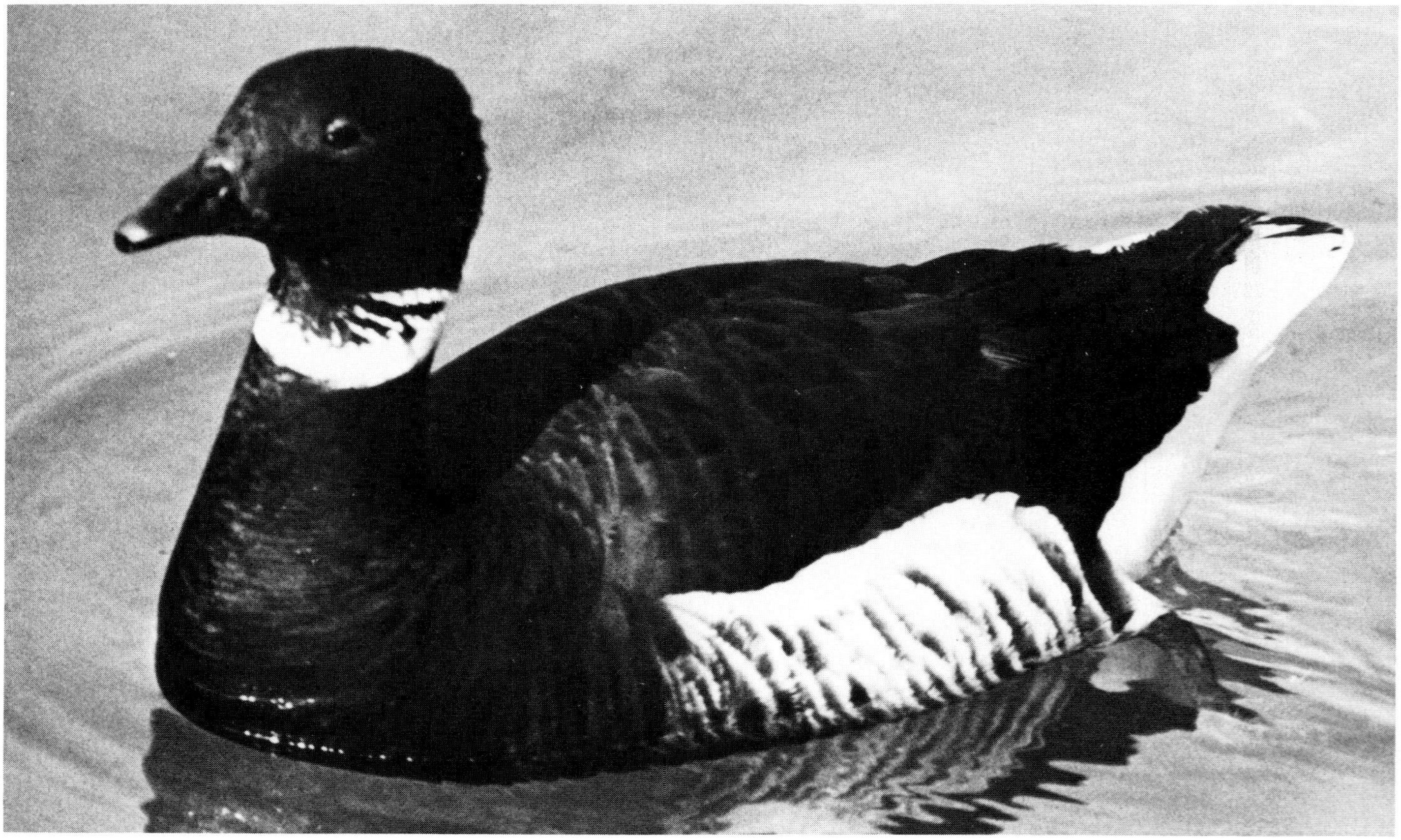

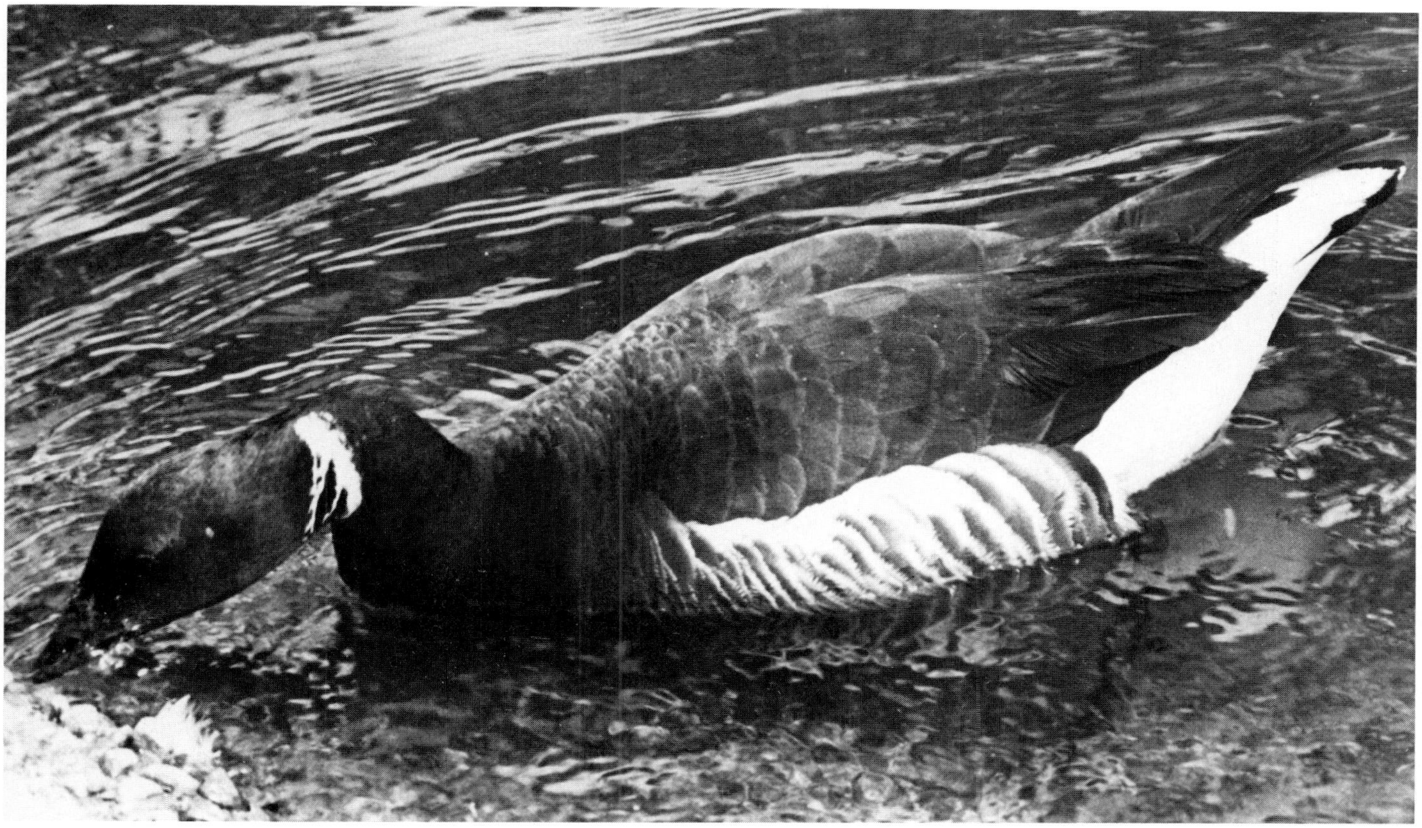

34-17

Pacific brant dabbling in the water.

34-18

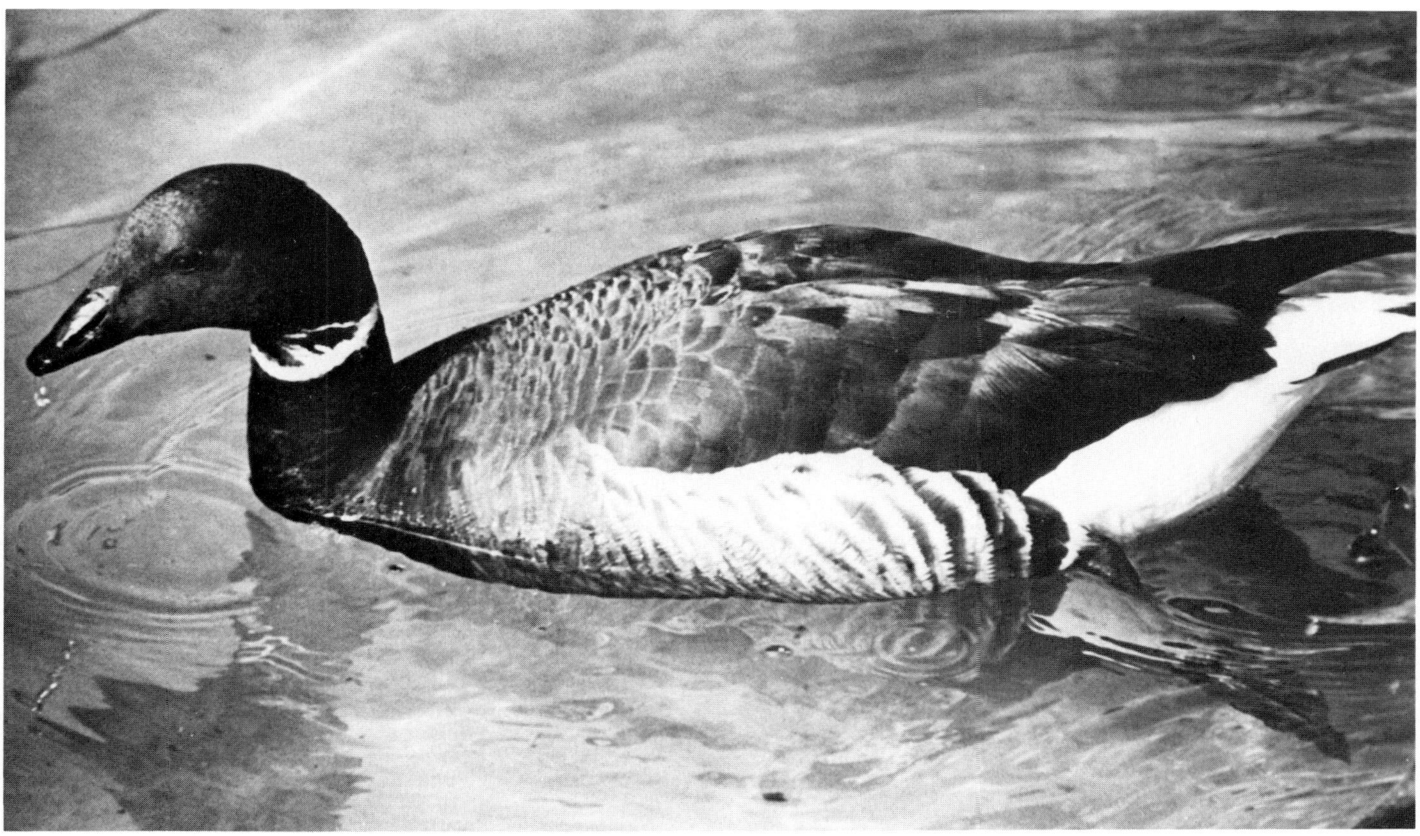

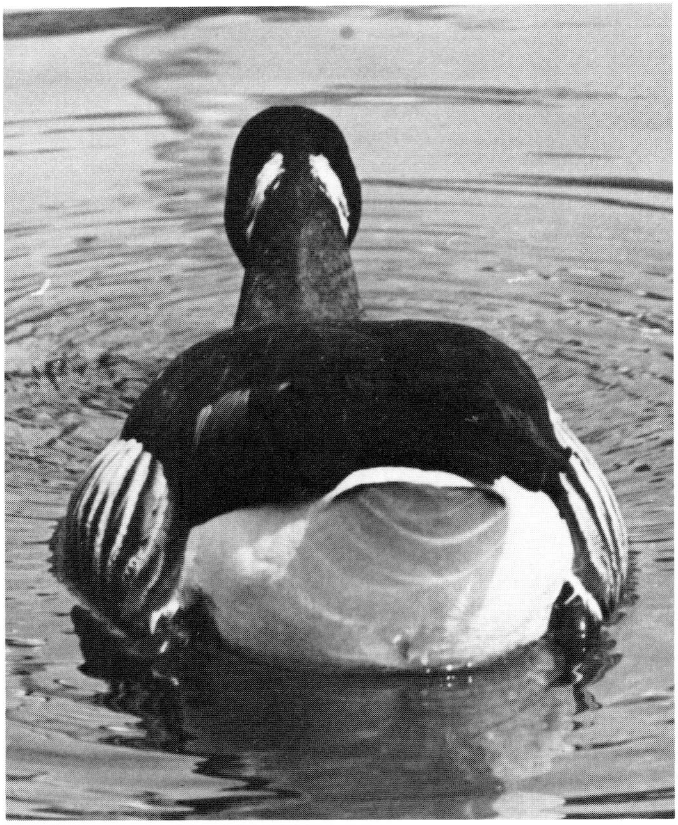

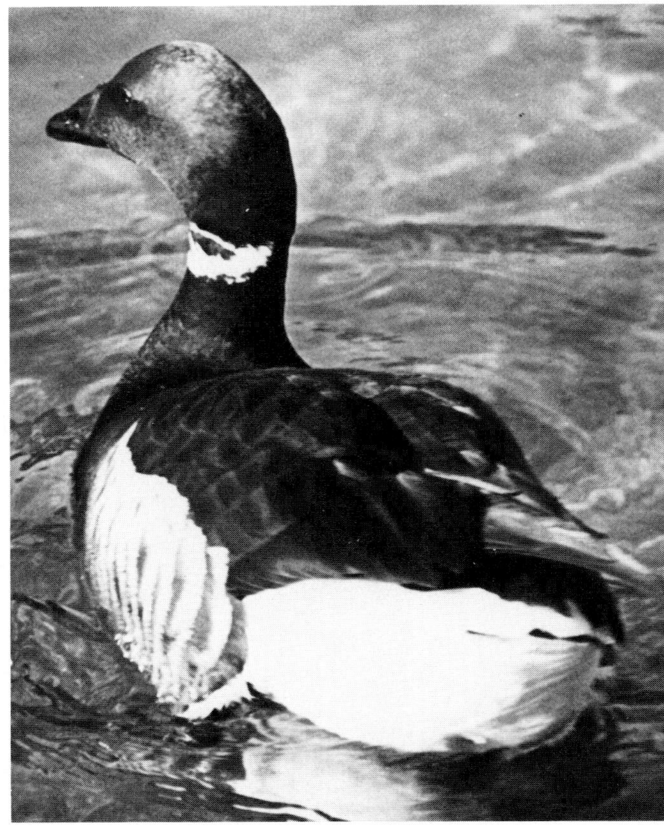

34-19 Rear views of the Pacific brant. Note body shape and extent of his white collar. 34-20

34-21 An alert, mated pair of Pacific brant.

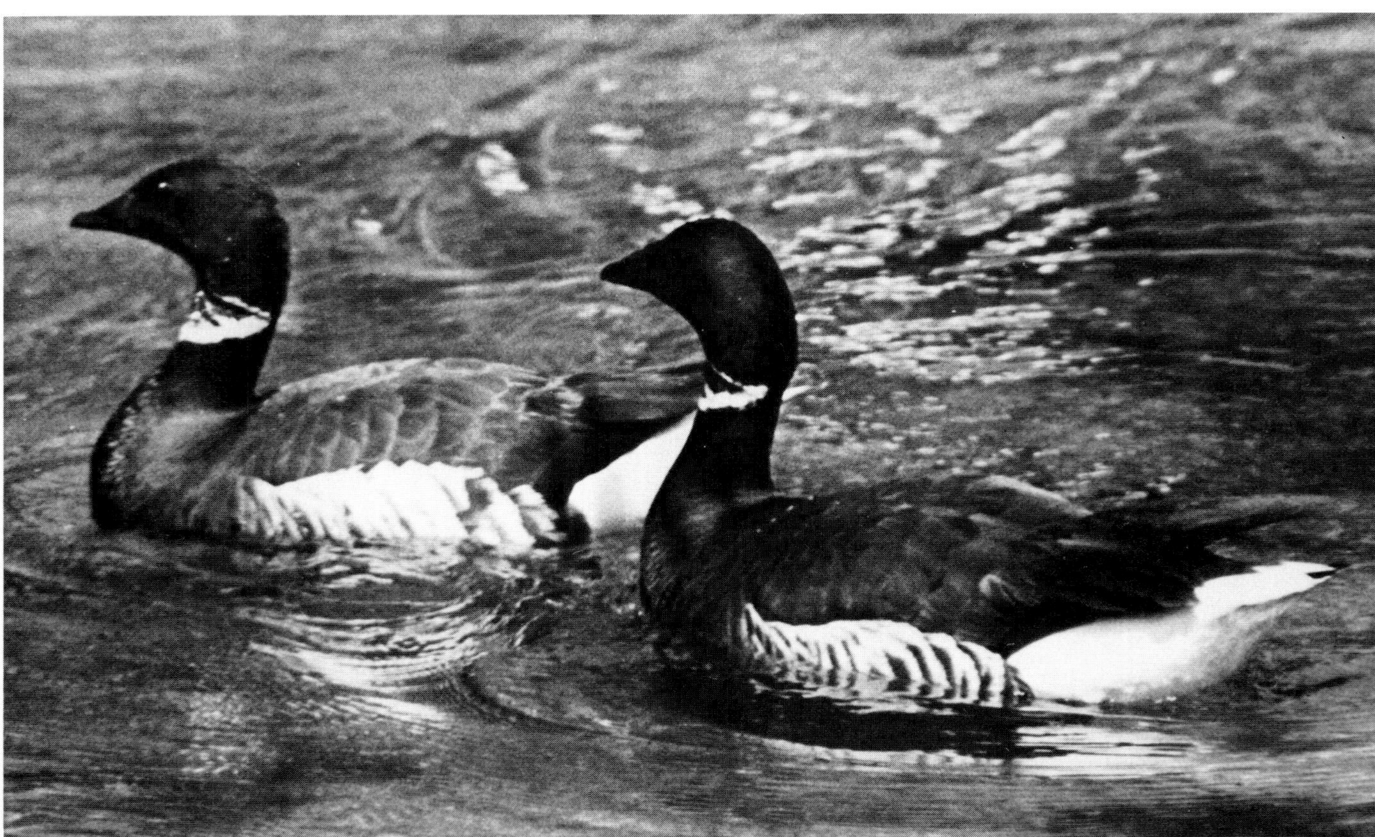

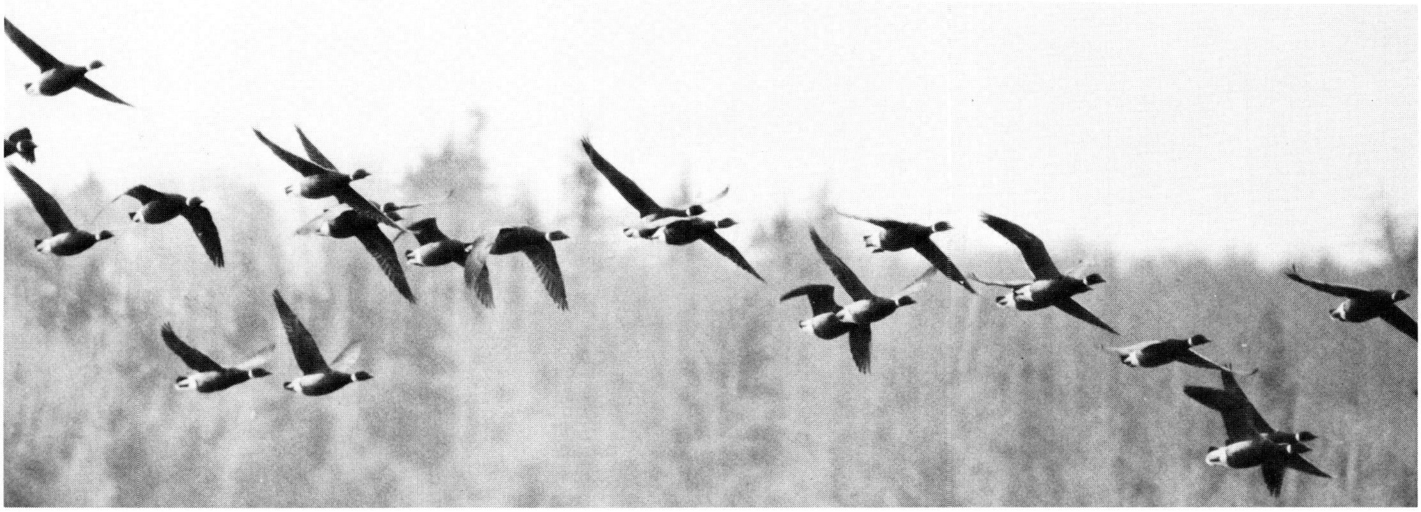

34-22 Group of Pacific brant. They usually fly in wide, undulating lines.

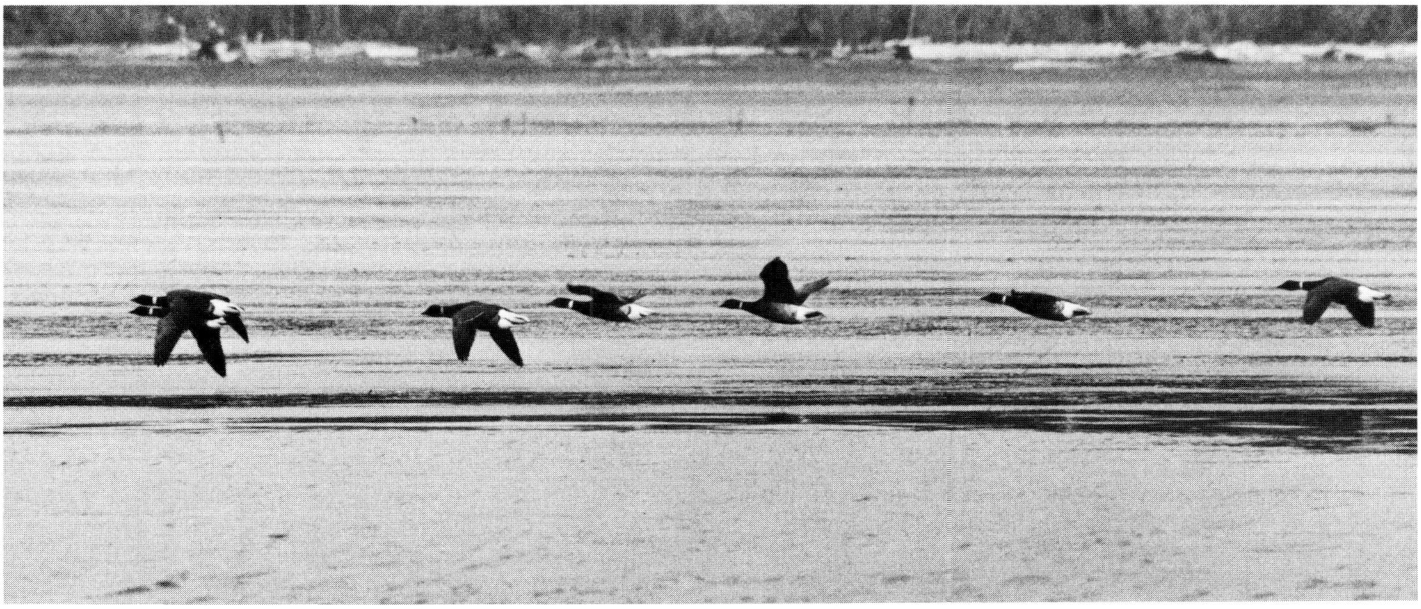

34-23 Brant are strong flyers. They fly low, often just above the waves.

34-24 Five different flight positions.

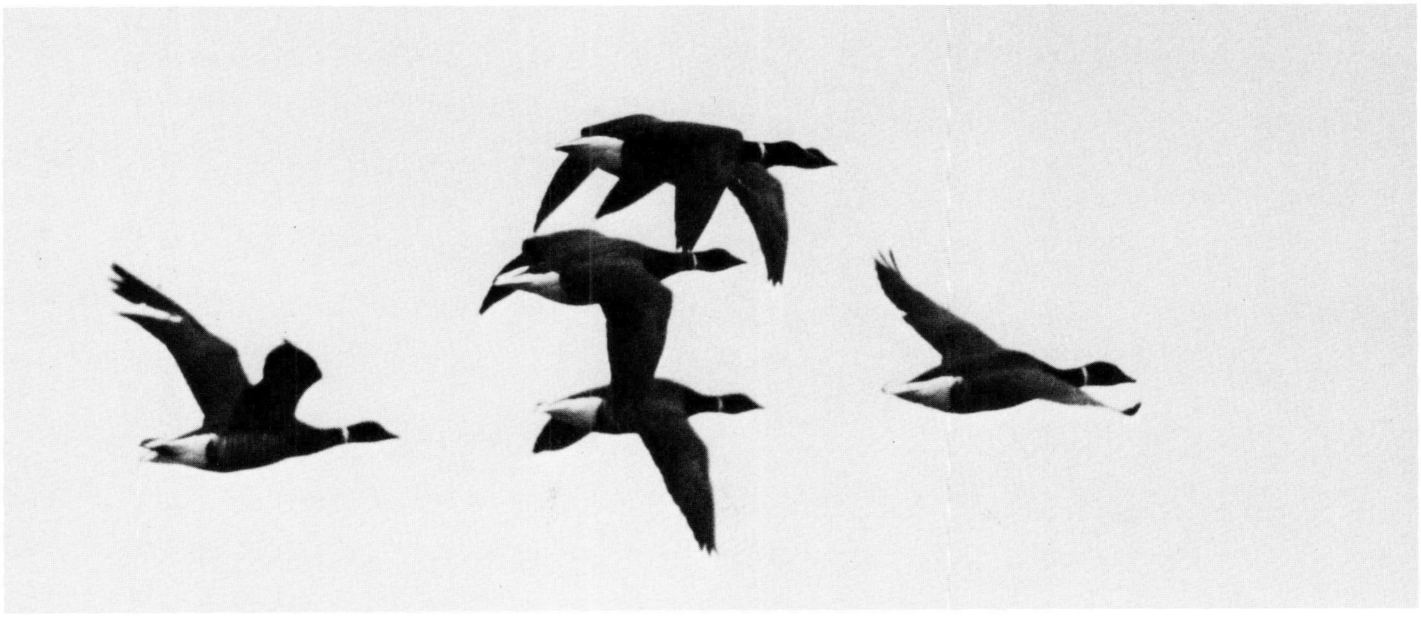

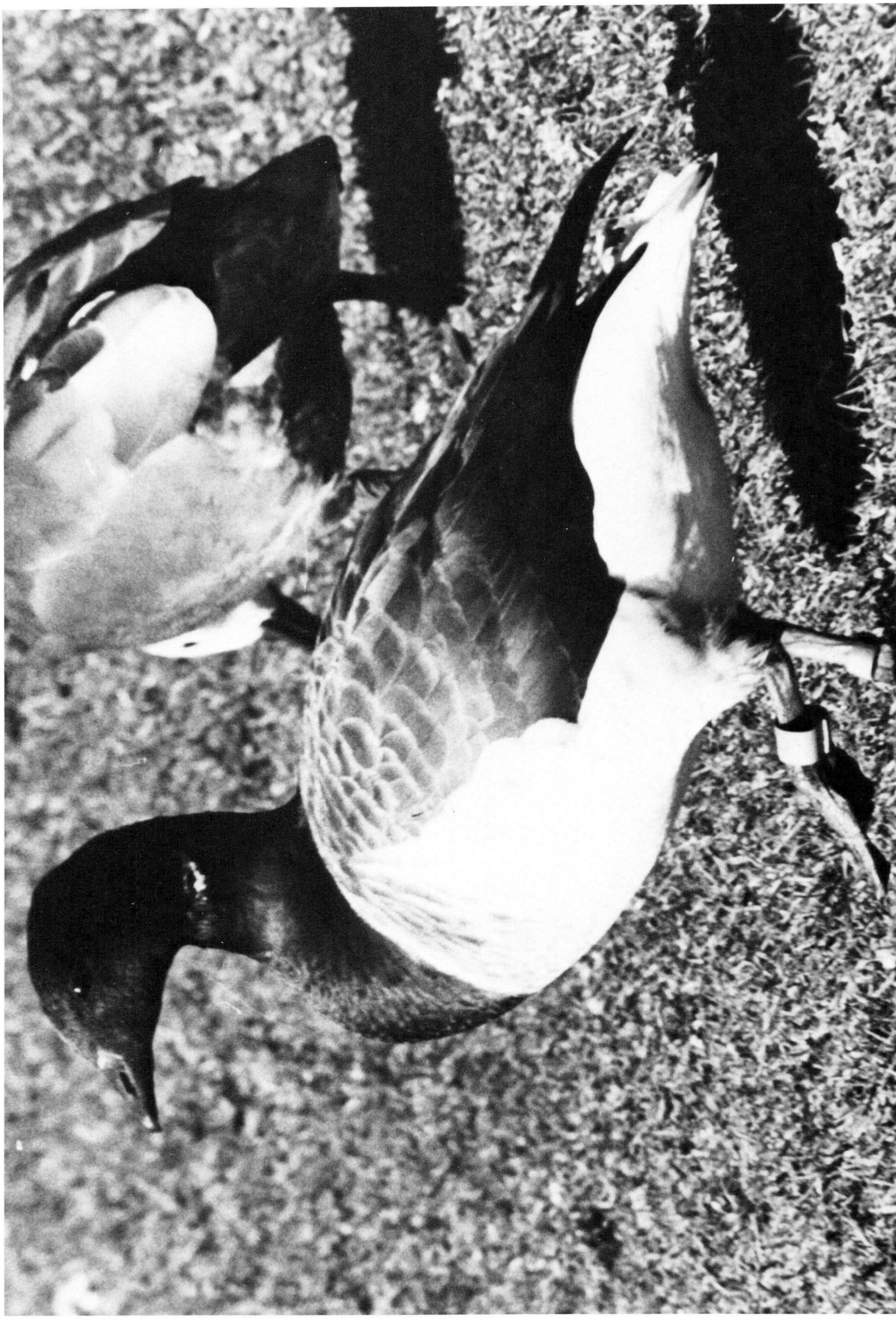

34-25 The Atlantic, sometimes called the American, brant is identical structurally to the Pacific brant, but has lighter sides and breasts. In addition, his chokerlike collar is smaller and discontinuous on both the front and back of his neck.

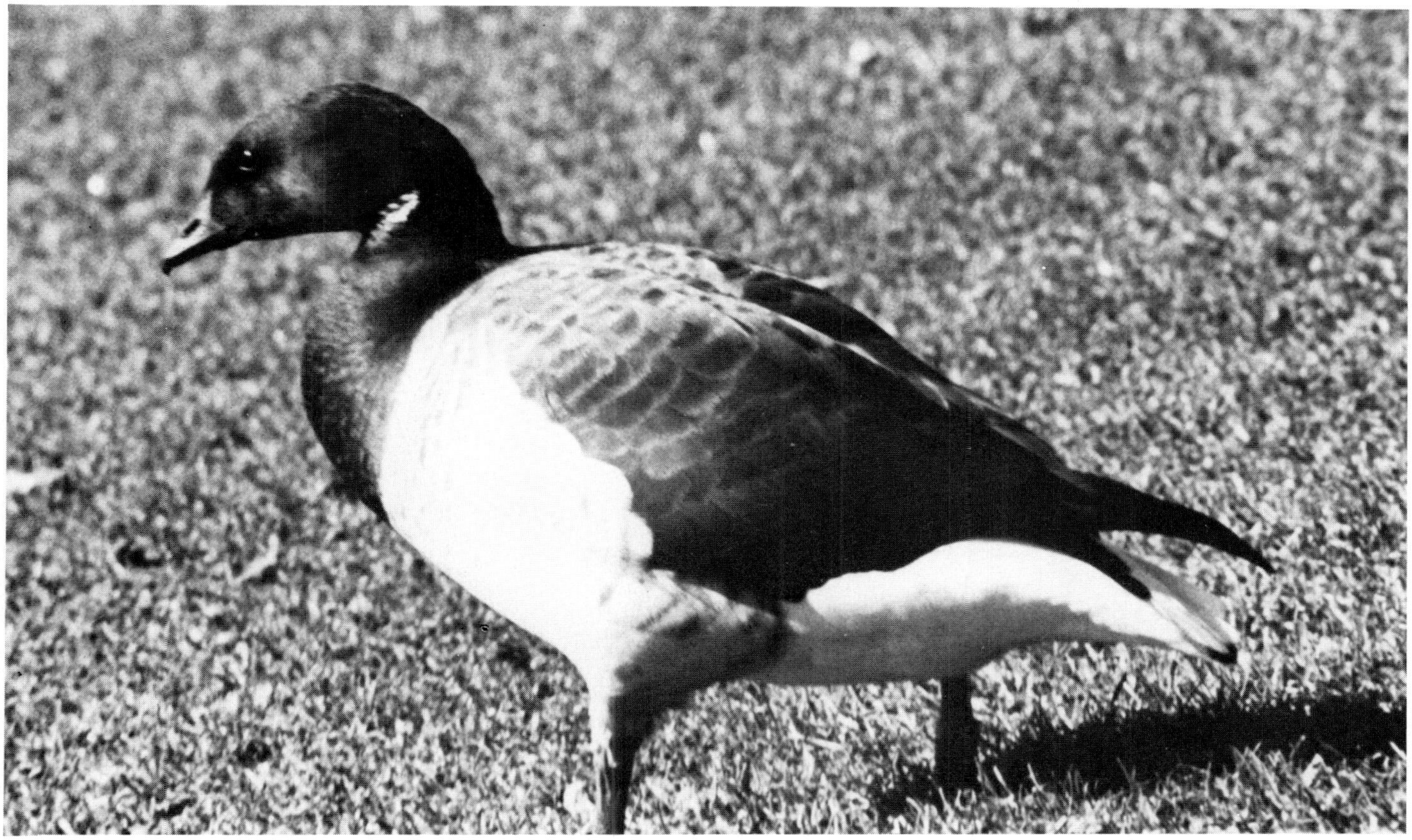

34-26 Atlantic brant in a graceful, striding pose.

34-27 Pair of Atlantic brant come down for a drink.

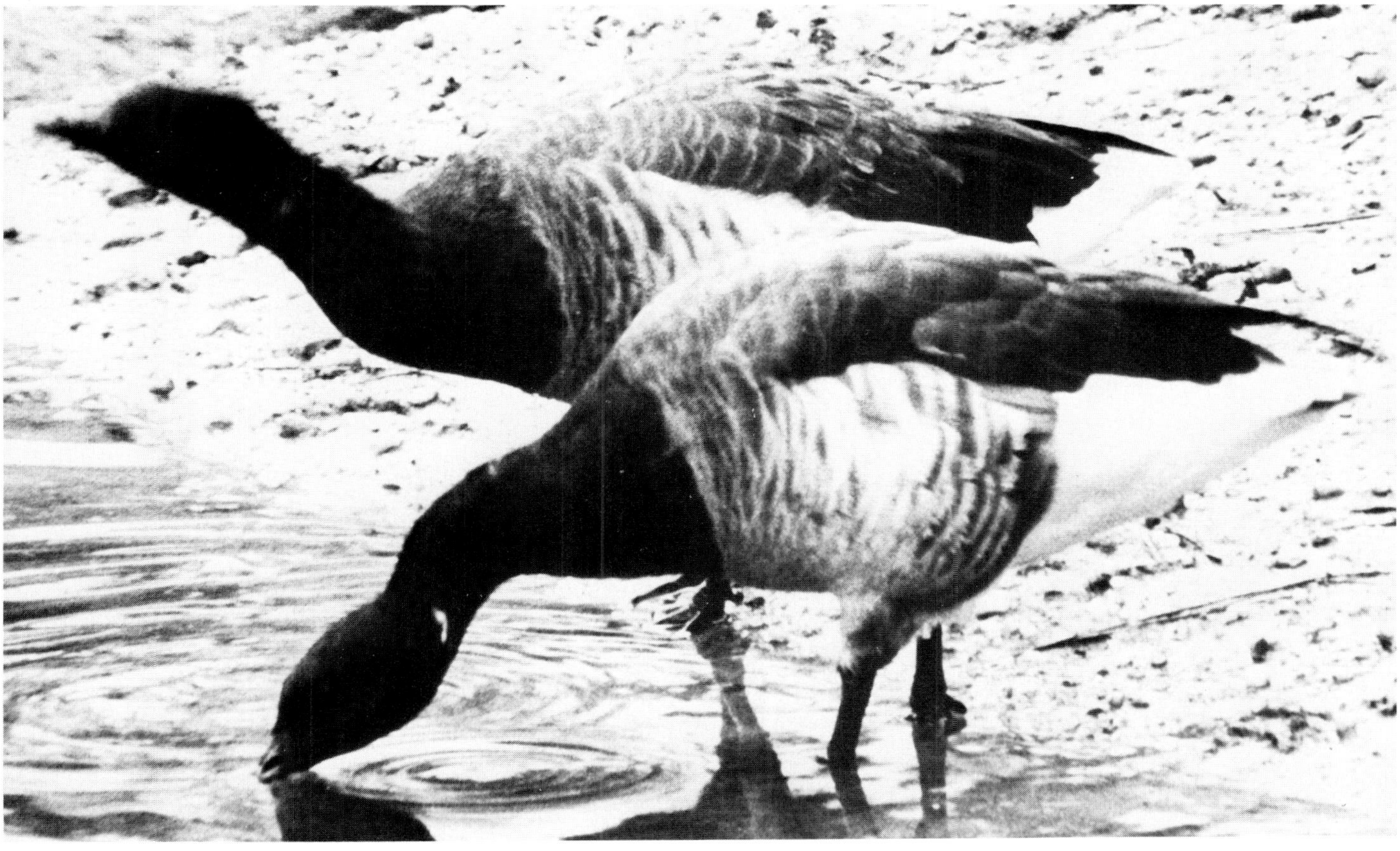

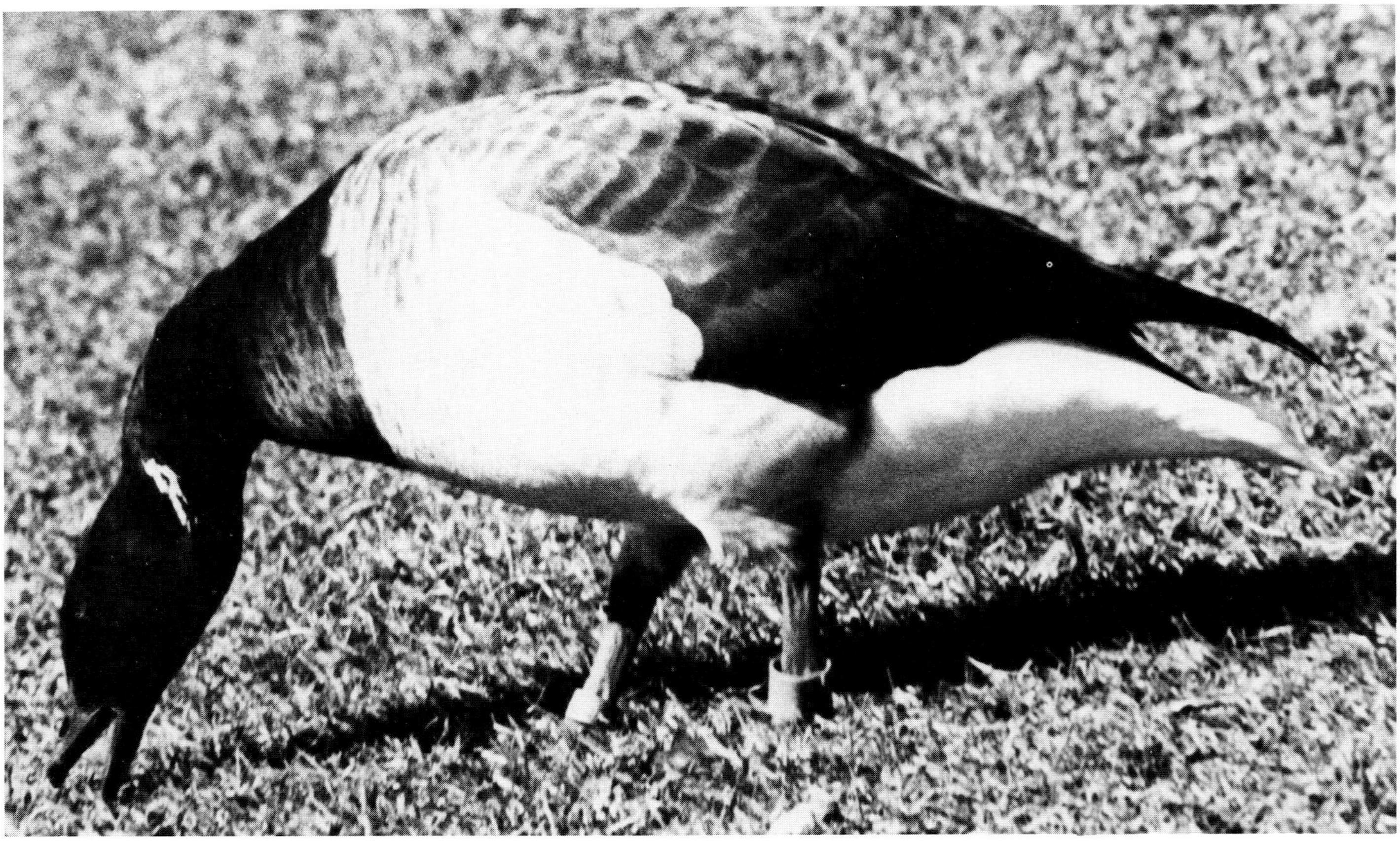

34-28

American brant cropping grass. They are vegetarians like most geese.

34-29

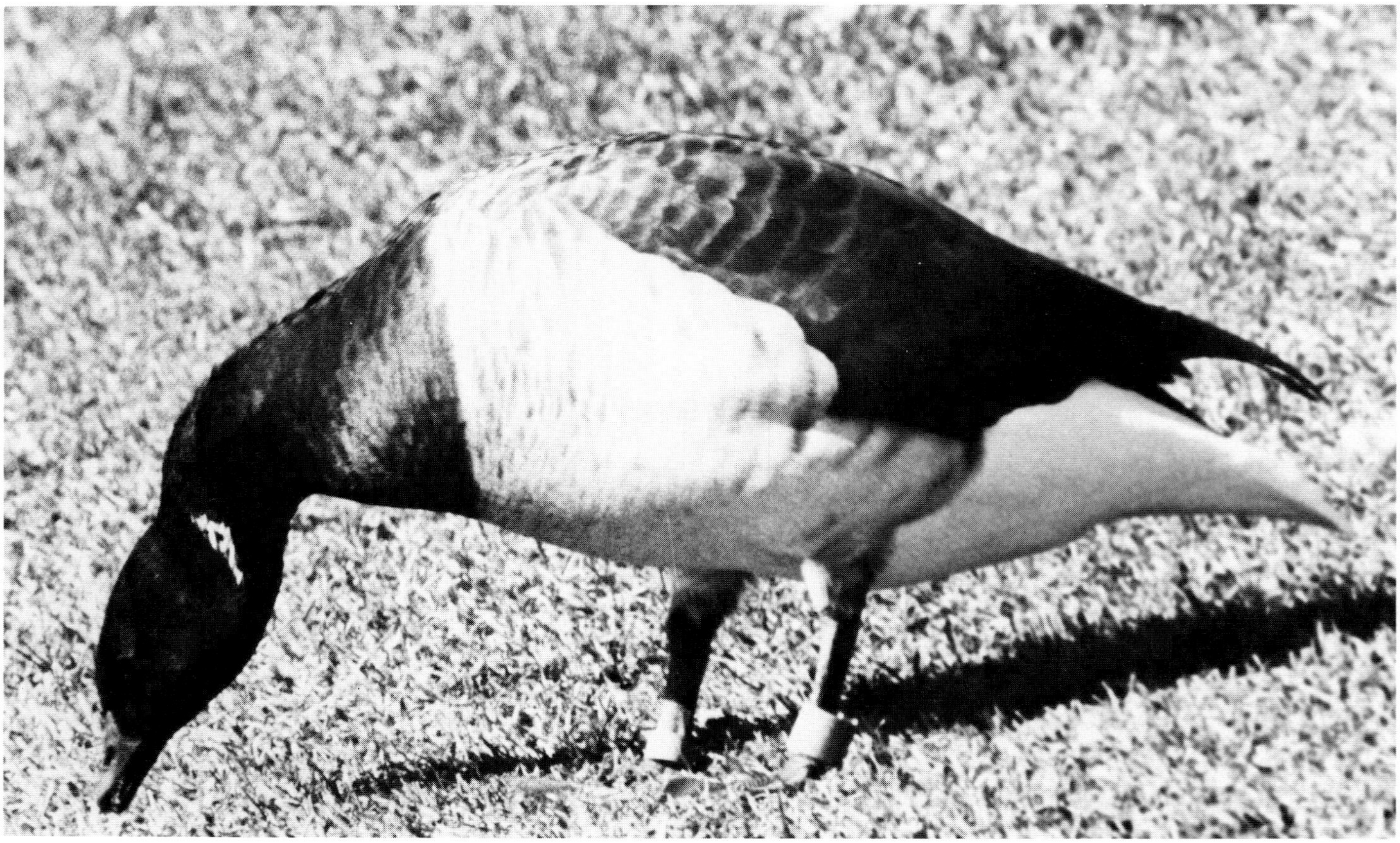

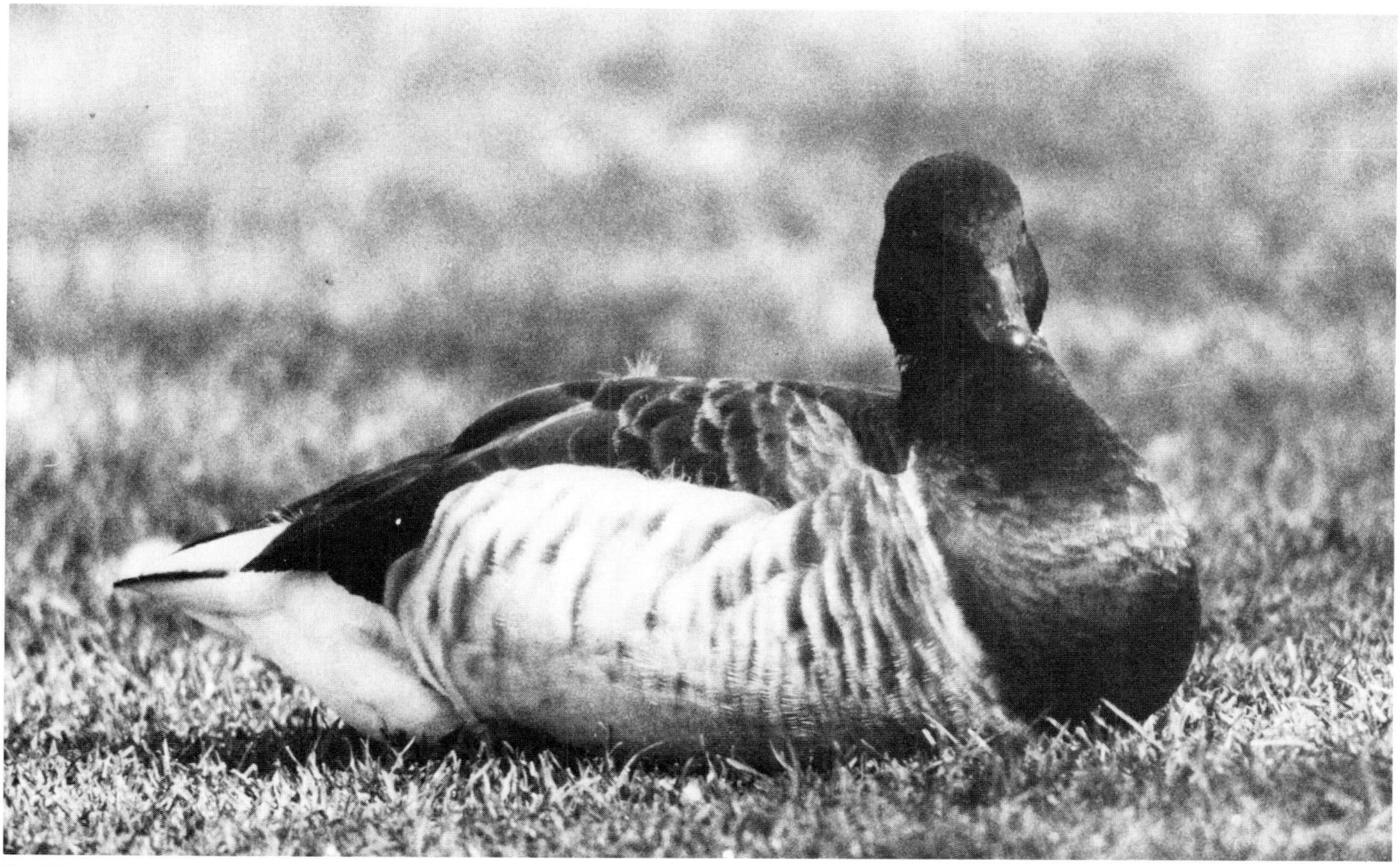

34-30

Two studies of resting Atlantic brant.

34-31

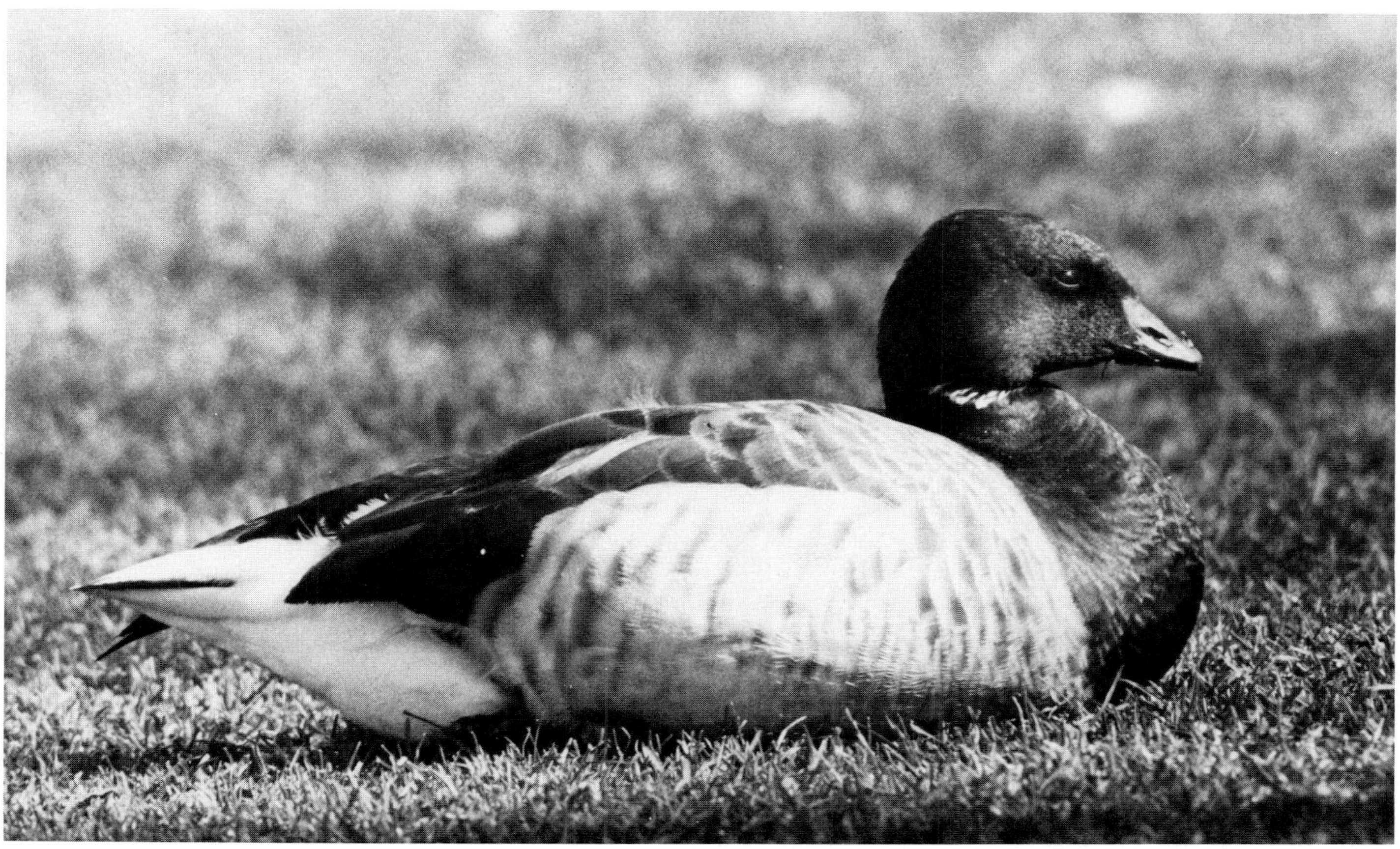

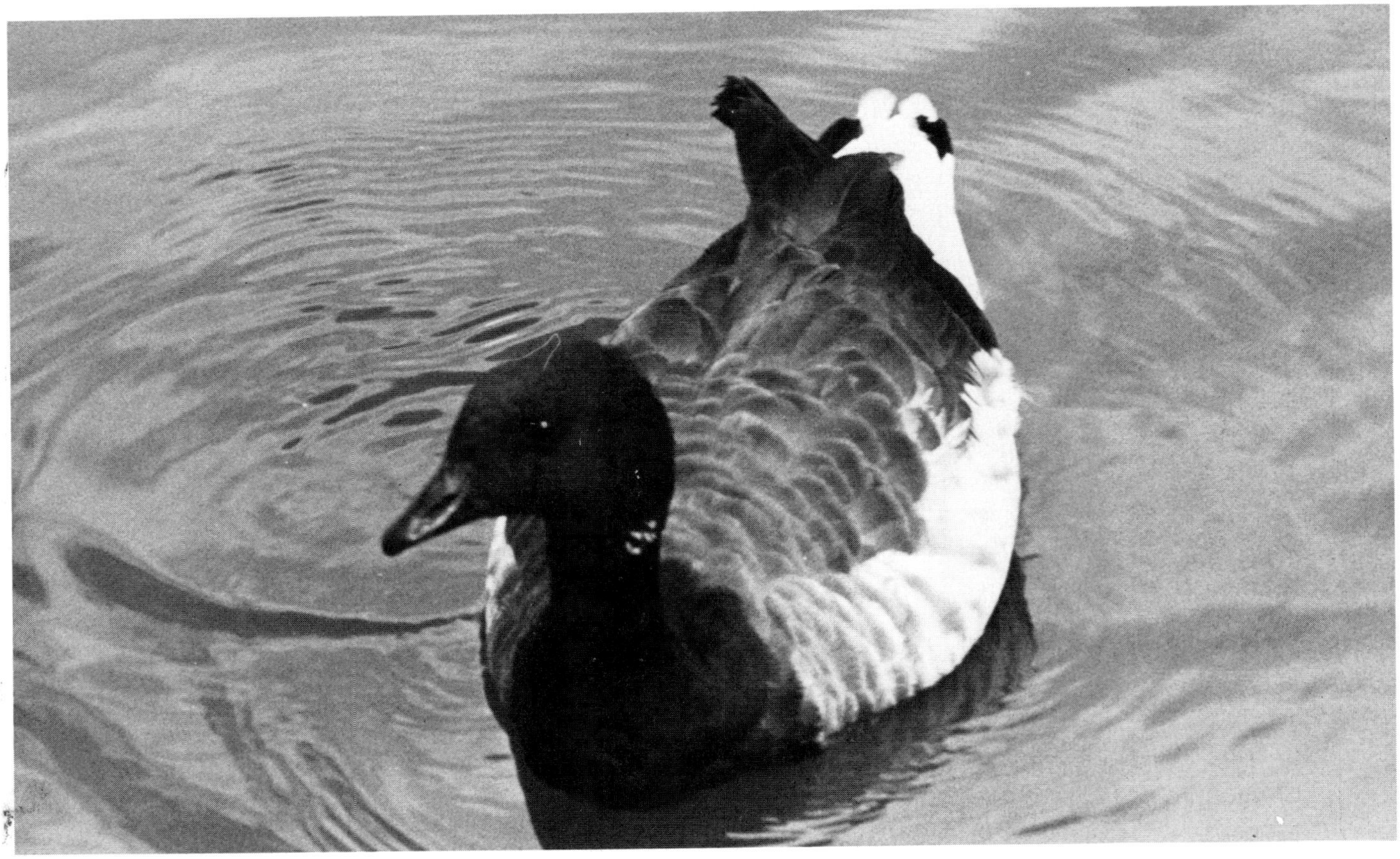

34-32

Atlantic brant, like their Pacific cousins, love eel grass and roll it into balls before swallowing. Their well developed salt glands enable them to subsist entirely on salt water and coastal vegetation.

34-33

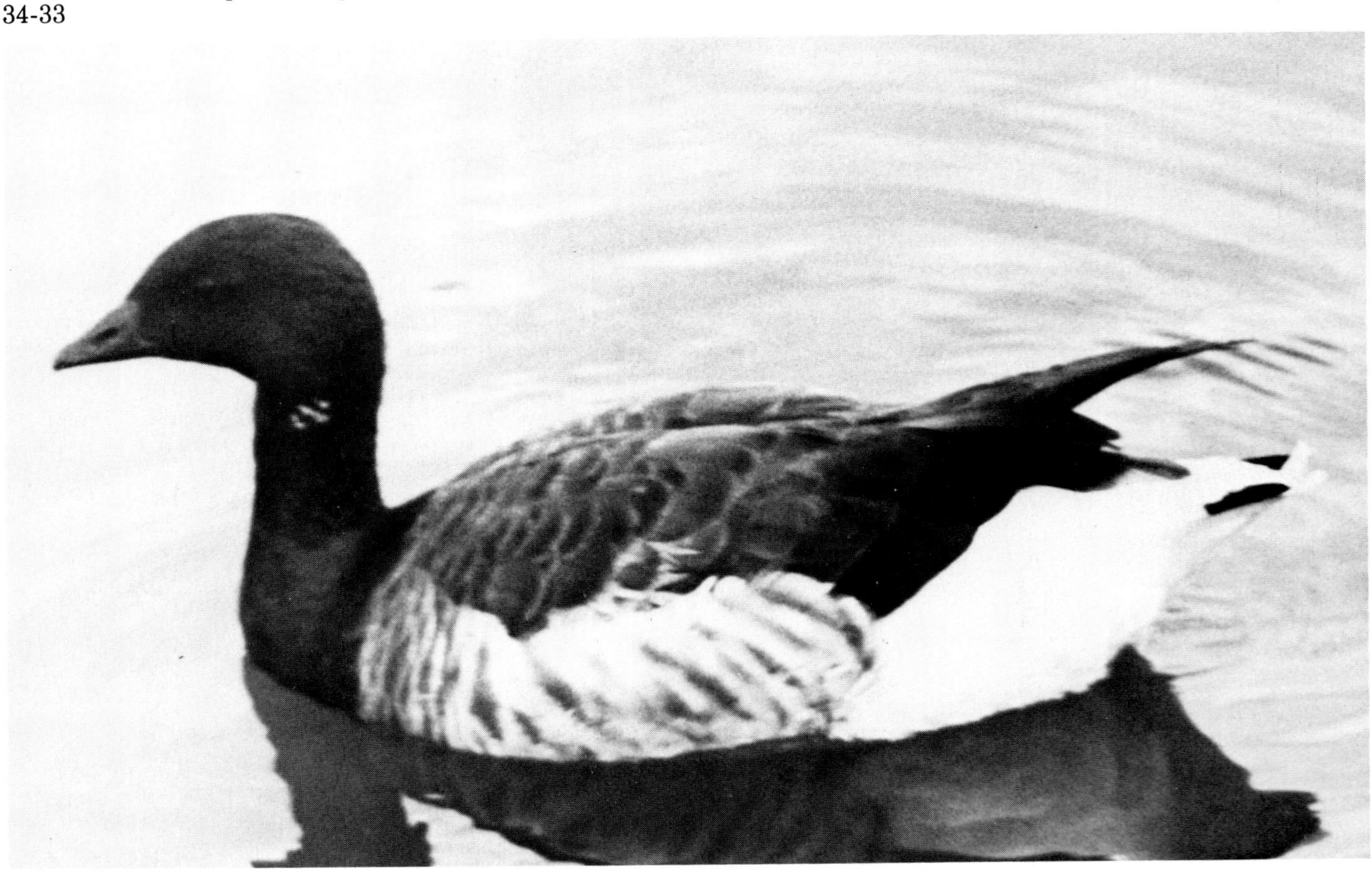

CHAPTER 35

The Emperor Goose

Anser canagicus
(Color Photos—page 93)

Bent describes the emperor goose as the "handsomest and least known of American geese." Van Campen Hellner (*Duck Hunting*) states they are the "wariest of waterfowl." Whether they are the handsomest and wariest of geese may be argued by many; but, without doubt, due to their very limited range, they are seen by fewer hunters and bird watchers than any other goose species in North America.

In some respects, the emperor goose resembles the blue goose; however, the dark, brownish-black underneck and orange-yellow tarsi and feet of the emperor are prominent featurs which help reduce possible confusion in identification. Also, because of the wide separation of their ranges, there is very little likelihood of these two species being seen together.

Emperor geese breed along the almost inaccessible coastal marshes of western Alaska in the Seward Peninsula and Morton Sound areas. Some breed along the eastern coast of Siberia at about the same latitudes. They are already mated when they arrive at their breeding grounds during the last part of May. During this period, the males are very jealous and strongly resent any approaches made toward their mates. Nesting sites are usually selected in the driftwood debris that marks the high tide line along the coasts, although some nests are located 10 miles or so inland. The young are hatched in late June or early July. About two or three weeks after the young appear, the adult birds molt and become flightless. During this period, both young and old are very vulnerable to depredation by their natural enemies, and at least in the past, by natives who captured some of these very helpless birds for food. By early August, the adults have again acquired their flight feathers and are able to fly, as are the young birds.

Emperor geese are almost as much at home in the ocean and on the coast as black brant. Unlike the plant-loving brant, their food during the winter consists mainly of mussels and shellfish. In the spring, they forage on grasses and berries like other geese. As previously mentioned, Eskimos take some birds, also their eggs, for food during the nesting season. However, these geese remain at all times far from most humans. The population of emperor geese is estimated at approximately 200,000, and their survival is not threatened. An occasional straggler (probably separated from his group by strong, northwest gales) is seen as far south as California. In the winter of 1970, a large number of bird watchers were delighted to spot three emperor geese on a tidal flat near Huntington Beach, California.

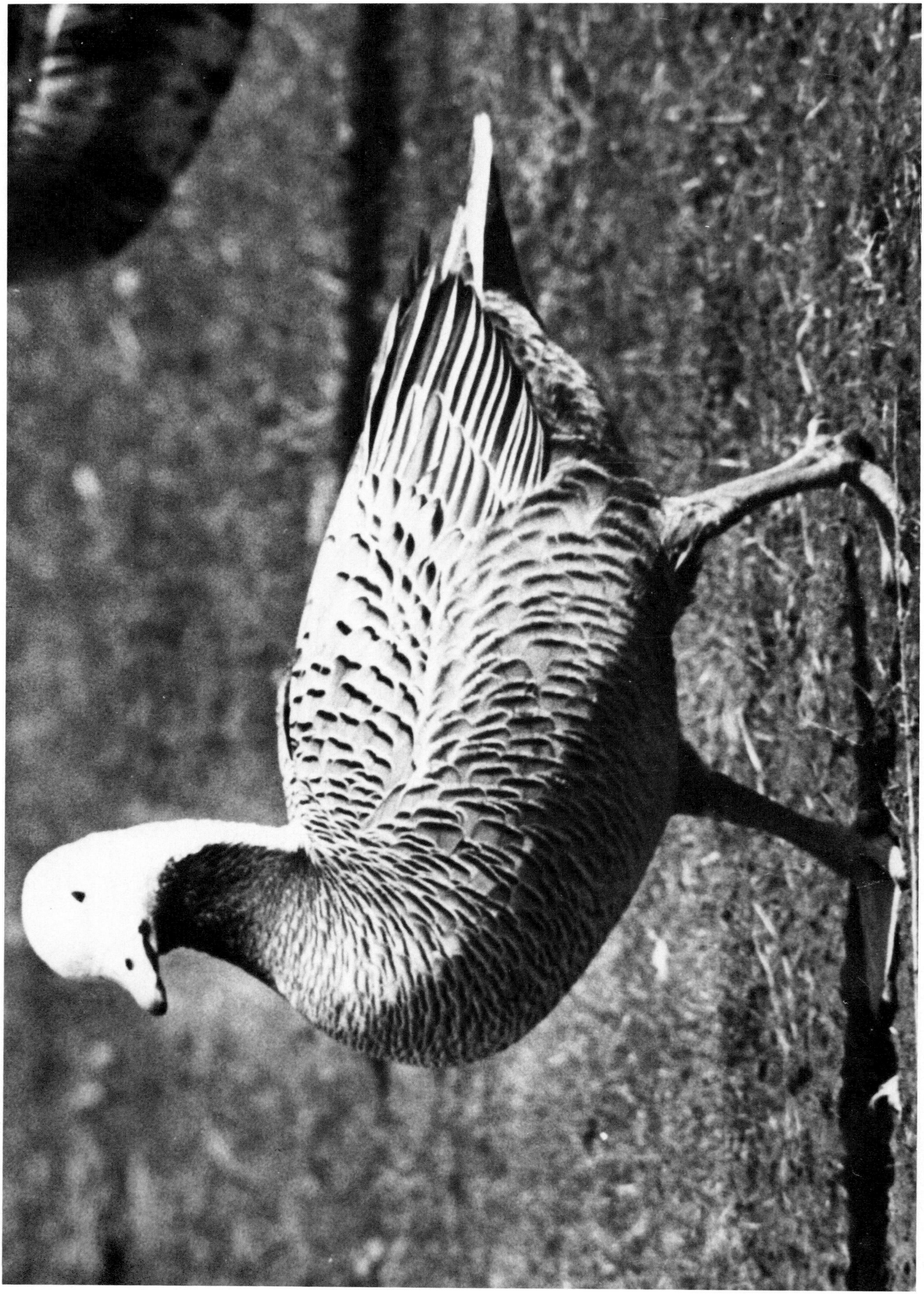

35-1 The beautifully marked and colored emperor goose. Because of his extreme northern range, he is rarely seen in the contiguous United States.

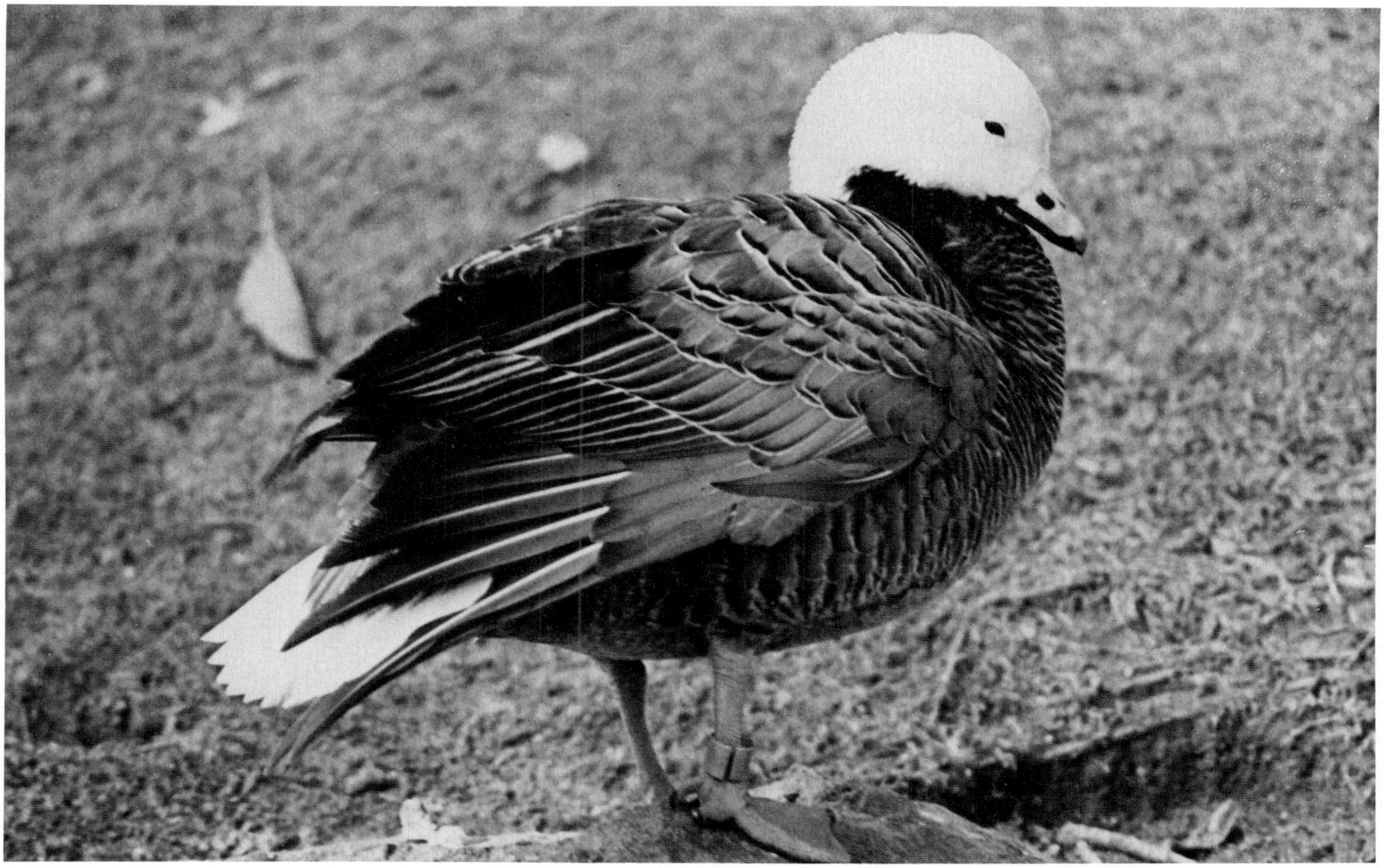

35-2 Emperor goose with one wing partially extended and the other raised.

35-3 Front and rear views of the emperor showing body cross-sectional shape, tail shape, and lateral leg placement. 35-4

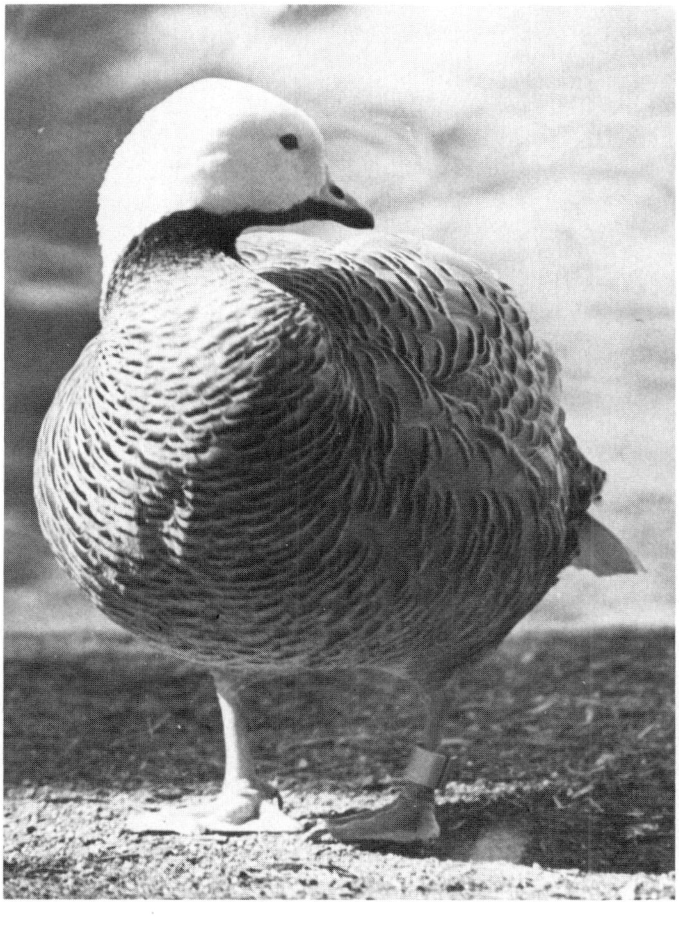

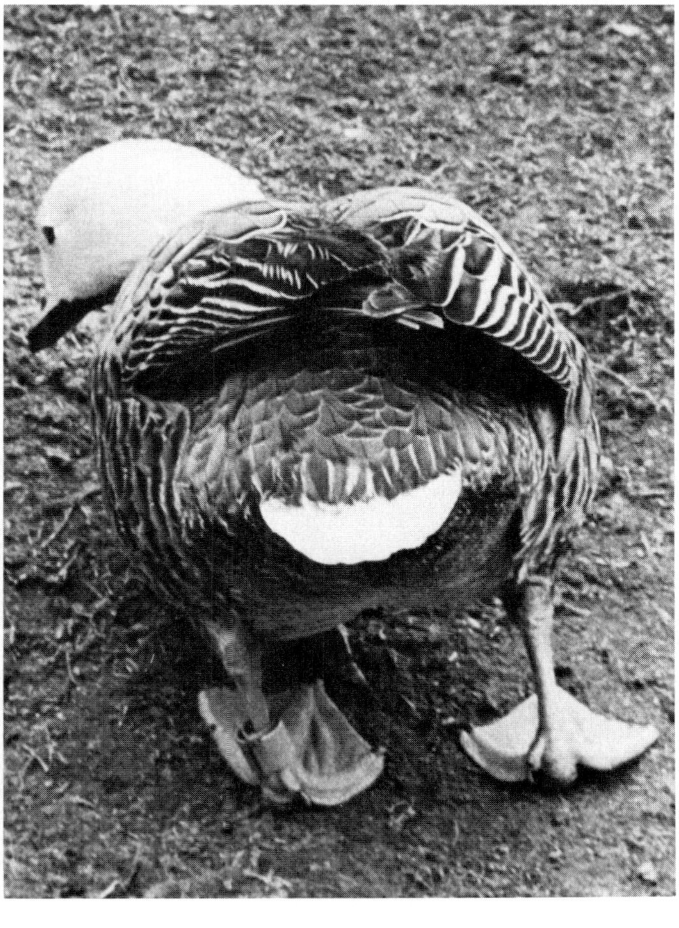

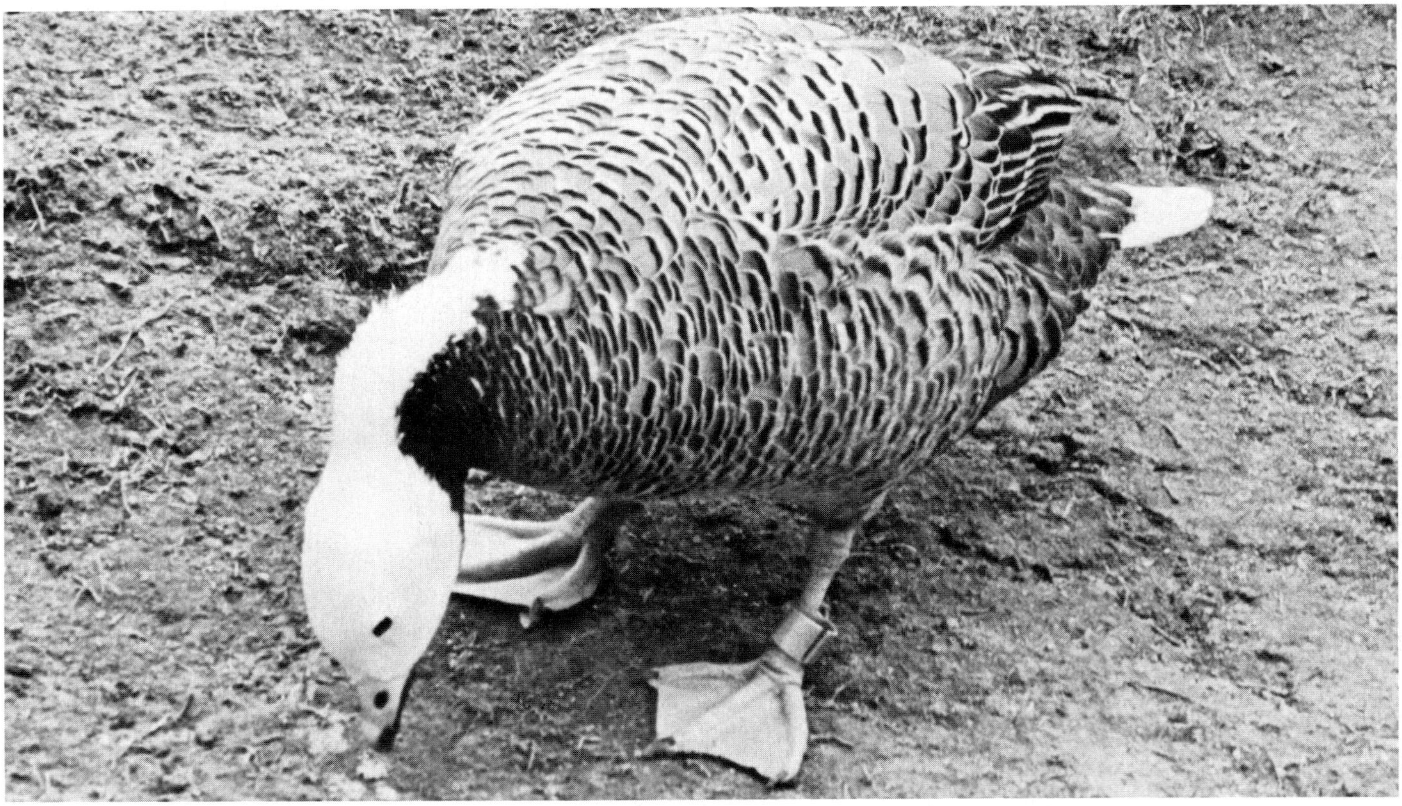

35-5 Emperor goose in a typical feeding position. Note the markings of his feathers.

35-6 Emperor goose in a threatening pose.

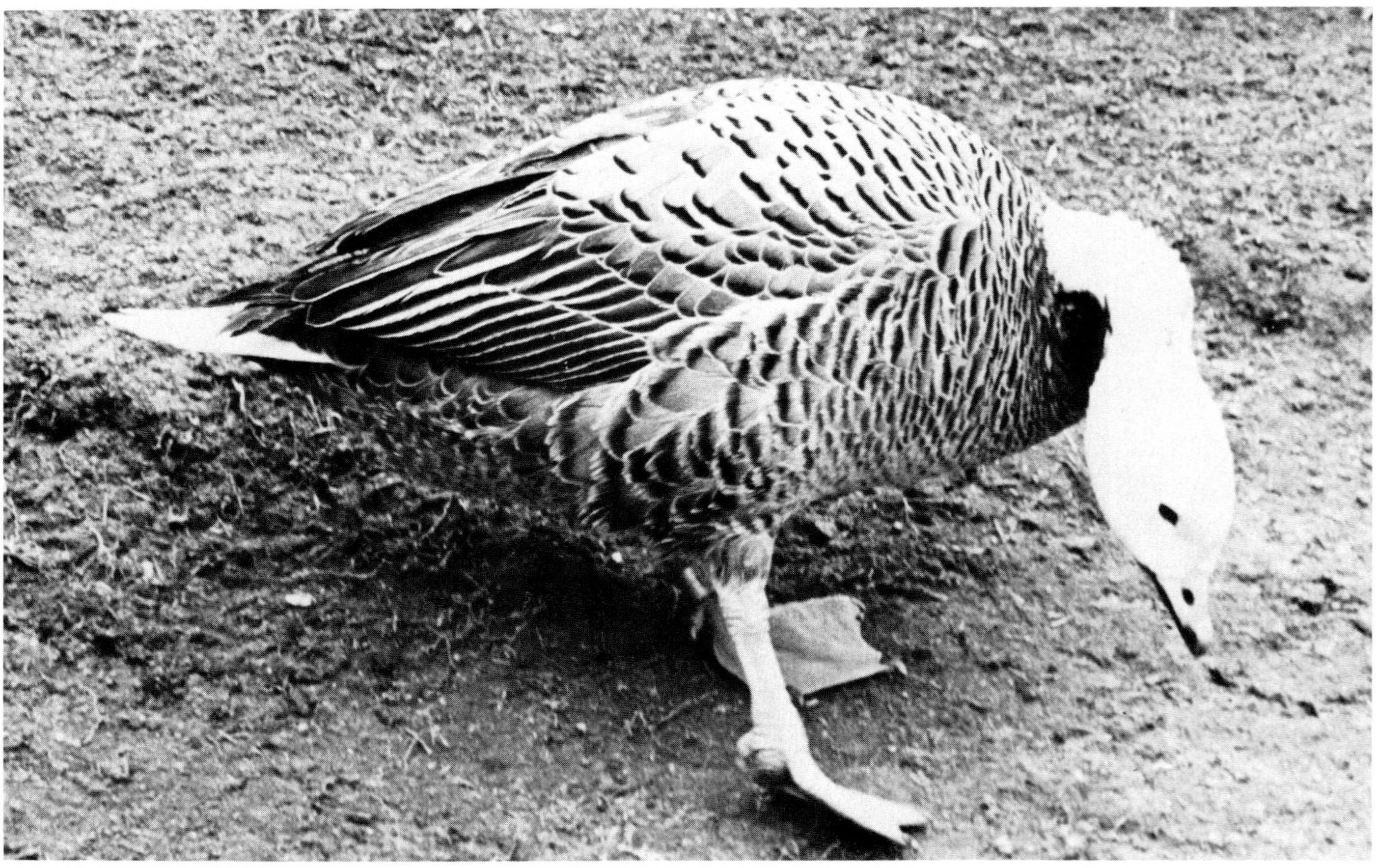

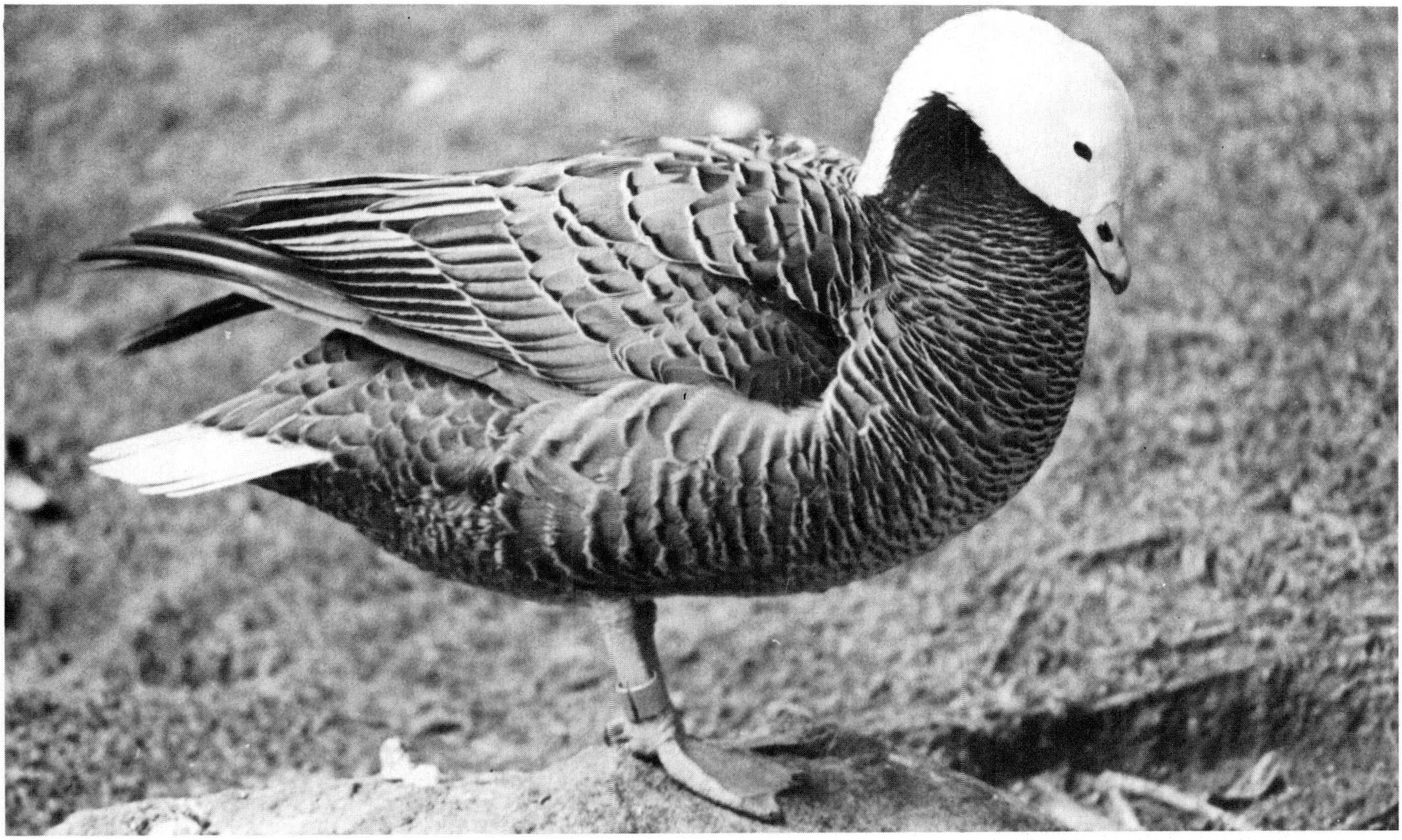

35-7 Profile study of the emperor. Note raised wings and how the scapulars and side feathers stand out.

35-8 Same pose from a different angle.

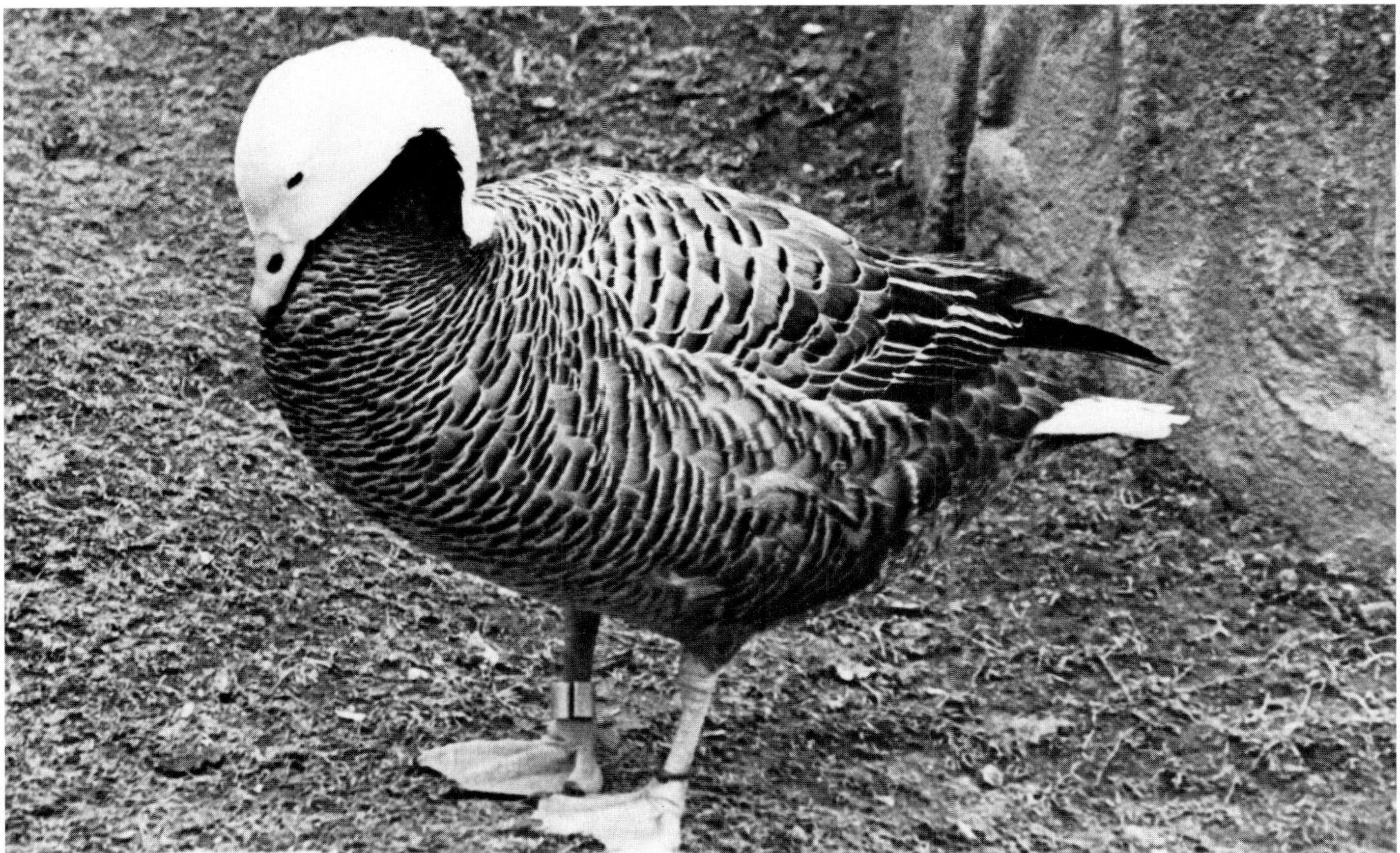

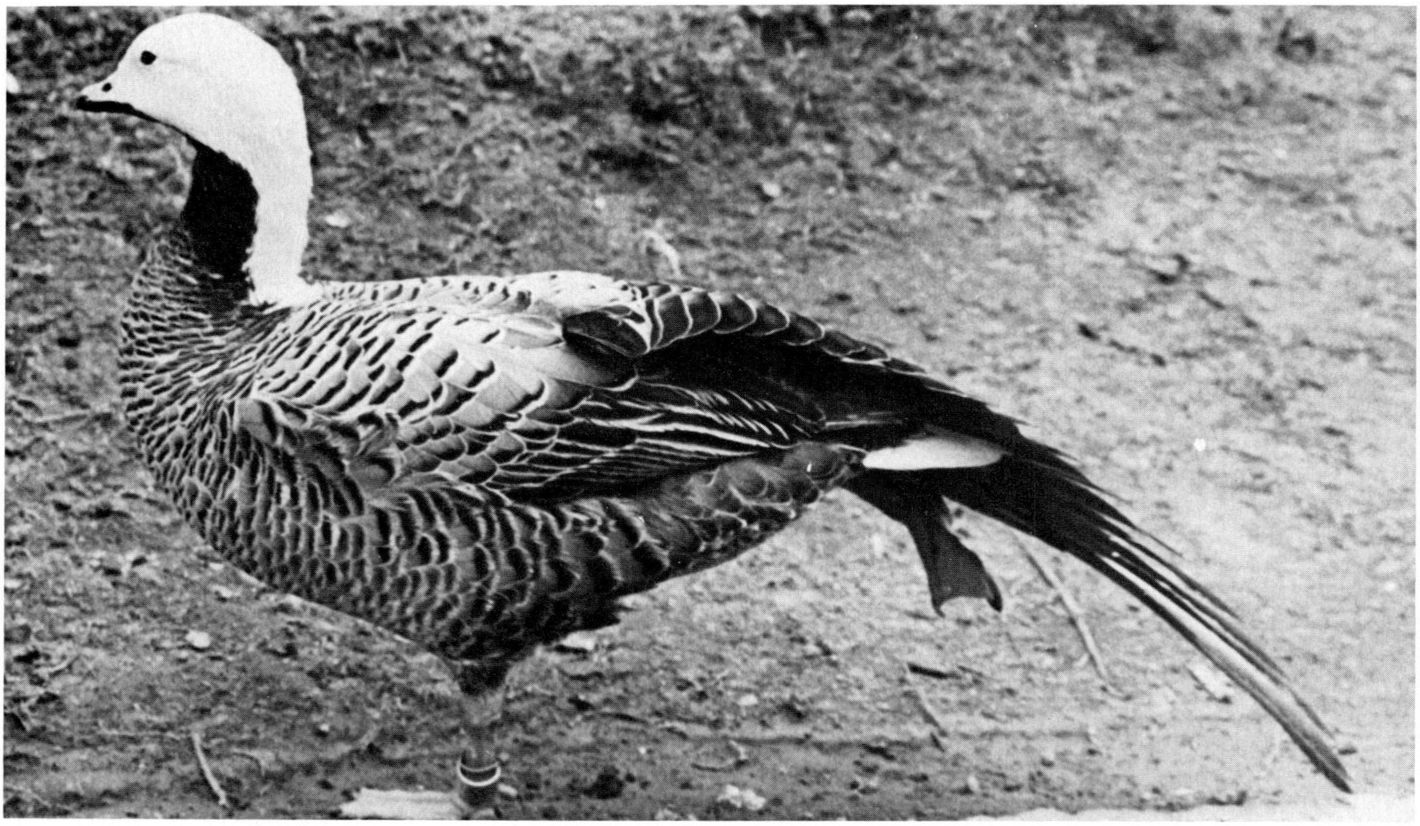

35-9 Emperor goose stretches one leg and wing.

35-10 Emperor goose stretches his wings. Good view of underside wing details.

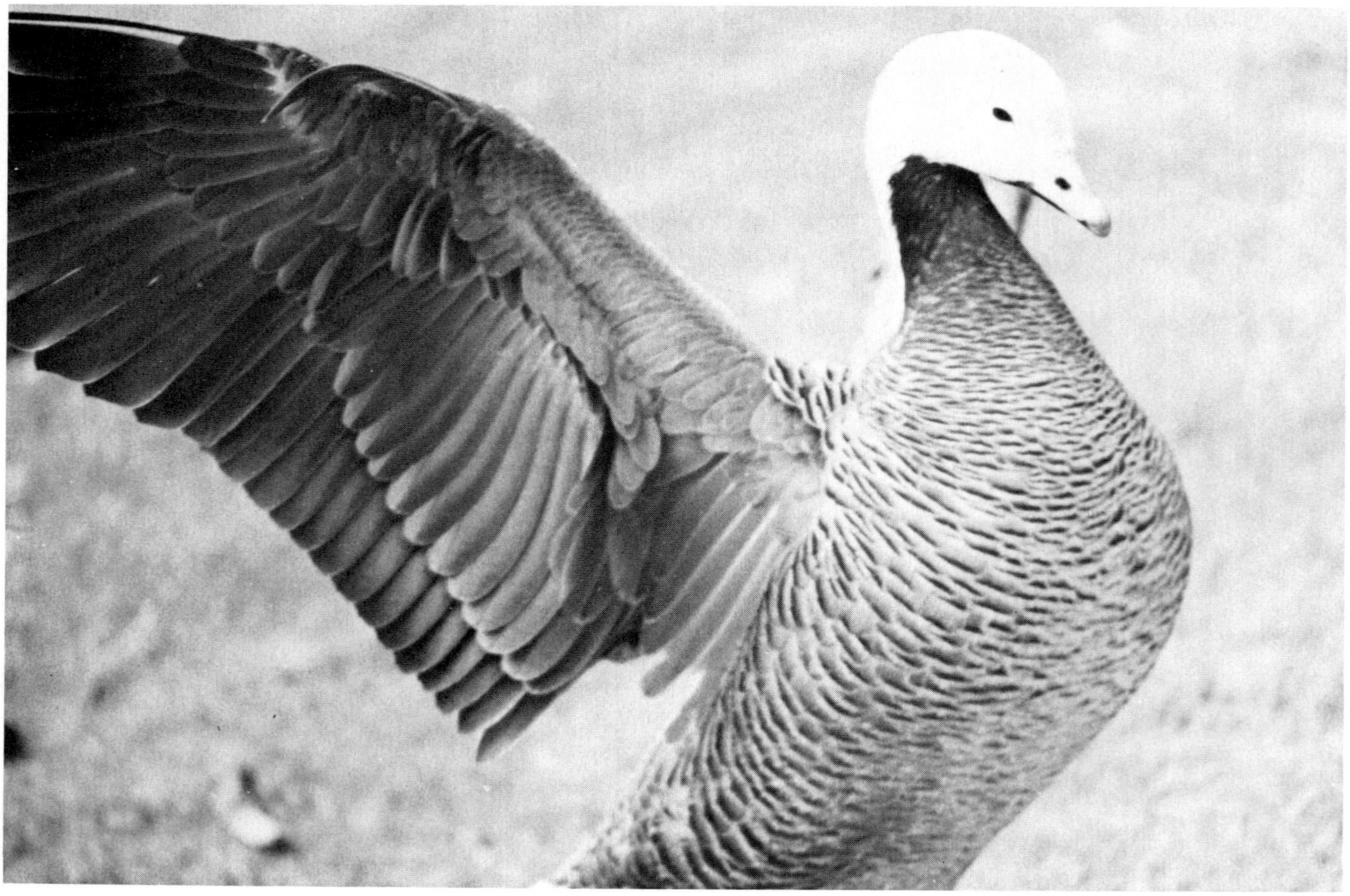

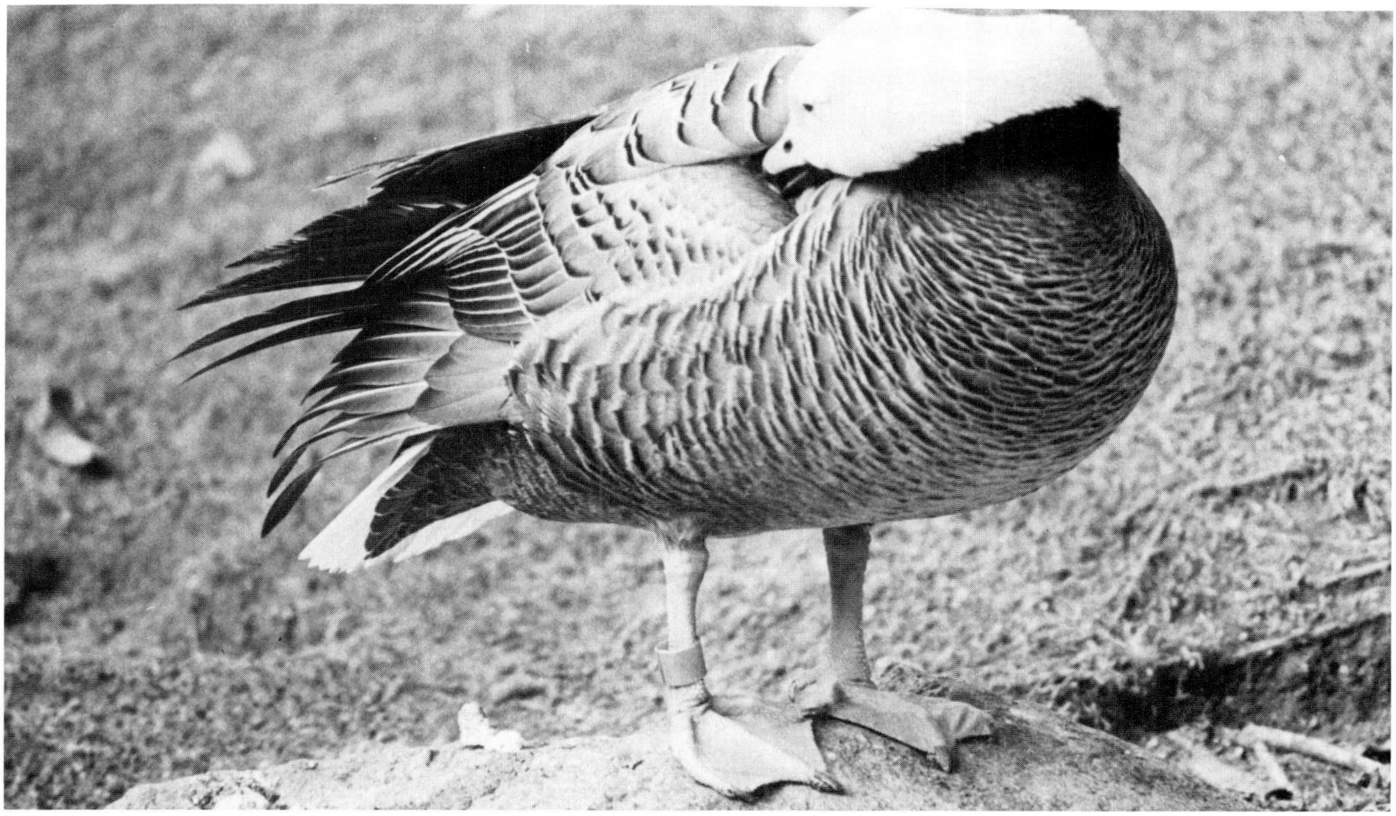

35-11 Emperor preens his upper wing coverts.

35-12 Nice preening poses. Notice expanded tail in left photograph. 35-13

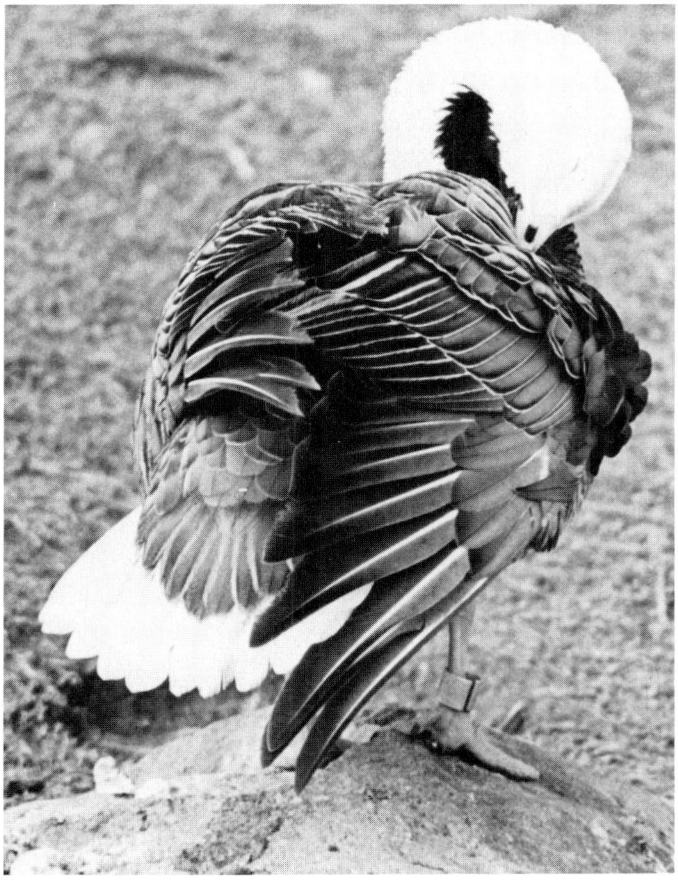

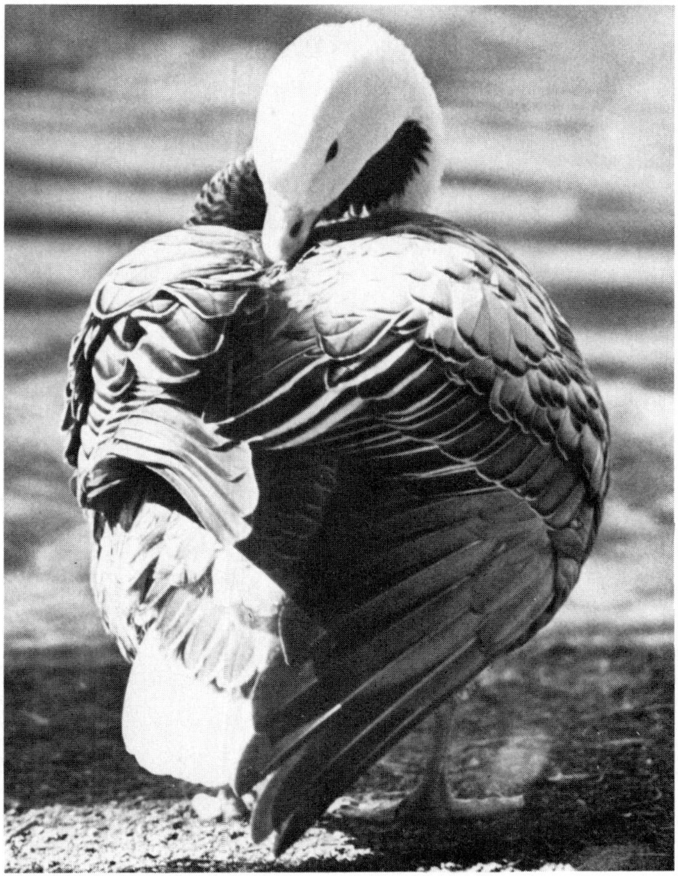

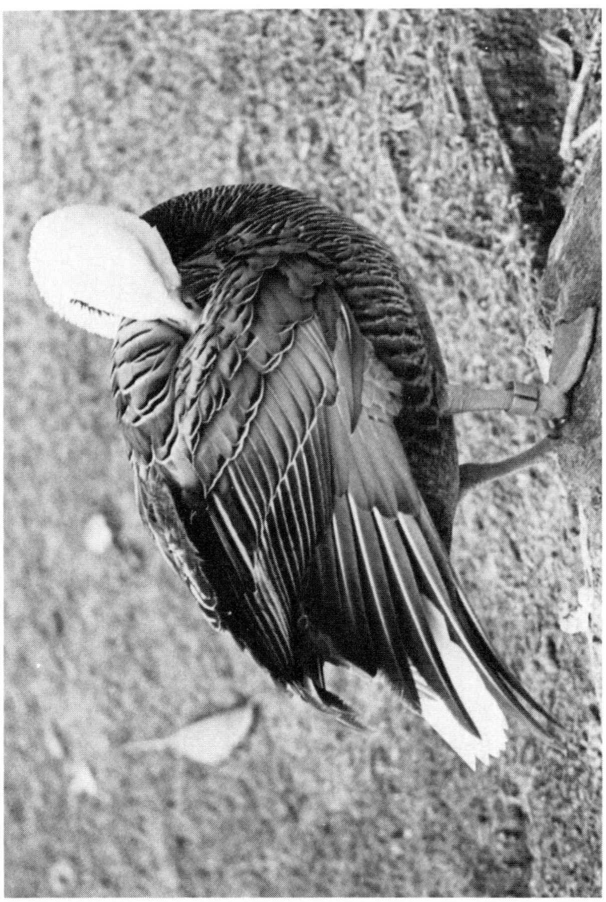

35-14

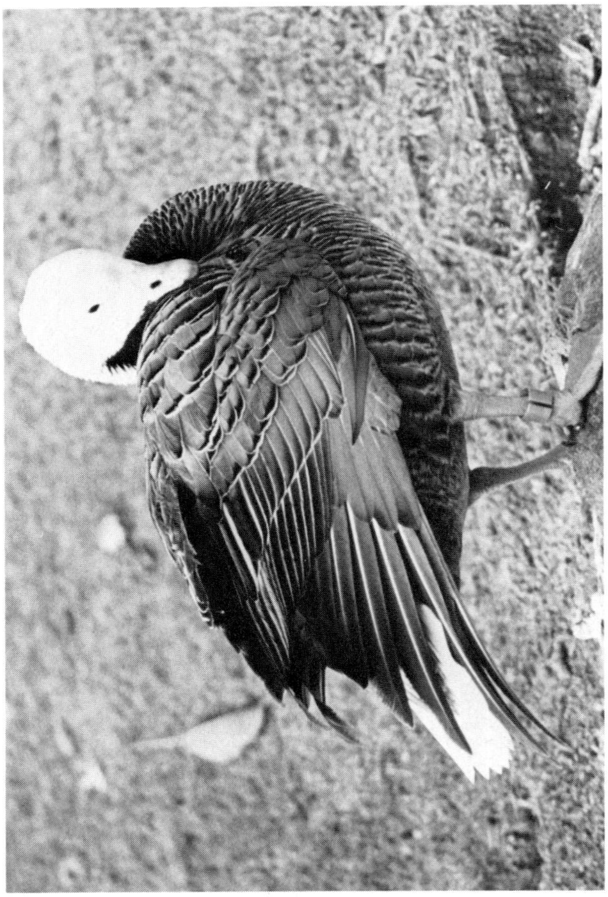

35-15

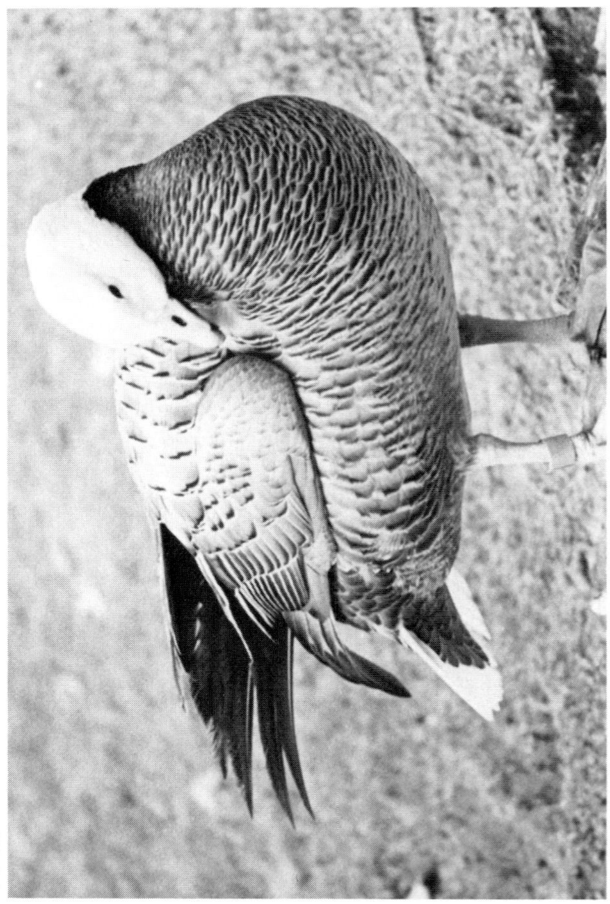

35-16

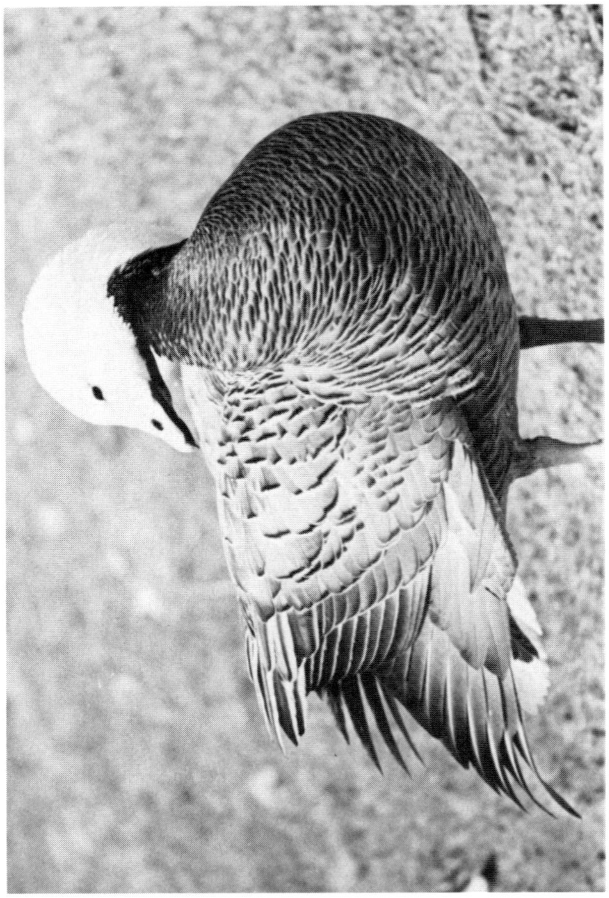

35-17

Four more preening poses.

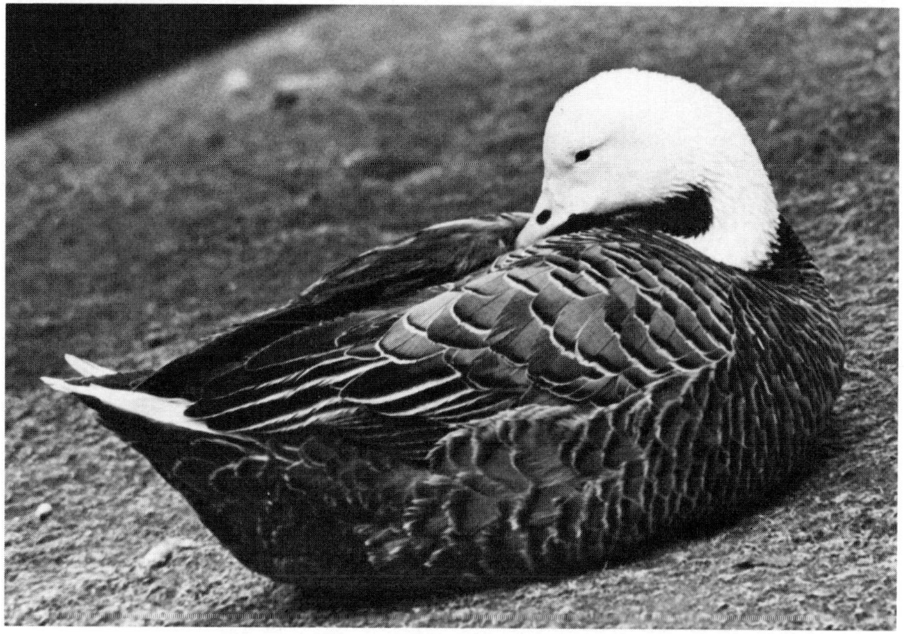

35-18 Resting emperor preens her back feathers prior to napping.

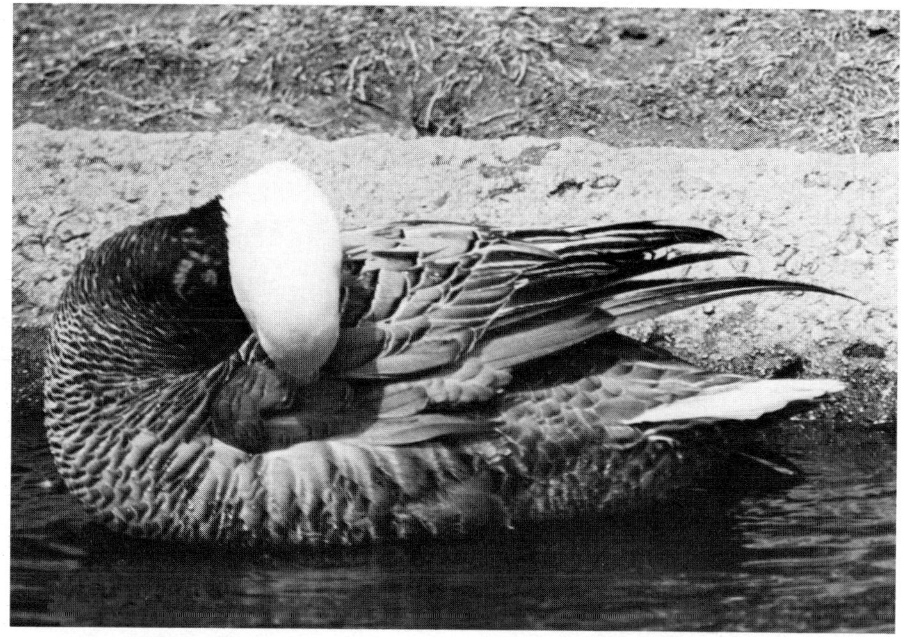

35-19 Emperor preens wing feathers after bathing.

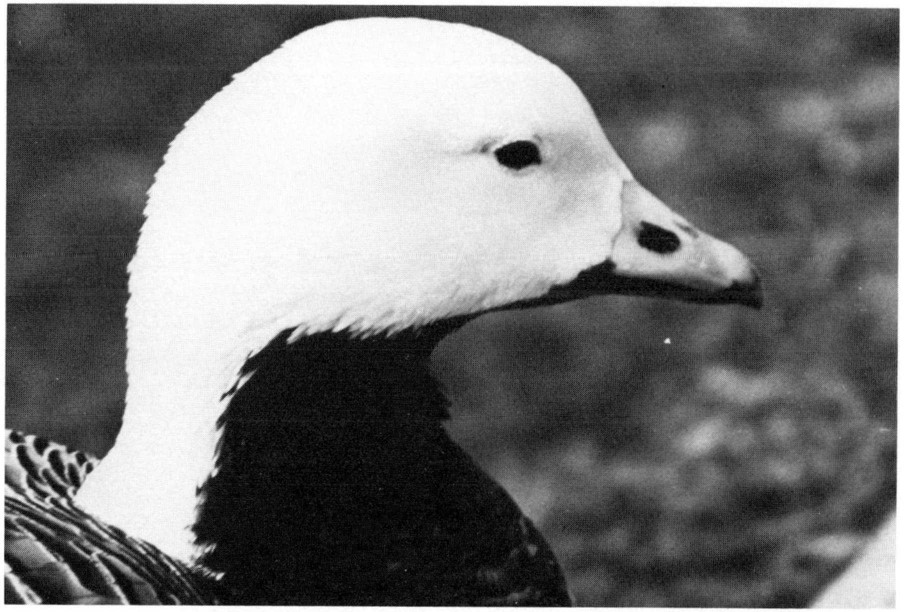

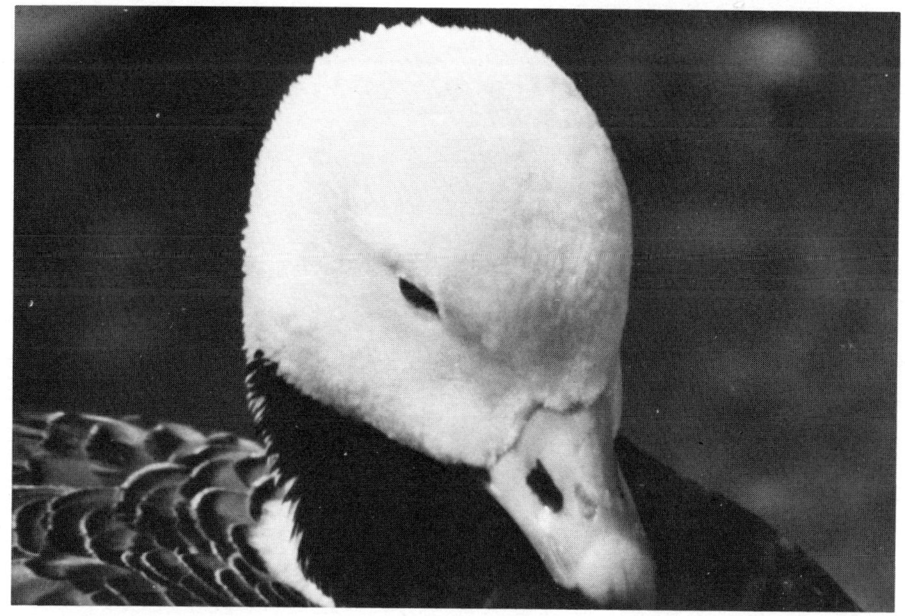

35-20 Profile and three quarter front views of the head and bill. 35-21

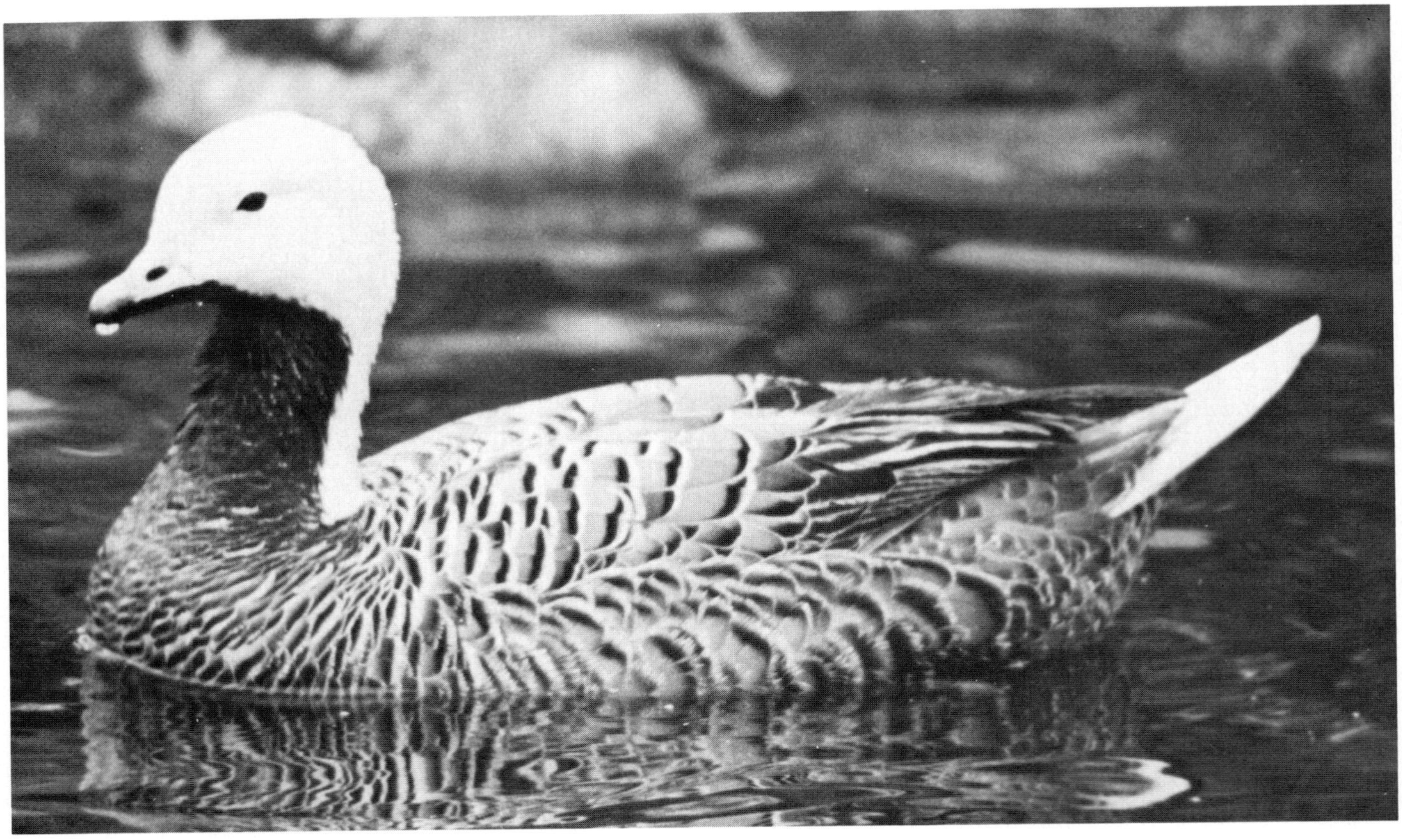

35-22 Good profile of a floating emperor goose.

35-23 Front and rear views of swimming emperor geese. 35-24

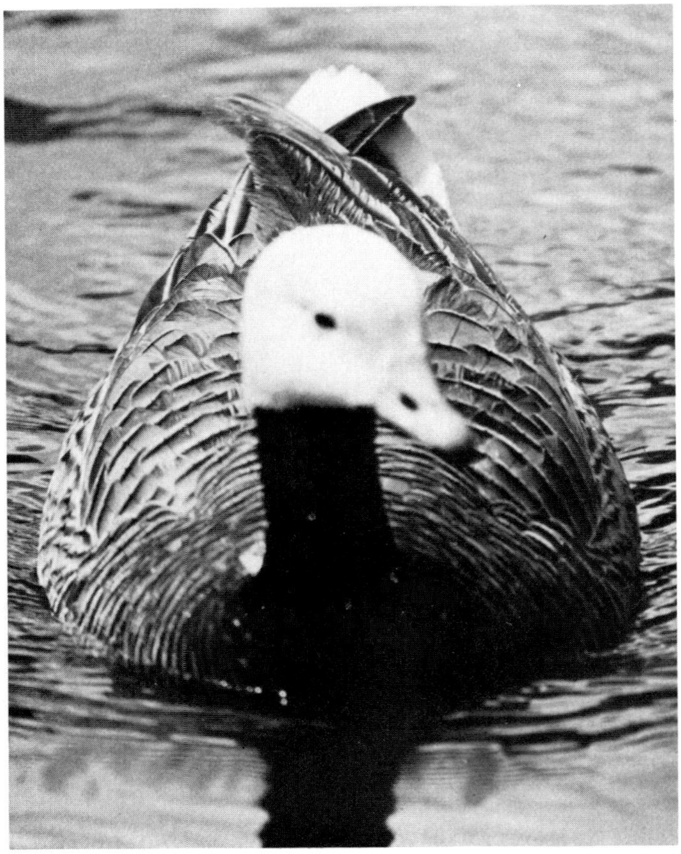

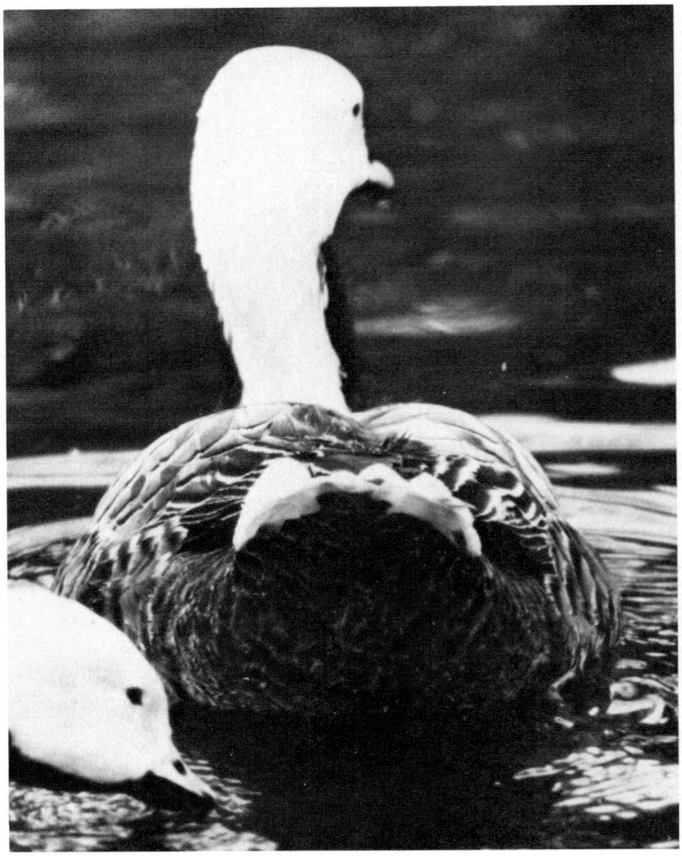

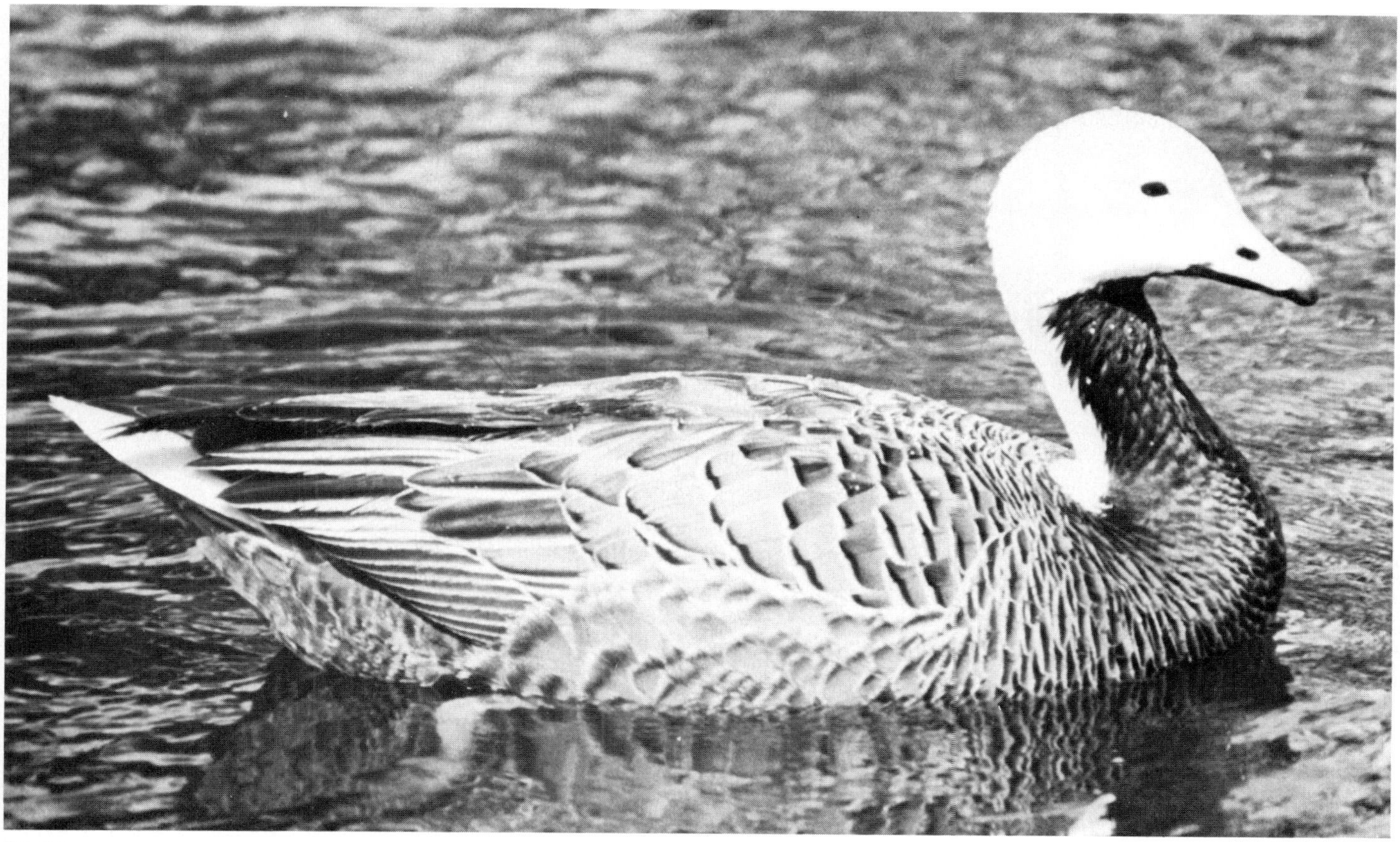

35-25

More profiles of floating emperor geese.

35-26

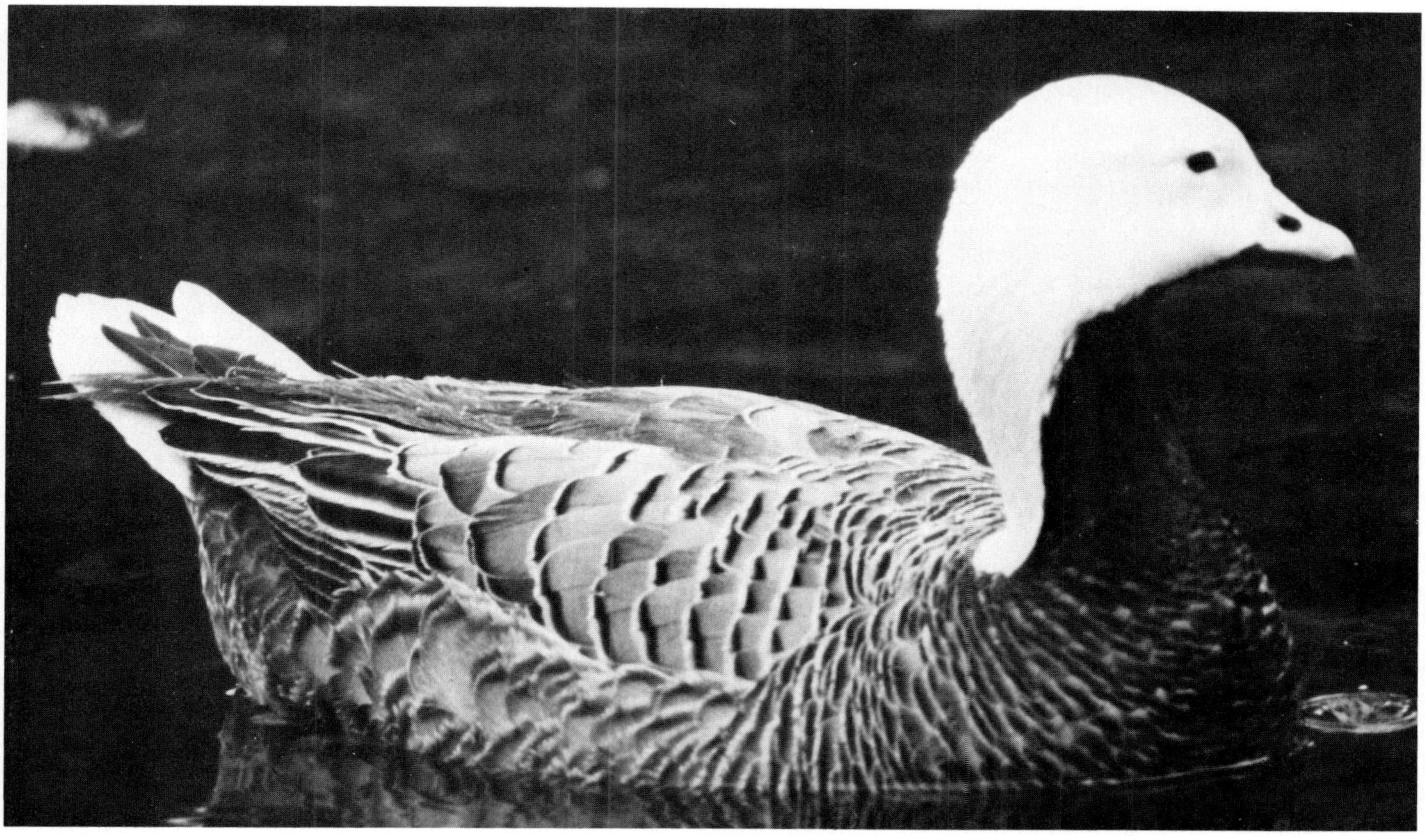

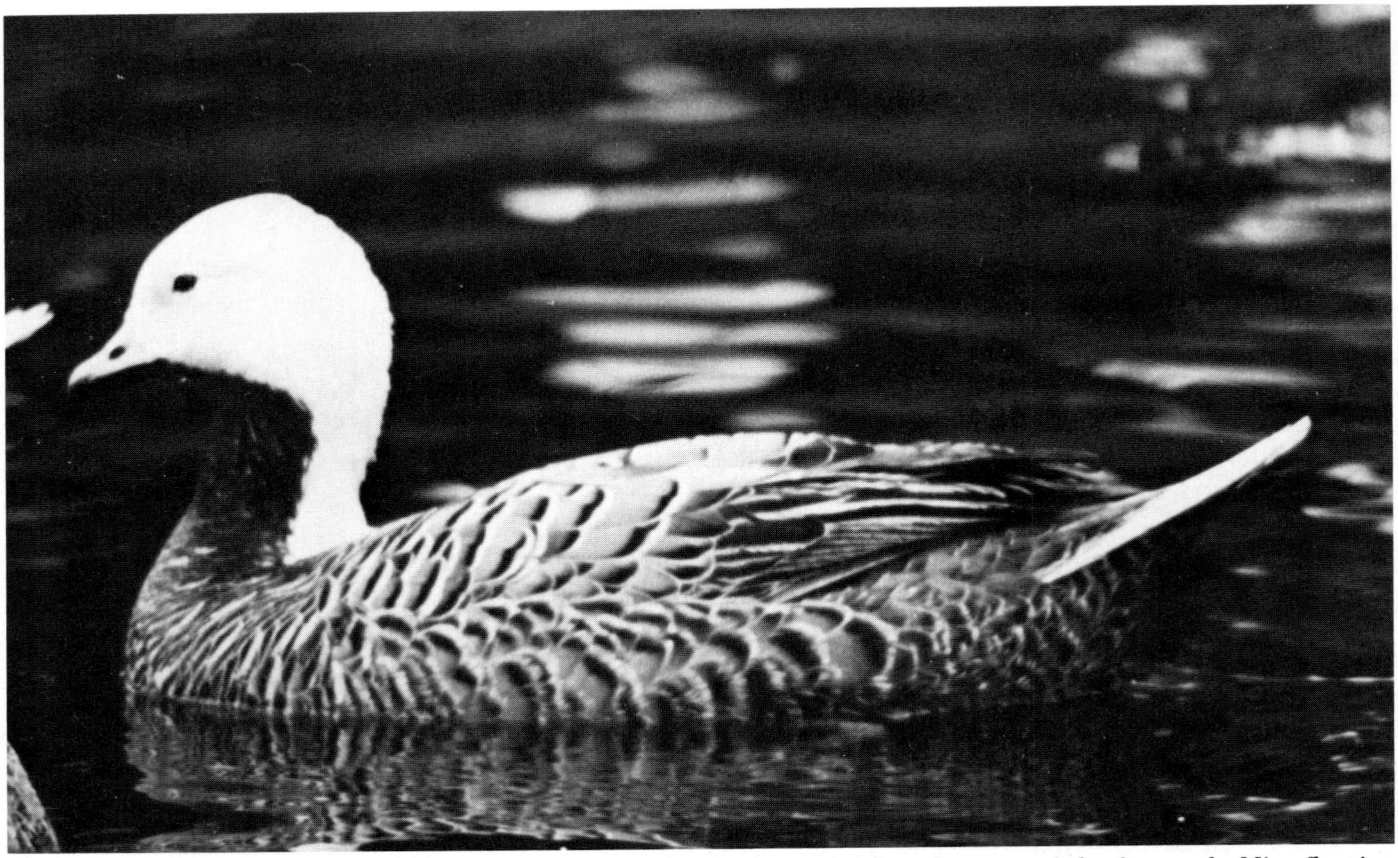

35-27 Emperors are hardy sea geese and spend most of their time in the salt water of the far north. Nice floating pose.

35-28 Another floating, preening pose.

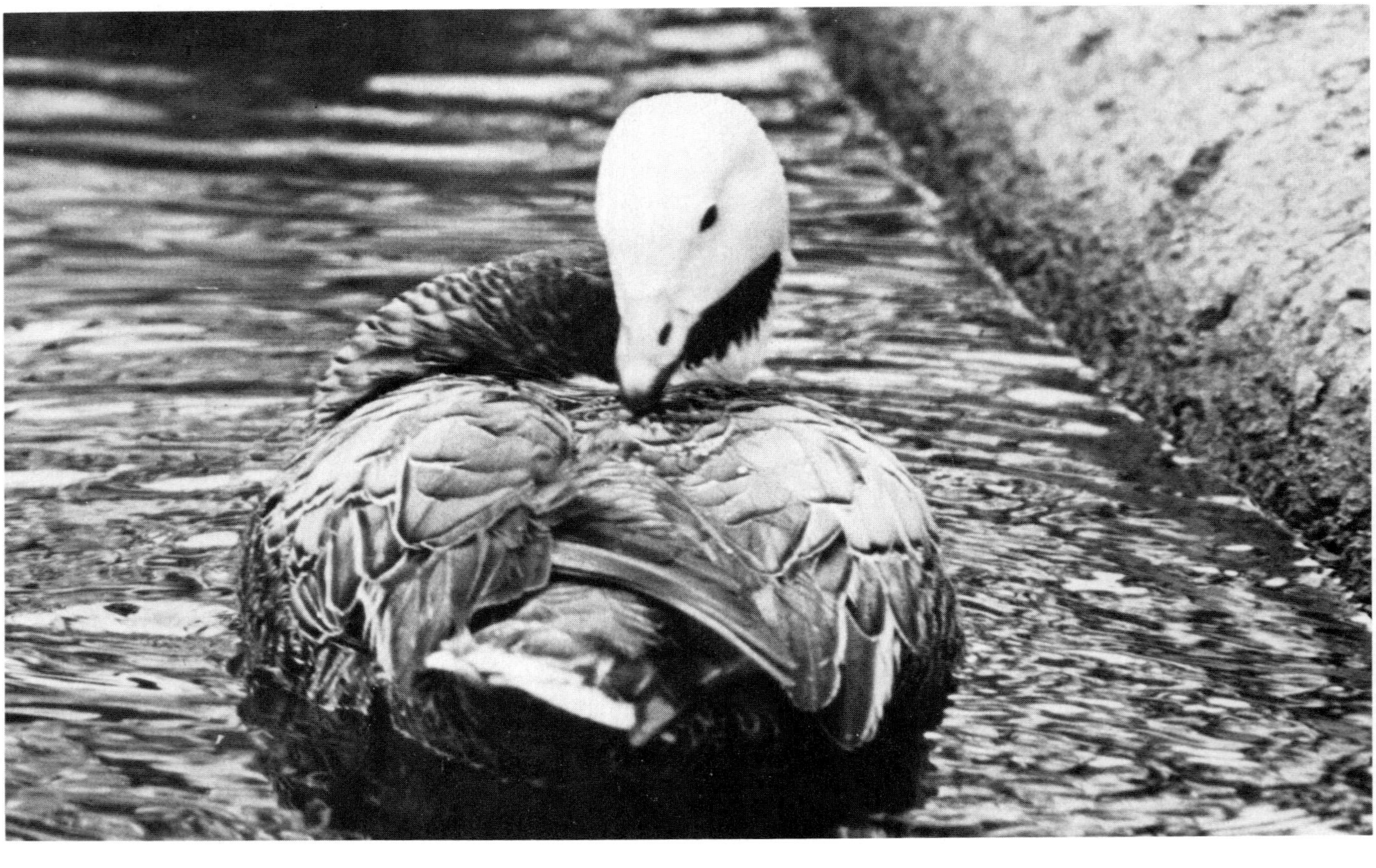

CHAPTER 36

Pacific White-Fronted Goose

Anser albifrons frontalis
(Color Photos—page 94)

Although rarely found east of the Mississippi River, the beautiful Pacific white-fronted geese are fairly abundant winter residents in California, along the coasts of Texas and Louisiana, and in parts of Mexico. During migration, whitefronts make many stops in Alberta, Manitoba, and the Great Plains states of the Central Flyway and parts of Washington and Oregon in the Pacific Flyway. They breed in the Arctic tundra of Alaska, from the Bering Sea eastward to central Arctic Canada, and in northeastern Siberia.

''Specklebelly'' or ''speck,'' as the Pacific white-fronted goose is commonly called, is a medium-size goose—males have an average weight of about 5½ pounds, an average wing span of 63 inches, and an average overall length of 29 inches. The adult goose is strikingly marked with a pink bill shading into pale blue at the base, a white band around the front of the face at the base of the bill, yellow to yellow-orange feet, and variable black and white markings on the breast. Immature birds (most whitefronts do not mature until their second, sometimes third year) lack the white facial band and the black and white breast markings, and their feet and bills are duller in color.

Whitefronts are the only geese on this continent whose heads (except for the white face), necks, chests, and upper parts are solidly brown. Due to this color characteristic, they are normally easy to identify when on the water. The yellow feet and variable black and white breast markings make the adults quite conspicuous in flight; and even the immature whitefronts are easy to identify when flying at close range. At greater distances, however, whitefronts are much more difficult to identify, as they tend to resemble Canada geese in color. This is because aerial perspective causes the brown to appear gray. Also, the V-shape flight formation of the white-fronted geese is similar to that of the Canadas. Groups of whitefronts are often seen flying with flocks of snow geese or the small-to-medium-size Canadas.

Another species of the white-fronted goose, the tule goose (Anser albifrons gambelli) winters in the Sacramento Valley of California. The tule goose is larger and heavier and weights up to 10 pounds have been recorded, and has similar markings to those of the Pacific white-fronted goose, but is somewhat darker in coloration. Its neck is longer in proportion to its body than the Pacific whitefront, and its bill is considerably longer (approximately 40 per cent) and heavier. The population of the tule goose is dangerously small, possibly under 1500.

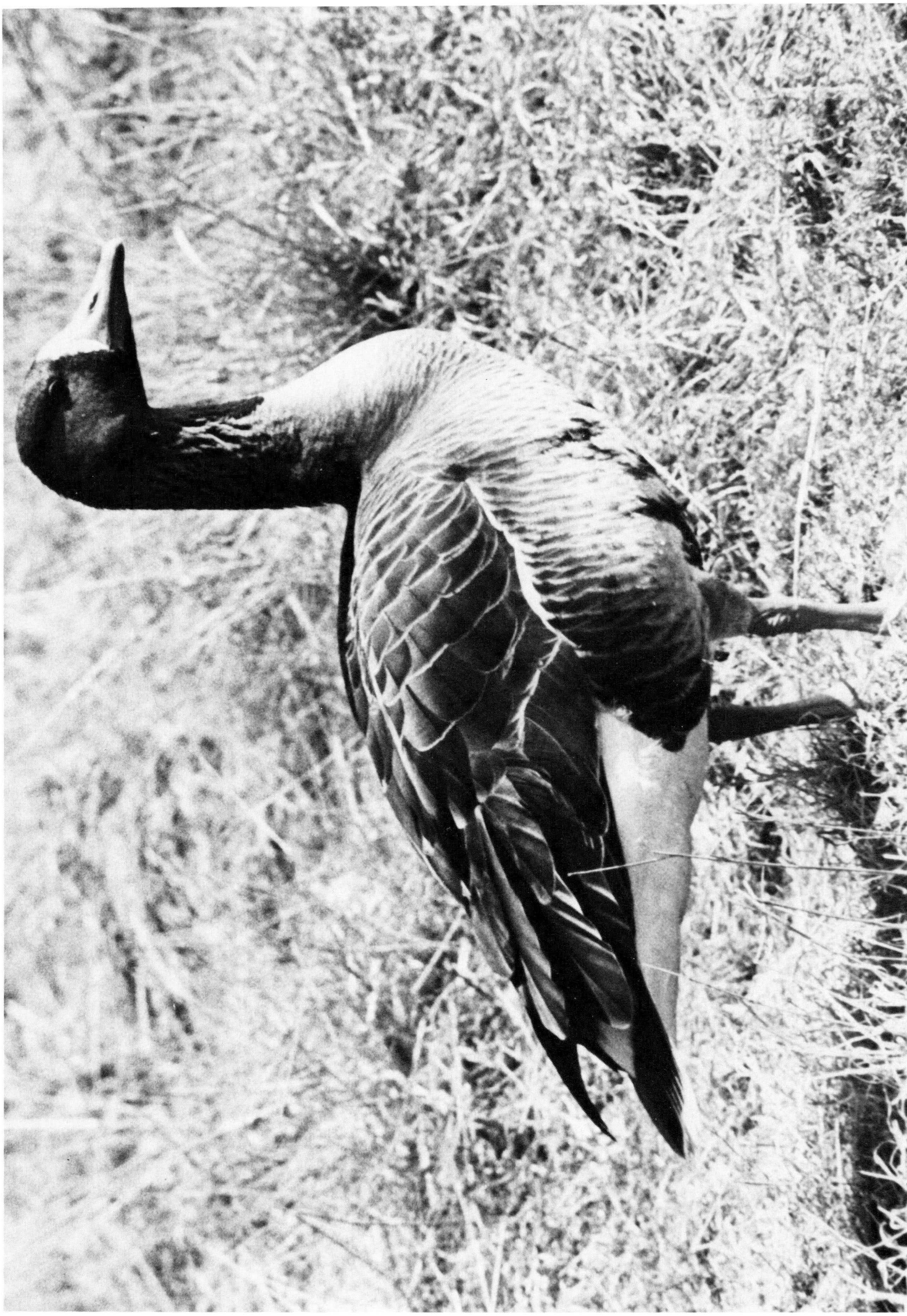

36-1 The strikingly marked and beautifully colored Pacific white-fronted goose. He is rarely seen east of the Mississippi River.

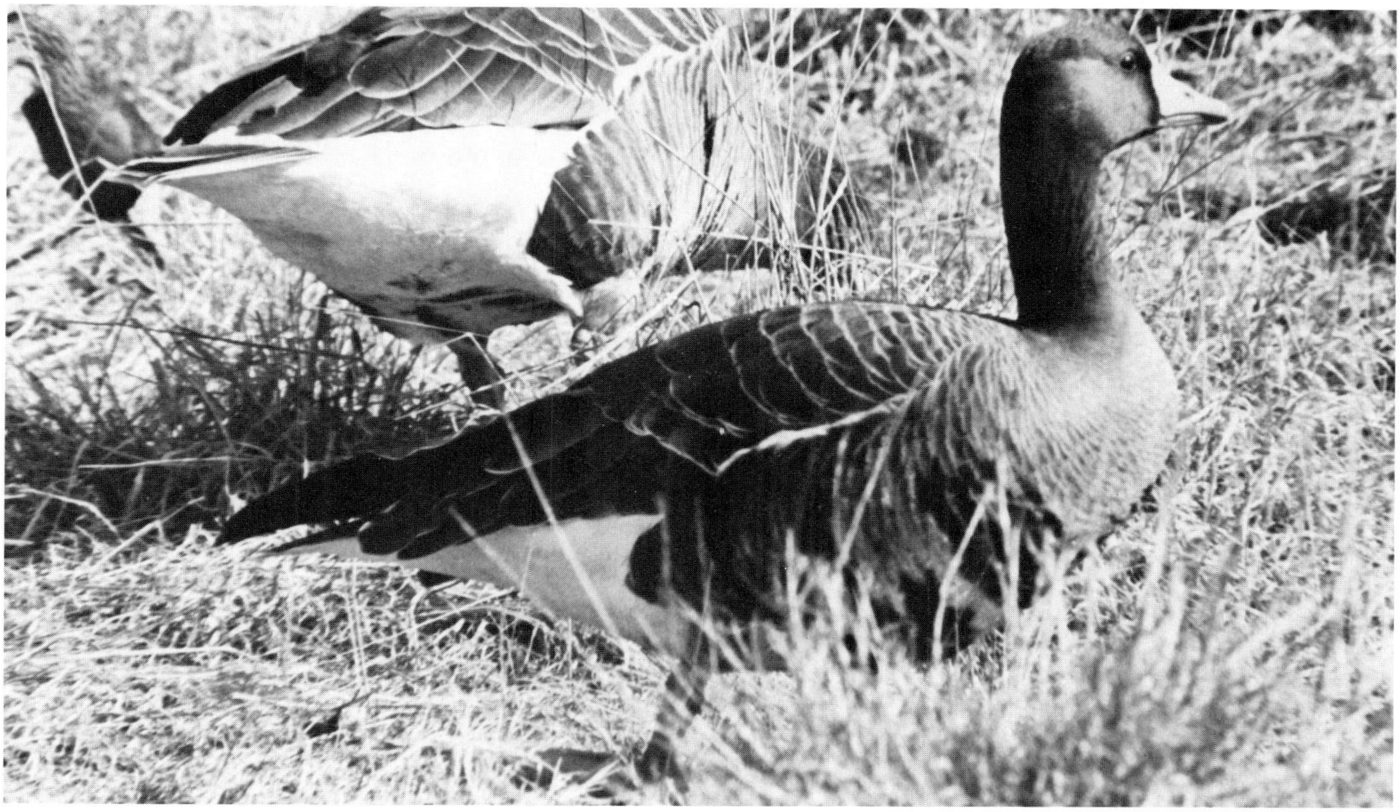

36-2 Whitefronts grazing on new grass shoots. Like Canadas, one goose is usually on the alert.

36-3 Drinking white-fronted goose shows off his body cross-section and lateral leg placement.

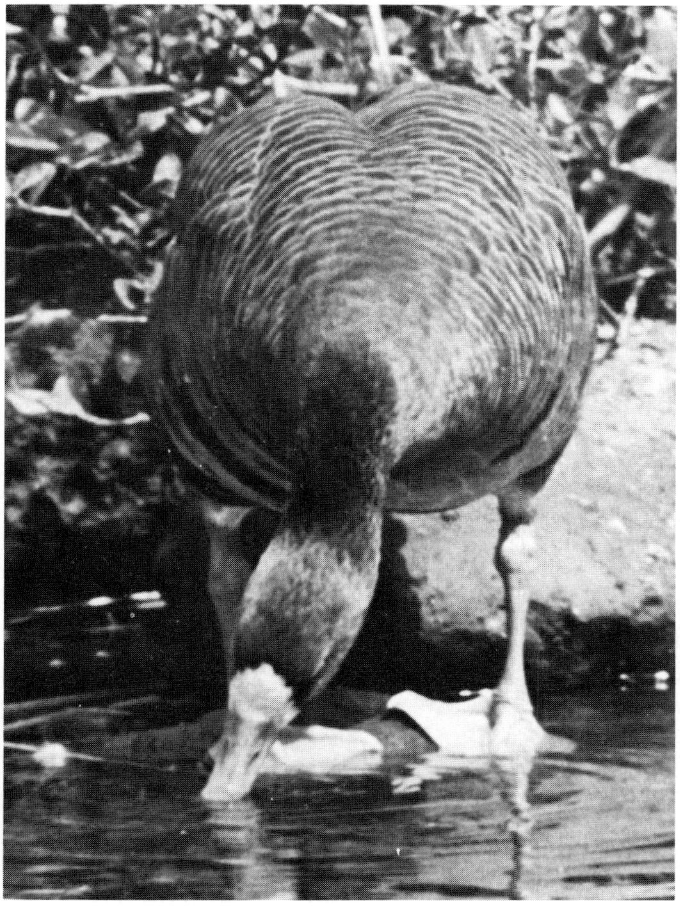

36-4 Rear view of the white-fronted, often called "specklebelly" goose.

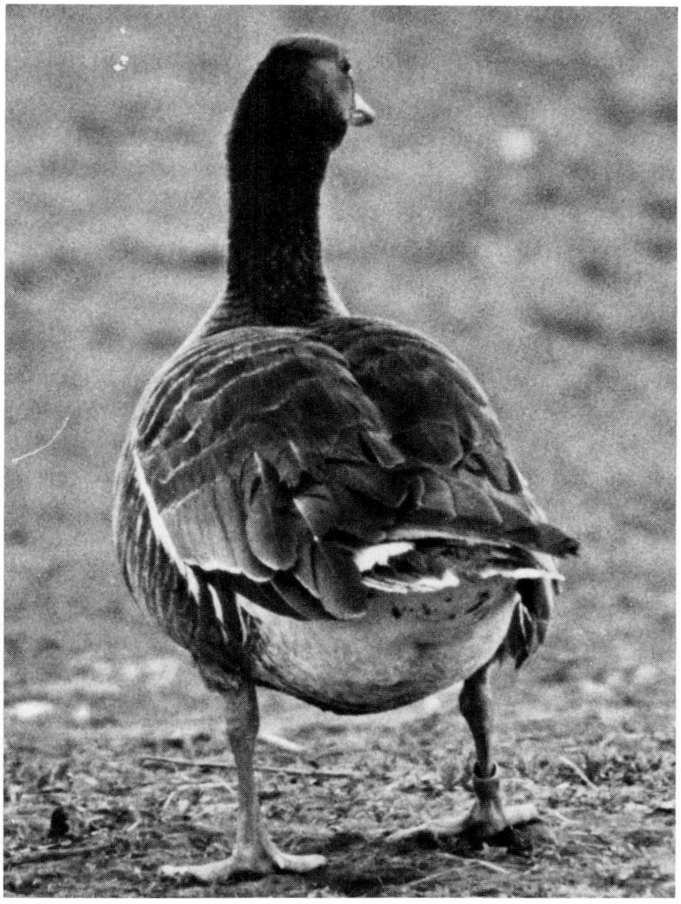

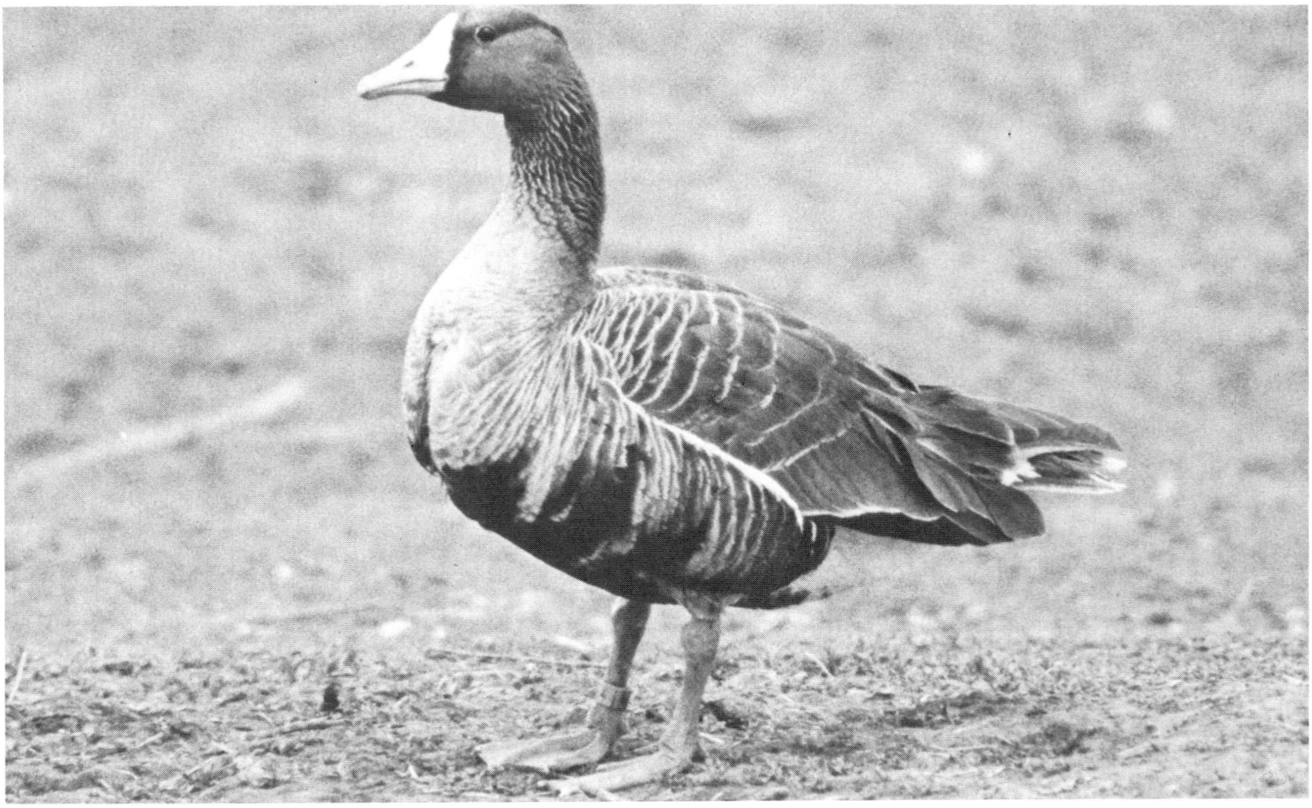

36-5 Good profile of a male white-fronted goose. These geese do not acquire their white faces and black belly markings until the second or third year.

36-6 The black markings on the belly of these geese are variable.

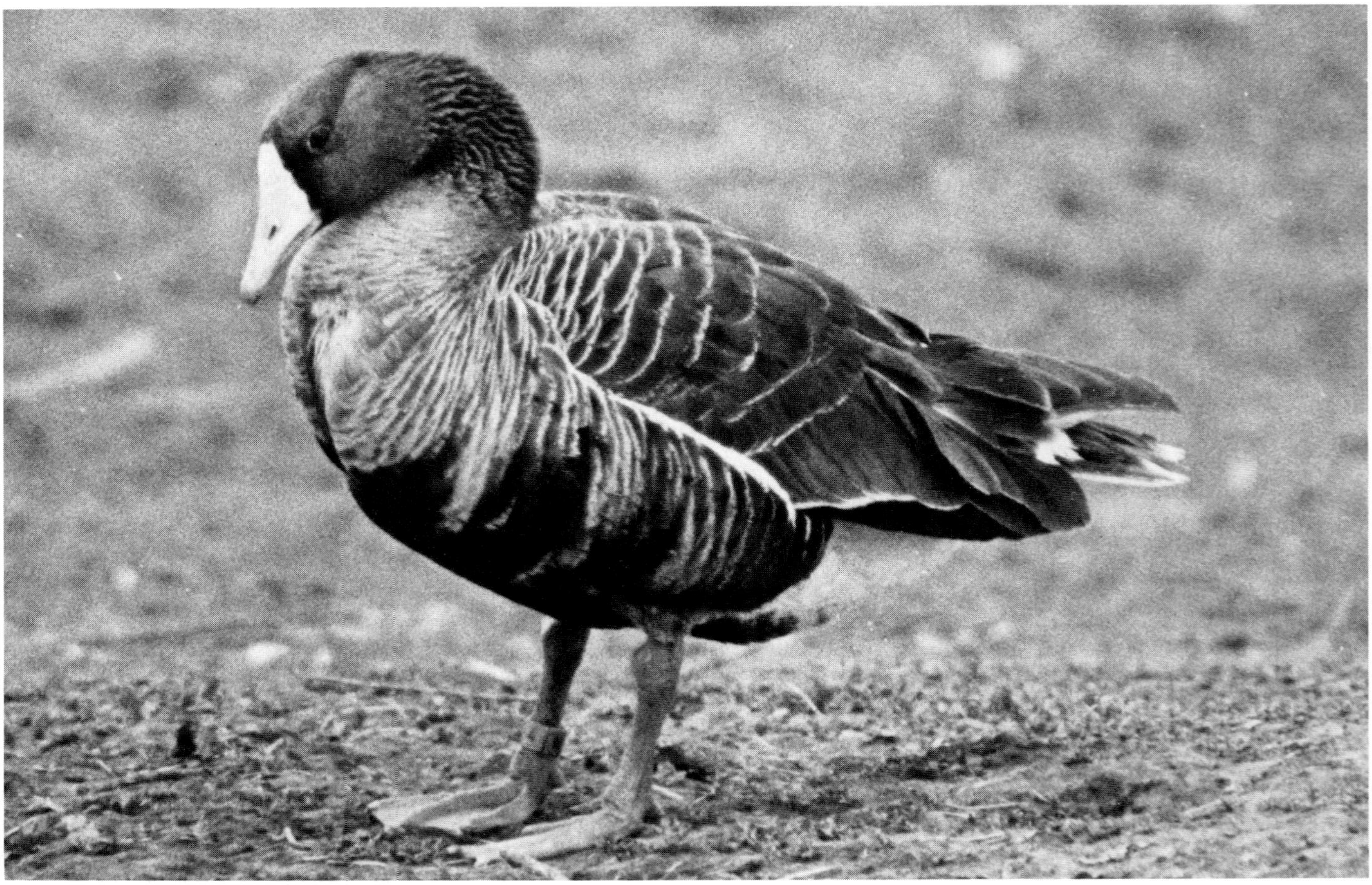

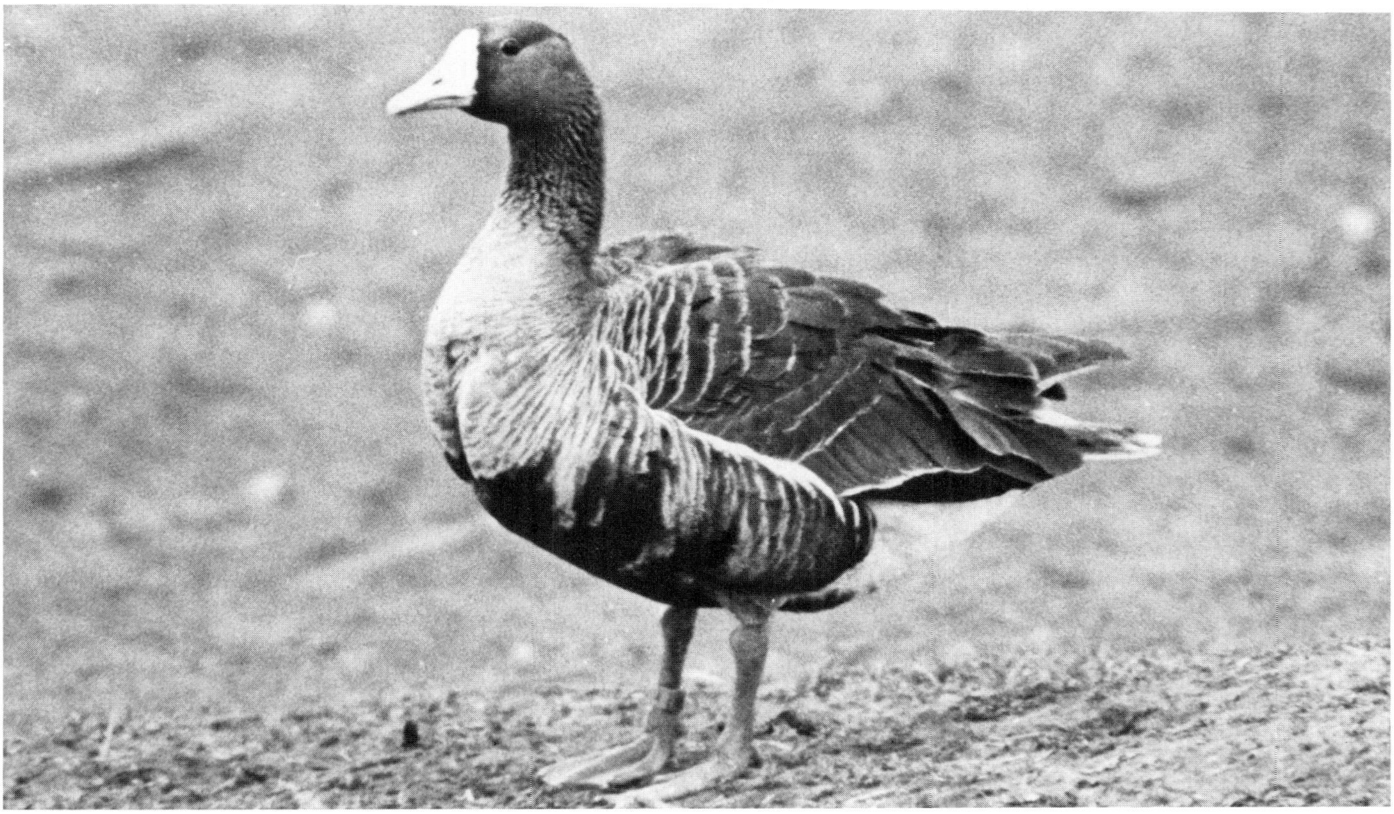

36-7 Another profile shot of the whitefront.

36-8 A white-fronted goose stretches his wings.

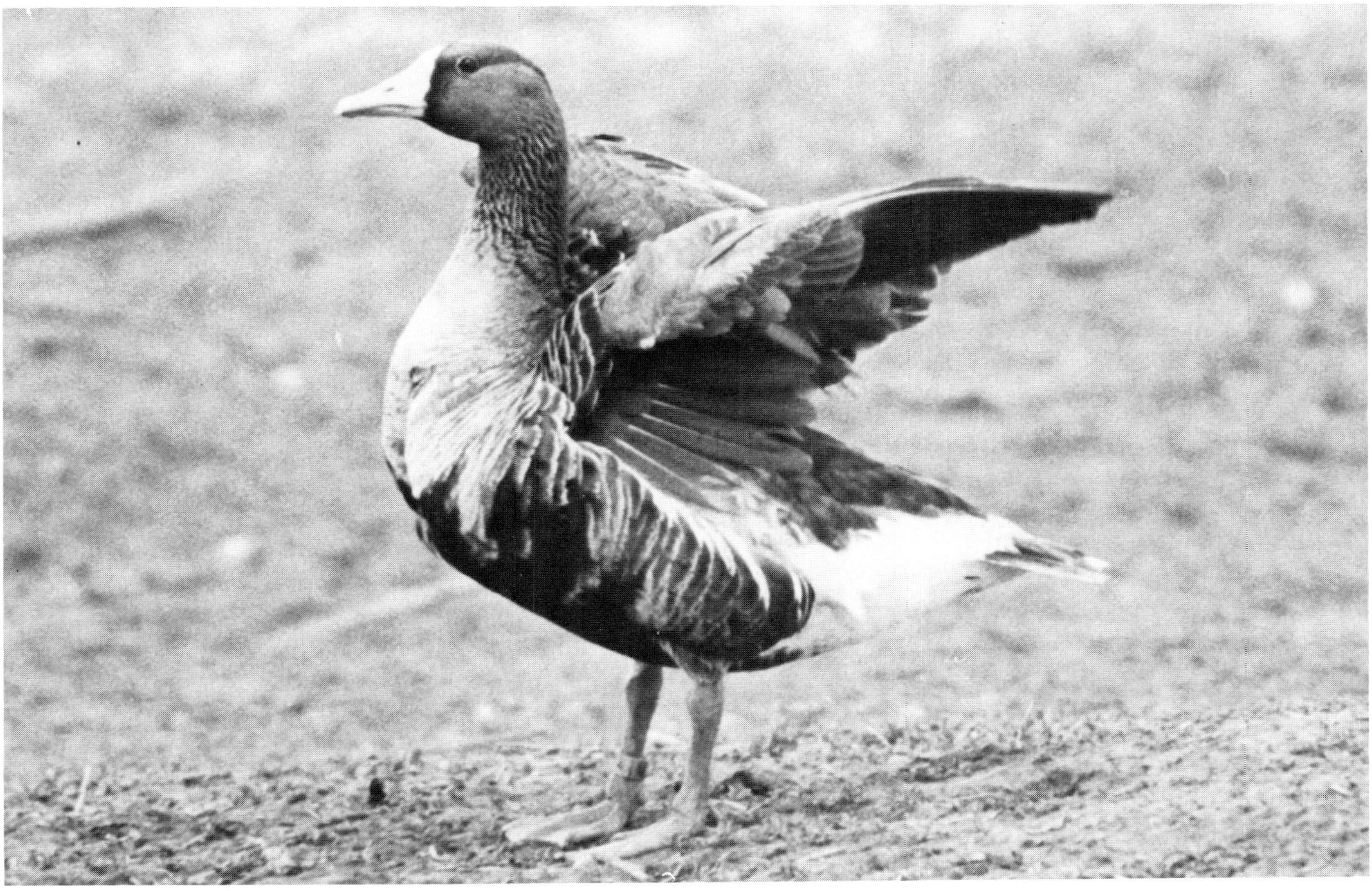

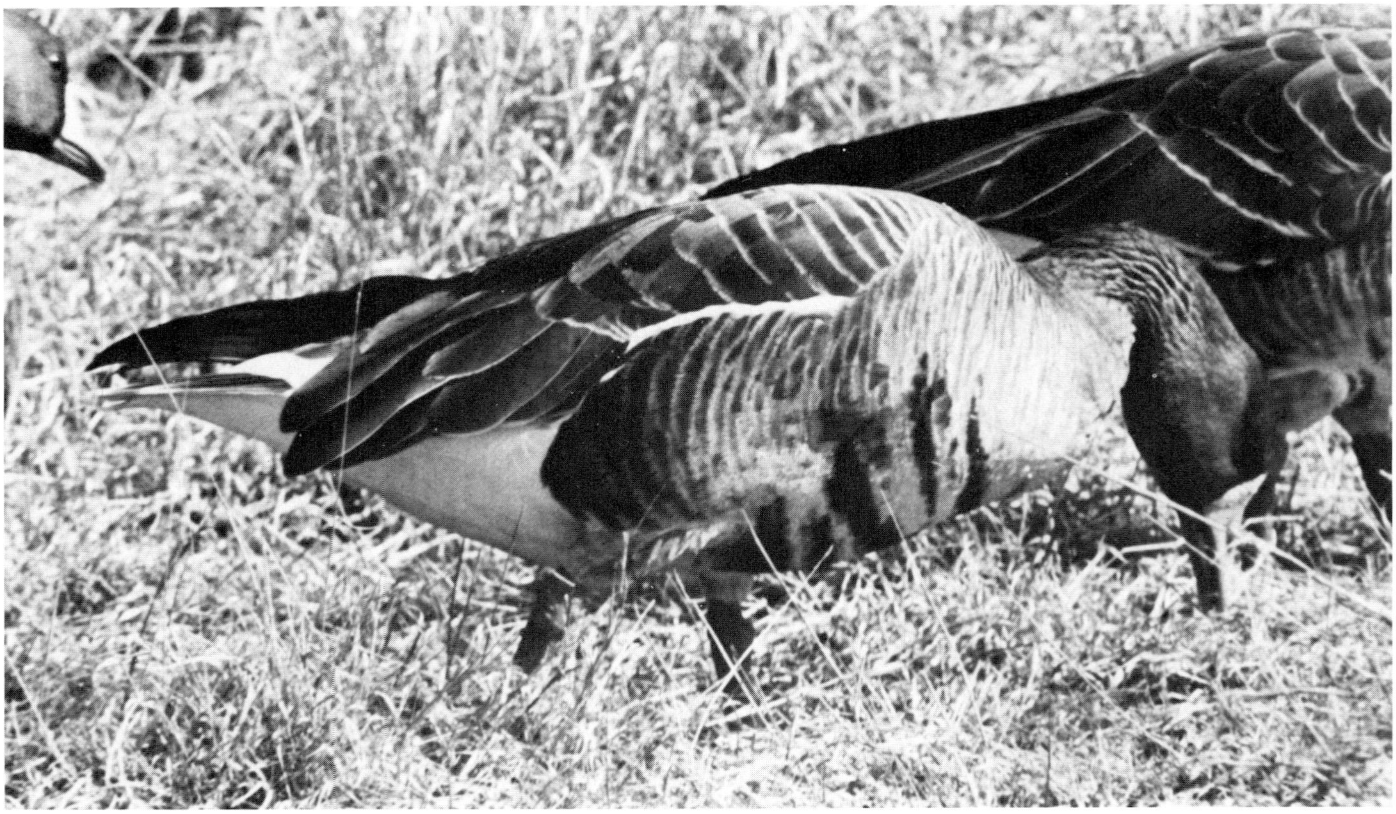

36-9 Specklebelly in a feeding position.

36-10 Whitefront in an alert position. He has much less black on his belly than the goose pictured in Fig. 36-6.

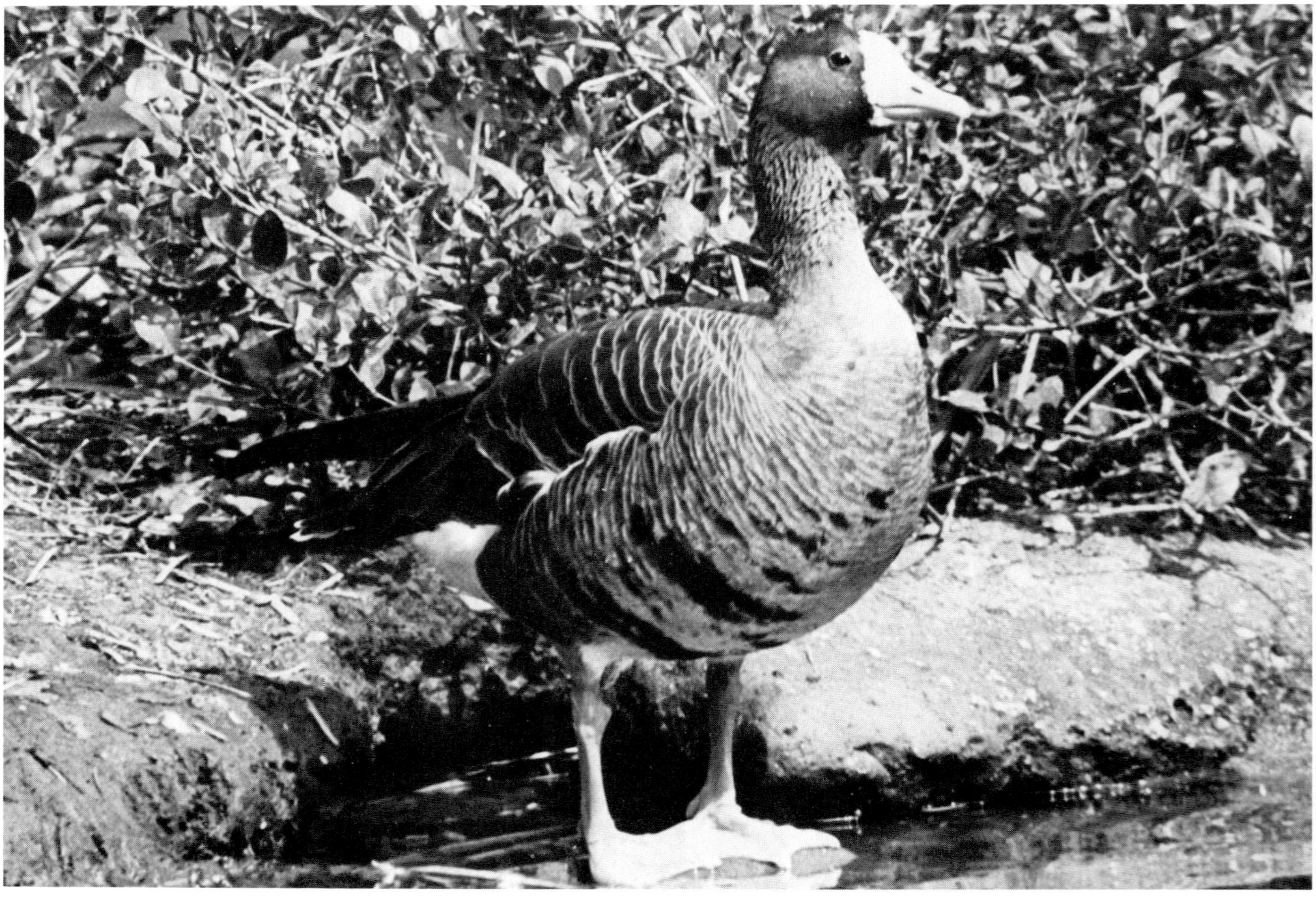

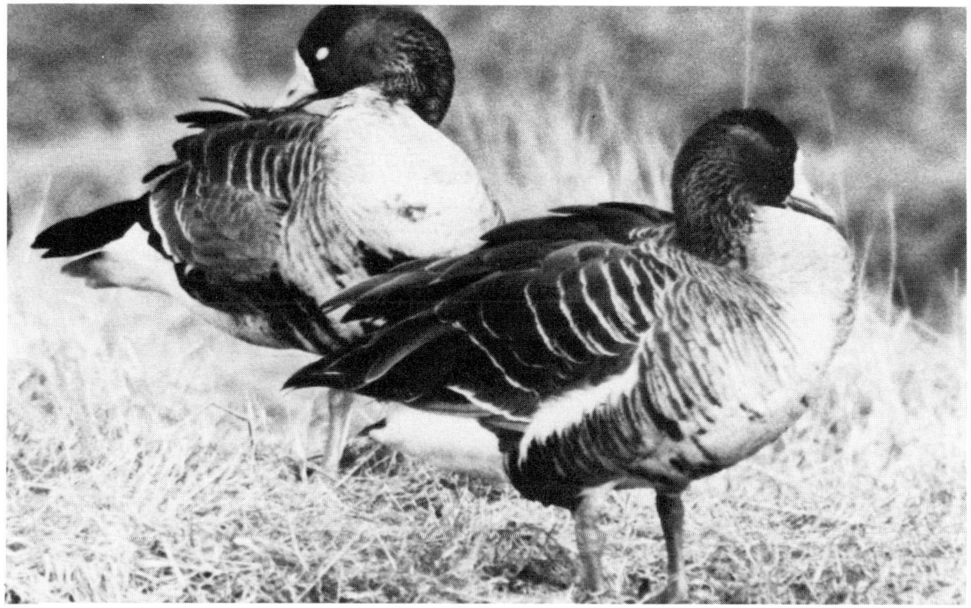

36-11

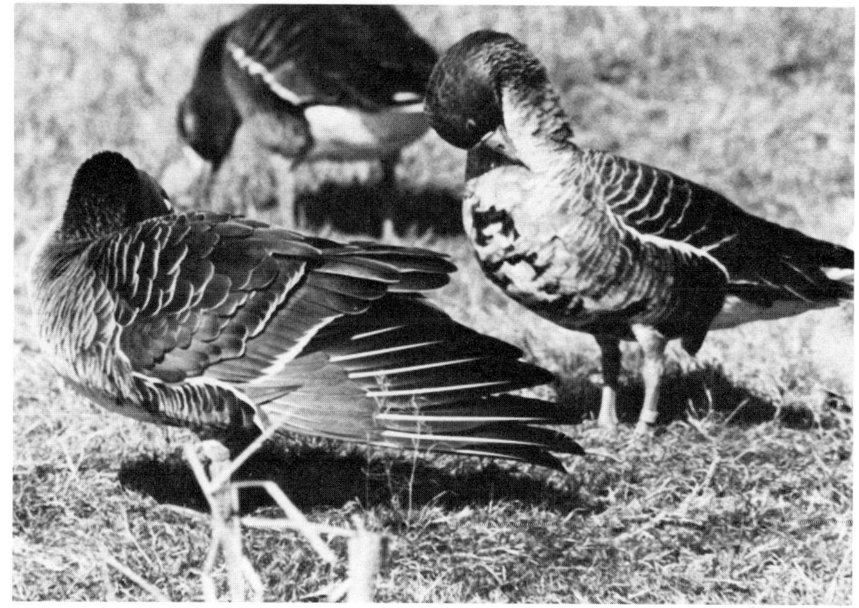

36-12

Whitefronts in preening positions.

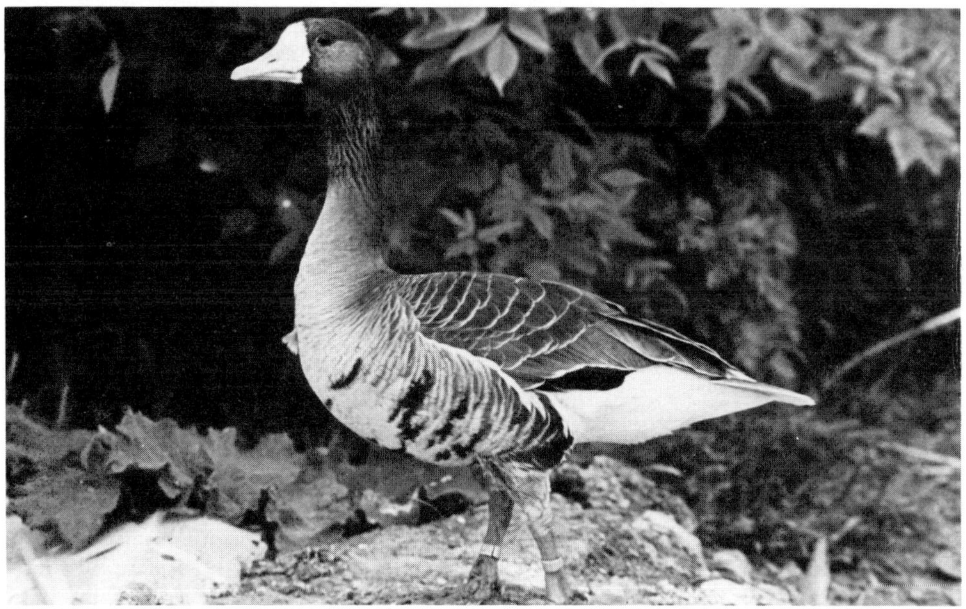

36-13 Nice profile of an alert white-fronted goose.

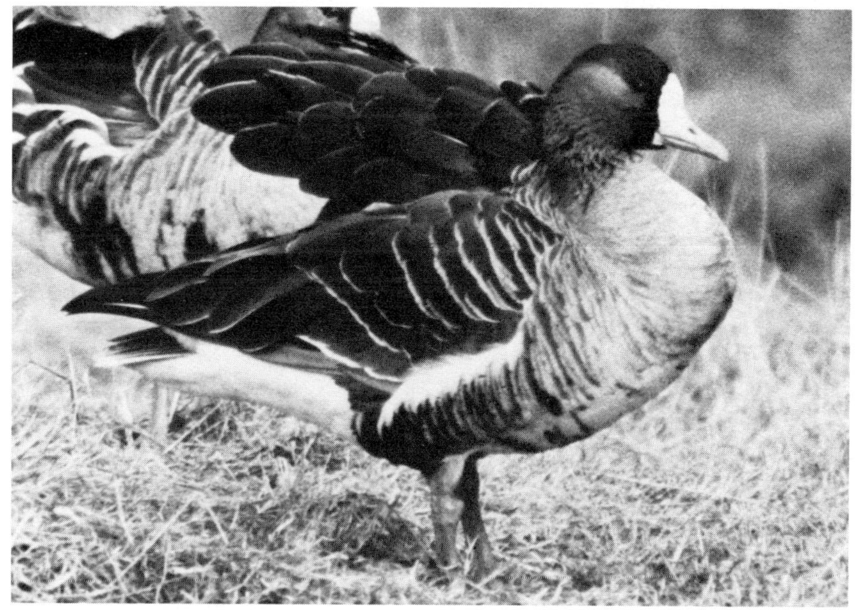

36-14 This white-fronted goose has raised his pinioned wing. Note scapular feather pattern.

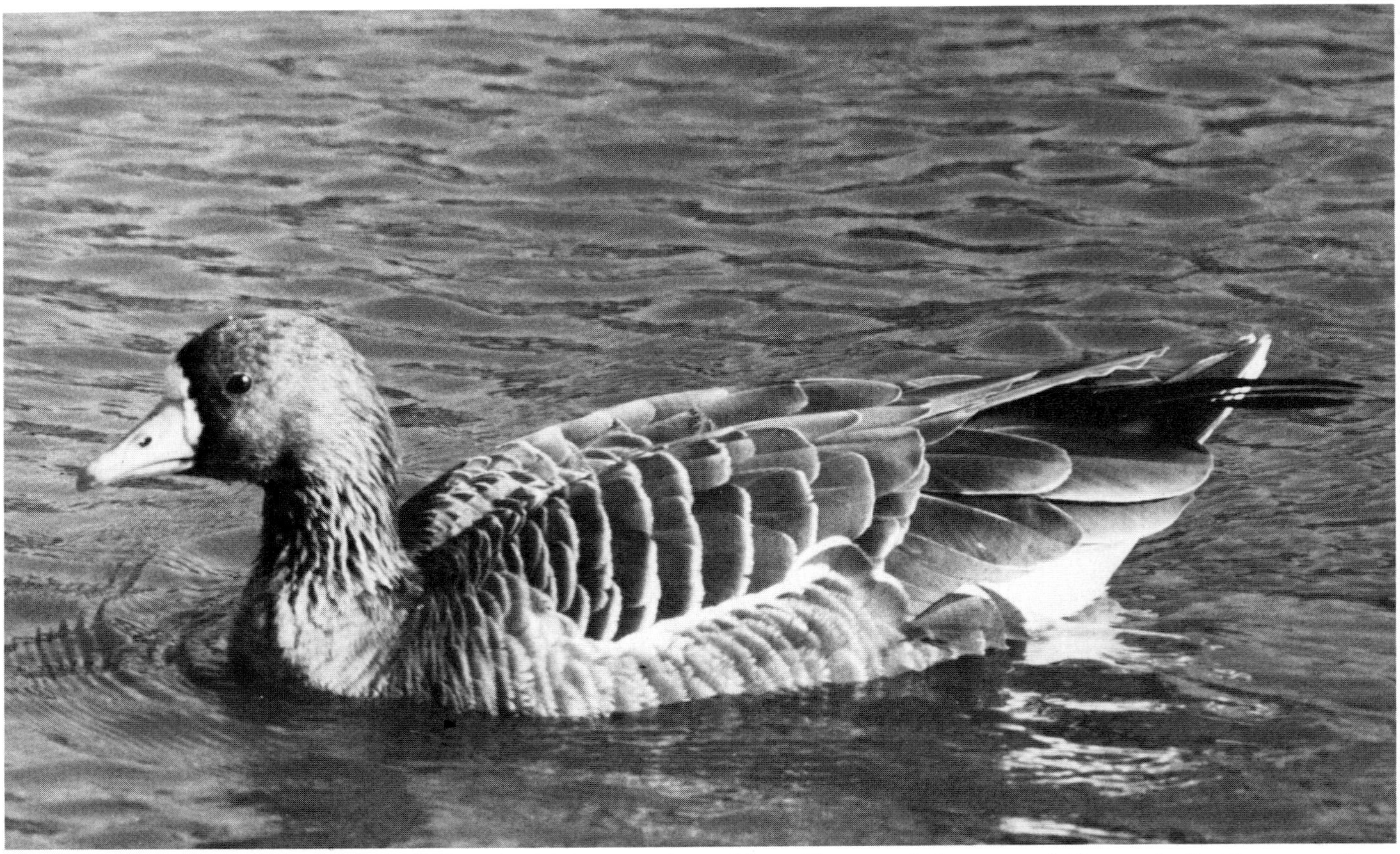

36-15 Observe individual feather detail of his scapulars. The ridges and furrows of the neck feathers on these geese are more irregular than those of snow geese.

36-16 Good profile of a floating white-fronted goose. Note definite intersection line between side feathers and scapulars. Bird in background is stretching for food.

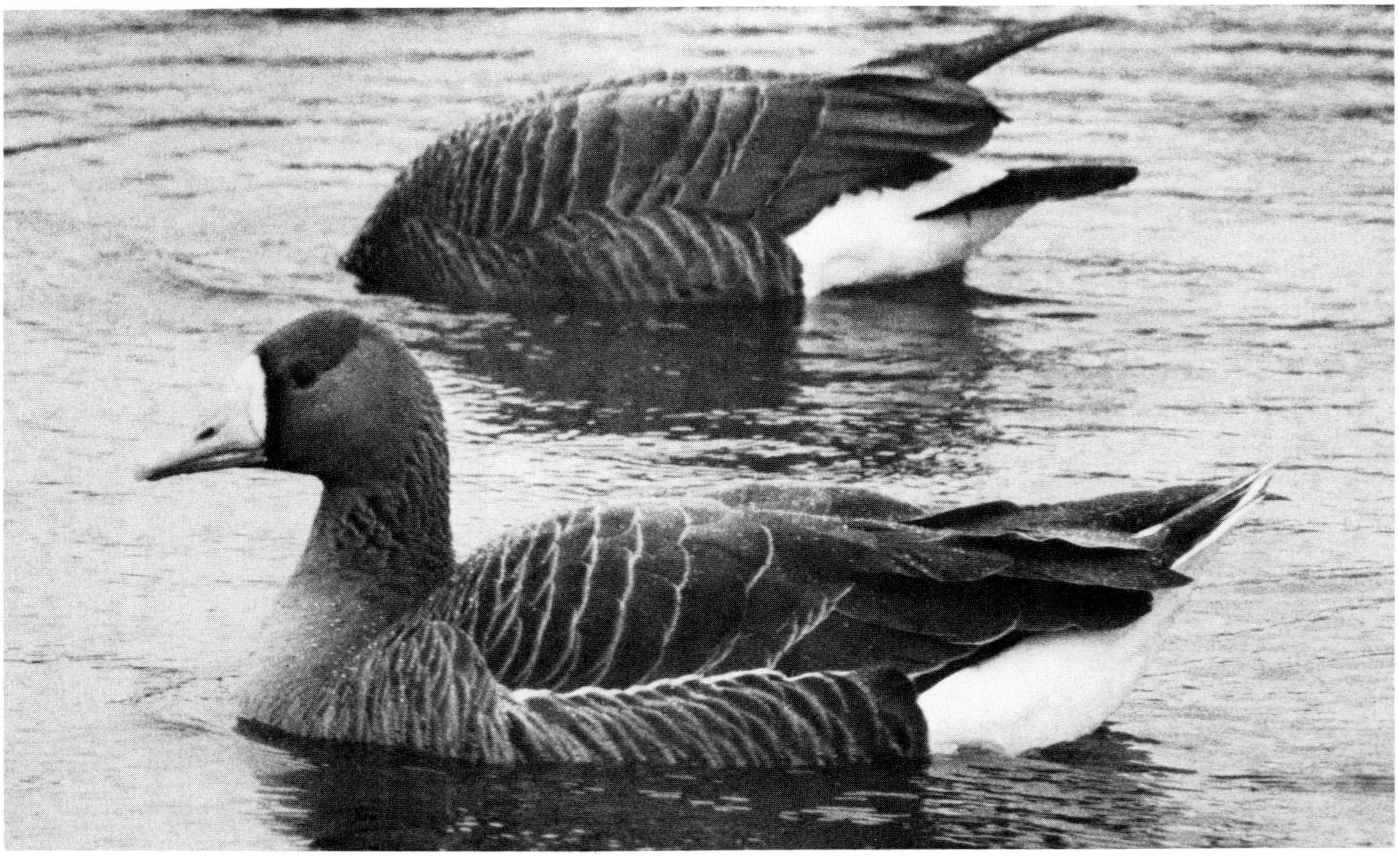

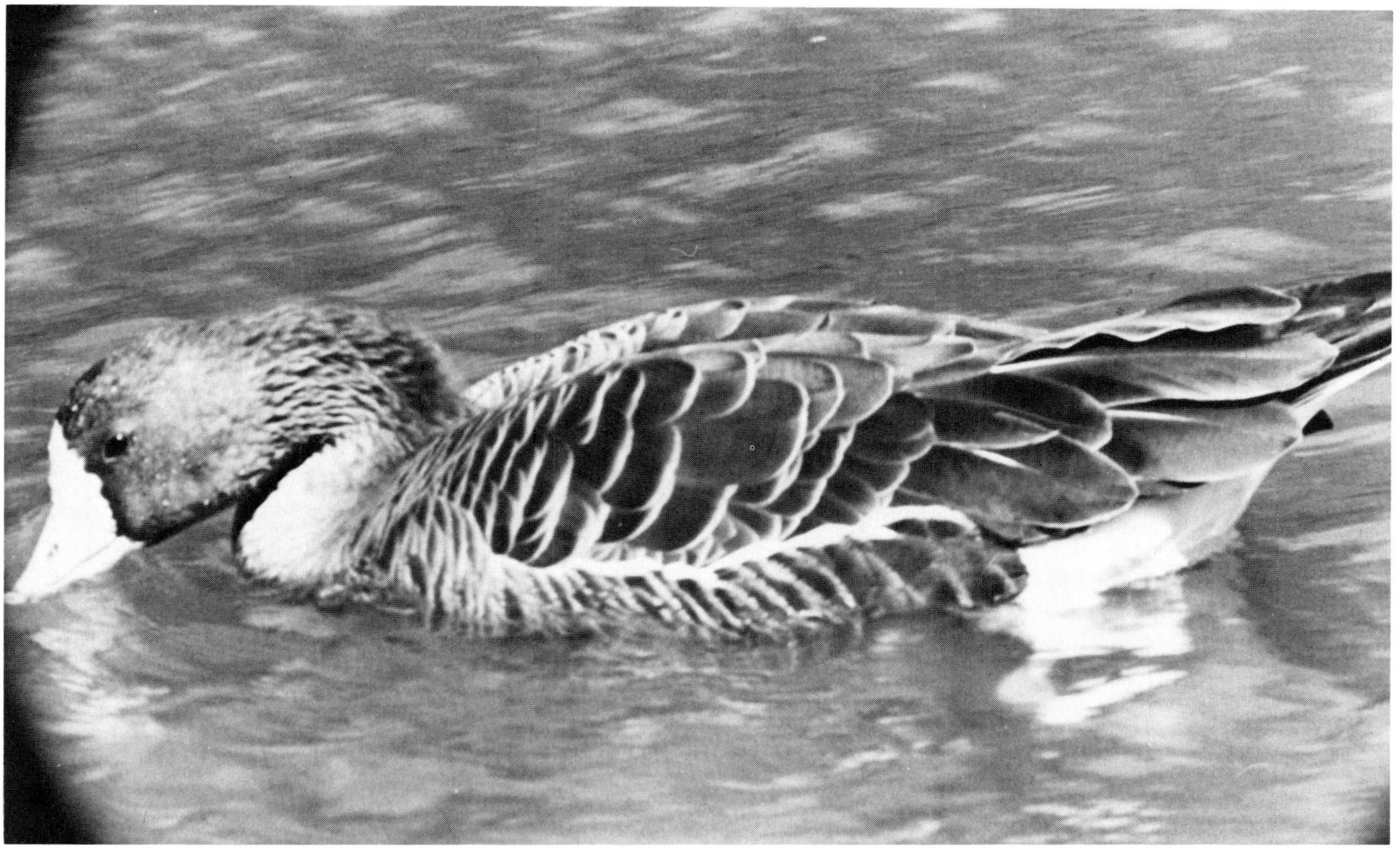

36-17 White-fronted goose takes a drink.

36-18 Another profile study of a floating white-fronted goose.

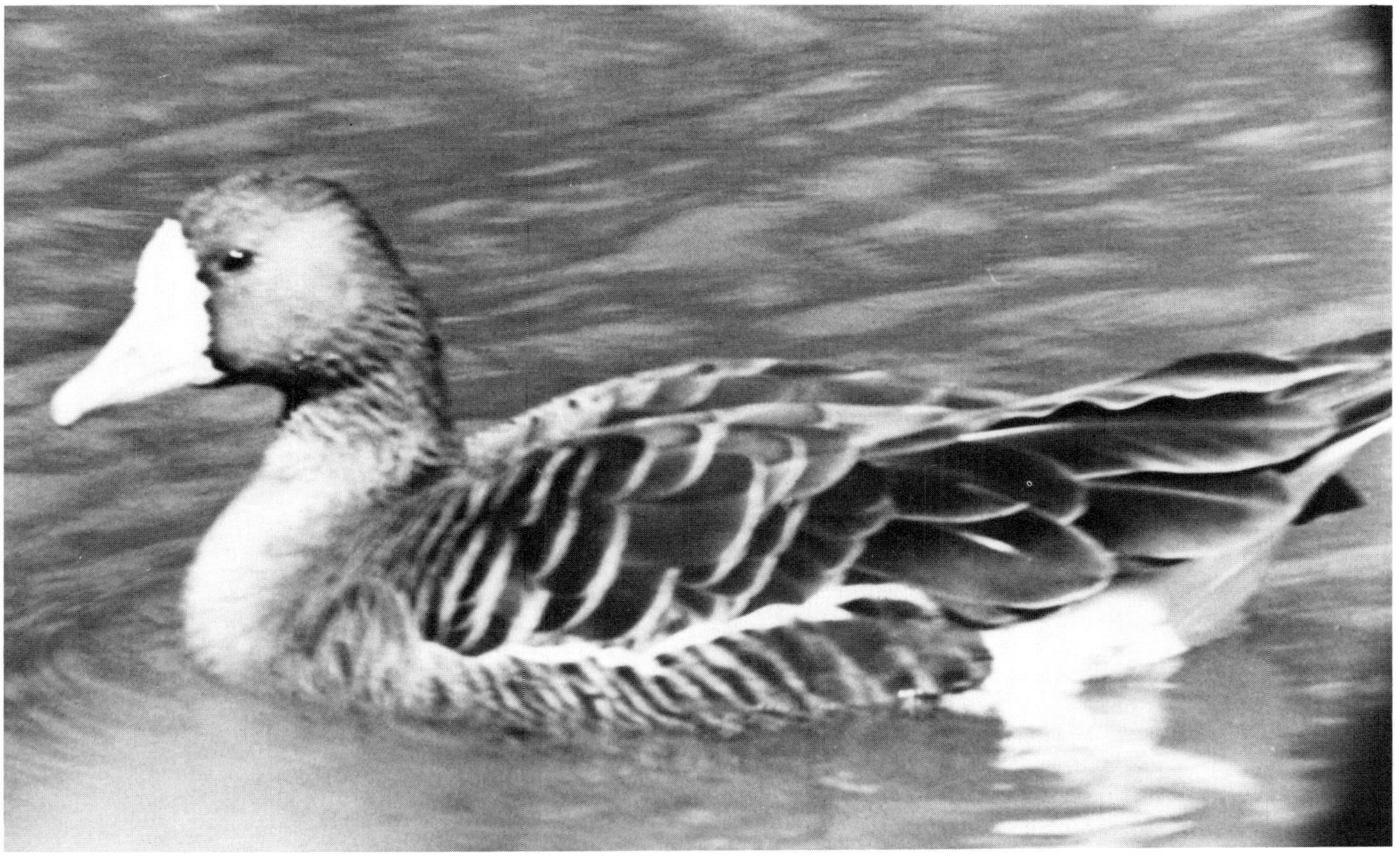

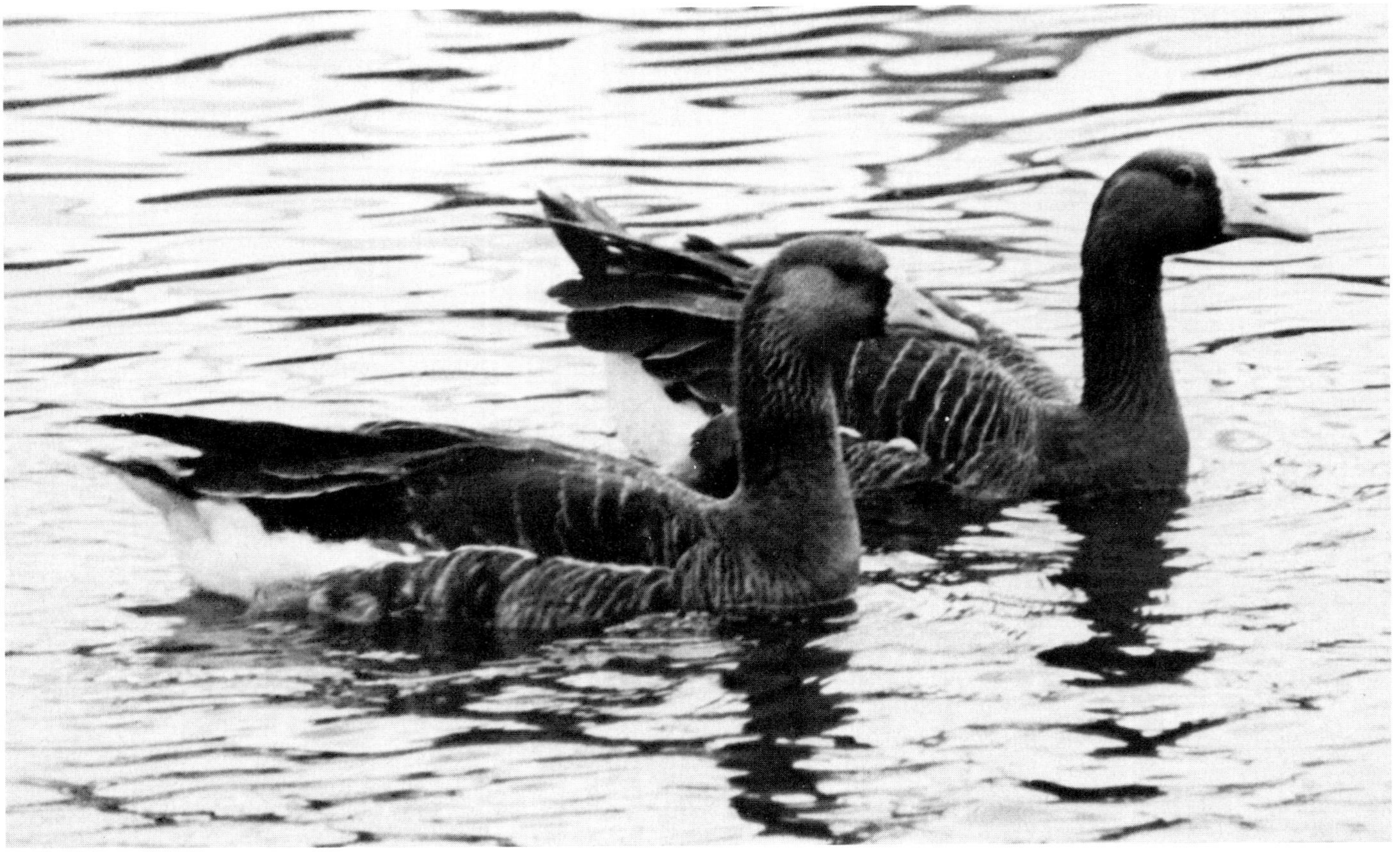

36-19

Mated pair of "specs" swim about leisurely.

36-20

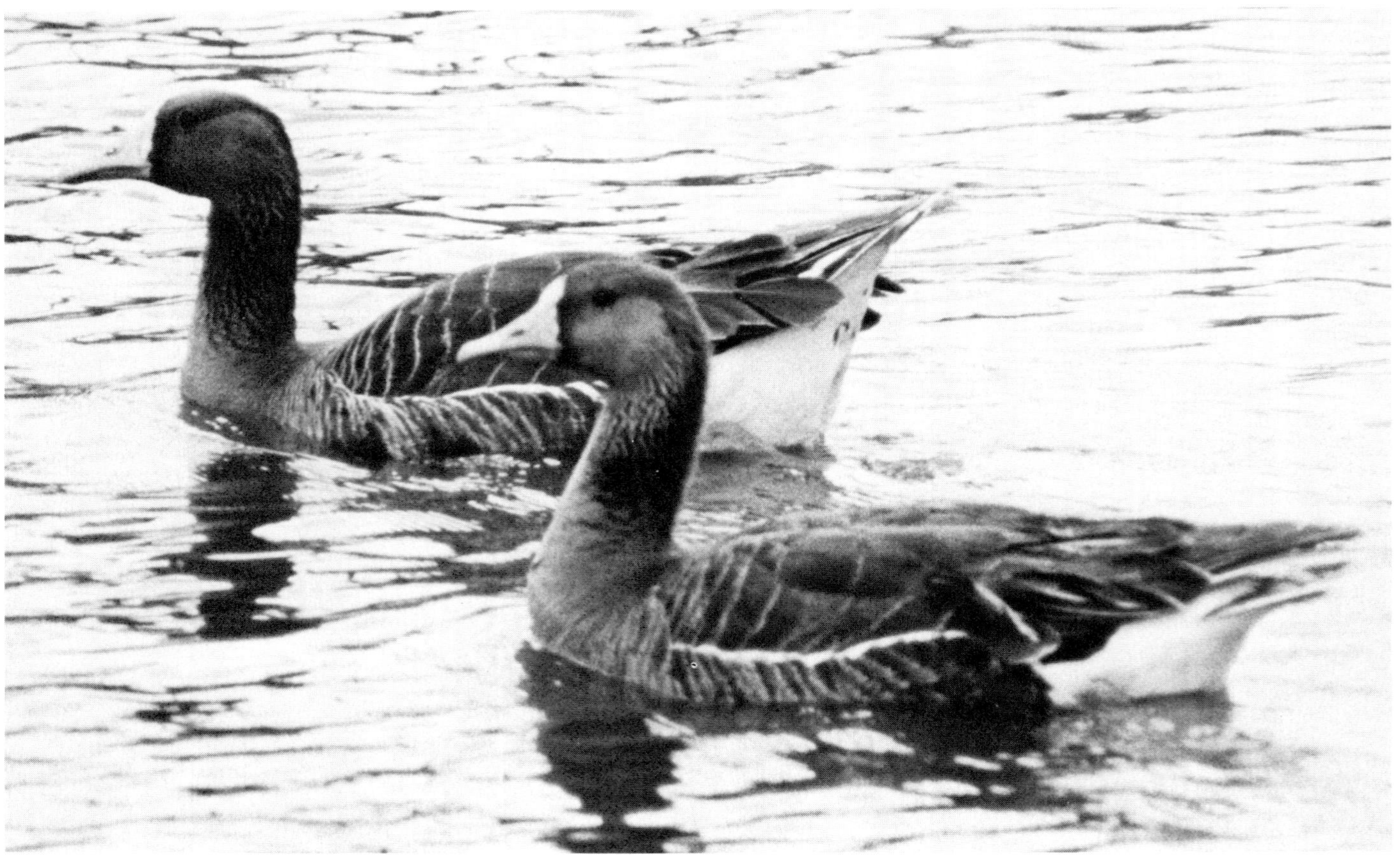

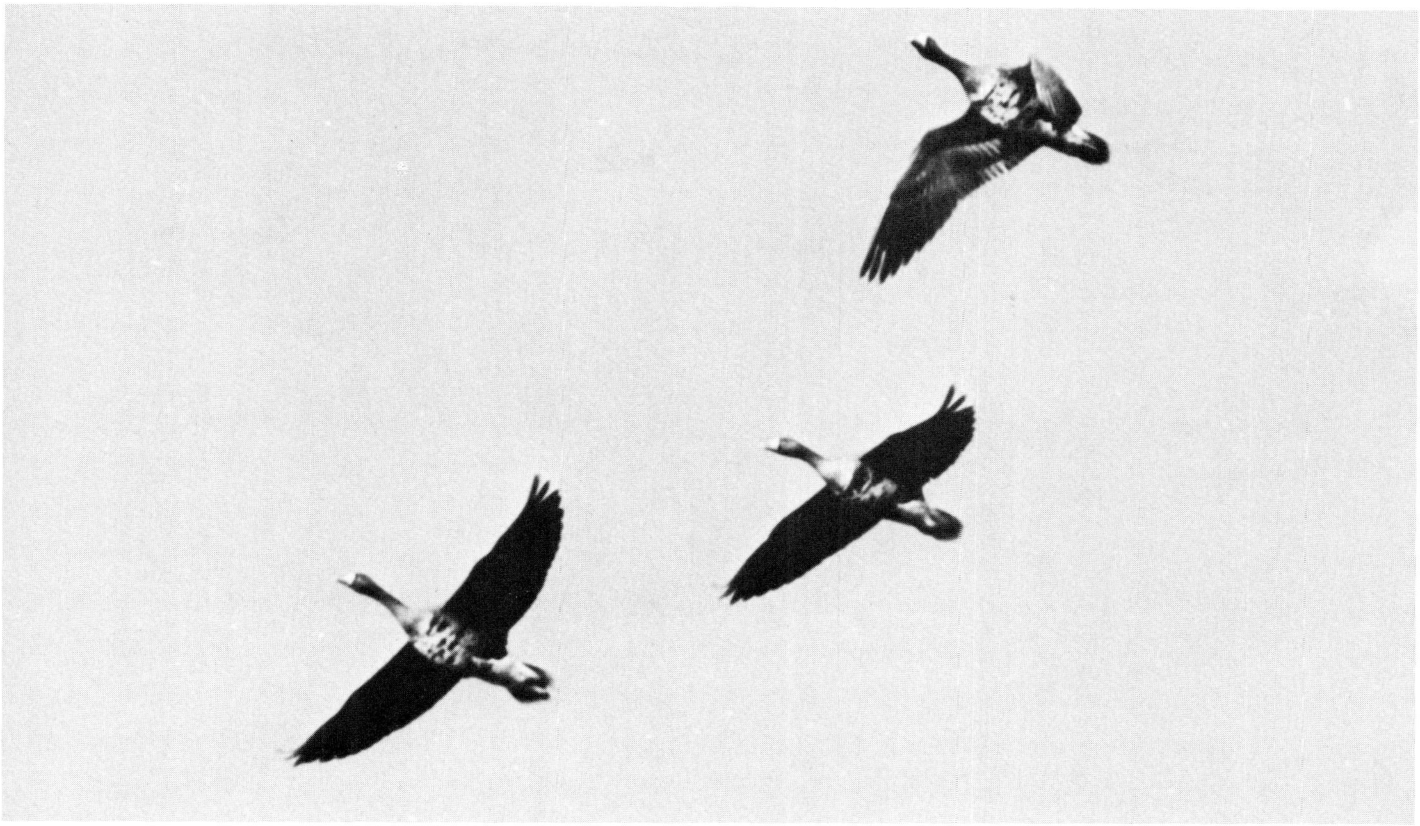

36-21

Two groups of Pacific white-fronted geese show off some of their flight positions.

36-22

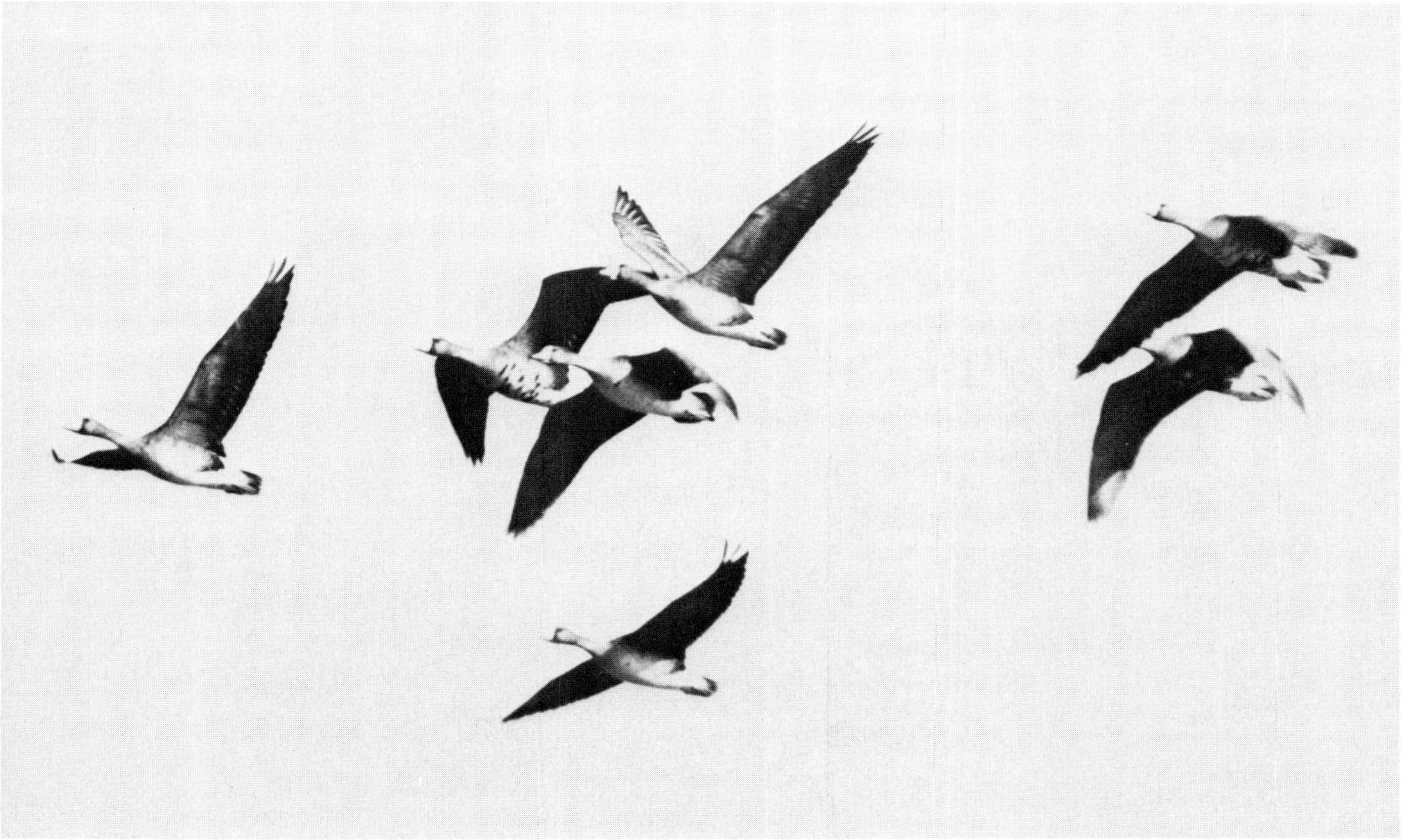

CHAPTER 37

Lesser White-Fronted Goose

Anser erythropus
(Color Photos-Page 95)

Although strictly an Old World species, the dainty and graceful lesser white-fronted goose, like the red-breasted goose, has been included in these pictorial studies for aesthetic reasons as the lesser white-fronted geese are ideal subjects for the artist. These little geese are much smaller than our Pacific white--fronted geese—proportionately about the same as the Ross's goose is to the lesser snow goose. With the exceptions of a yellow ring around their eyes, smaller bills relative to their heads, and folded wings which extend past their tails, the lesser white-fronted geese are miniature Pacific whitefronts. Their calls are similar to the *ca-leek-aleek'* or *ca-lee-leek-leek'* of our whitefronts but are higher pitched.

The lesser white-fronted geese breed along the northern parts of the Scandinavian Peninsula, Finland, Russia, and Siberia. They normally nest on higher and more wooded grounds than the European and Greenland white-fronted geese. Their wintering range is extensive, covering most of Europe and Asia. They are still a common species in Central Siberia but one group, which in former years migrated to Japan in large numbers, has been decimated.· Lesser whitefronts are never seen on this continent except in private and public aviaries where they are a favorite of many aviculturists.

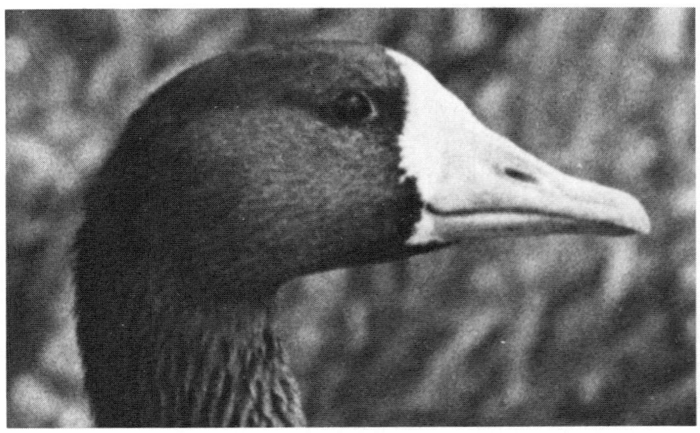

Pacific white-fronted goose.

Lesser white-fronted goose.

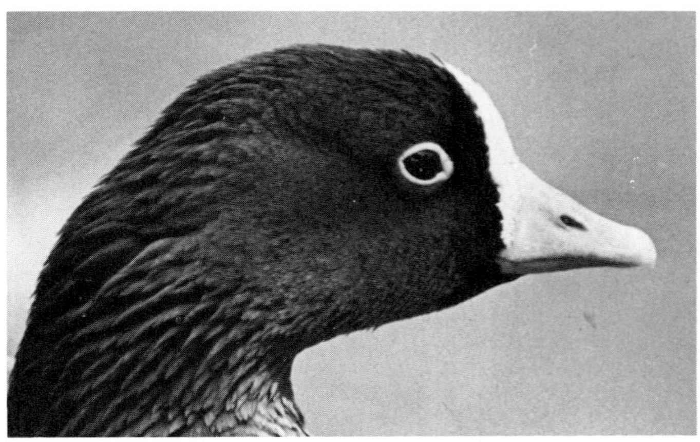

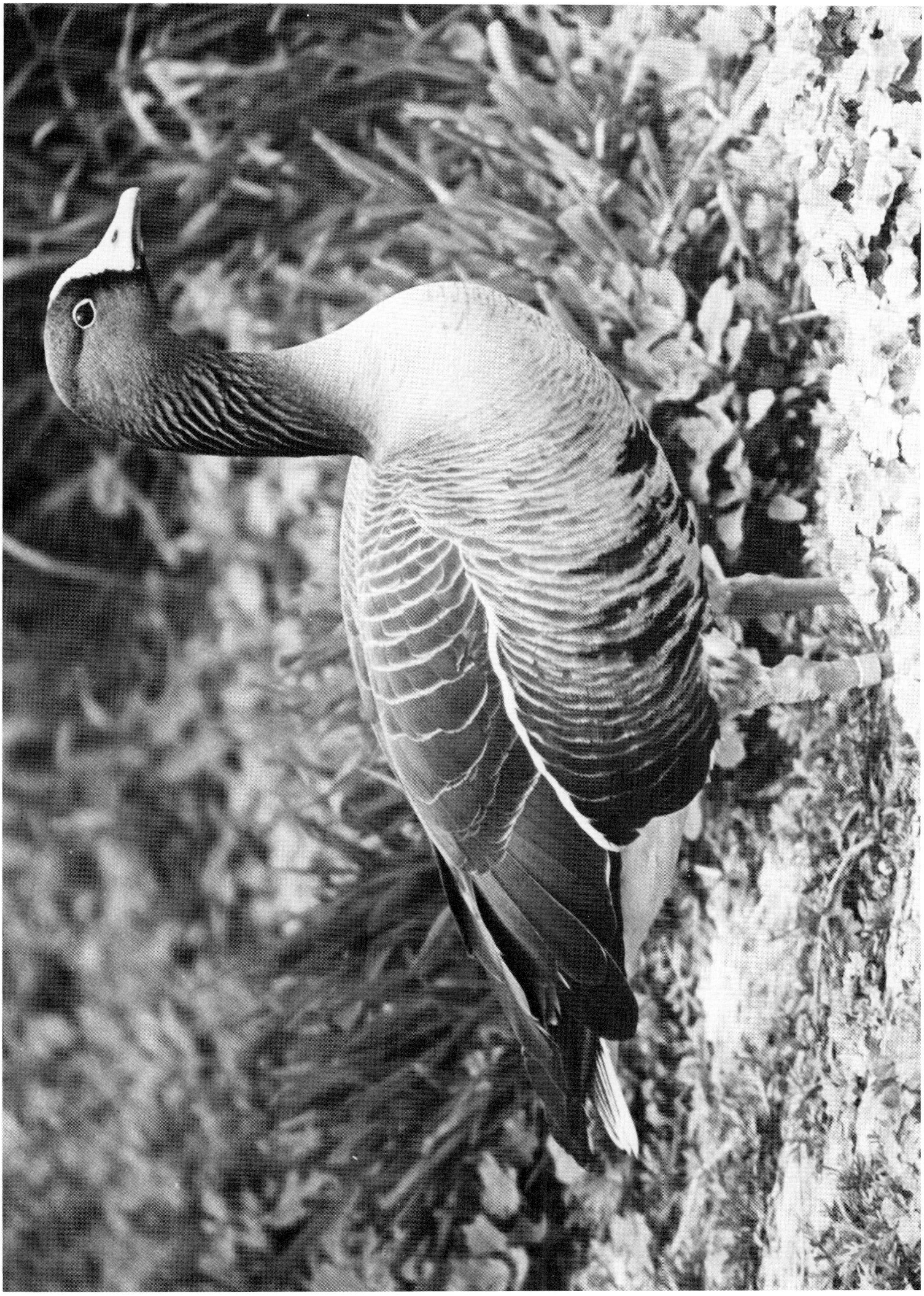

37-1 The lovely little lesser white-fronted gander. Except for his size which is about that of a large Cackling Canada goose, he is almost identical with his Pacific white-fronted cousin.

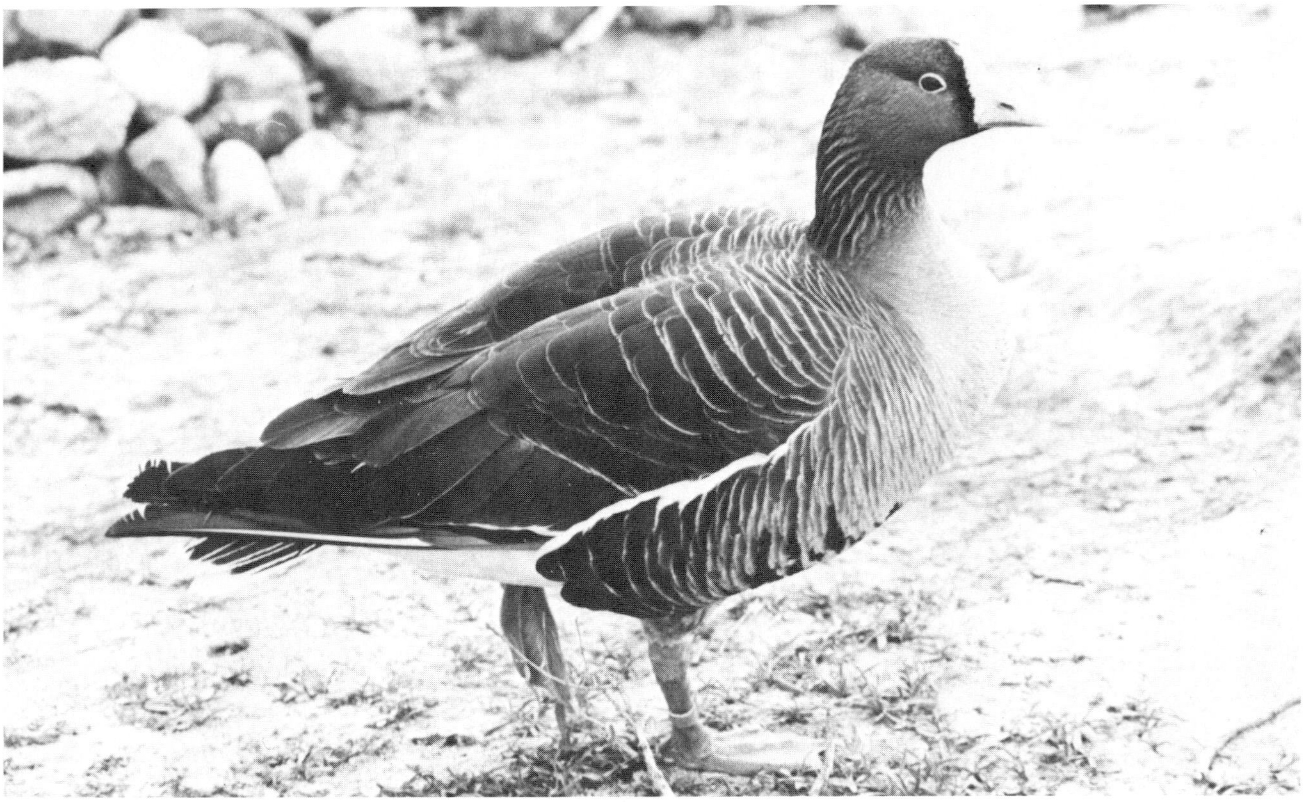

37-2 Little lesser white-fronted, an Old World goose, about to take a step.

37-3 Three-quarter rear view shows considerable feather detail.

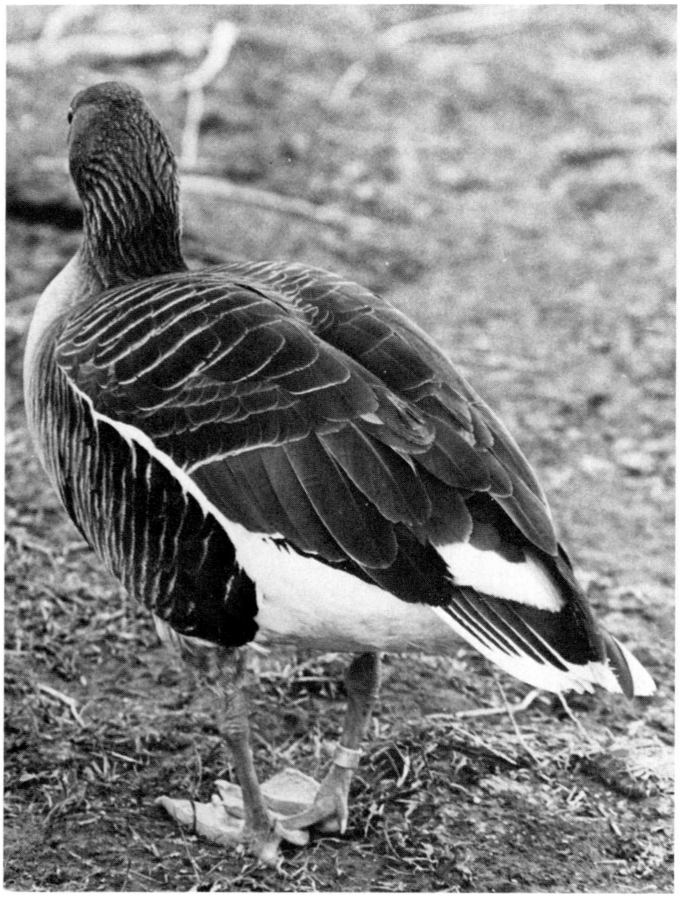

37-4 Good front view of the lesser white-fronted goose. Note the narrow yellow ring around his eye. This marking is unique among the white-fronted goose species.

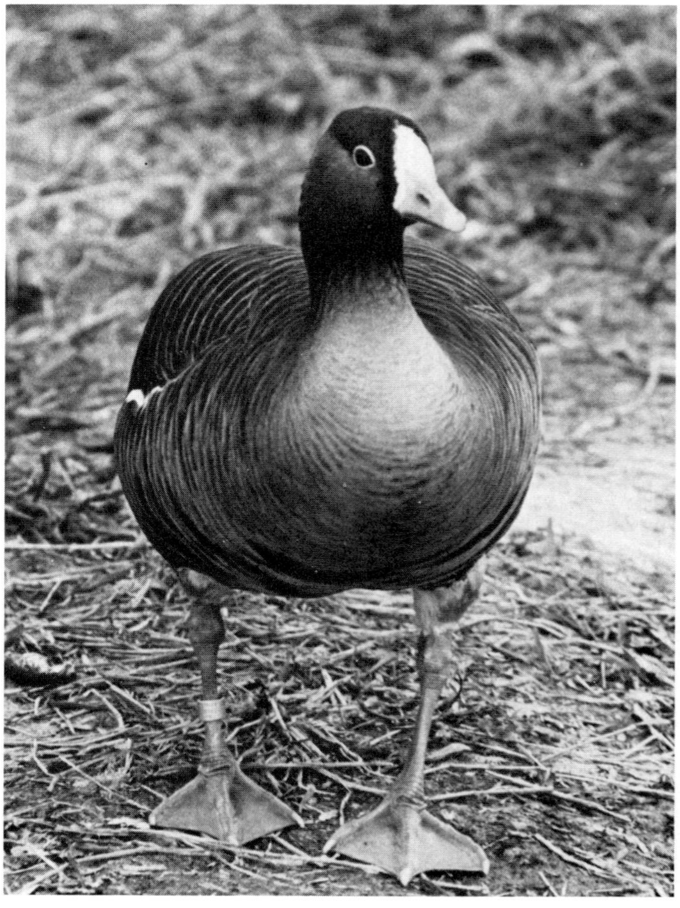

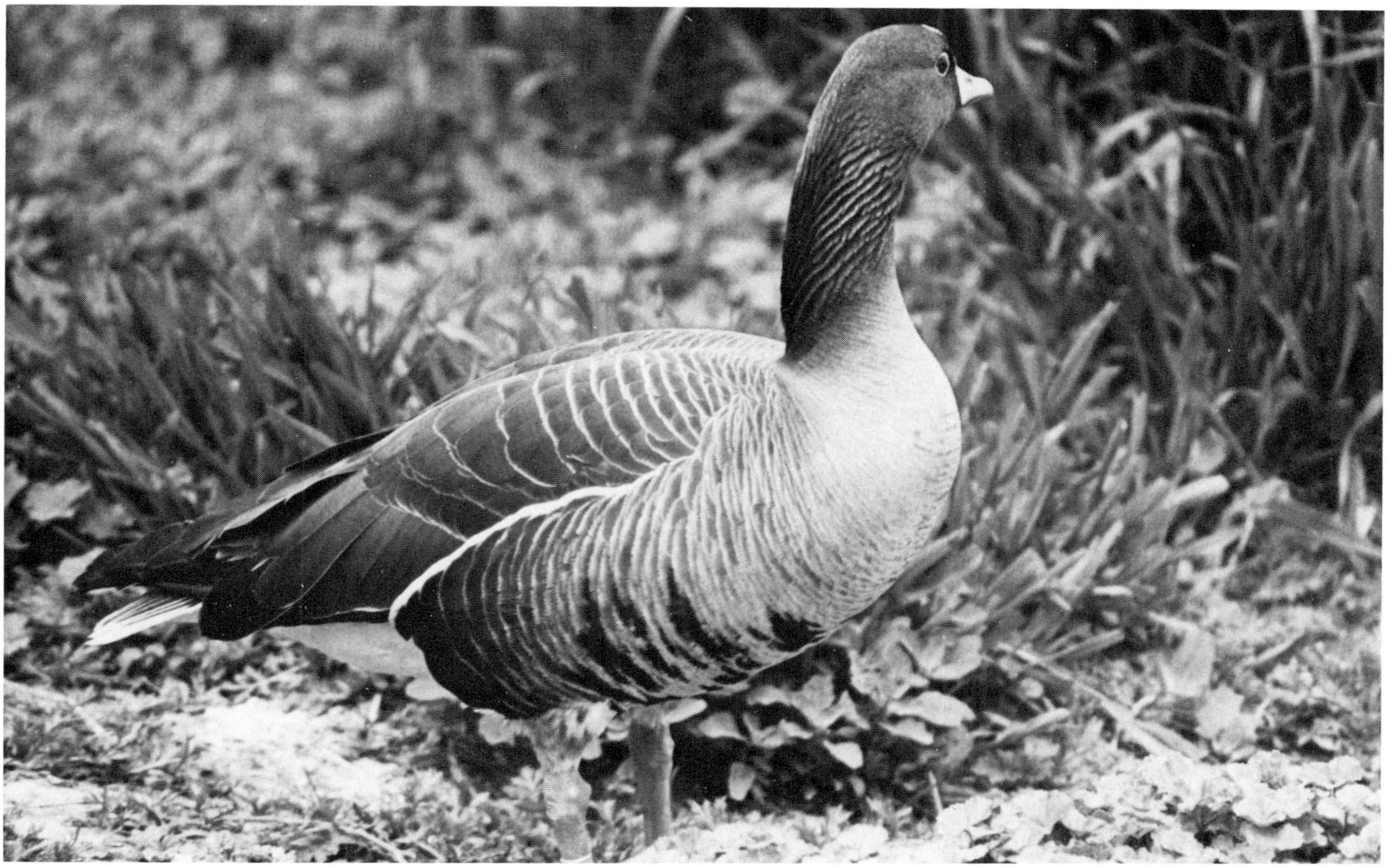

37-5

Lesser whitefronts in alert positions. Notice how their neck feathers lie in ridges and valleys.

37-6

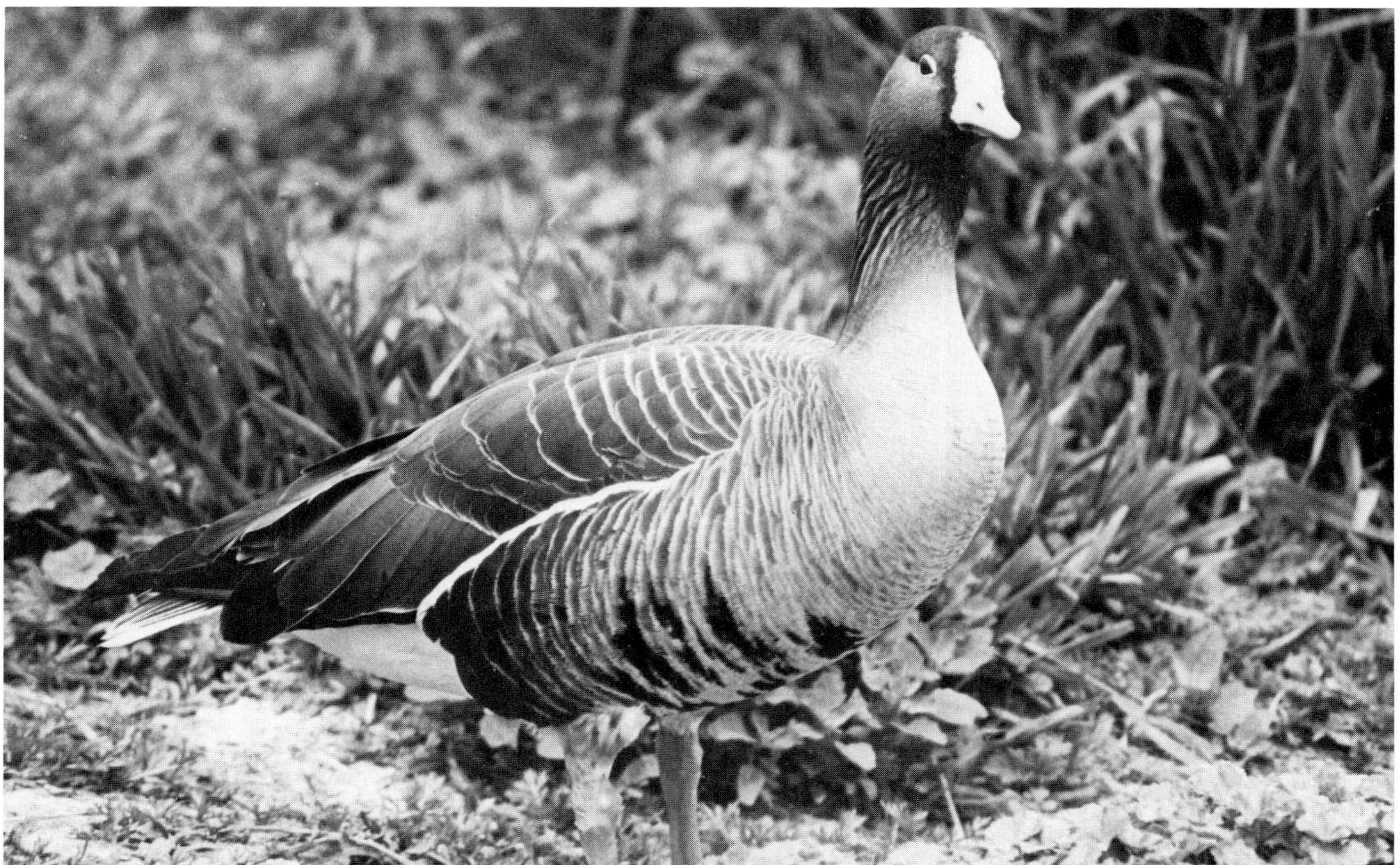

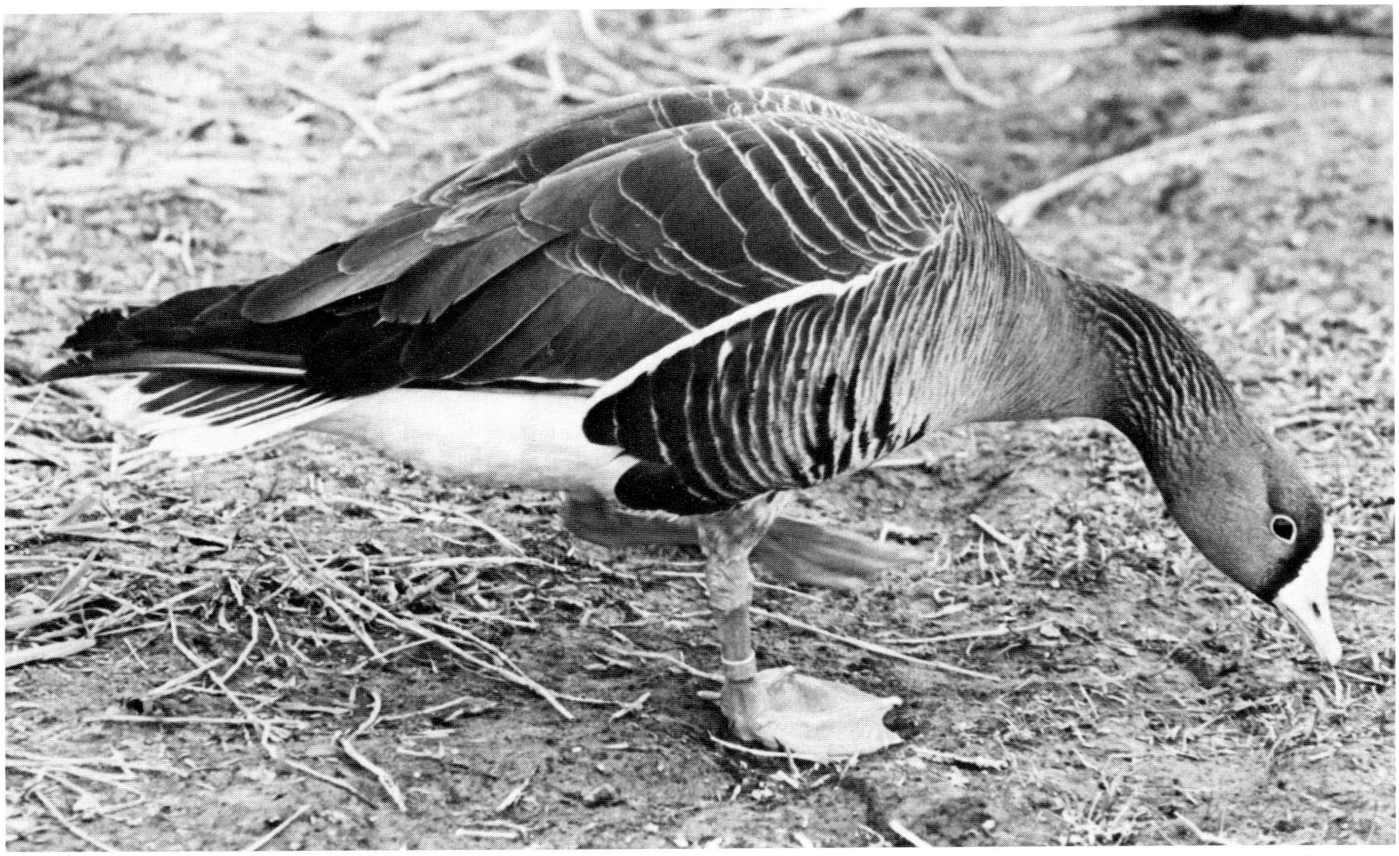

37-7

Lesser white-fronted geese in feeding positions.

37-8

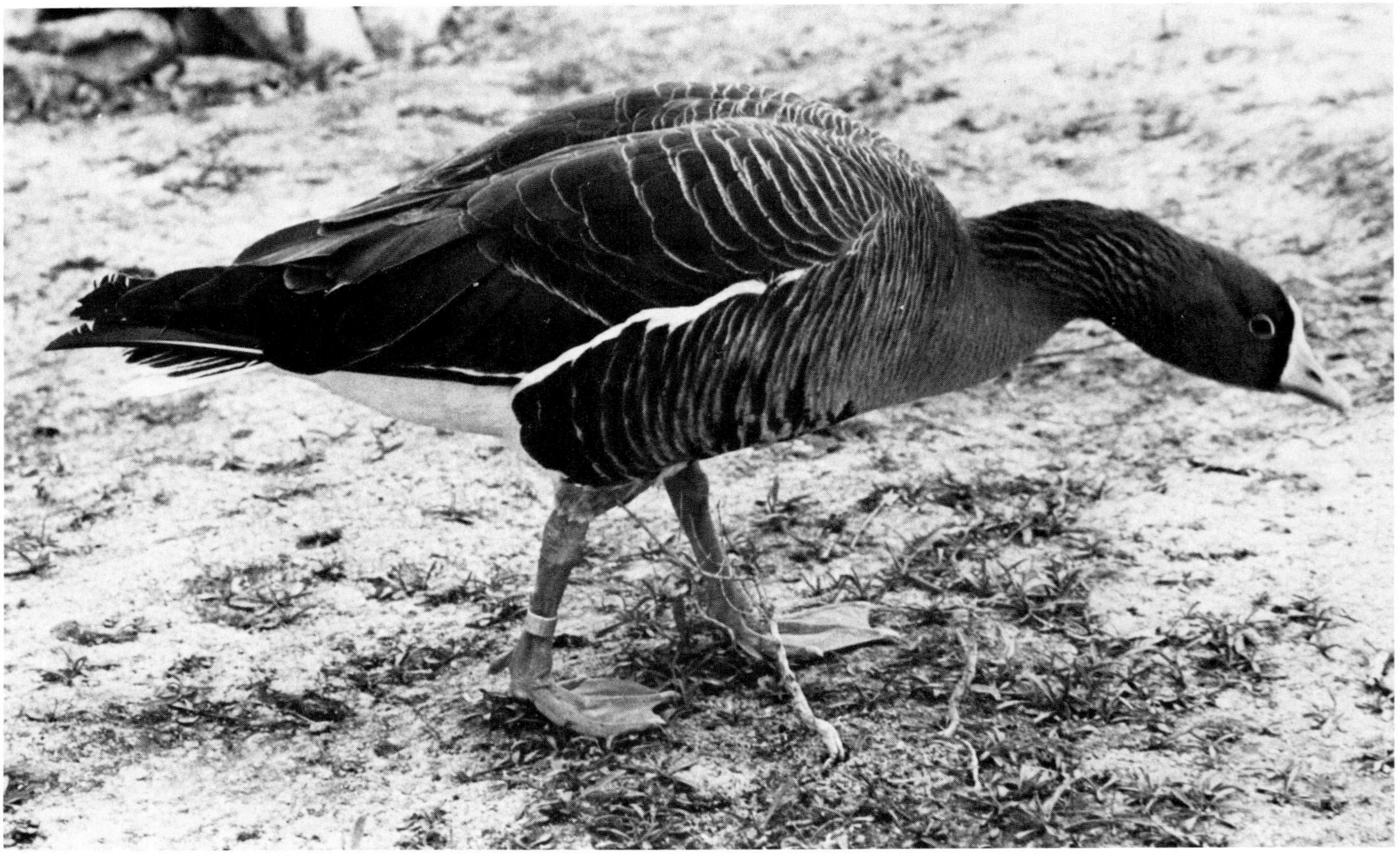

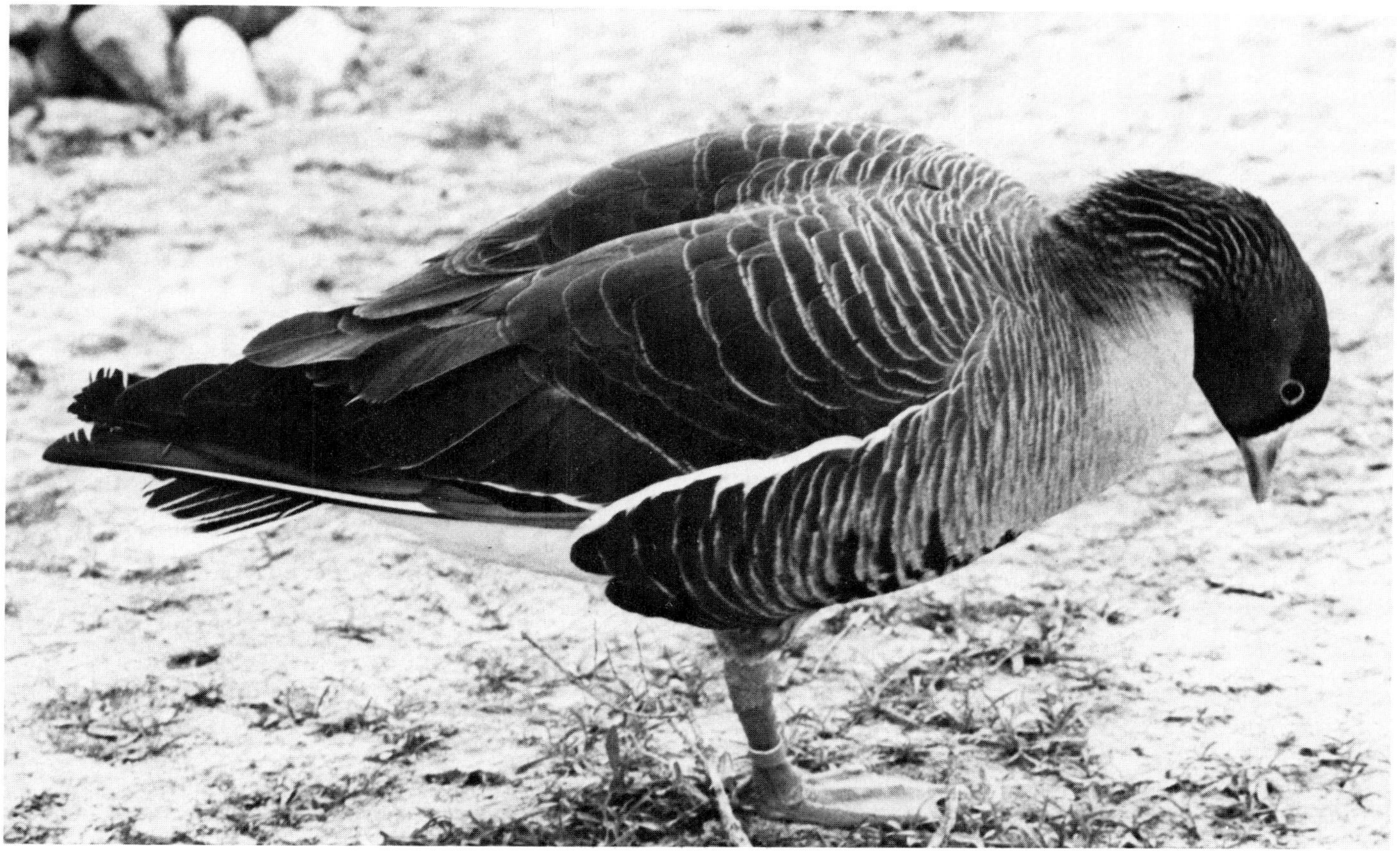

37-9

Two more studies of lesser whitefronts in feeding positions.

37-10

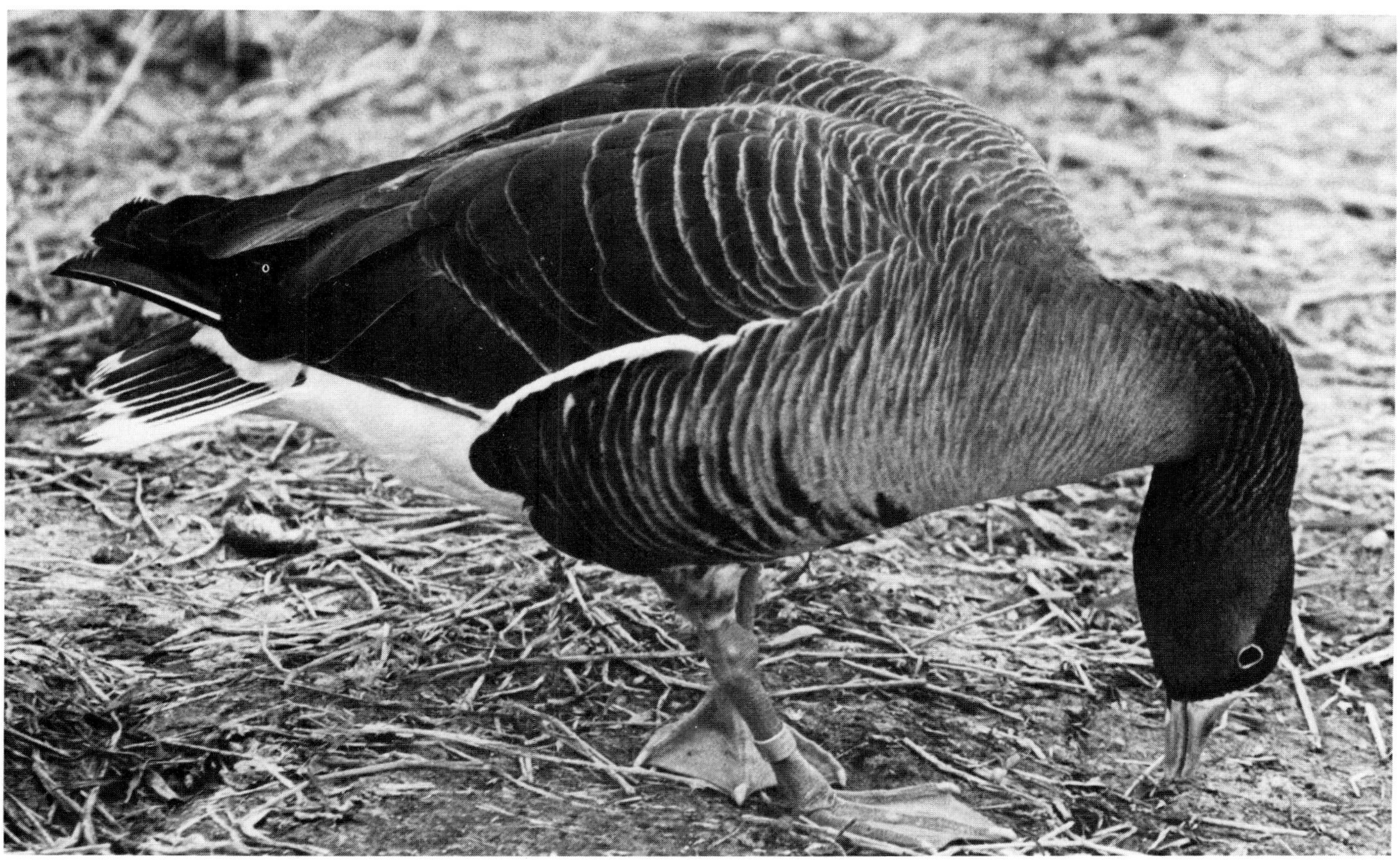

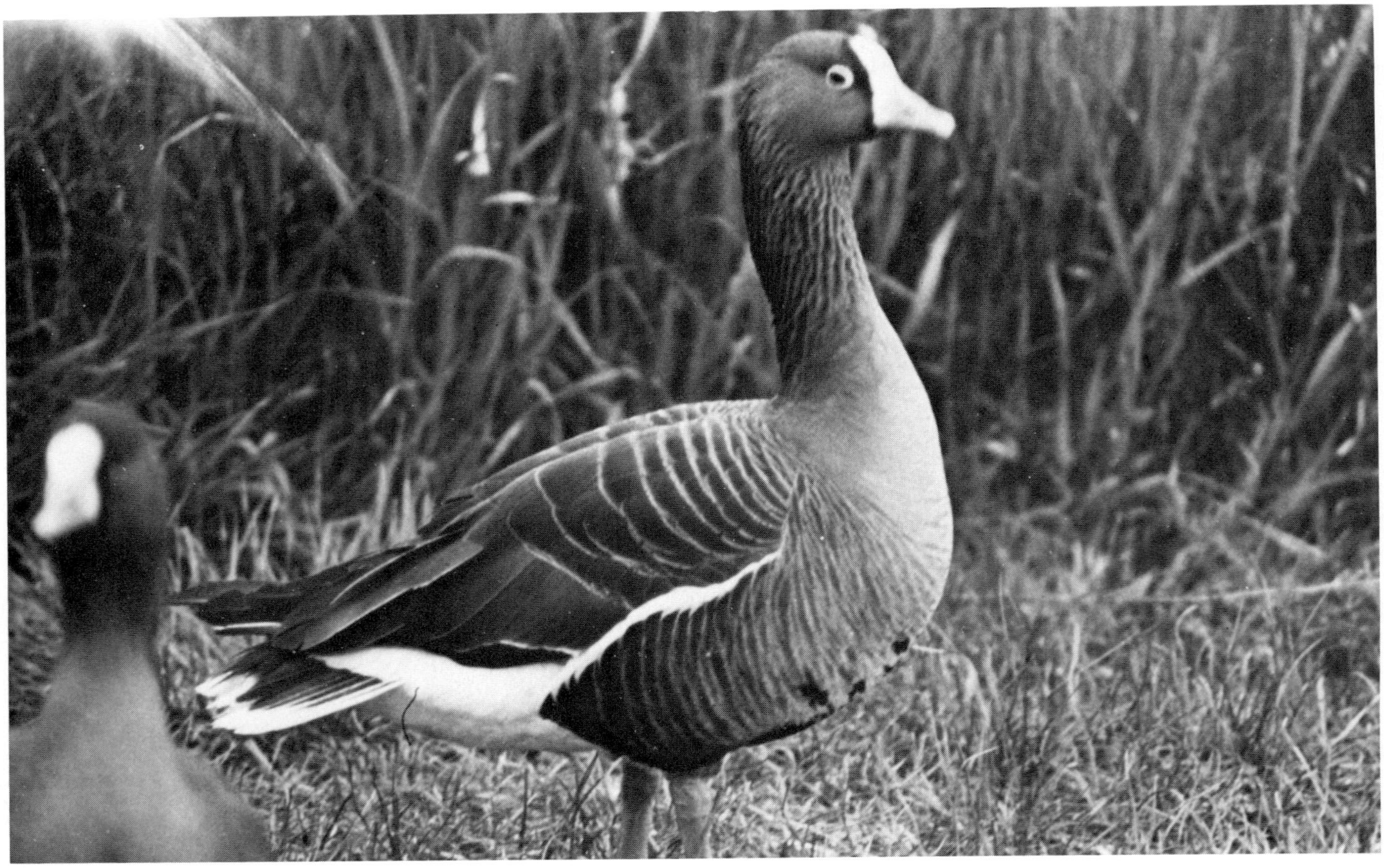

37-11

This little whitefront assumes two alert poses.

37-12

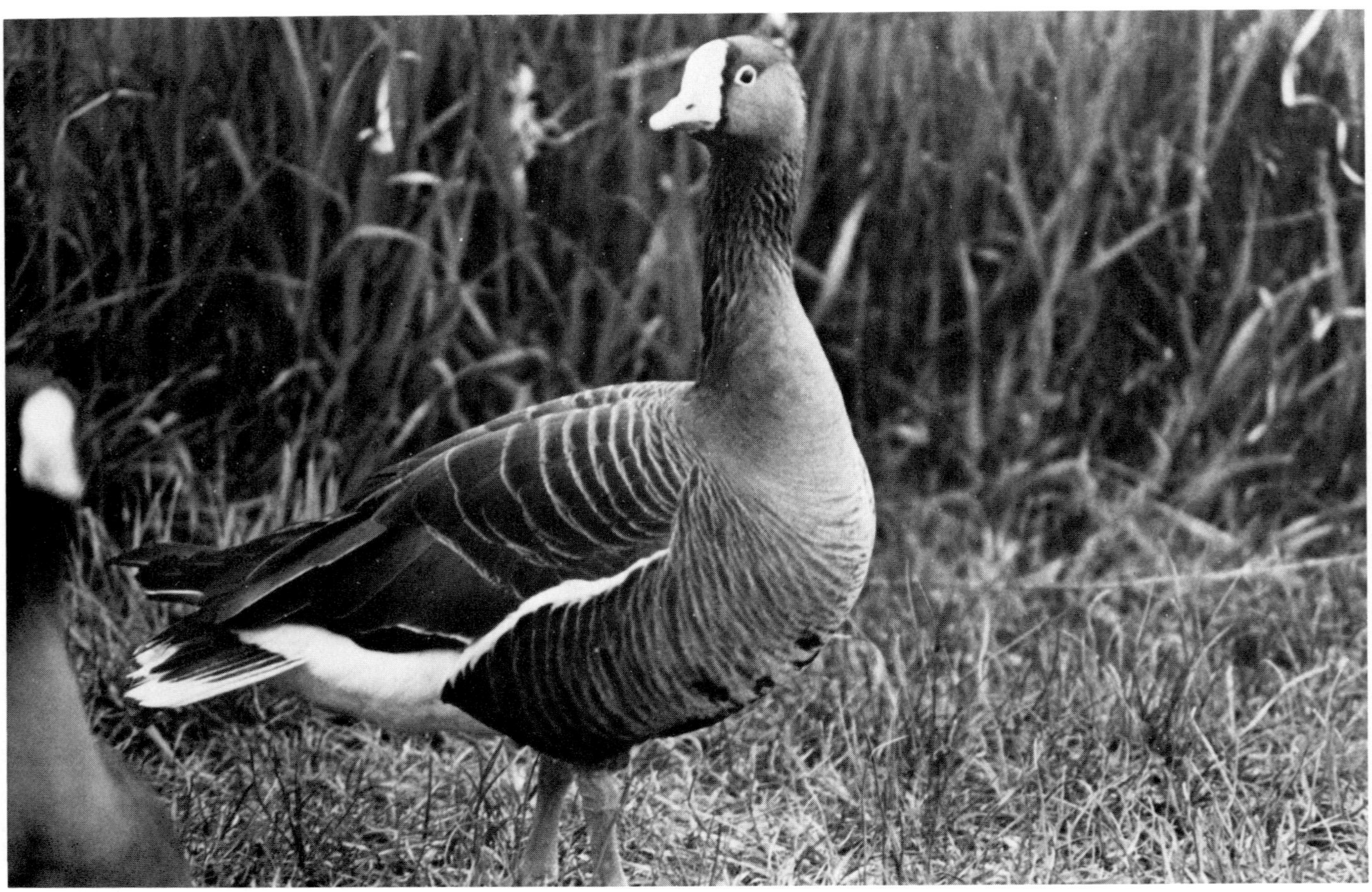

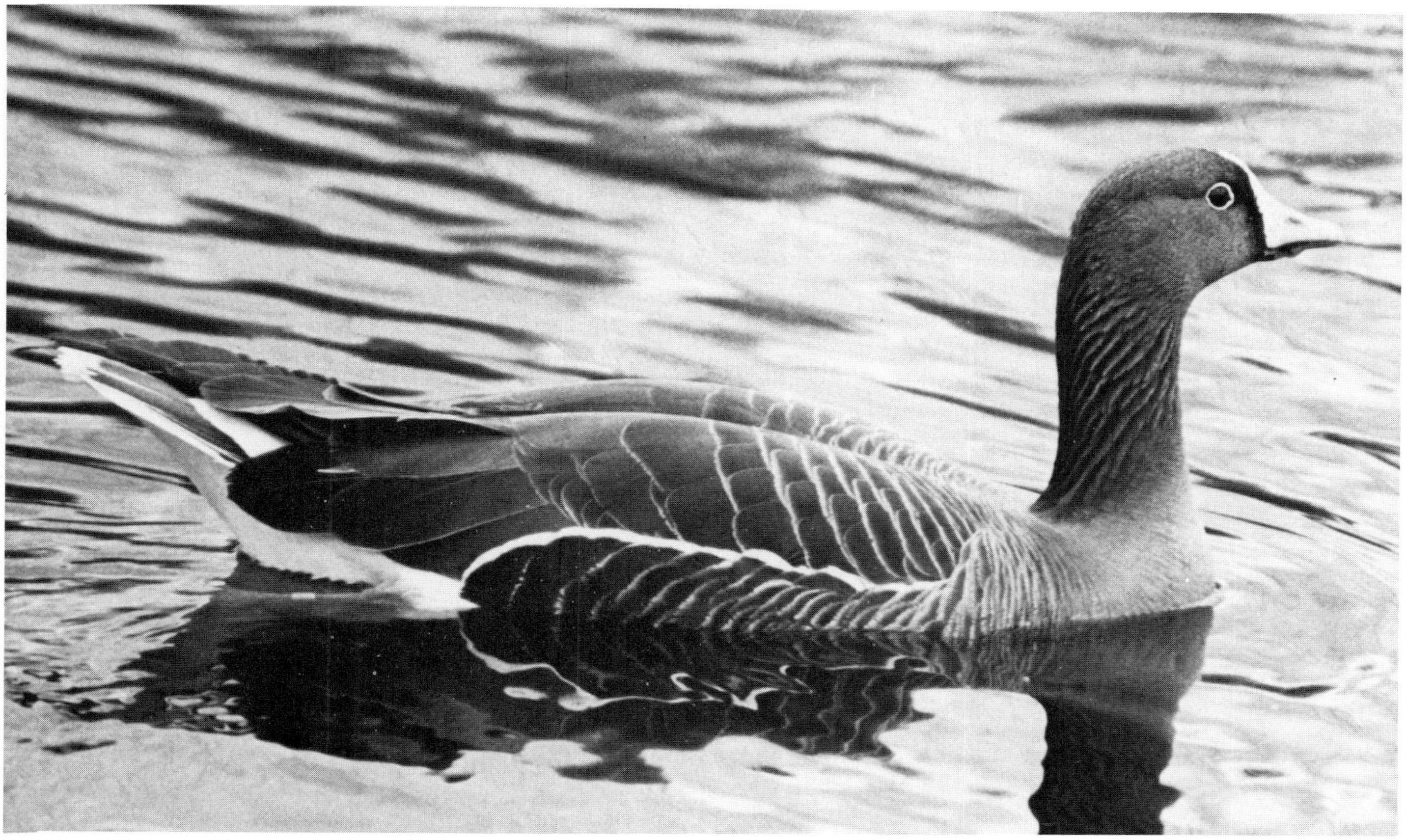

37-13 Nice profile of an alert floating lesser whitefront.

37-14 Front and rear views of the lesser whitefront. They ride quite low in the water. 37-15

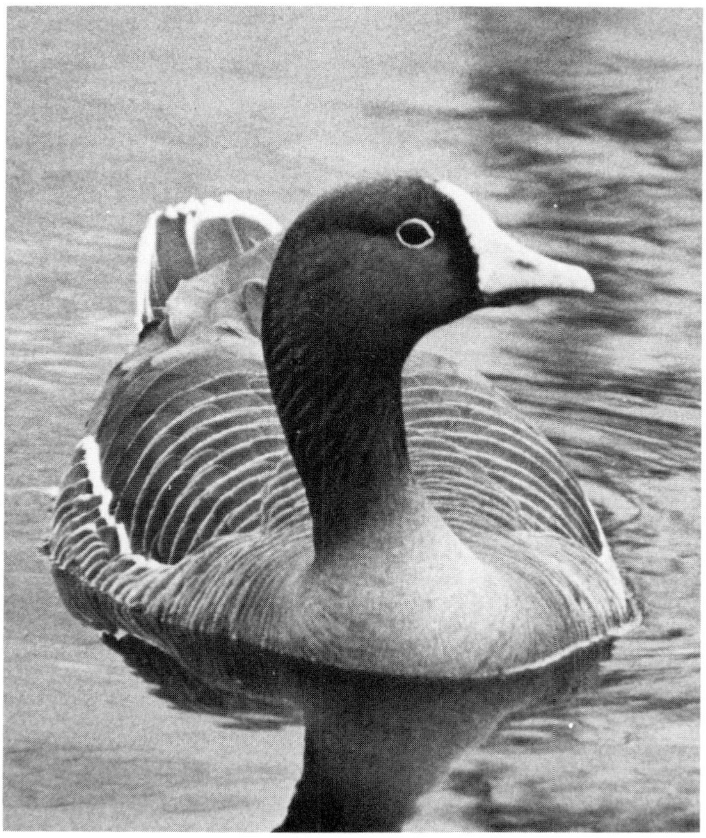

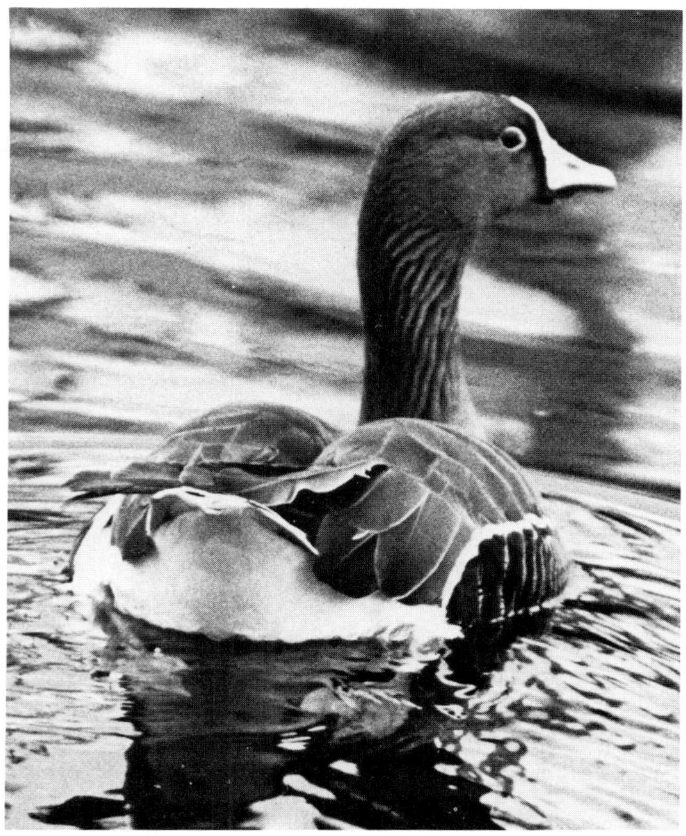

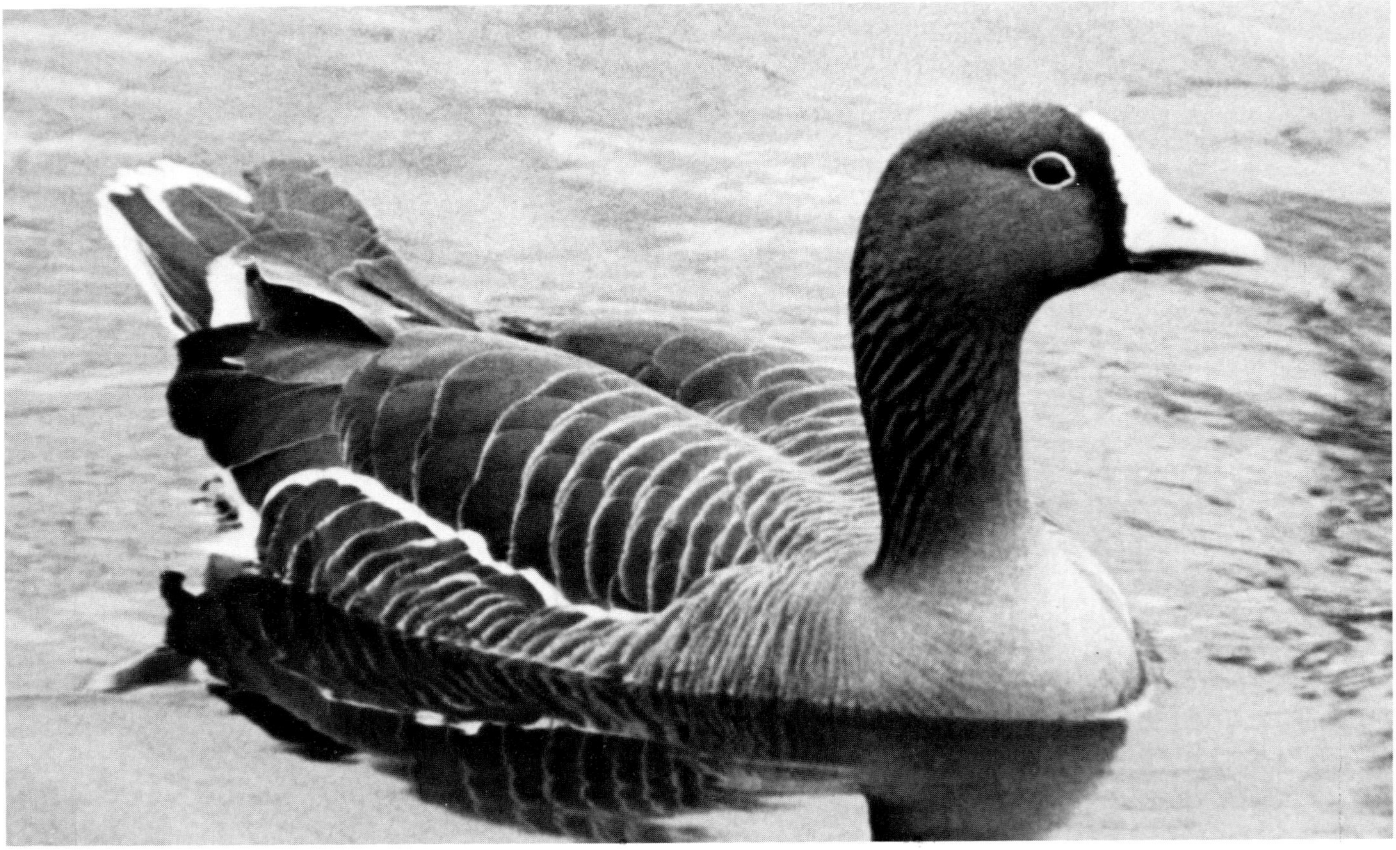

37-16

Additional shots of floating lesser white-fronted geese.

37-17

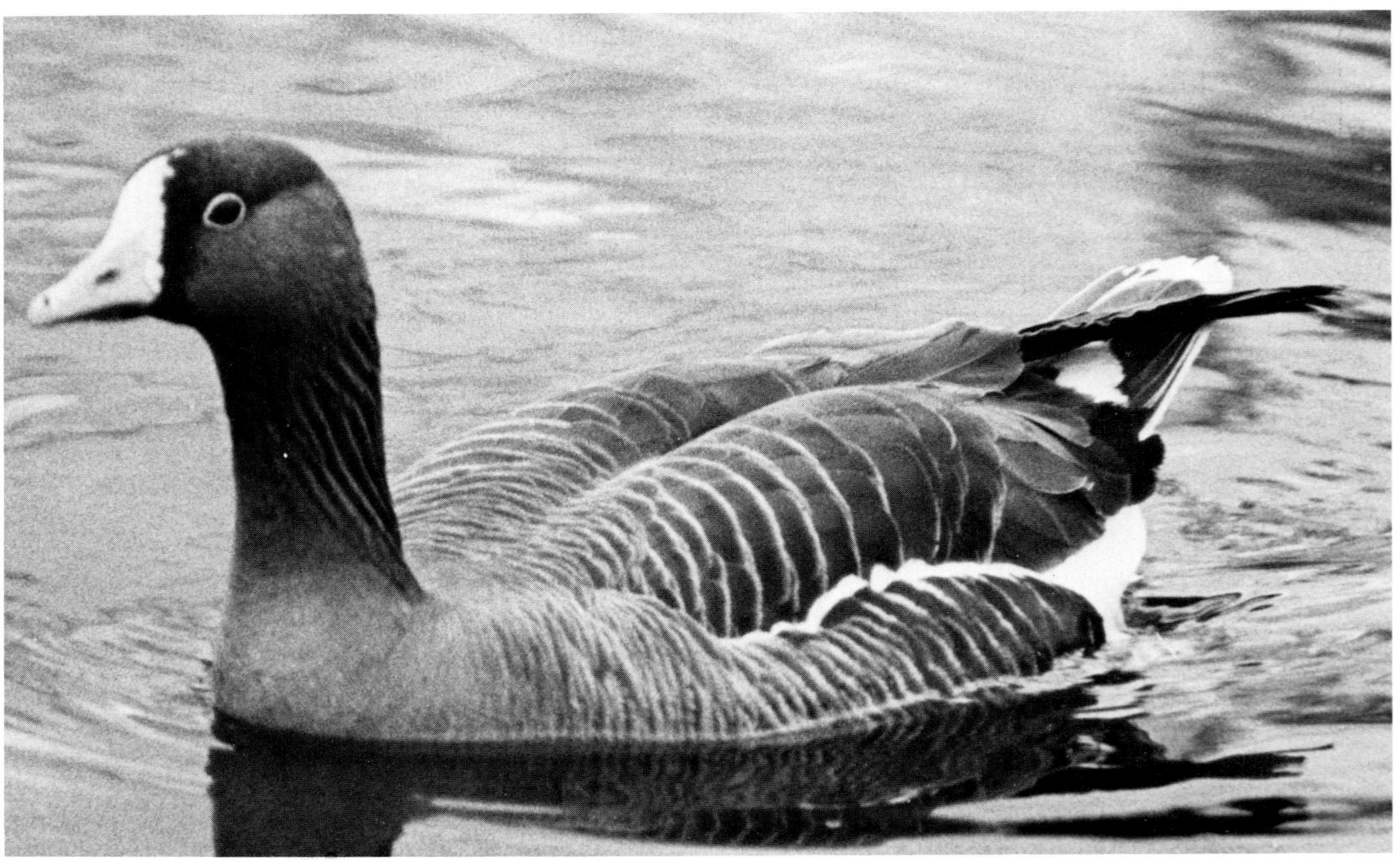

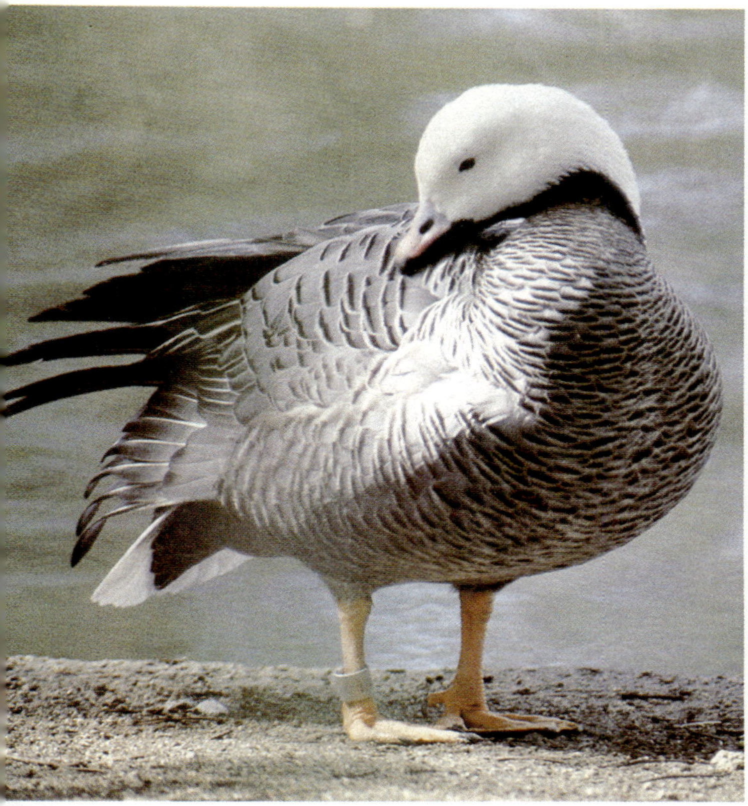

III-15

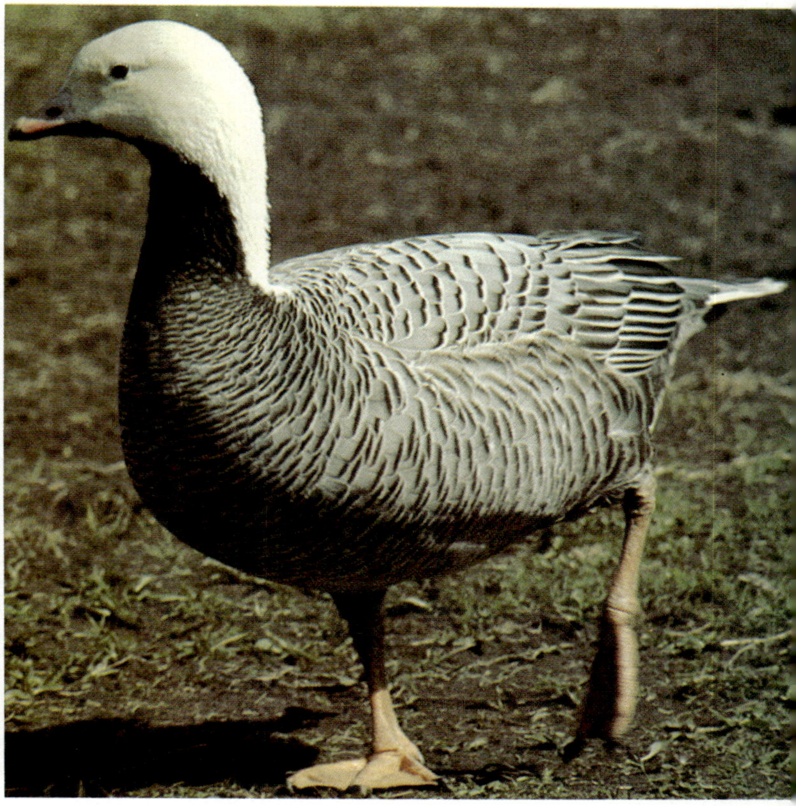

III-16

Emperor Geese. (Chapter 35)

III-17

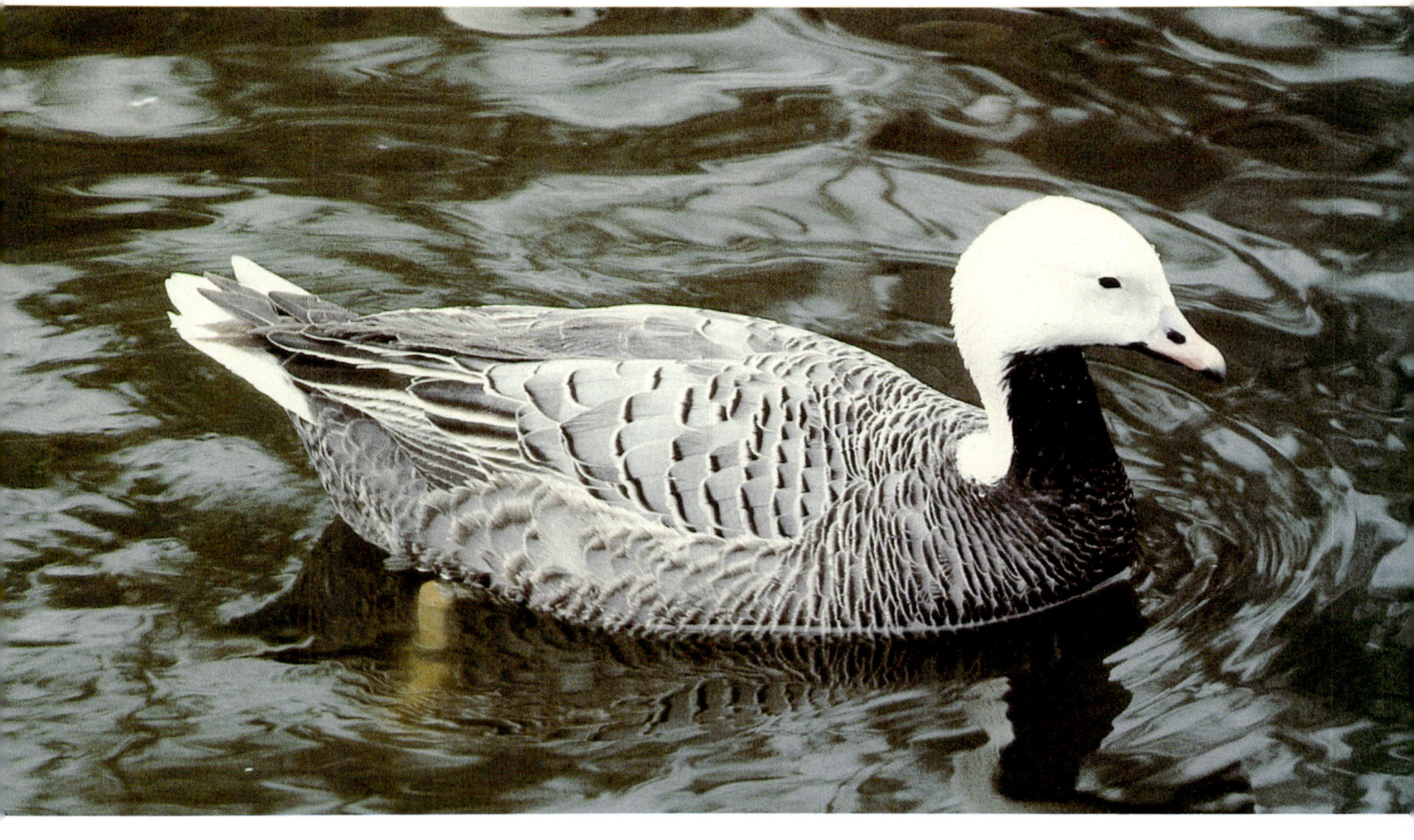

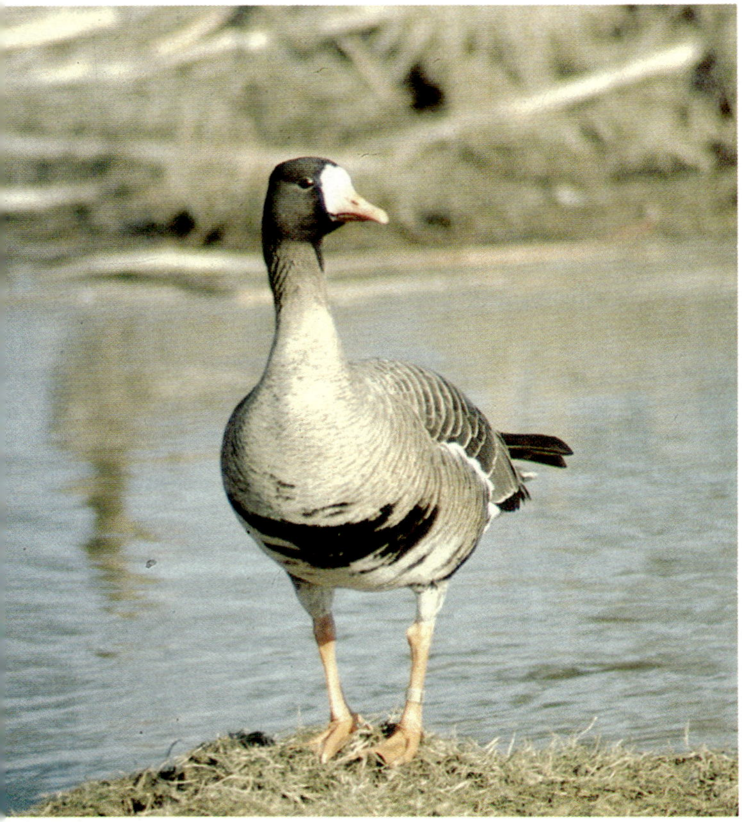

III-18

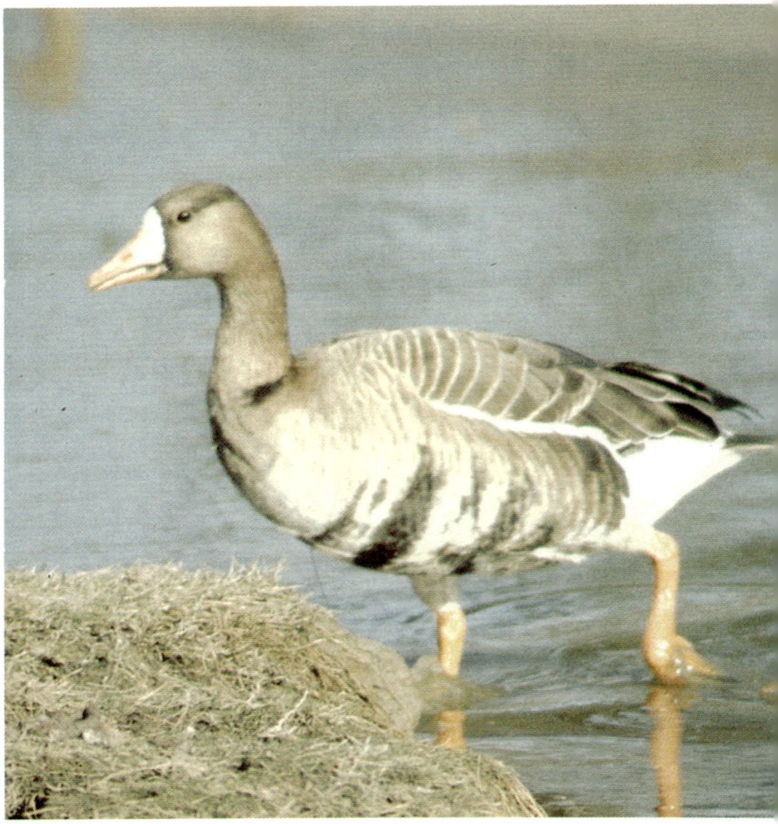

III-19

Pacific White-Fronted Geese. (Chapter 36)

III-20

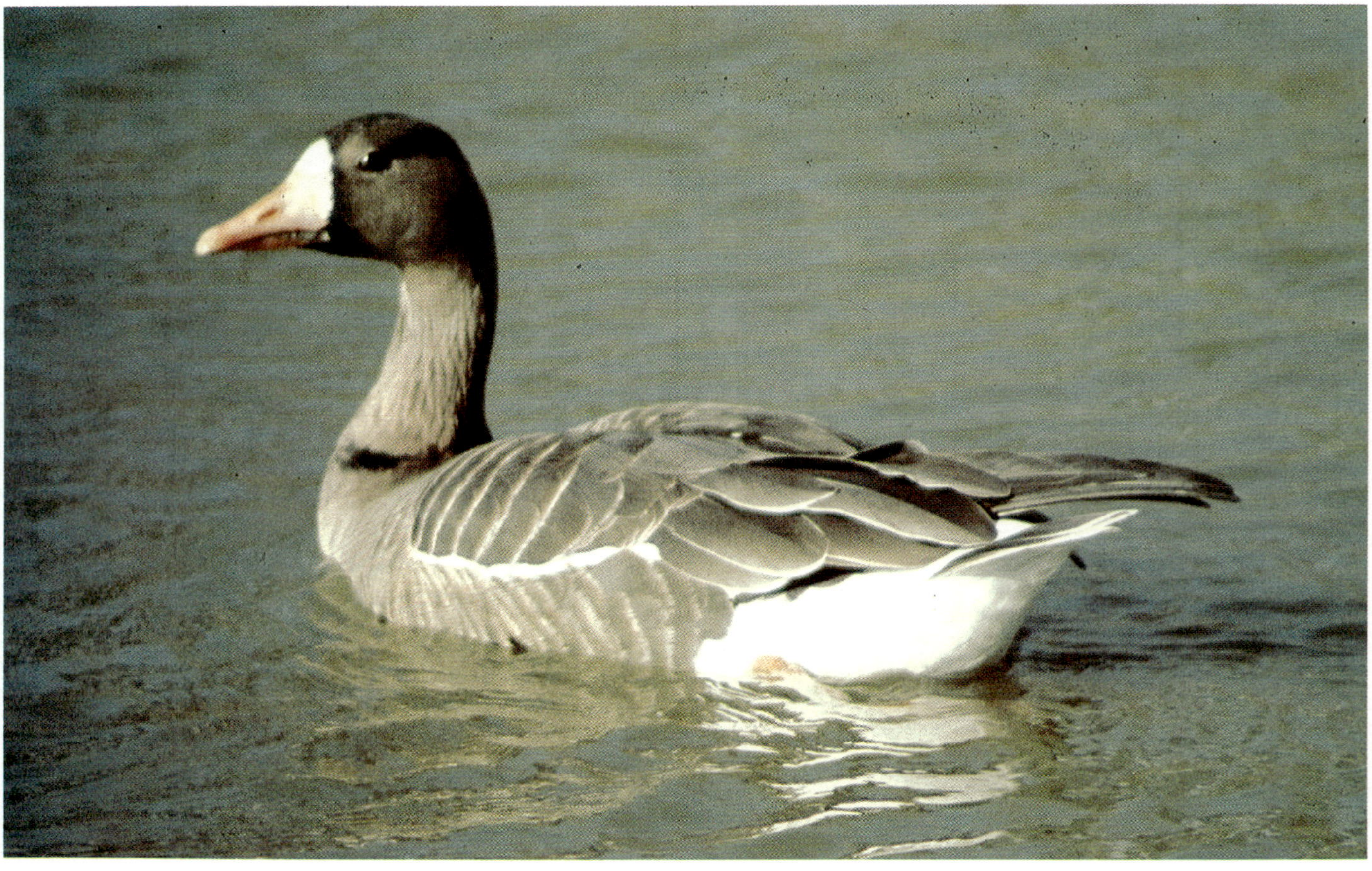

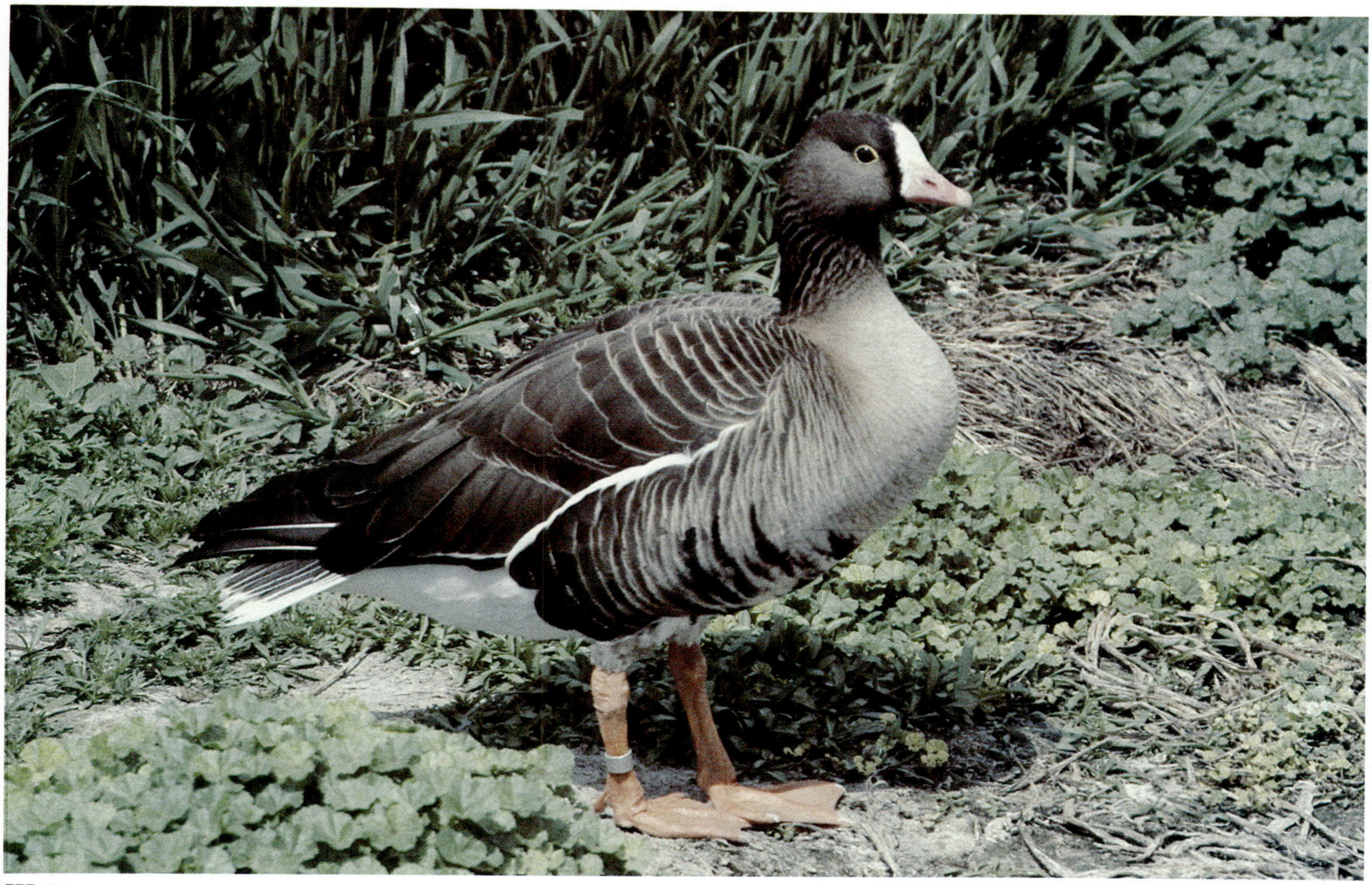

III-21

Lesser White-Fronted Geese. (Chapter 37)

III-22

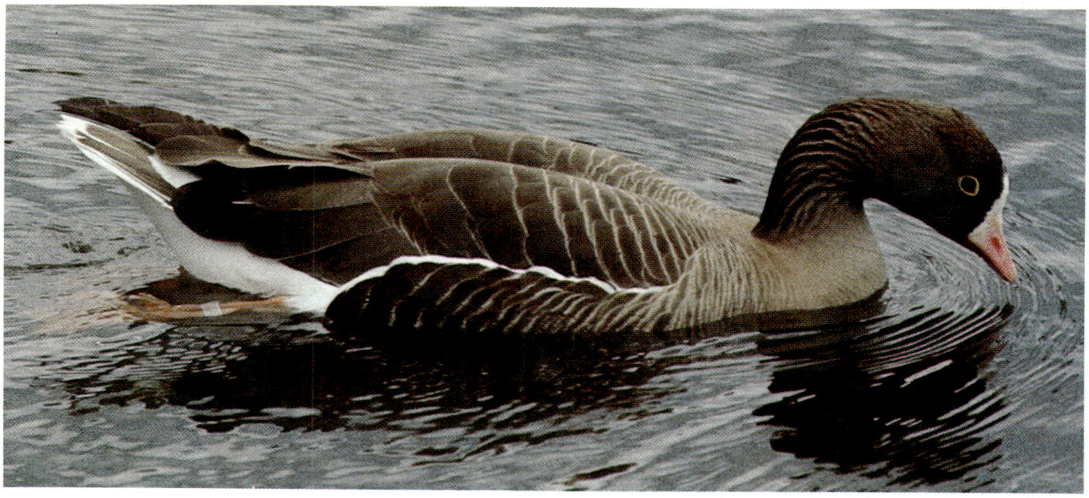

III-23 Lesser White-Fronted Goose. (Chapter 37)

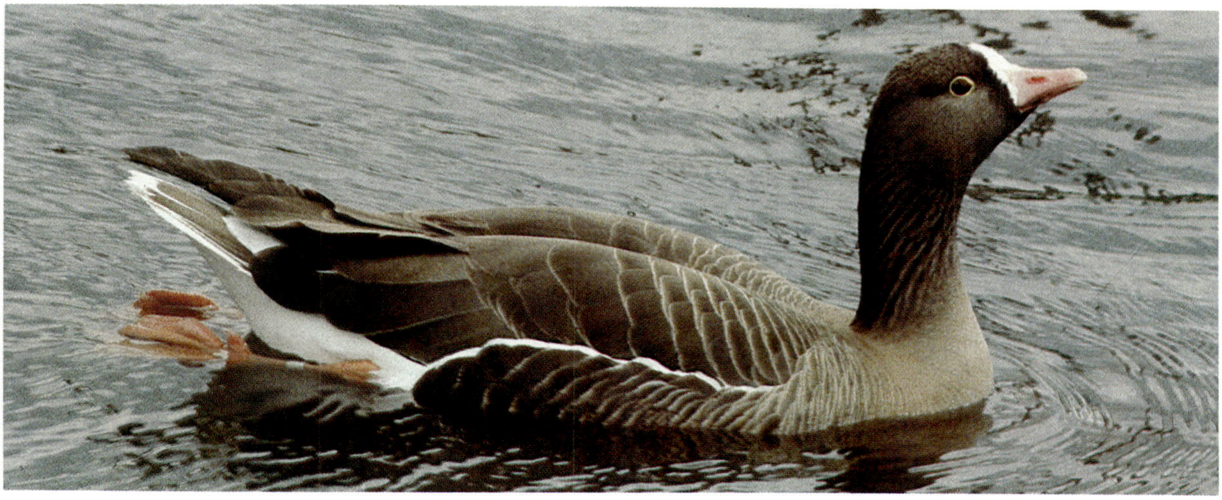

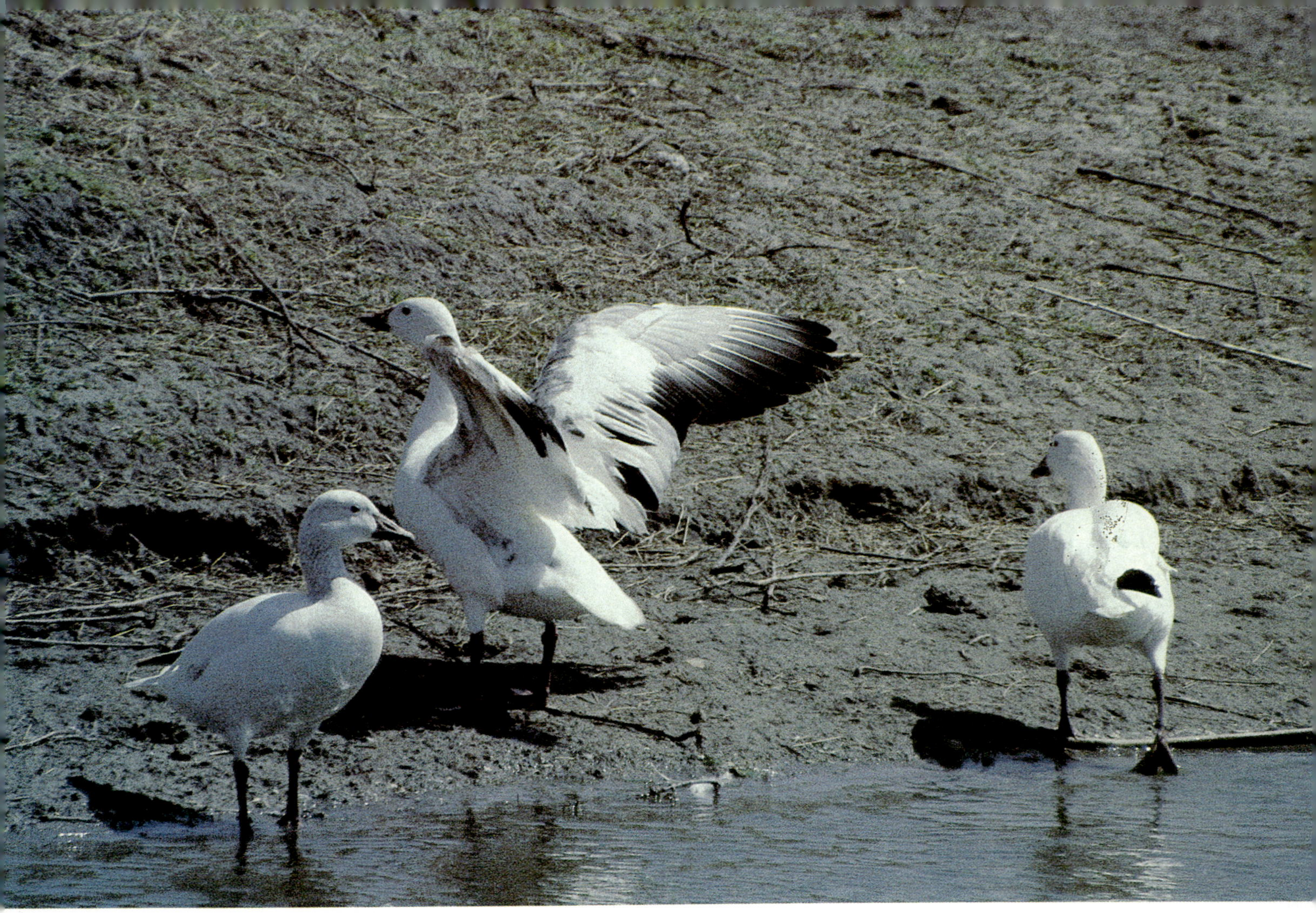

III-24
III-25

Lesser Snow Geese. (Chapter 38)

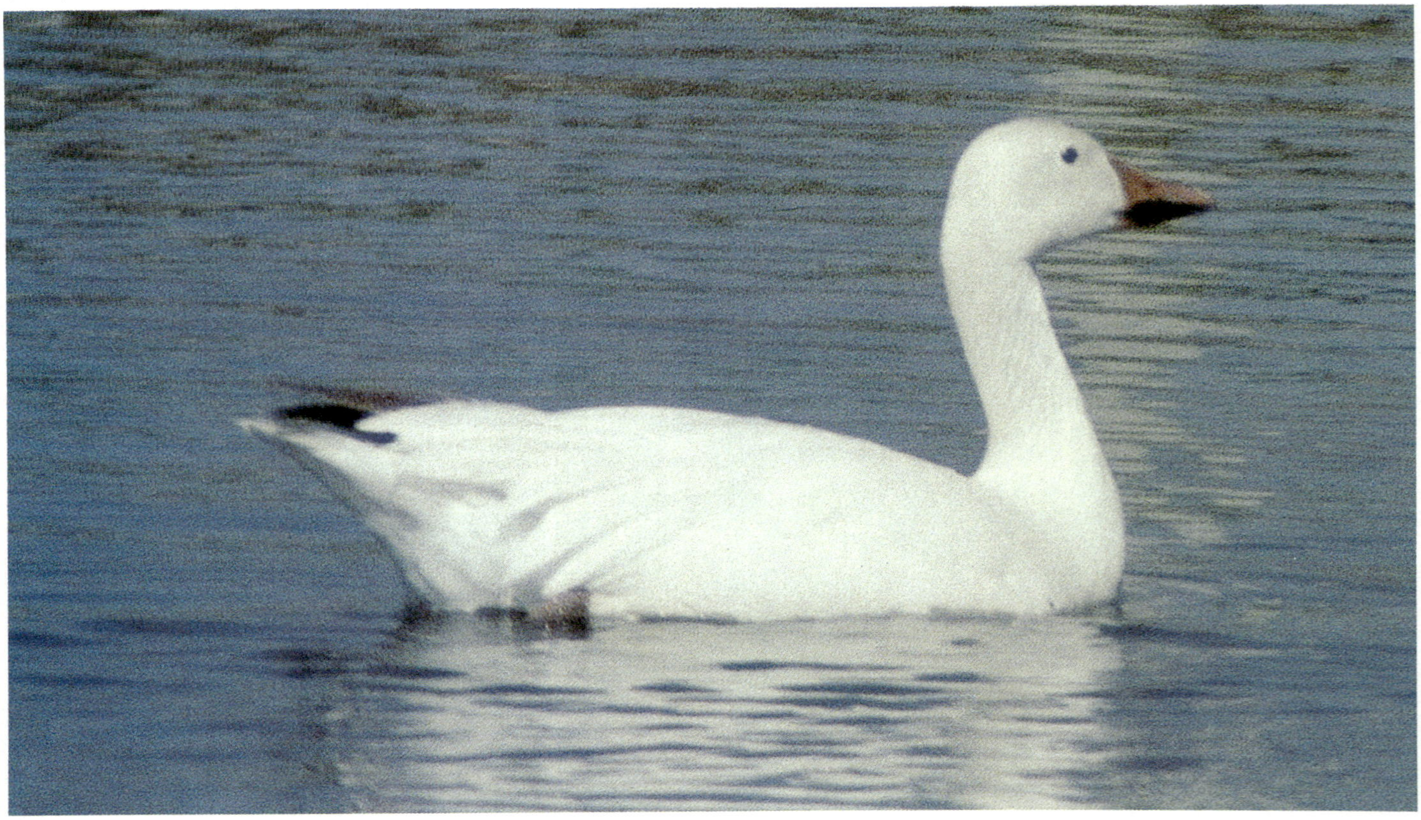

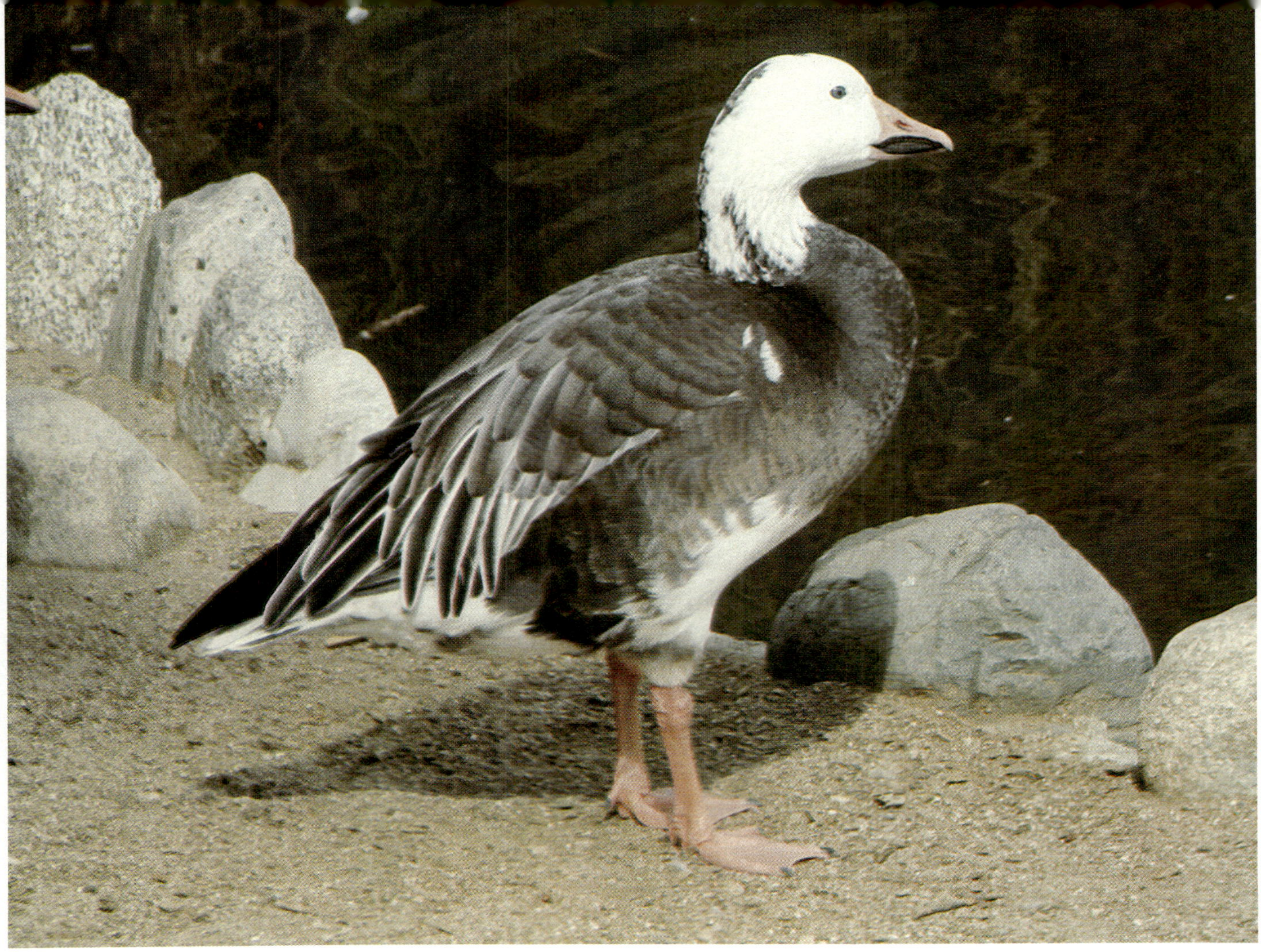

III-26

III-27

Blue Geese. (Chapter 38)

III-28

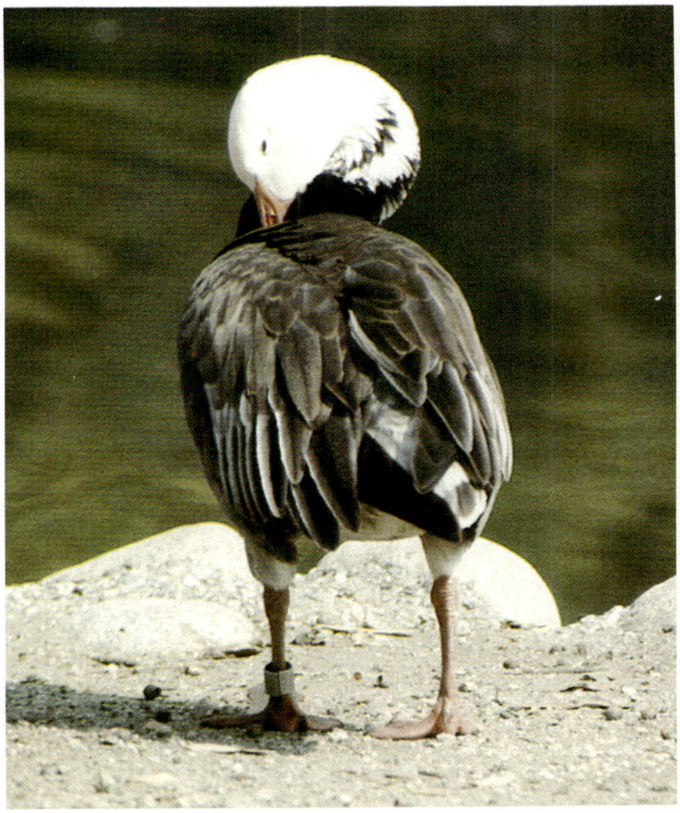

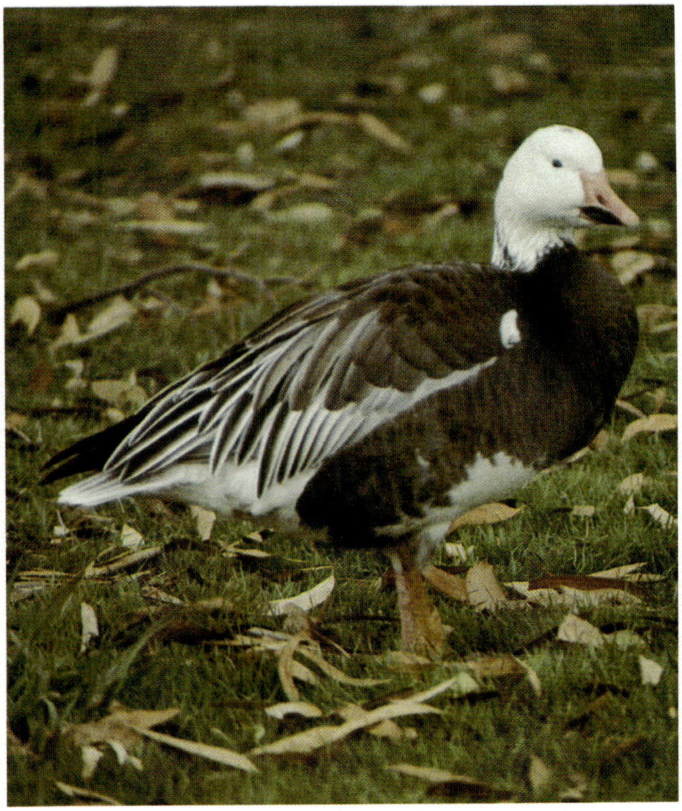

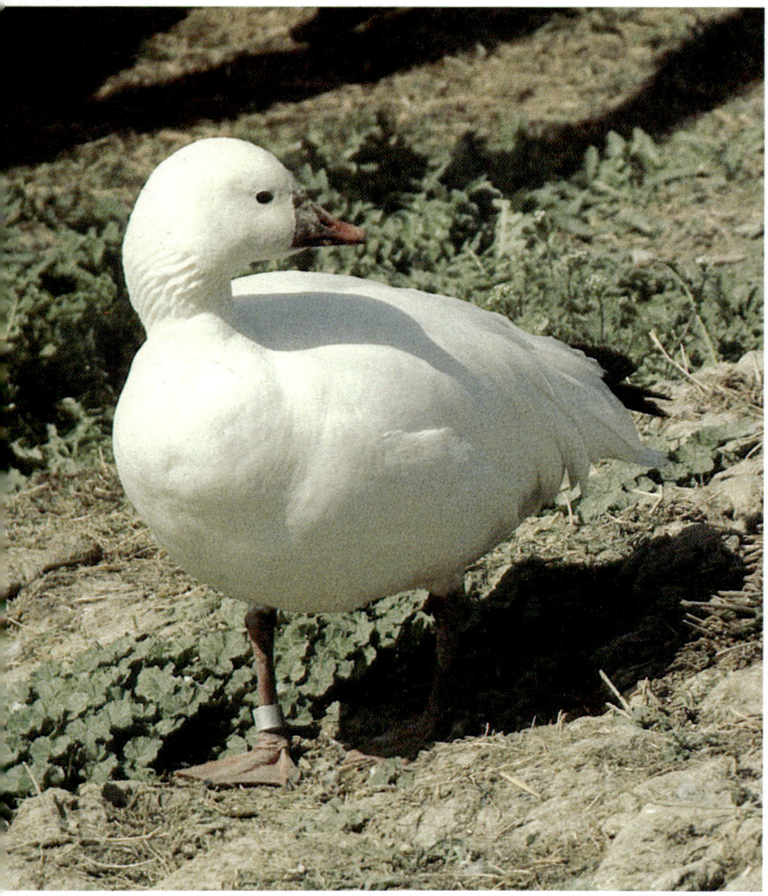

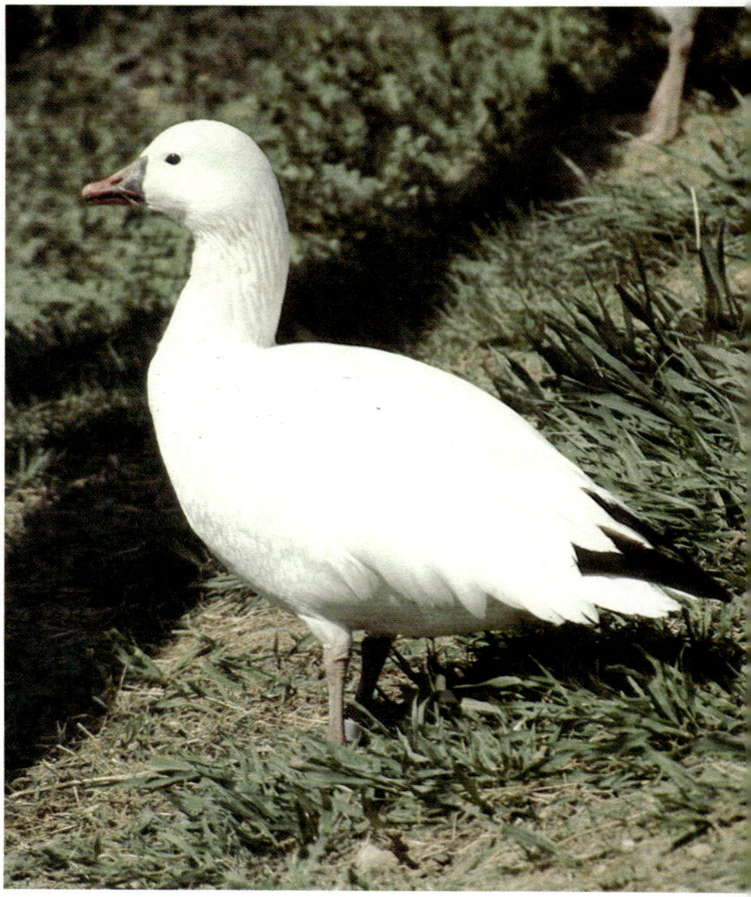

III-29

II

III-31

III-32 Ross's Geese, Pair. (Chapter 39)

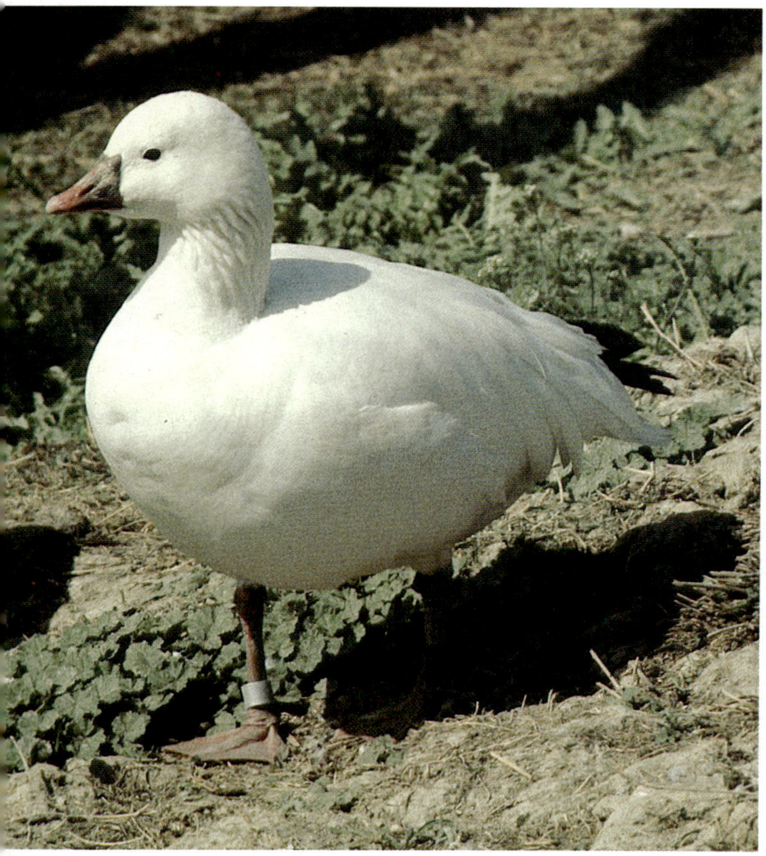

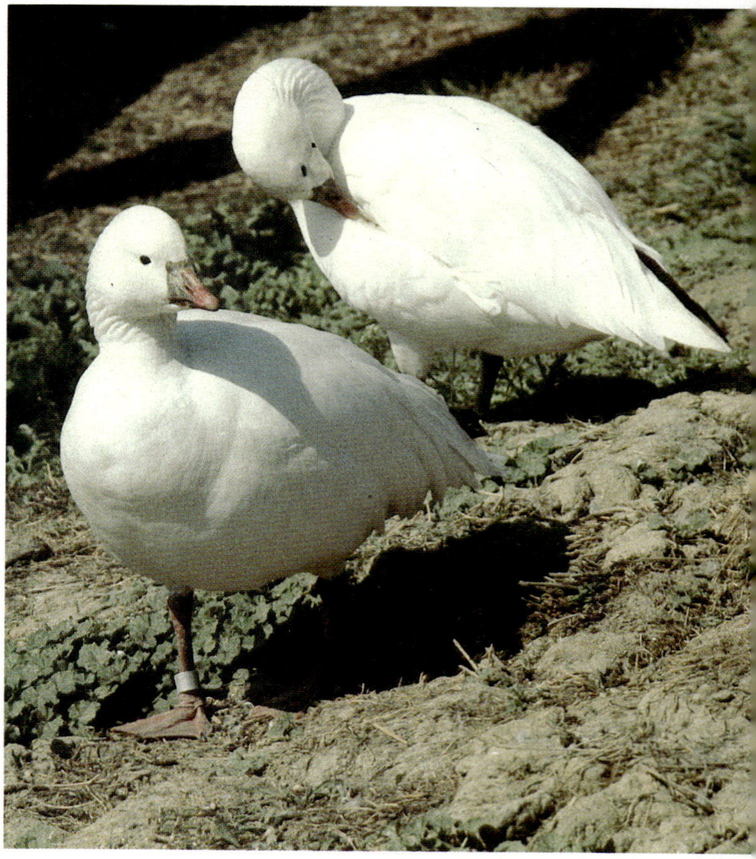

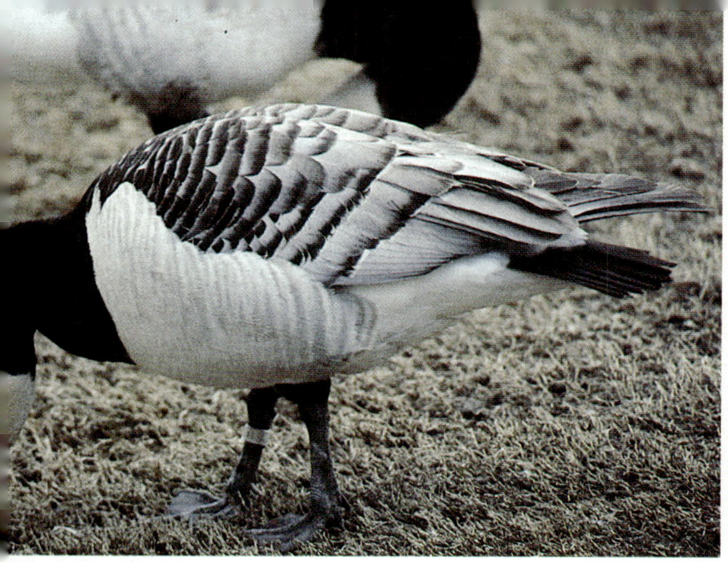

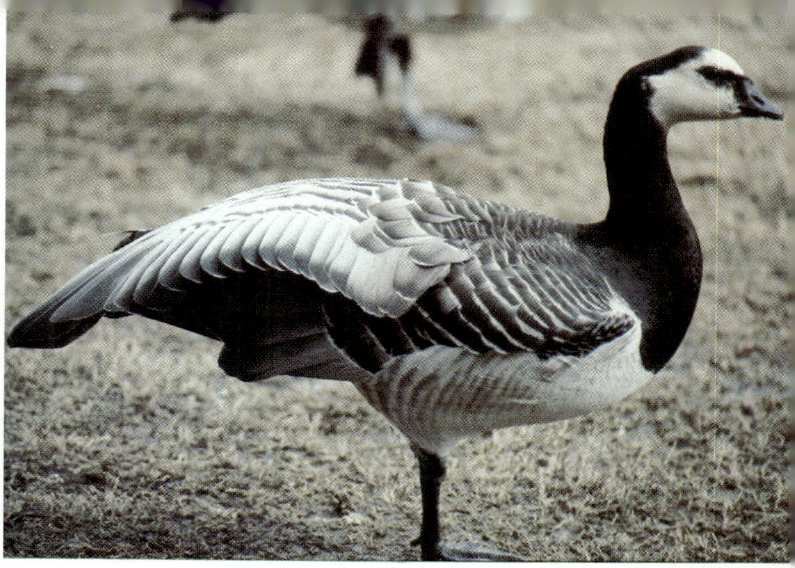

III-33

III-34

Barnacle Geese. (Chapter 40)

III-35

III-36

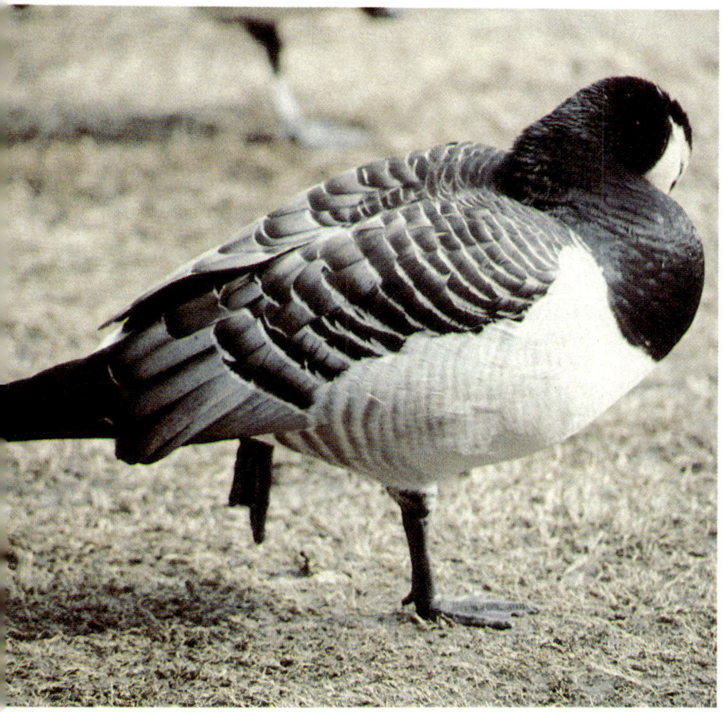

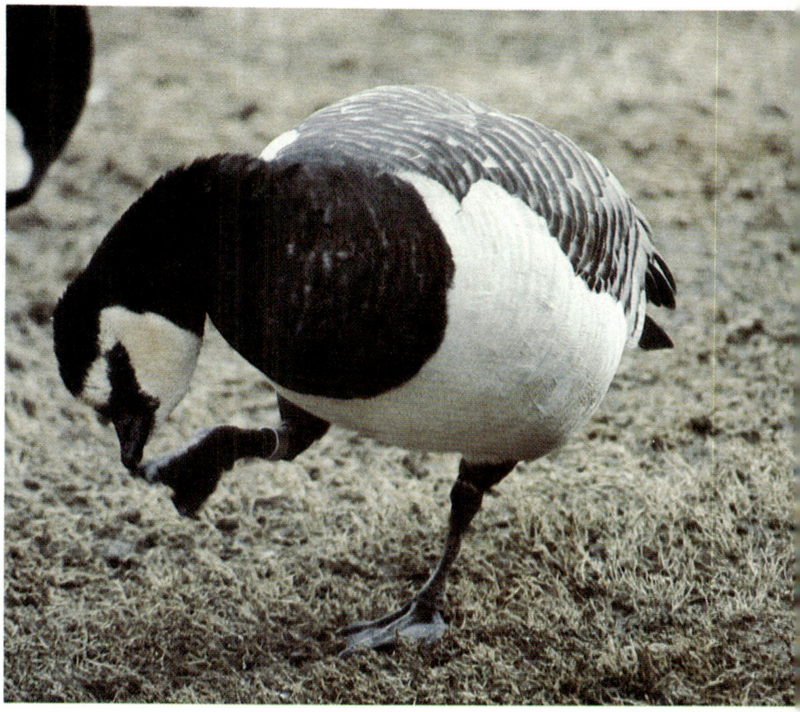

III-37 Barnacle Geese (Chapter 40)

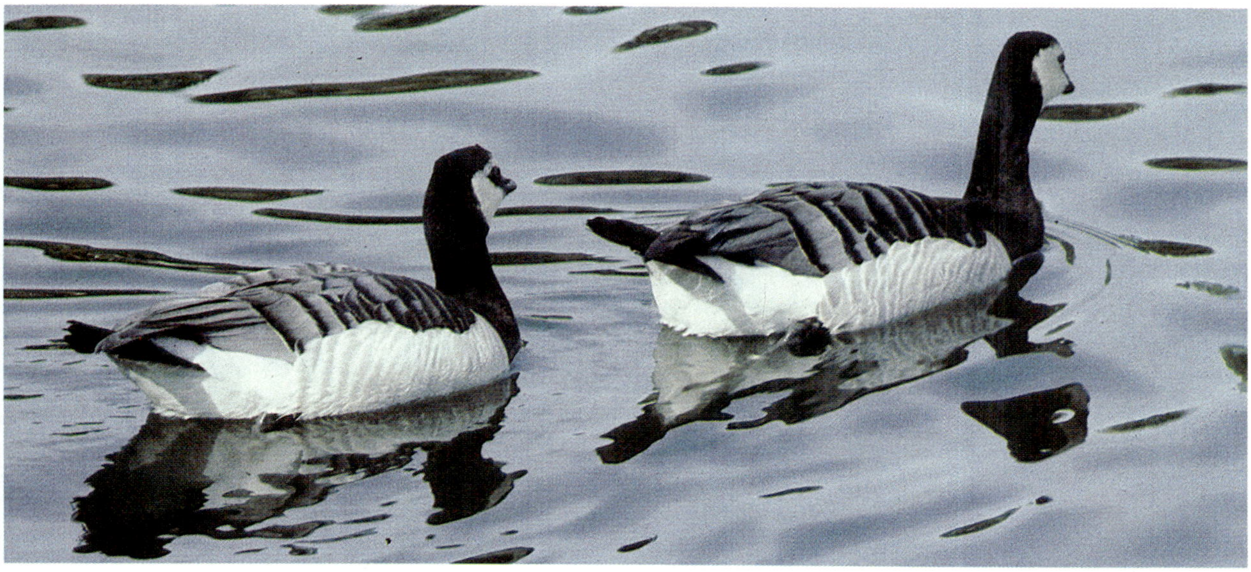

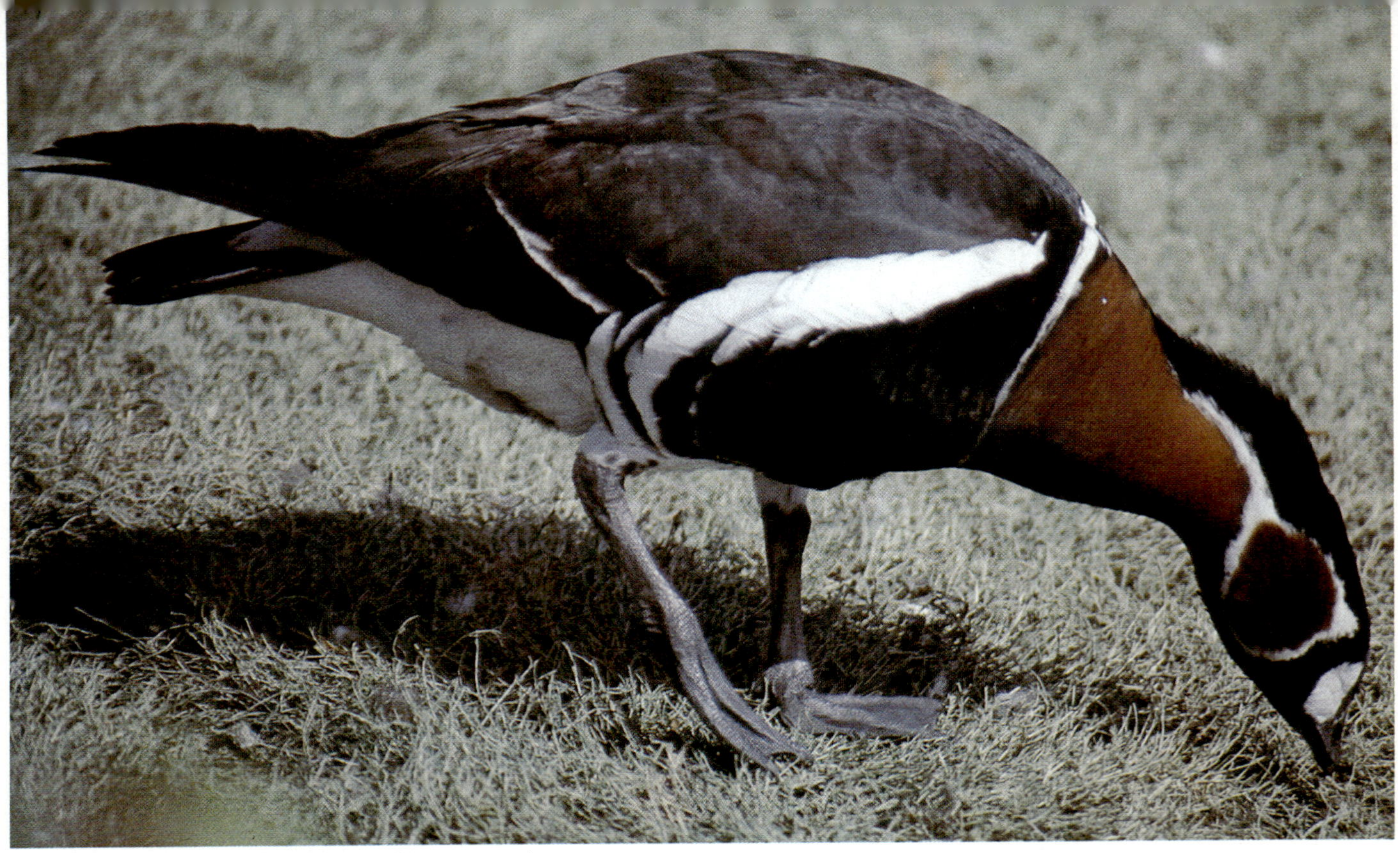

III-38 Red-Breasted Goose. (Chapter 41)

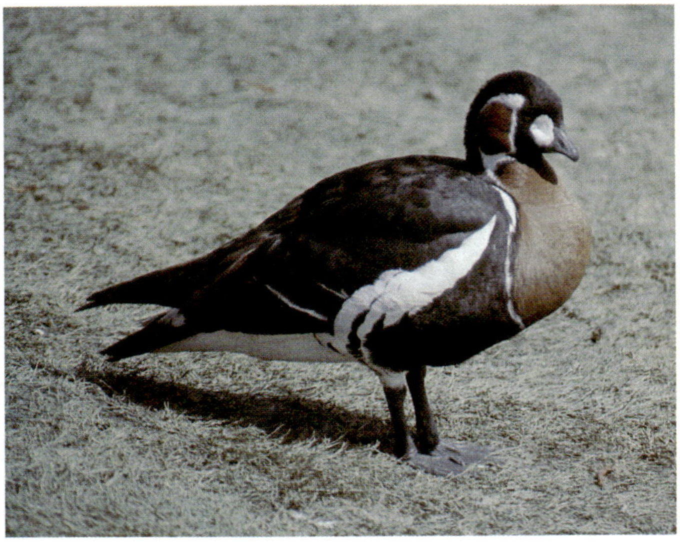

III-39

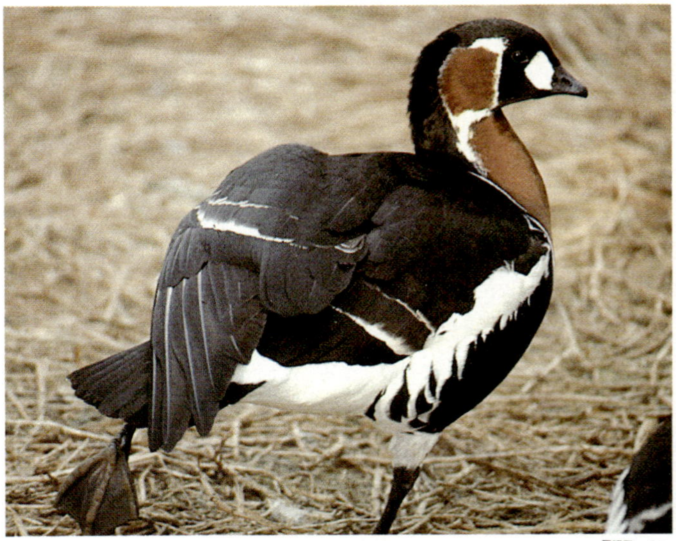

III-40

Red-Breasted Geese. (Chapter 41)

III-41

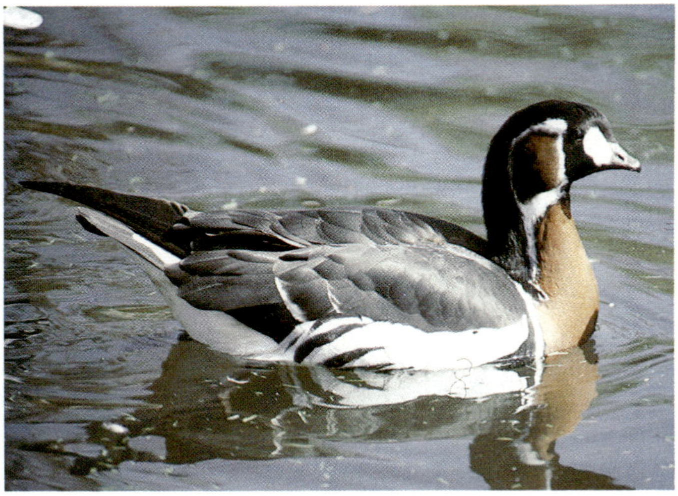

III-42

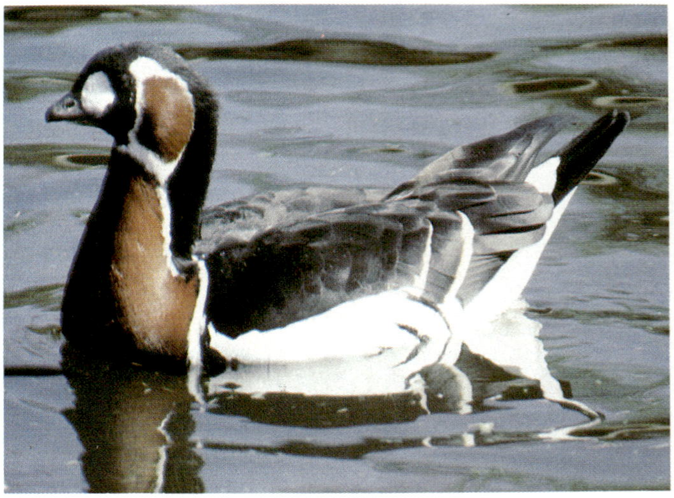

CHAPTER 38

Lesser Snow and Blue Geese

Anser coerulescens coerulescens
(Color Photos-Page 96 & 97)

Lesser snow geese and blue geese are identical except for coloration. Most ornithologists now believe they are color phases of the same species. A smaller group still maintains the birds are two distinct subspecies and the intergrading between them is a result of hybridism, as snow and blue geese readily interbreed. Regardless of whether they are separate subspecies or color phases, these geese are colorful birds and make most interesting subjects for the artist.

Snow and blue geese are the most abundant geese in North America. Although they winter in several concentrated areas—the Sacramento, San Joaquin, and Imperial Valleys of California (white phase only); along the southeast coast of Texas (white phase predominant); and the Louisiana coast (blue phase predominant)—they are seen during migration along all of the flyways. White phase snow geese breed in Arctic Siberia, the Arctic coast of Alaska, and the Arctic islands east to the Baffin Islands. The blue phase birds nest in the Baffin and Southampton Islands.

These geese, when migrating or flying to feeding areas, maintain long, diagonal lines or V-shaped formations. Their constant talking can be heard for considerable distances.

As recently as 50 or 60 years ago, the blue phase goose was relatively rare. Now, there are more blues in the Mississippi Flyway than white birds and they are increasing at a rate of about 2 percent per year. Although there have been a few specimens taken, the blue phase is a rarity along the Pacific Flyway. It is very possible we are witnessing evolution—survival of the fittest—between these two color phases. F.G. Cooch (*Waterfowl Tomorrow*) reports blue geese have a higher rate of survival at the nesting grounds, possibly because they nest later than white phase geese and their nests are less likely to be subject to flooding during the incubation period. Also, by then the predators have had an opportunity to satiate their appetites somewhat at the expense of the earlier white birds. Cooch further states that the survival rate of the blue phase birds is higher during hunting season as hunters seem to favor the big white birds. According to John Lynch, U.S. Fish and Wildlife biologist, blue phase birds predominate in family groups of mixed color by a ratio of 1.78 to 1. In families where the parents were a blue goose and a snow goose, the ratio of young blues to young whites was 2.46 to 1. Another important factor contributing to the increase in blue phase geese is that male snow geese are reluctant to mate with female blue geese, while female snows readily breed with male blues. All of these factors point to an eventual takeover of the white phase by the blue phase in the Central and Mississippi Flyways. There appears to be little likelihood of blue geese becoming predominant in the Pacific Flyway in the foreseeable future.

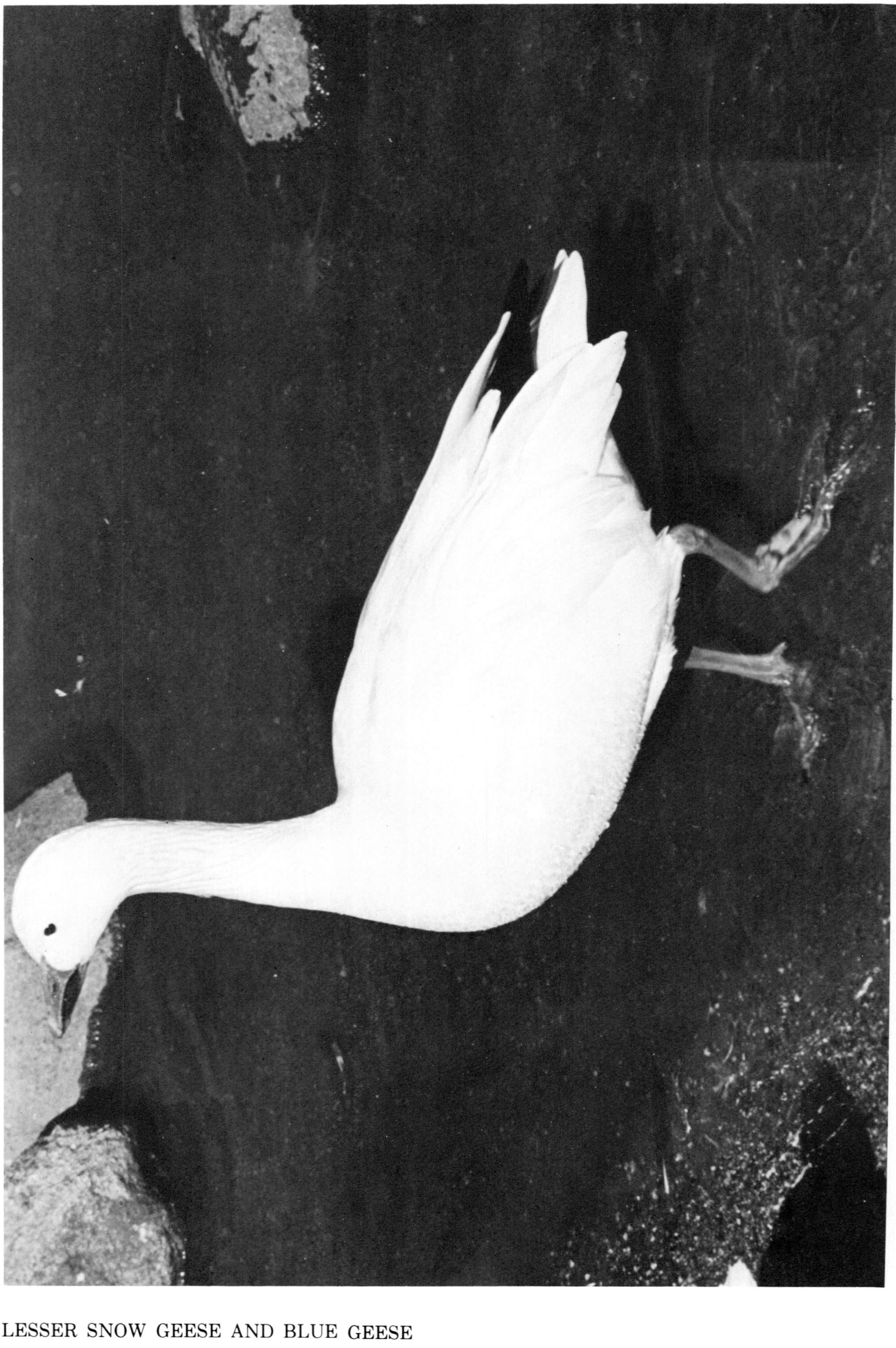

38-1 Lesser snow goose. Except for weight and size, he is very similar to the greater snow goose which winters exclusively on the East Coast.

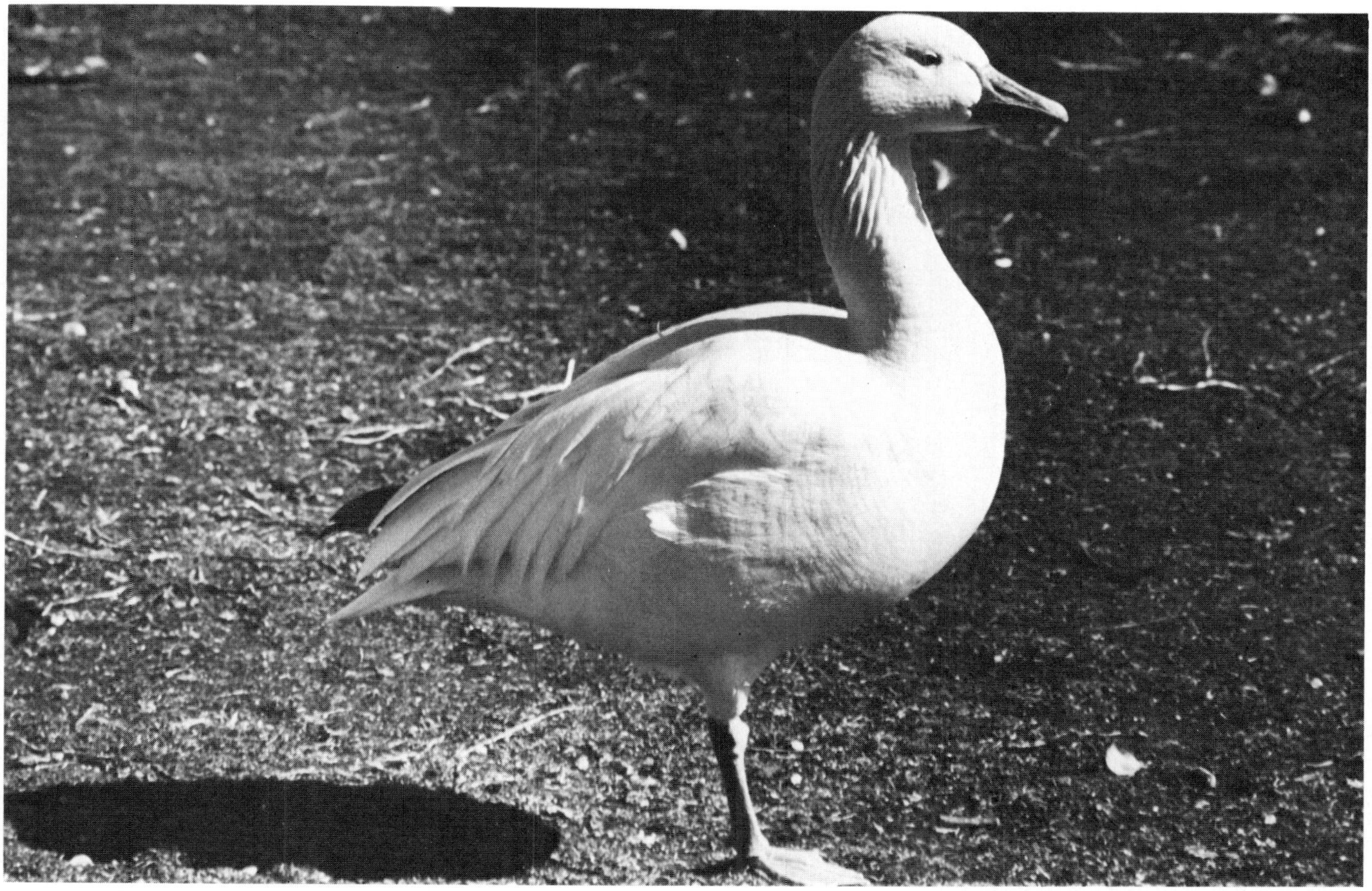

38-2 Good profile view of the lesser snow, who is relaxing on one leg. Take particular notice of his long greater wing coverts.

38-3 Rear and front views of the lesser snow goose. 38-4

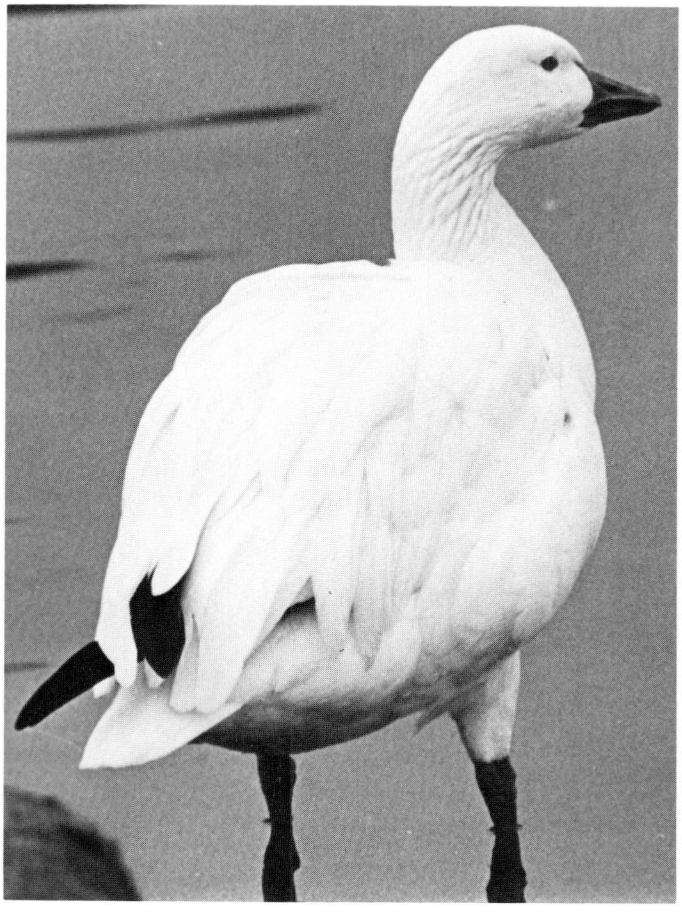

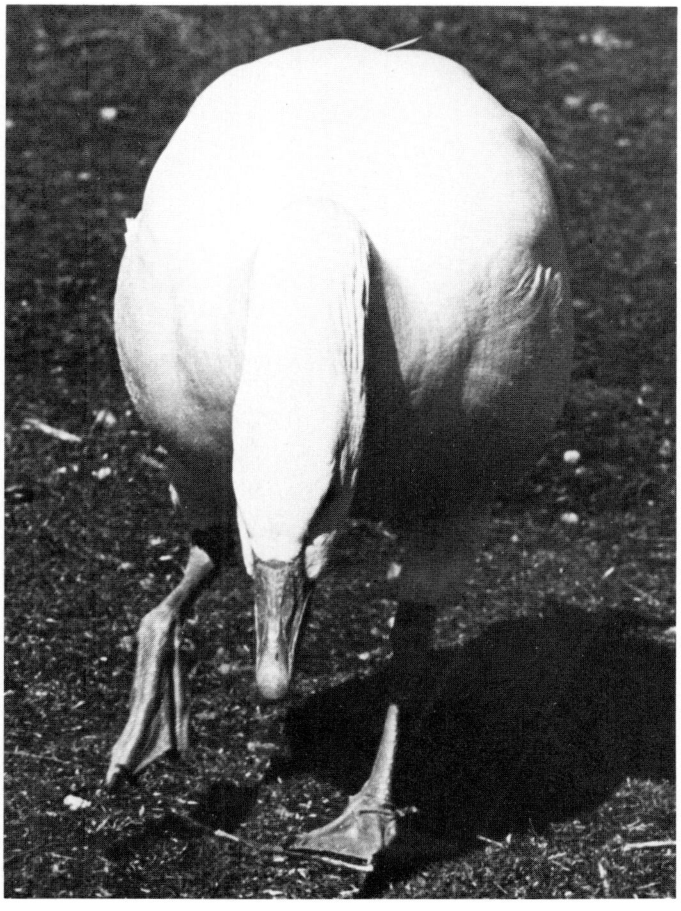

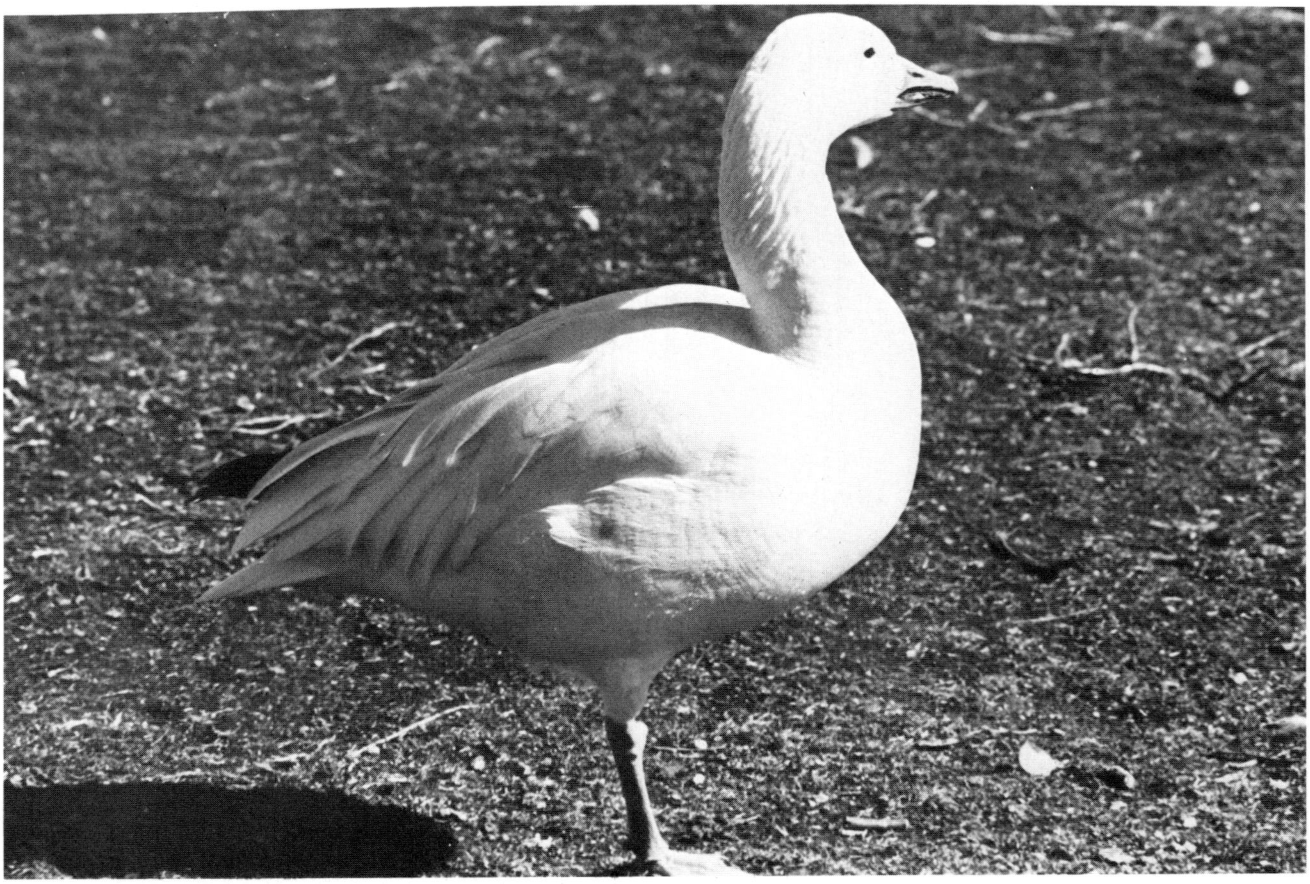

38-5 Another view of the goose shown in Fig. 38-2—nice pose.

38-6 Rear views of a striding lesser snow goose. 38-7

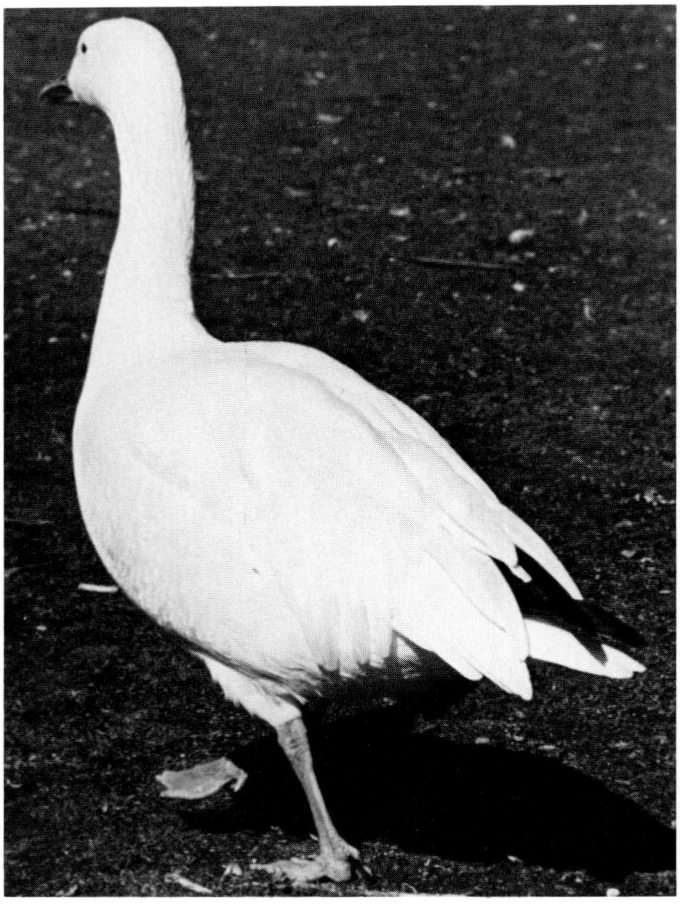

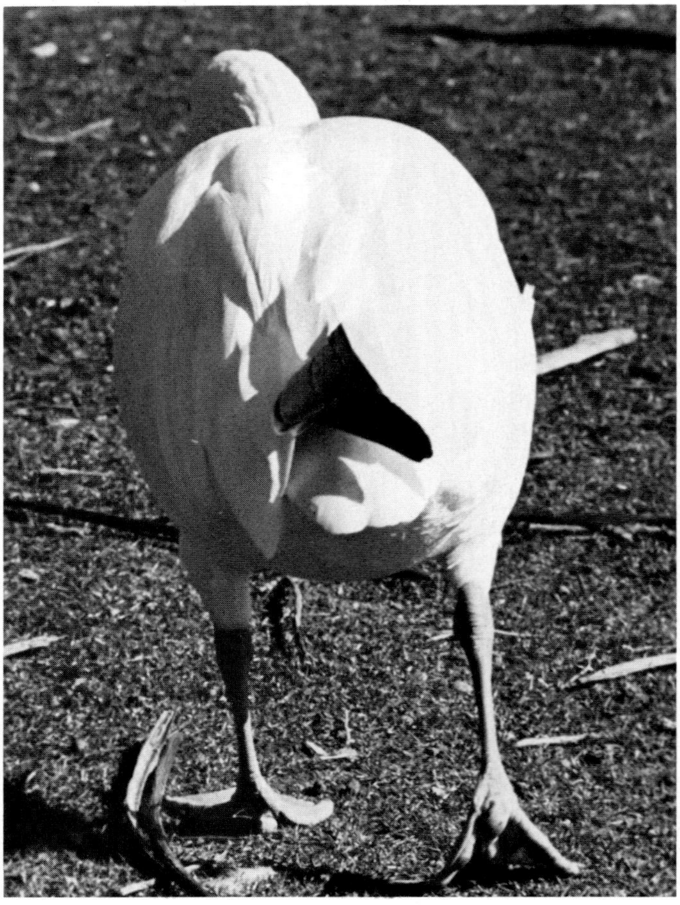

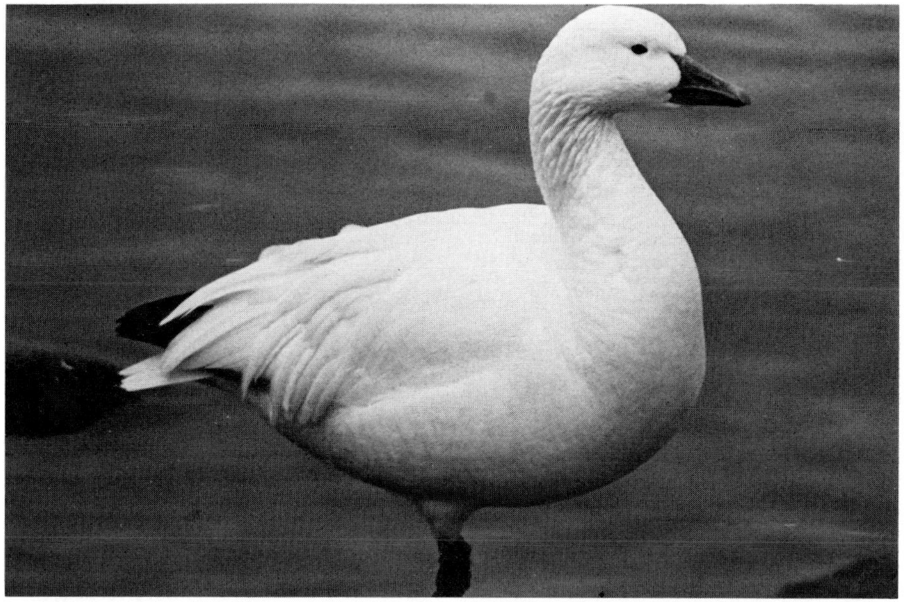

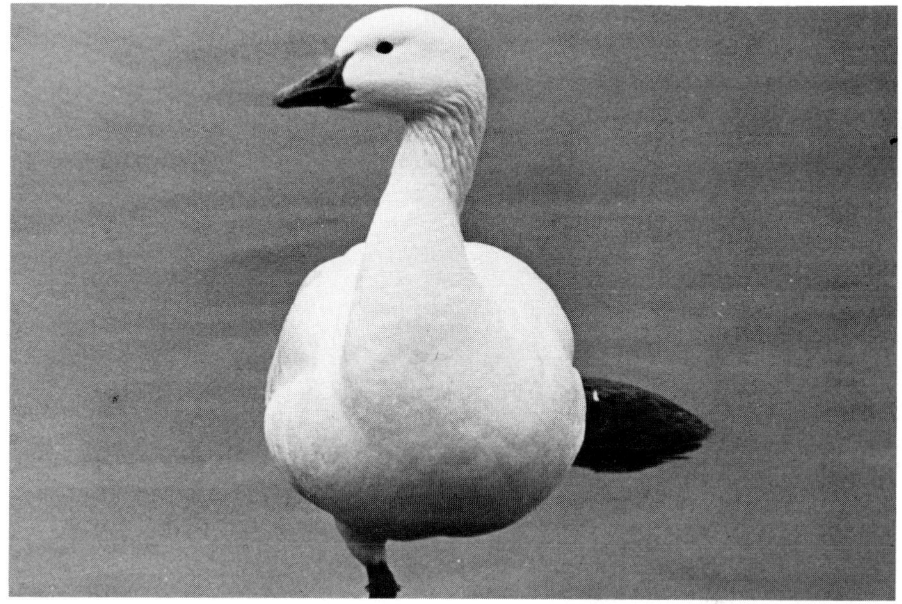

38-8 Profile and front views of a snow goose resting on one leg. 38-9

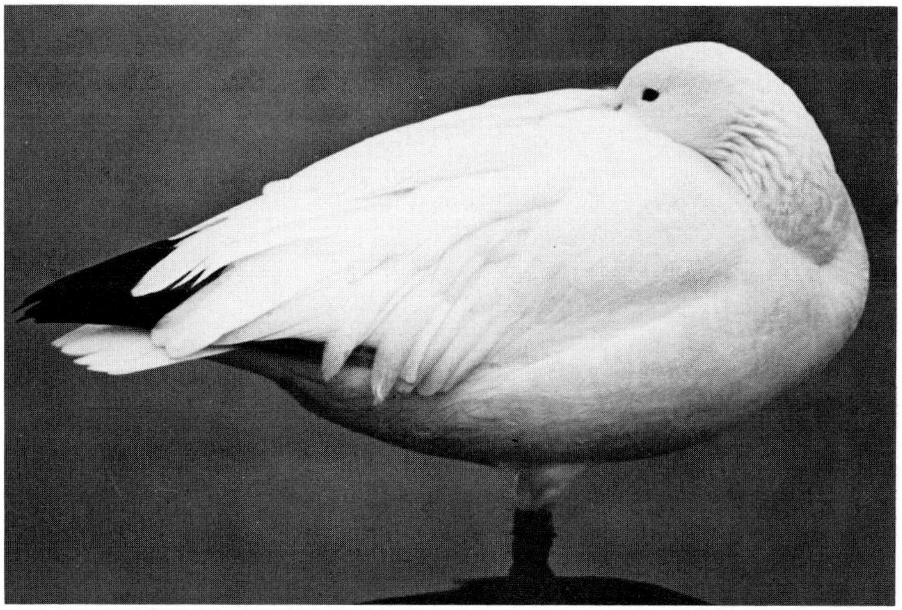

38-10 Snow goose in the classic sleeping position.

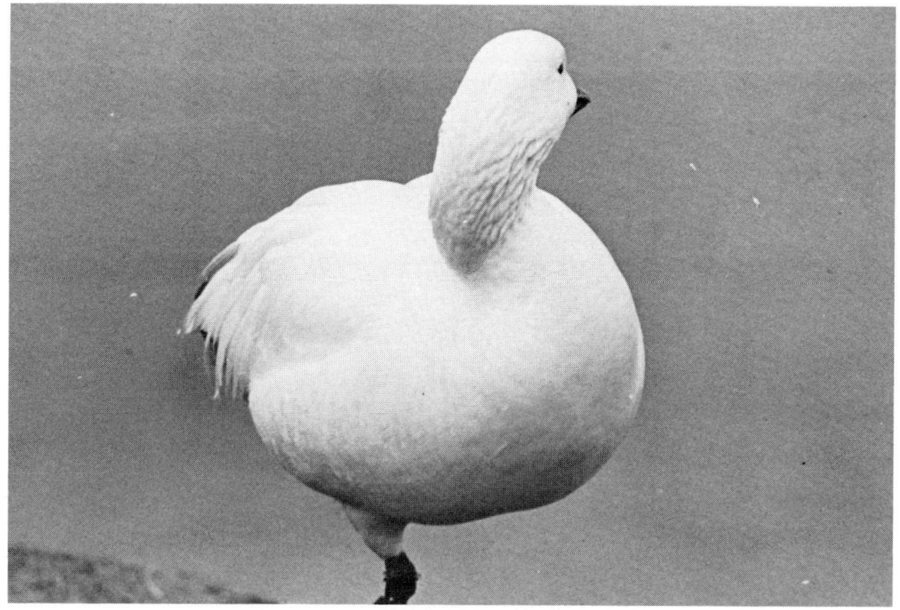

38-11 Another view of a snow goose resting on one leg.

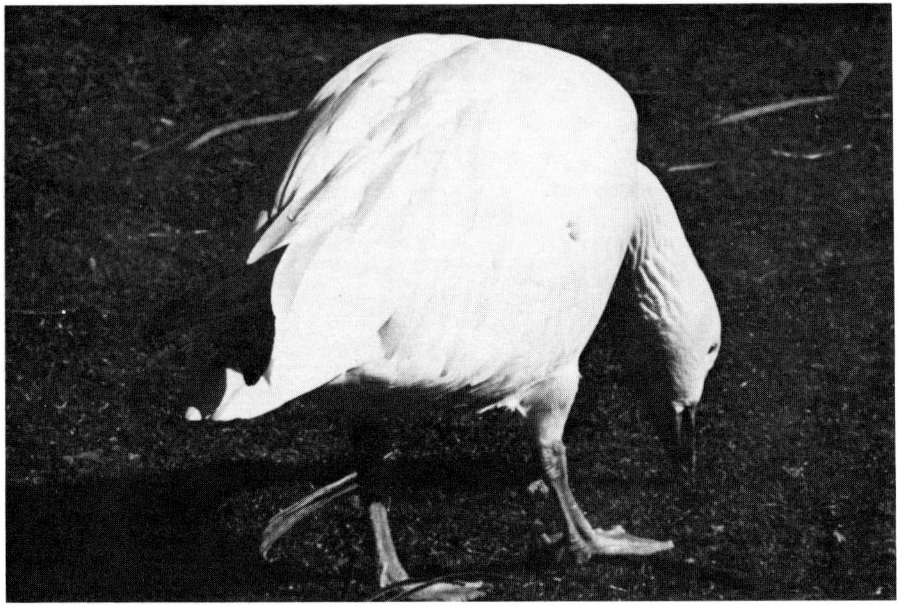

38-12 Lesser snow goose in the feeding position as viewed from the rear.

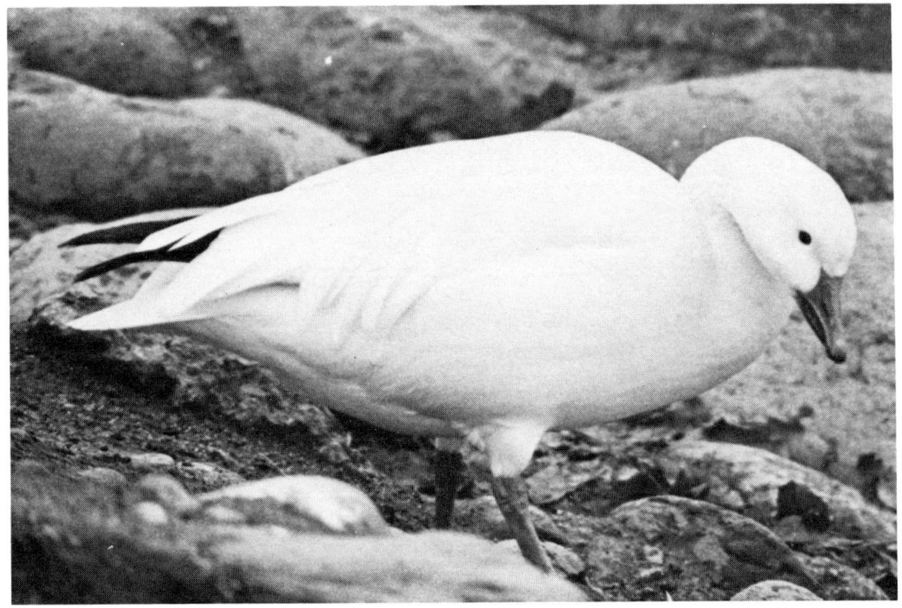

38-13 Nice striding profile shot of a snow goose.

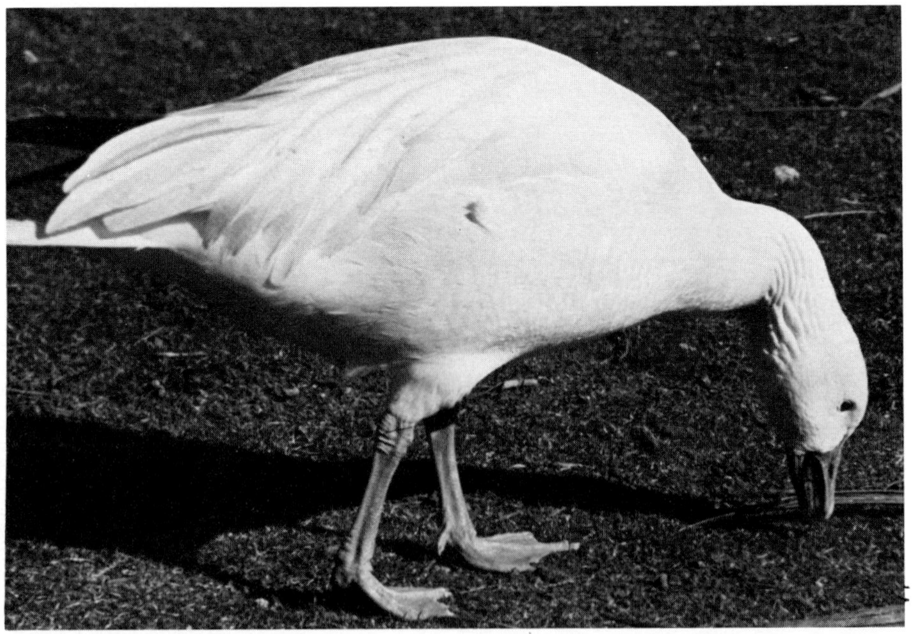

38-14 Good profile view of a striding snow goose in the feeding position.

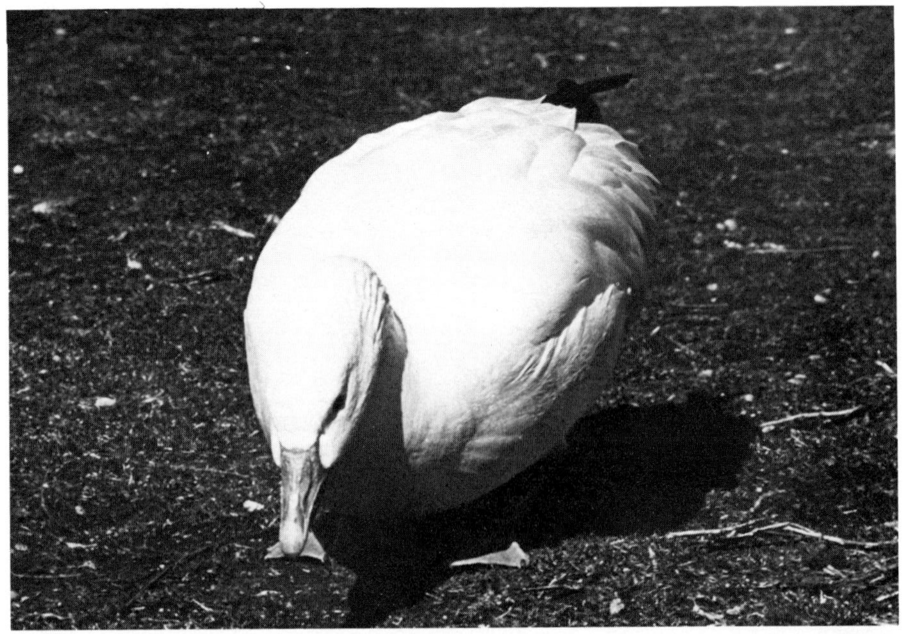

38-15 Snow goose in the feeding position as viewed from the front.

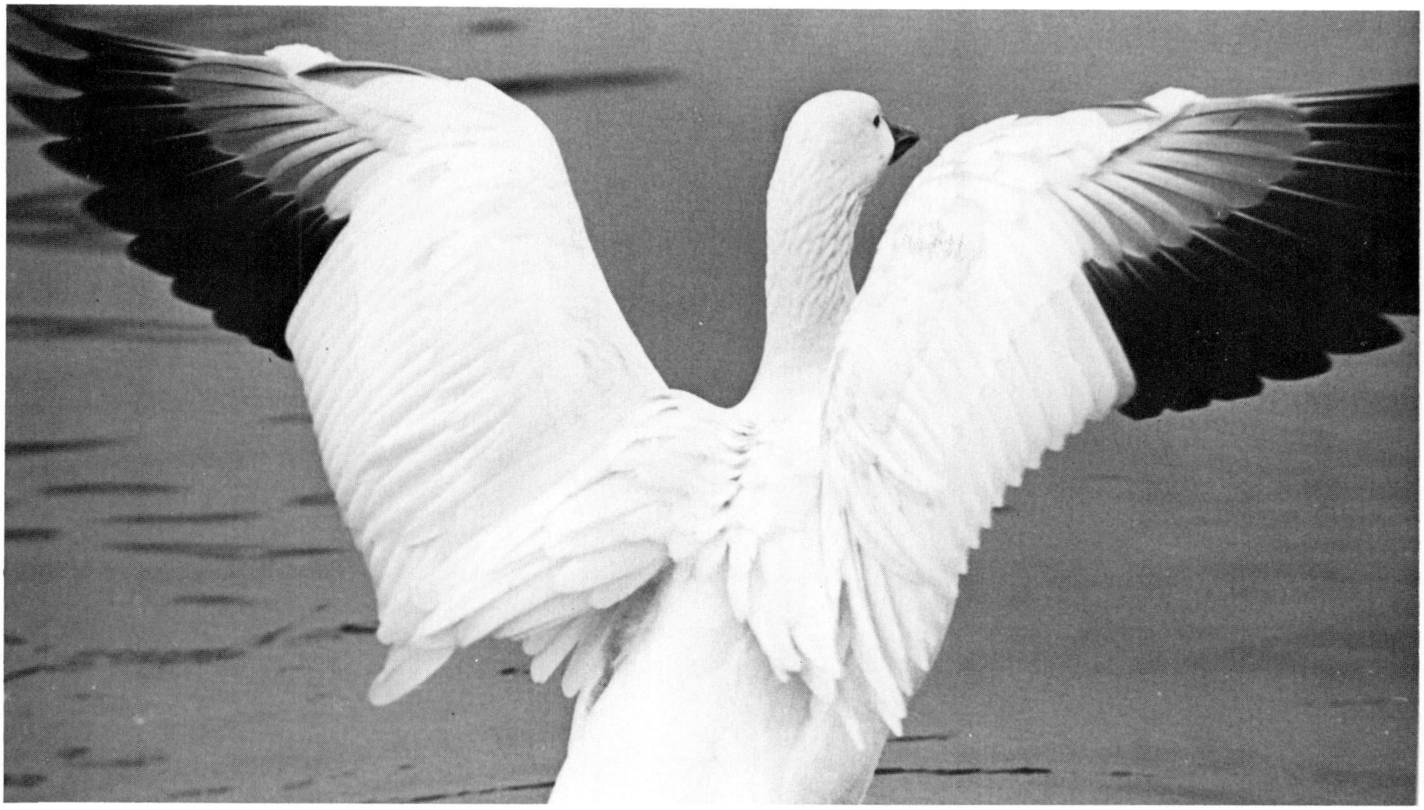

38-16

Lesser snow goose stretches his wings. A great deal of feather detail information can be obtained from these views. Especially note raised scapulars.

38-17

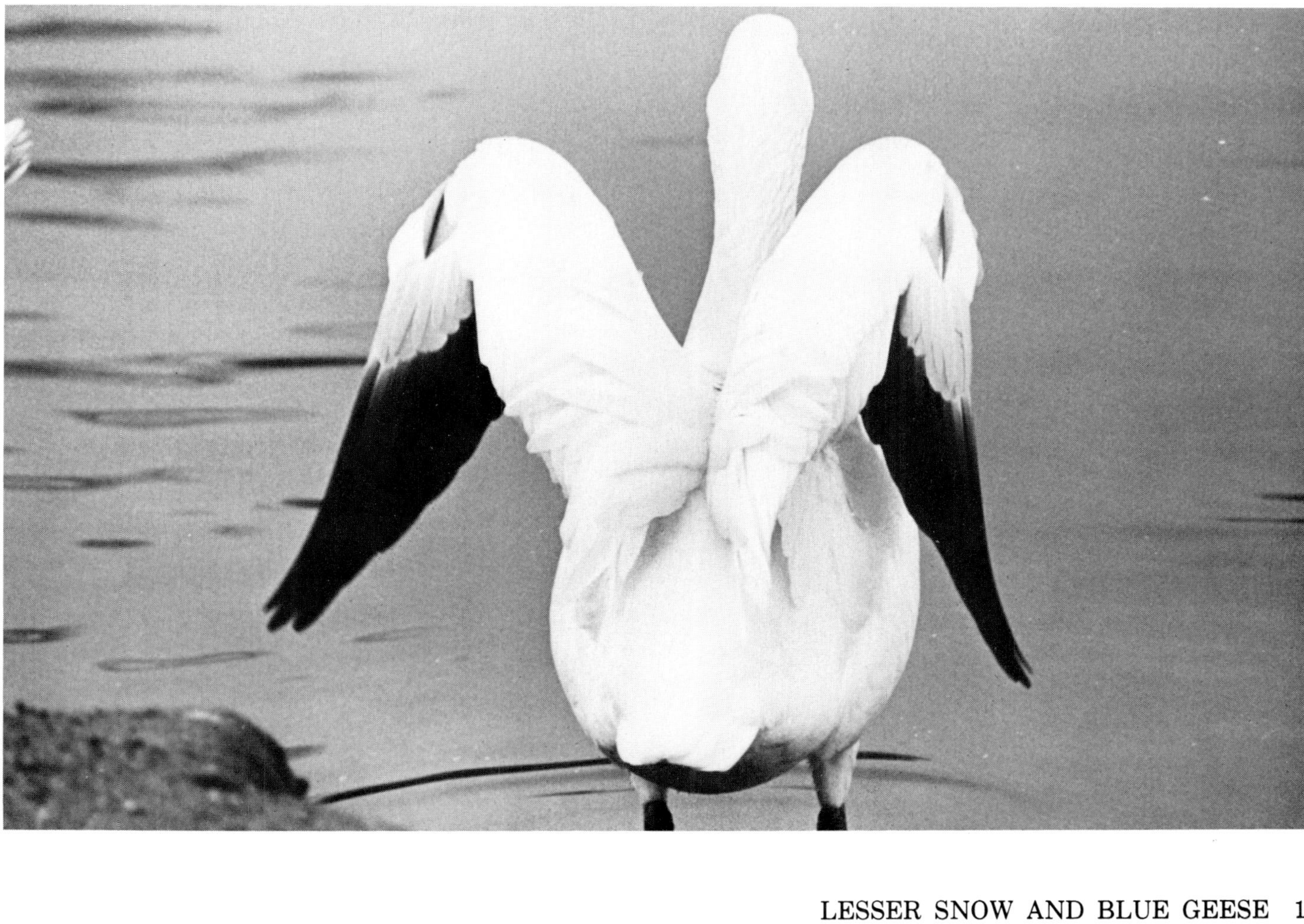

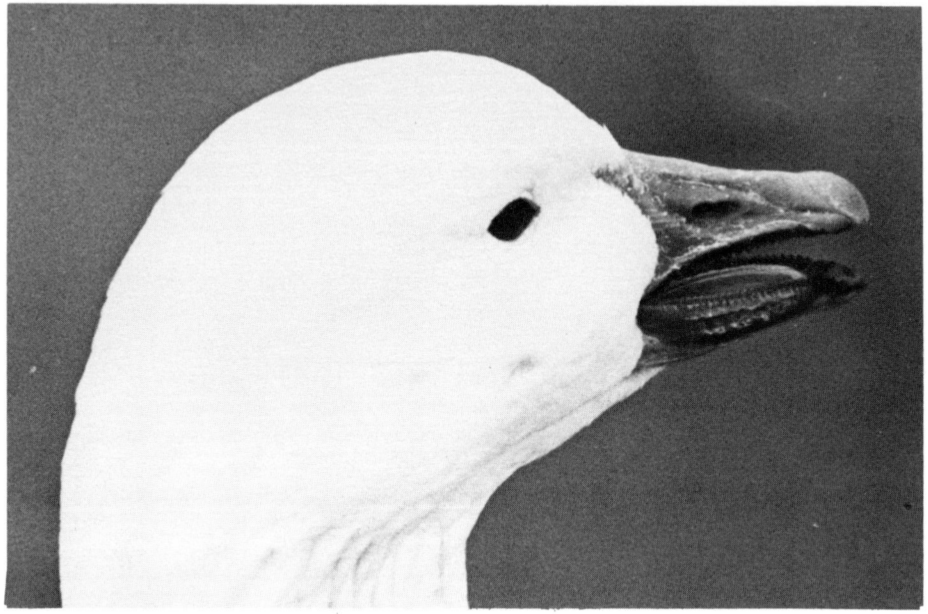

38-18 Snow goose calling. Notice the lamellae, or comb-like projections, on his lower mandible.

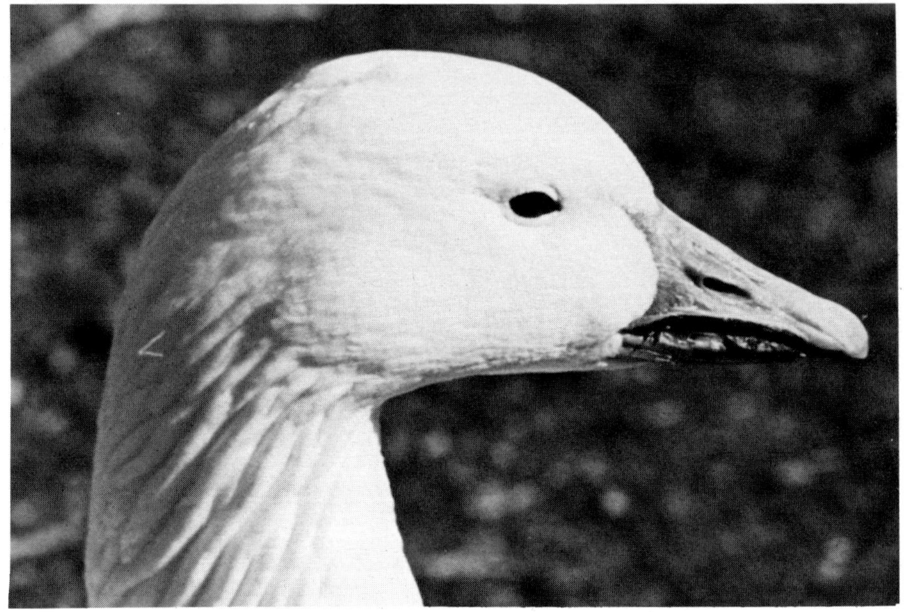

38-19 Profile of a snow goose's head and bill. His neck feathers lie in ridges and valleys.

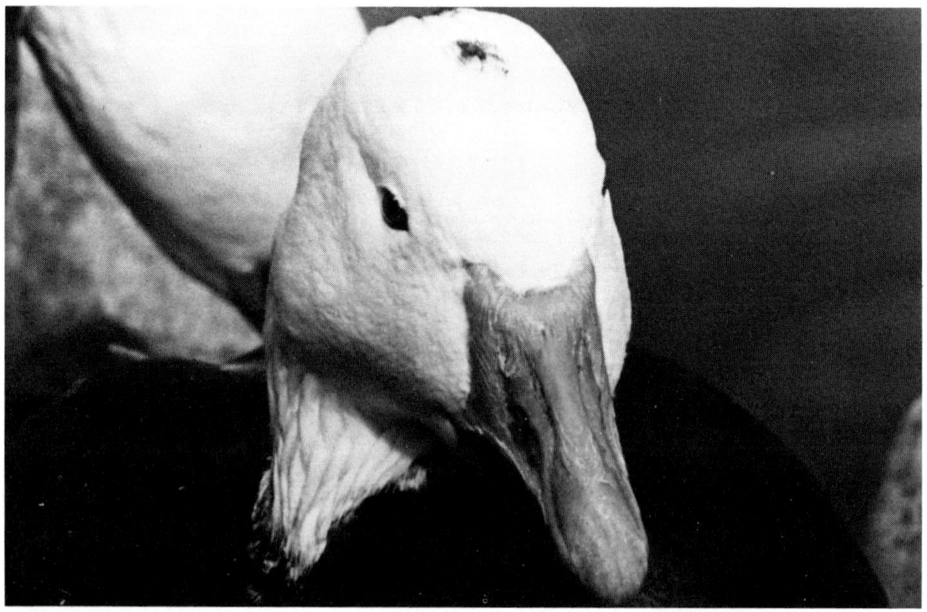

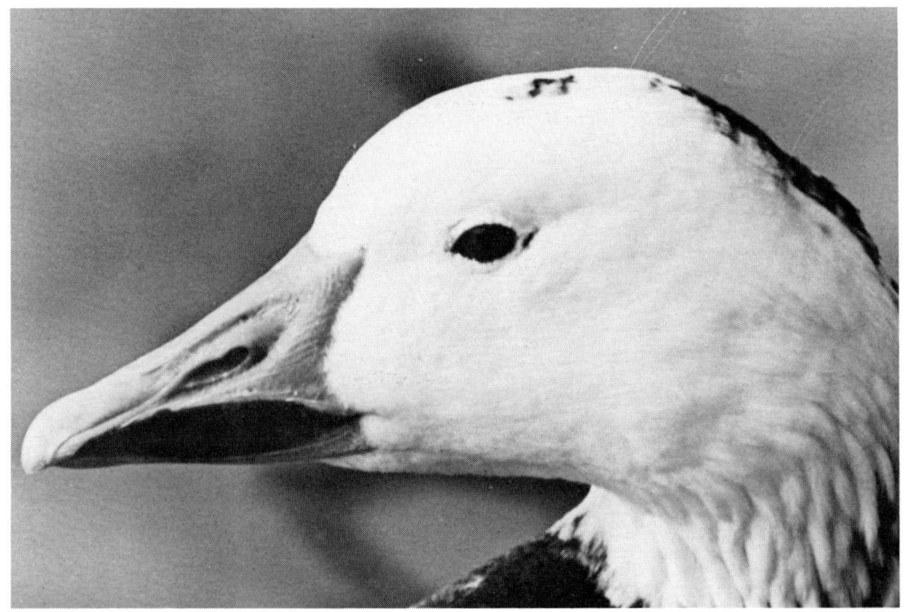

38-20 Front and profile views of a blue goose's head and bill. 38-21

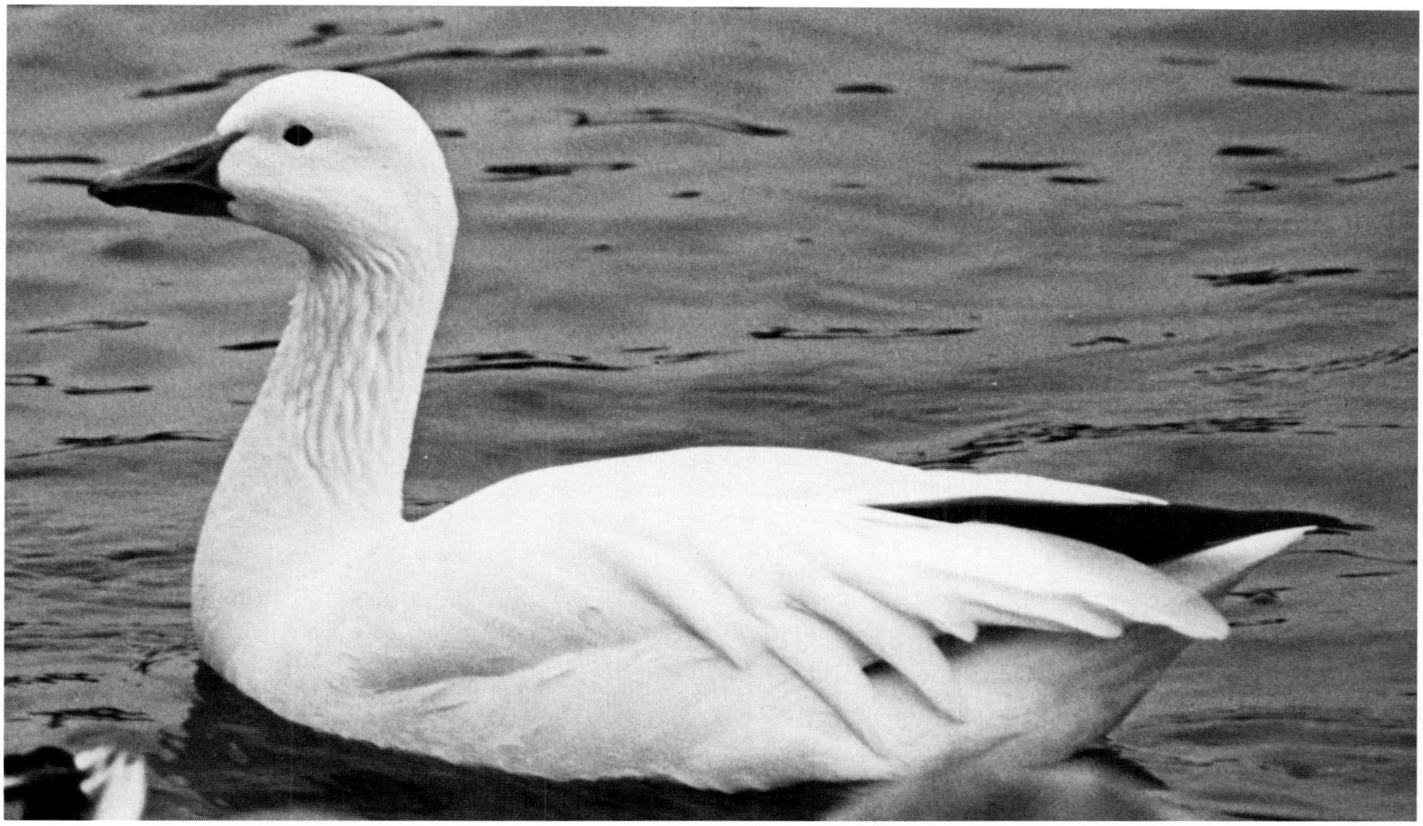

38-22

Profile and front views of a lesser snow goose in an alert floating pose.

38-23

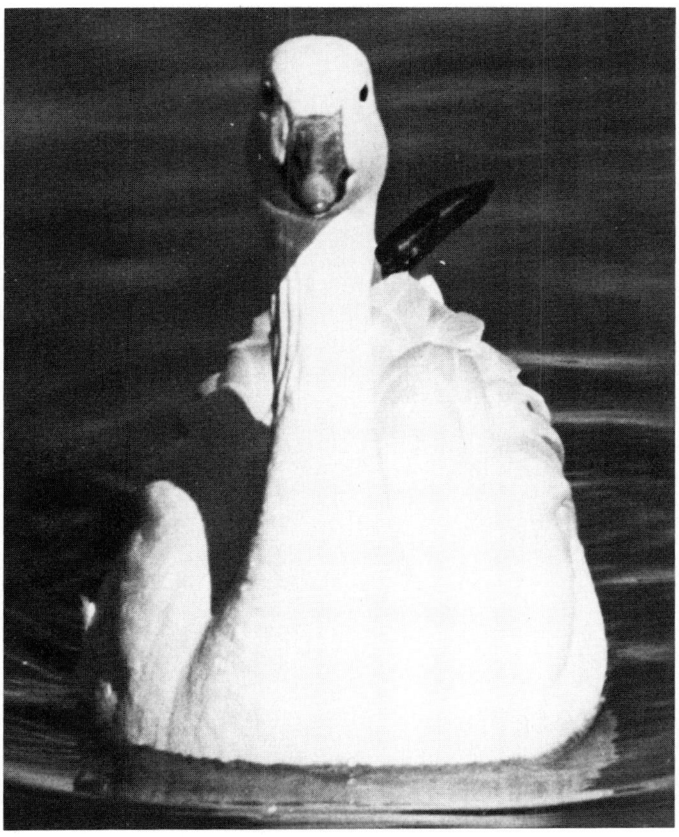

38-24

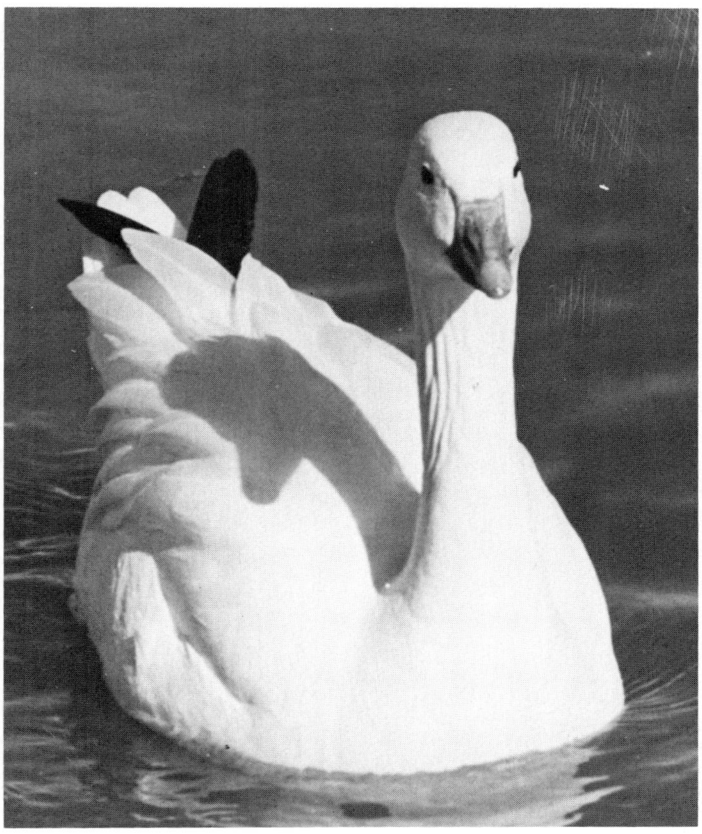

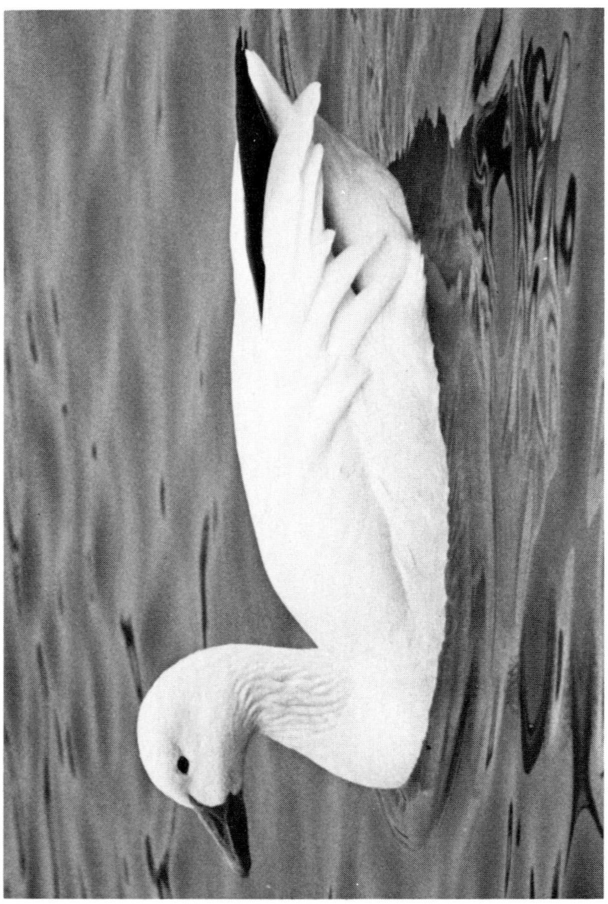

38-25 Nice profile of a floating snow goose.

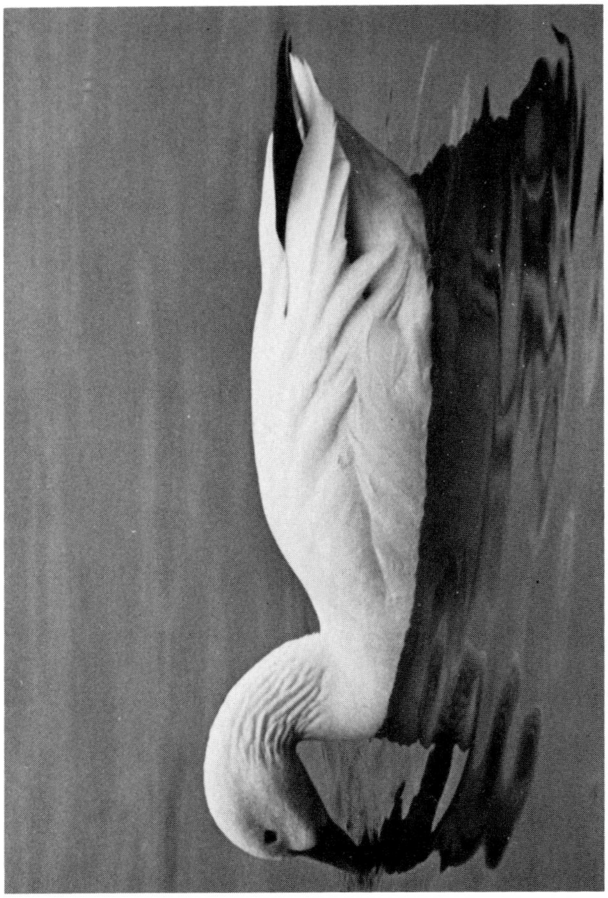

38-26 Snow goose takes a sip of water.

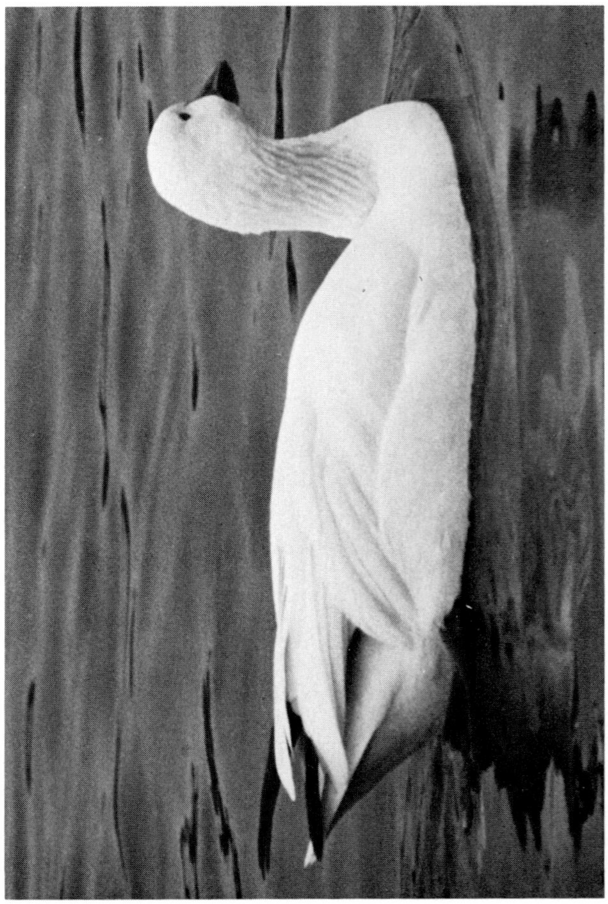

38-27

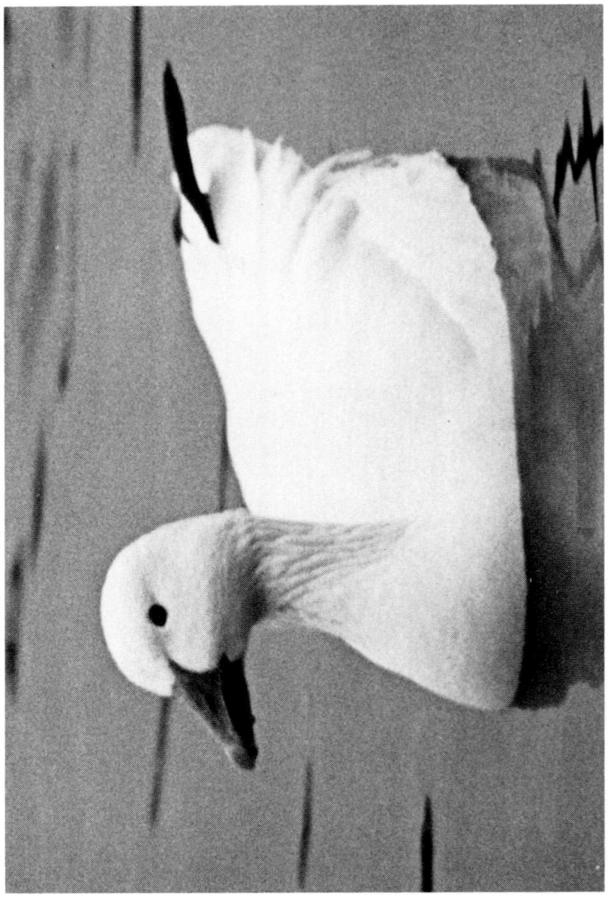

38-28

Two more studies of floating snow geese.

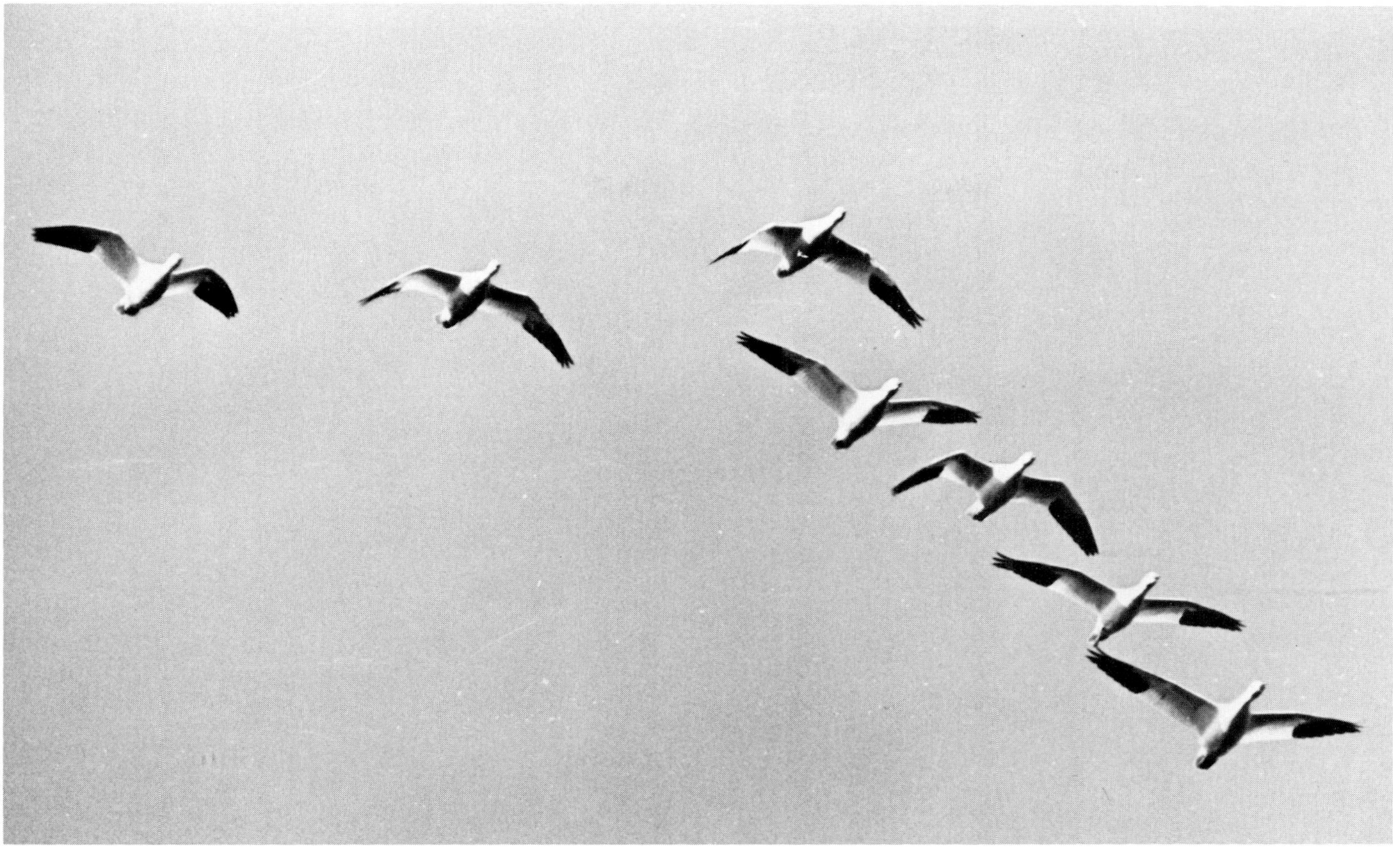

38-29 Small group of lesser snow geese coming over the blind in a typical formation.

38-30 A lone blue goose climbing shortly after takeoff.

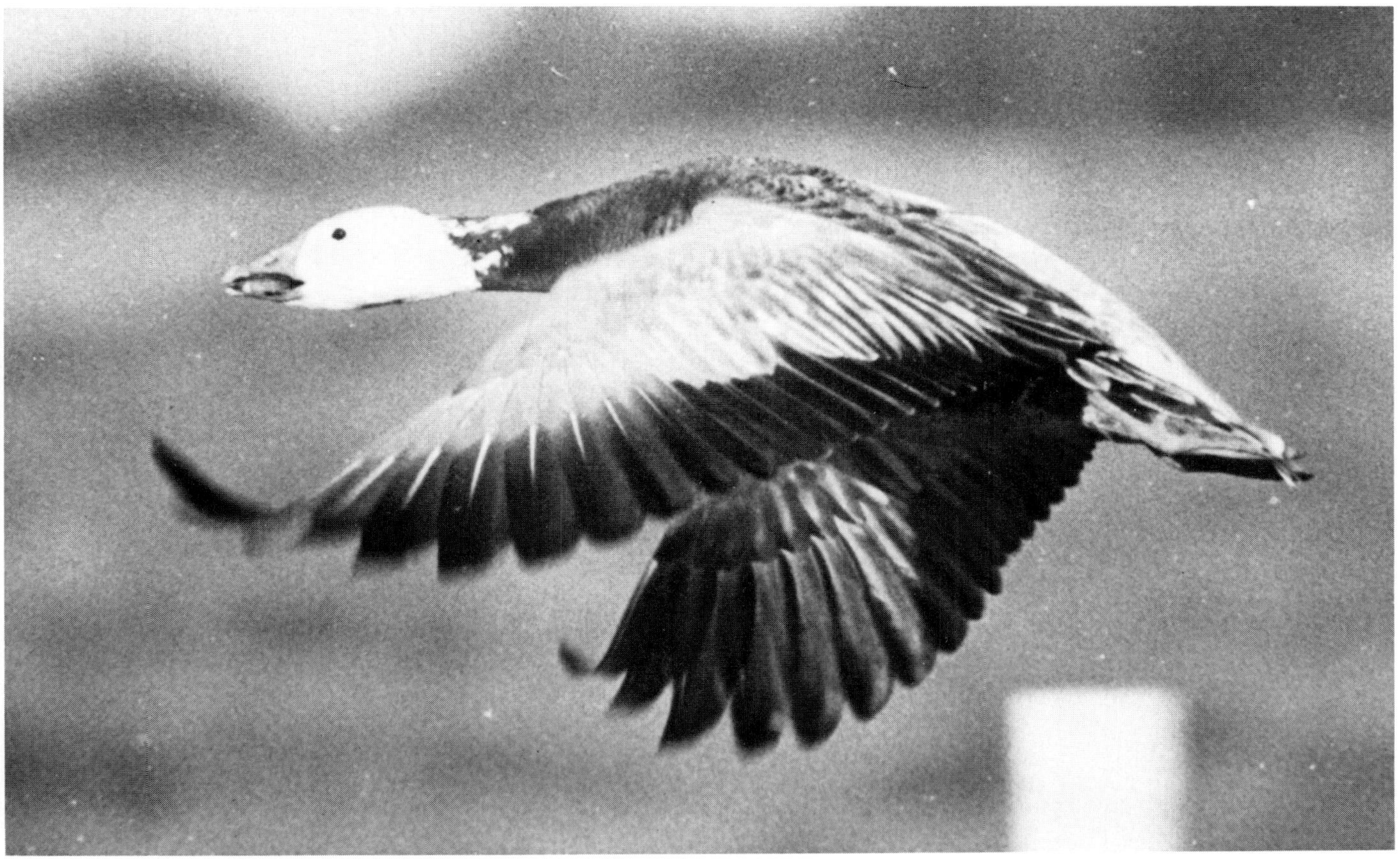

38-31

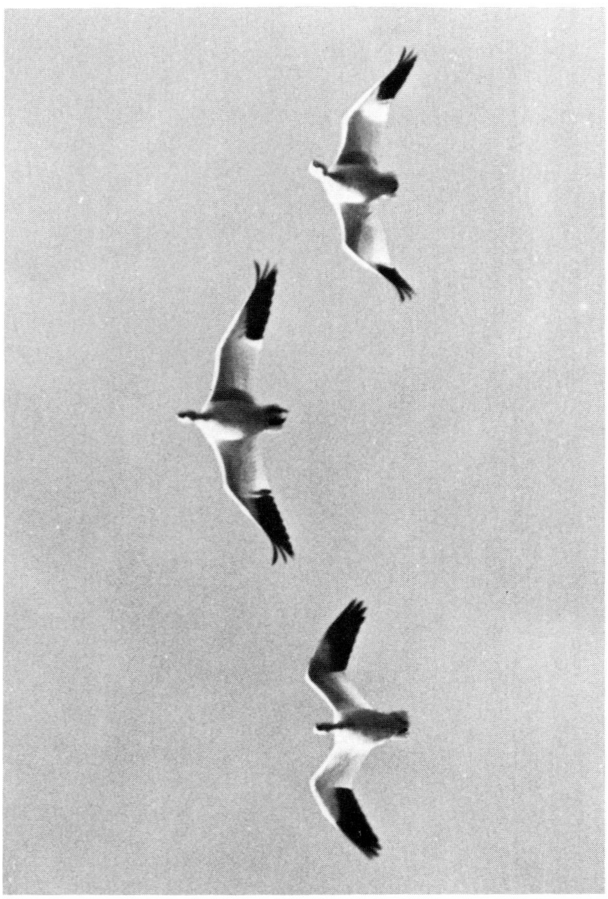

38-32

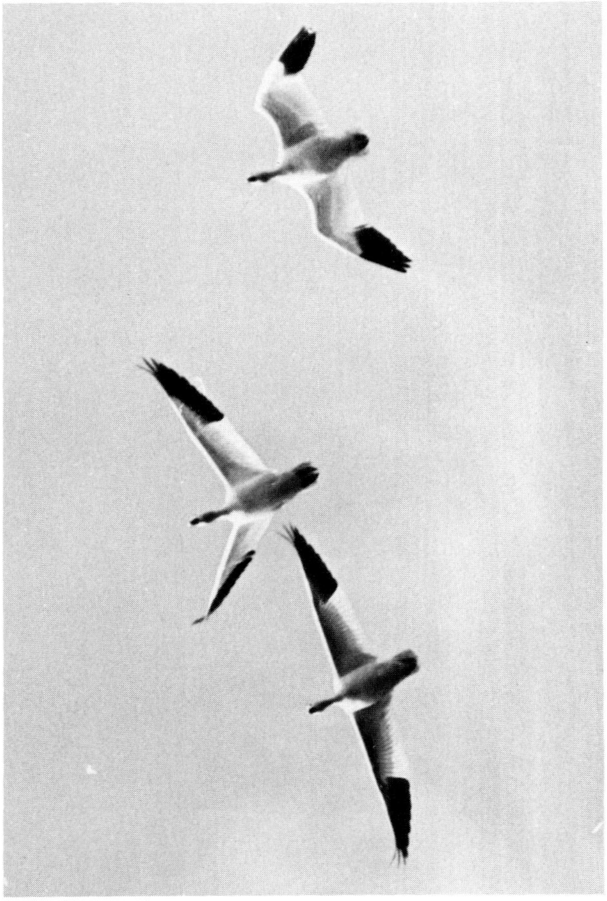

38-33

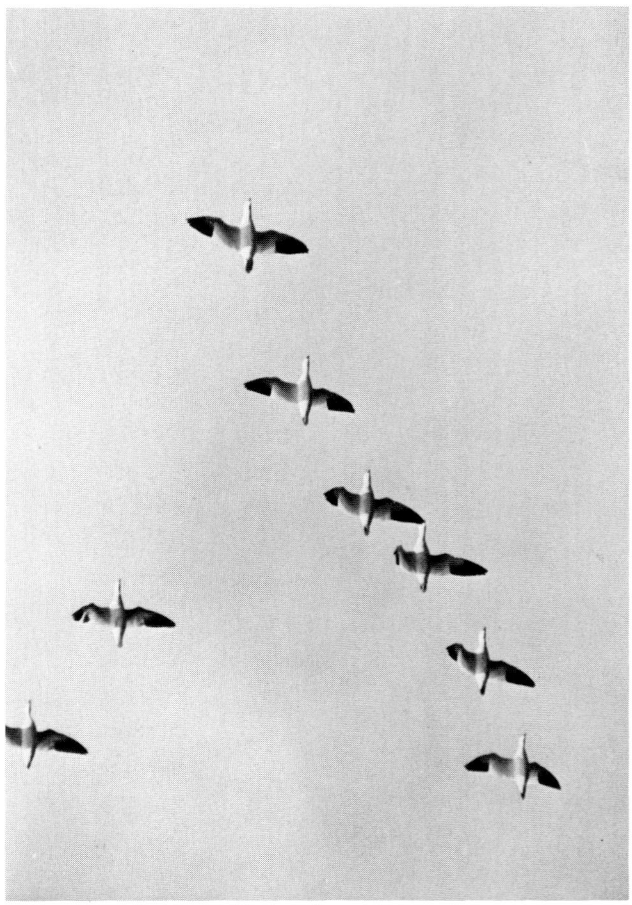

38-34

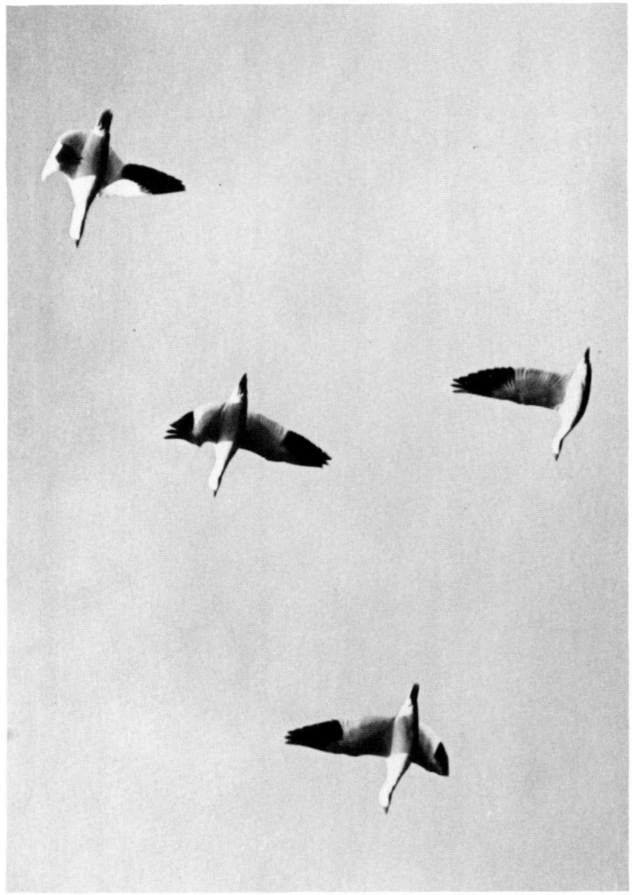

Four studies of lesser snow geese in flight.

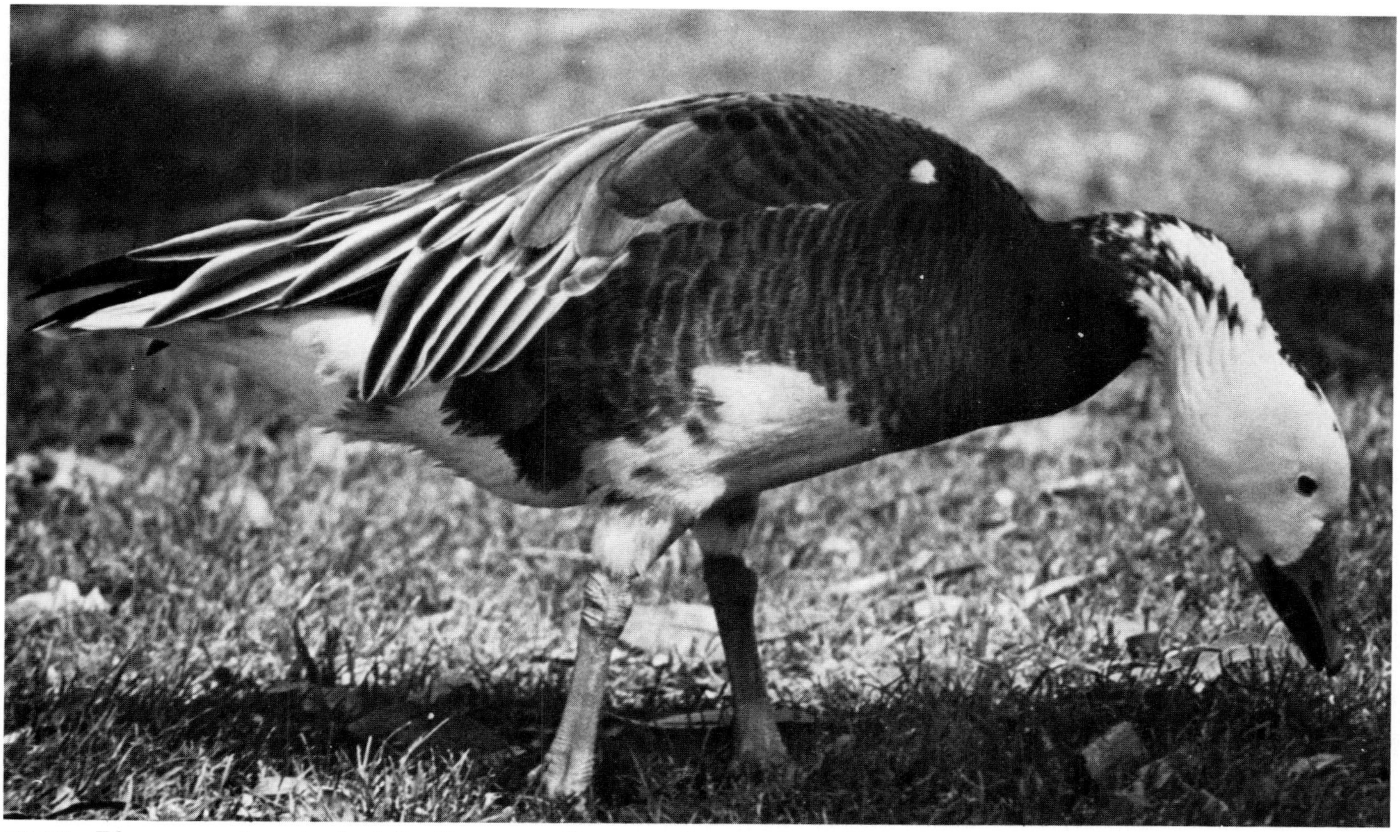

38-35 Blue goose in a typical feeding pose. Structurally, they are identical to snow geese. Again, note his long greater wing coverts.

38-36 Good rear and front views of a feeding blue goose. 38-37

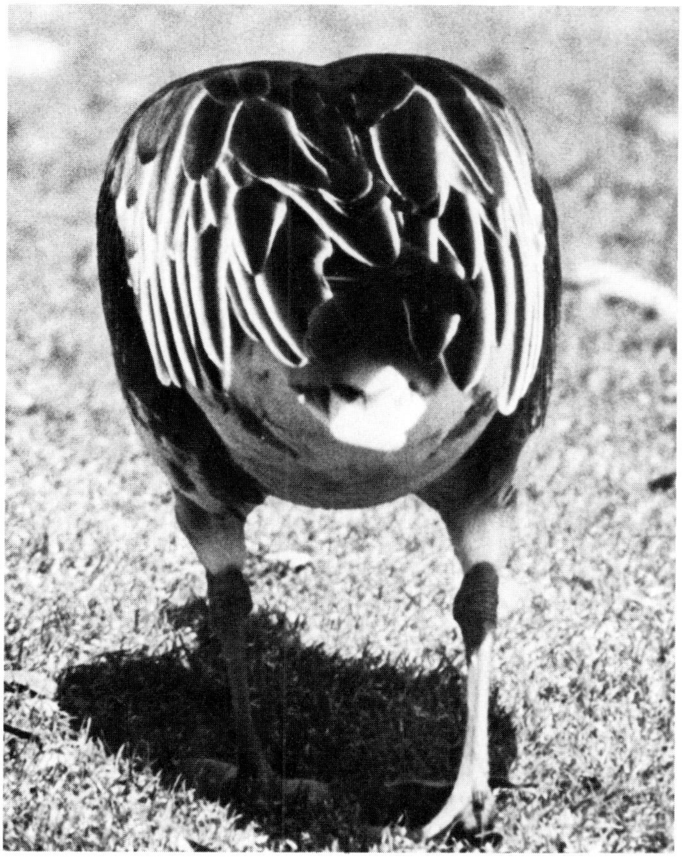

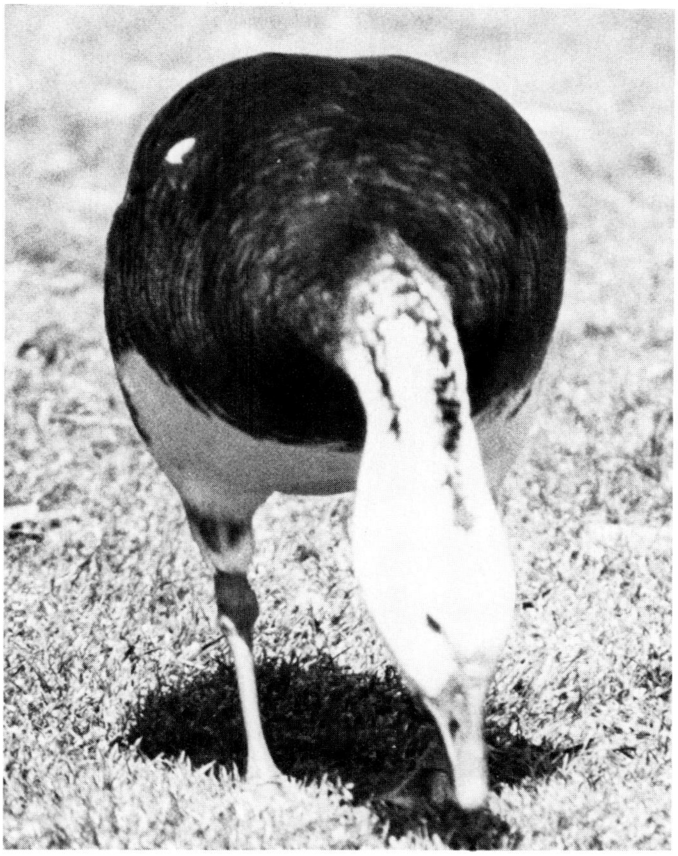

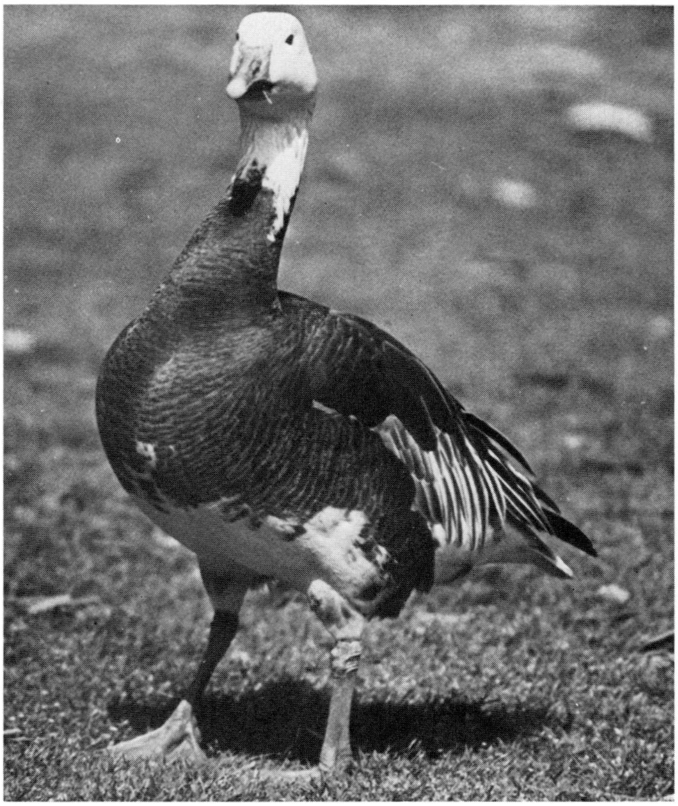

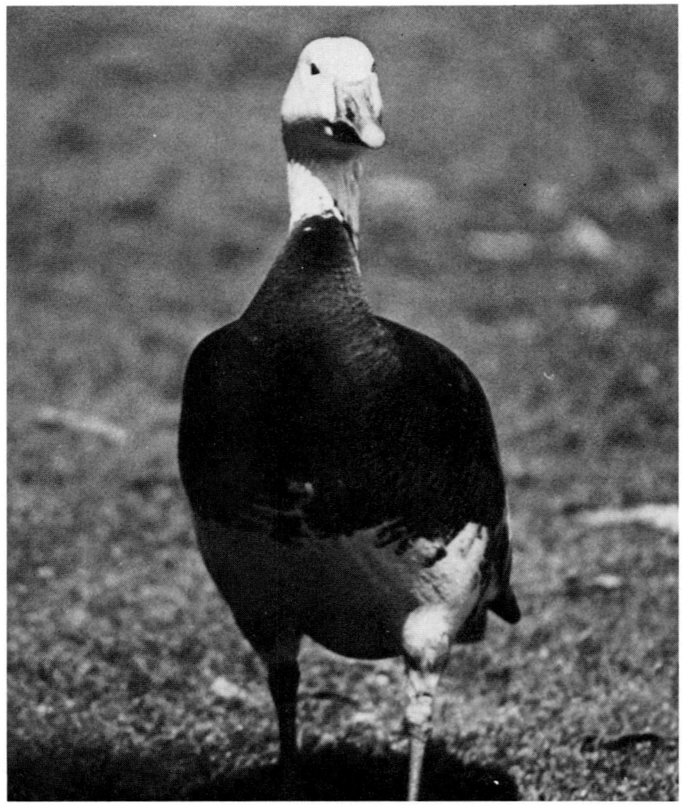

38-38 Two studies of a very alert blue goose. 38-39

38-40 These two rear views not only show body shape but also a great deal of feather detail. 38-41

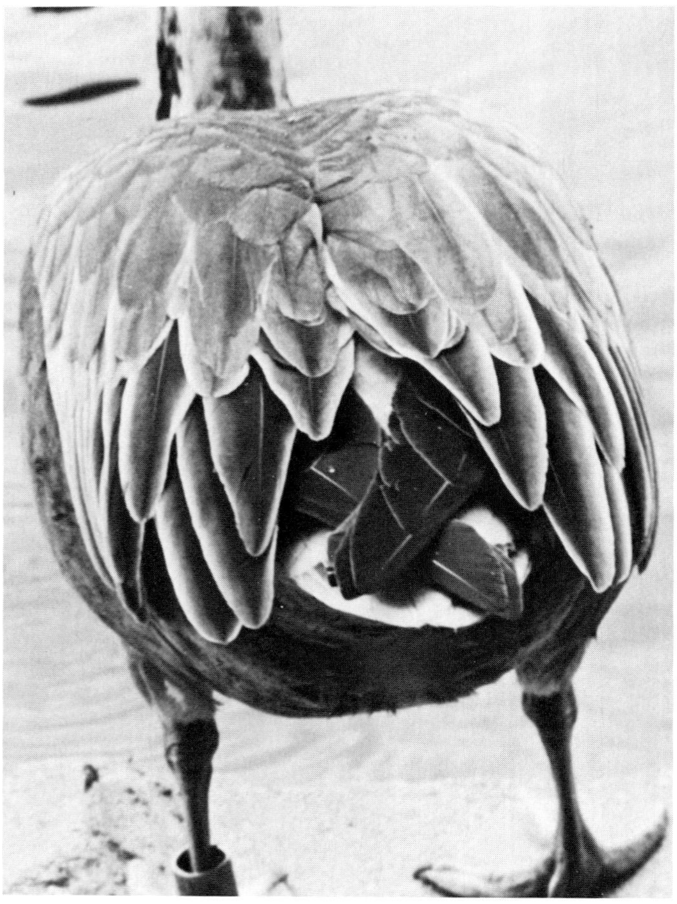

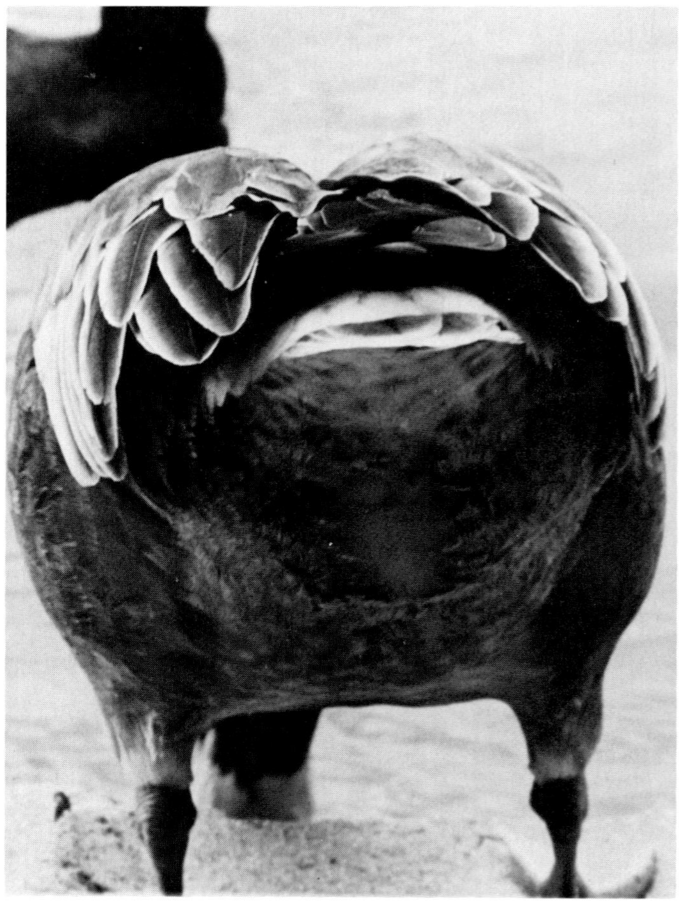

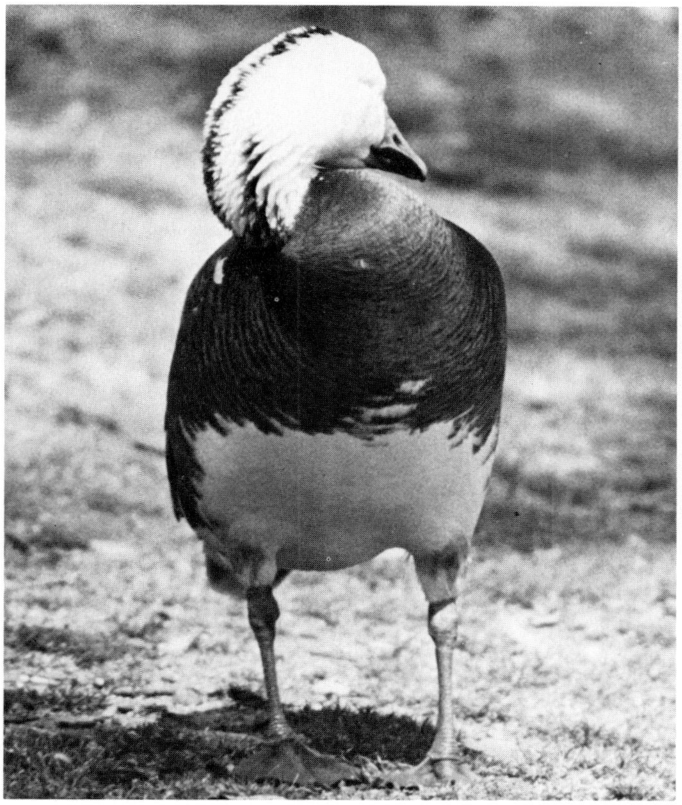

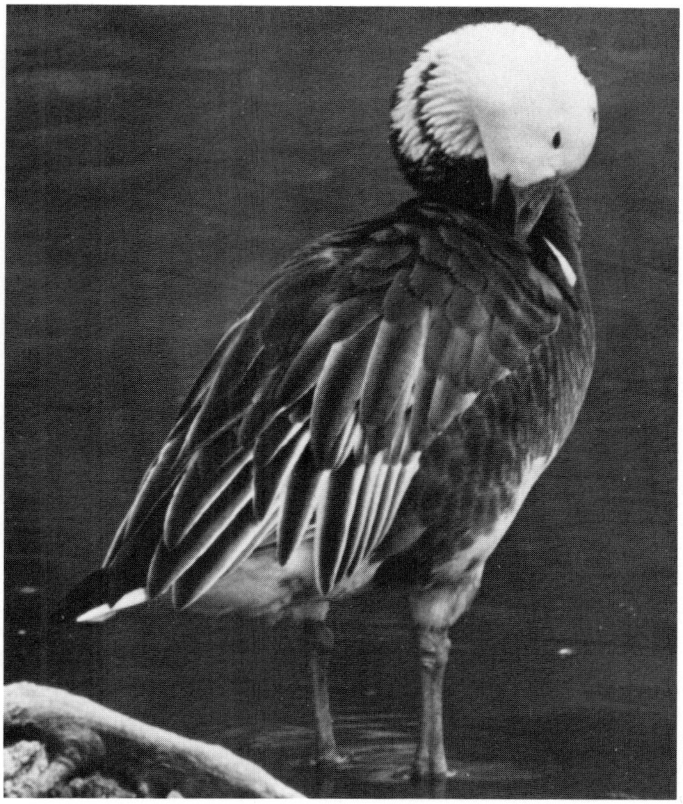

38-42 Two studies of preening blue geese as viewed from the front and the rear. 38-43

38-44 Blue goose preens his scapulars. Interesting pose.

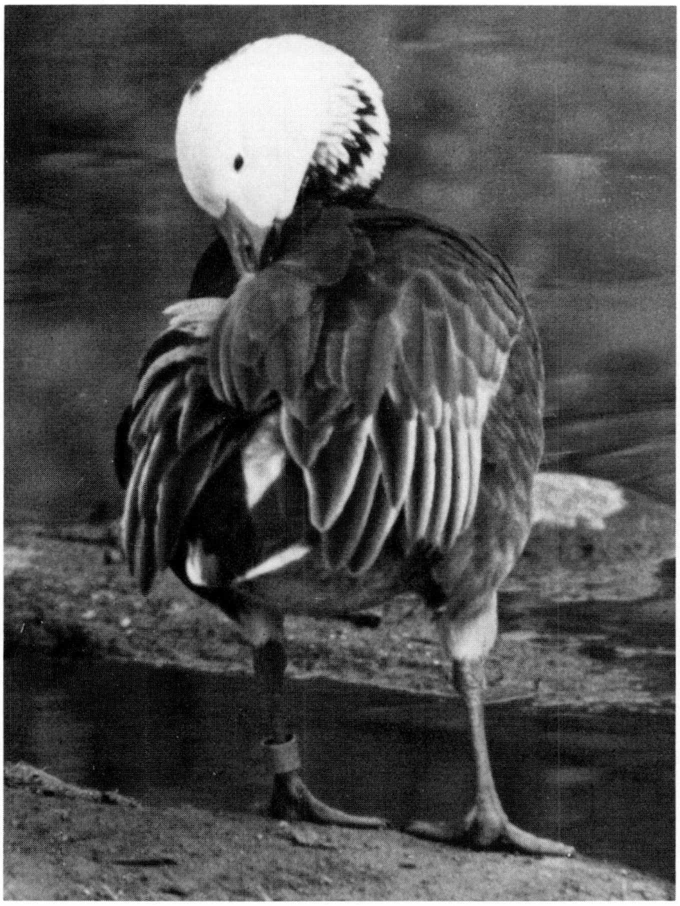

38-45 Blue goose raises his head to allow water to run down his throat after taking a drink.

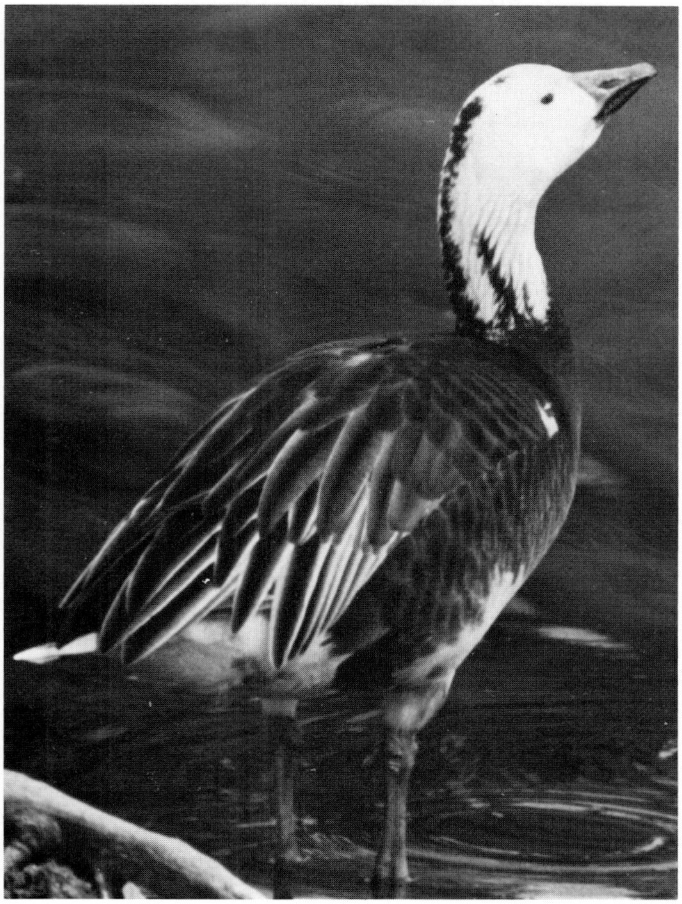

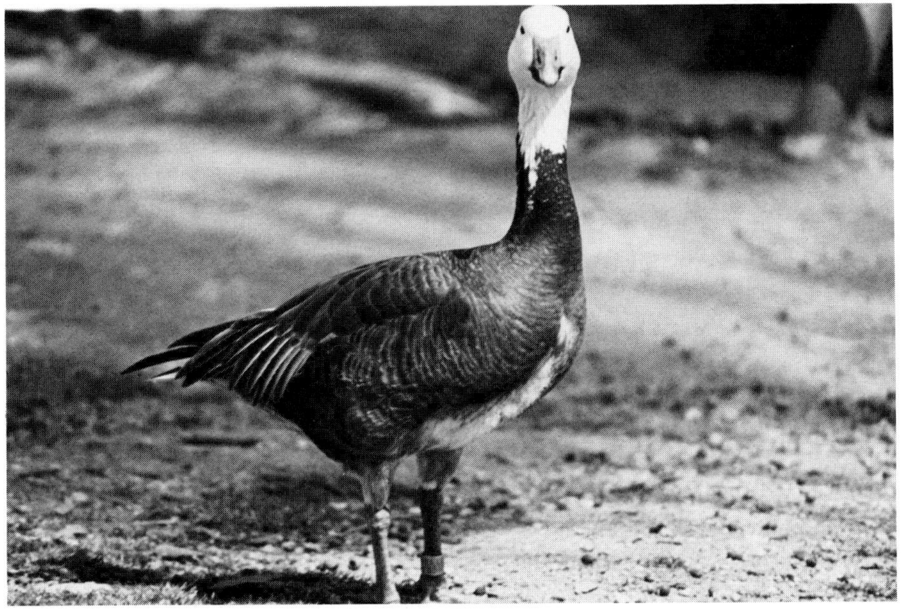

38-46 This blue goose cranes his neck for a better view.

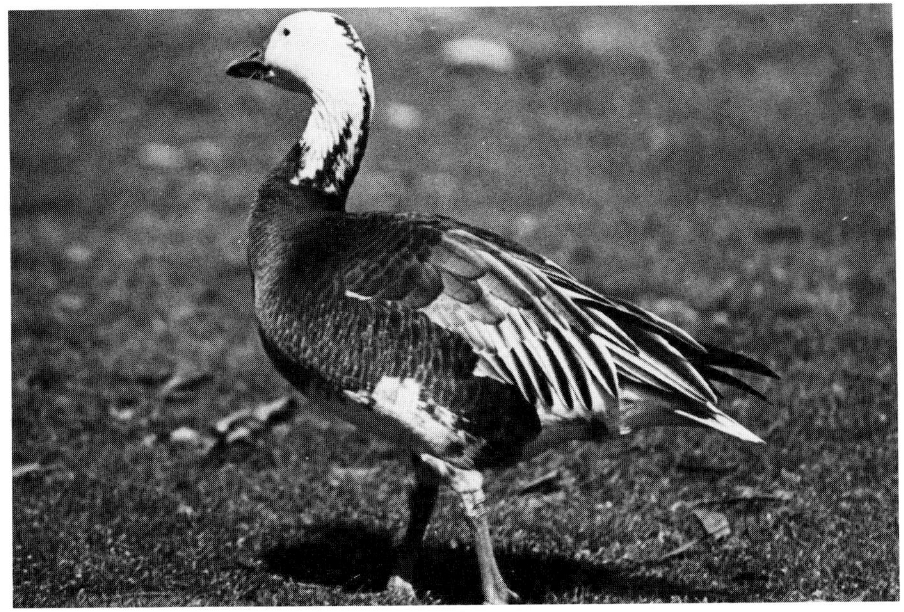

38-47 Nice profile of a striding blue goose.

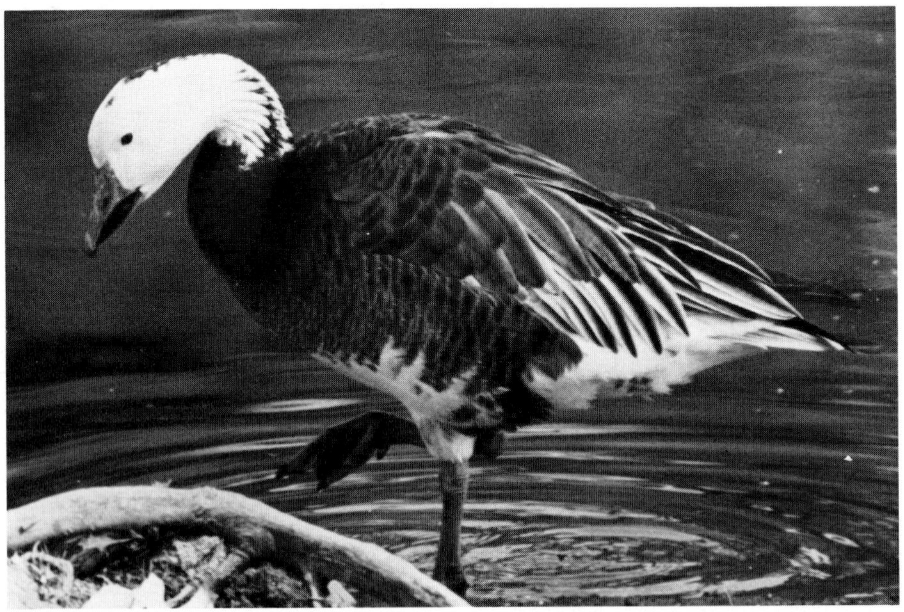

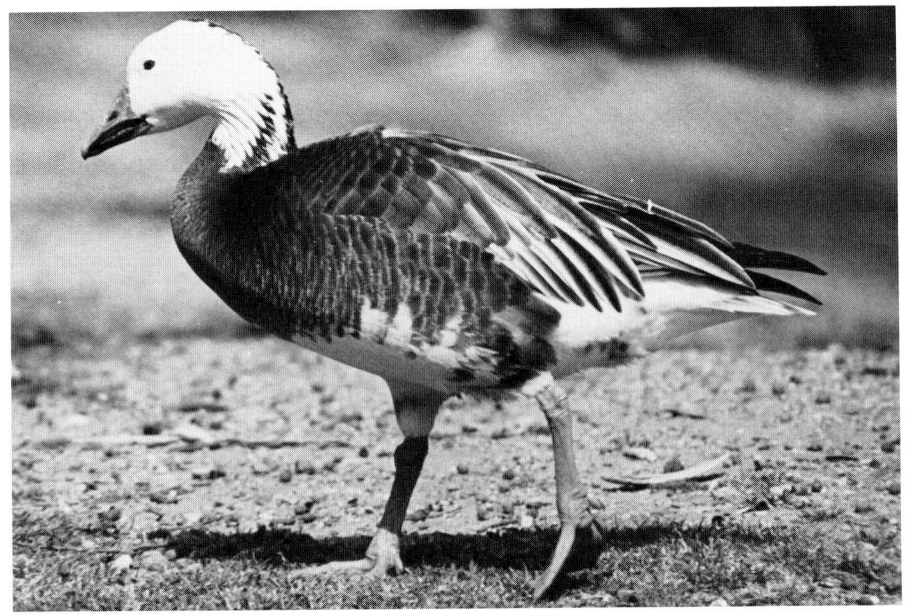

38-48 Two studies of striding blue geese. Note leg and foot positions. 38-49

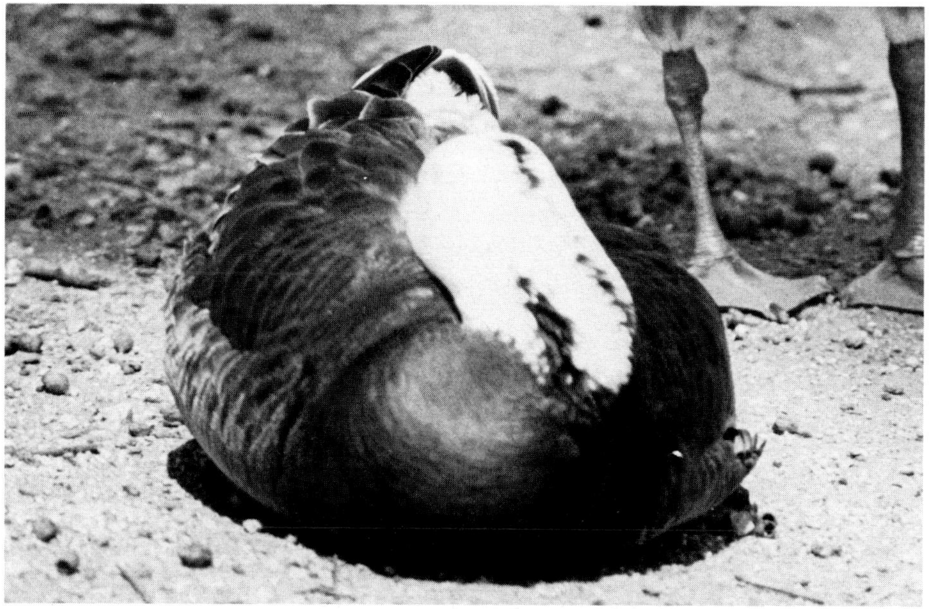

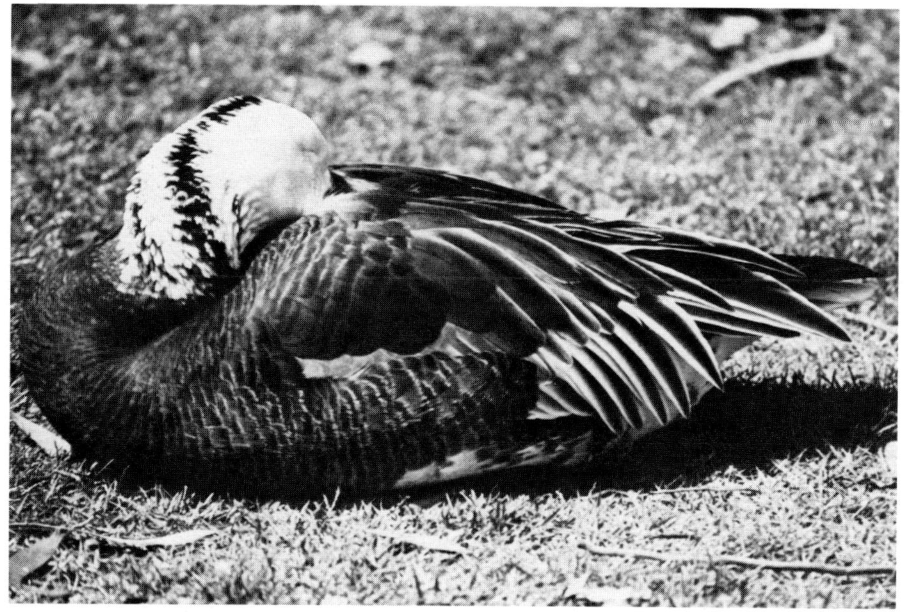

38-50 Resting blue goose as viewed from three different angles. 38-51 38-53

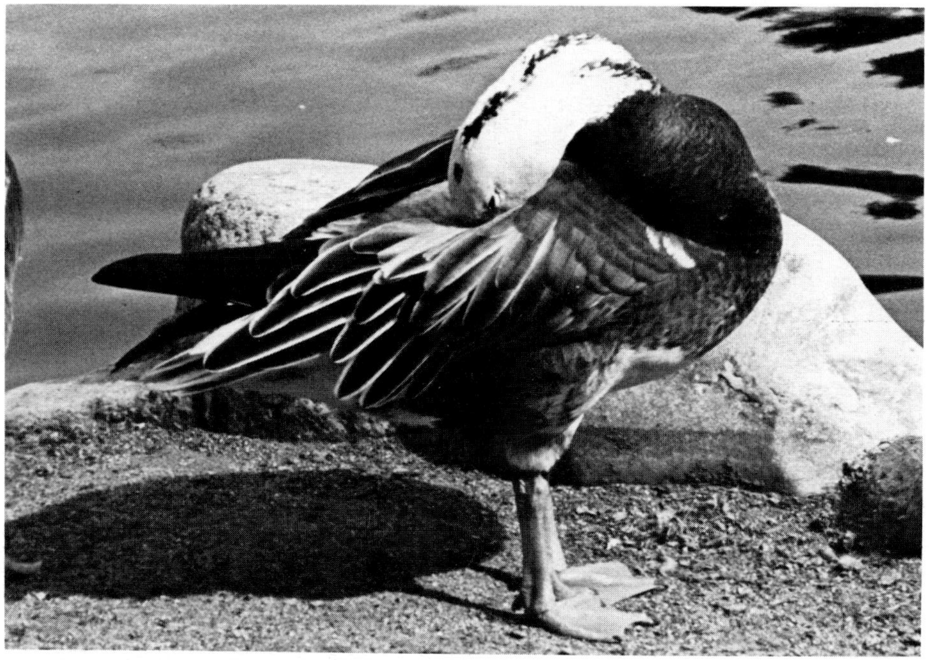

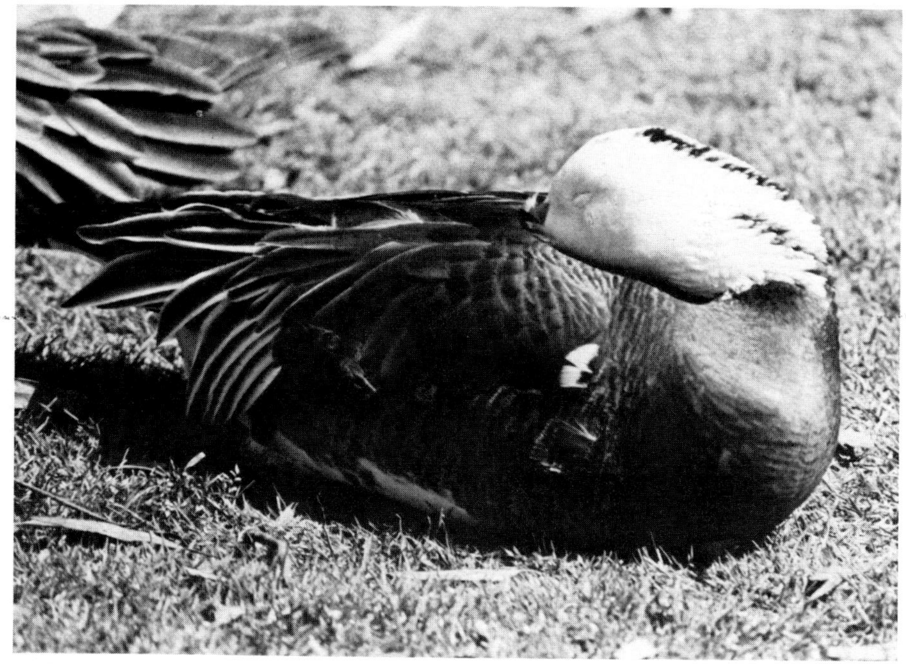

38-52 Blue goose preens under his scapulars. Note neck and upper chest convolutions.

CHAPTER 39

Ross's Goose

Anser rossi
(Color Photos-Page 98)

The lovely little Ross's goose, the rarest and one of the smallest of North American geese, is seldom seen except in California and only during the winter. Although scientifically described and named in 1861 by John Cassin after Bernard Rogan Ross, Chief Factor of the Hudson's Bay Company, little was known of the Ross's goose except its wintering habits. In 1938 or 1940 (there appear to be two different accounts), Angus Gavin of the Hudson's Bay Company at last found its breeding grounds near the Perry River, almost 50 miles north of the Arctic Circle. In 1949, this area was again visited by Hanson, Gueneau, and Scott who reported there were no Ross's geese nesting on the lakes where they were previously found by Gavin (Delacour). From the number of nests found in the general area, it was determined by these three that the world populationf Ross's geese may have been less than 2,000. However, in 1960, Thomas W. Barry (*Waterfowl Tomorrow*) surveyed a larger area and counted at least 9,000 Ross's geese, most of which were nesting approximately 100 miles east of the Perry River. Snow geese were also nesting in this area and, because of the difficulty in making positive identification between these two species, Barry reports that considerably more of these little geese could have been nesting there. Other nesting areas have been found in the Southampton Island area (northwest part of Hudston Bay). It is Barry's belief that Ross's geese may also be found nesting with snow geese along the south central shores of Baffin Island.

The Ross's goose is classified as one of the group of threatened species—its present population is somewhat more than 30,000. This bird, except for having a shorter bill in proportion to its head, appears to be a miniature snow goose and is commonly mistaken for one. Because of difficulty in identification, hunters are now allowed a bag limit of one bird a day in the Central and Pacific Flyways. The Ross's goose has at least two characteristics which make identification at a distance possible—they are considerably less talkative when flying than snow geese and their flight is much more erratic. These little geese often dart from side to side and change altitude slightly—their black-tipped, white wings flash in the sunlight as they bank rapidly, first one way and then the other. Also, they often fly in disorganized groups compared to the long, diagonal lines of snow geese. I have seen large groups—probably several hundred birds—of Ross's geese on a number of occasions that were easily identifiable over a distance of several miles by their flight mannerisms, flashing wings, and tight grouping. They often intermingle with snow geese and are then somewhat easier to identify by comparison in size.

Immature Ross's geese, like immature snow geese, are much grayer on their upper parts than their pure-white parents; their feet and bills are also paler in color. According to Bent, immature birds acquire their adult plumage when they are about 10 months old.

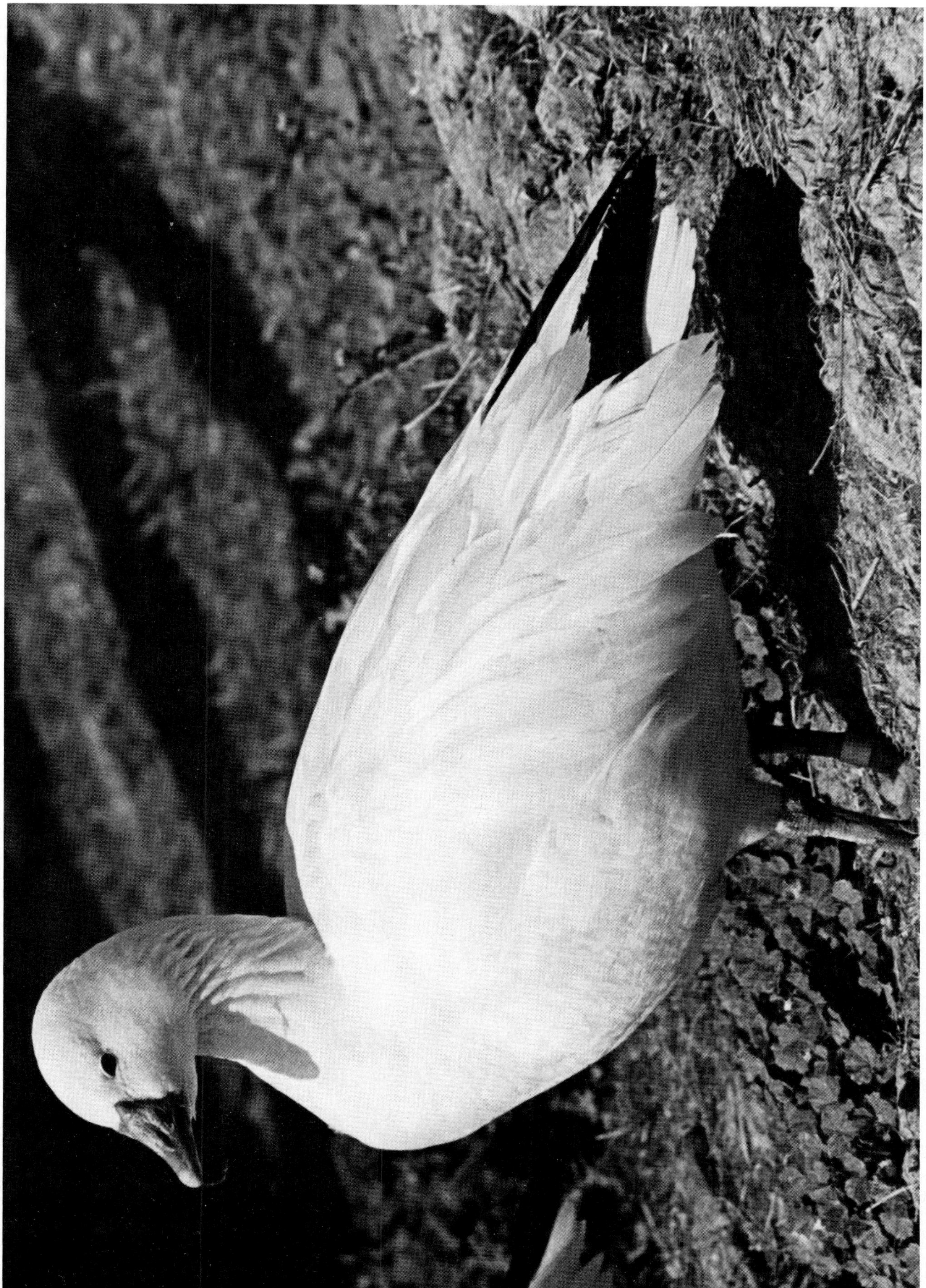

39-1 The pretty and dainty little Ross's goose. He is a miniature snow goose except that his bill is relatively smaller as compared to his head, also his neck is shorter and heavier.

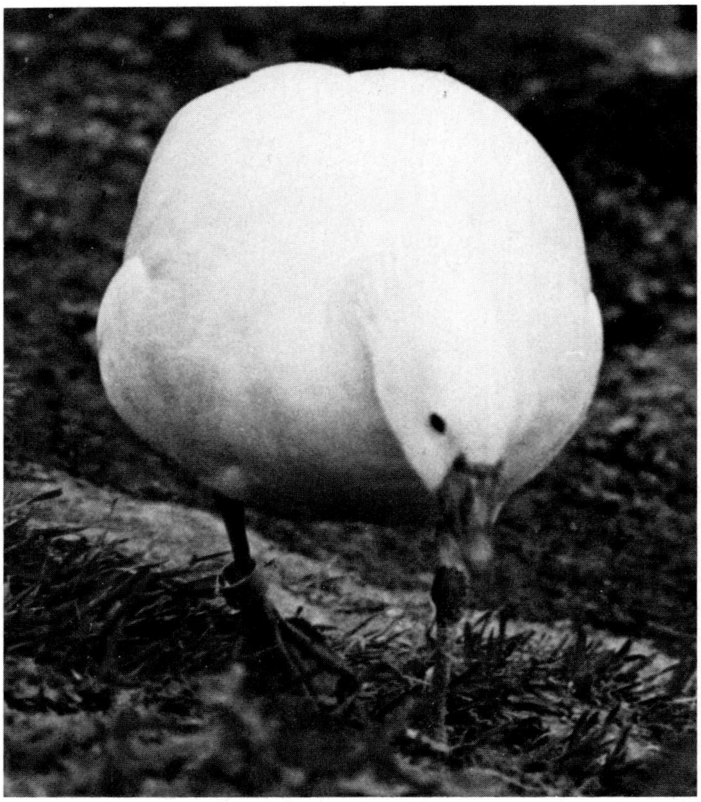

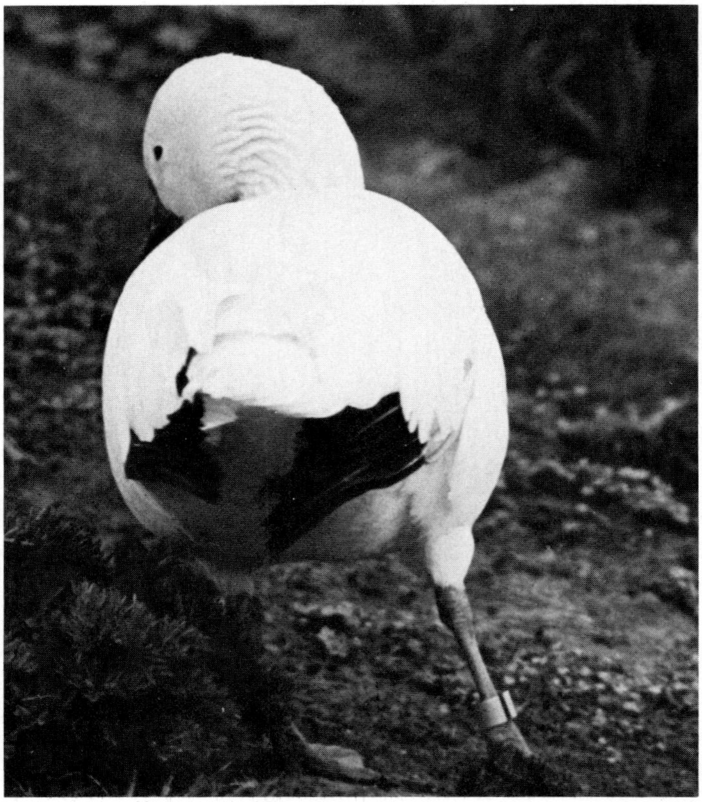

39-2 Front and rear views of the little Ross's goose. 39-3

39-4 The beautiful little Ross gander. Notice how his neck feathers lie in ridges and furrows.

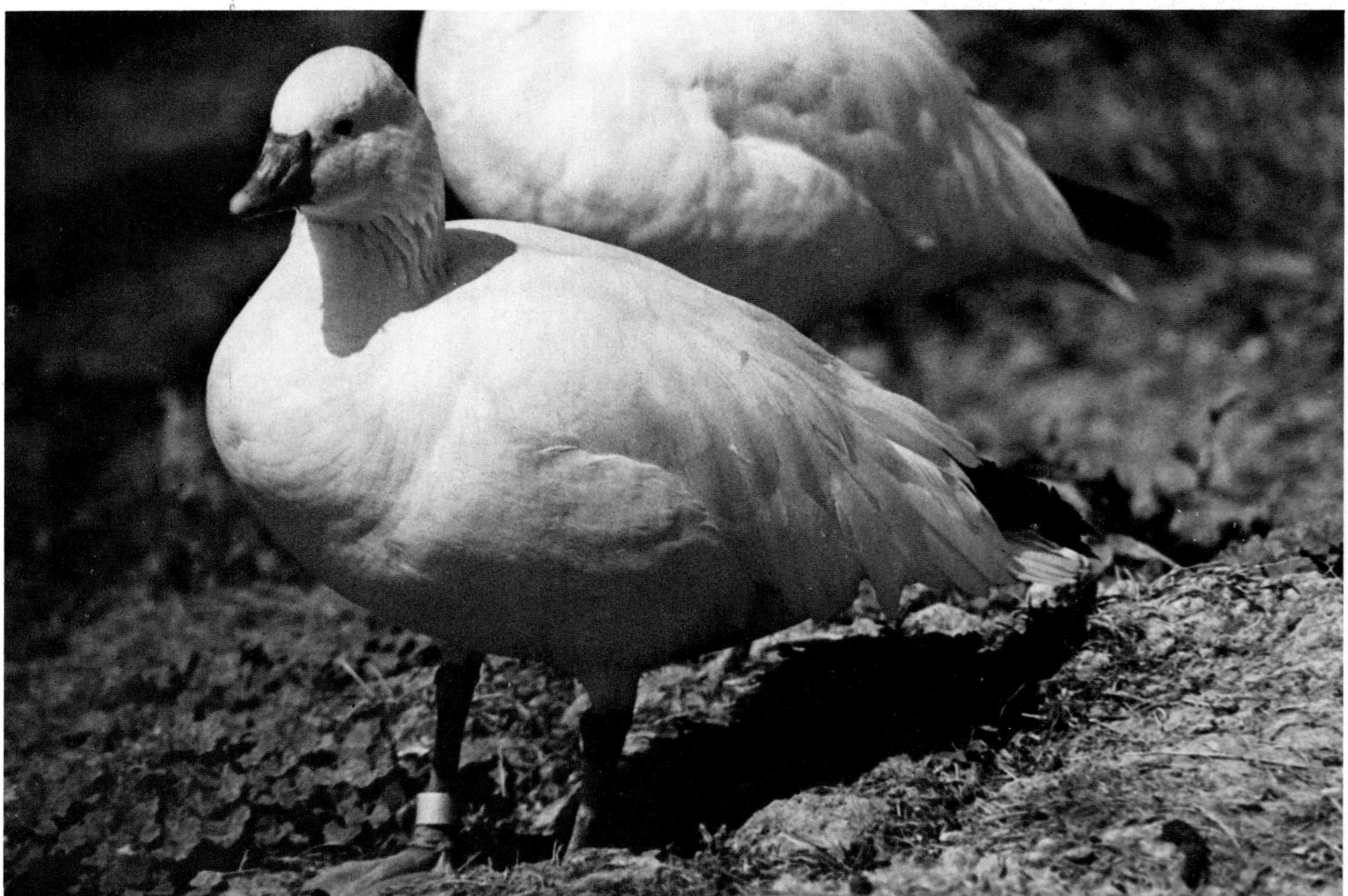

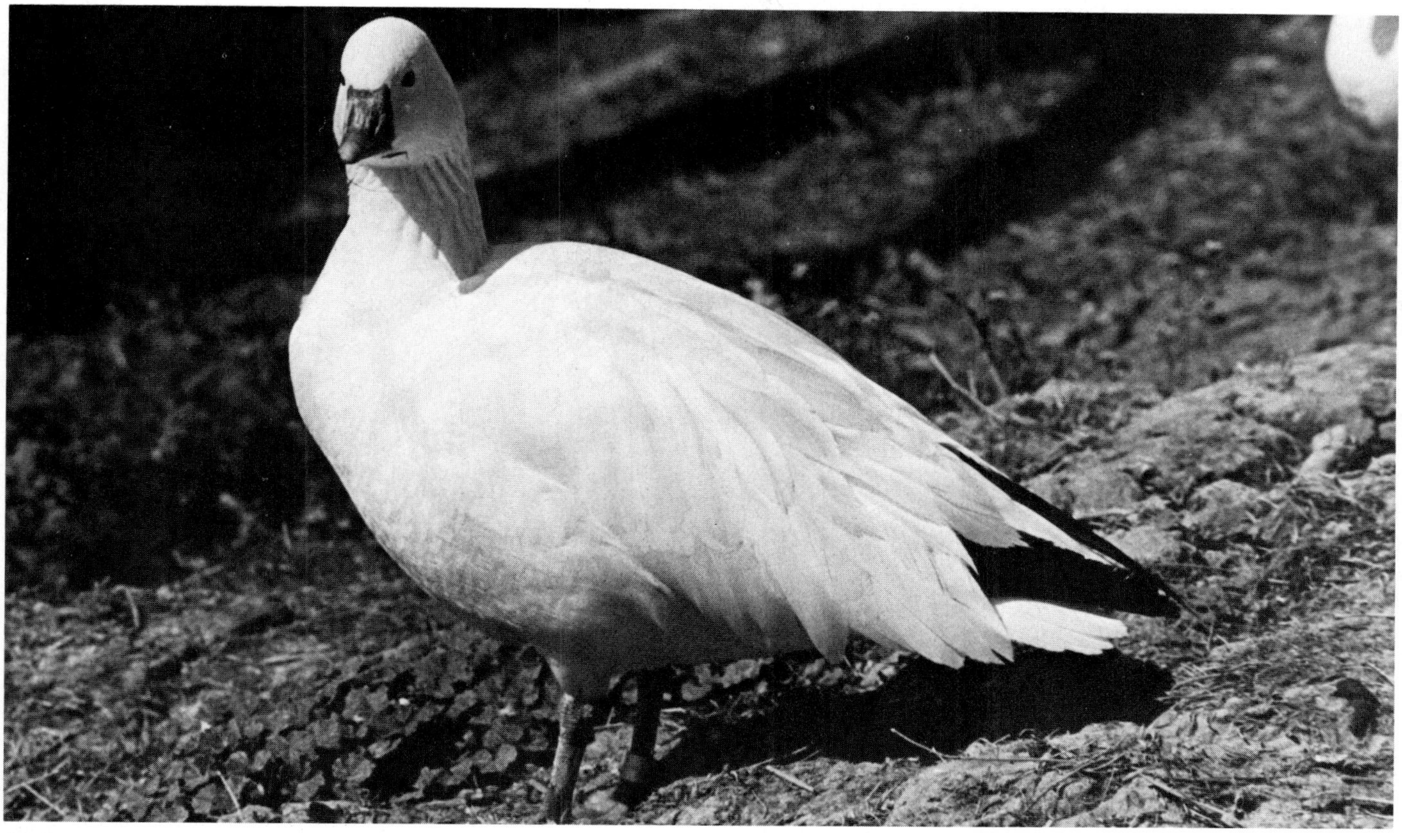

39-5

Two more profile studies of the Ross's goose.

39-6

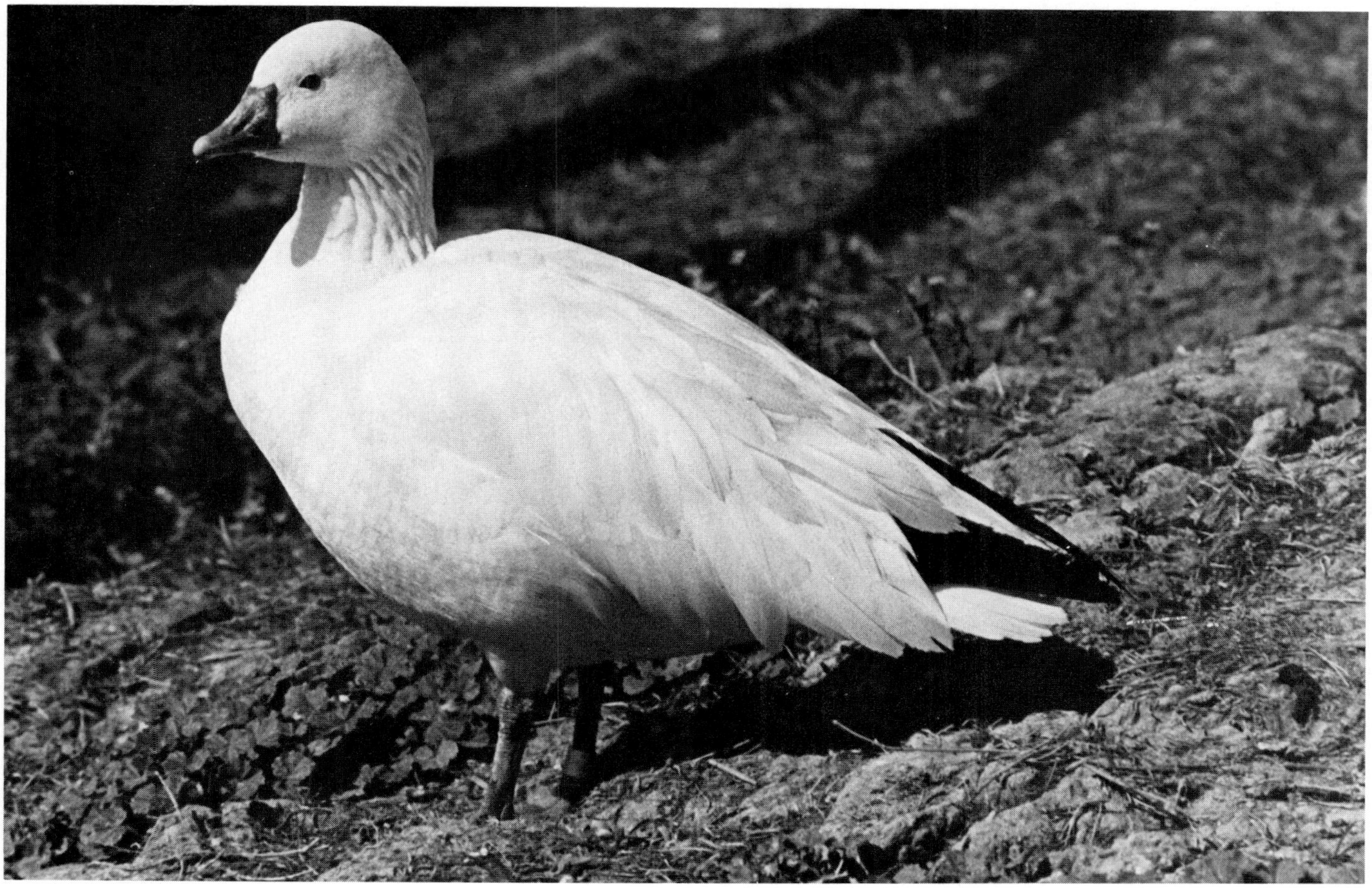

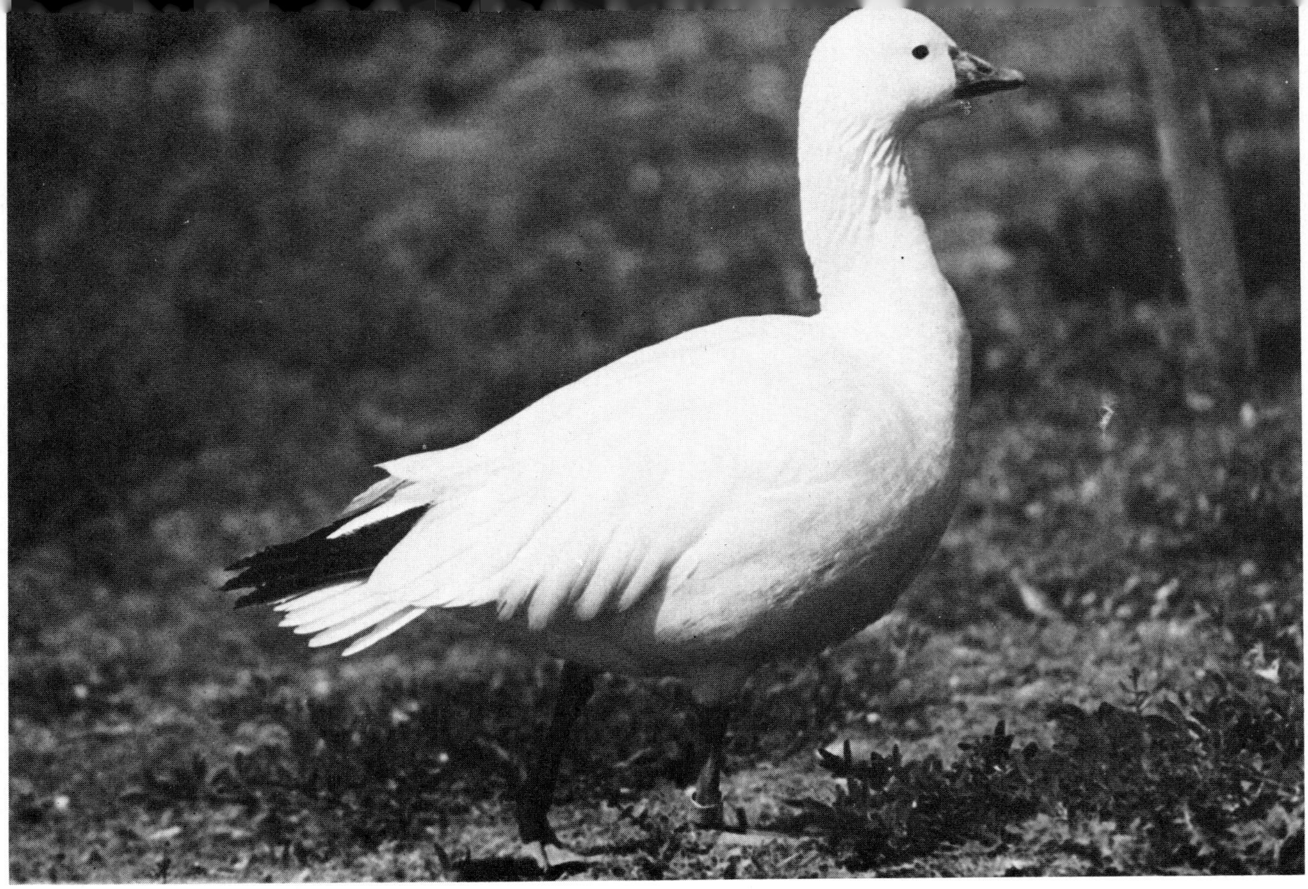

39-7

Ross's geese in alert positions.

39-8

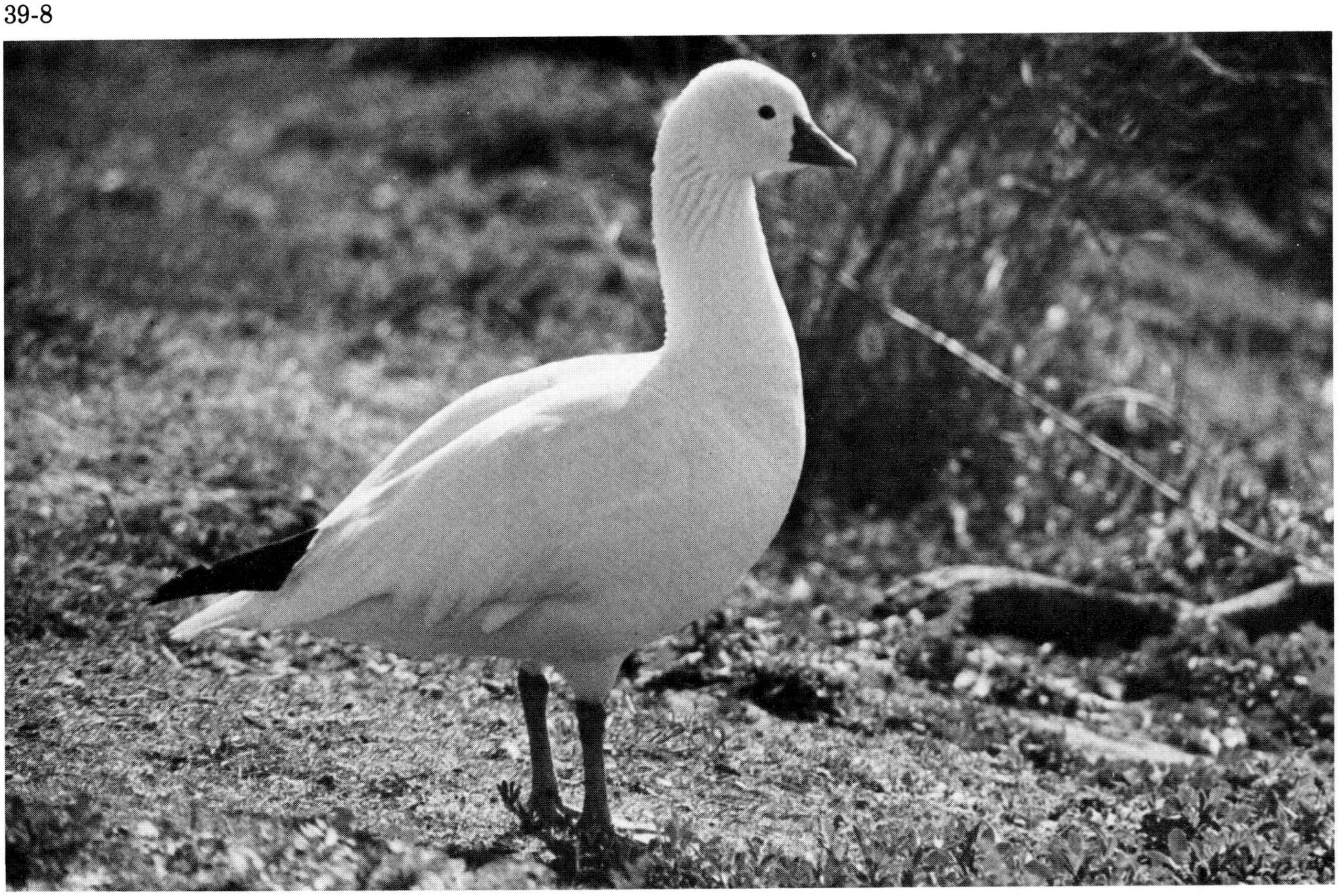

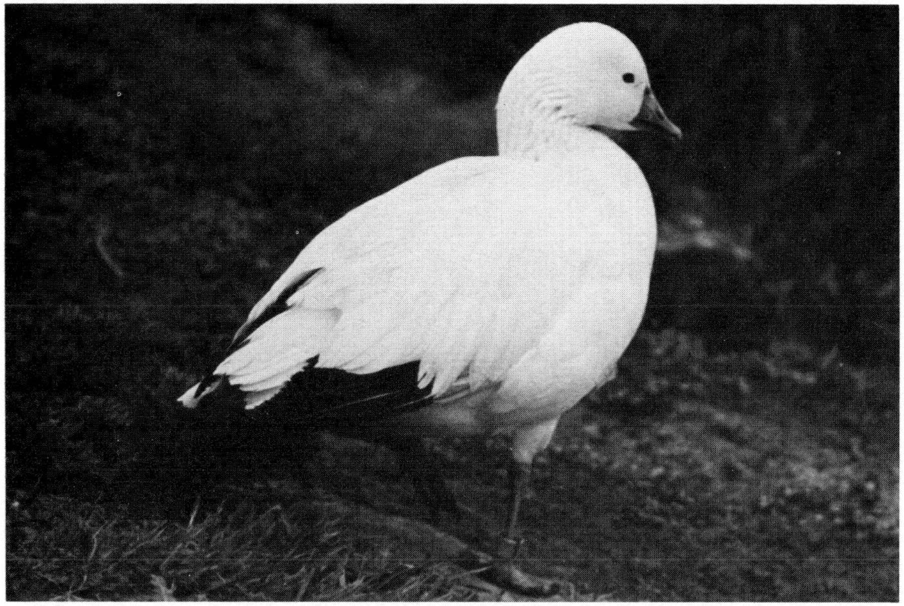

39-9

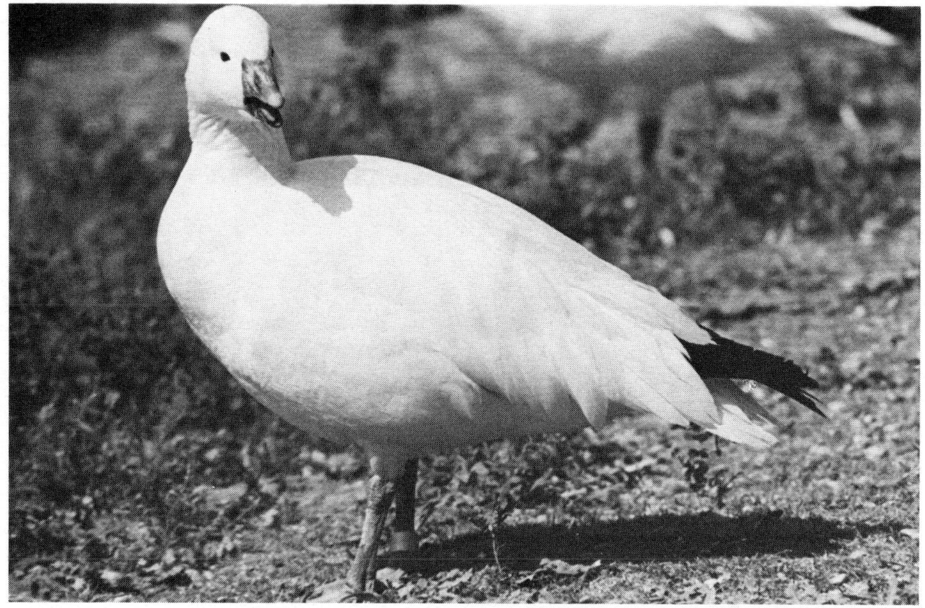

39-10

Lovely little Ross's geese in four different poses. Notice that the bird in the upper right photo is calling.

39-11

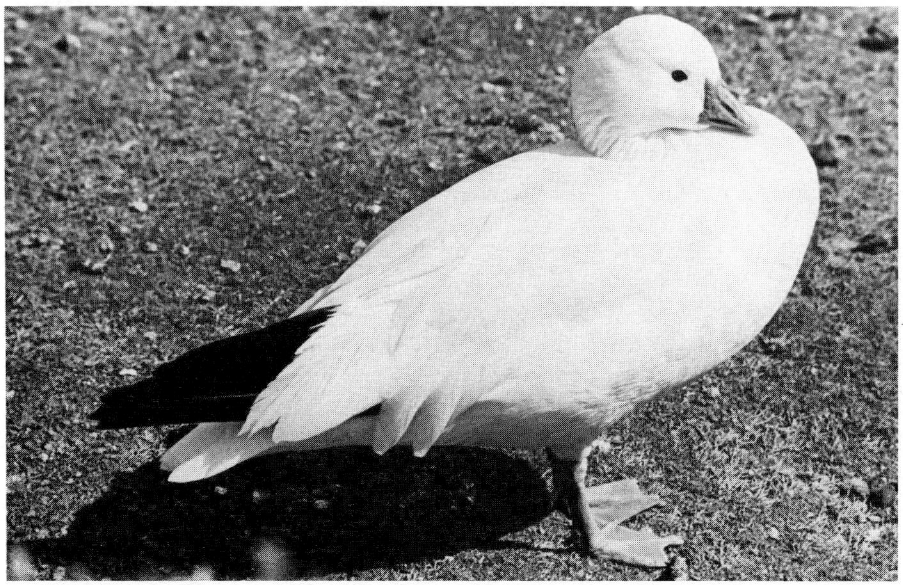

39-12

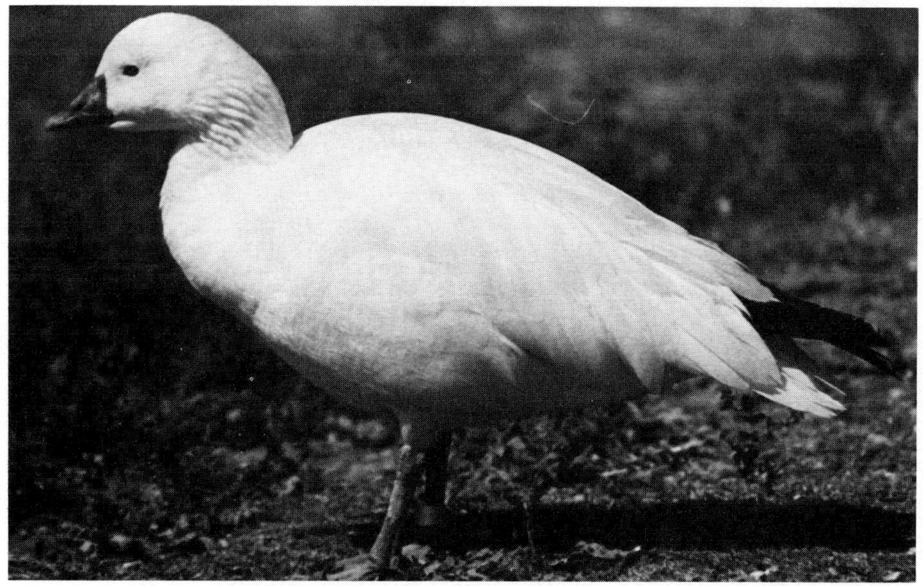

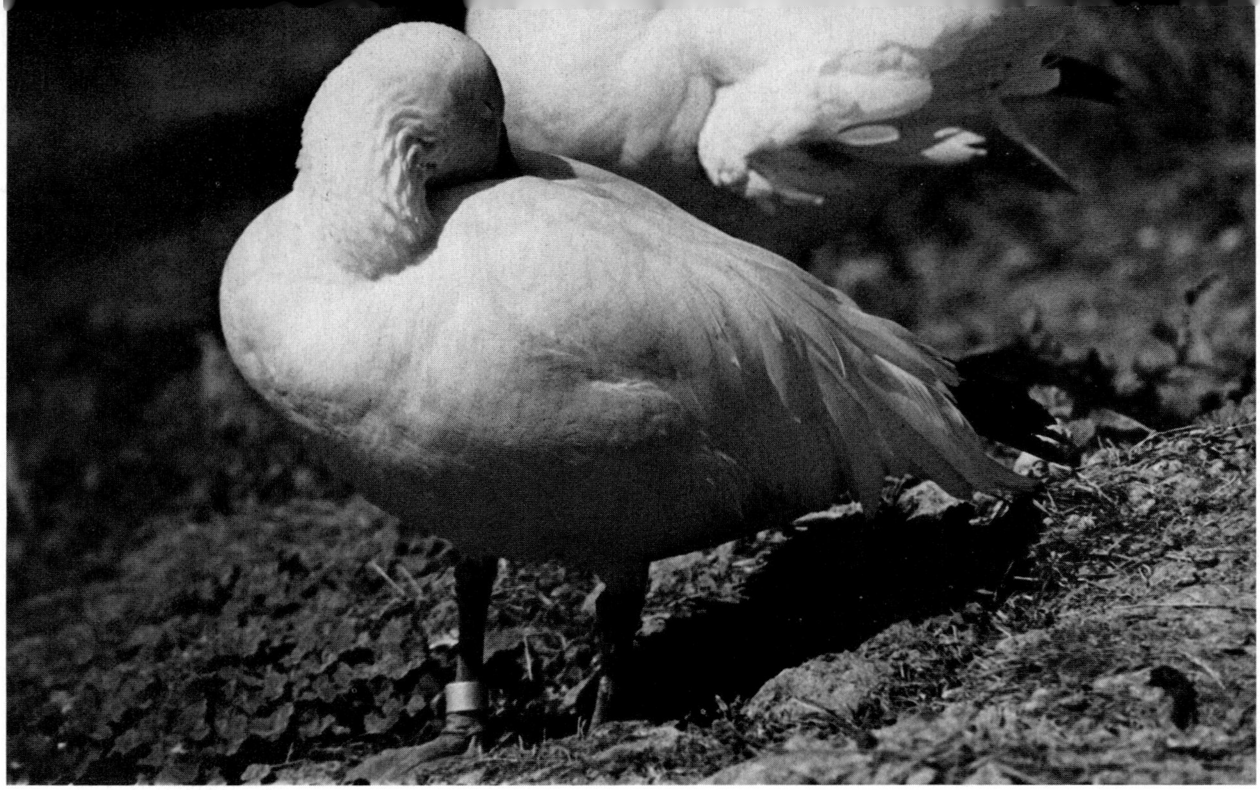

39-13 Little Ross gander takes a nap.

39-14 Ross's goose in a pleasing pose.

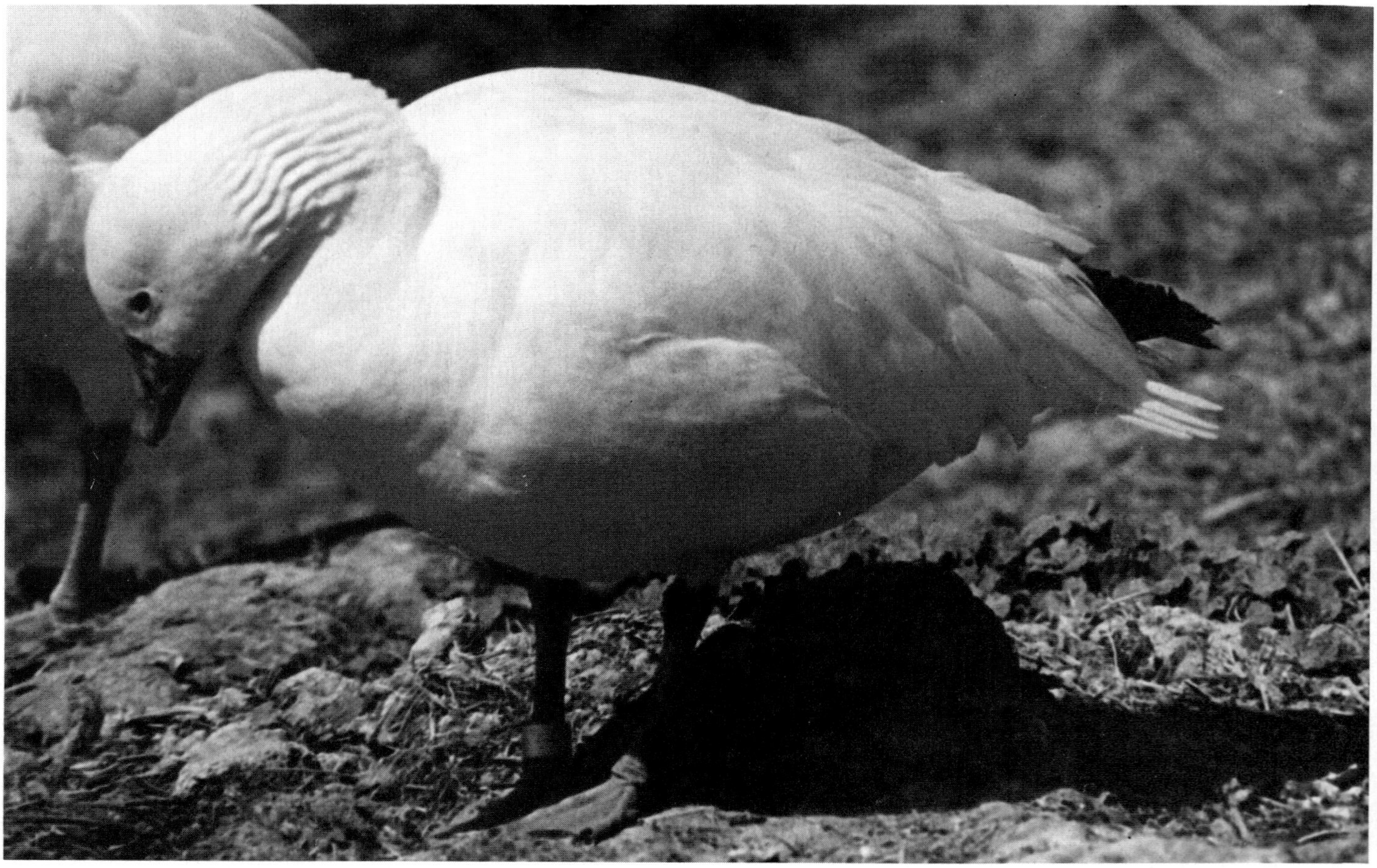

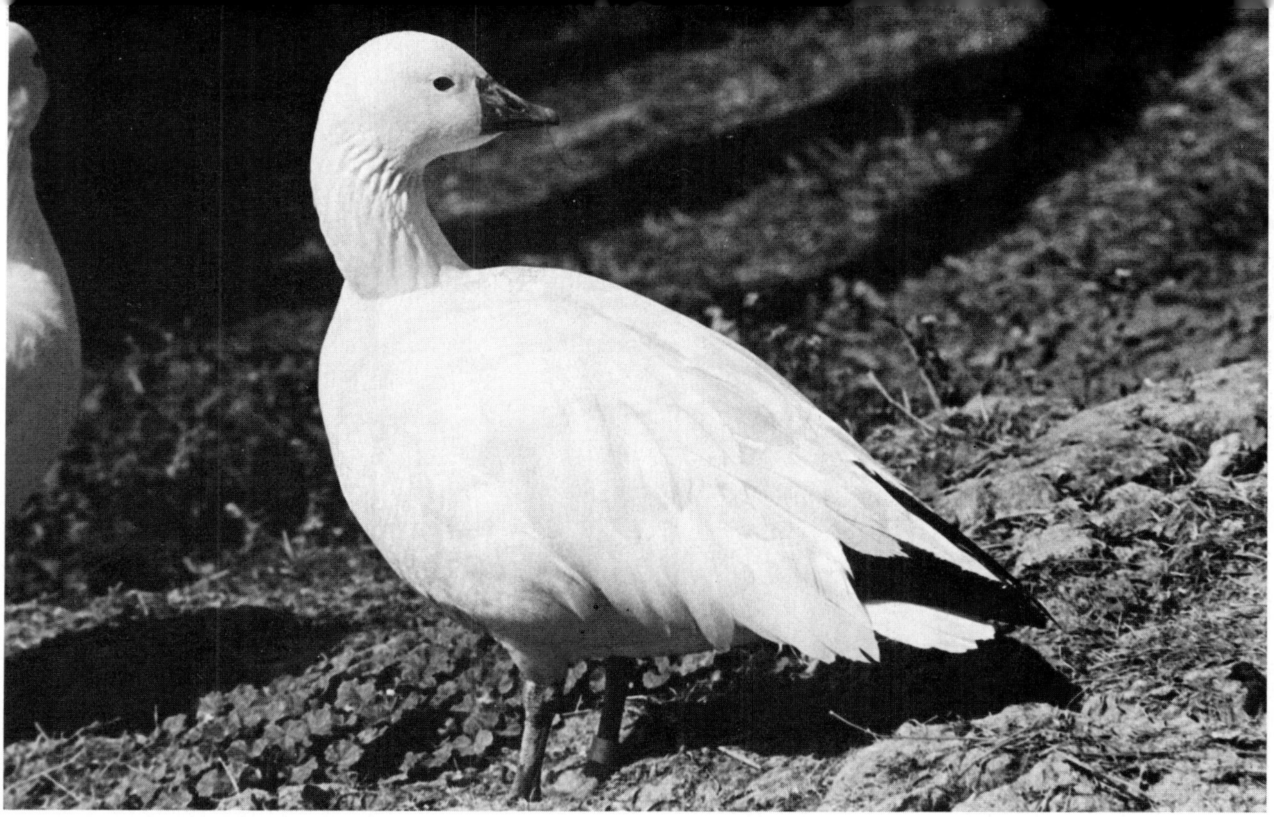

39-15 Little Ross gives a quizzical eye to the author. Nice pose.

39-16 Striding Ross's goose.

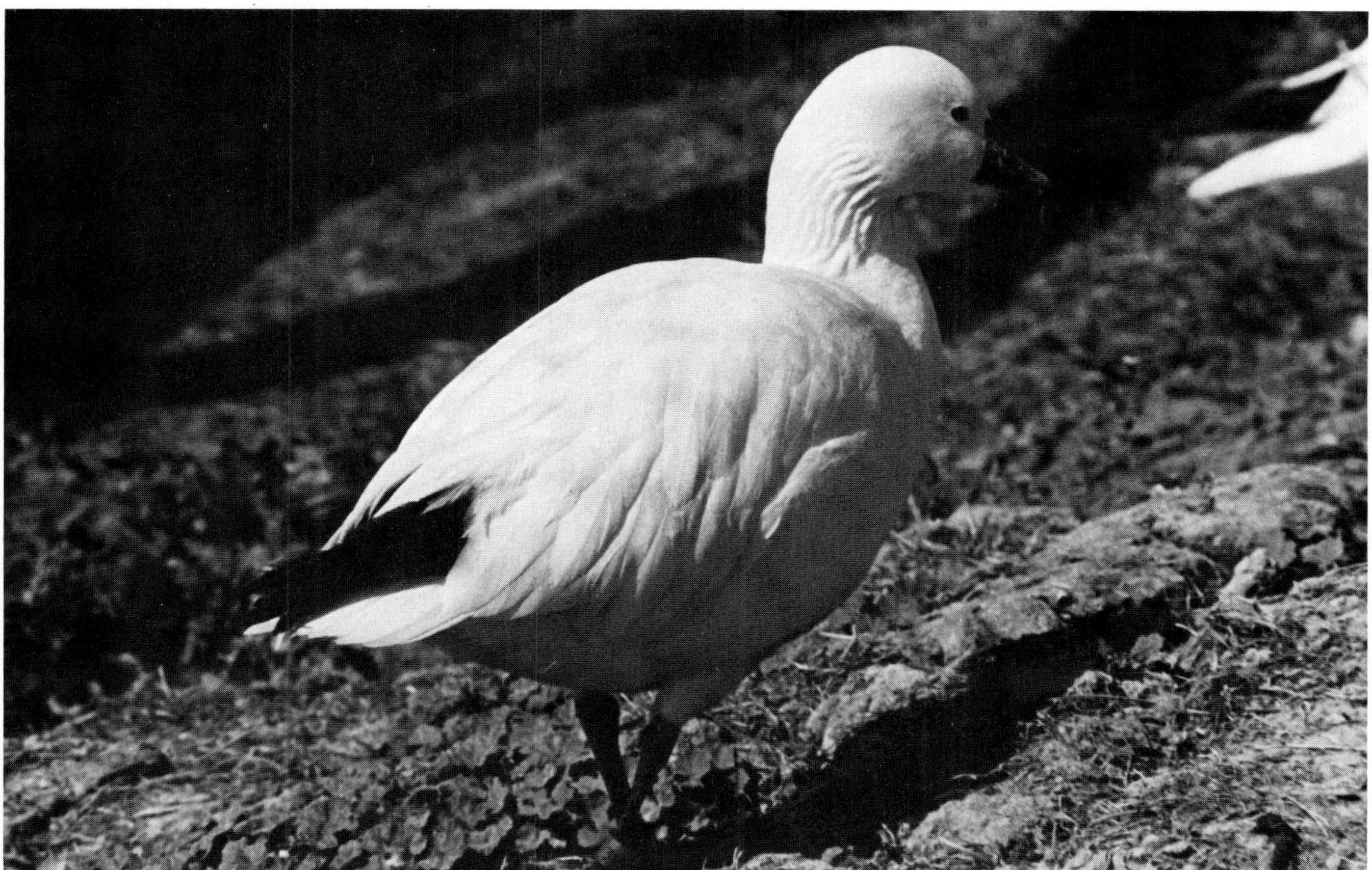

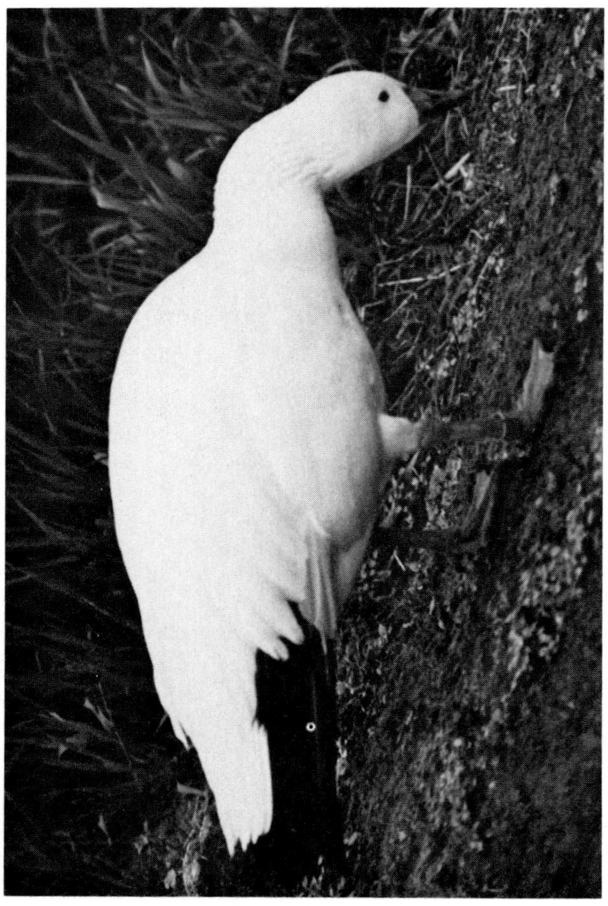

39-17

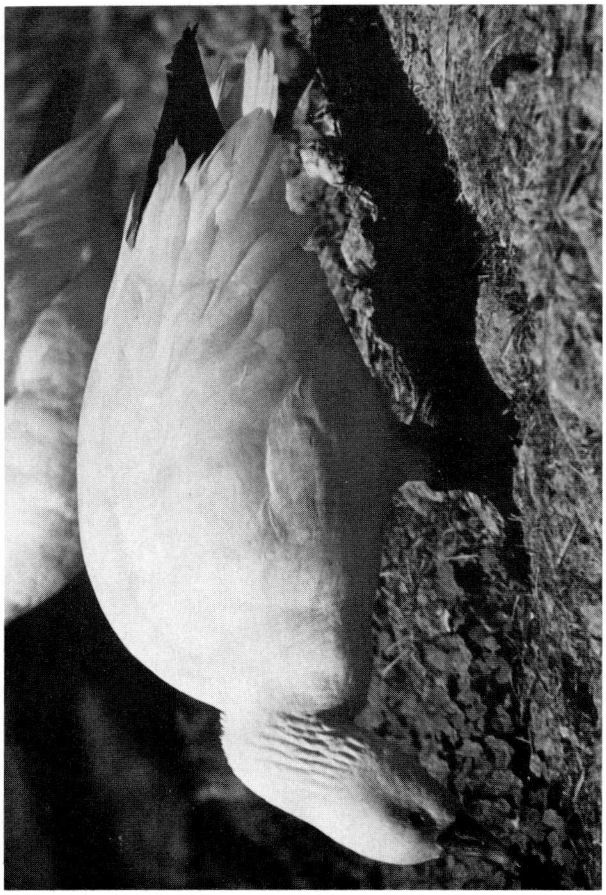

39-18

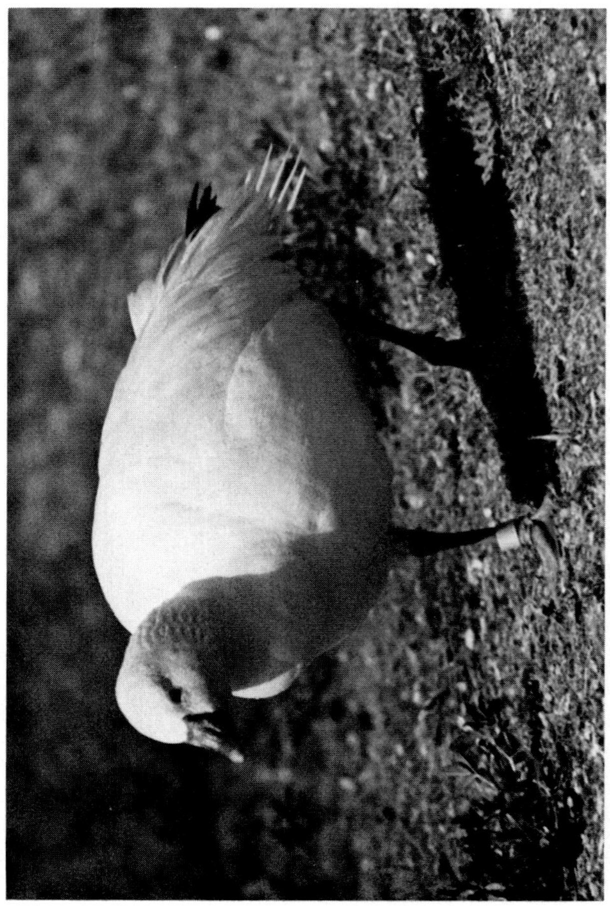

39-19

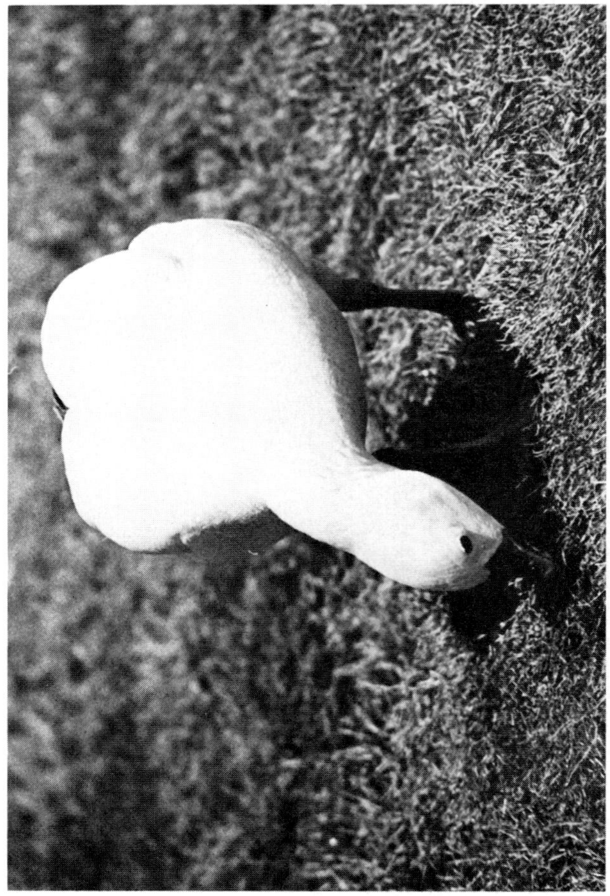

39-20

Ross's geese in feeding positions.

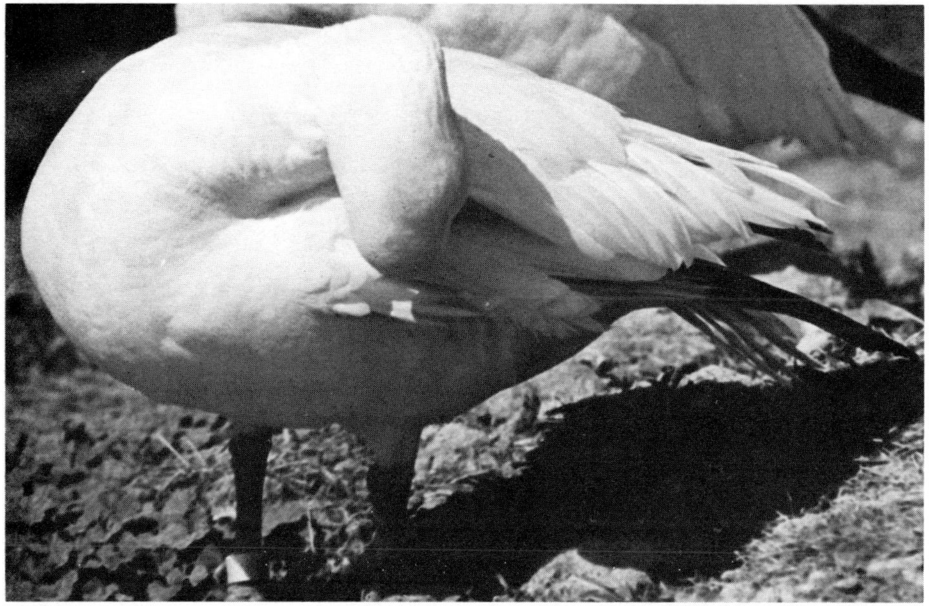

39-21

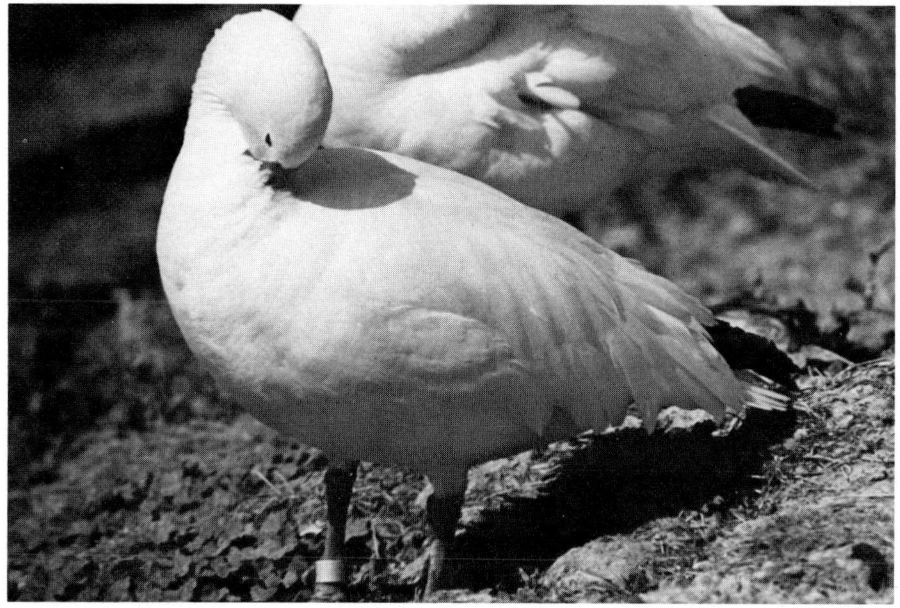

39-22

Four studies of preening Ross's geese. They are dainty little birds not much larger than a mallard duck.

39-23

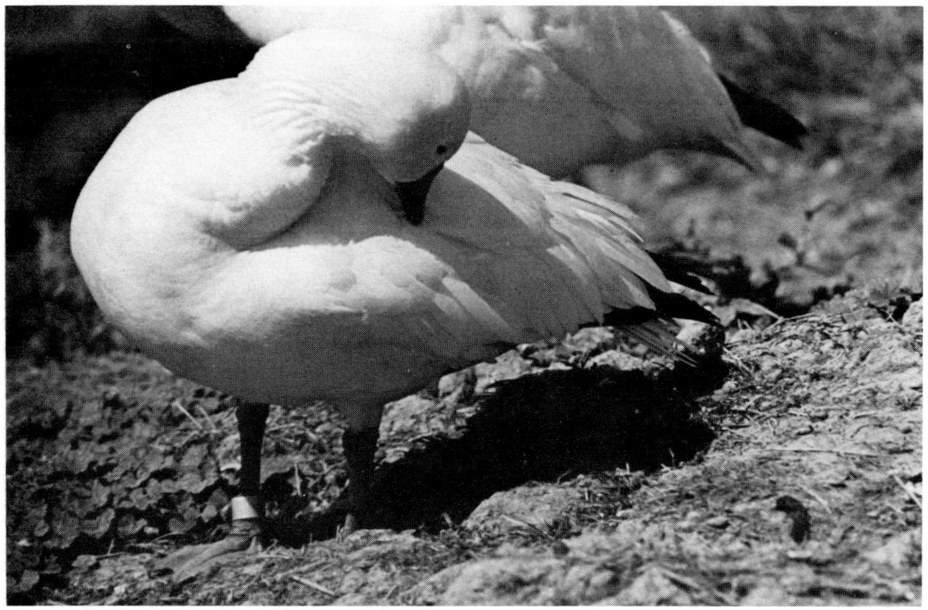

39-24

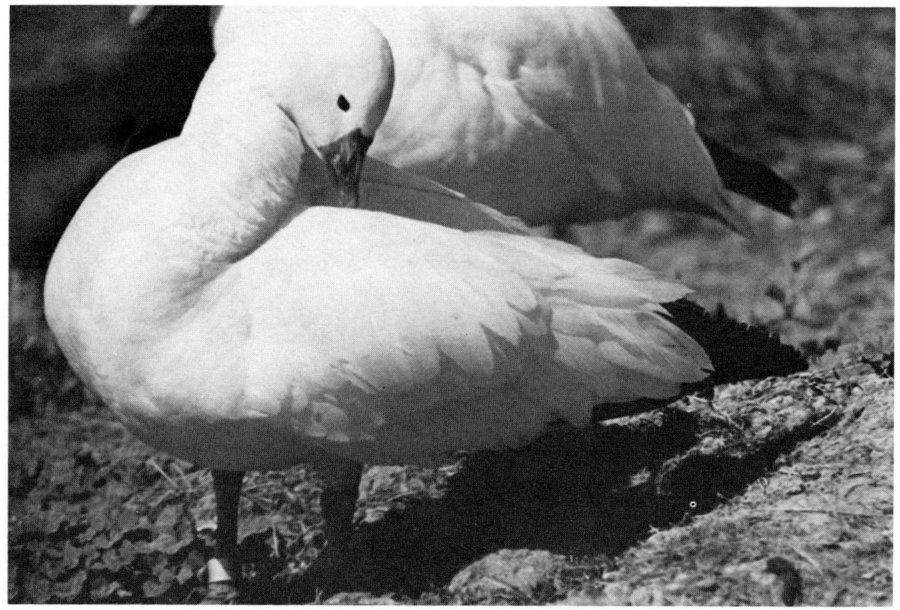

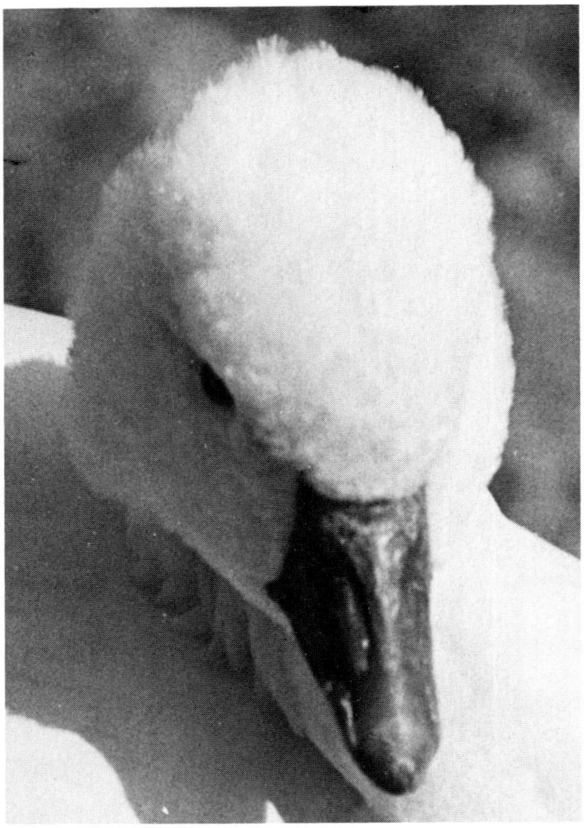

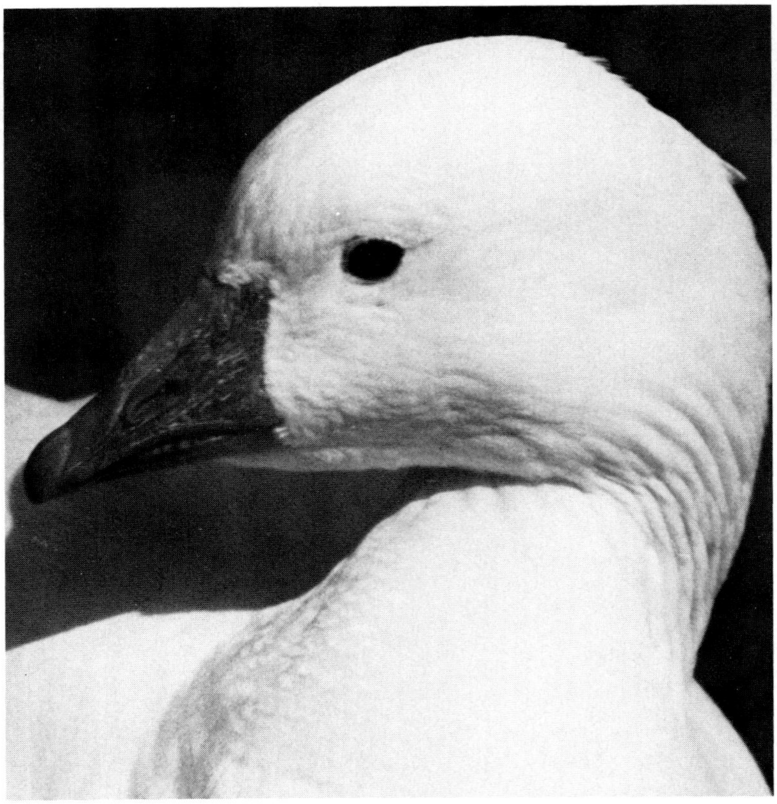

39-25 Front and profile views of the Ross's goose's head and bill. The older birds have warty protuberances on their bills between the base and the nostril. 39-26

39-27 Ross's goose in the sleeping position as viewed from the front.

39-28 Little Ross in a pleasing, resting pose.

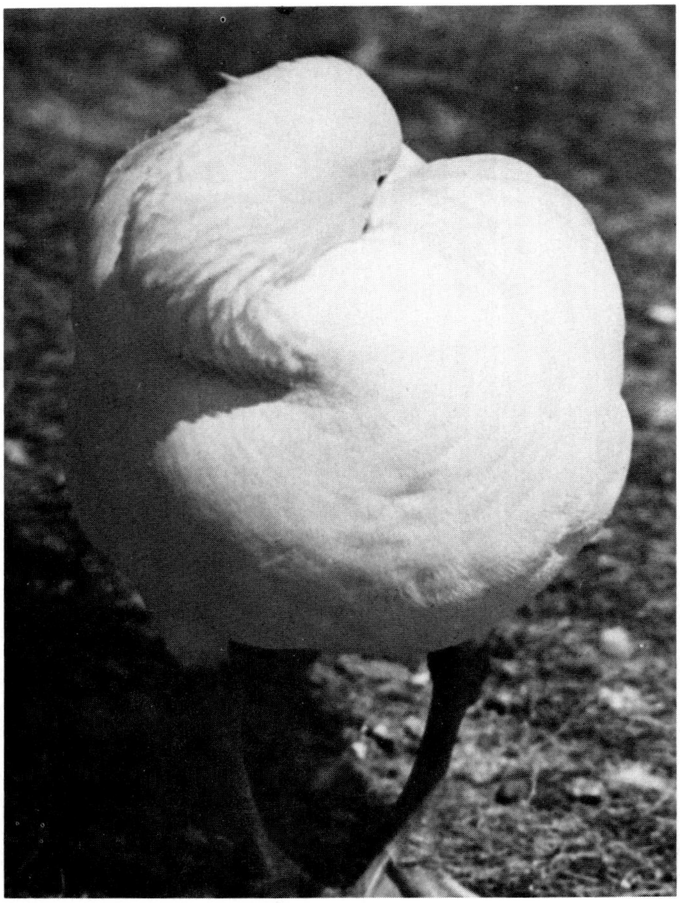

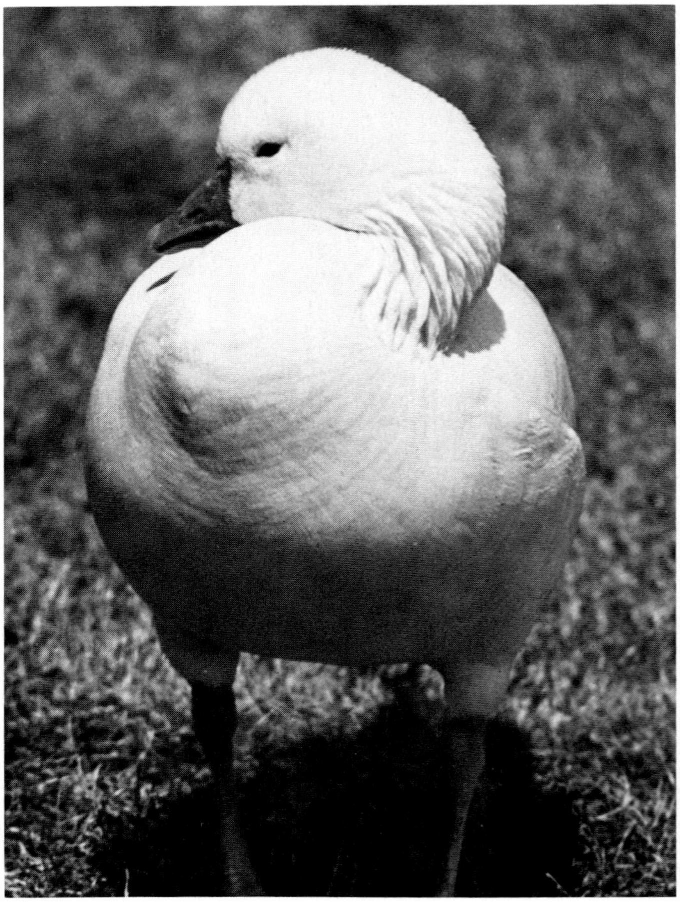

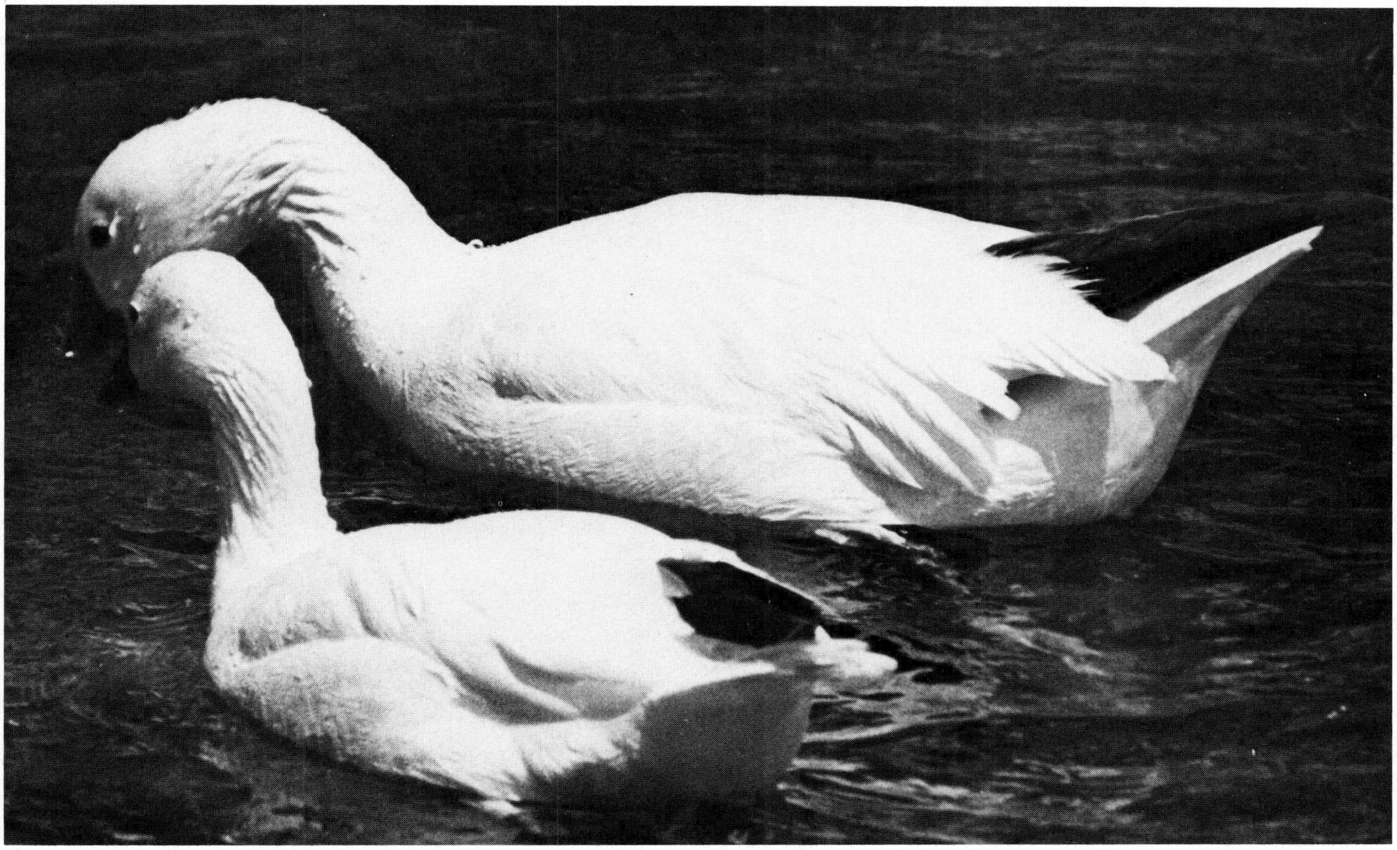

39-29 Ross geese dabble in the water.

39-30 Little Ross's goose in an alert floating position.

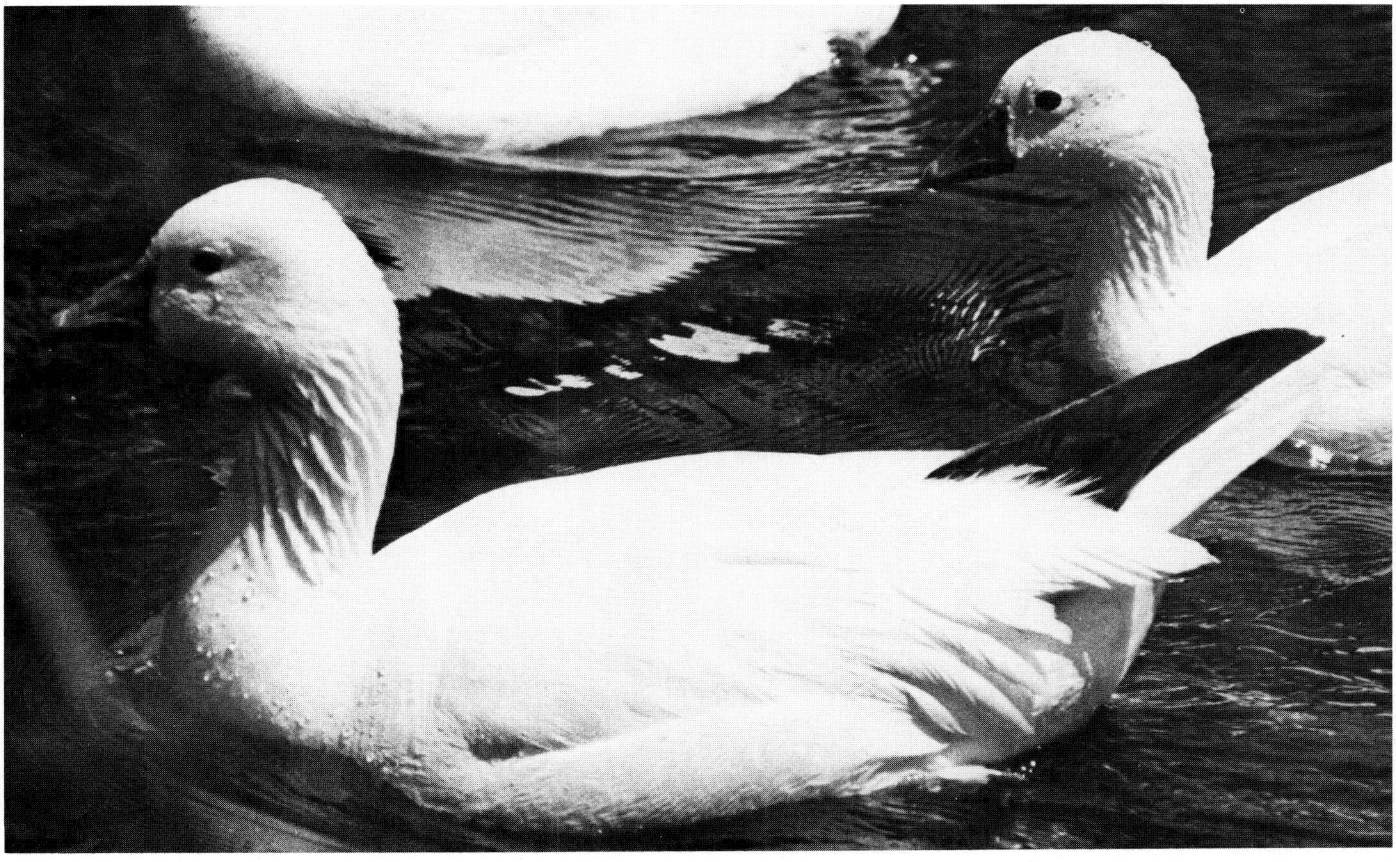

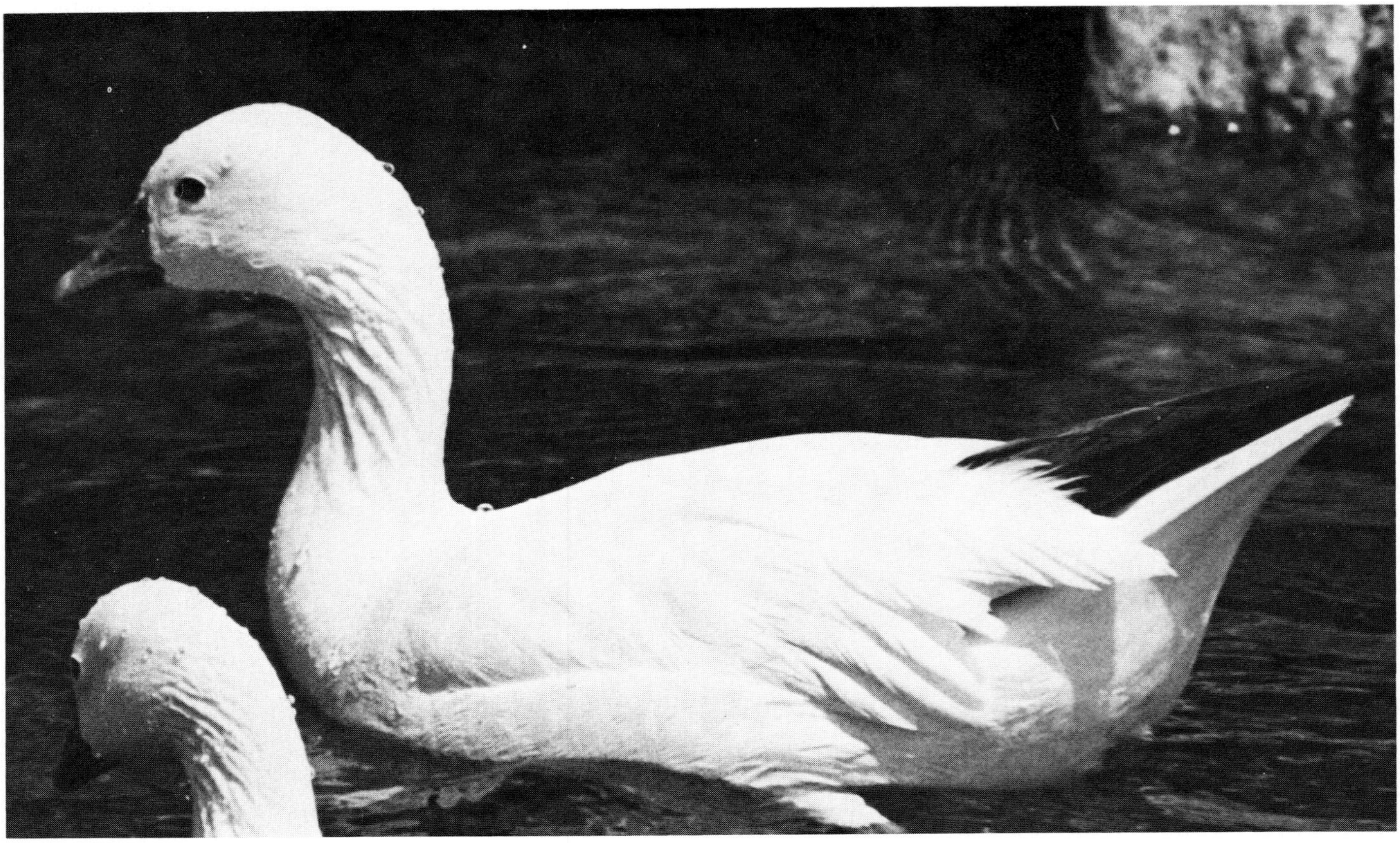

39-31 Another view of the floating Ross's goose. Note how gracefully he holds his head.

39-32 Little Ross preens as he rests.

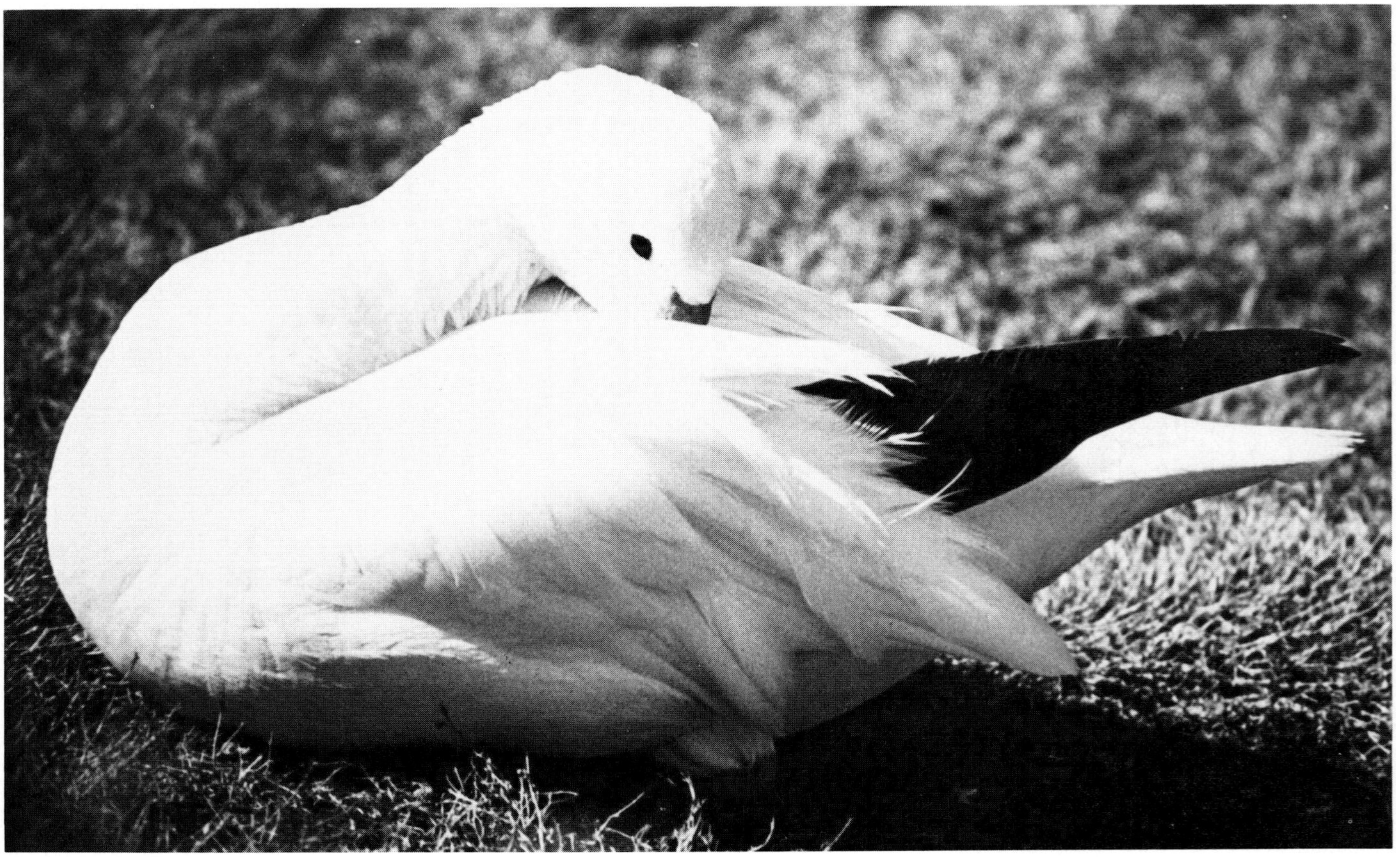

CHAPTER 40

Barnacle Goose

Branta leucopsis
(Color Photos-Page 99)

Barnacle geese, although natives of Europe, are fairly frequent visitors to eastern North America. They breed along the northeastern coast of Greenland and on the Spitsbergen Islands north of Norway. Their wintering range includes most of the extreme northwestern part of Europe, but on occasion they are seen inland as far south as Switzerland and Austria. Barnacle geese are very common winter residents of the west coast of Scotland and depart this area in large numbers for their breeding grounds.

When arriving at their nesting areas, most mated pairs select nesting sites high up on ledges of precipitous cliffs and, in some cases, atop pinnacles of rock. Inasmuch as there is little or no feed or water at these nesting locations, the newly hatched goslings must somehow reach the valley floors in order to survive.

There has been conjecture as to whether the parents carry the young down or if the downy puffballs make the almost vertical descent, sometimes several hundred feet, by floating down, the speed of the fall being possibly lessened by strong air currents flowing up the face of the cliffs. According to Salomonsen (*The Birds of Greenland*), both means of making the descent have been witnessed. An adult male, and also female barnacle geese have been seen carrying goslings down, one at a time, in their bills. In another instance, a gosling was carried on the back of one of the parents. They have also been observed floating down unaided from heights of 100 feet and landing safely in the water. Other families, where the terrain permitted, were seen walking down to a lake. After spending one to two weeks on the inland ponds and lakes, the young are led to the coast where they are joined by numbers of other families.

Although barnacle geese somewhat resemble brant, feed on tidal mud flats and in the shallow, offshore waters on occasion, and are seldom found far from the coast, they are as much land geese as brant are sea geese. Their favorite food is the short, sweet grass found in the coastal areas fed by fresh water.

The breeding grounds of the barnacle goose in northeastern Greenland is fairly close, or may even possibly overlap, the breeding grounds of the Atlantic, or American, brant. It is possible a few barnacle geese may somehow get separated from their own kind and migrate to the eastern seaboard of North America with the brant. Another possibility, of course, is that these occasional visitors are carried inadvertently far south and west of their normal migration routes by strong winds during violent storms.

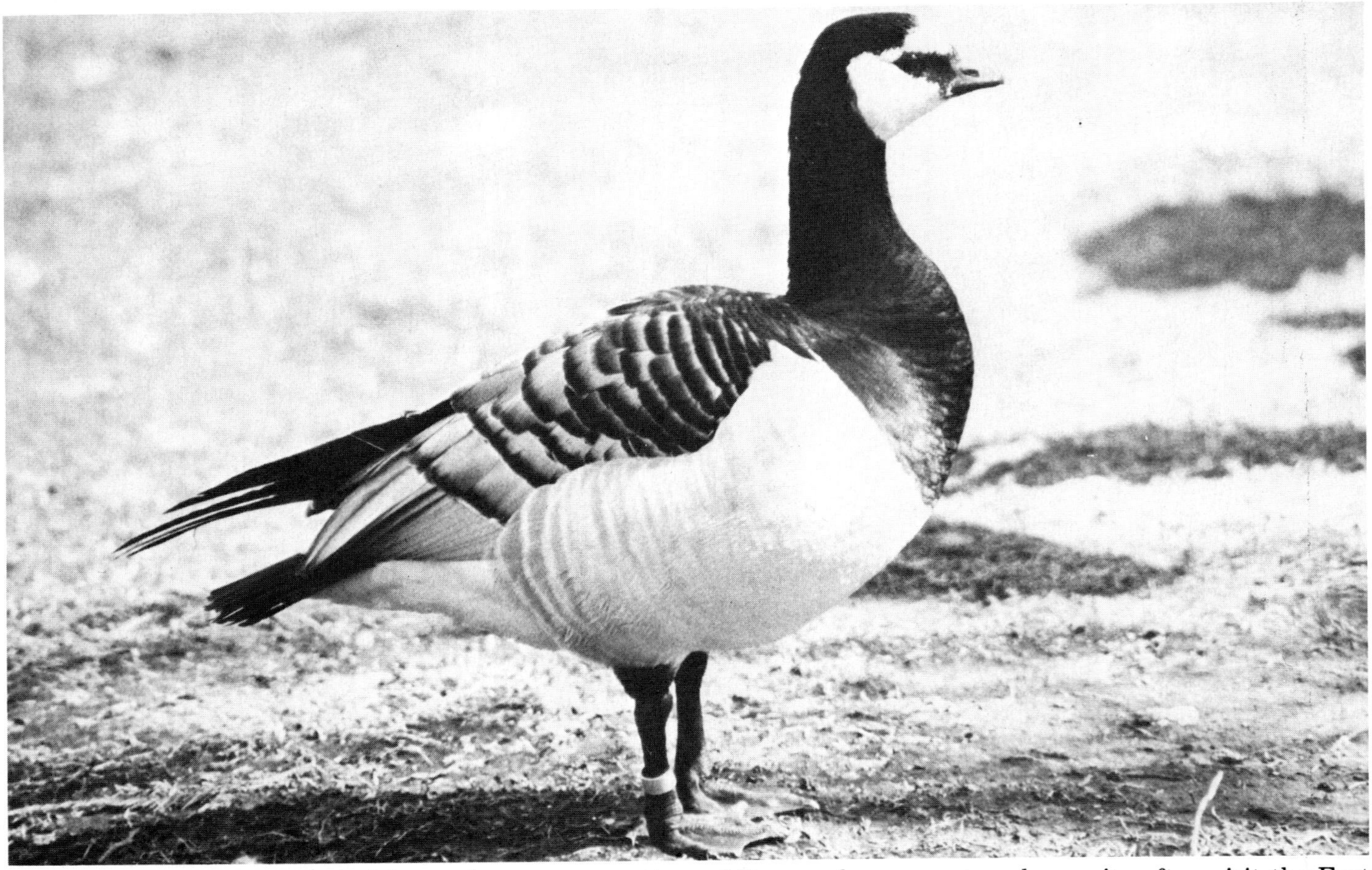

40-1 The distinctively marked barnacle geese are natives of Europe; however, stragglers quite often visit the East Coast.

40-2 Barnacle goose raises one foot prior to tucking it under his side feathers.

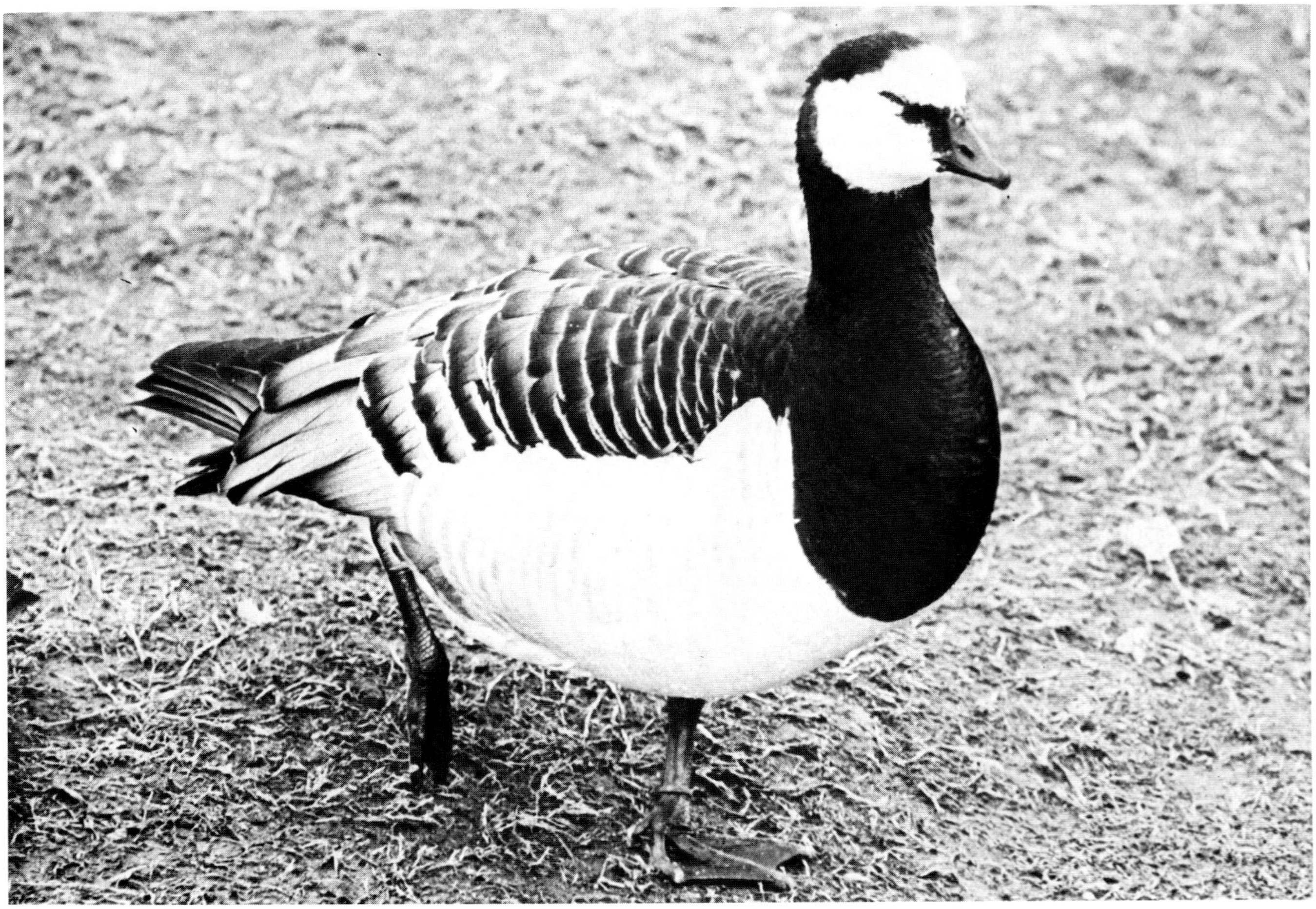

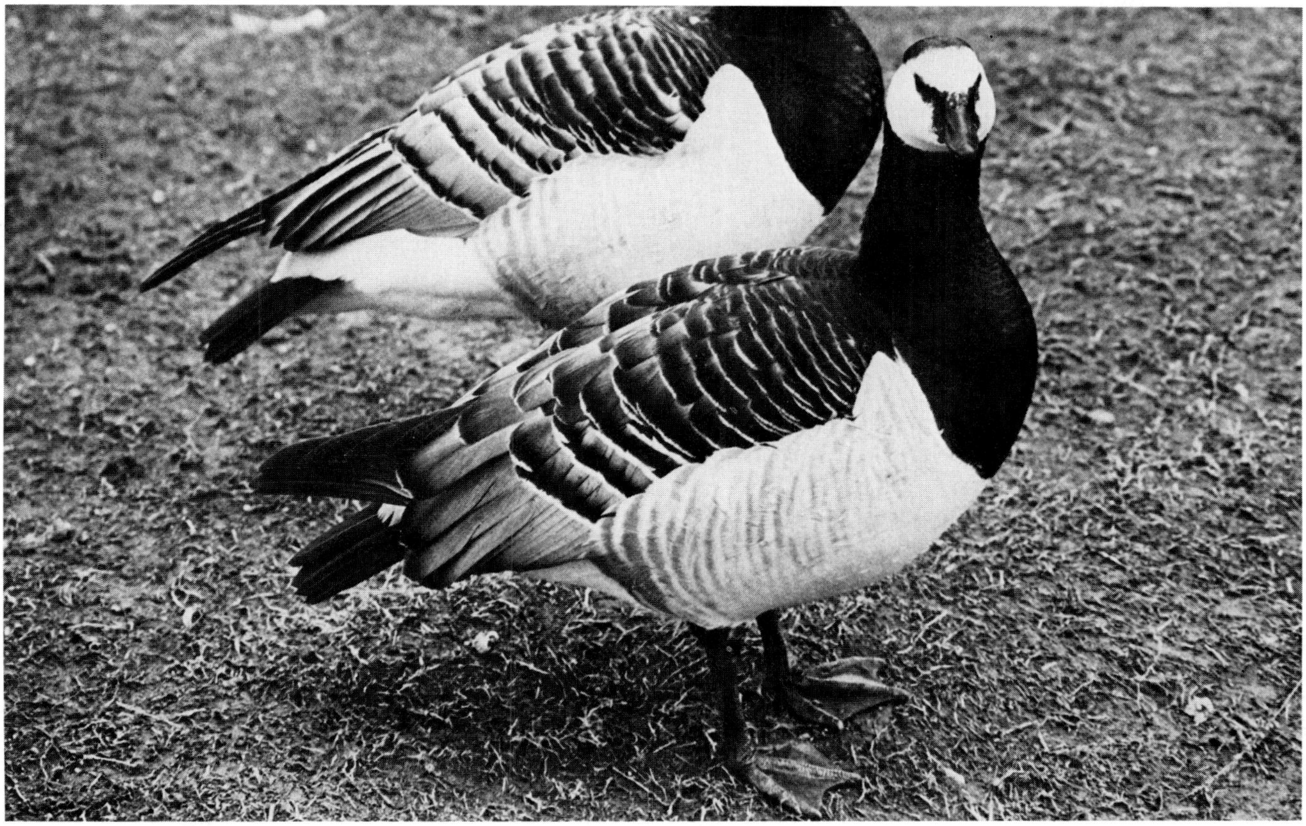

40-3

Profile studies of barnacle geese. They are small, a little larger than our brant.

40-4

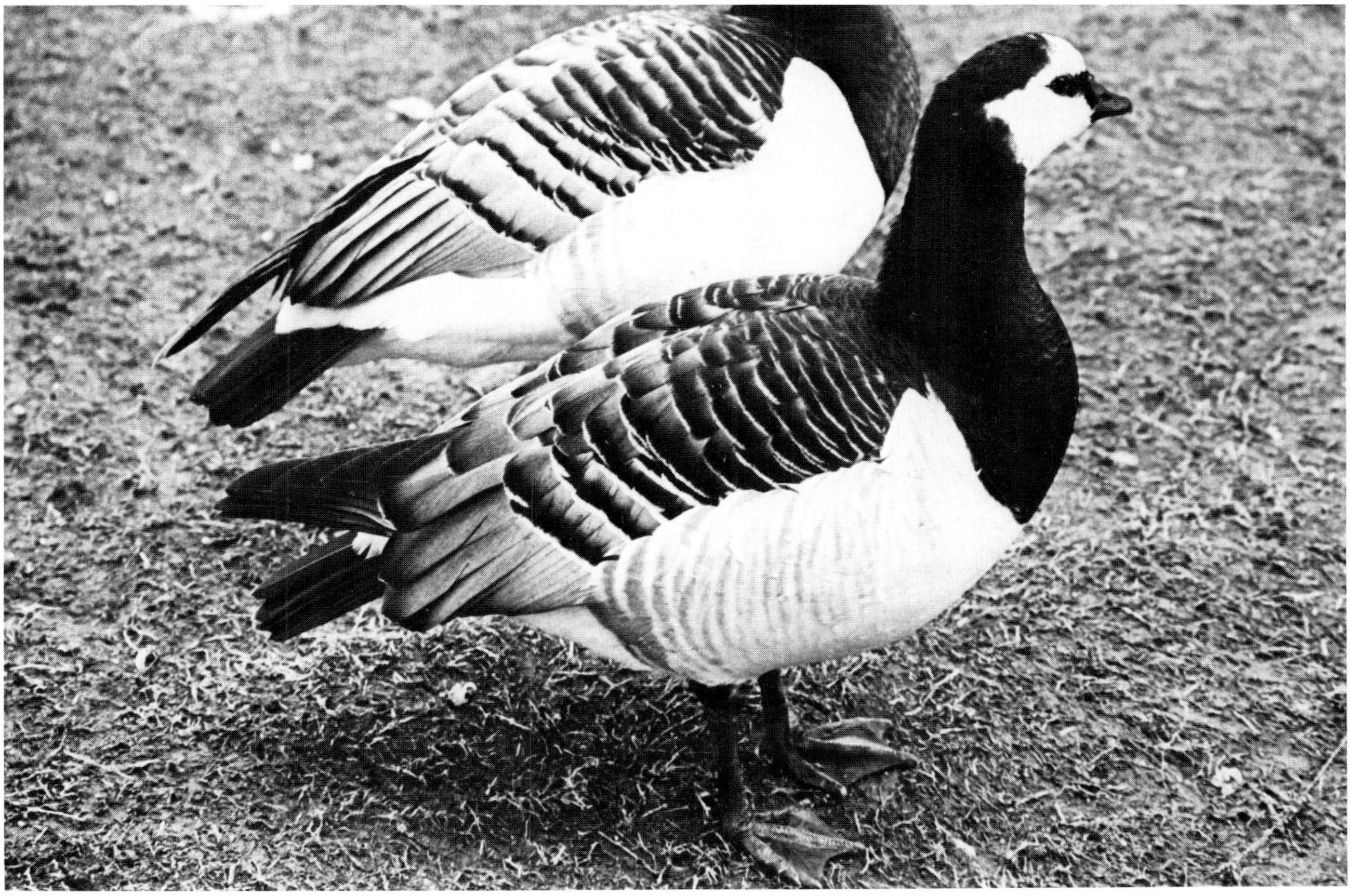

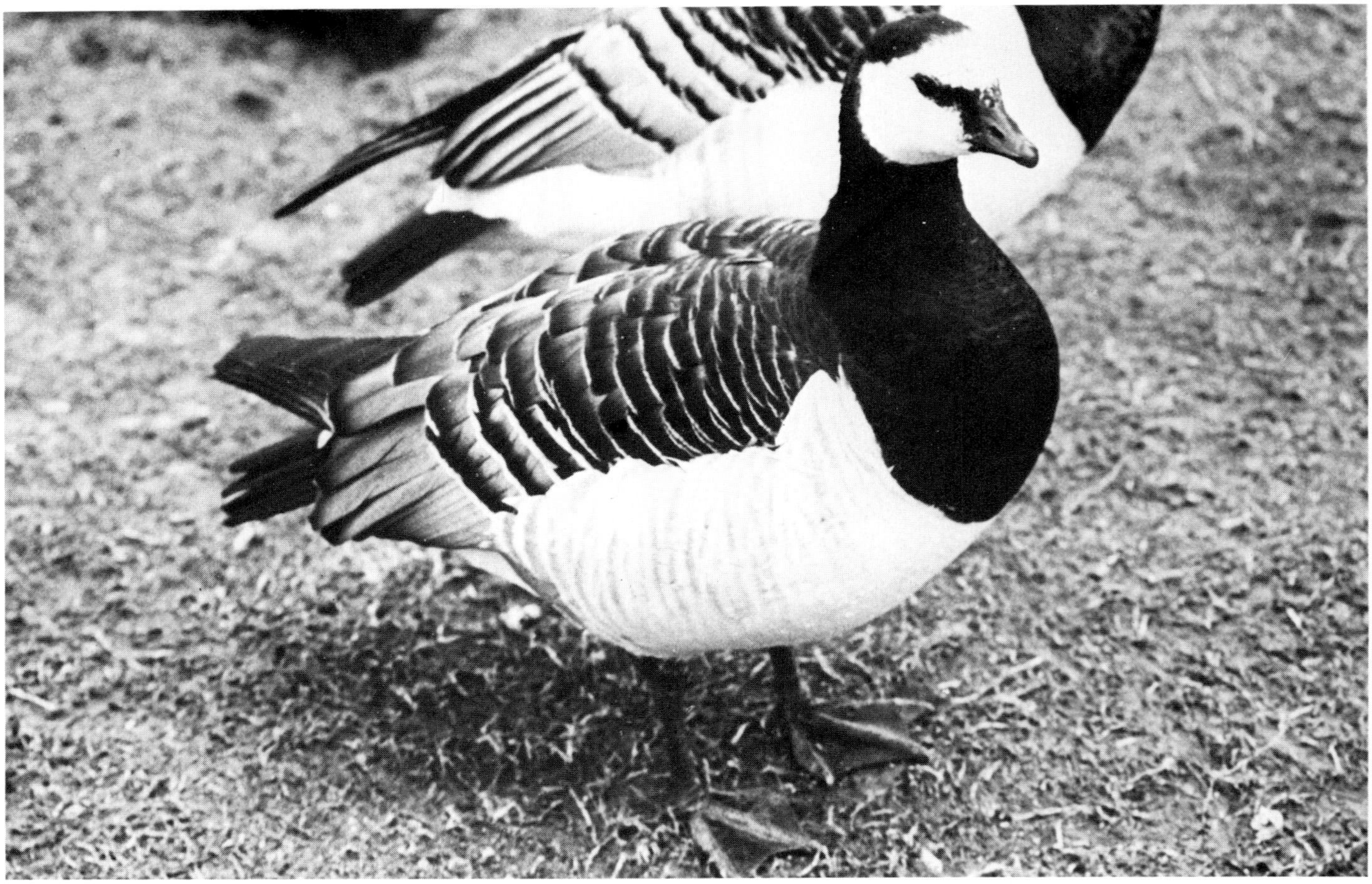

40-5 Barnacle goose. Although they feed on tidal flats, they are as much land geese as brant are sea geese.

40-6 Front and rear views of the barnacle goose. 40-7

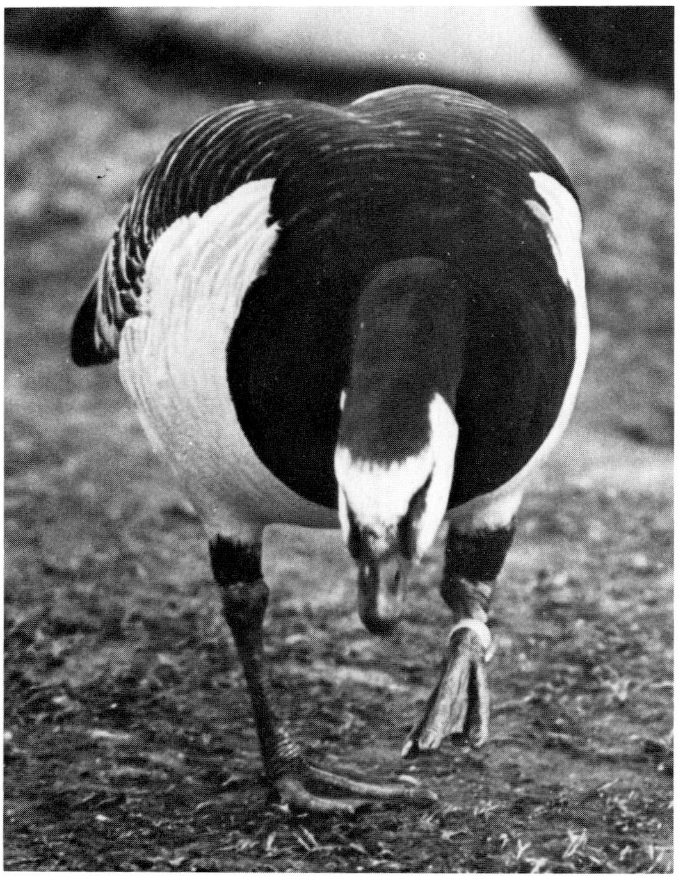

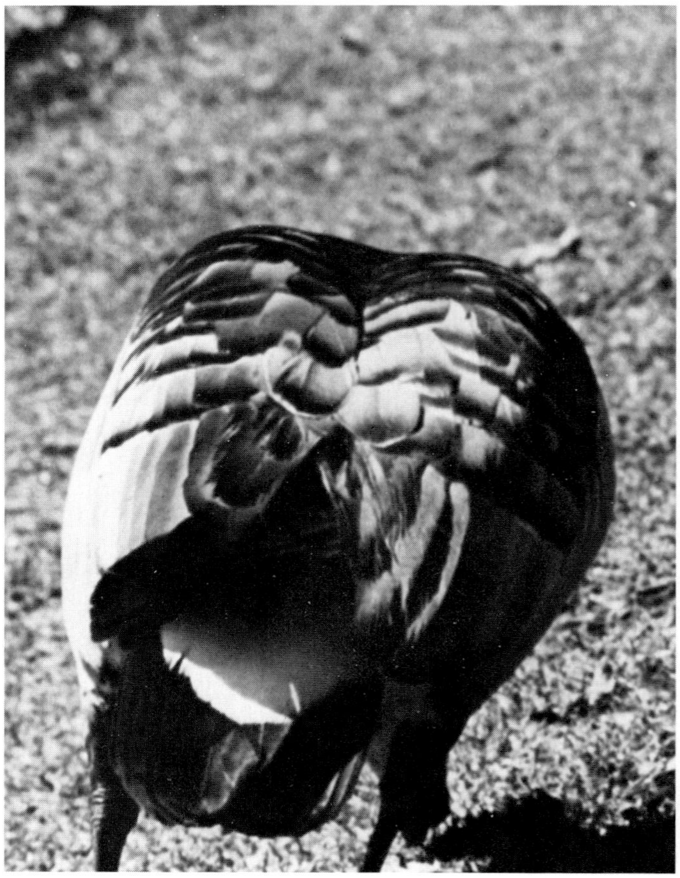

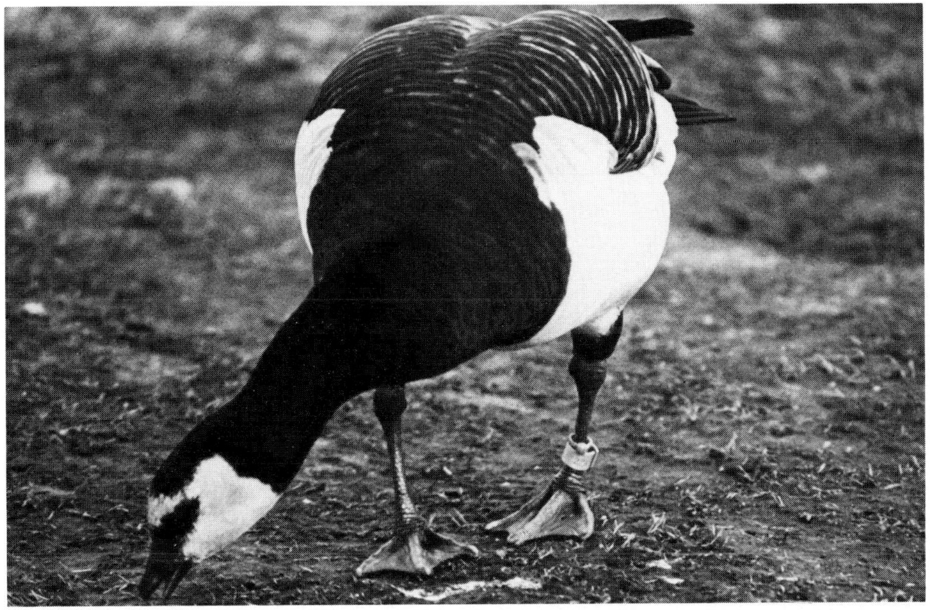

40-8

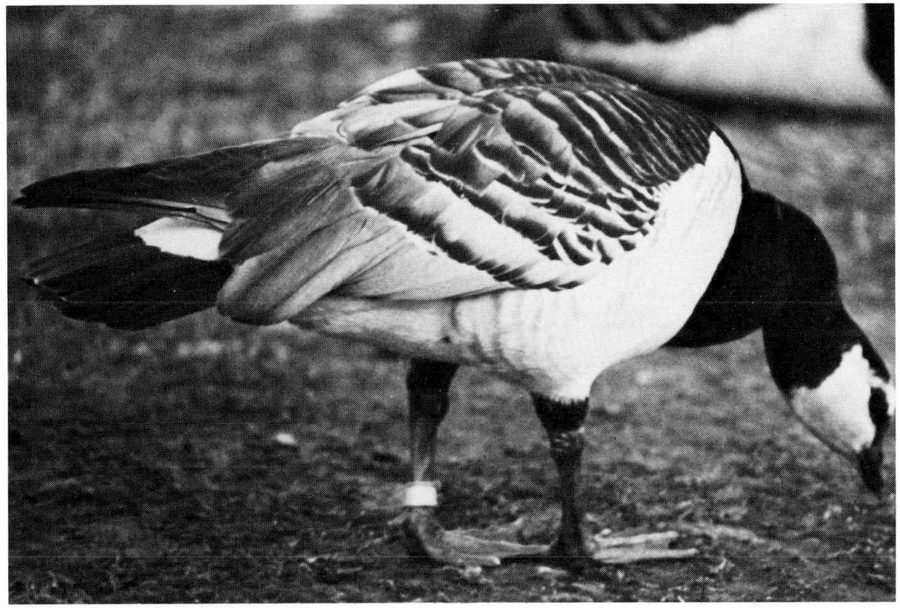

40-9

Barnacle geese in the feeding position photographed from different angles.

40-10

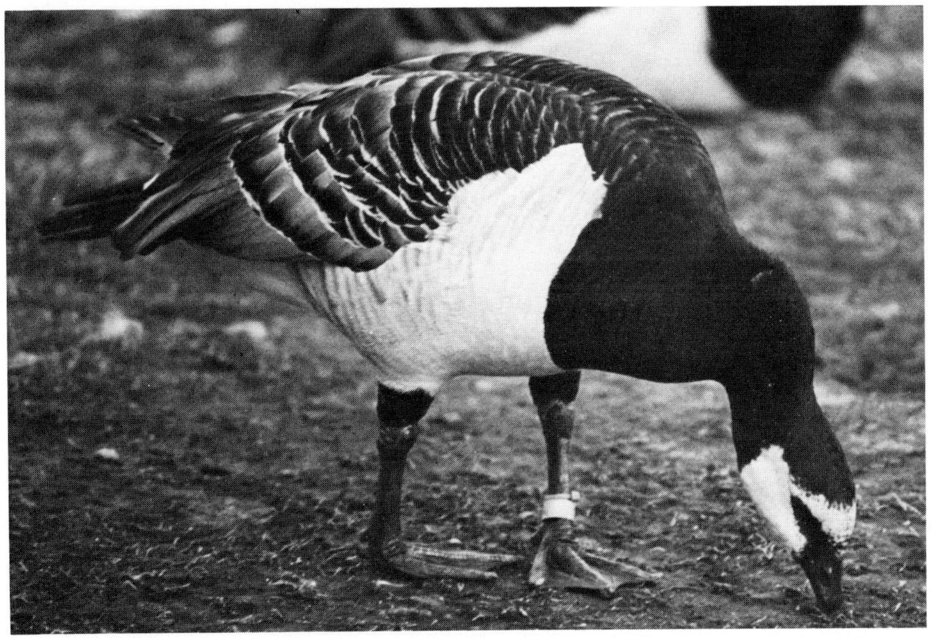

40-11

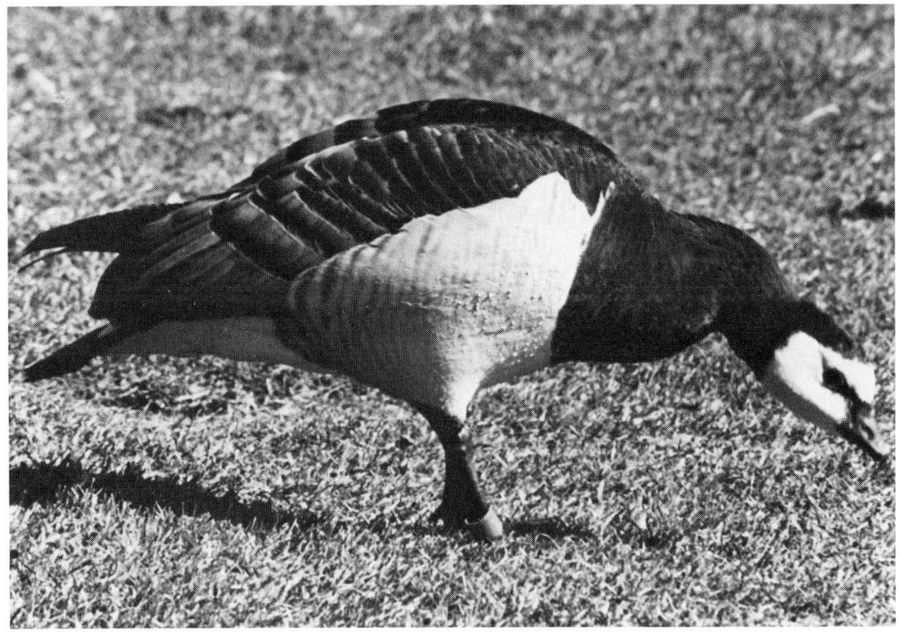

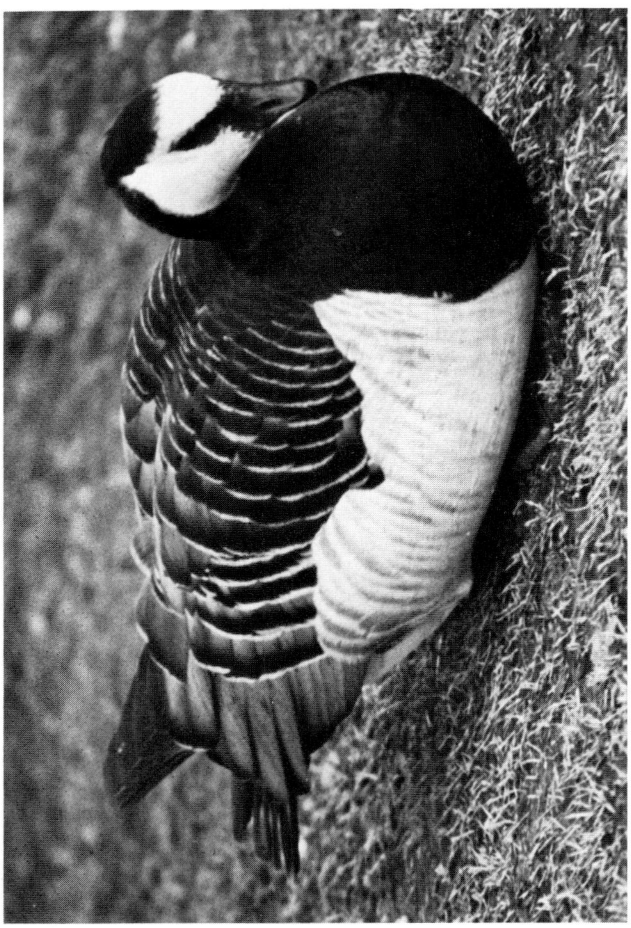

40-12

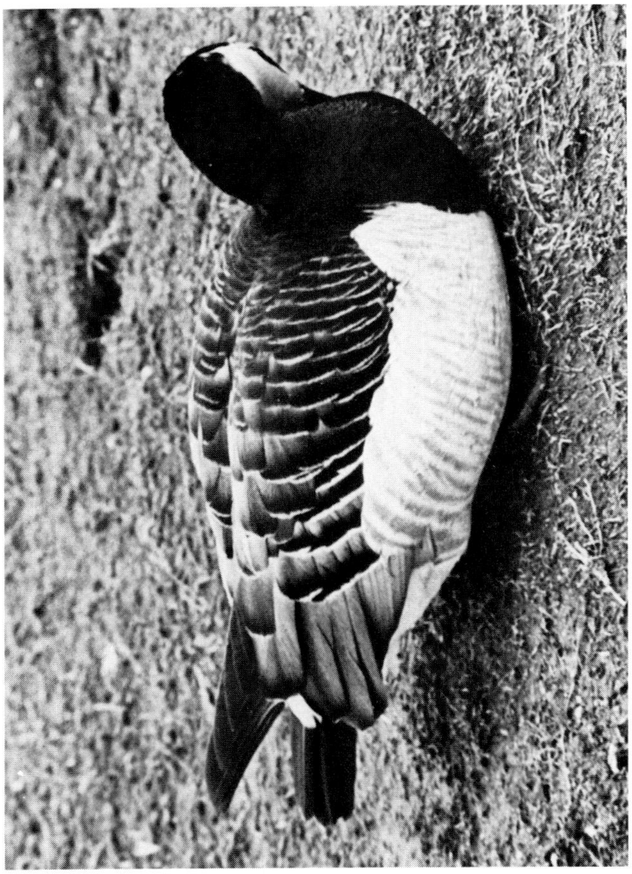

40-13

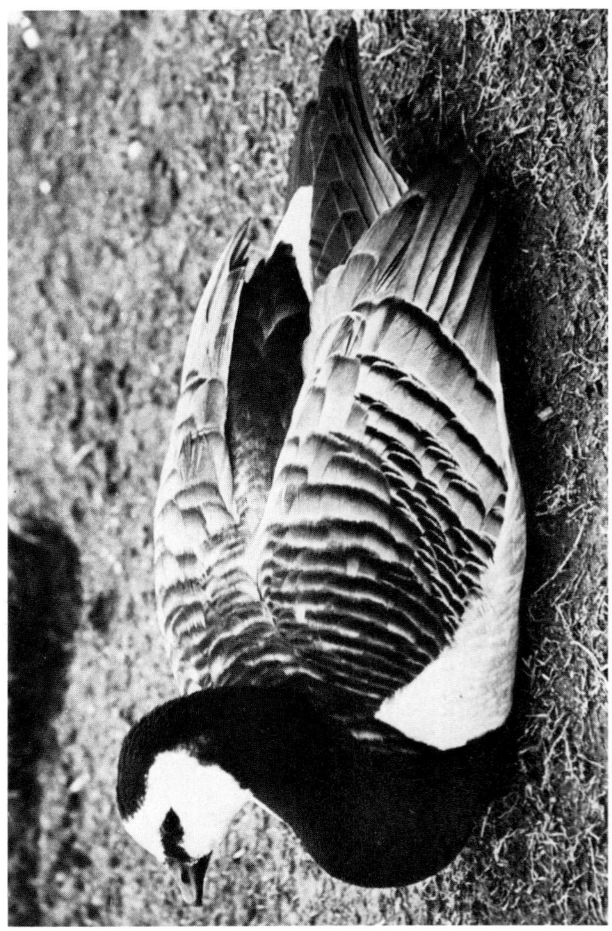

40-14

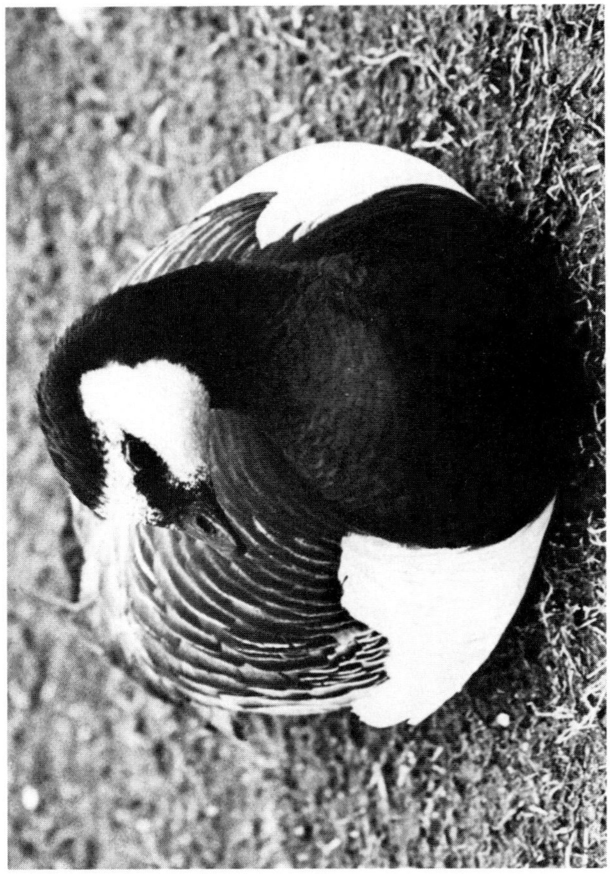

40-15

Little barnacle goose relaxes on the ground. Four studies.

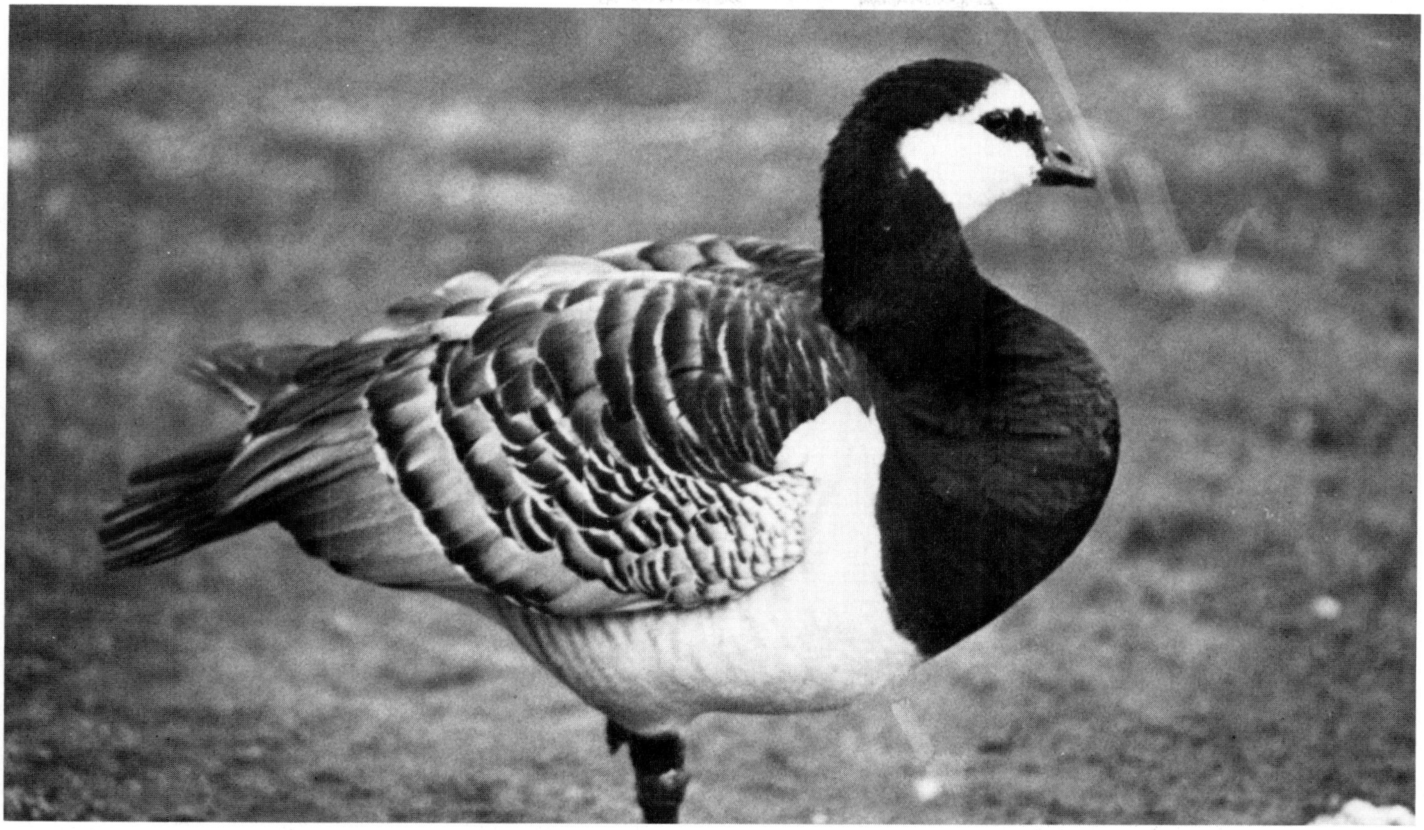

40-16

Profile and front views of a barnacle goose resting on one leg.

40-17

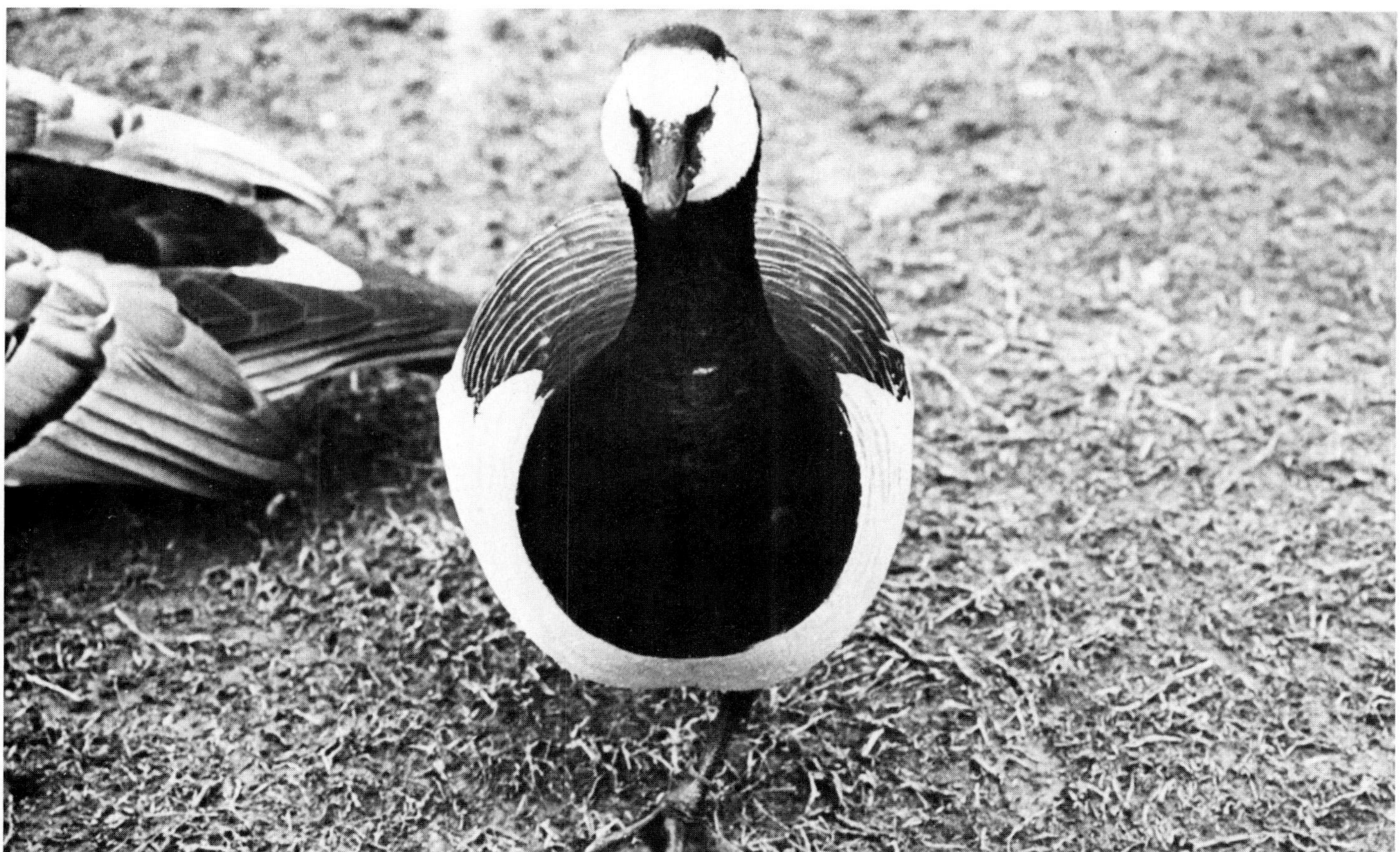

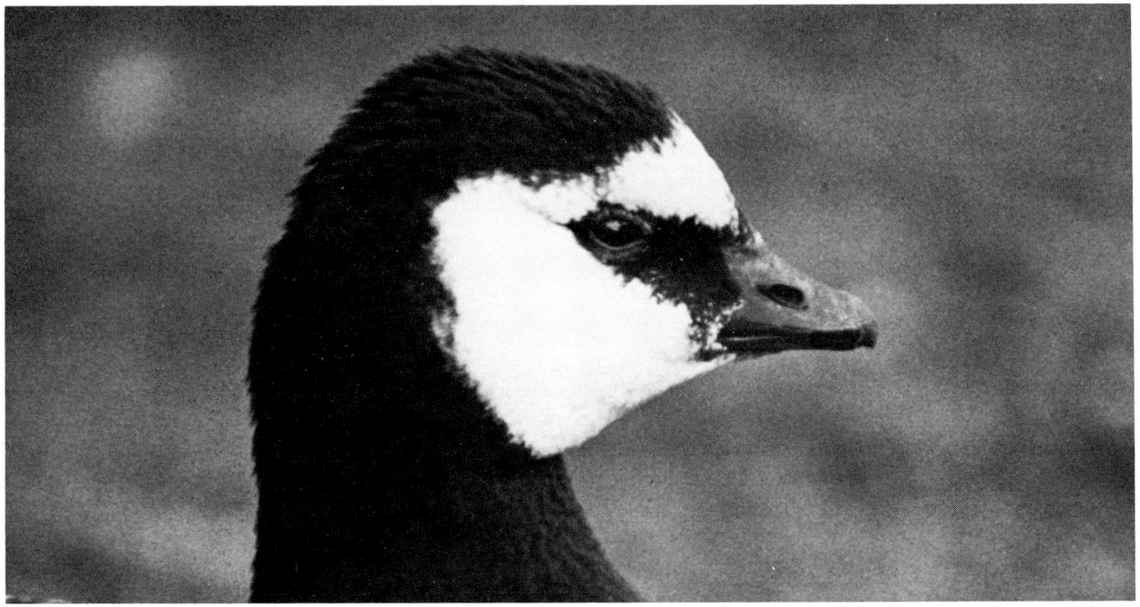
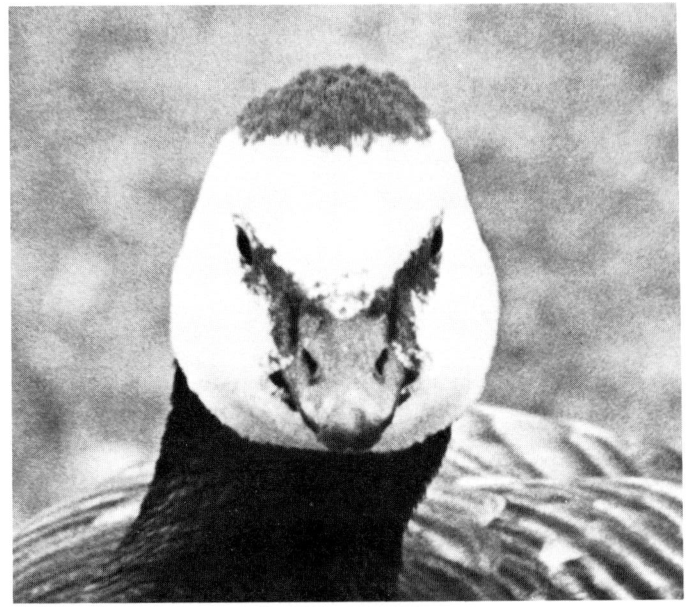

40-18 Profile and front views of the barnacle goose's head and bill. 40-19

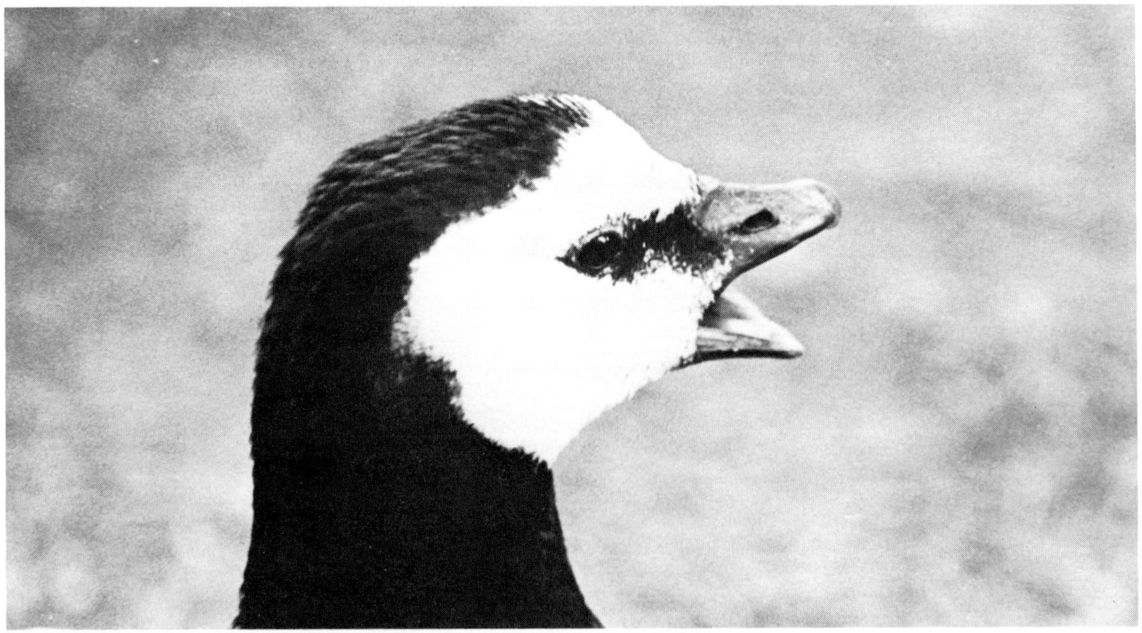

40-20 Little barnacle goose in a talking mood.

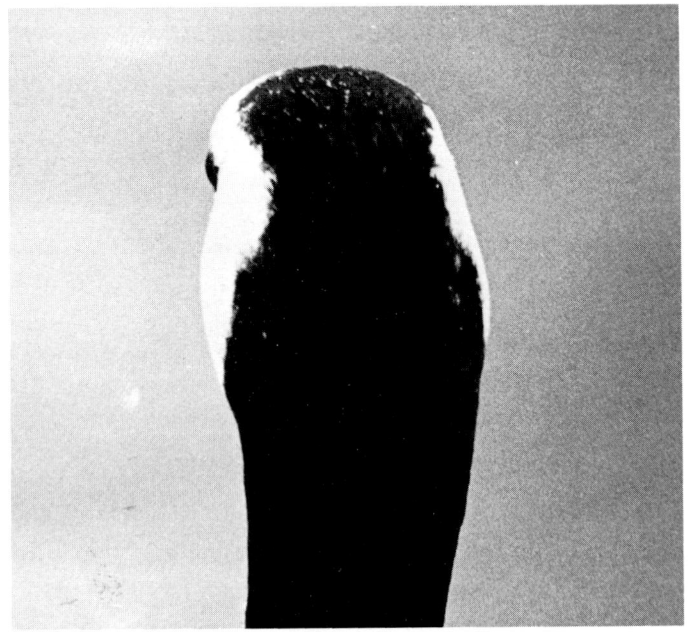

40-21 Rear view shows his smooth head and neck lines.

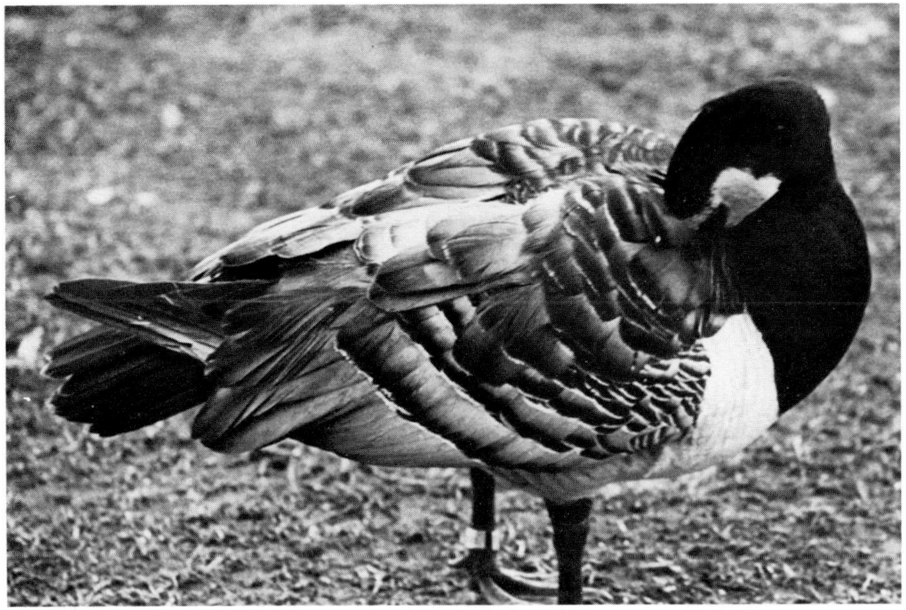

40-22

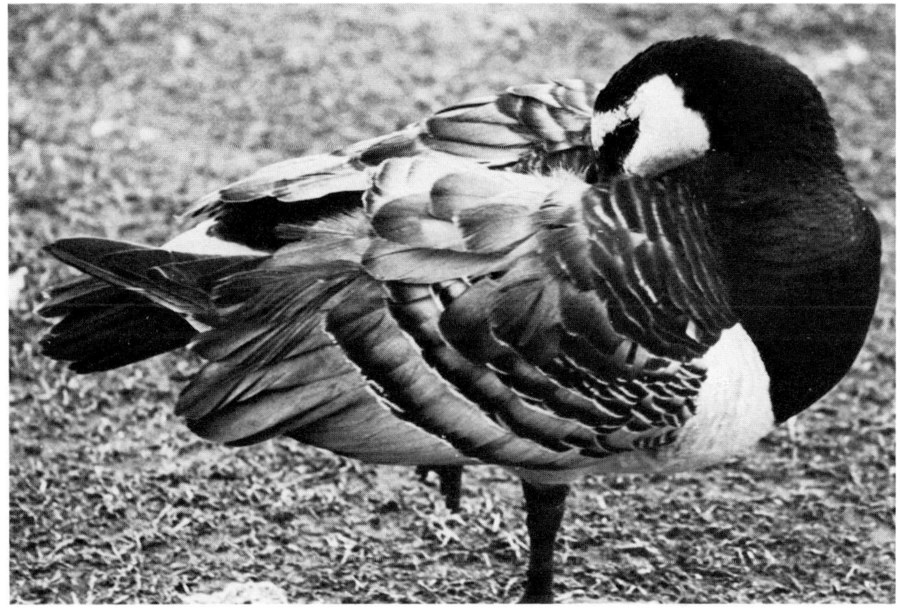

40-23

Four studies of a barnacle goose industriously preening his feathers.

40-24

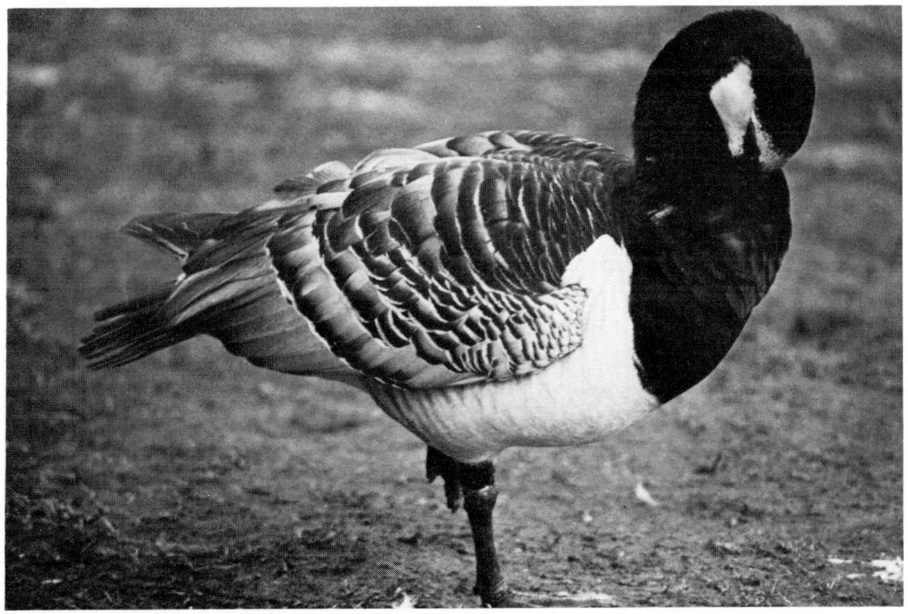

40-25

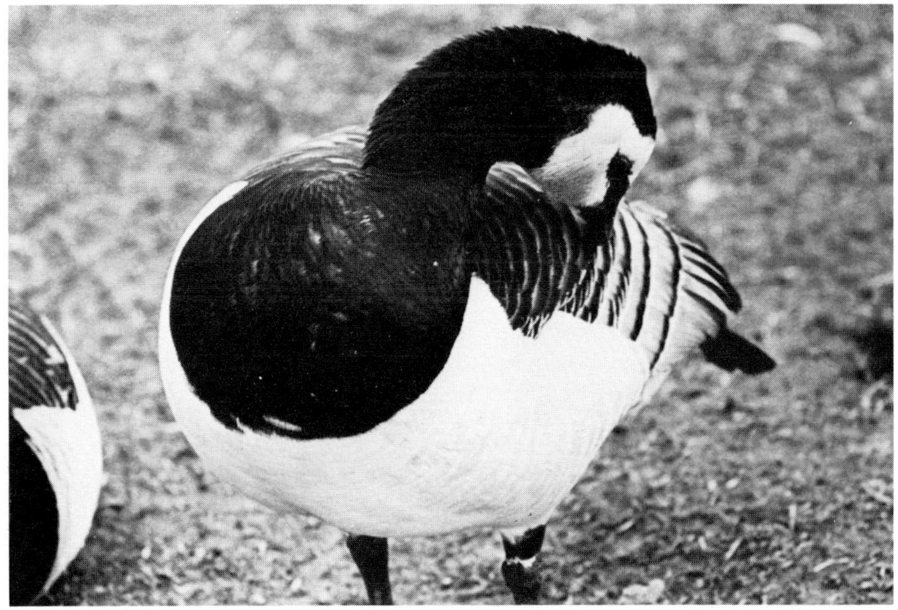

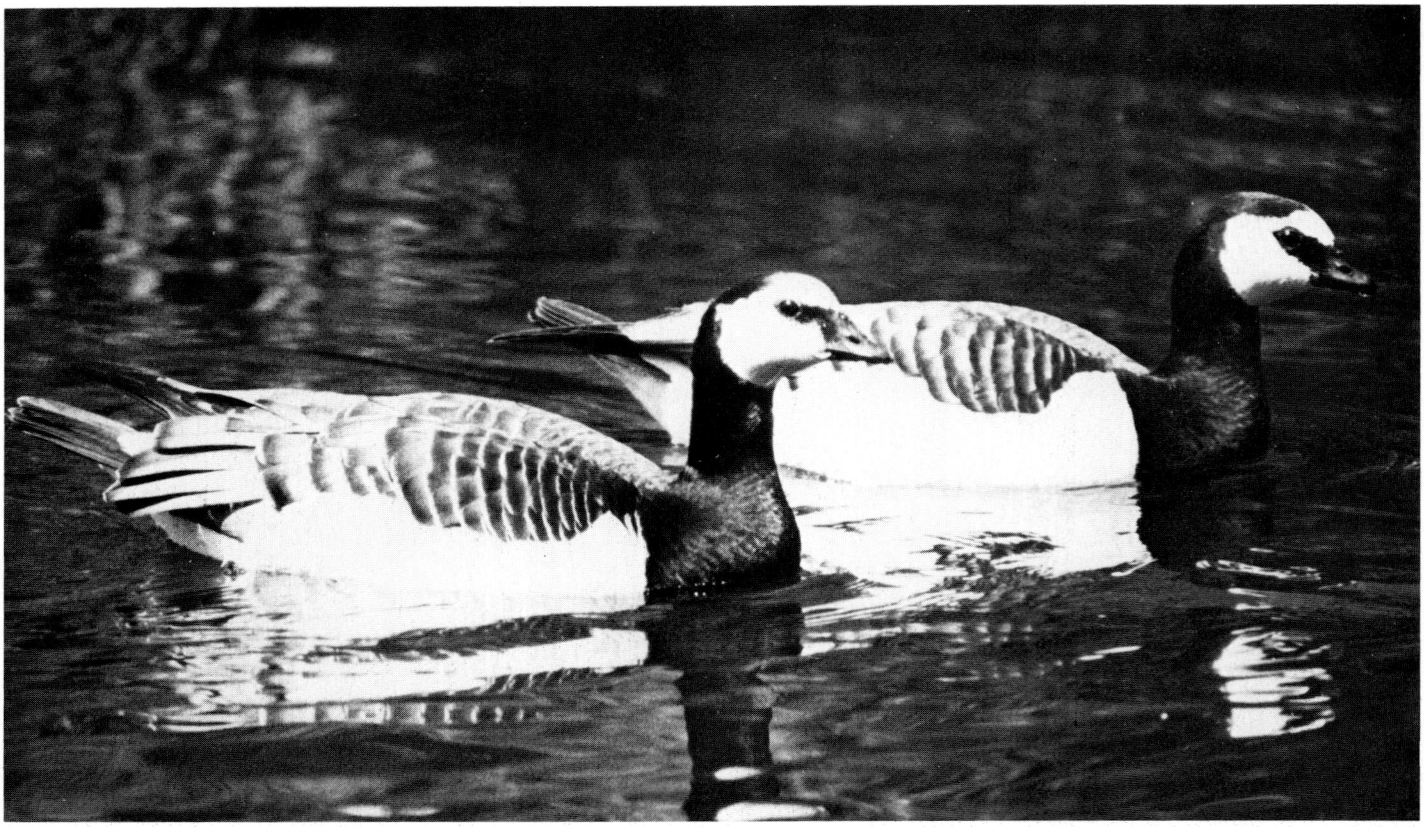

40-26

Pair of barnacle geese paddle slowly around.

40-27

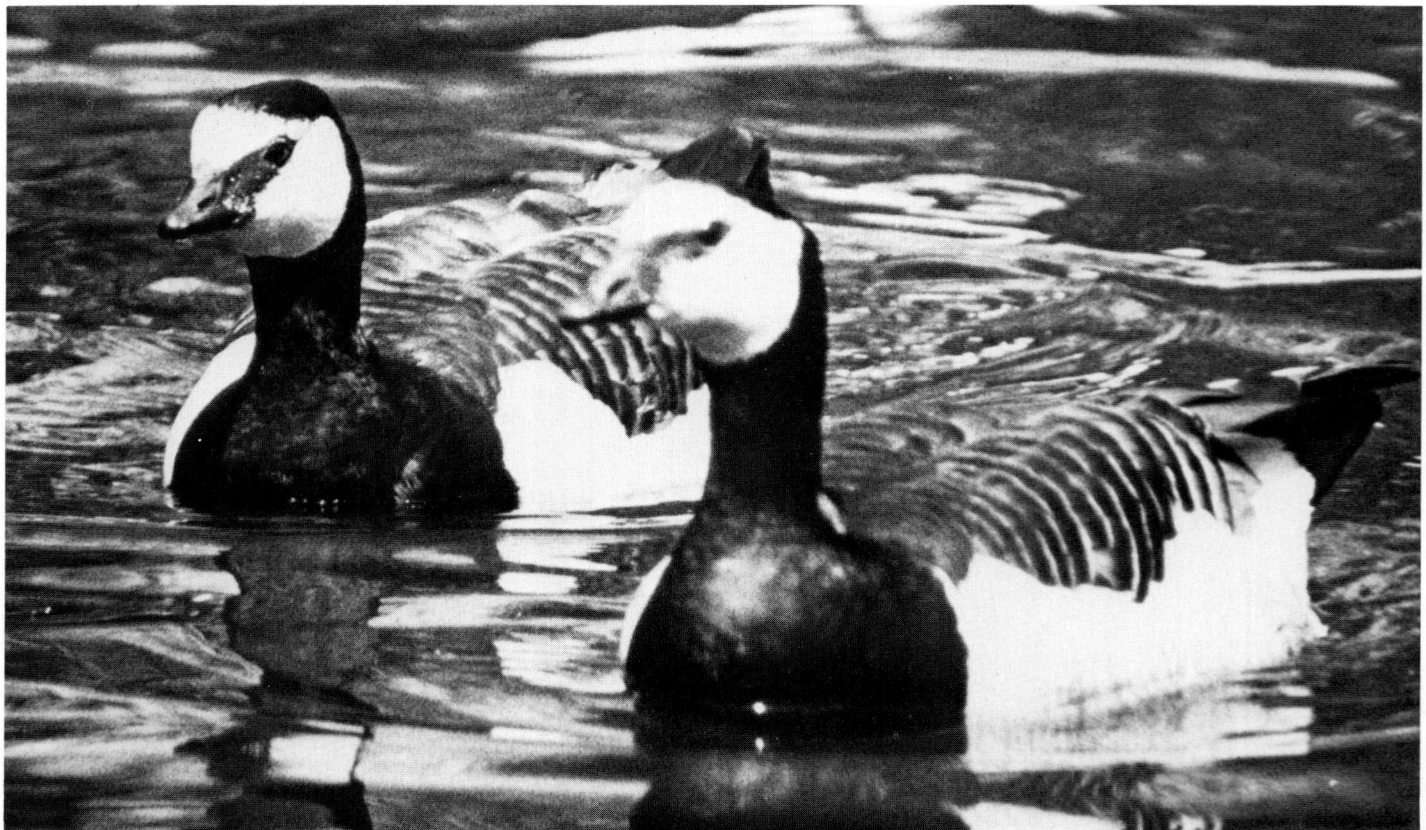

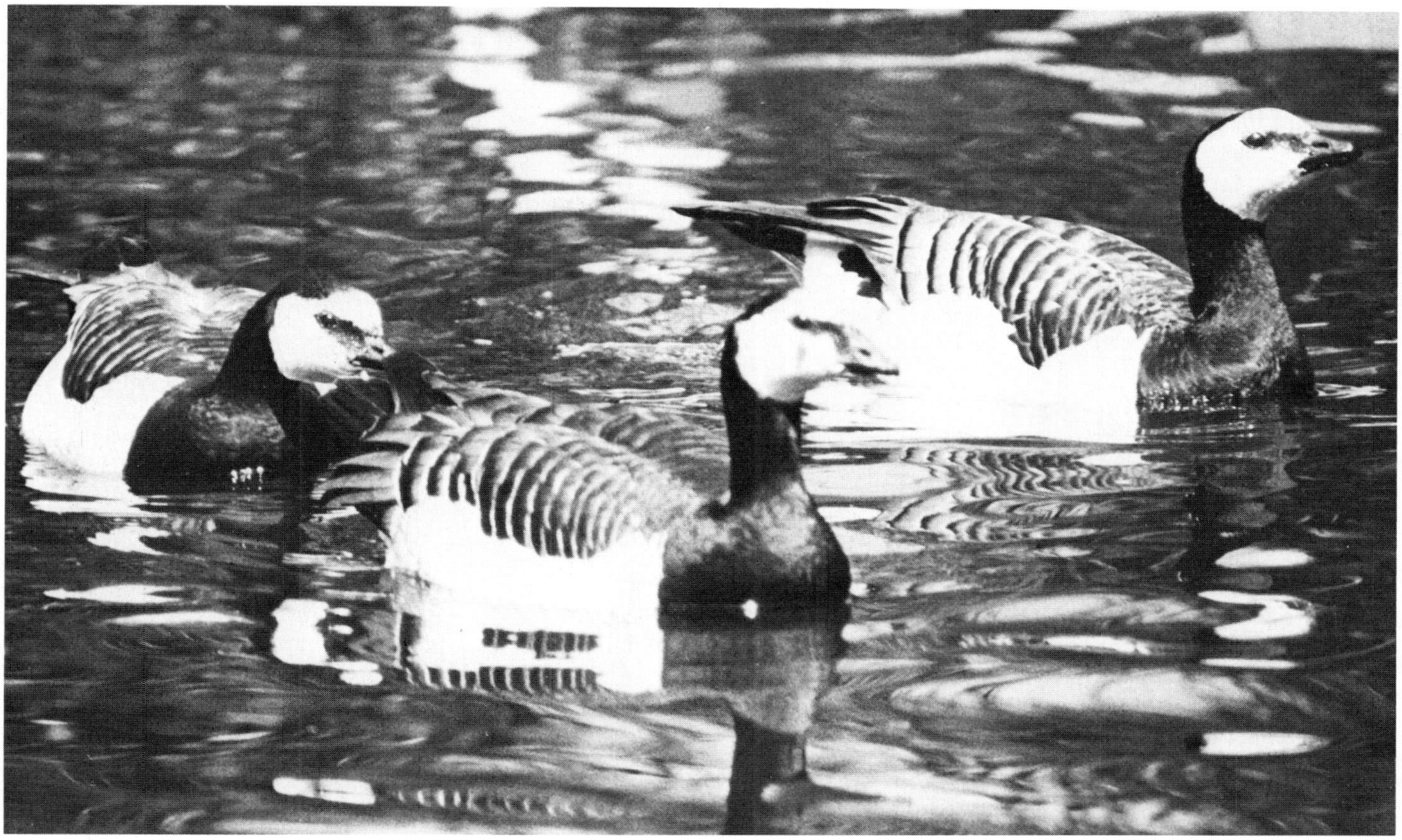

40-28 Three barnacle geese. Notice difference head positions.

40-29 Nice profile of a floating barnacle goose.

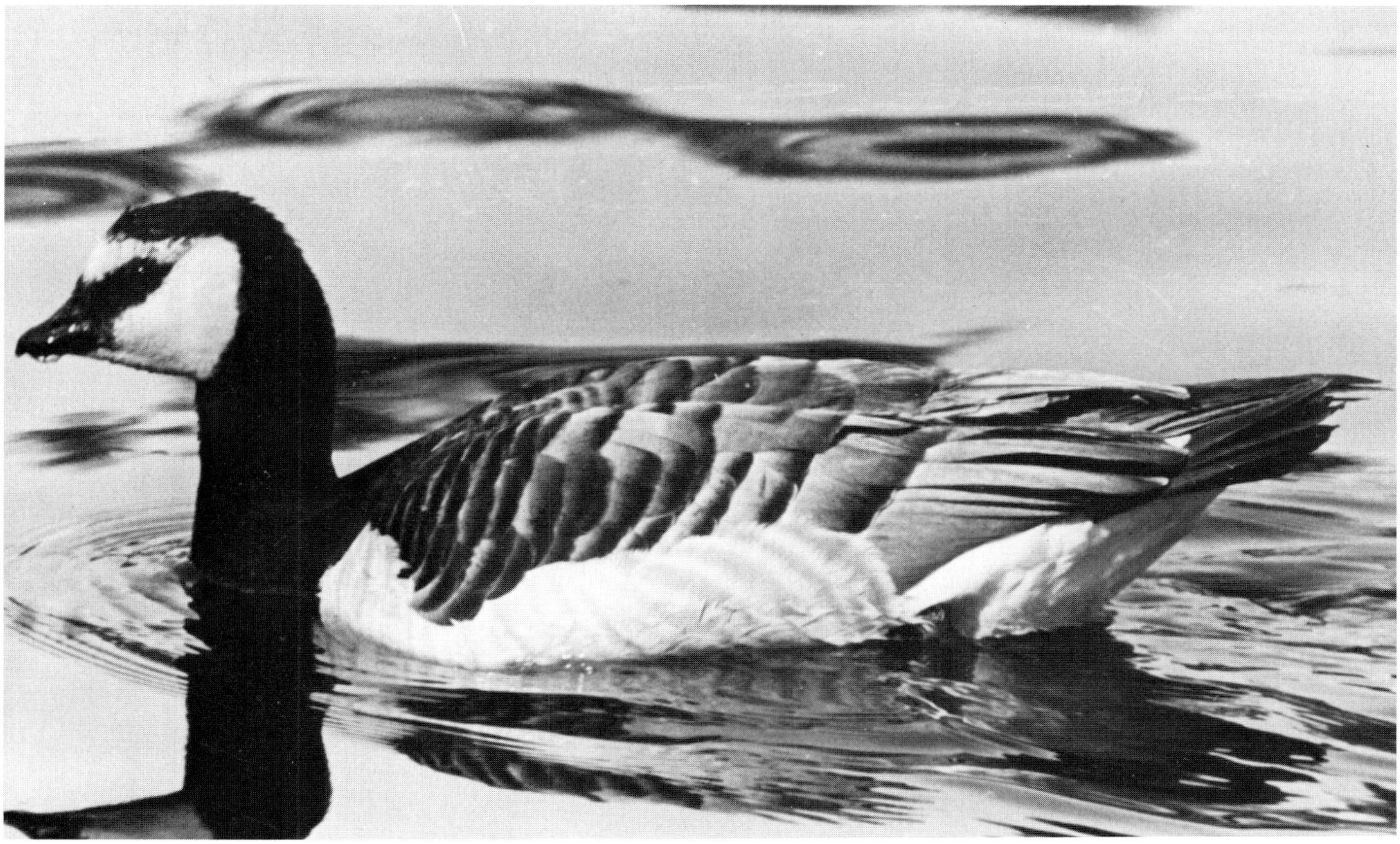

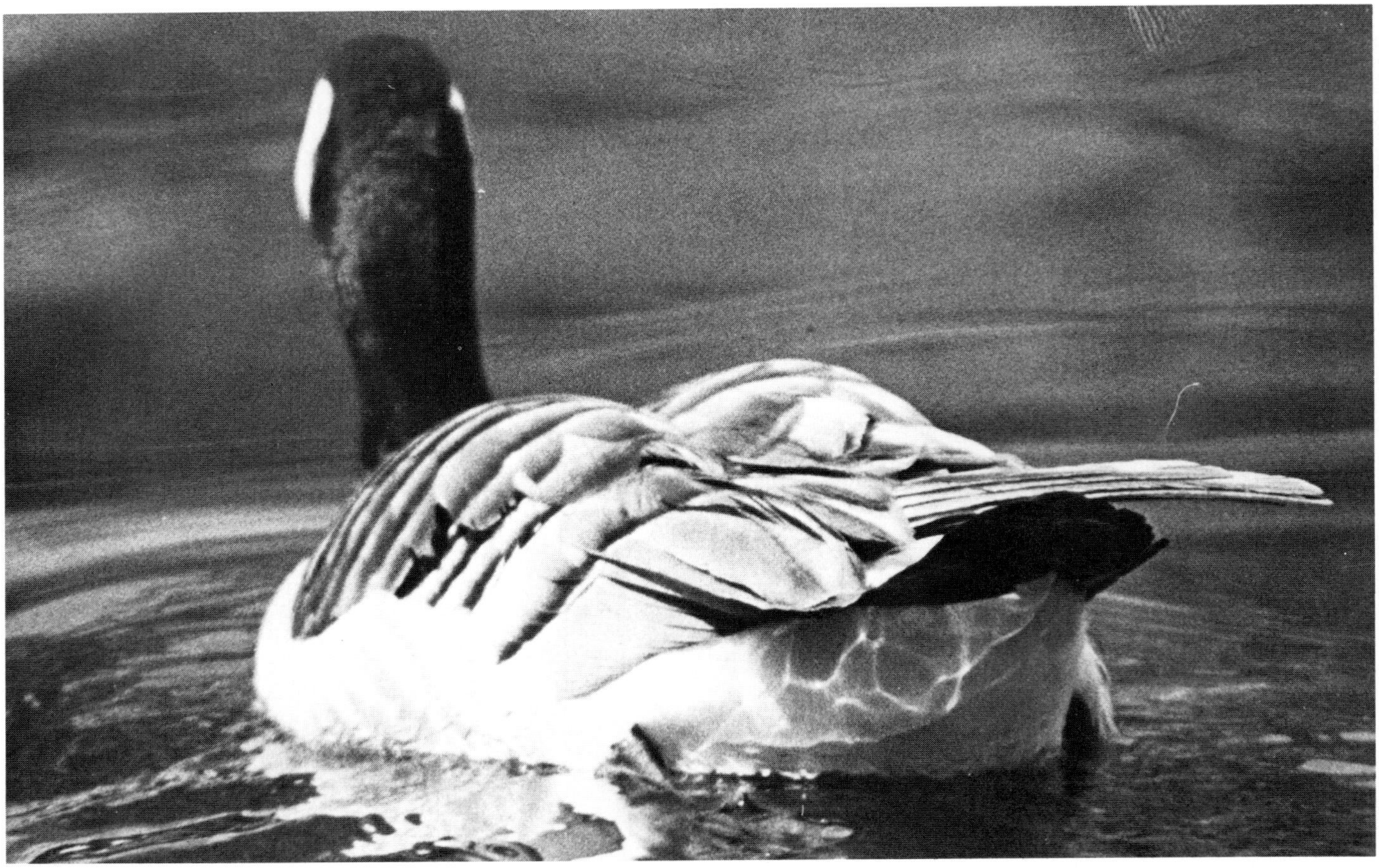

40-30

Two additional studies of floating barnacle geese.

40-31

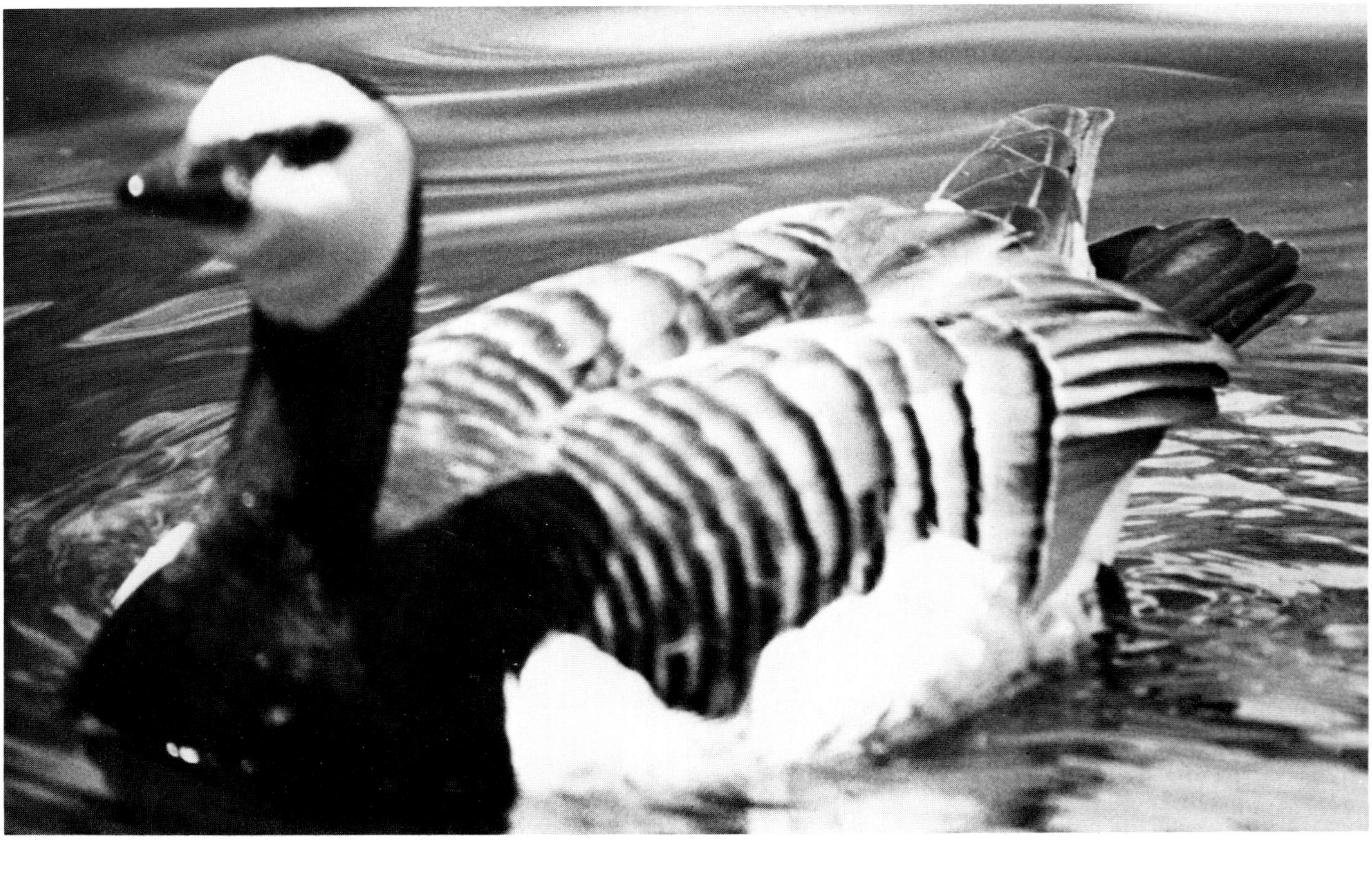

CHAPTER 41

Red-Breasted Goose

Branta ruficollis
(Color Photos-Page 100)

Unfortunately for us, this most colorful and lovely little goose is an extremely rare visitor to western North America. However, it is now being more commonly sought after and propagated by aviculturalists and can be seen quite often in parks, zoos, and in private collections. The red-breasted goose, sometimes called the Siberian goose, is the most beautiful of all the geese, which is the reason it has been included in these pictorial studies of North American waterfowl.

They breed in northern Siberia, generally between the Ob and the Katanga Rivers and in their deltas. Their wintering grounds are around the southern shores of the Caspian and Aral Seas, where they feed on crops and grasses like other geese, but move back to the salt water at night and spend their resting period on sand bars or islands. Red-breasted geese are often seen in the company of lesser white-fronted geese. Northward migration starts in February and March and they reach their breeding grounds in early June. These little geese have somewhat similar nesting habits to those of barnacle geese, preferring holes in cliffs and banks that are protected by brush or shrubs.

Redbreasts are graceful and dainty little birds—very nearly the size of cackling Canada geese. Their necks are probably about the same length as the cacklers, but because of manelike feathers on the hind neck and nape, they appear to be considerably thicker. Also like the cackler, their wing span is about twice their overall body length. Johnsgard (*Waterfowl*) lists the redbreasted's overall length as 21-22 inches. According to Delacour, his bill size and length of tarsi are about 15 per cent smaller than those of the cackler.

This little goose is exquisitely marked and colored—a beautiful study of contrasts. His bright, chestnut-red chest, neck front and sides, and cheeks are demarcated from his rich, black head, hind neck, upper body parts, sides, and breast with white stripes. The upper side feathers are heavily edged with white. His black tail is strikingly offset by snow white coverts, flanks, and belly. His large wings are of the same deep, shiny black with the greater and a few middle coverts edged, with white.

Delacour writes: "Their voice is high-pitched, pleasant and rather musical, if a little harsh, their calls consisting of a two-syllabled staccato 'kee-kwa,'' 'Kik-wit,' 'ti-che' and so forth, the second note a little broken. They hiss frequently and squeak constantly in an irritated way while feeding."

Red-breasted geese adapt extremely well to captivity—even those that are captured in the wild become tame in a short time. They are a lovely addition to any collection of waterfowl.

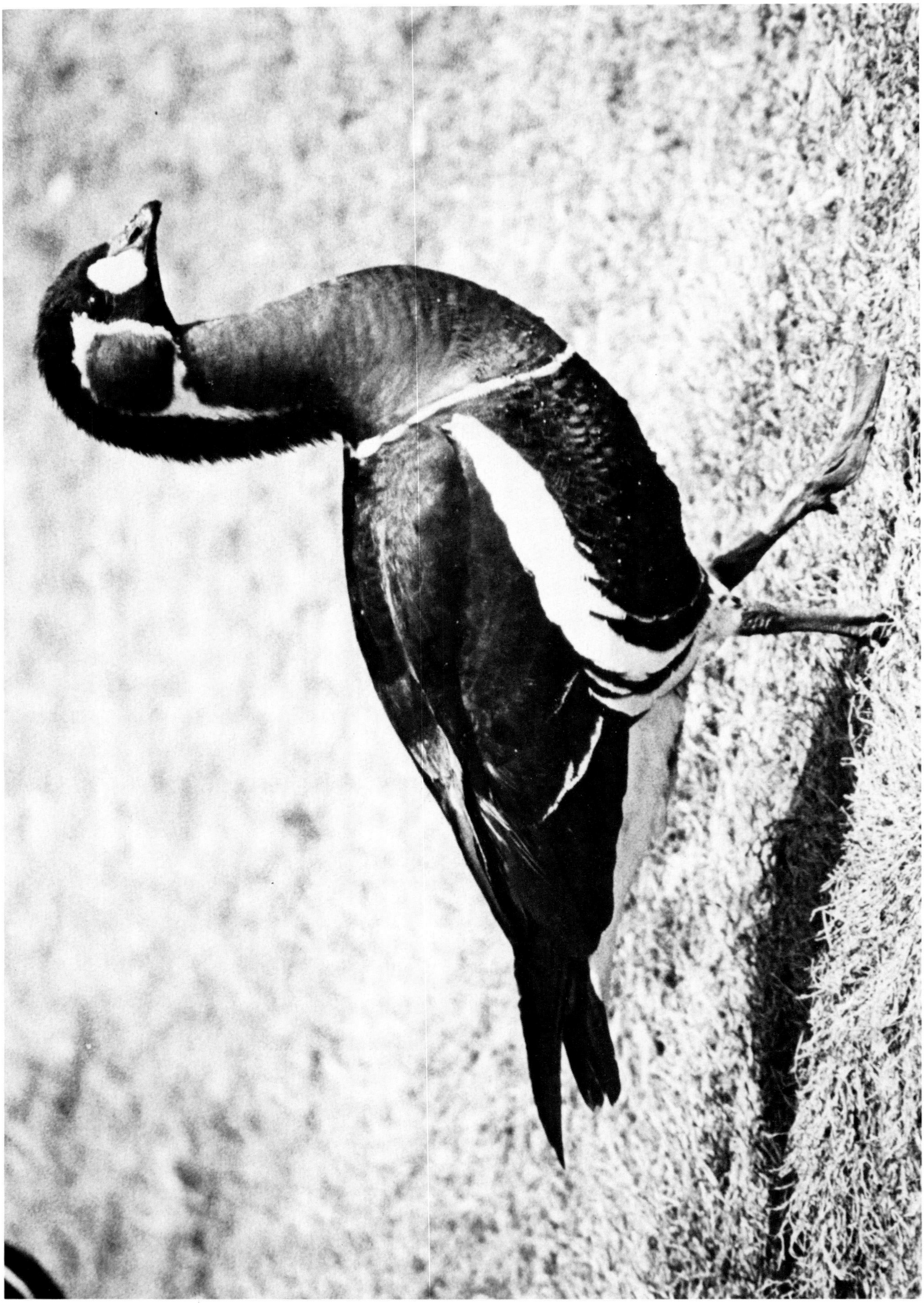

41-1 The extraordinarily marked and colored red-breasted goose in an alert, striding pose. He is the most beautiful of all the geese.

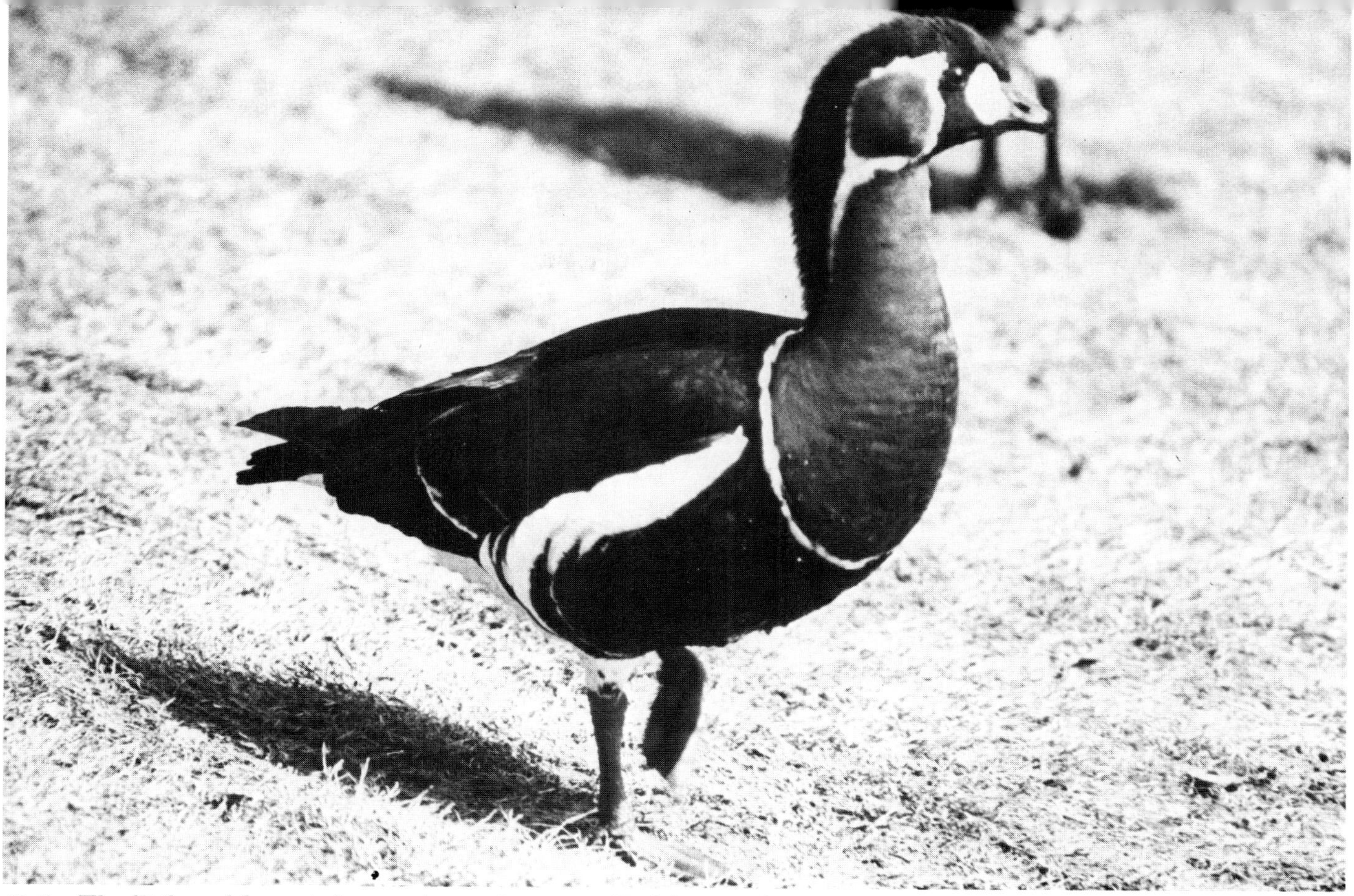

41-2 The little red-breasted goose in an alert pose. Red-breasted geese breed in western Siberia and are extremely rare visitors to this country.

41-3 Nice front view of the red-breasted goose.

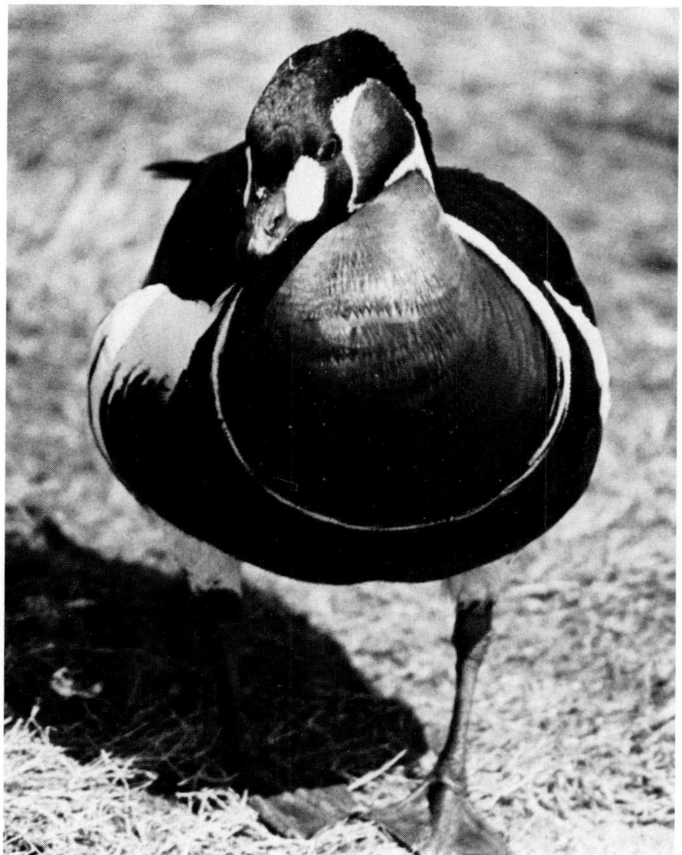

41-4 Alerted red-breasted goose strides away.

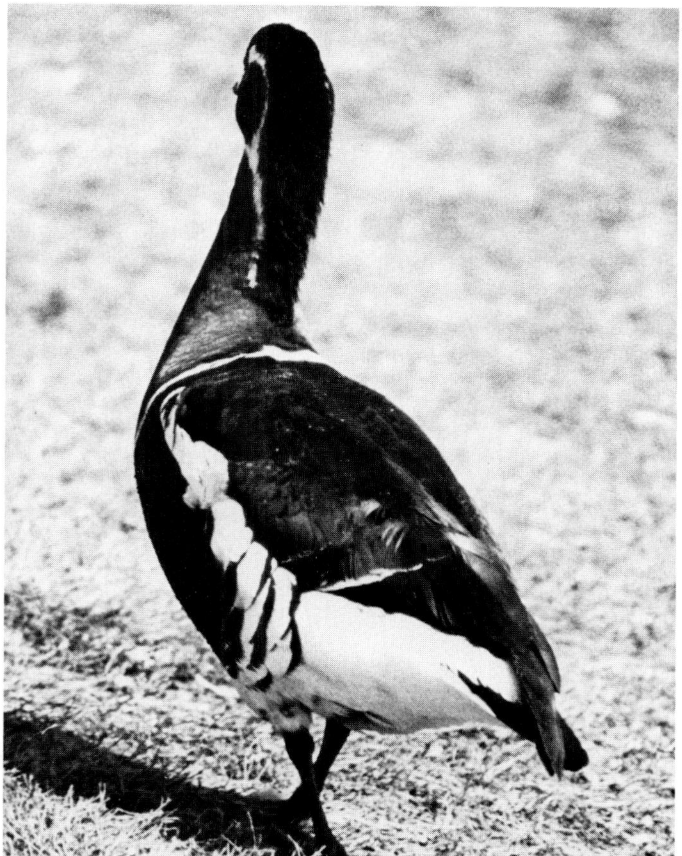

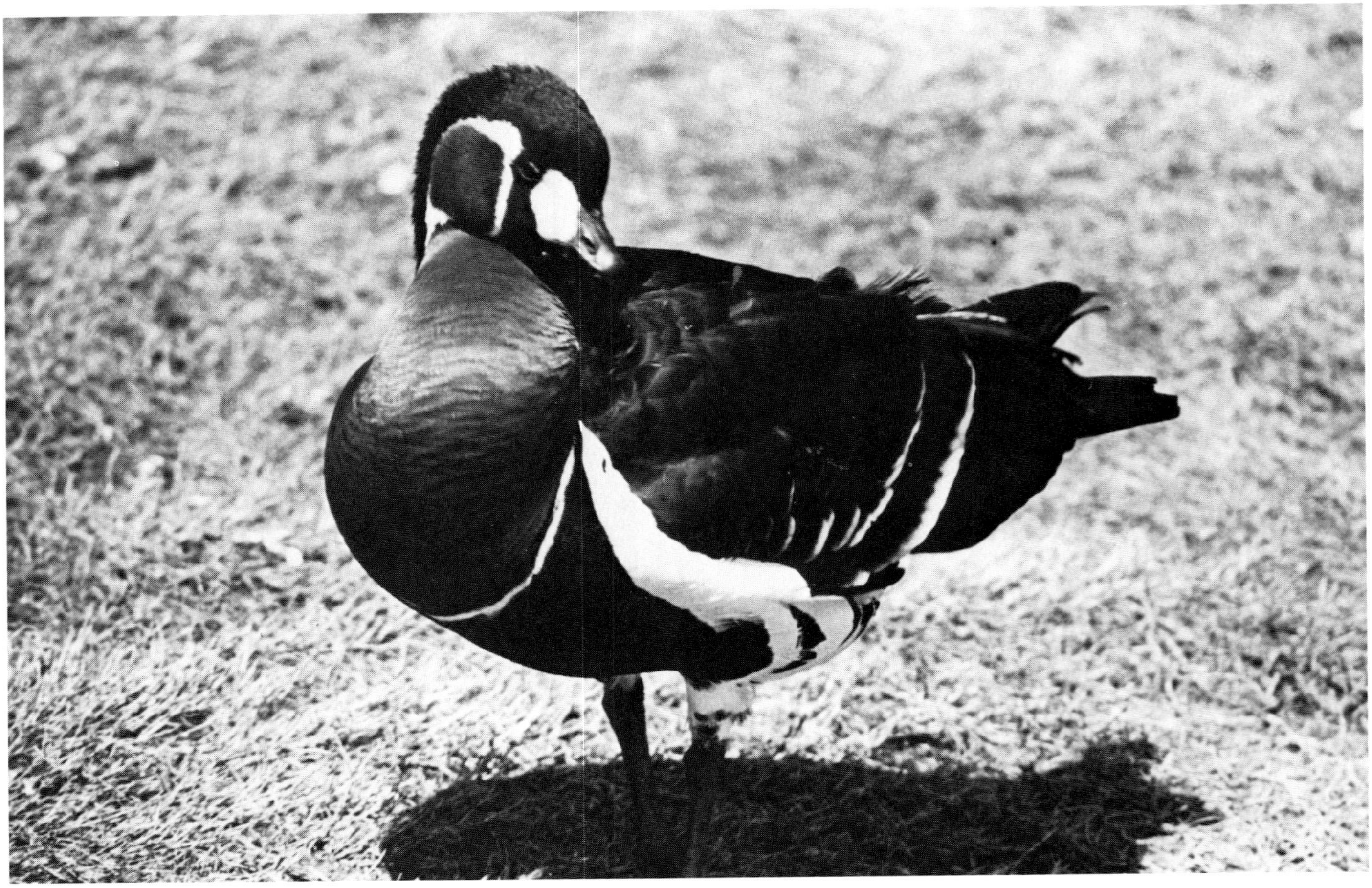

41-5

Two studies of the red-breasted goose. Notice how he has partially exposed one wing, forcing his side feathers down.

41-6

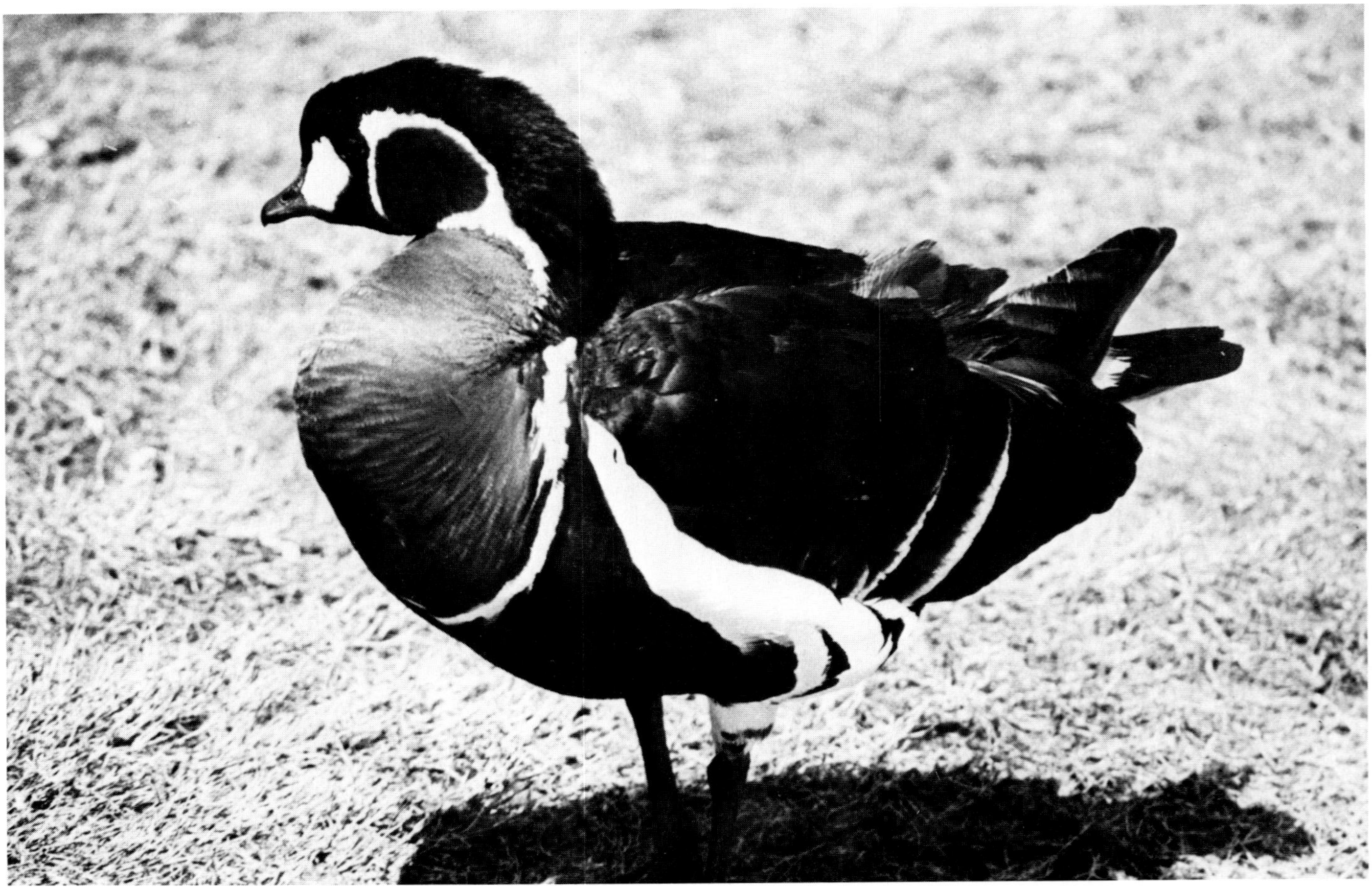

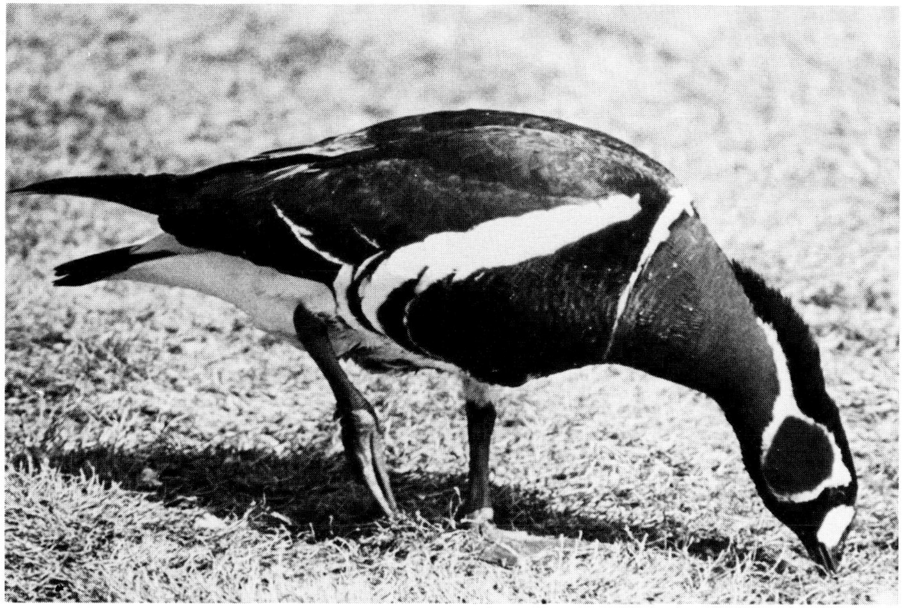

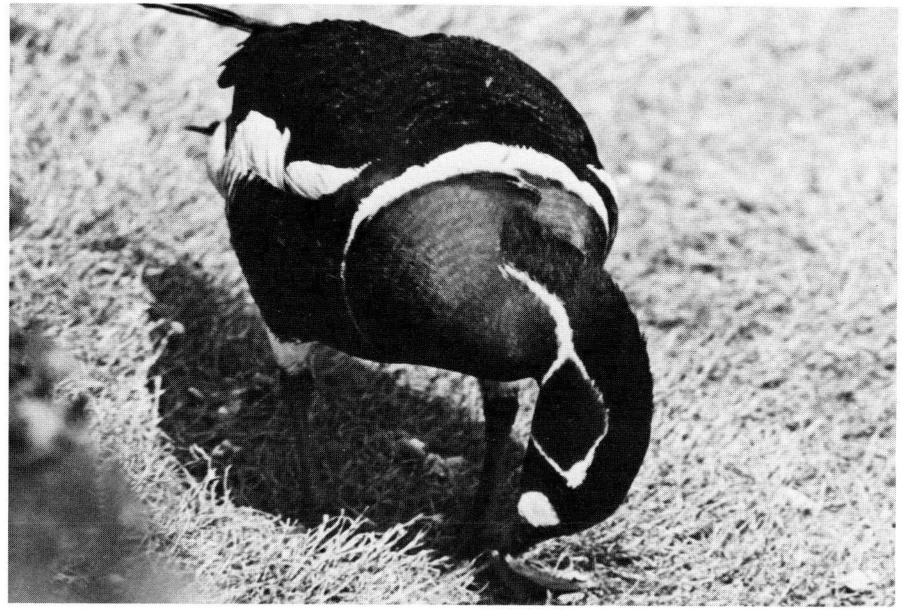

41-7 Four studies of feeding red-breasted geese as viewed from different angles. Like most geese, they are fond of grass. Especially notice 41-8
41-9 the mane-like feathers on the back of their necks. 41-10

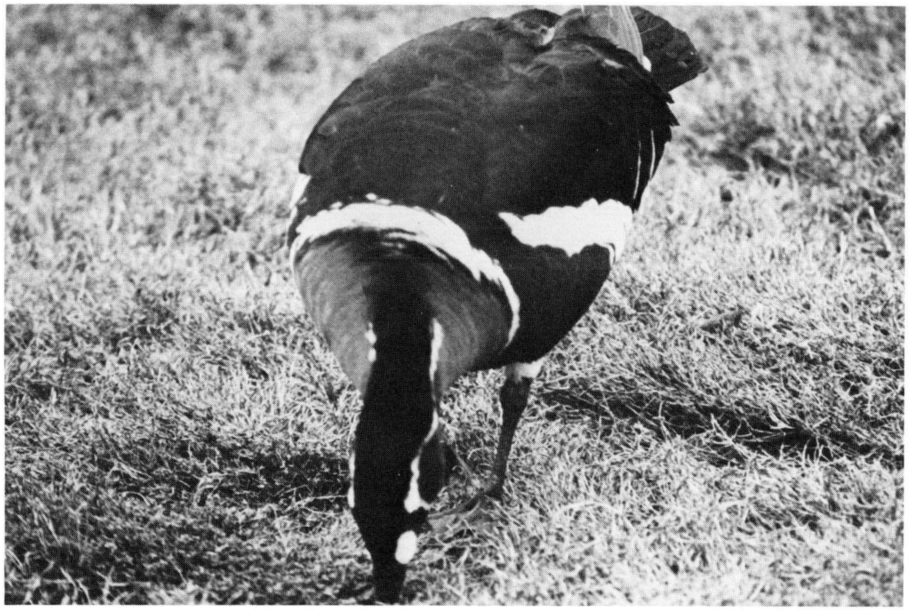

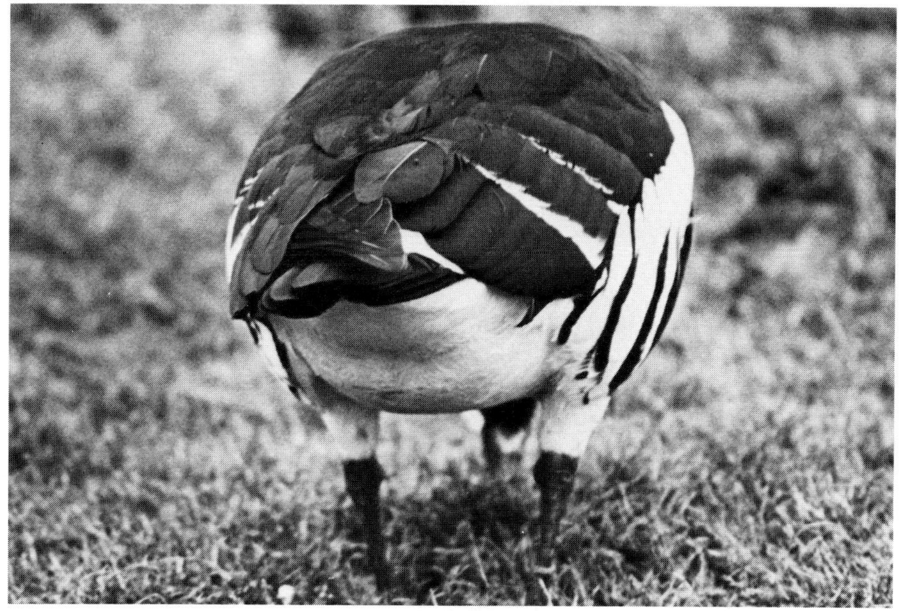

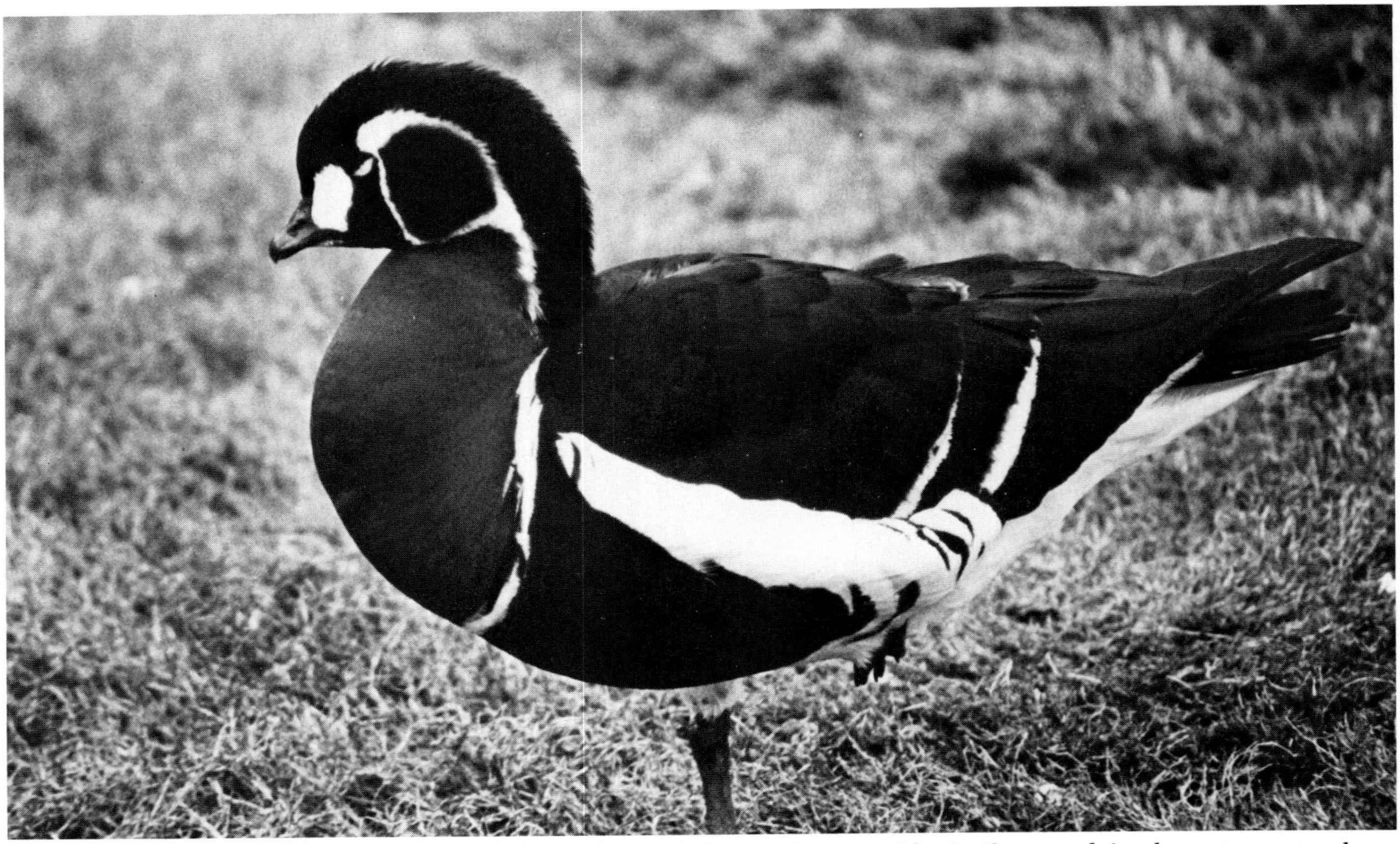

41-11 This red-breasted goose has pulled one leg and foot under his side feathers and is about to go to sleep.

41-12 Two studies of the red-breasted goose's head and bill. His bill is almost identical to a Cackling 41-13
Canada goose's.

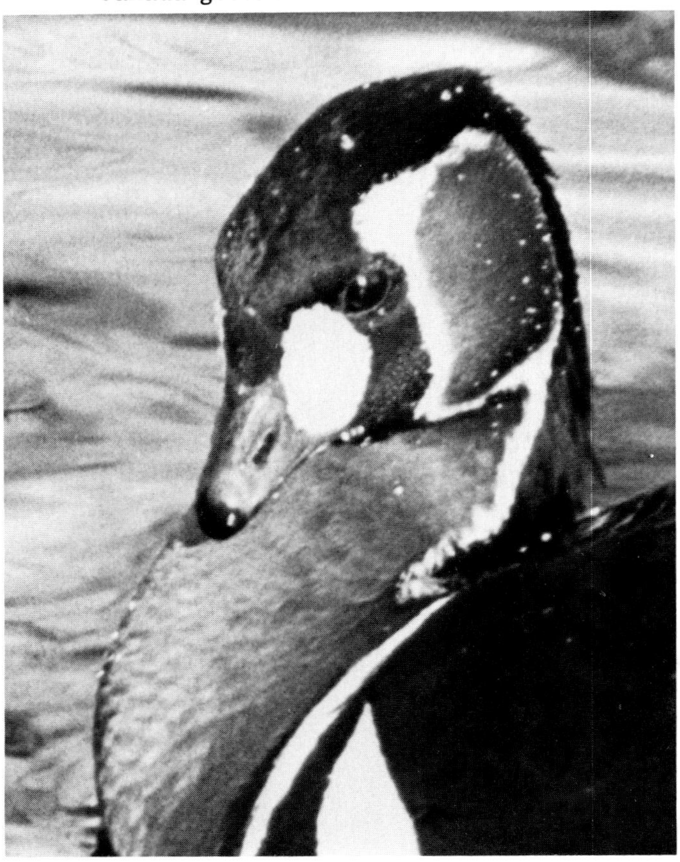

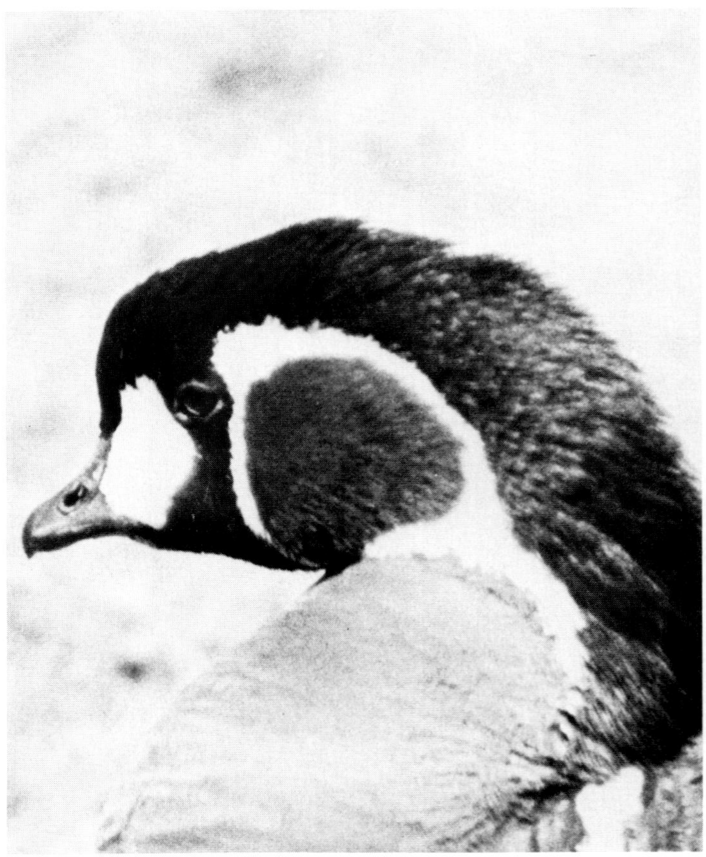

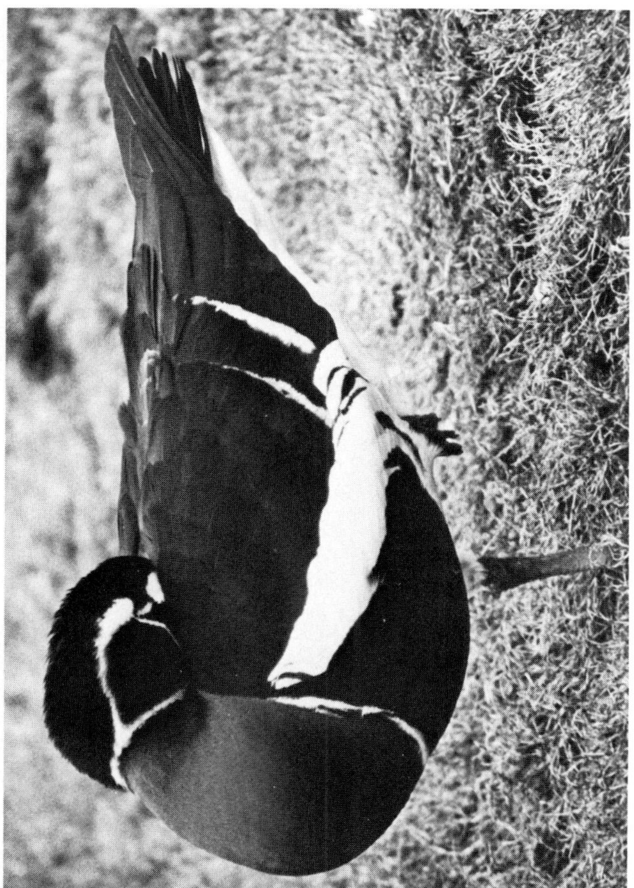

41-14

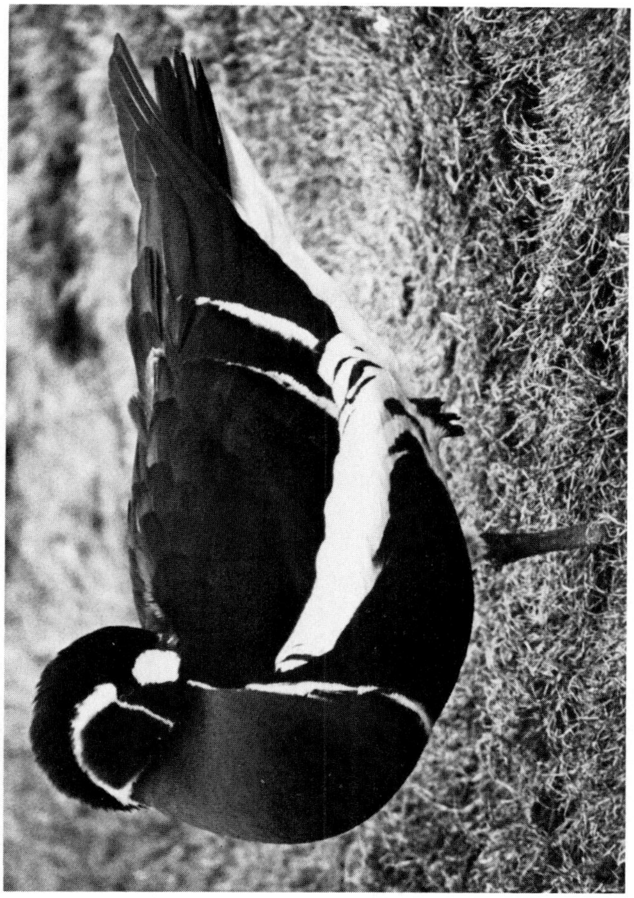

41-15

Four studies of a sleeping red-breasted goose.

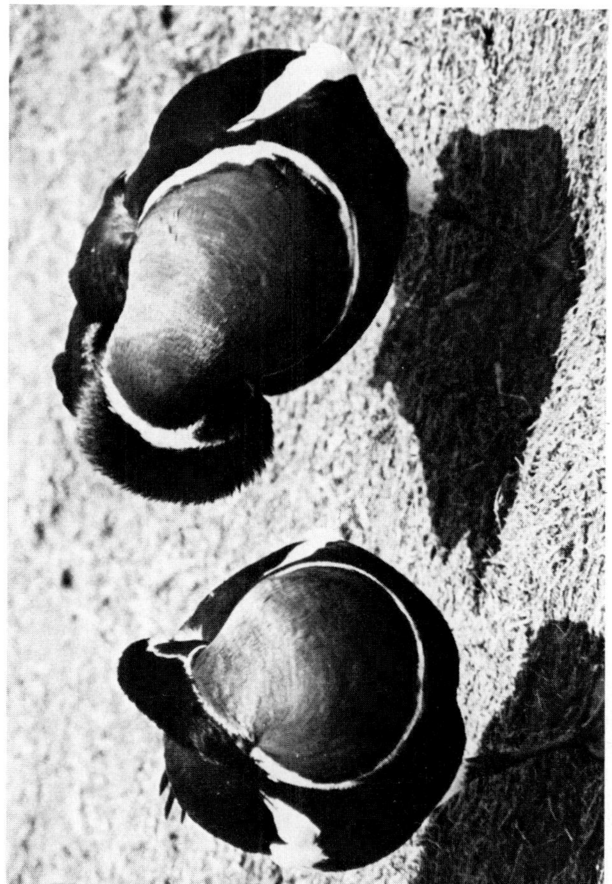

41-16

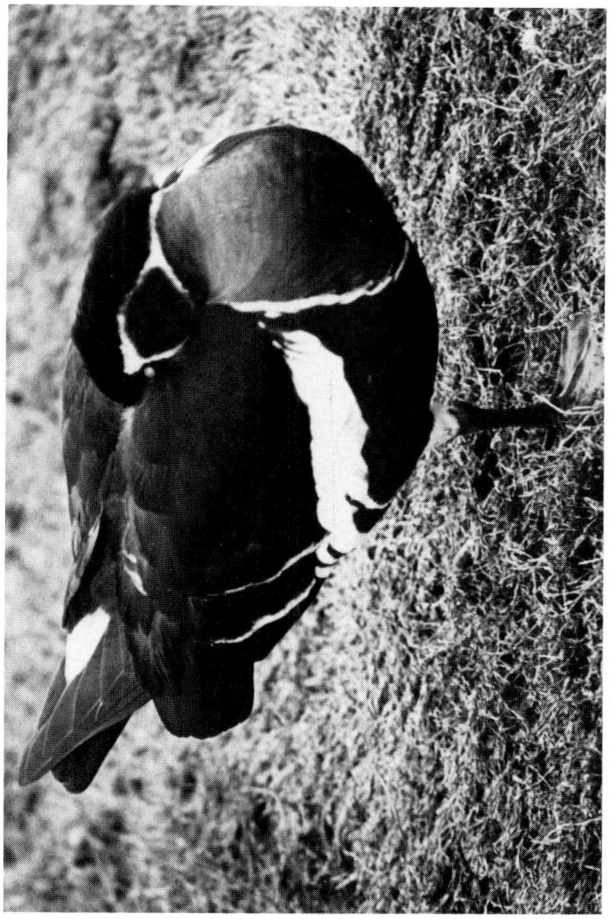

41-17

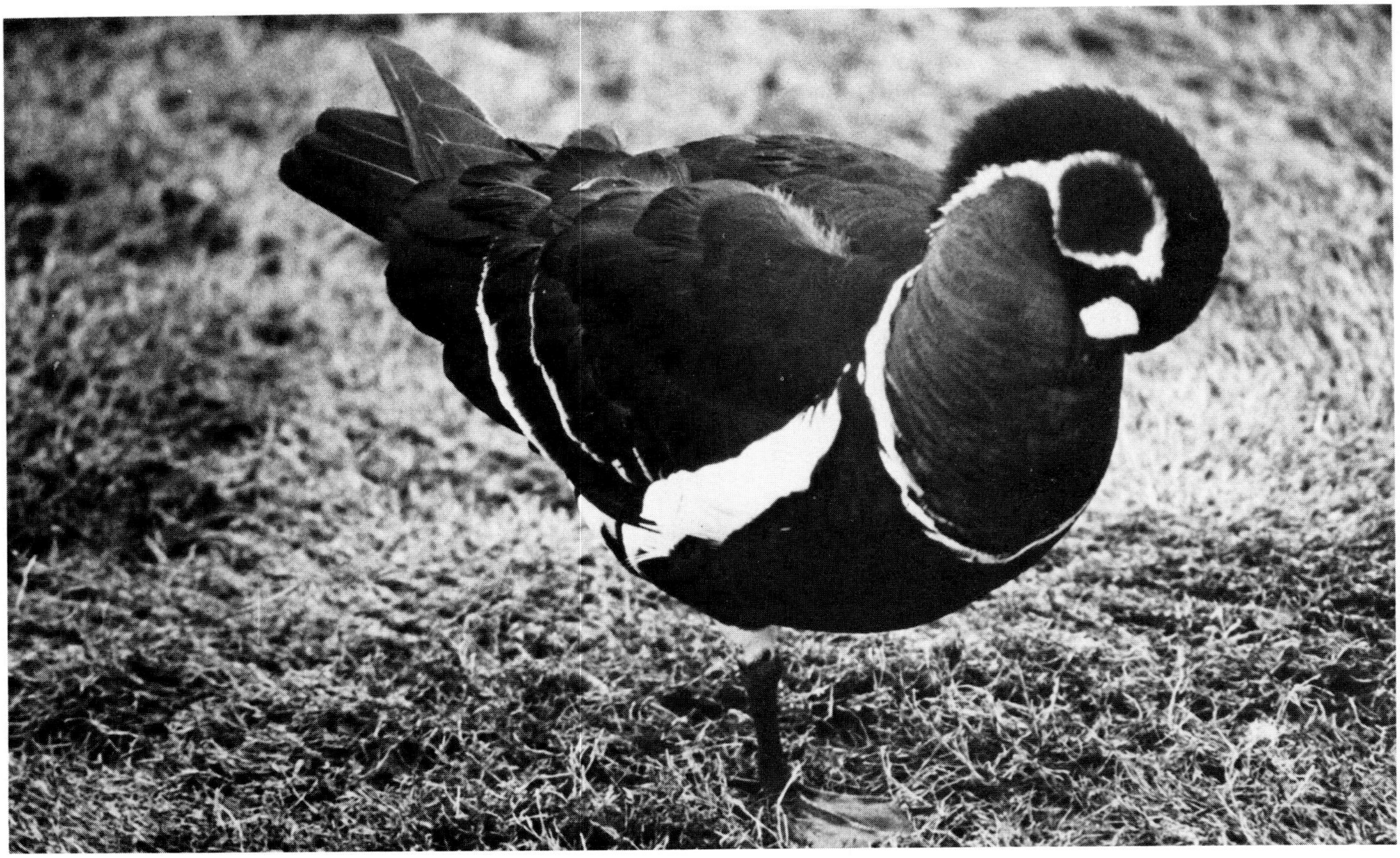

41-18

Little goose preens his chest feathers.

41-19

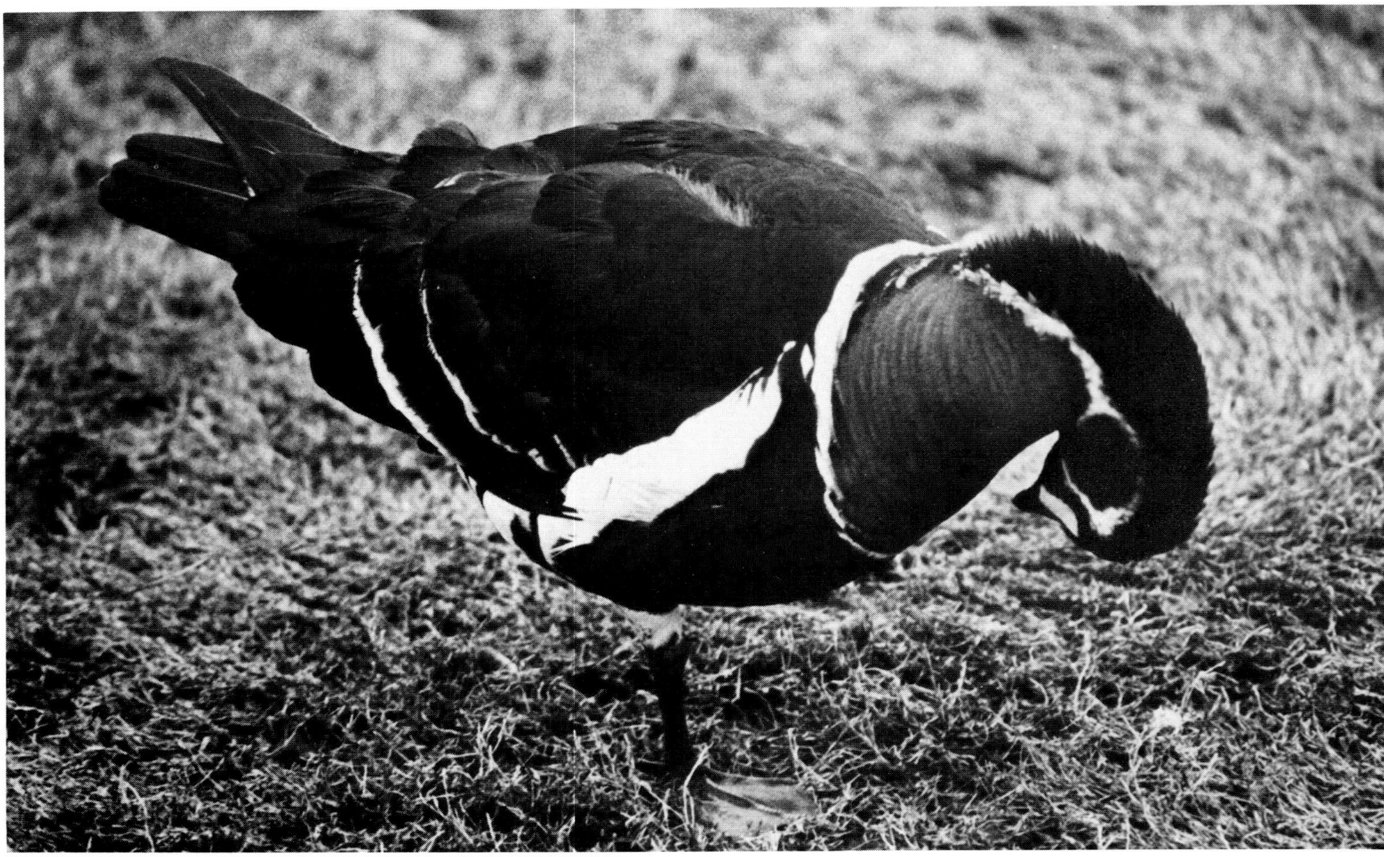

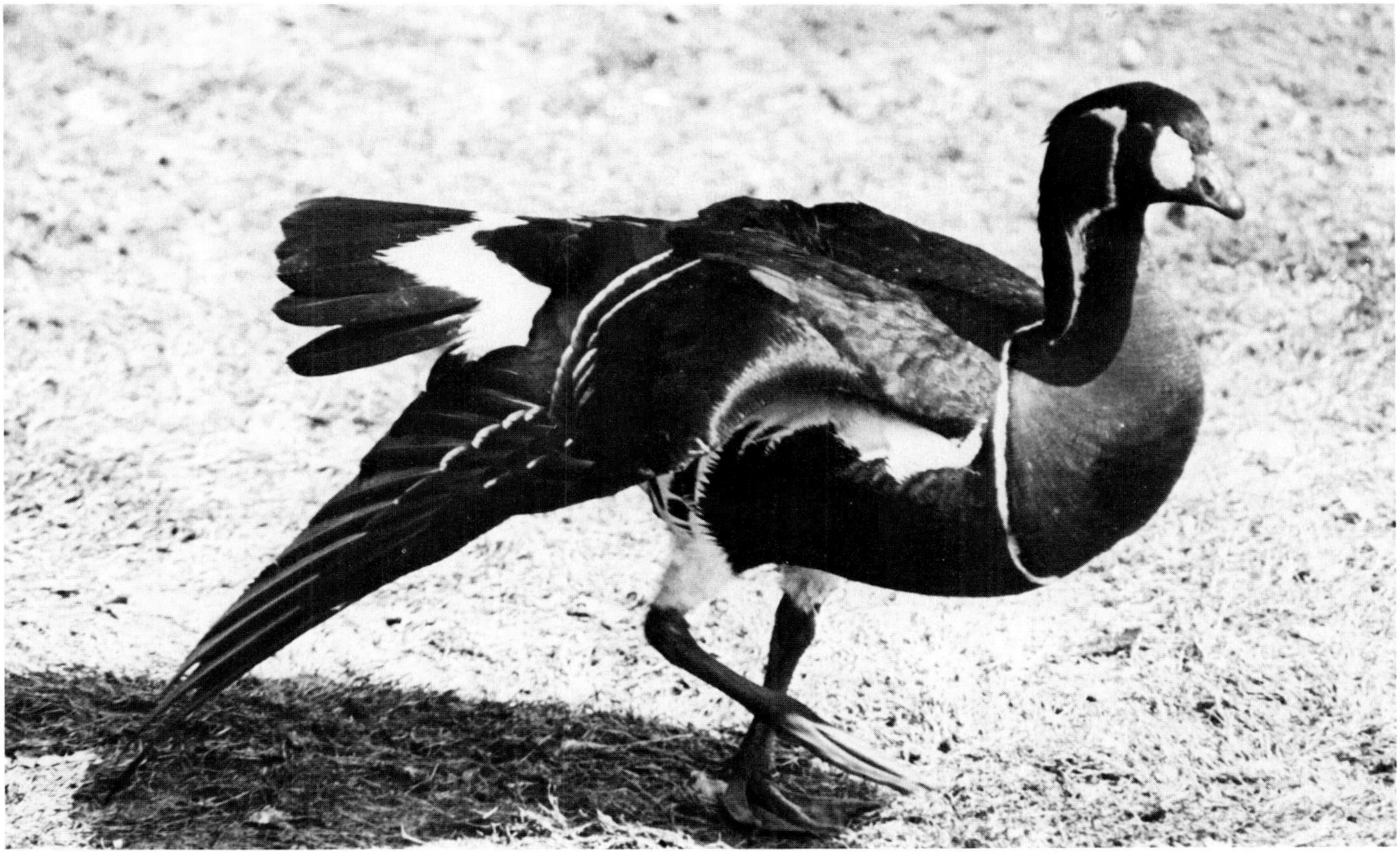

41-20

Red-breasted goose stretches one leg and wing. Notice how tightly he has pulled all of his feathers close to his body.

41-21

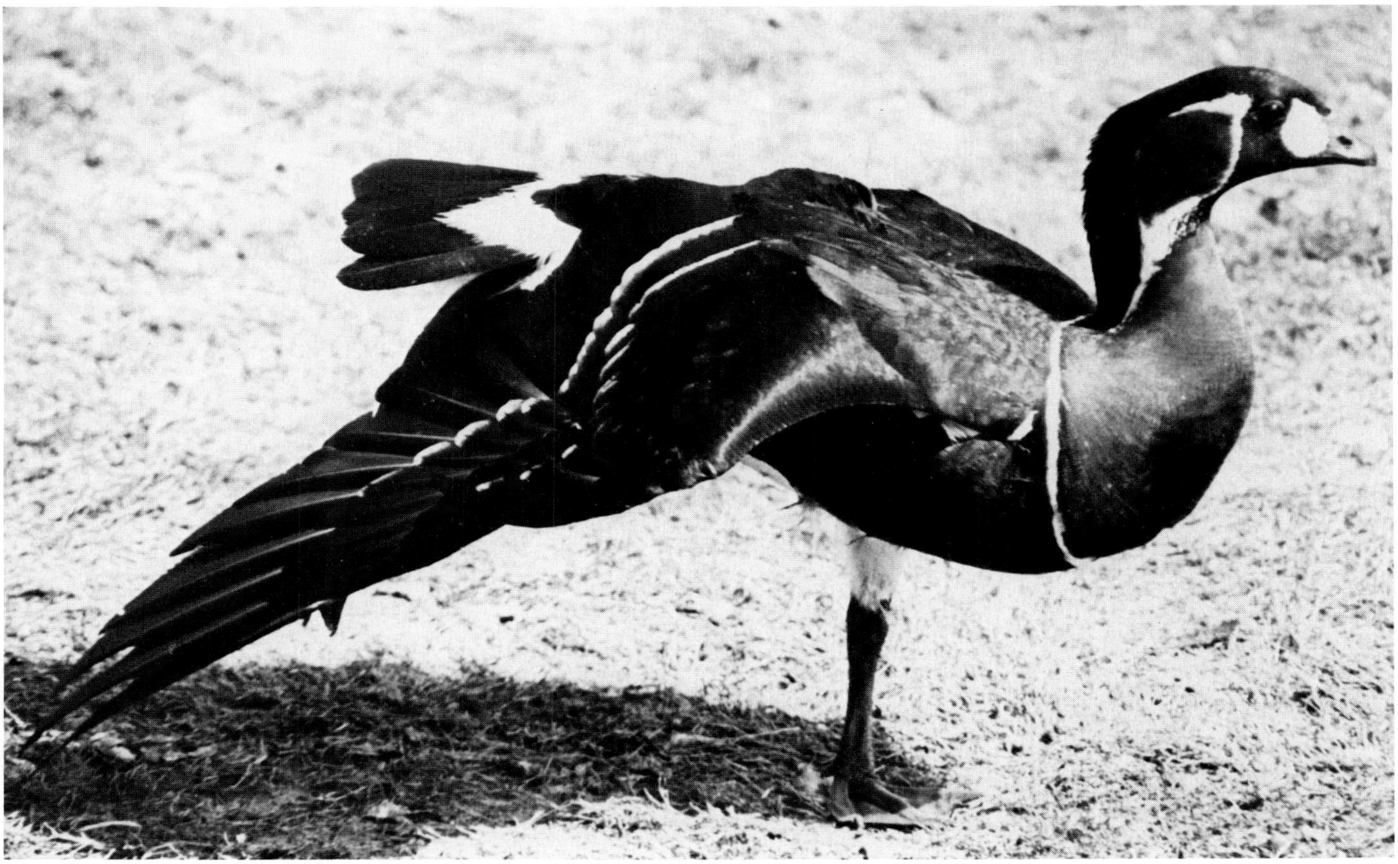

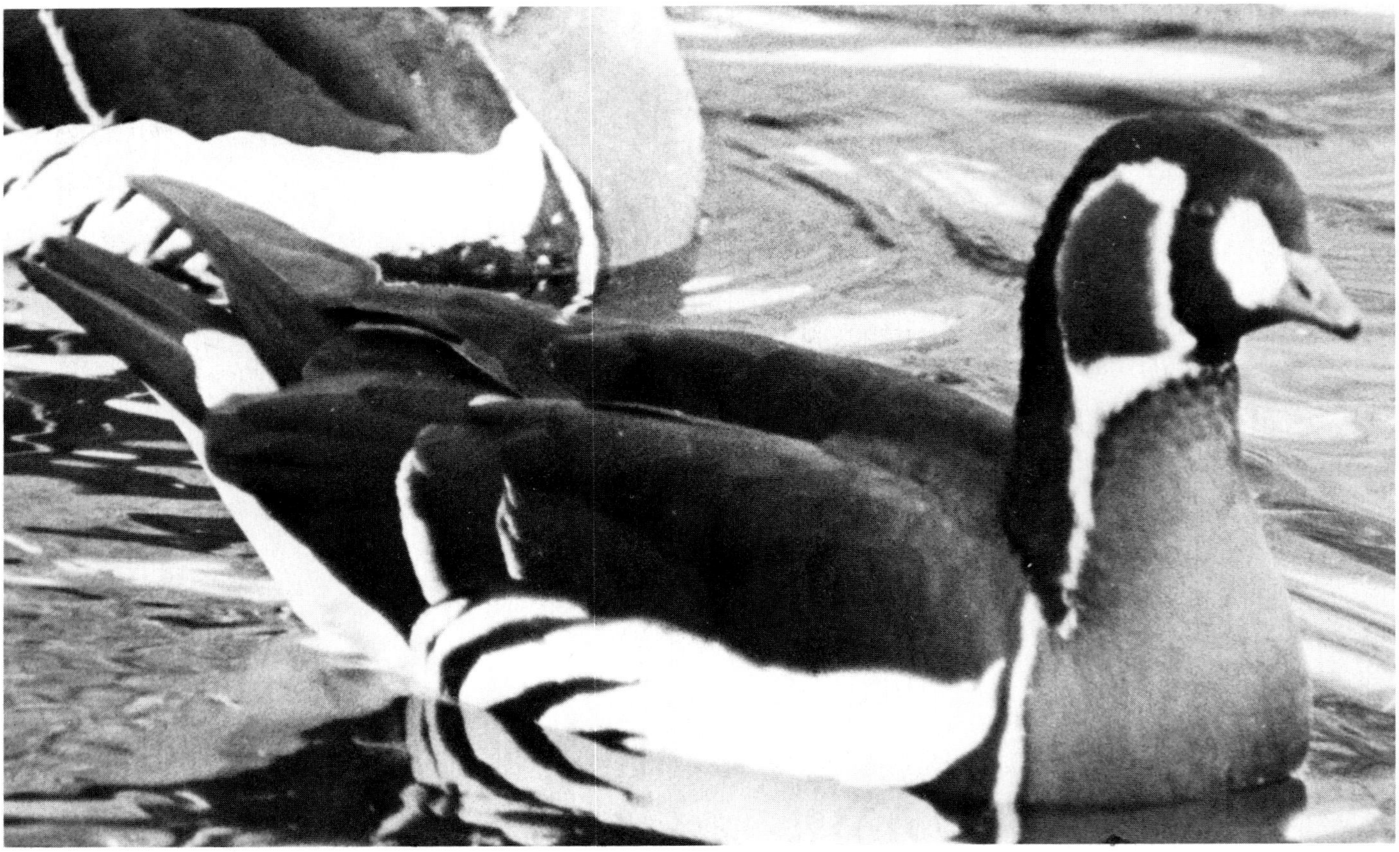

41-22 Good floating profile of the red-breasted goose.

41-23 Rear and front views show his body shape. 41-24

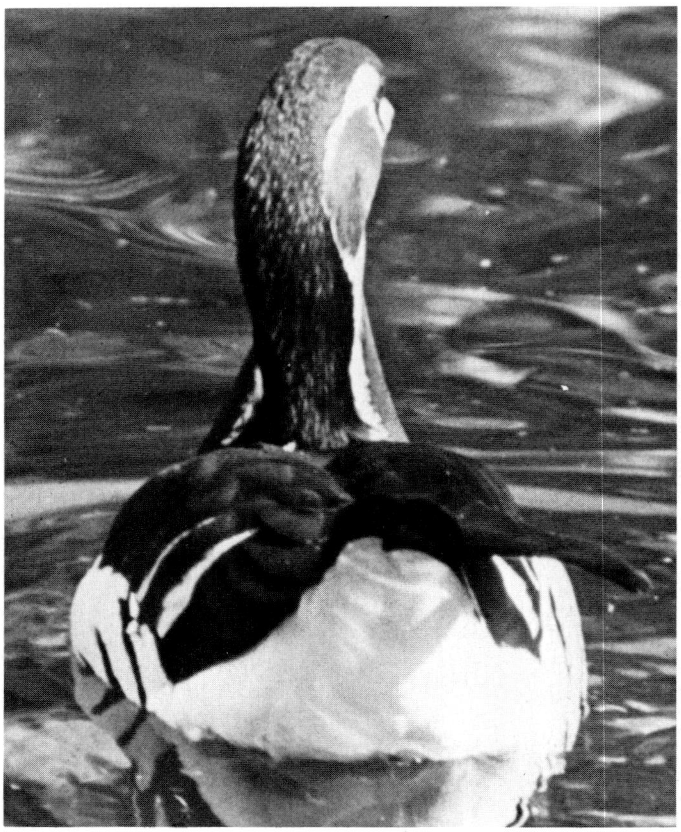

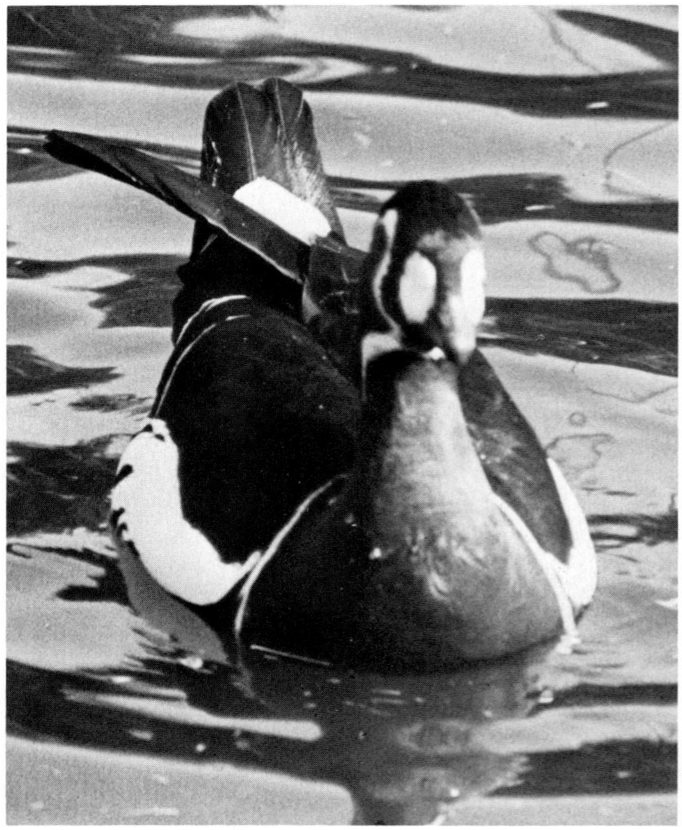

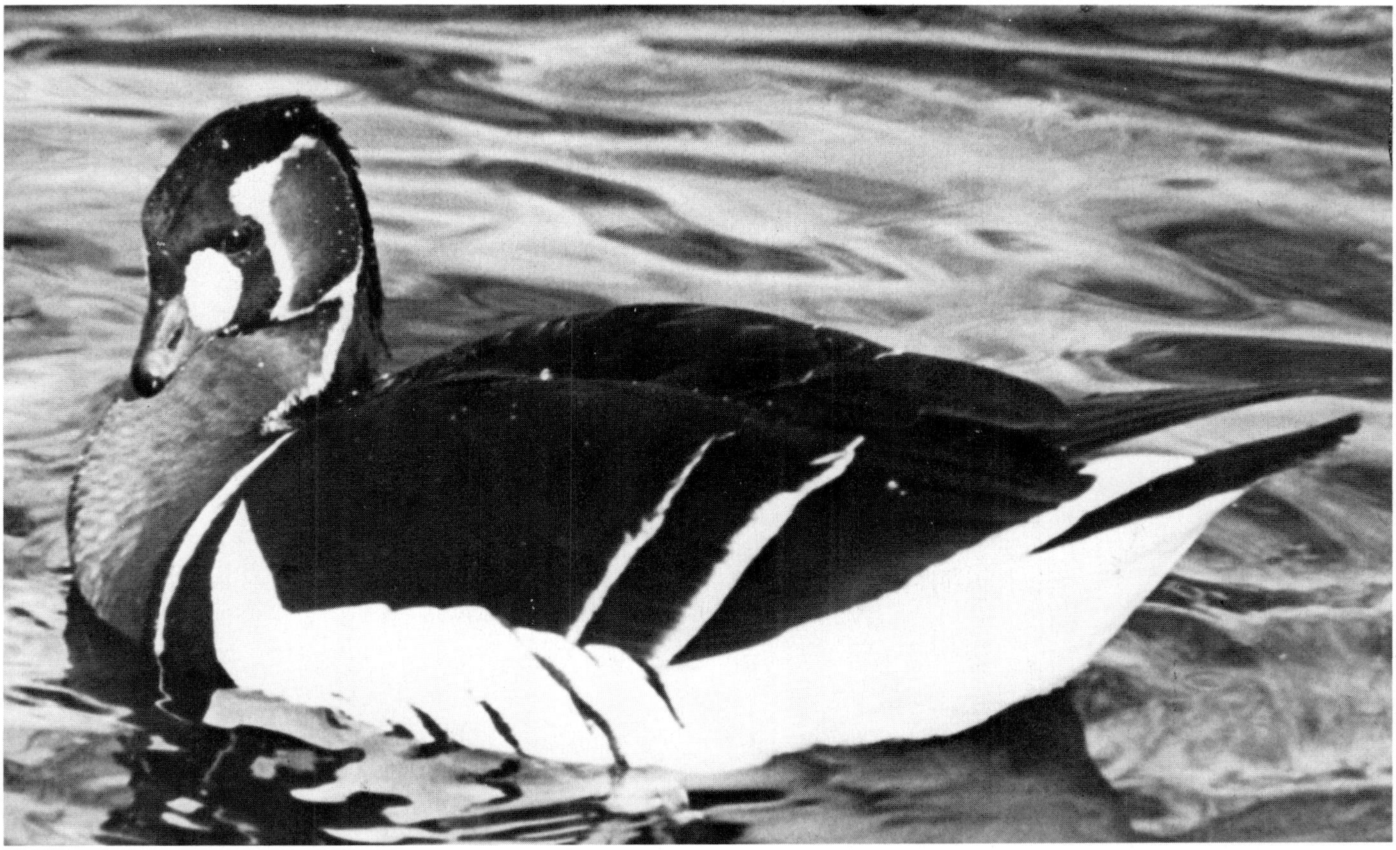

41-25 Red-breasted goose in an interesting pose.

41-26 Little goose looks for food in the water.

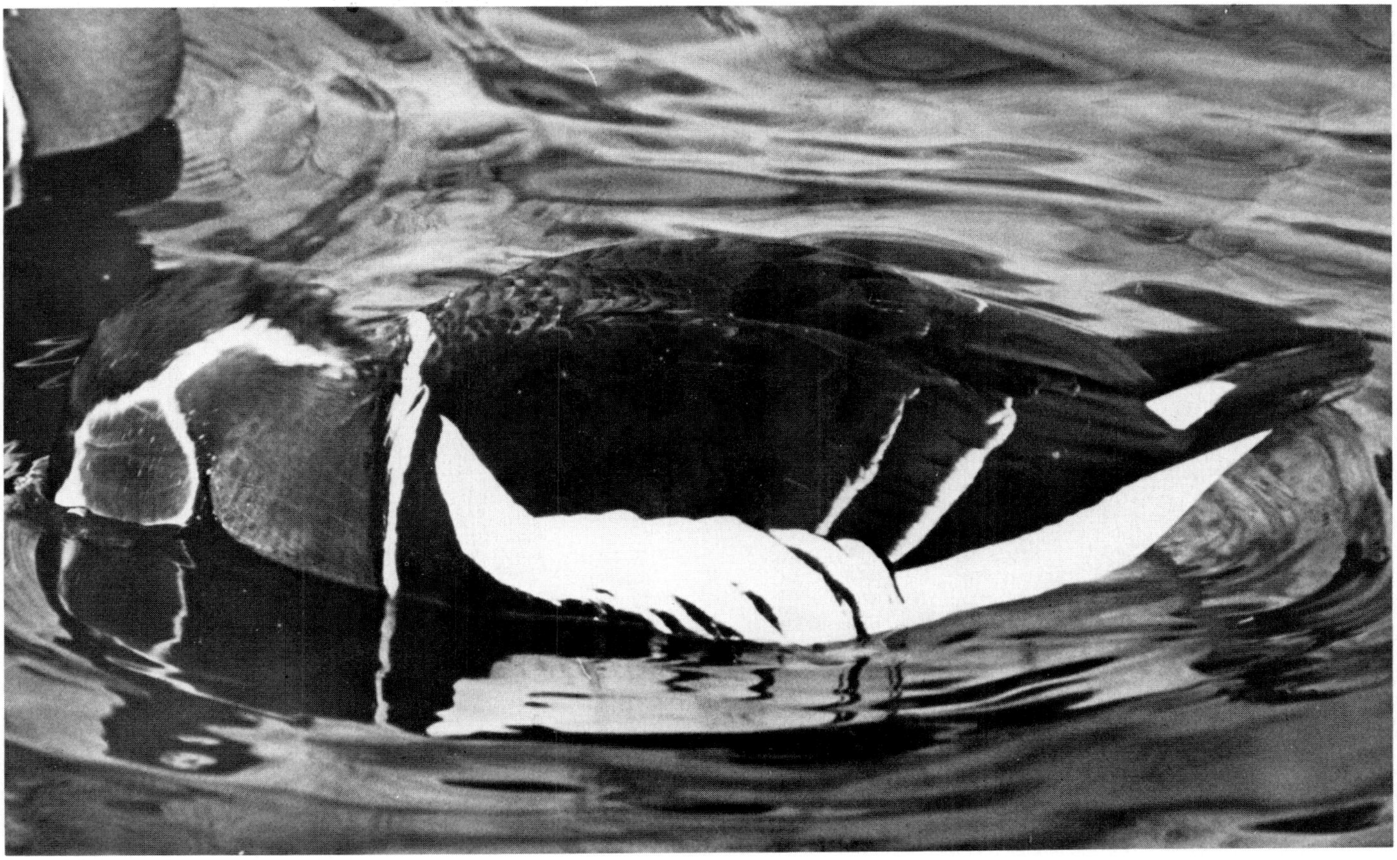

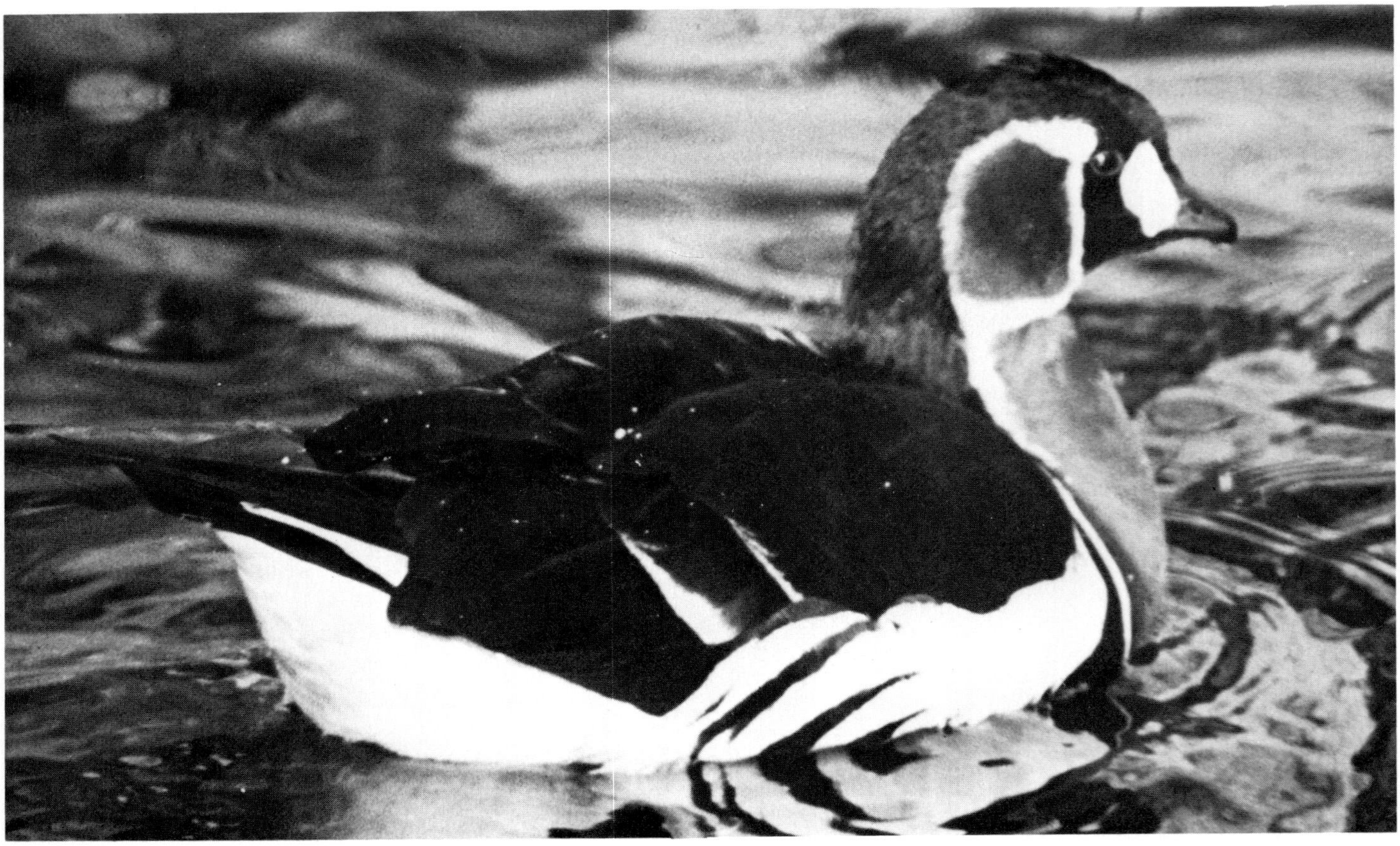

41-27

Two more interesting floating poses of red-breasted geese.

41-28

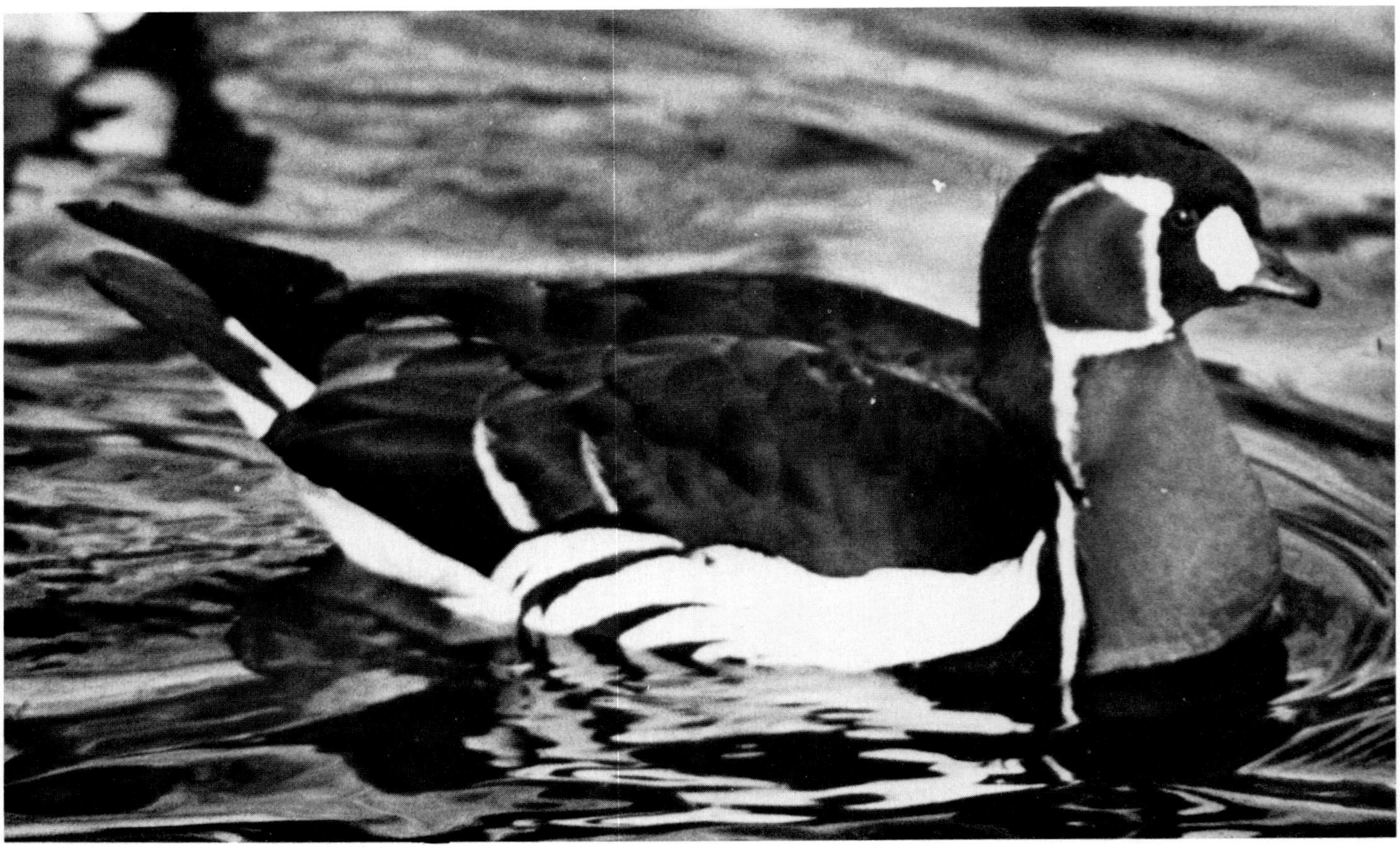

CHAPTER 42

Nene Goose

Branta sandvicensis
(Color Photos-Page 165)

Although the Nene (pronounced nay-nay), or Hawaiian, goose is closely related to the Canada goose, it has evolved under specialized habitat and climate conditions into a very distinct and non-migratory species. The Nene's behavior is similar to the Canada's except that members of this species are generally more jealous and quarrelsome, in some cases to the extent of even attacking their own mates. Their calls are considerably different—more like low, mournful moans.

Their native habitat is the mountain slopes of the Hawaiian Islands, primarily on the island of Hawaii, where there is little standing water except in the form of small, often temporary, pools. As a probable result of this semi-arid and often steep habitat, the webs of their feet are greatly reduced and the size and strength of their toes has increased.

It was estimated that in the late 1940s fewer than 50 Nene geese were in existence in the mountainous areas of the island of Hawaii. The population of this species was probably never great and during the 1800s, and possibly earlier, large numbers were slaughtered to provide food for the California Forty Niners and also whaling ships. Contributing also to their very near extinction was the introduction of non-native predators such as feral dogs, pigs, and the mongoose causing extensive depredation especially during the nesting season. Hunting of these geese was prohibited, although not rigidly enforced, in 1911 but at that late date much of the damage had been done and most of the geese were already gone. They were saved thanks to the efforts of an Hawaiian rancher, Harold Shipman, who first bred these birds in captivity as early as 1918. Three of his Nene geese were sent to the Wildfowl Trust in England and, as a result of this timely action, hundreds of Nenes were successfully reared and some 200 were eventually returned to their native habitat. In addition to the birds raised by the Wildfowl Trust, the Hawaiian Division of Fish and Game, numerous zoos, and private avaiaries are now producing hundreds of Nene geese annually—over 1600 have now been released on the islands of Hawaii and Maui. The continued existence of these fine birds in their native areas now appears to be assured. The Nene goose has been appropriately designated as the state bird of Hawaii.

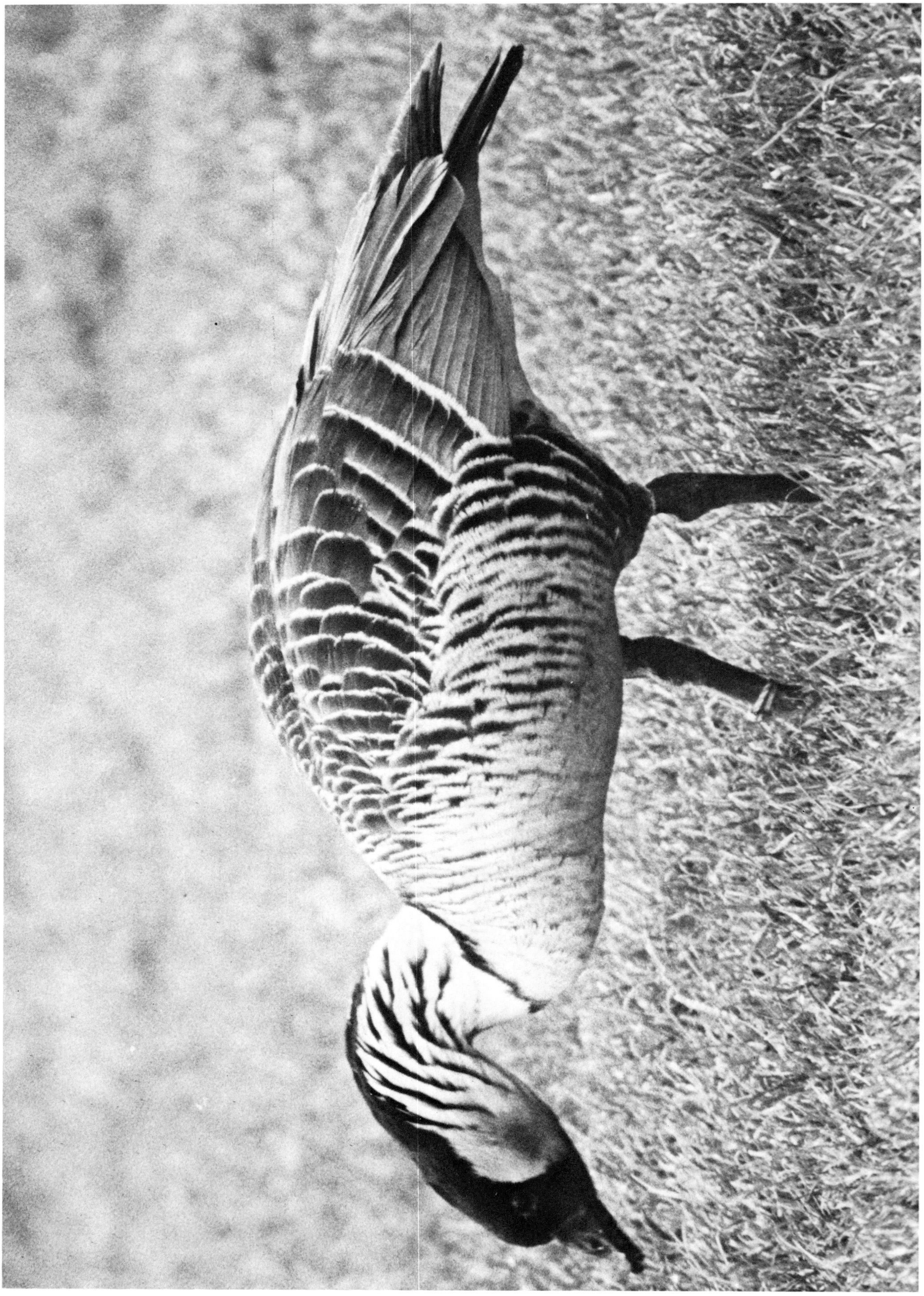

42-1 The attractive Nene, or Hawaiian, goose. The Nene are medium size geese—about the size of lesser Canadas. Almost on the verge of extinction, they are now gradually increasing in numbers with the help of captive breeding.

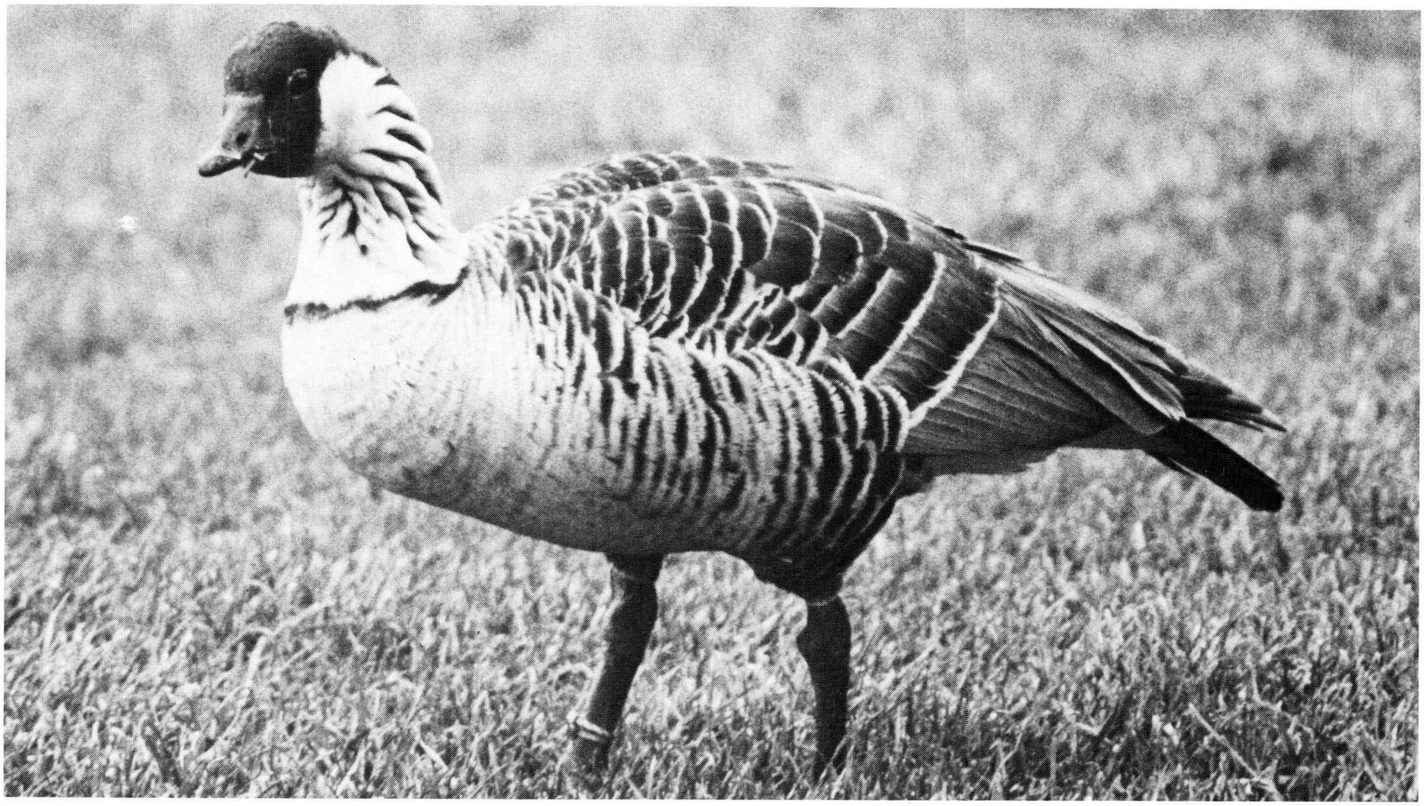

42-2 The Nene stops his feeding long enough to check out the author.

42-3 Front views of feeding Nene geese. 42-4

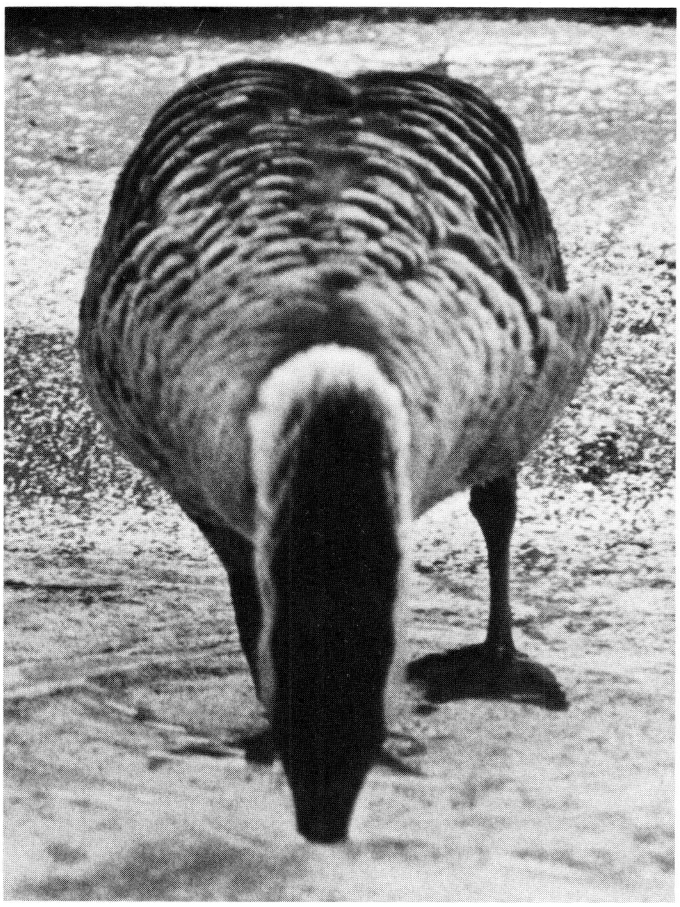

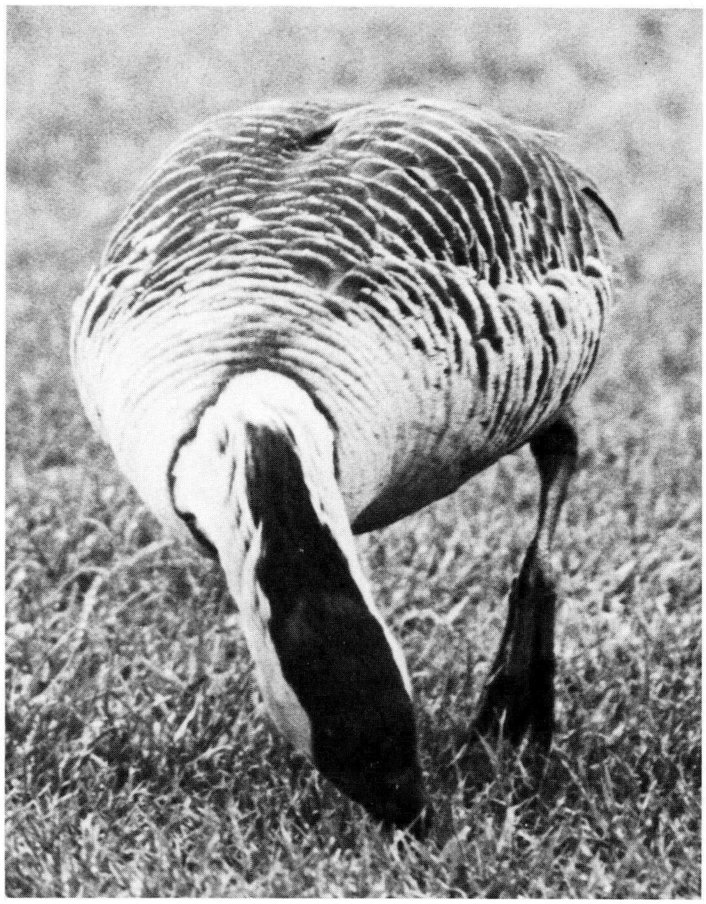

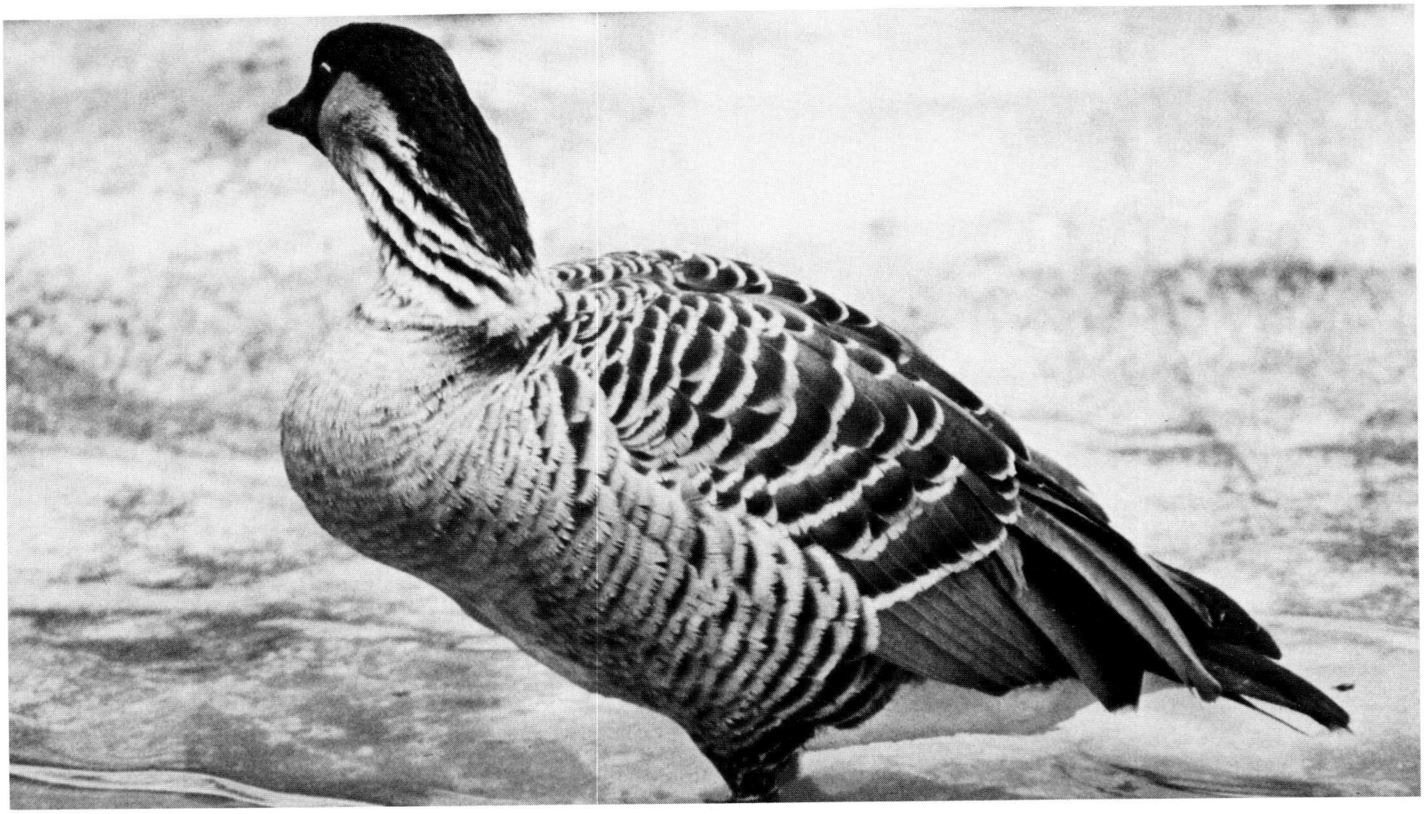

42-5 Unlike our other geese, the Nenes adapted to a habitat with little water except small, often temporary pools.

42-6 Nene geese are closely related to Canada geese. Their markings are somewhat similar, except that their "throat patch" extends down the length of their neck.

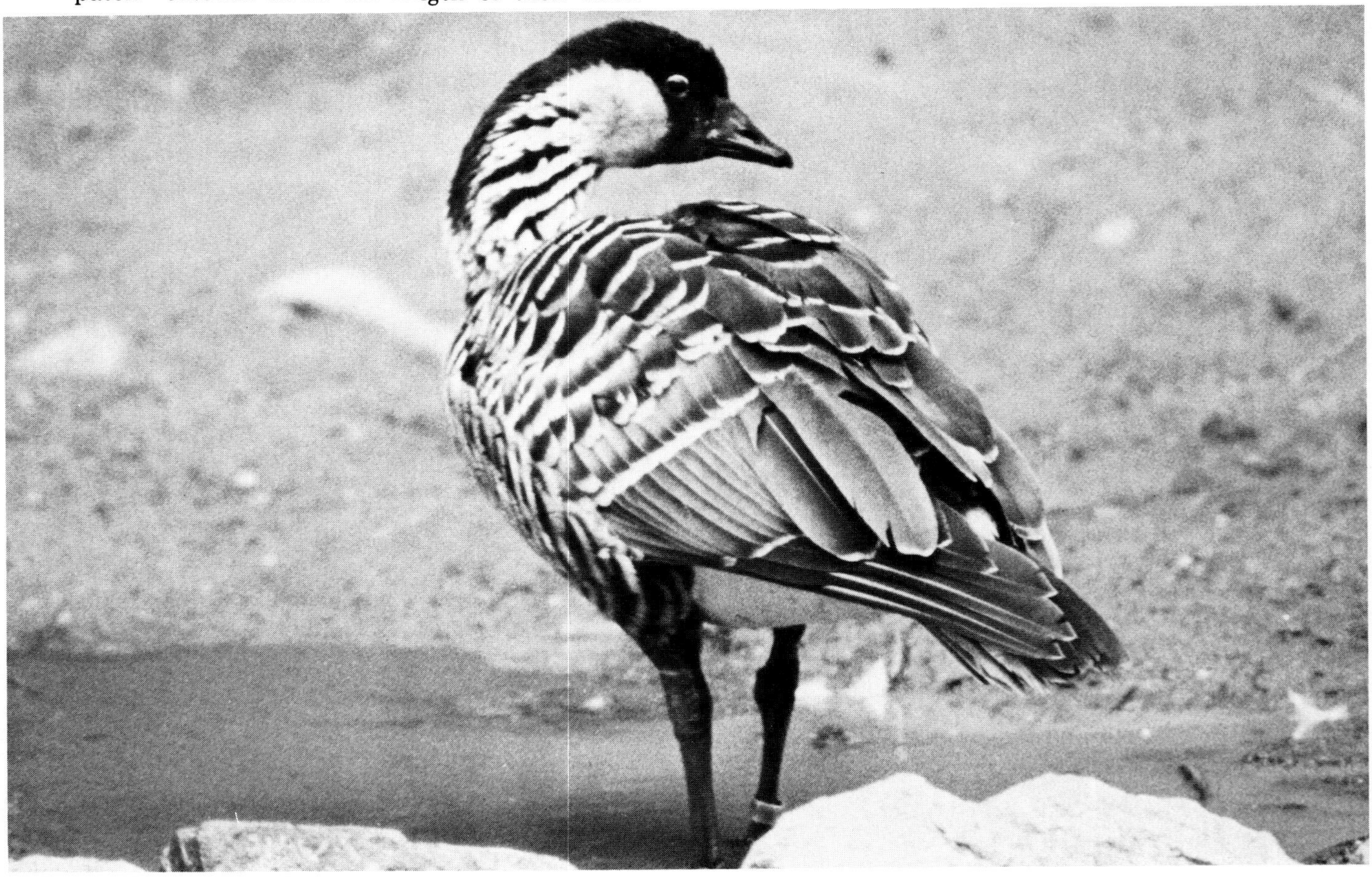

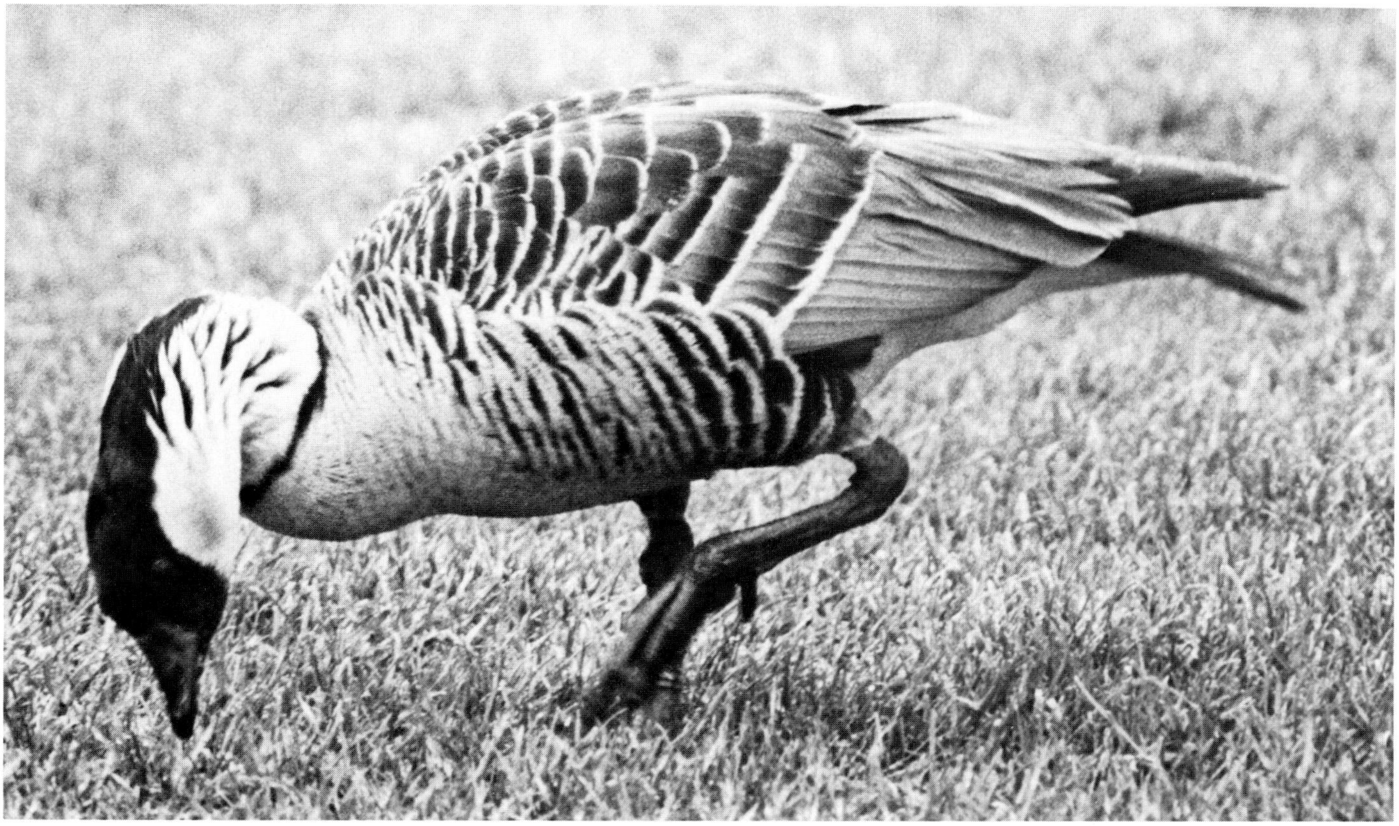

42-7

Two studies of Nene geese in feeding positions.

42-8

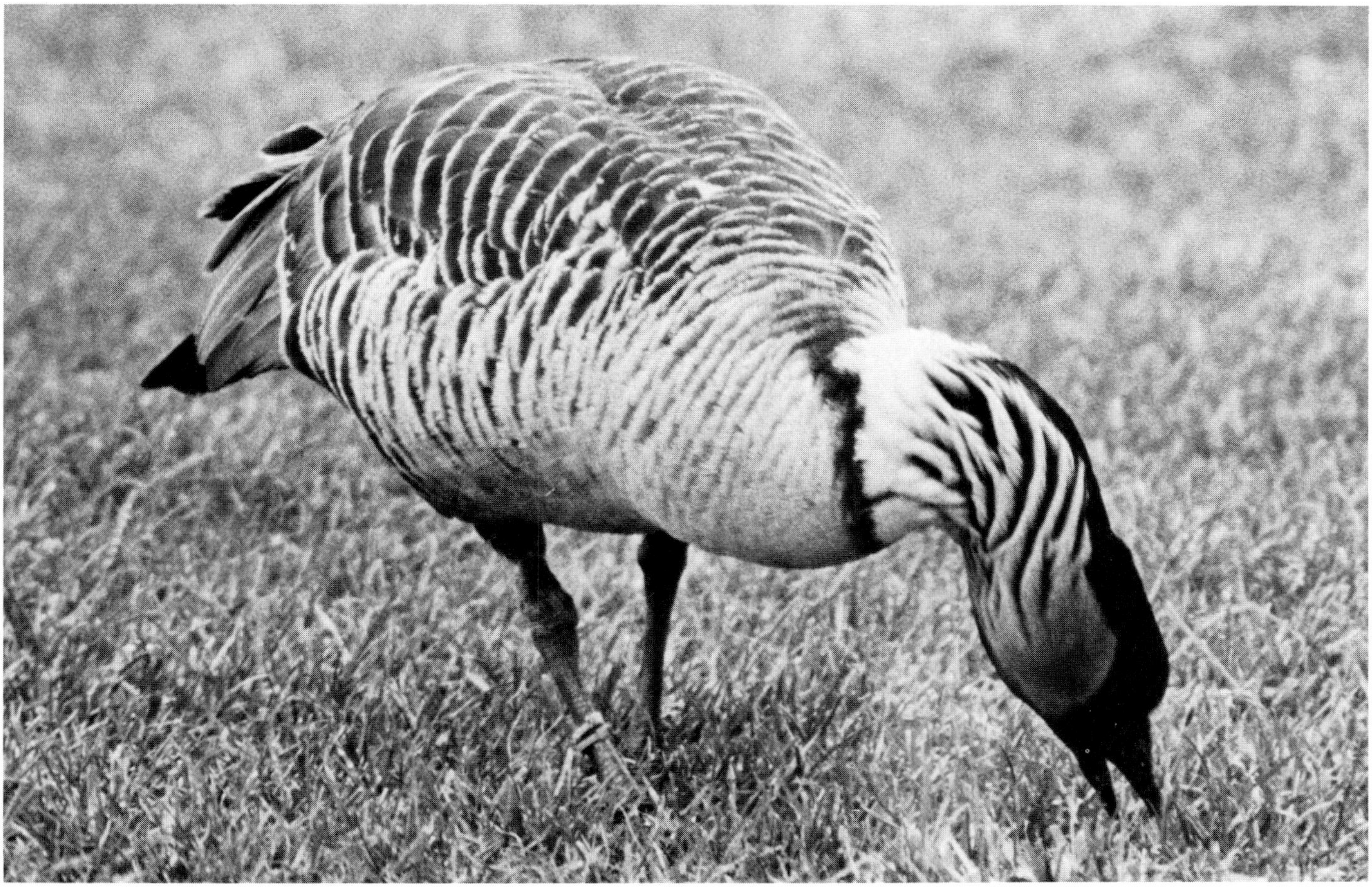

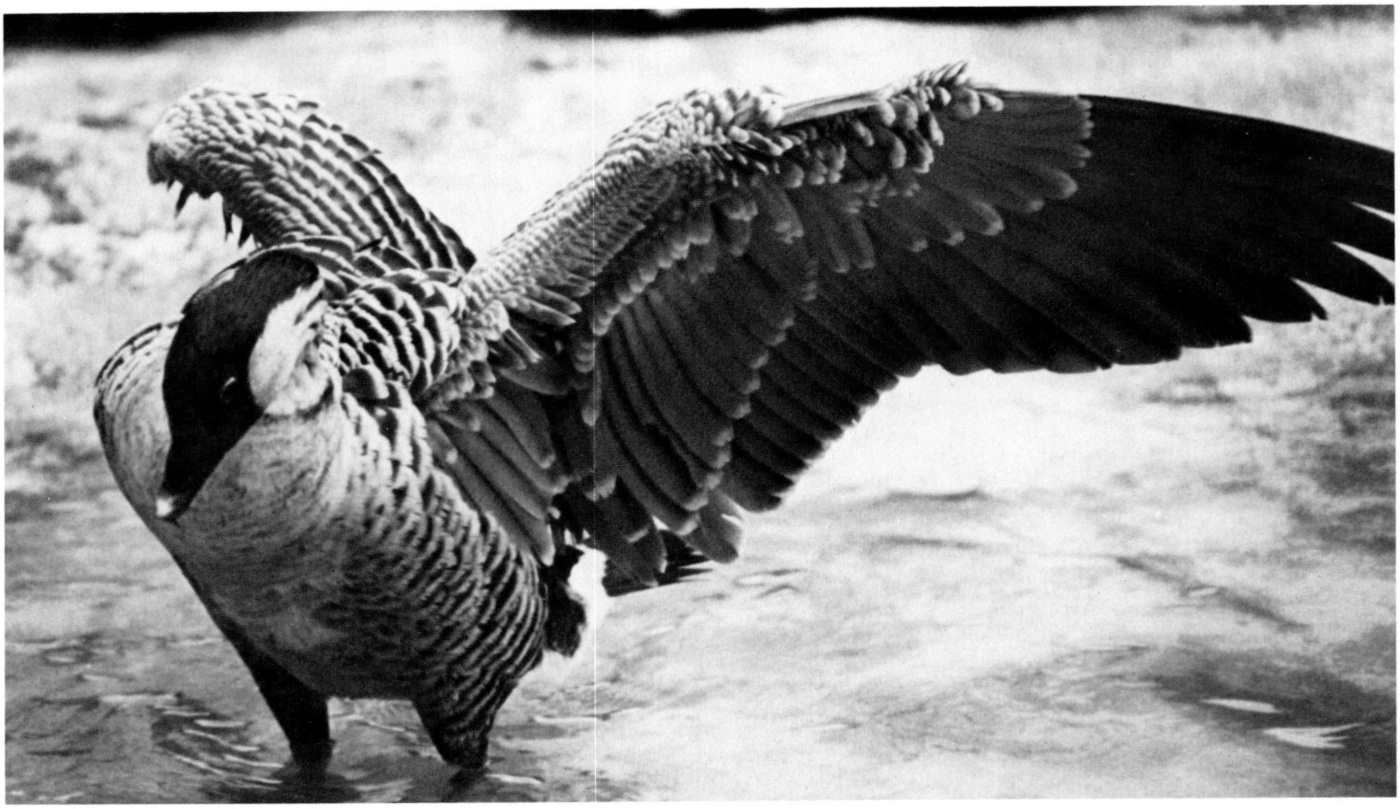

42-9

Nene stretches his wings. The Nene are good flyers but are non-migratory.

42-10

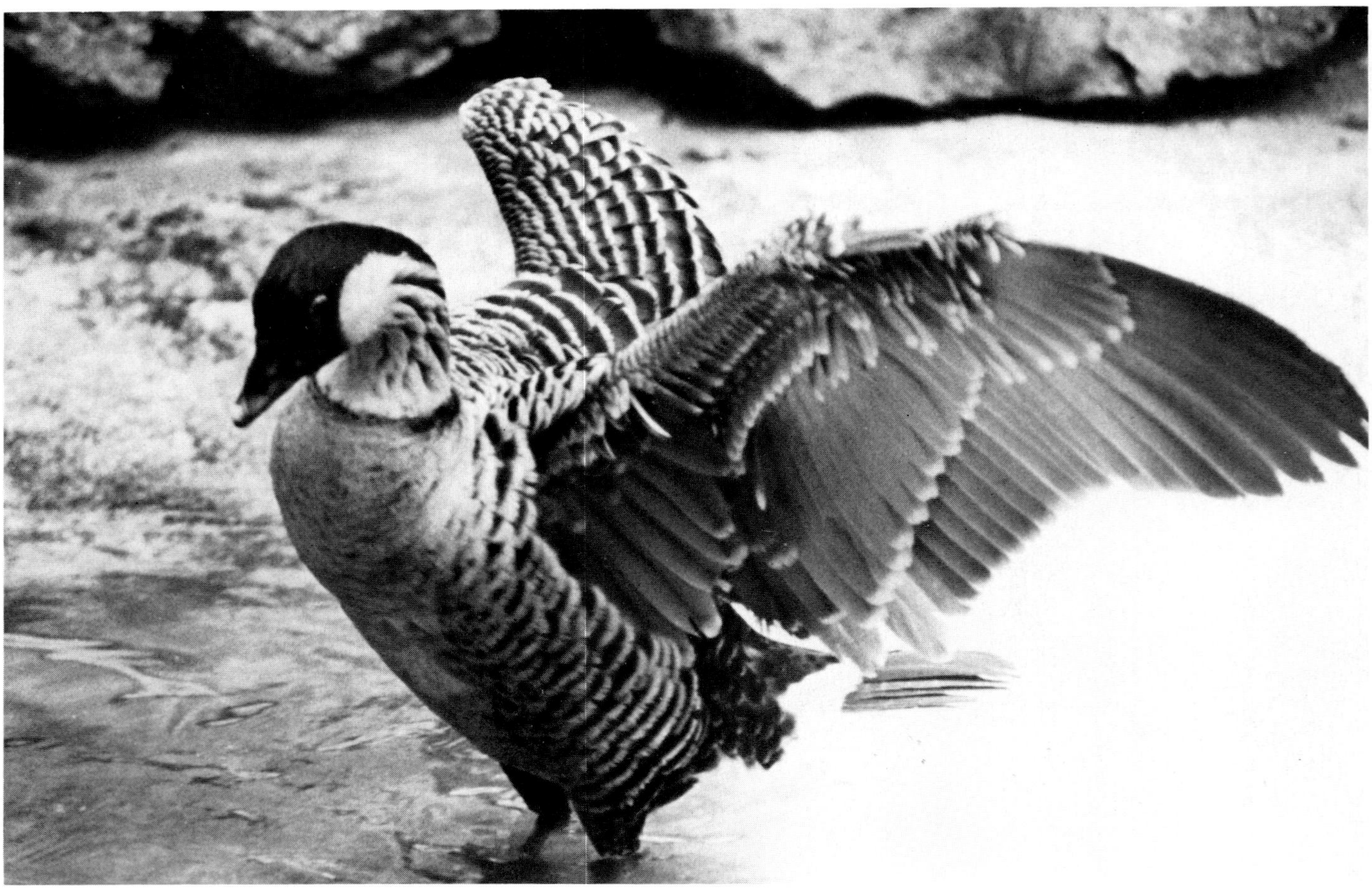

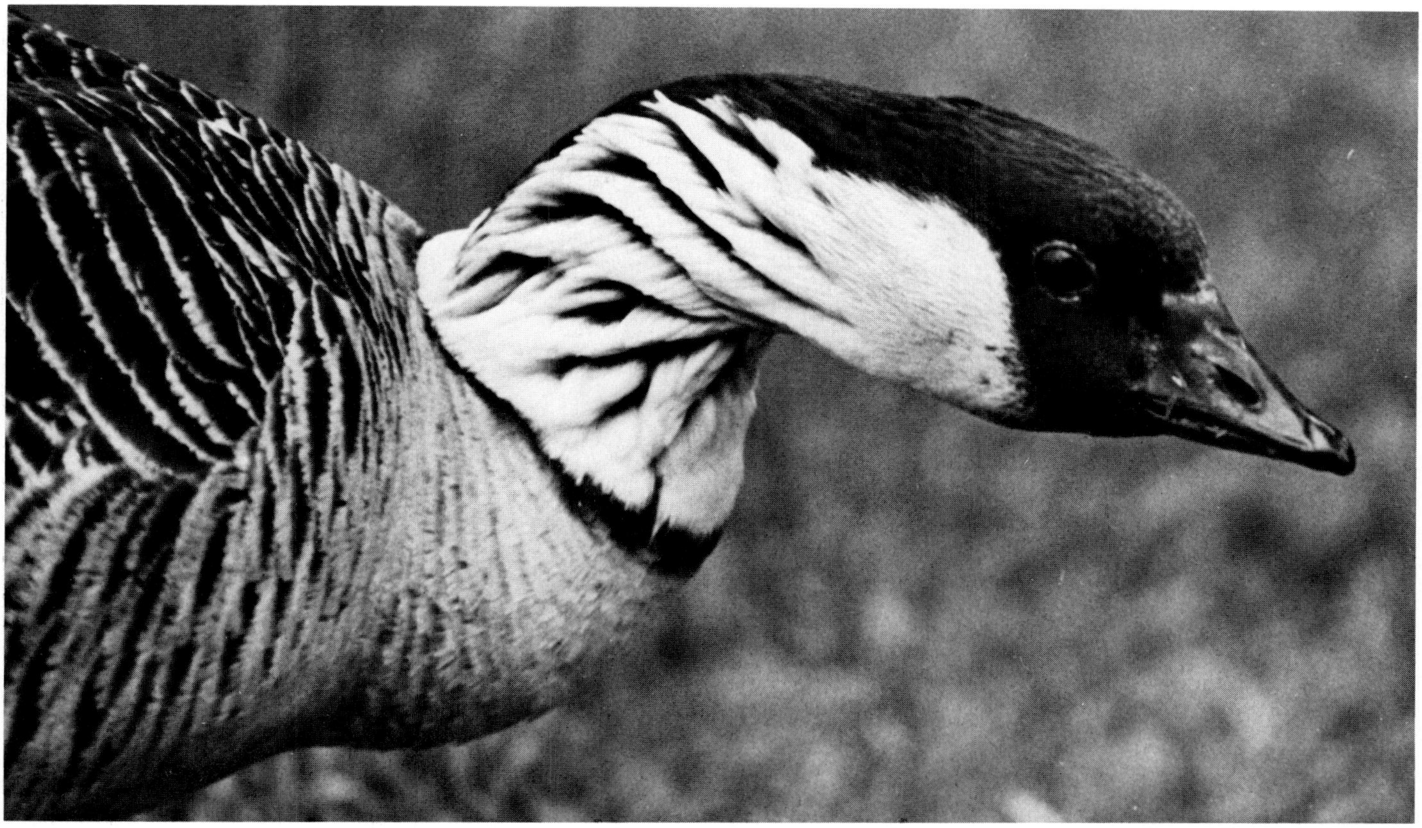

42-11

Profile, front, and rear views of the Nene's head, bill, and neck. Their neck feathers lie in deep furrows and ridges, much more pronounced than those of our other geese. Their head and bill are quite similar to Canada's.

42-12

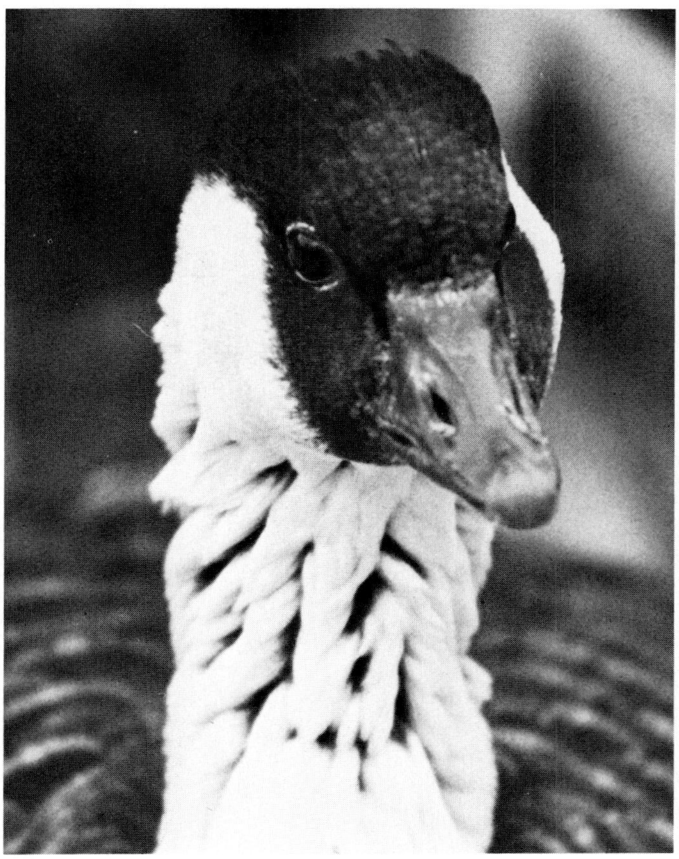

42-13

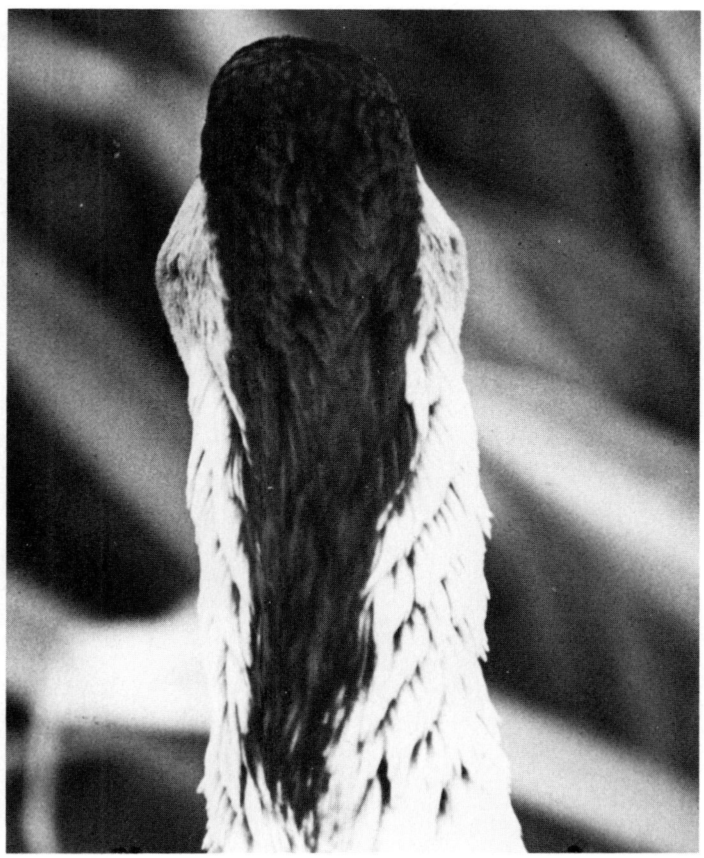

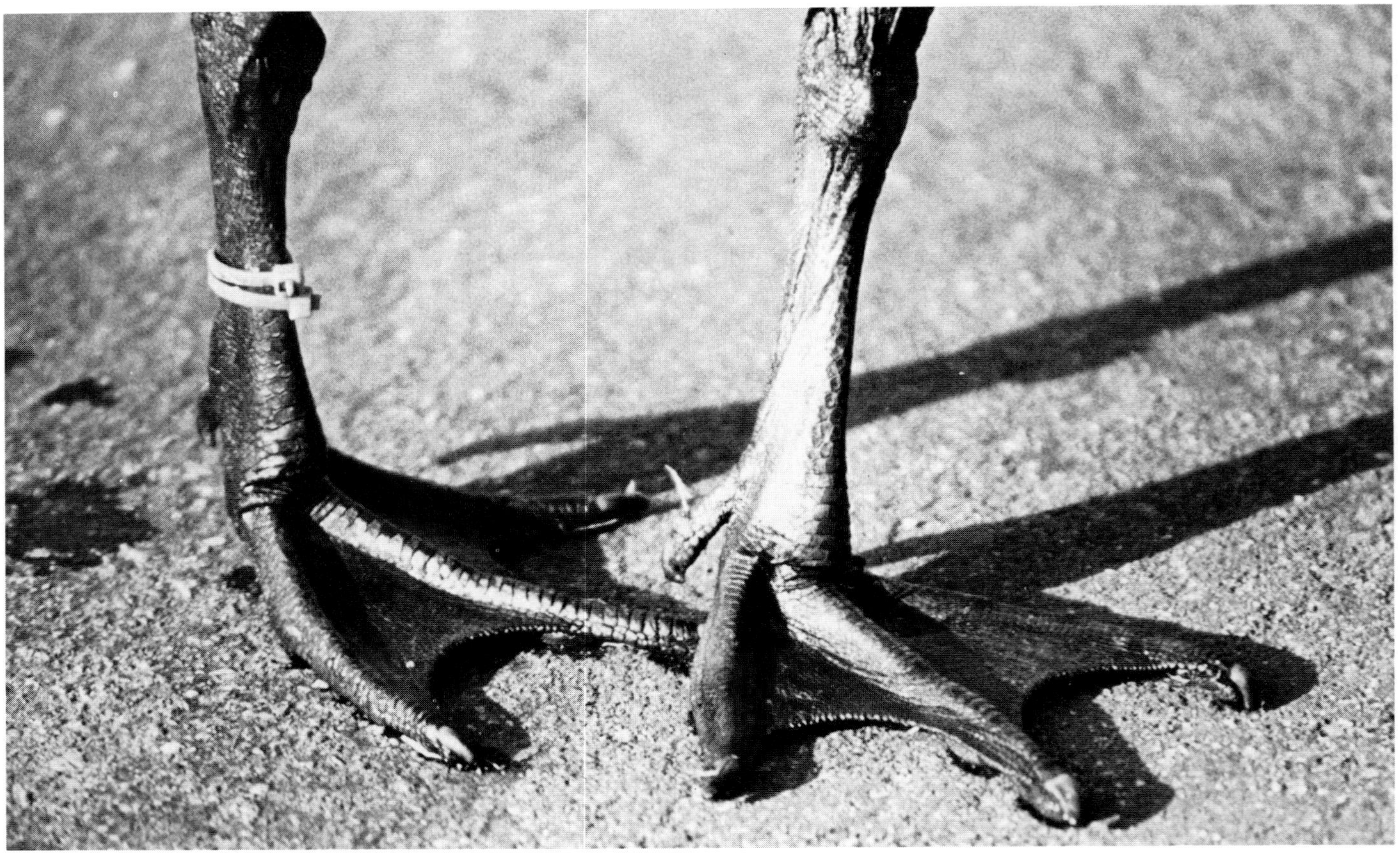

42-14 Feet of the Nene goose. Their webs have reduced in size greatly. Their long toes are very powerful as a result of their climbing and walking over rough terrain.

42-15 Nene goose takes an afternoon siesta.

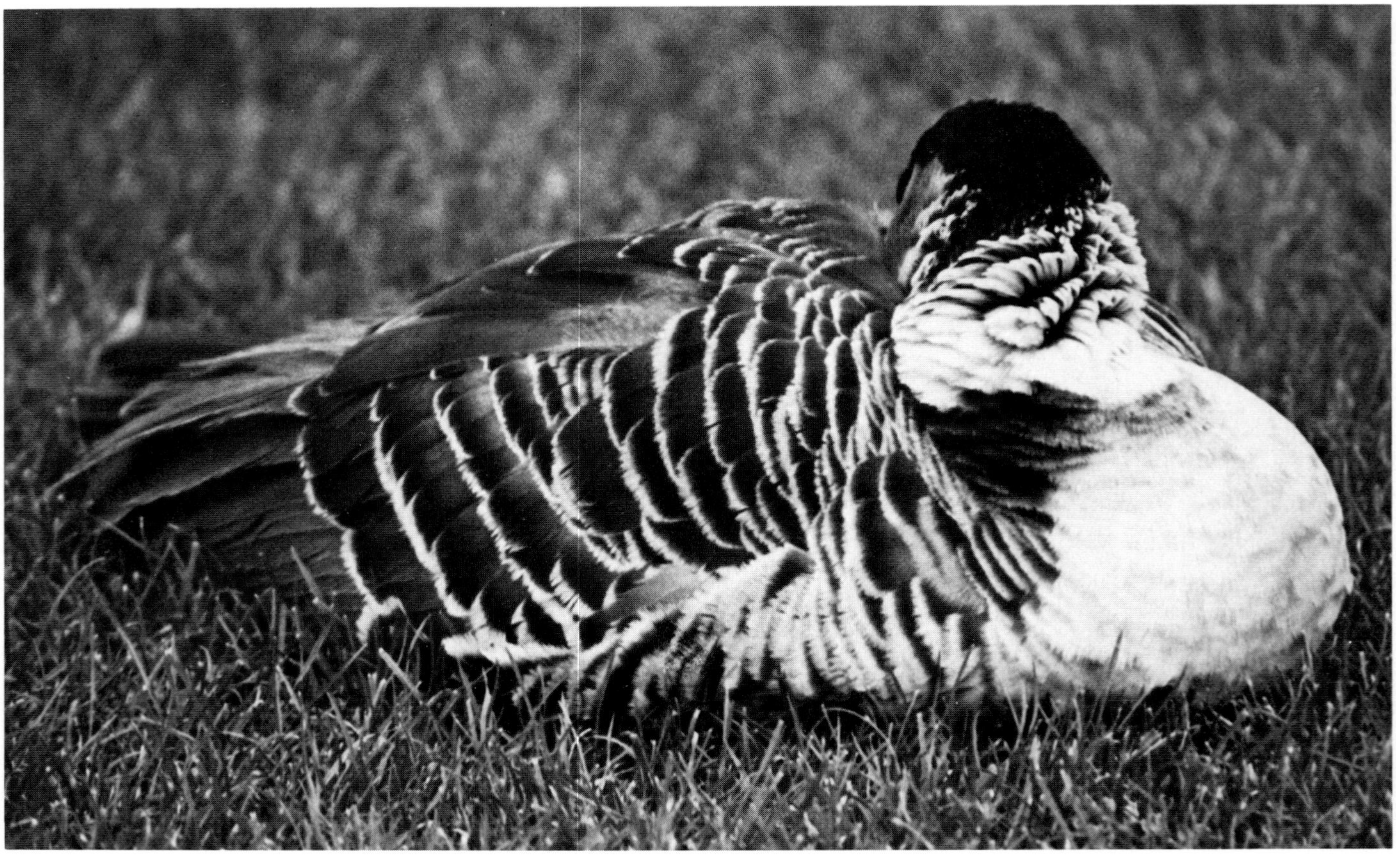

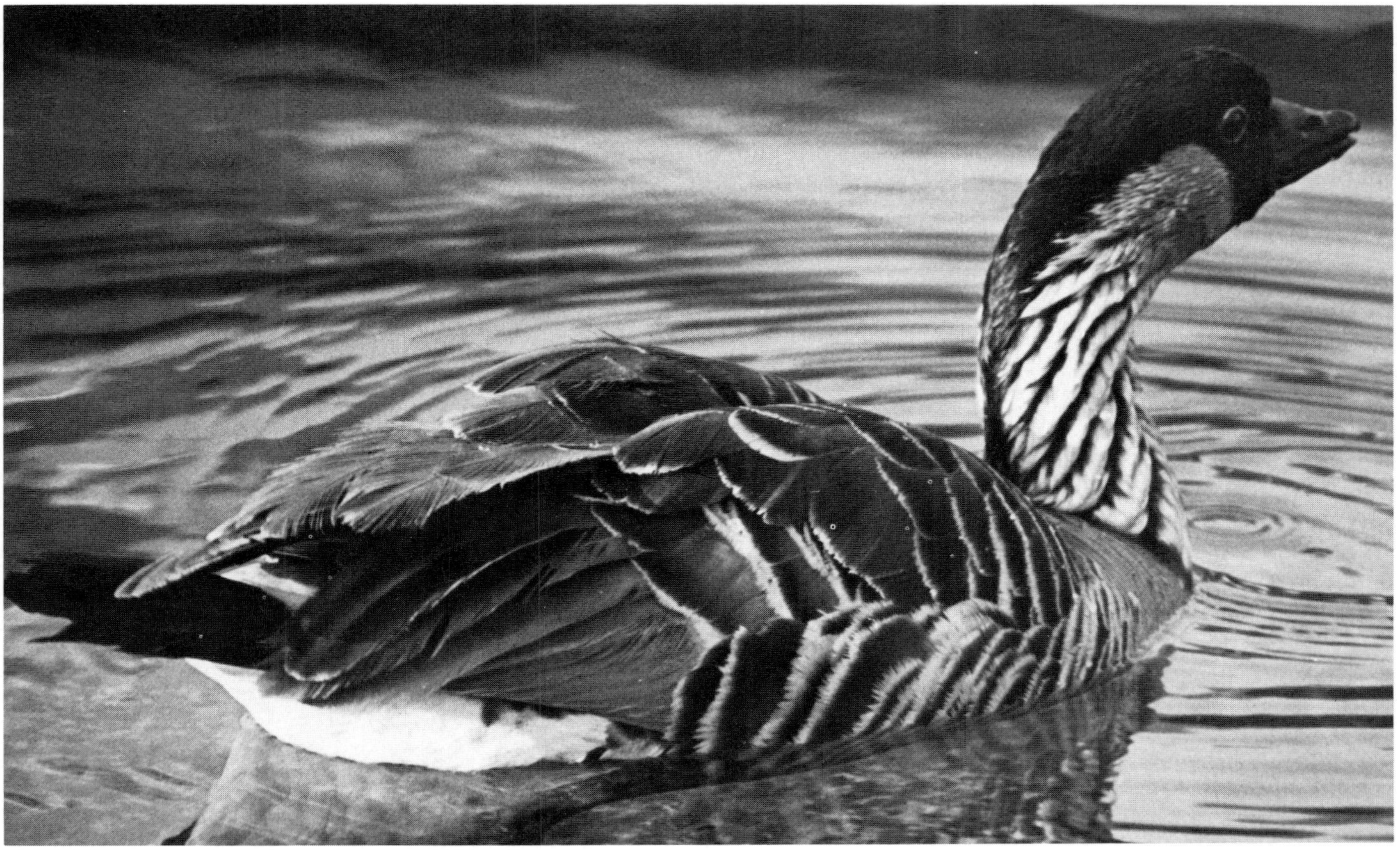

42-16

These smallish Hawaiian geese take to the water infrequently but are good swimmers.

42-17

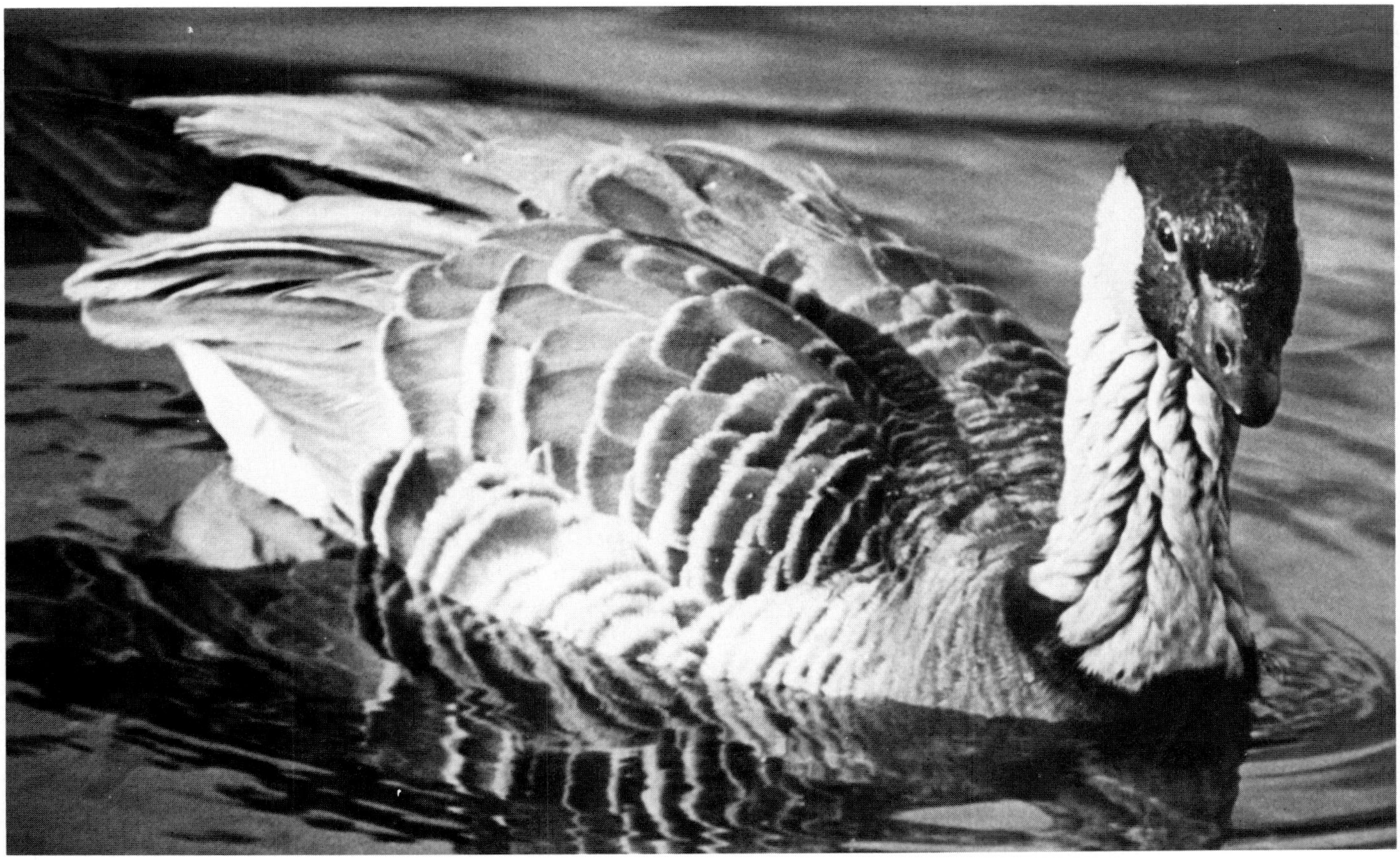

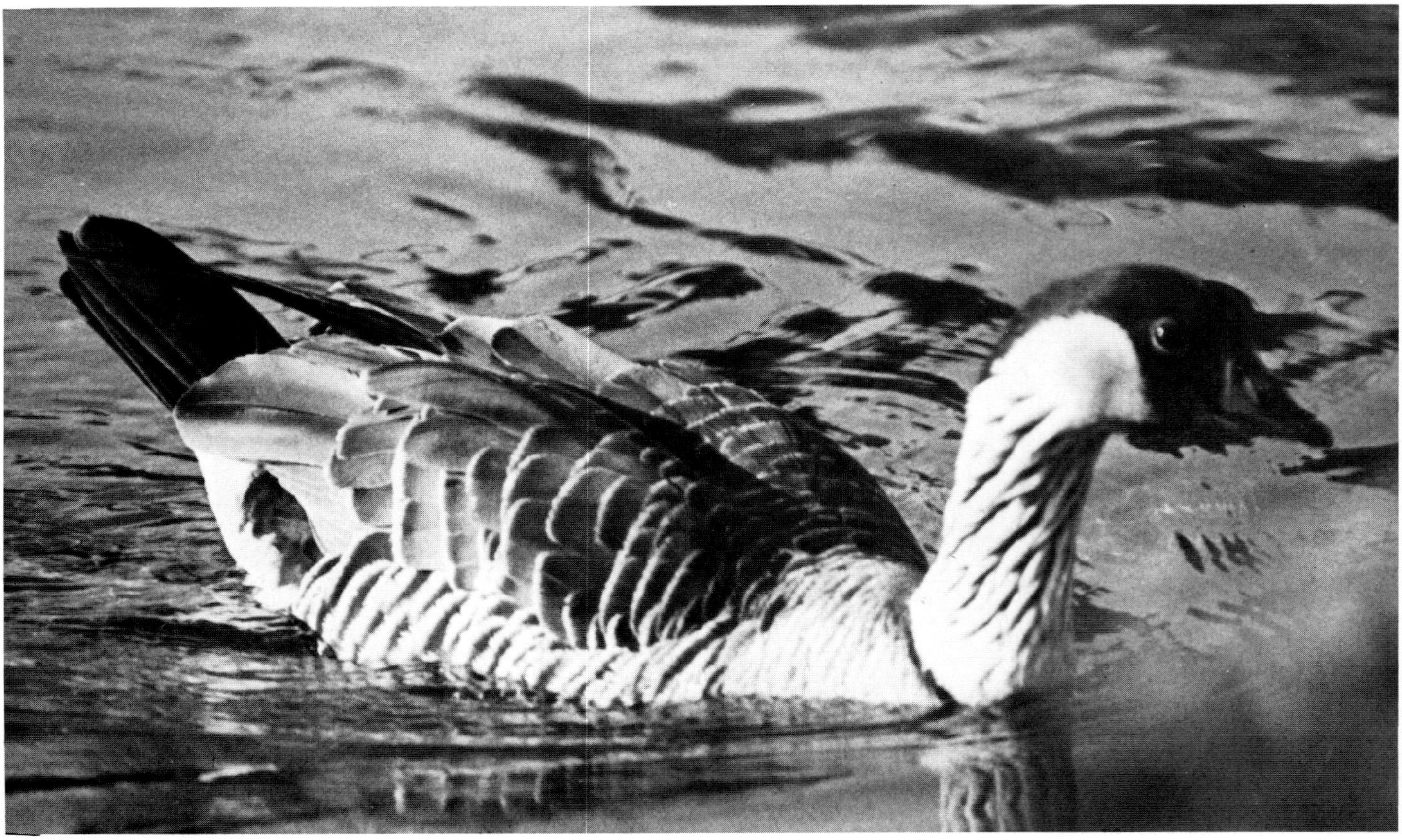

42-18

Two additional studies of swimming Nene geese.

42-19

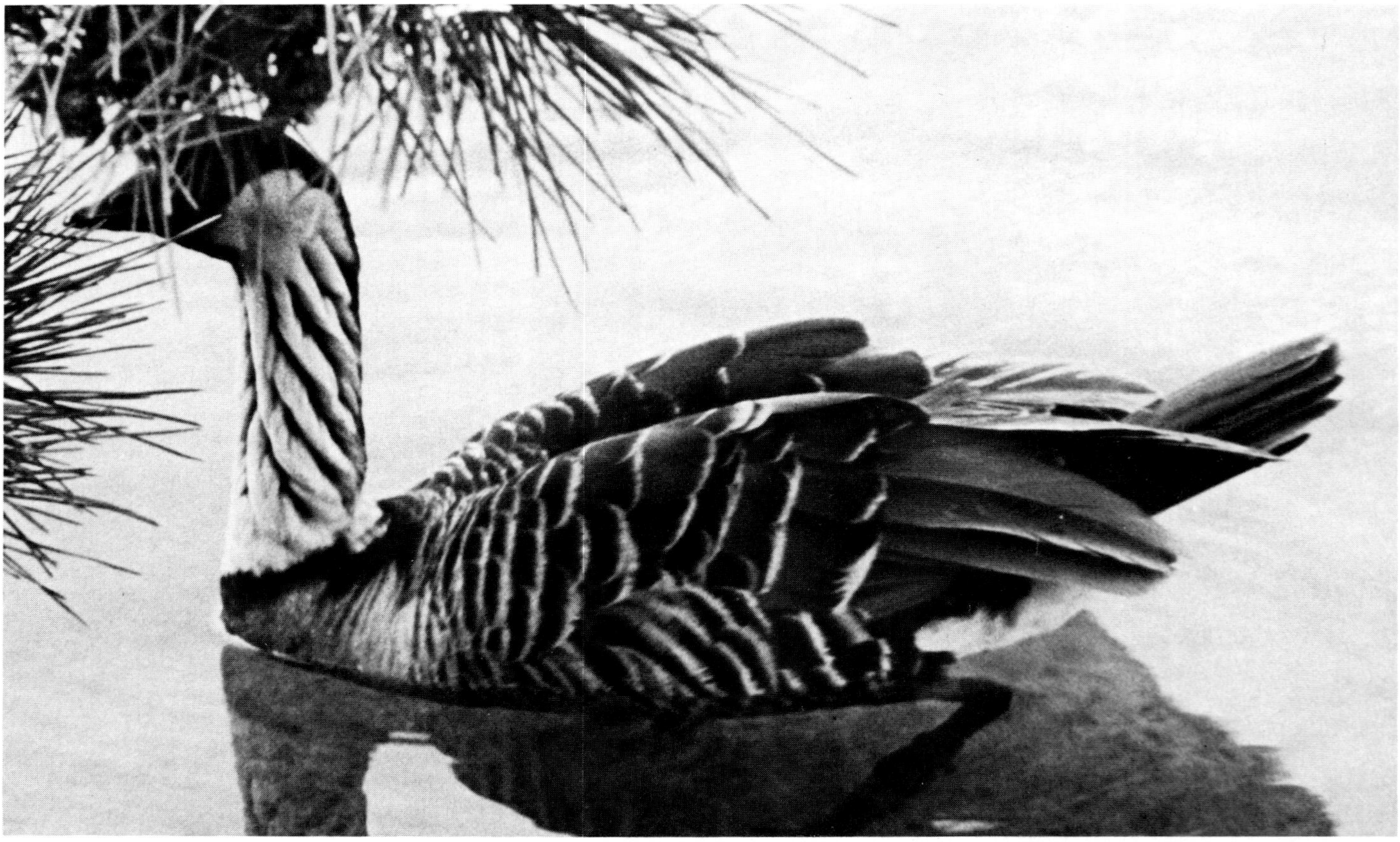

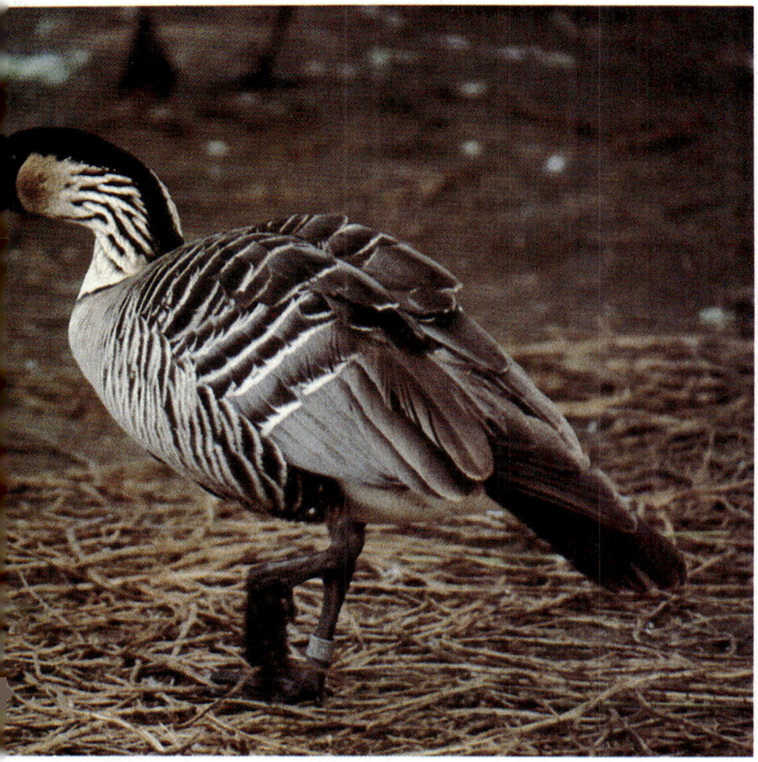

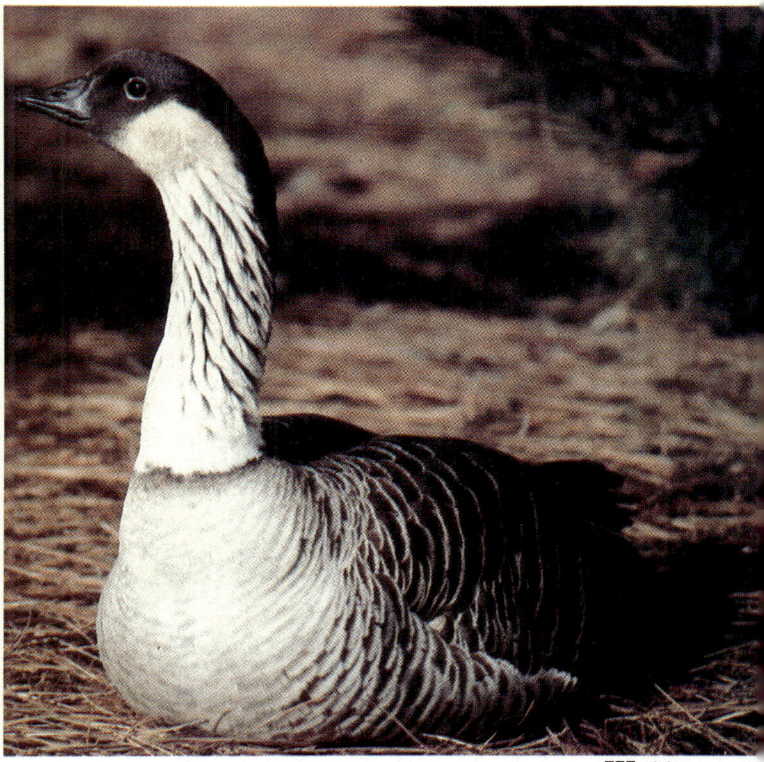

III-43

III-44

Nene Geese. (Chapter 42)

III-45

III-46

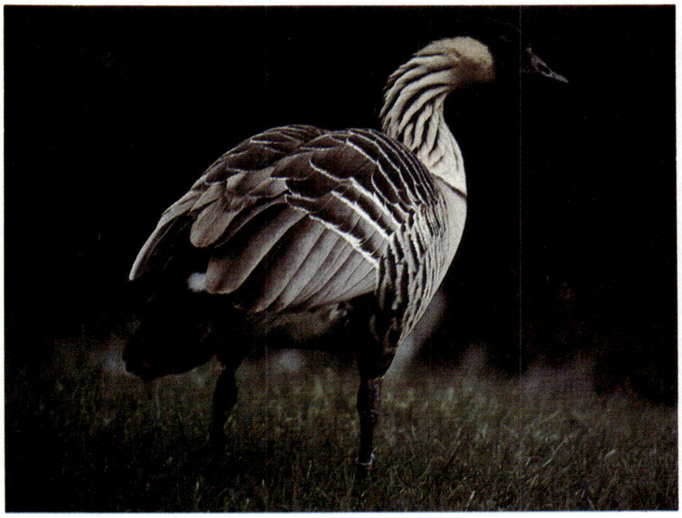

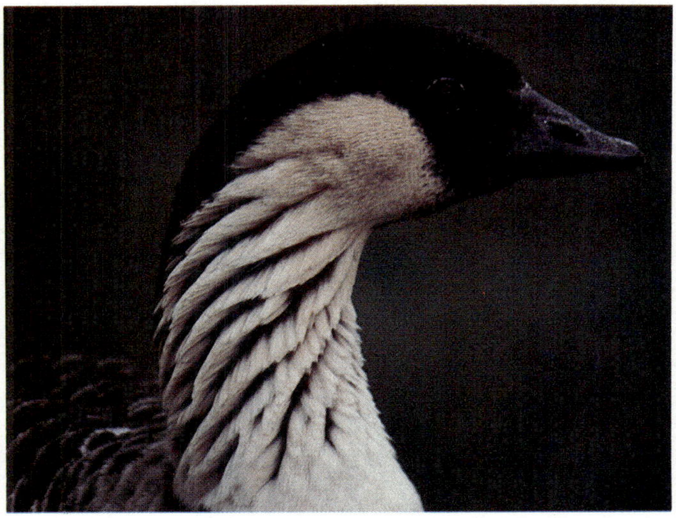

III-47

Nene Geese. (Chapter 42)

III-48

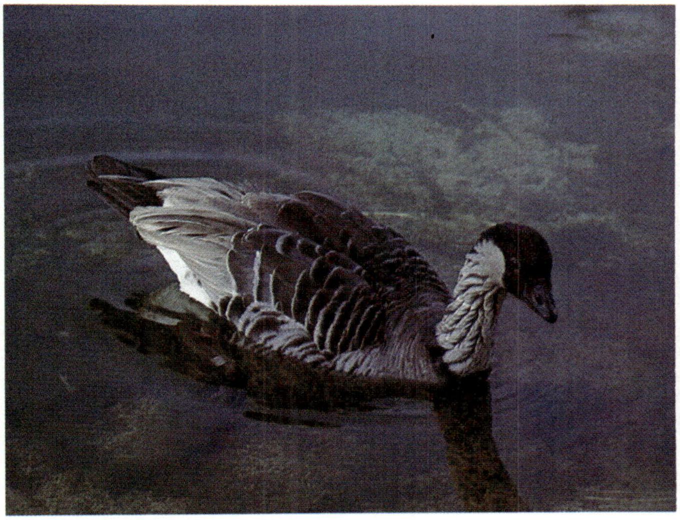

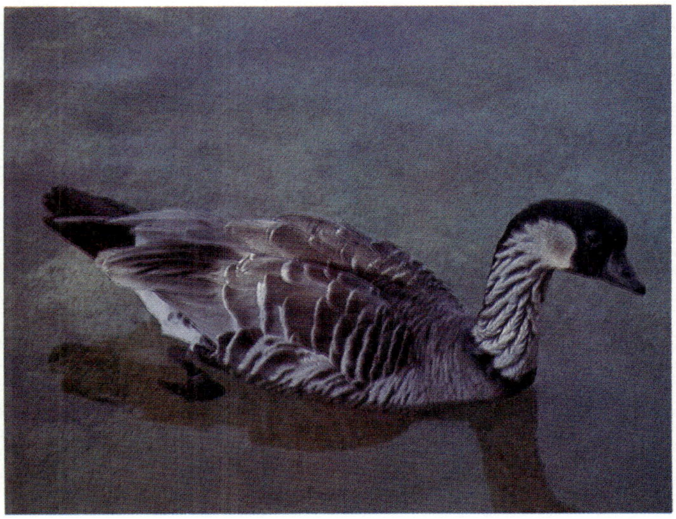

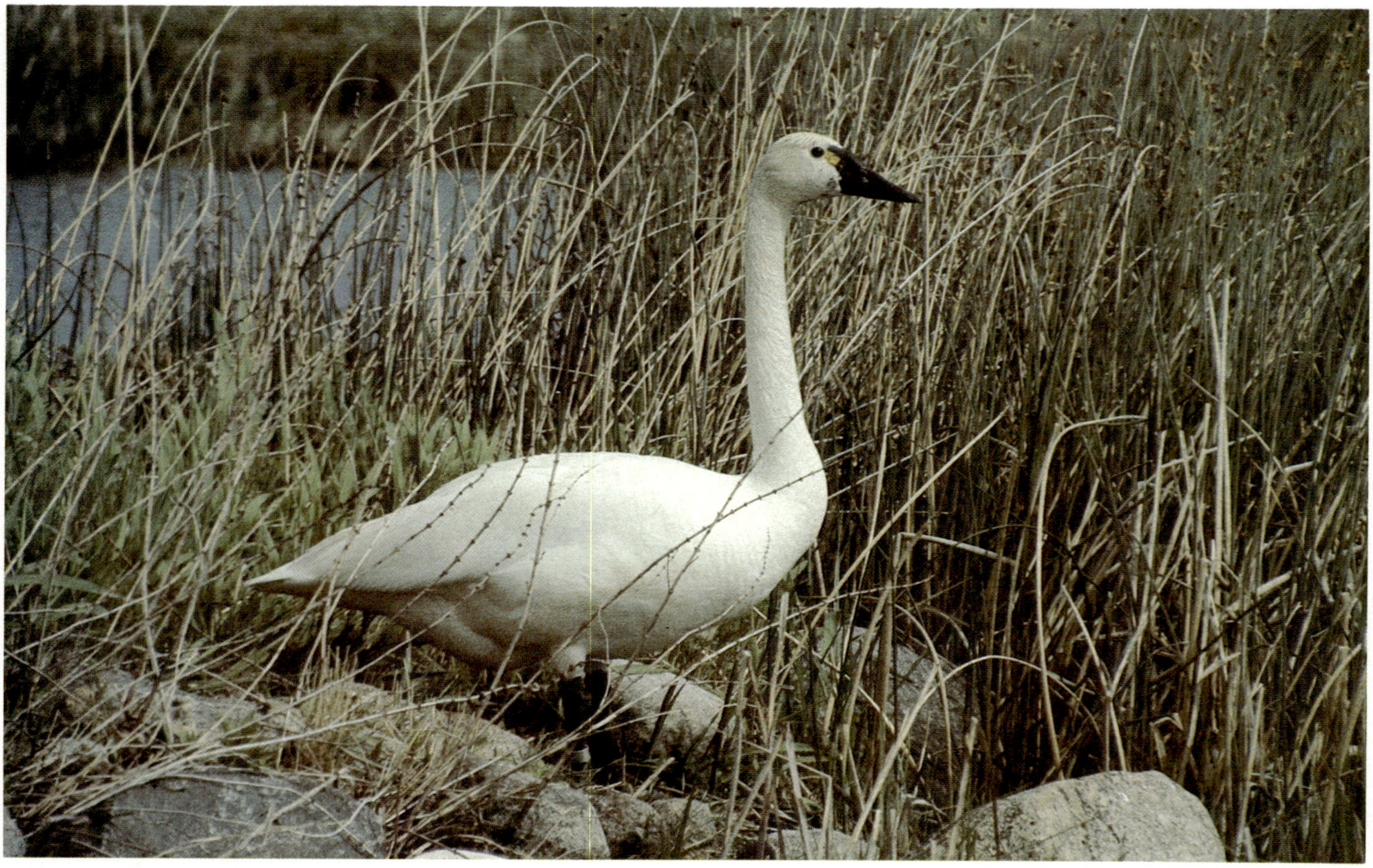

III-49 Whistling Swan. (Chapter 43)

III-50 Whistling Swans, Pair. (Chapter 43)

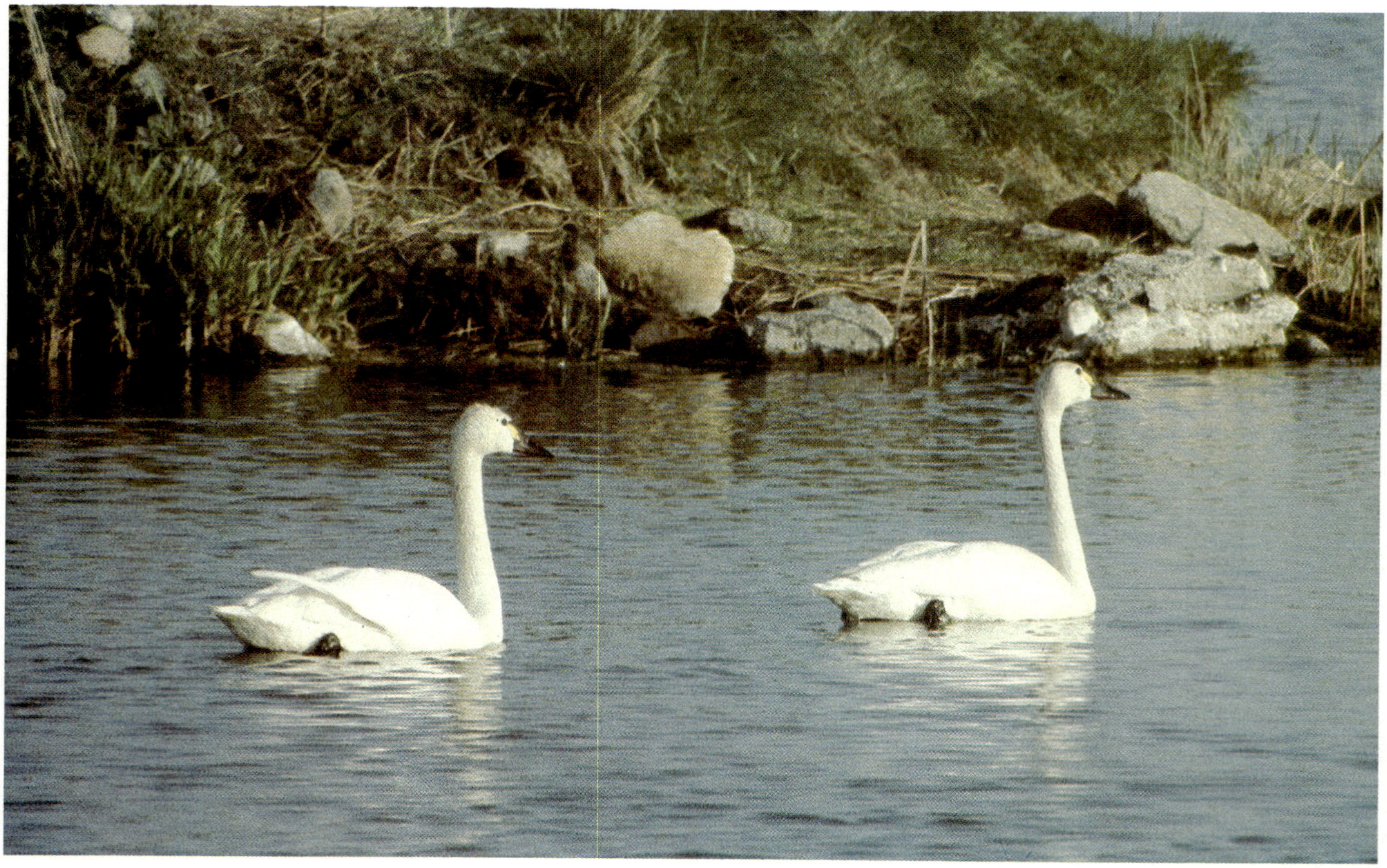

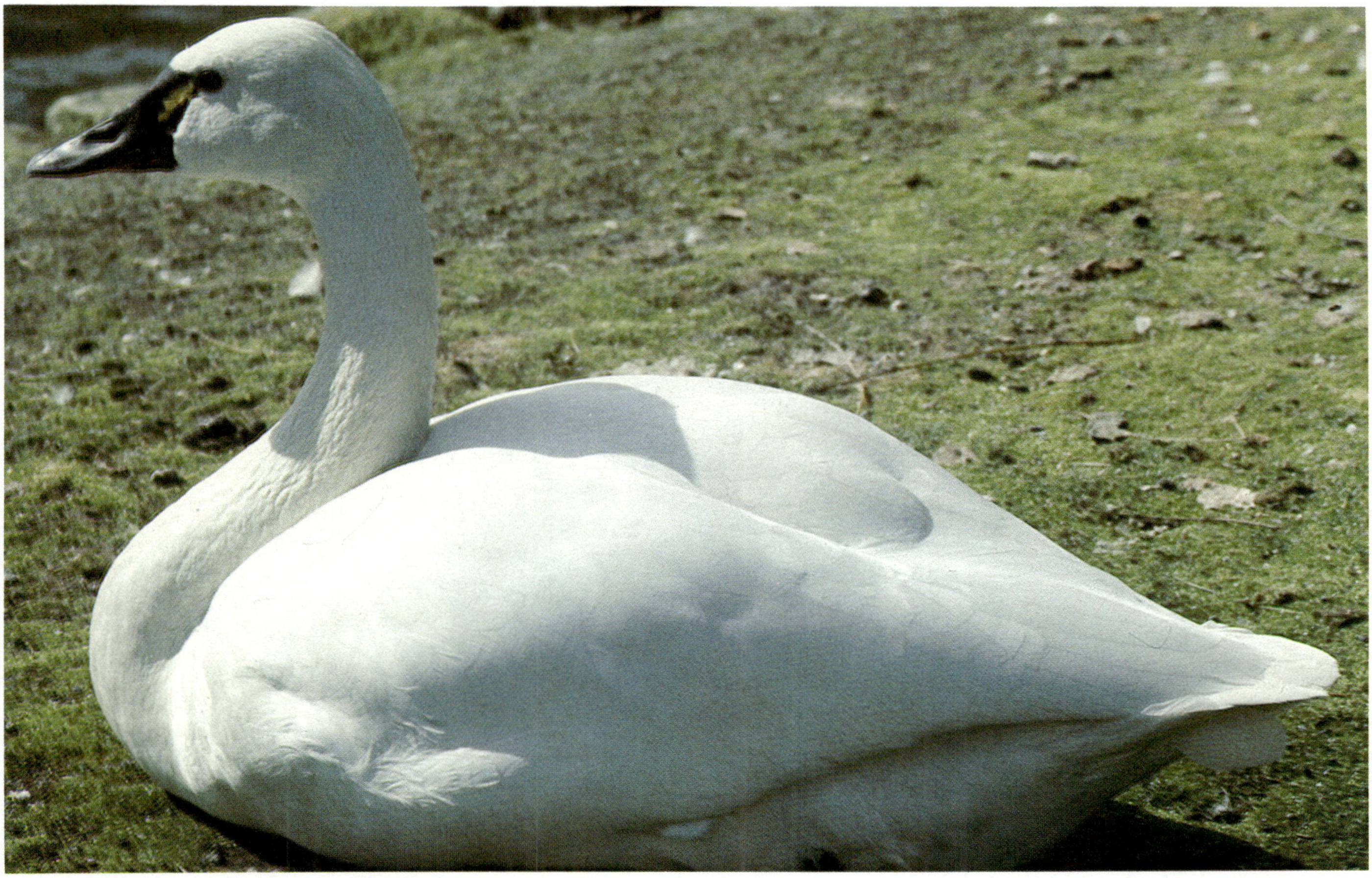

III-51 Whistling Swan. (Chapter 43)

III-52 Mute Swans. (Chapter 45) III-53

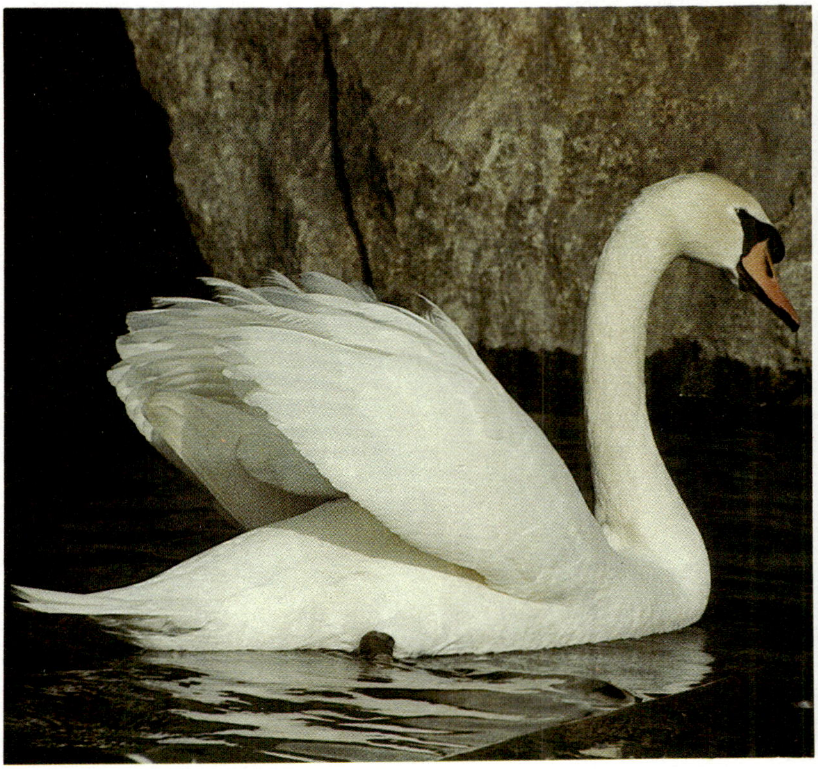

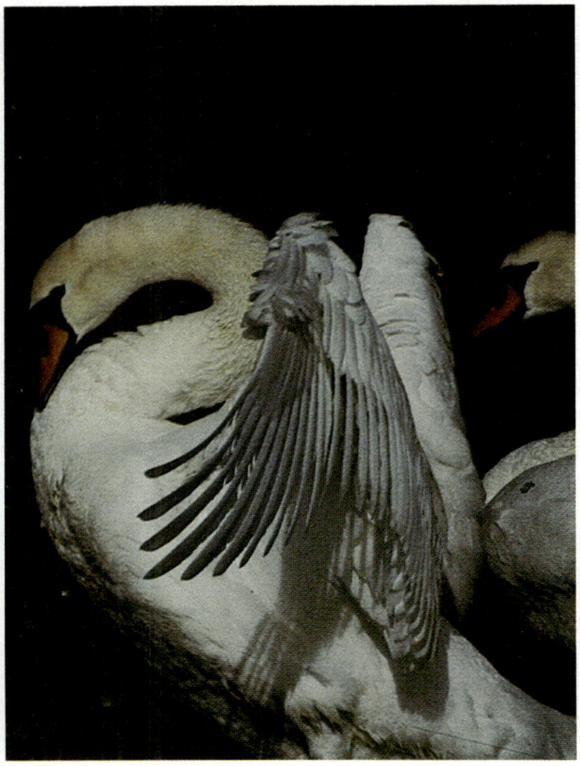

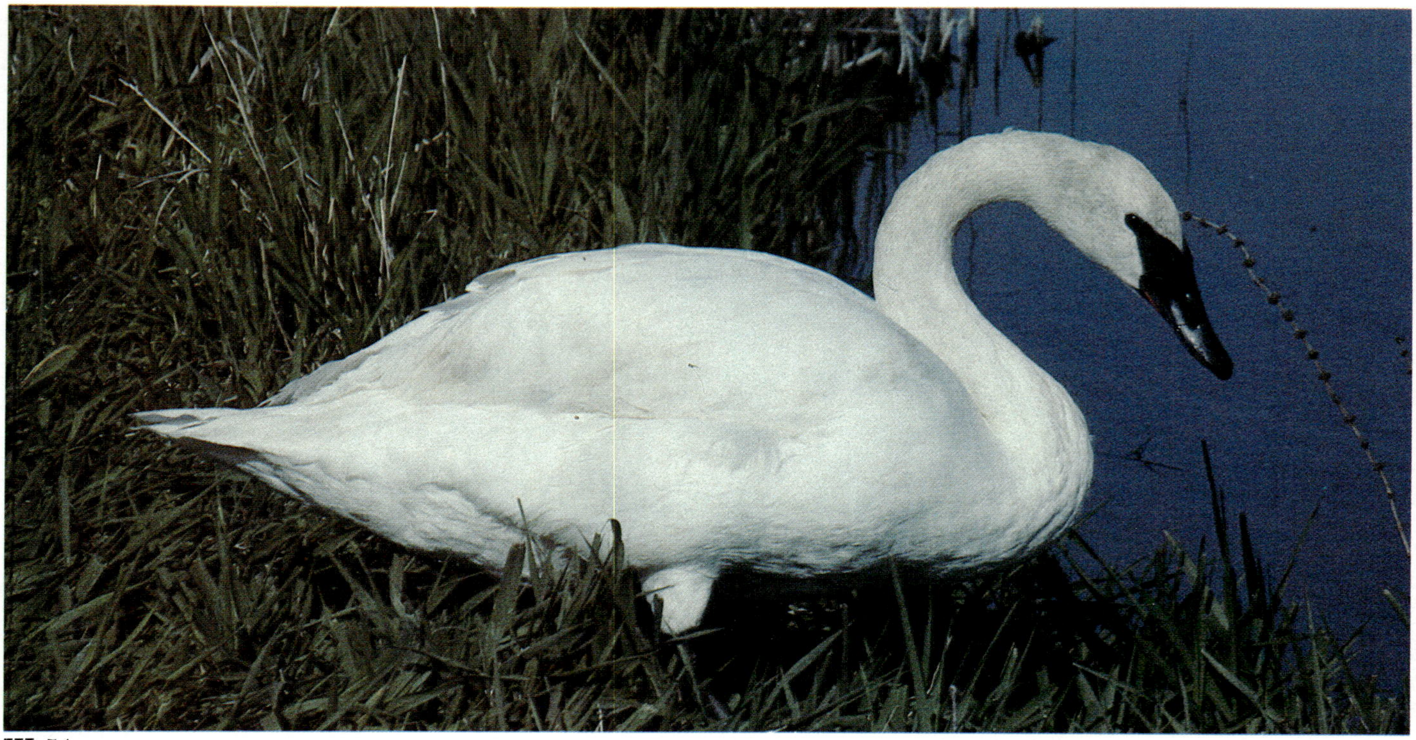

III-54

III-55

Trumpeter Swans. (Chapter 44)

III-56

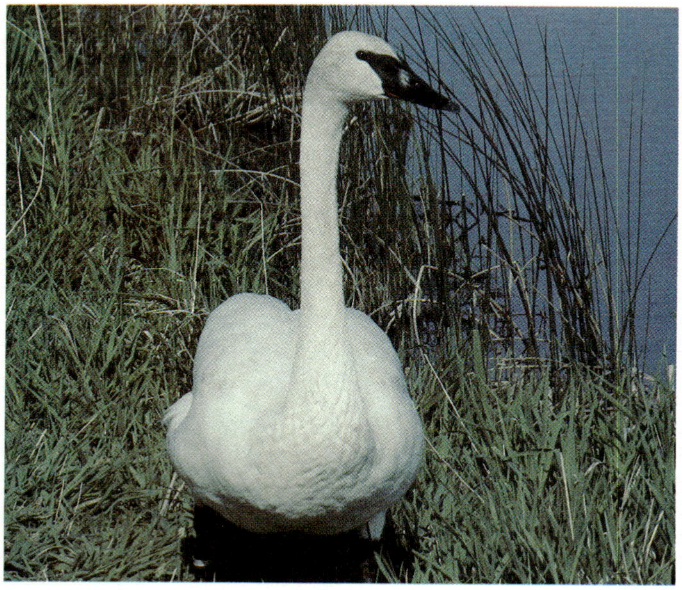

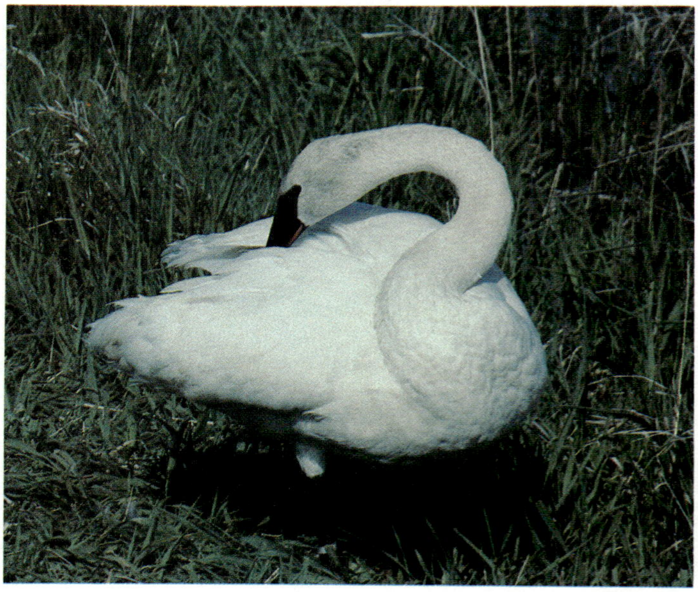

III-57

Trumpeter Swans, pair. (Chapter 44)

III-58

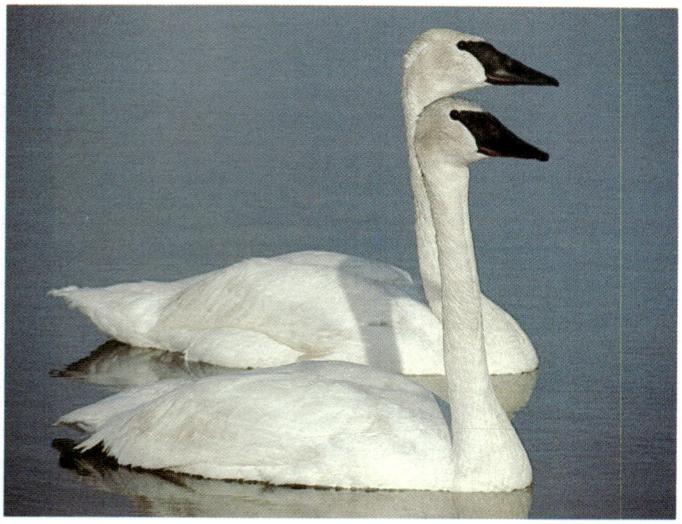

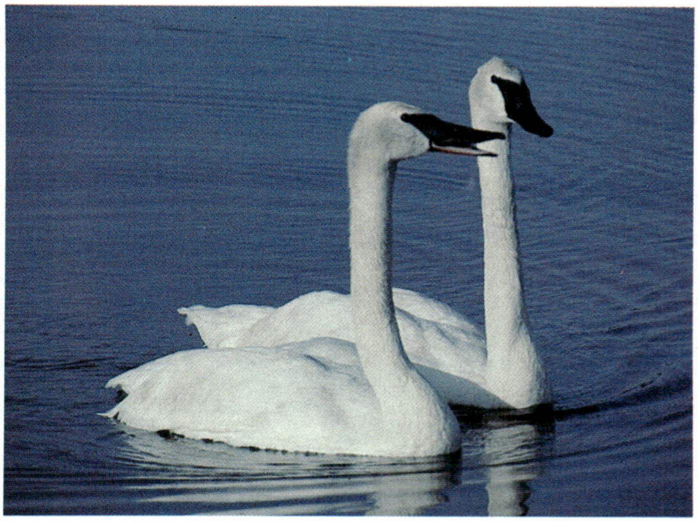

CHAPTER 43

Whistling Swan

Cygnus columbianus columbianus
(Color Photos-Page 166 & 167)

The elegant whistling swan, one of our two native swan species, while substantially reduced in numbers from earlier years, is still fairly common during the winter in areas on both the East and West Coasts. Whistlers nest in the most remote regions of arctic Alaska and Canada, places that are not likely ever to be disturbed by man to any great extent. These very wary birds have been protected since 1916; therefore, it is unlikely their present numbers will ever again be greatly diminished.

Although considerably smaller, whistling swans are not always easily distinguished from trumpter swans. Most whistling swans have a yellow patch on their bills, just forward of each eye, but, unfortunately, some do not. In flight, the two species can be identified by their voices. The call of the whistling swan is high-pitched as compared to the trumpeter's low, extremely resonant, hornlike call. Whistlers can be distinguished from snow geese by their longer necks, slower wing beat, and completely white wings.

Whistling swans in flight are the ultimate in gracefulness. They migrate in small V-shaped flocks, led by a strong mature male, or cob, as he is called. The young birds, or cygnets, normally fly farther back in the formation where less effort is required to maintain the speed of the group. When traveling to their feeding grounds, they fly in long, curving lines, or sometimes in irregular formation.

Whistling swans do not reach full maturity until they are five or six years old but occasionally mate when they are only three years of age. Like geese, they mate for life, but if one is killed, the other may take a new mate. Nests are usually made on a mound of moss or dried grass, often near the water but sometimes as far as a half mile from the shoreline. Sometimes, the female will lay as many as seven eggs, though four is the average number. The beautiful, downy young hatch in 32 to 35 days. Approximately two weeks after the cygnets are hatched, the female molts and becomes flightless. About the time she is able to fly, the cob molts his flight feathers, so, normally, one of the parents is capable of flight at all times. The cygnets are flying in about 2½ months, and are ready to migrate when they are 3½ months old. Usually only two or three of the young survive; they remain constantly with their parents for the first year.

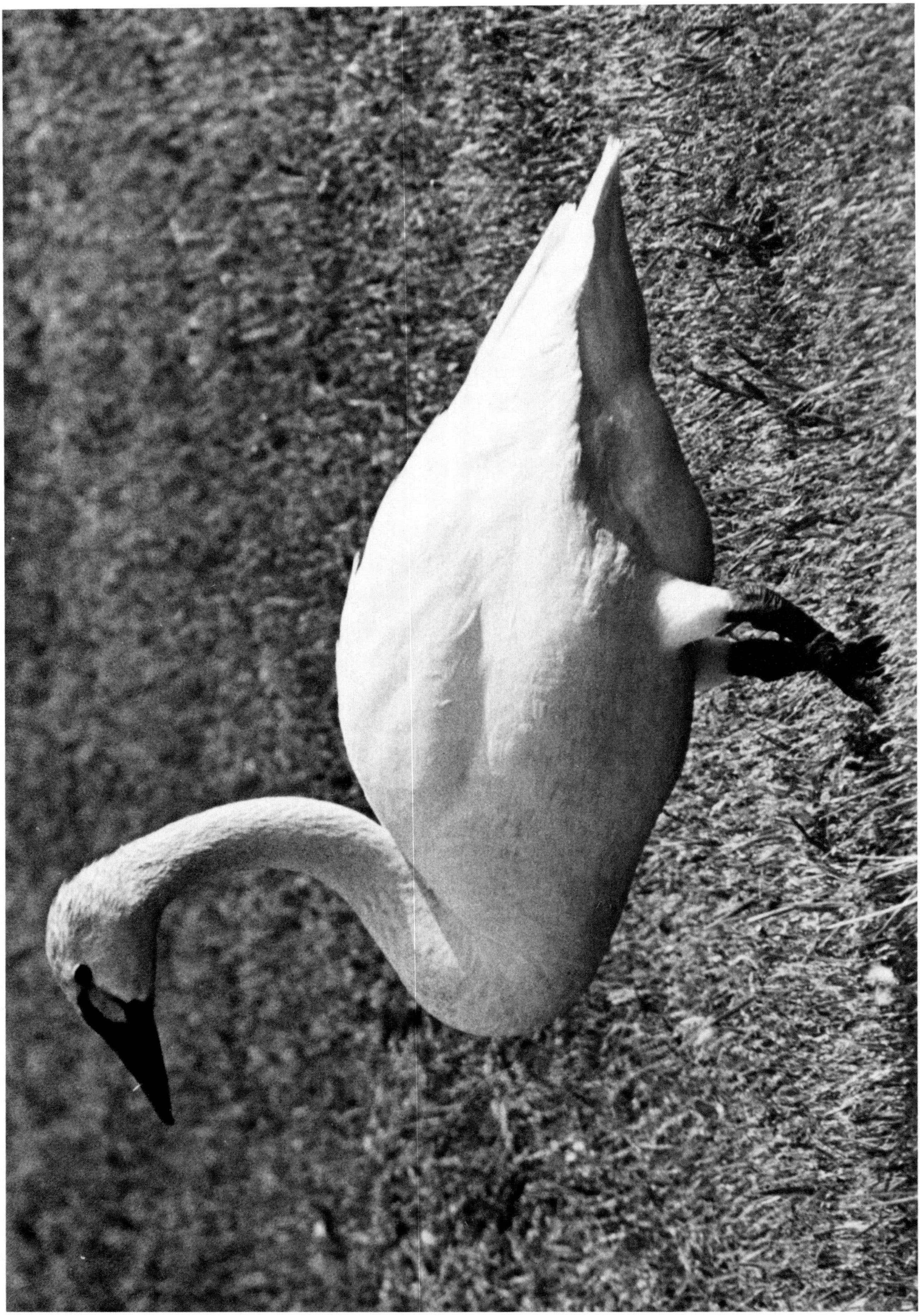

43-1 The magnificent whistling swan. Whistling swans are common winter visitors to both the East and West Coasts. These large birds are exceeded in size only by the trumpeter swan.

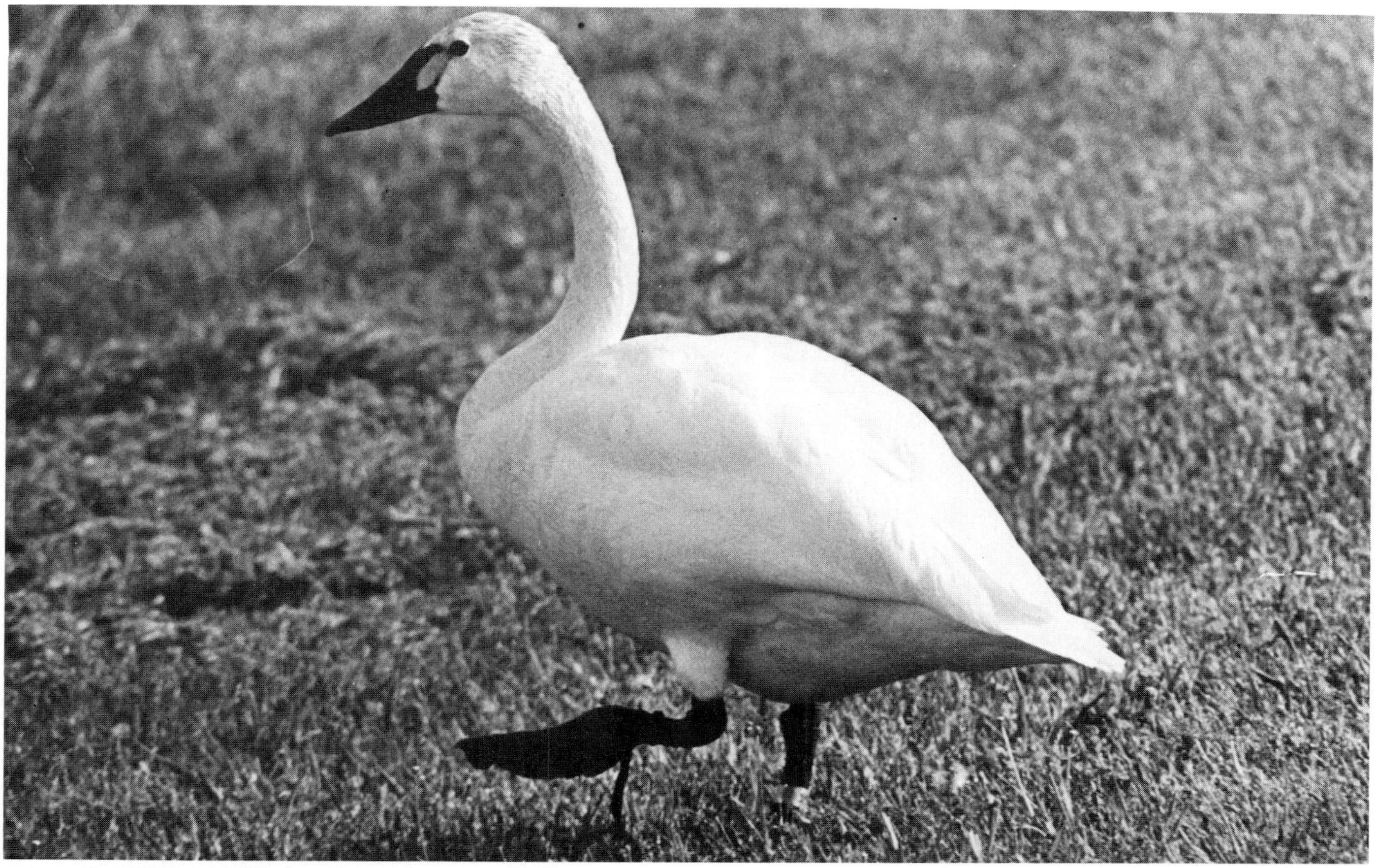

43-2 Striding whistling swan. Note large feet.

43-3 Front views of this graceful bird. Note body shape and the wide placement of his muscular legs. 43-4

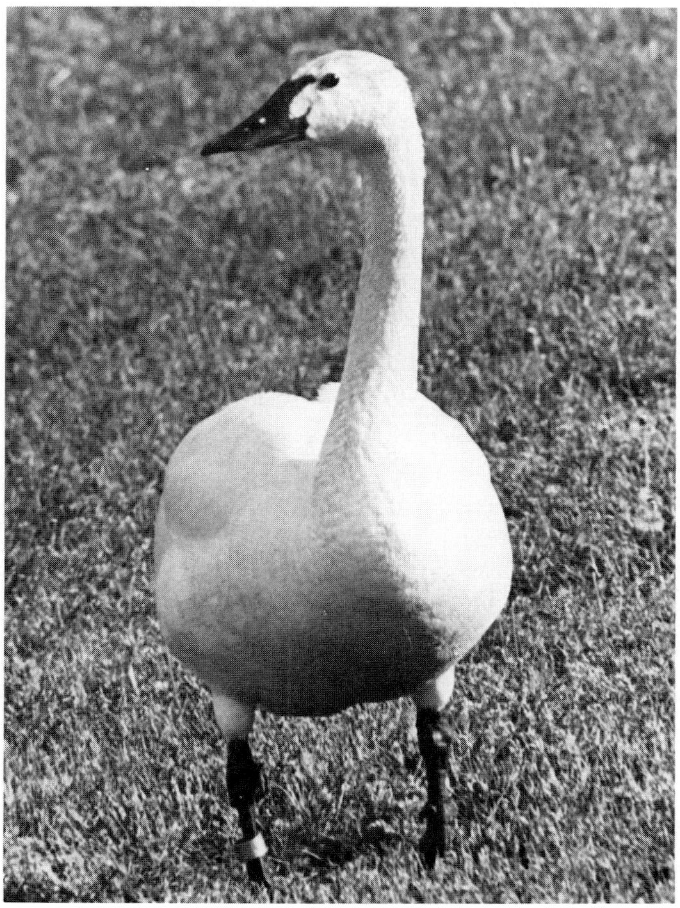

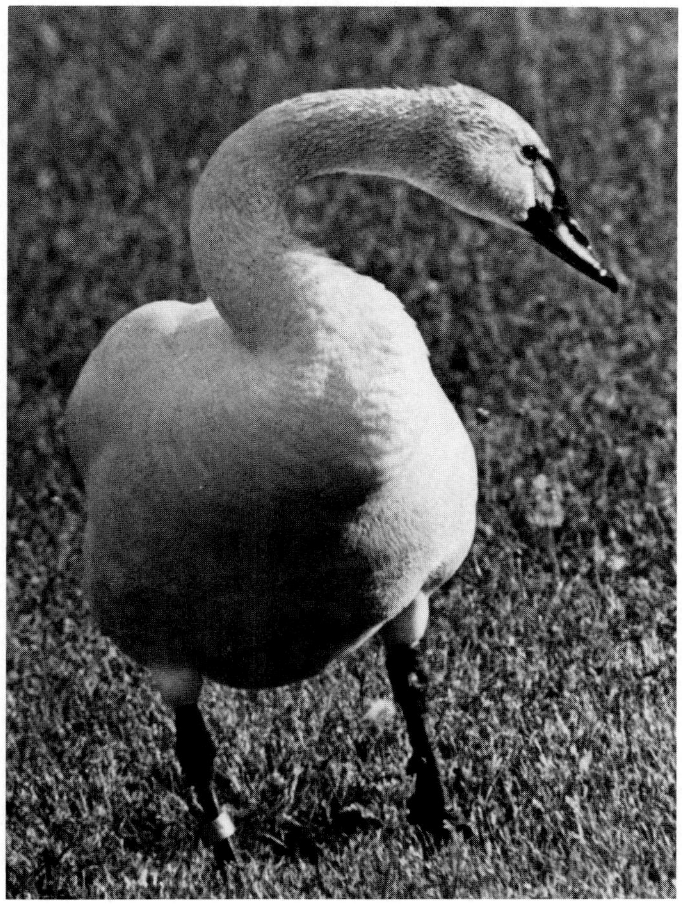

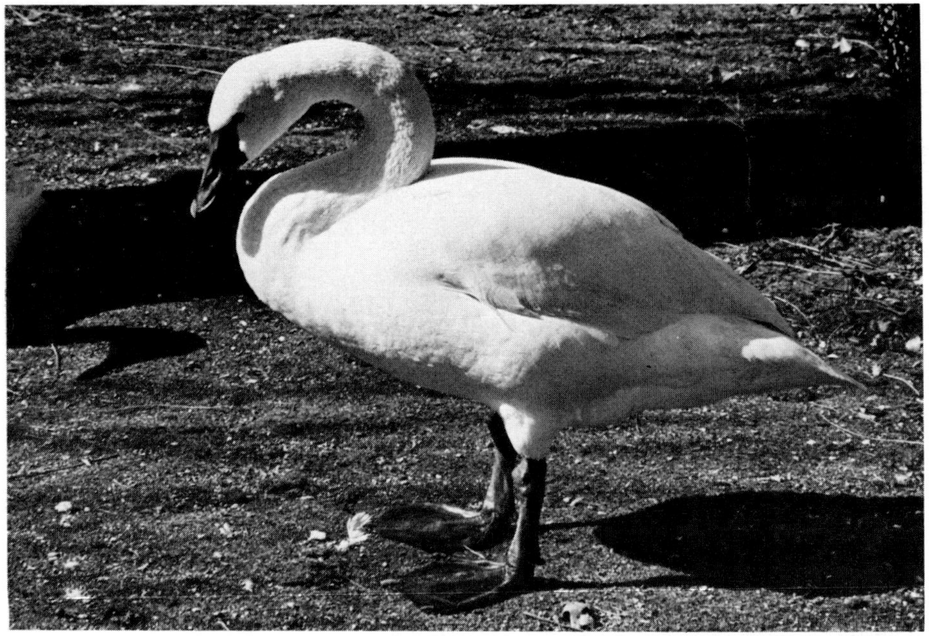

43-5

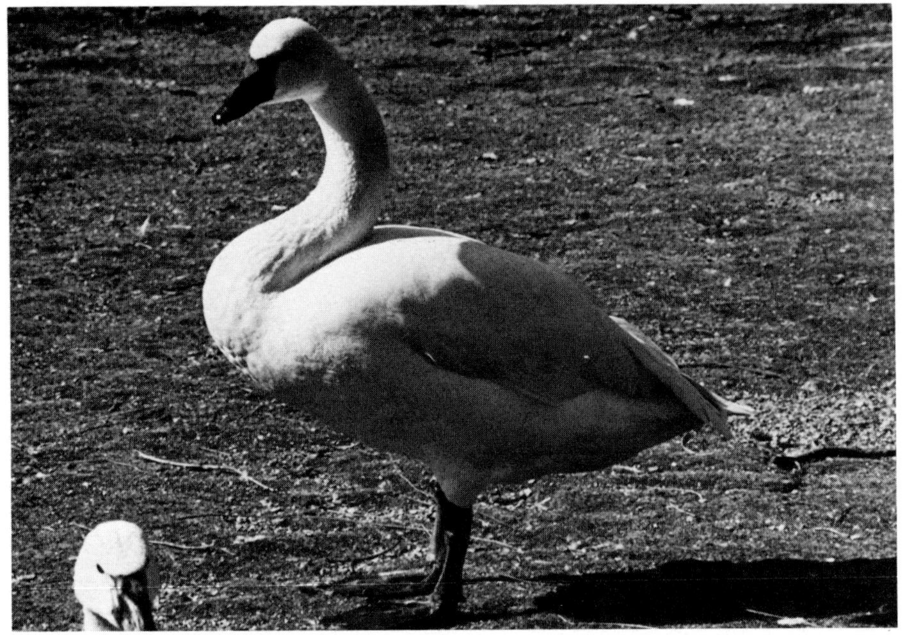

43-6

Four profile studies of whistling swans. Their necks are very flexible and are usually held in graceful, flowing lines.

43-7

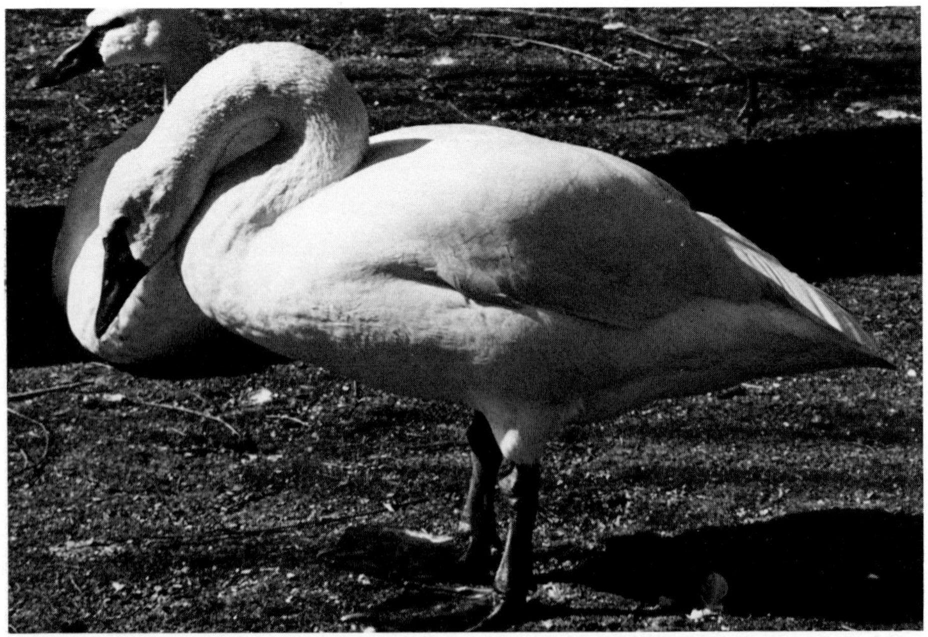

43-8

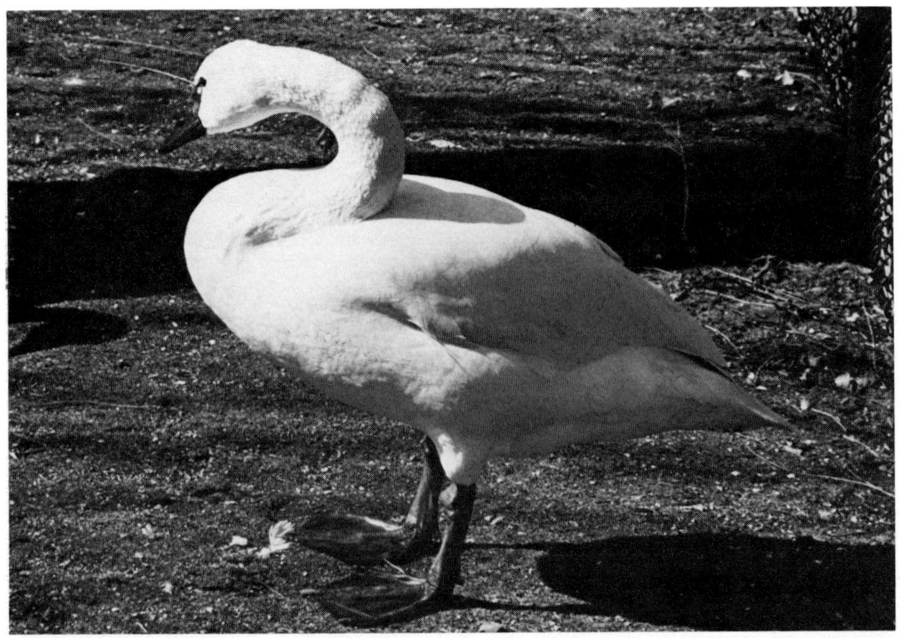

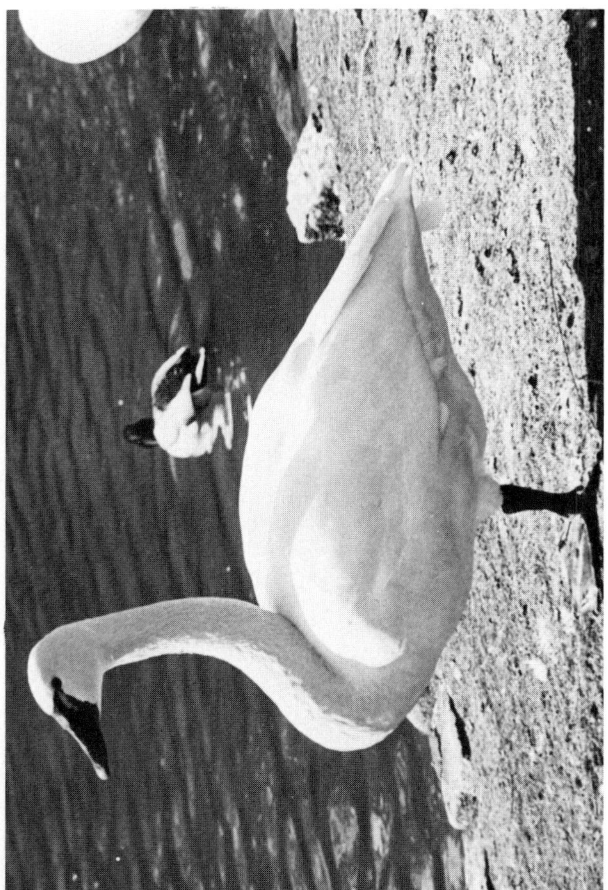

43-9

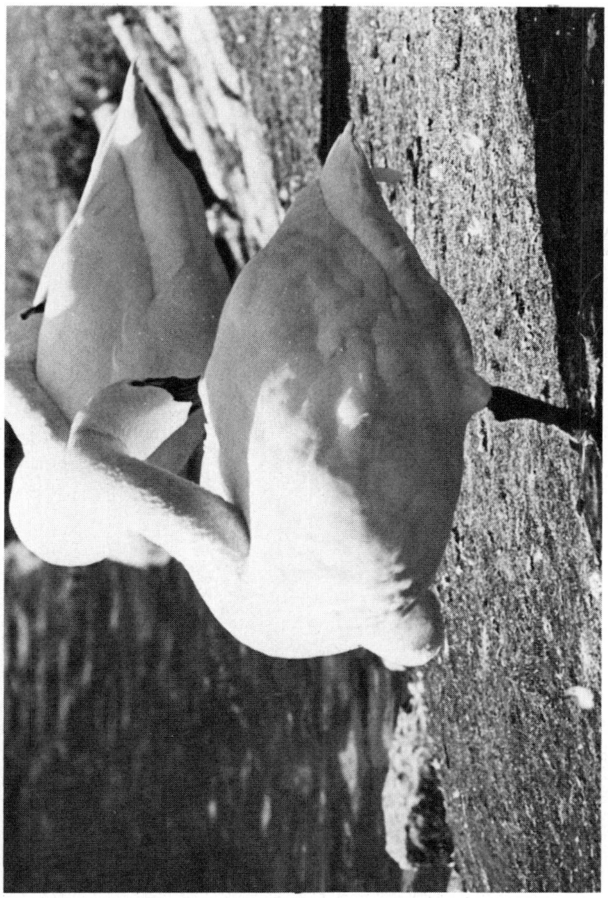

43-10

Nice profile of a whistling swan standing on one leg.

Whistling swans preen their feathers while resting on one leg.

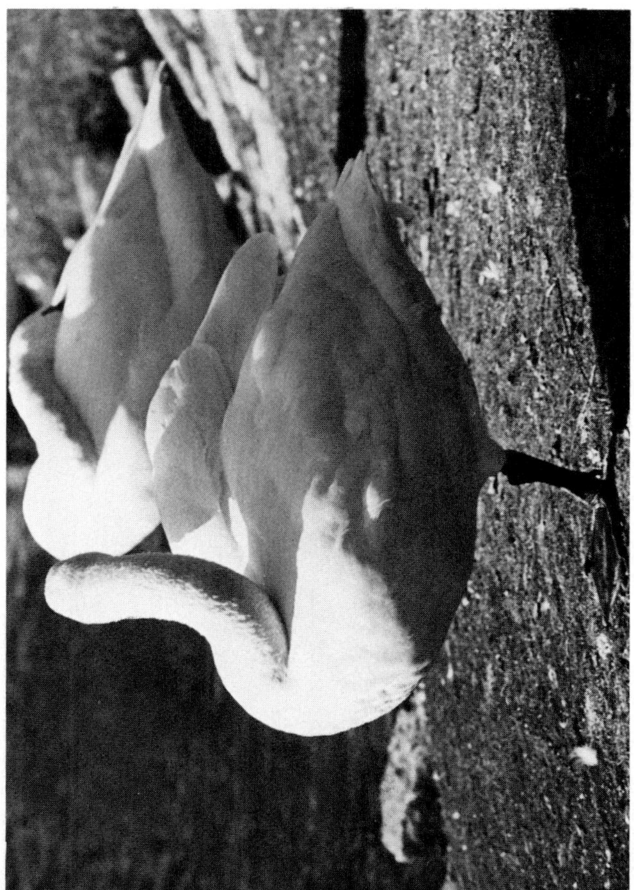

43-11

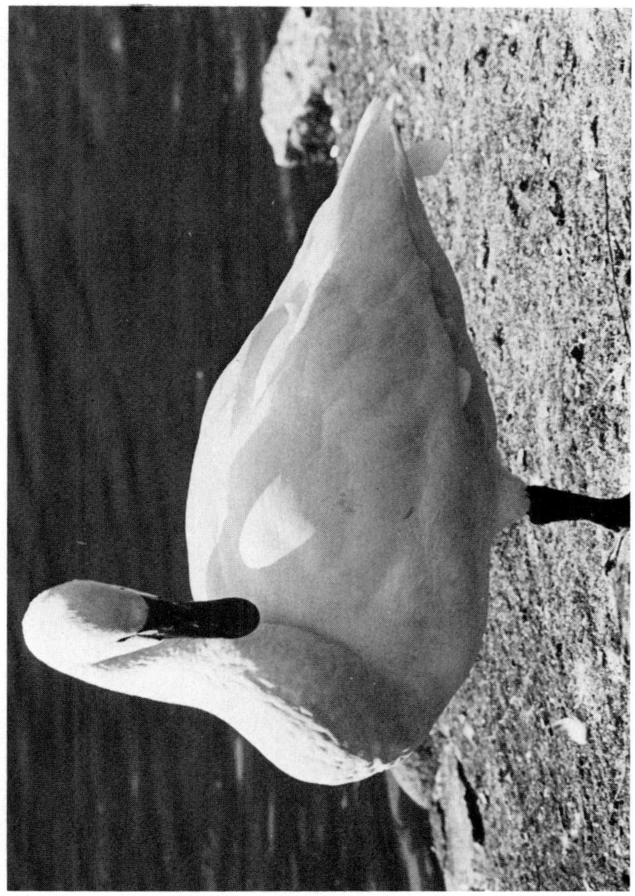

43-12

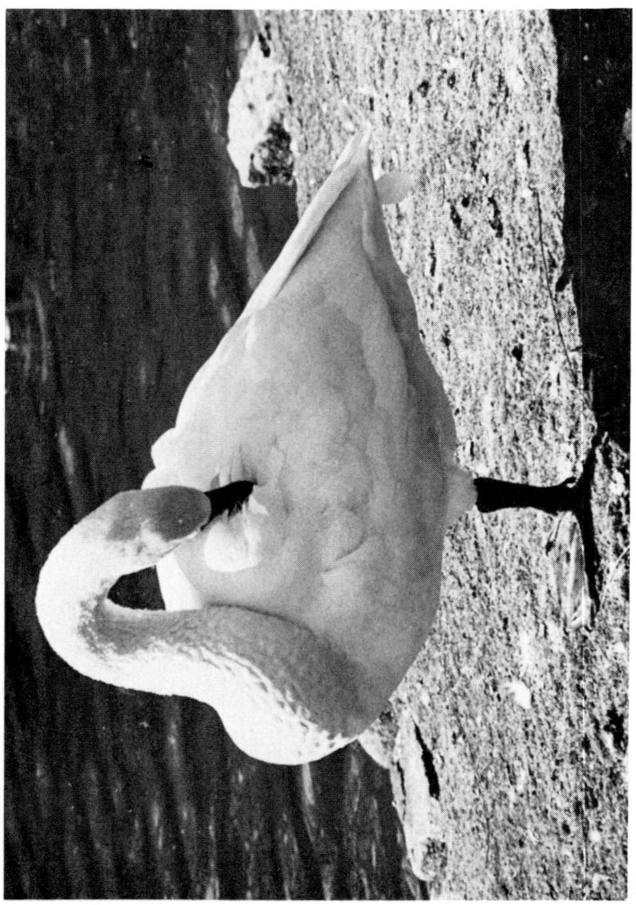

43-13

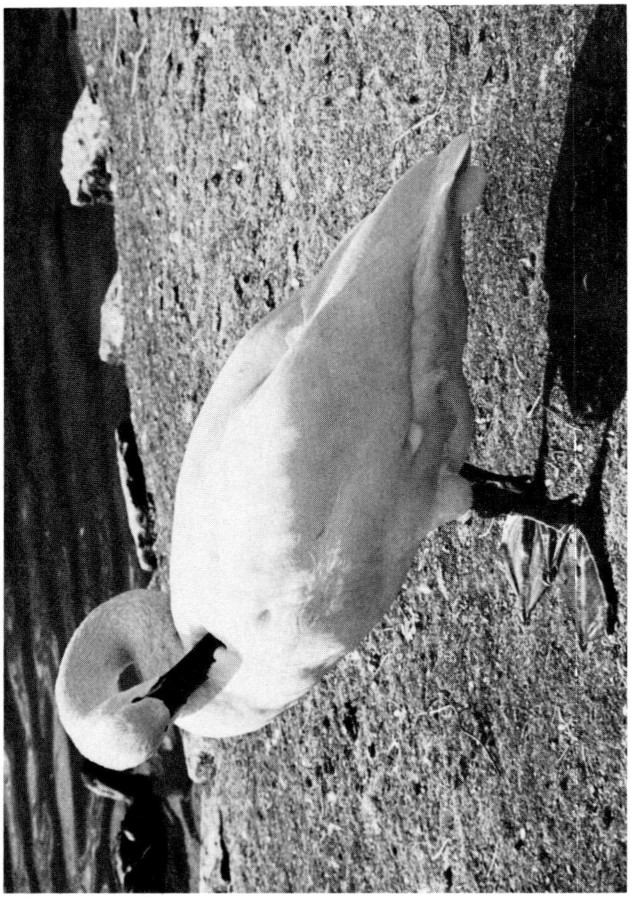

43-14

Whistling swans in four interesting preening poses. Notice graceful neck lines.

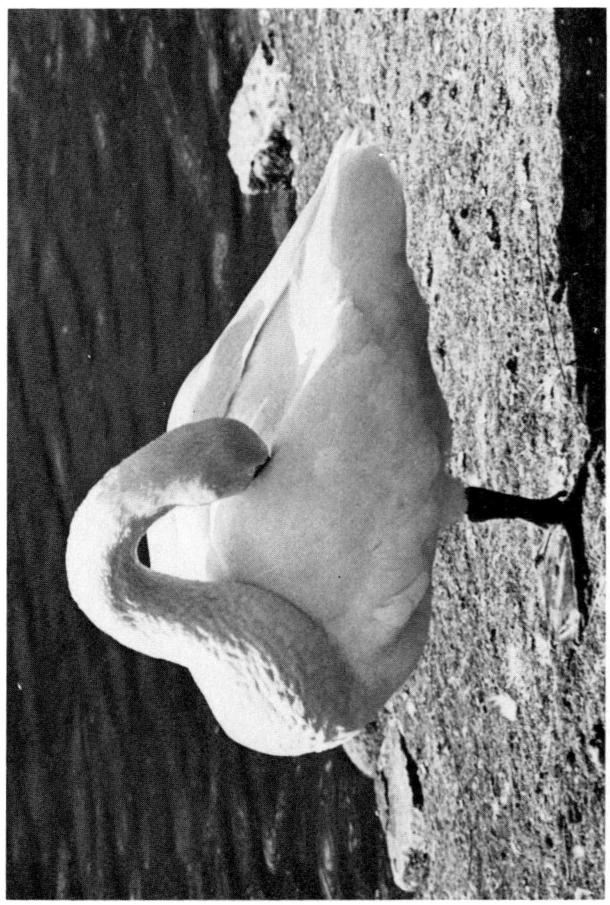

43-15

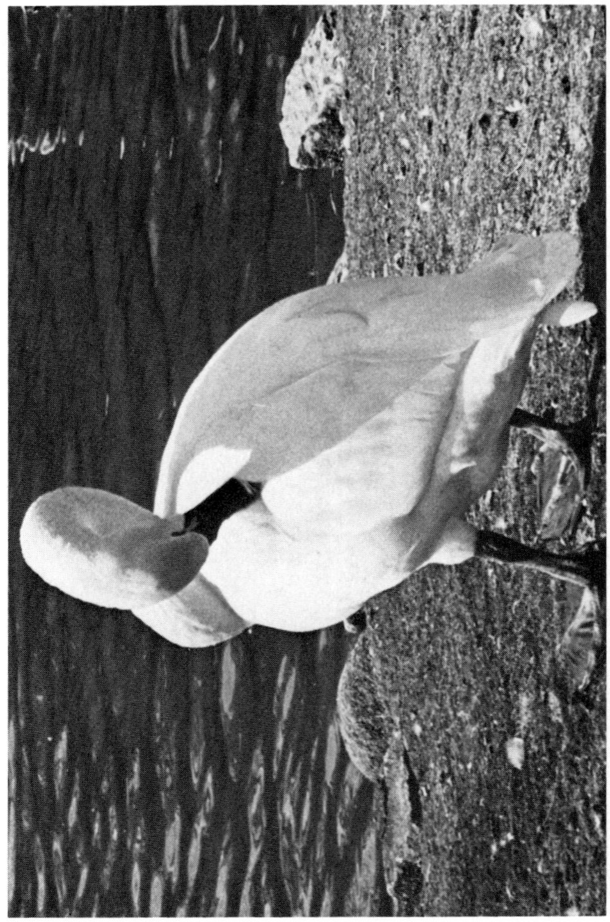

43-16

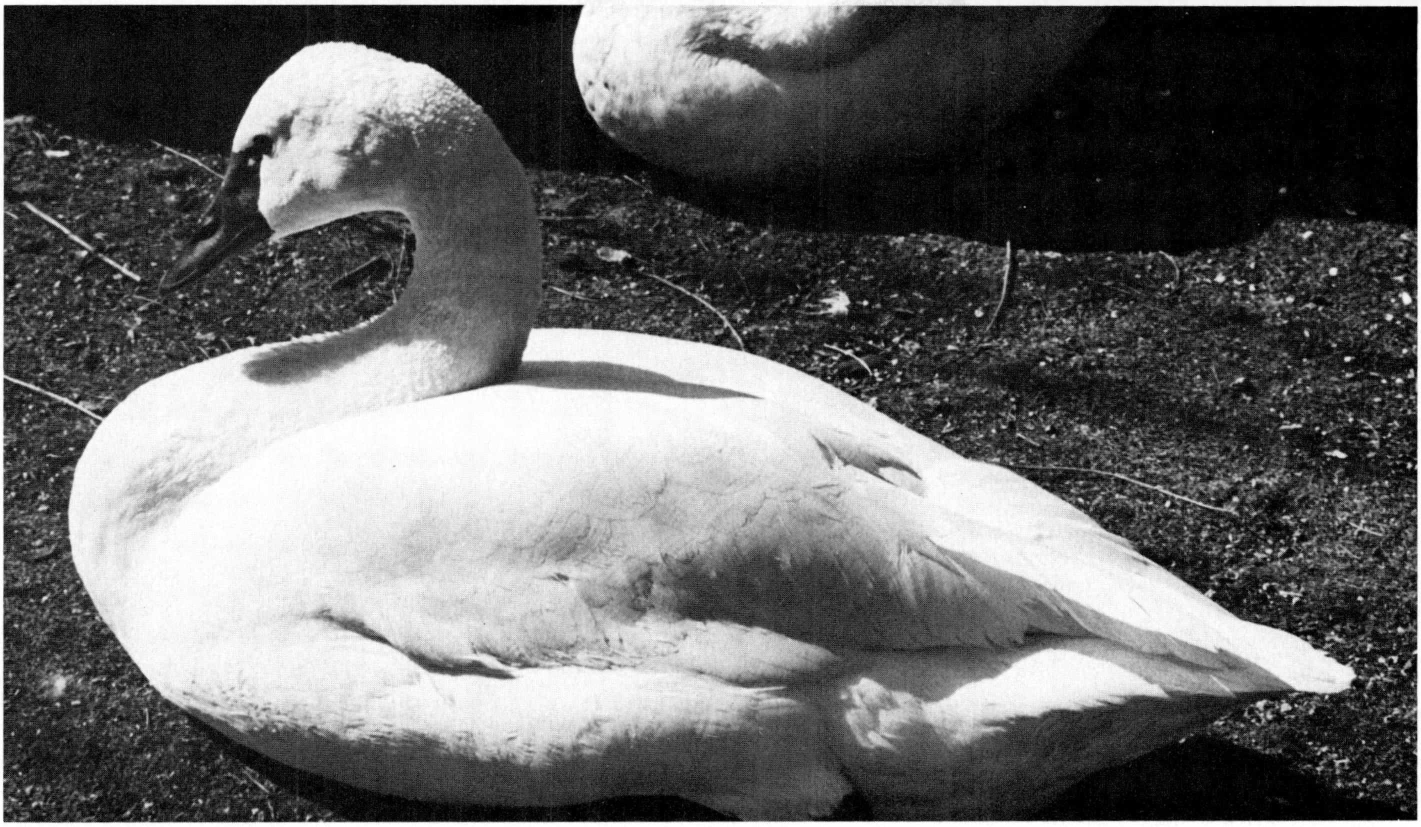

43-17

Whistling swans in resting poses.

43-18

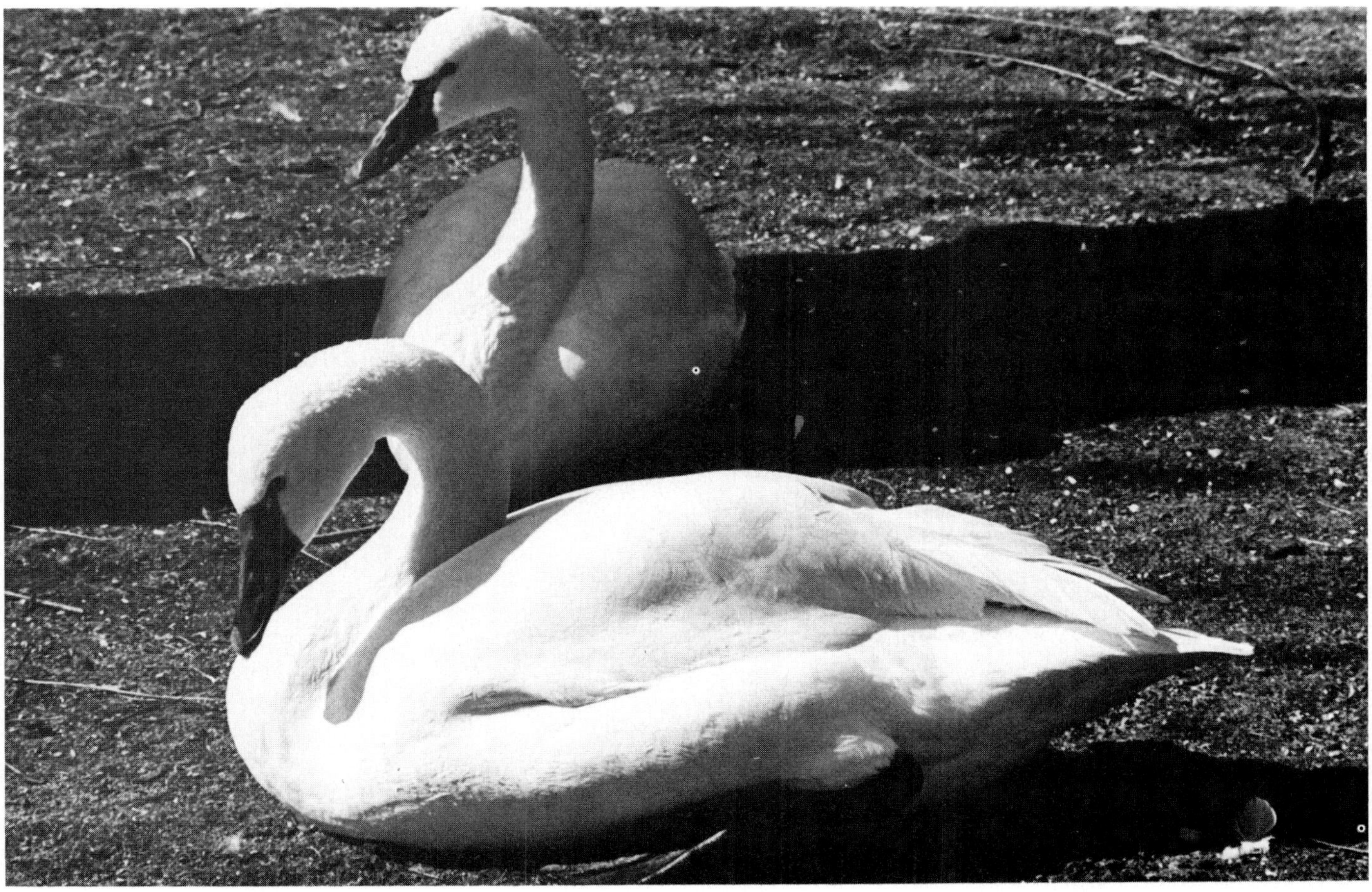

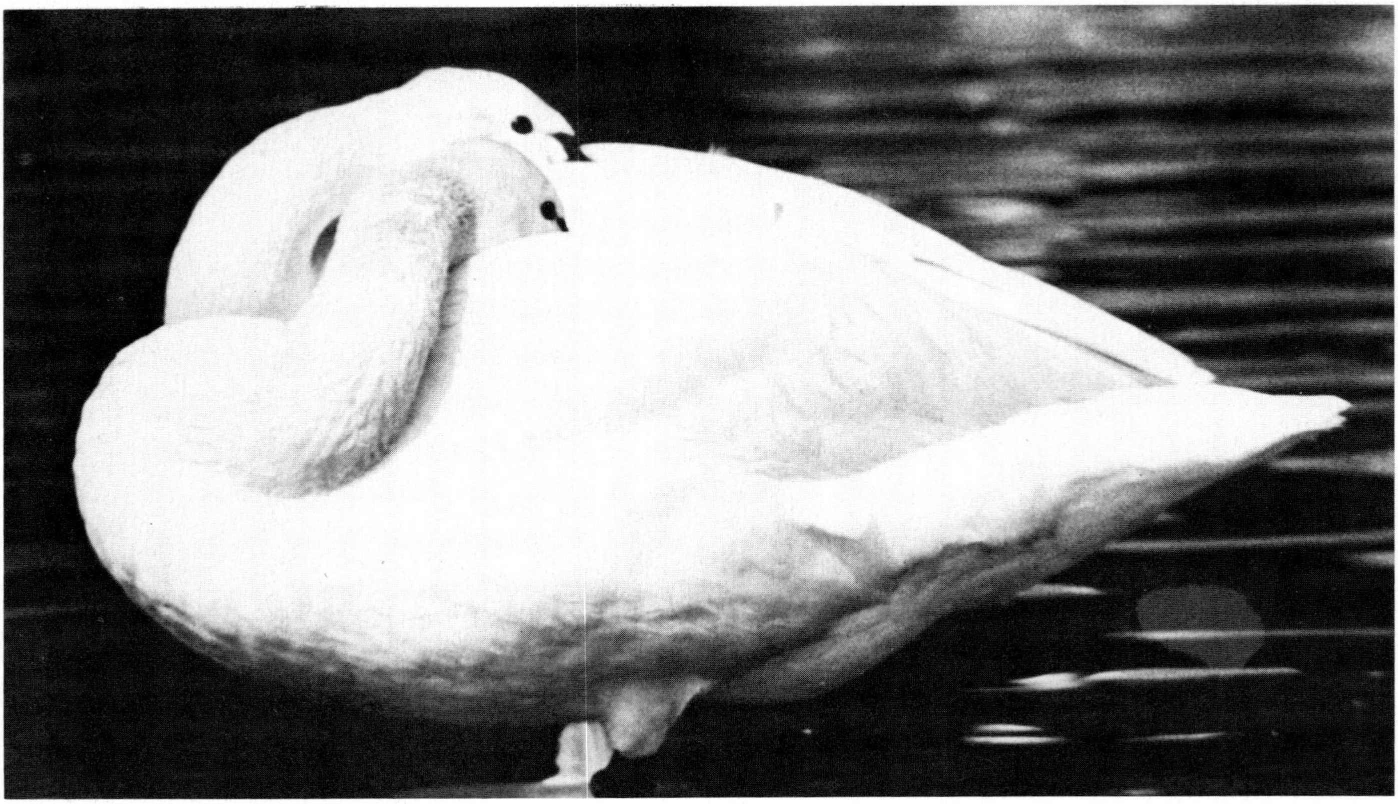

43-19 Pair of whistlers in sleeping positions.

43-20 Whistler preens his back feathers as he stretches one leg.

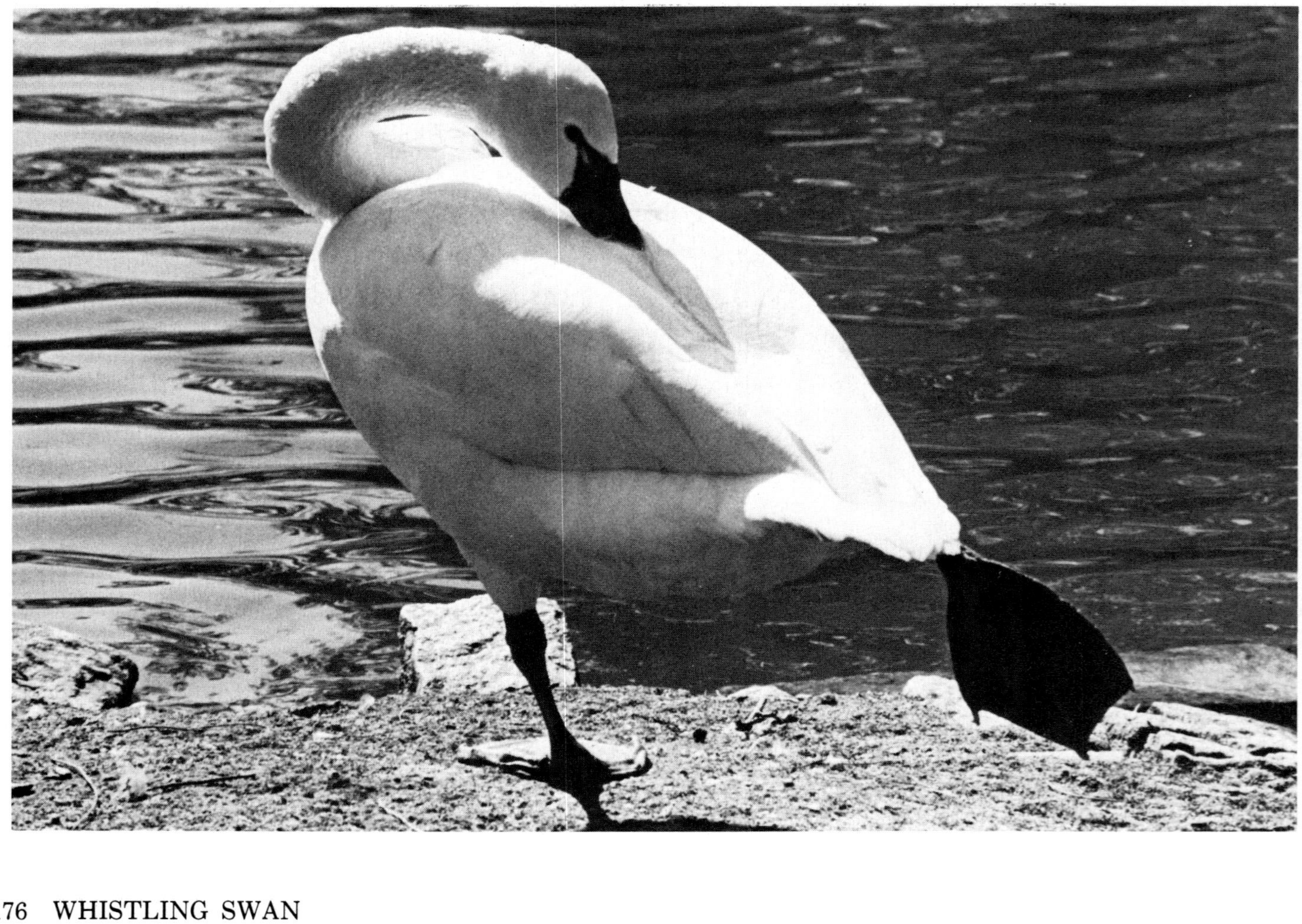

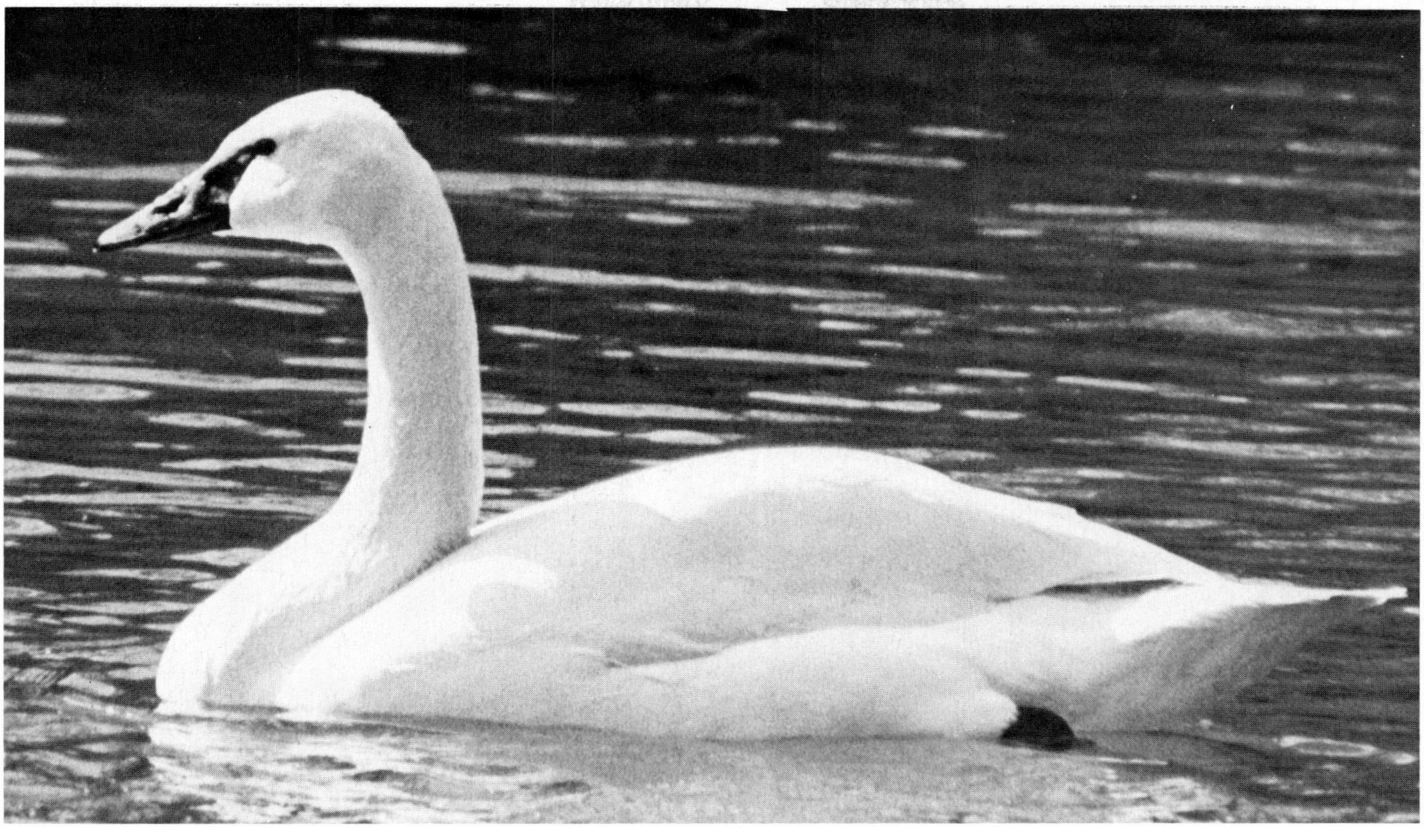

43-21 Nice profile of a swimming whistling swan.

43-22 Front and rear views. Notice how the bird on the right has raised his wings and scapulars. 43-23

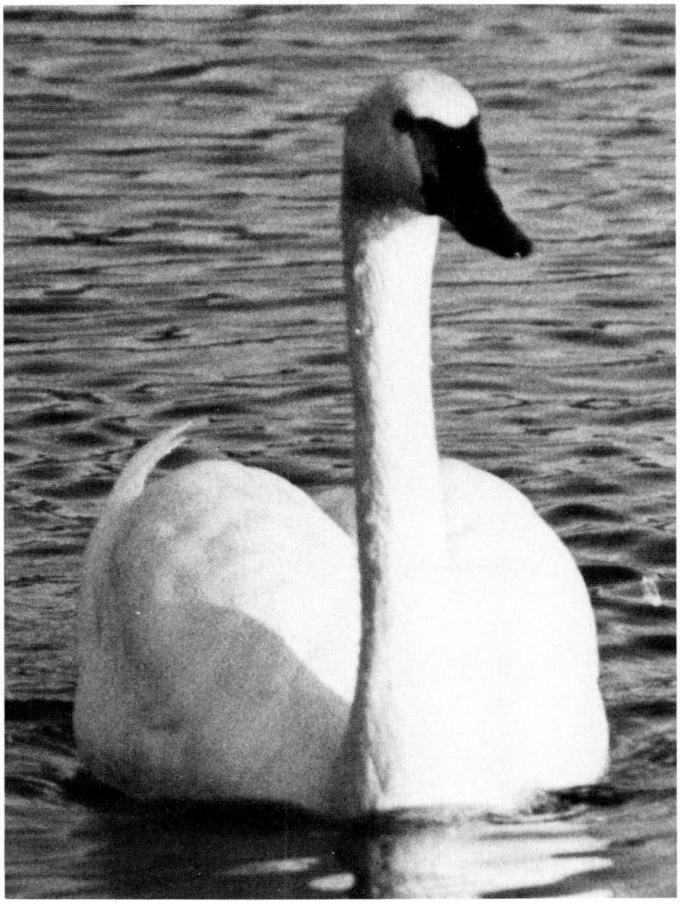

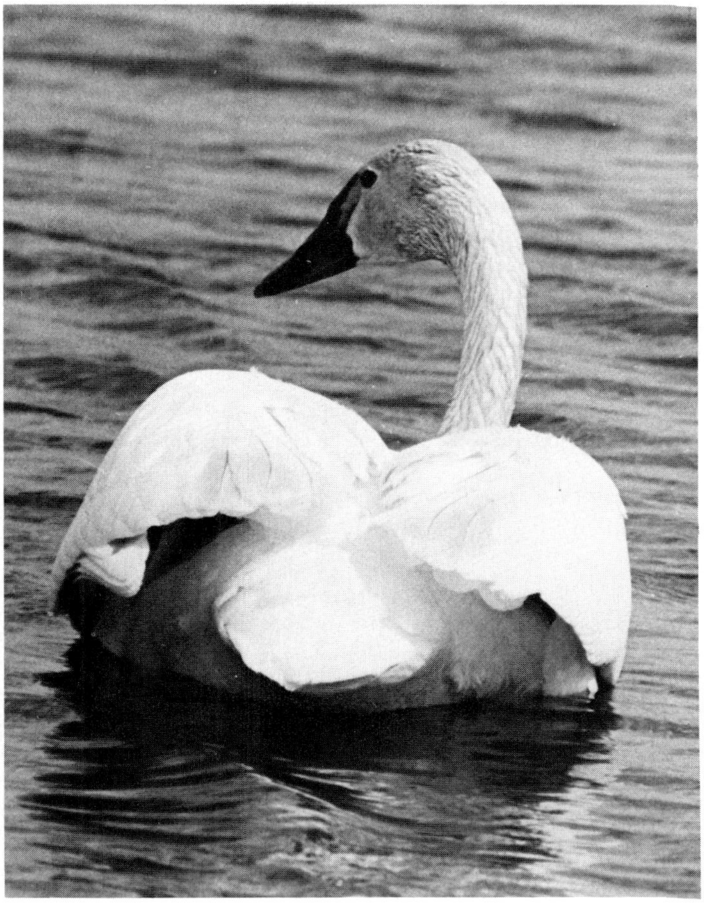

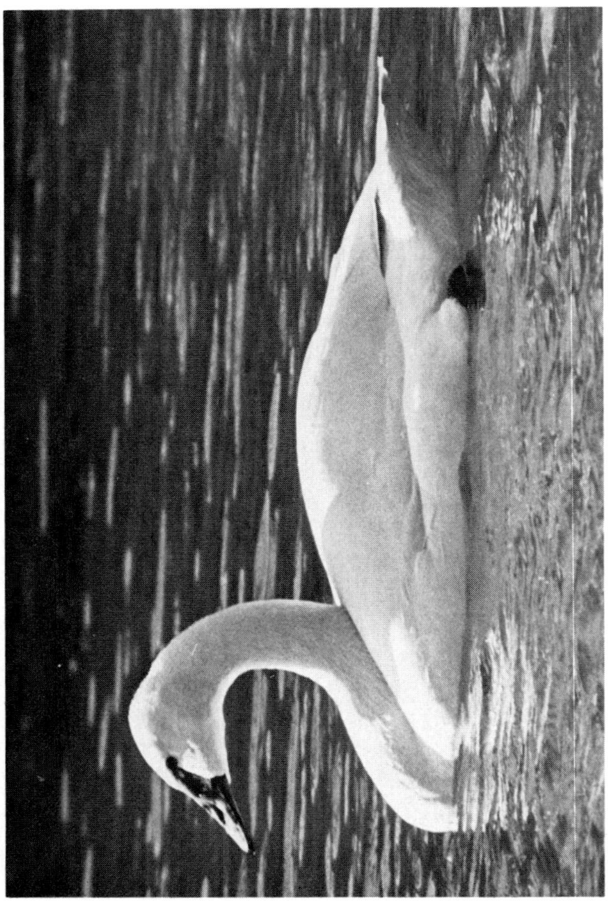

43-24

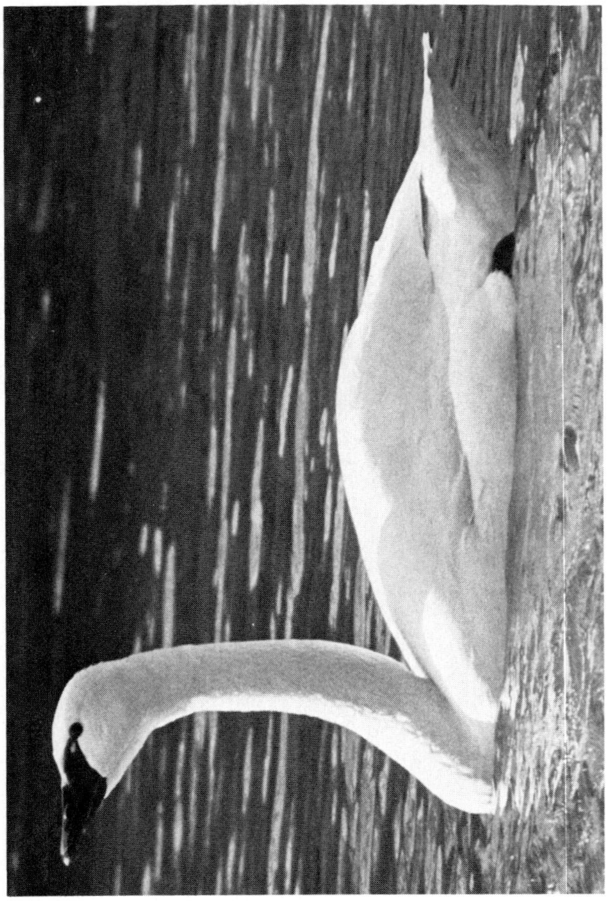

43-25

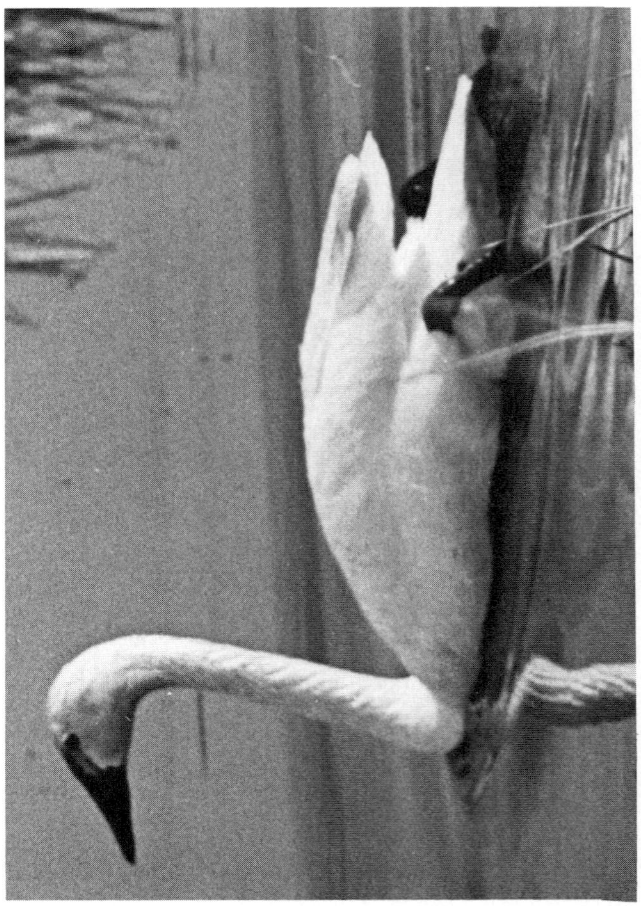

43-26

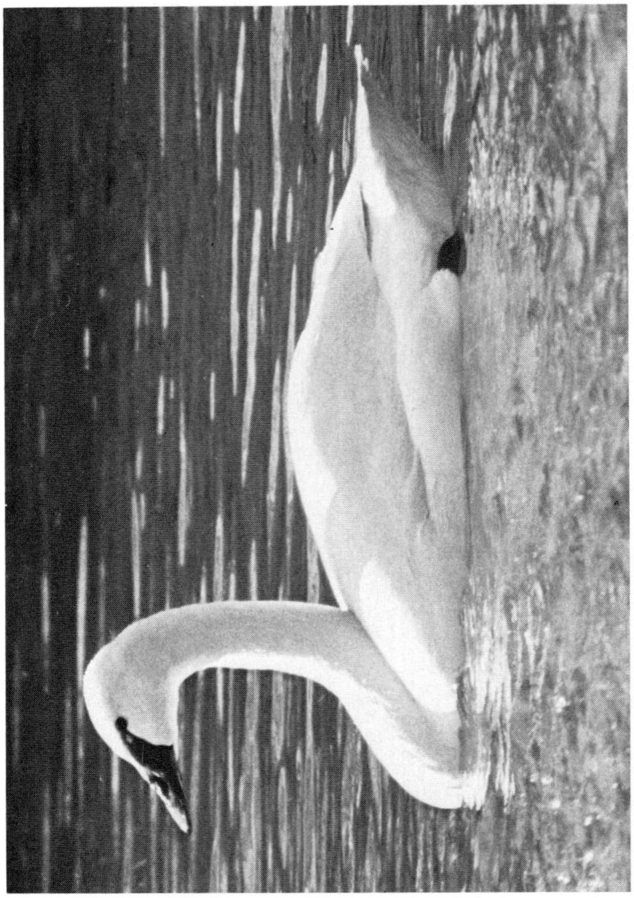

43-27

Four profile studies of floating whistling swans.

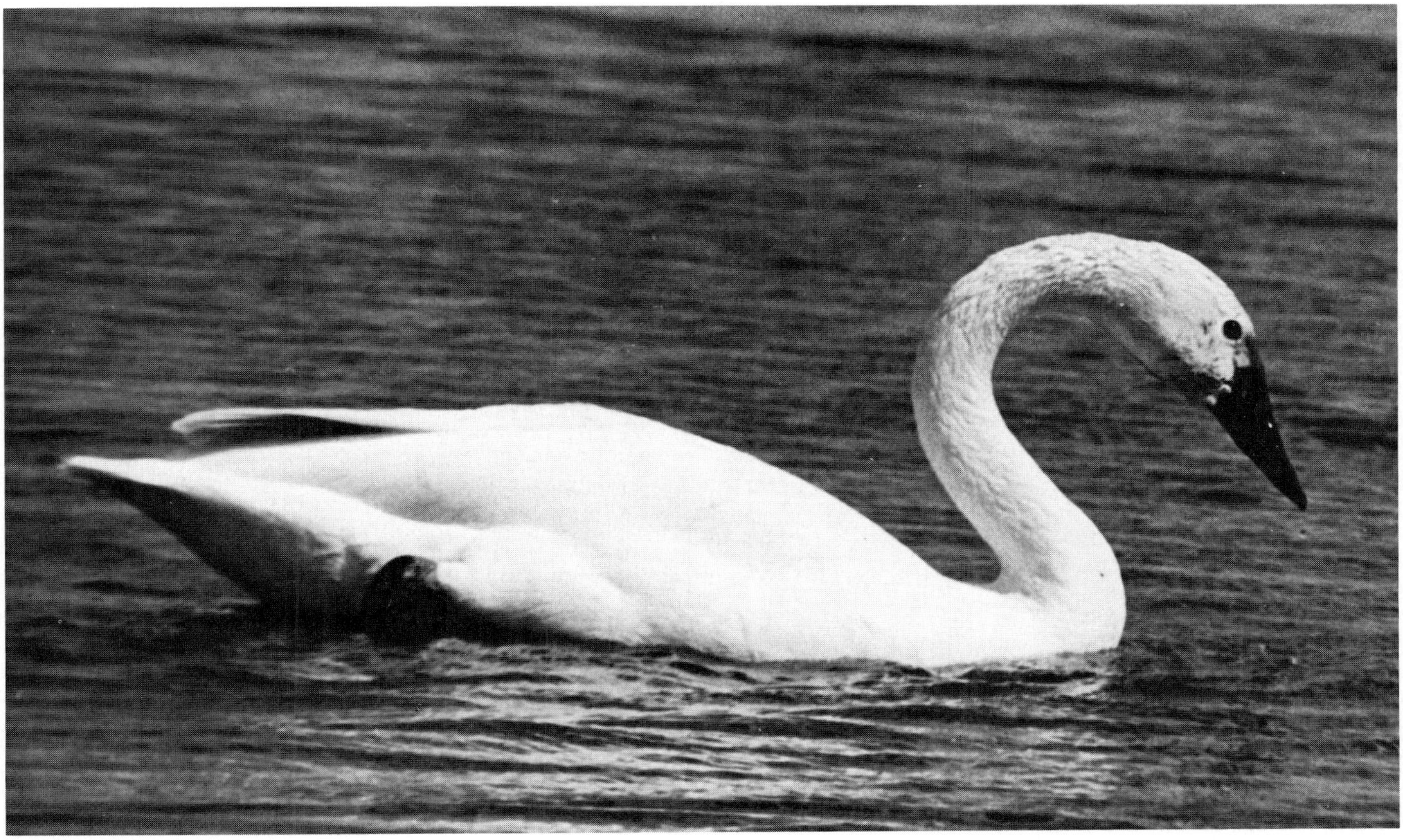

43-28

The elegant whistling swan in two very graceful poses.

43-29

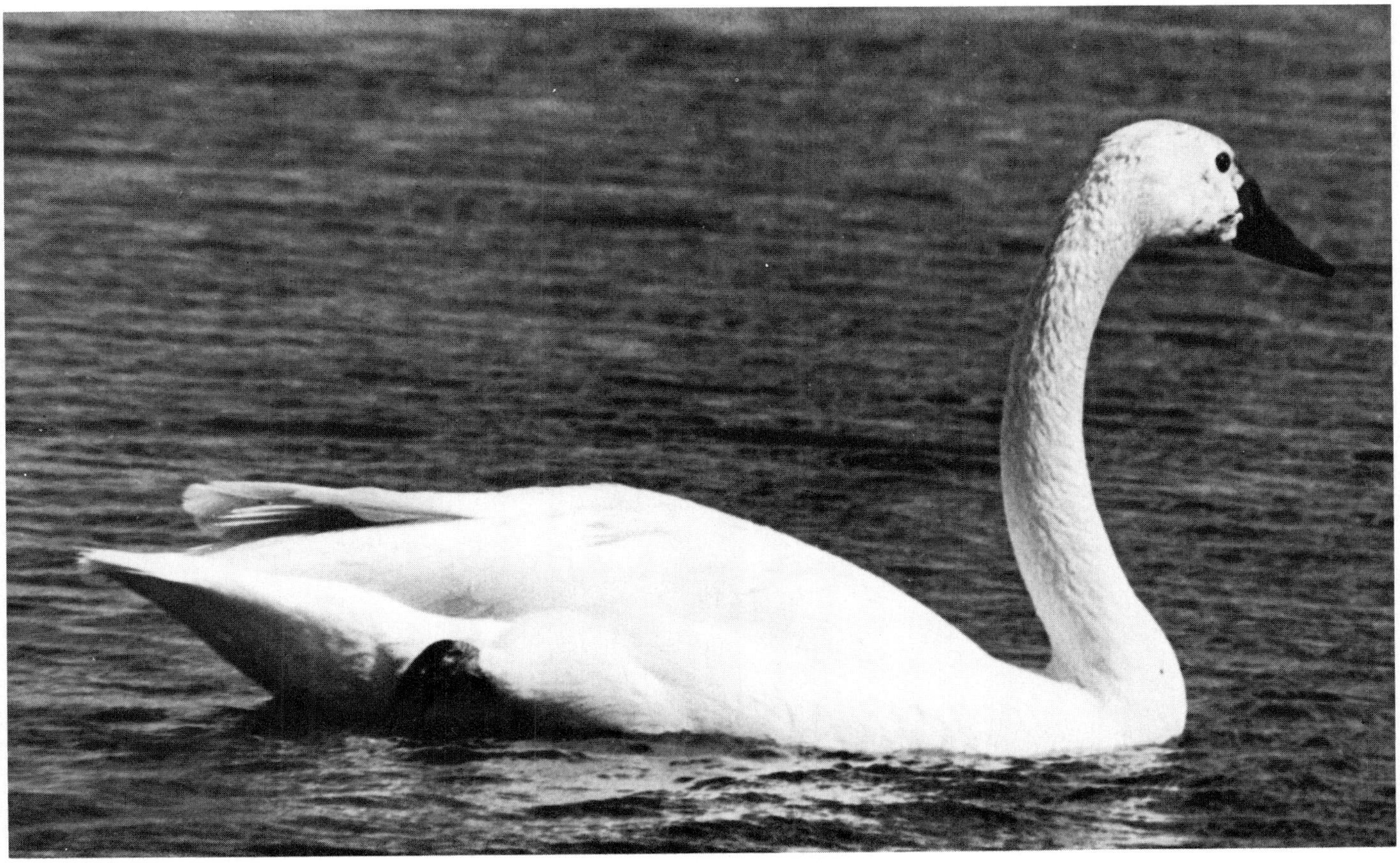

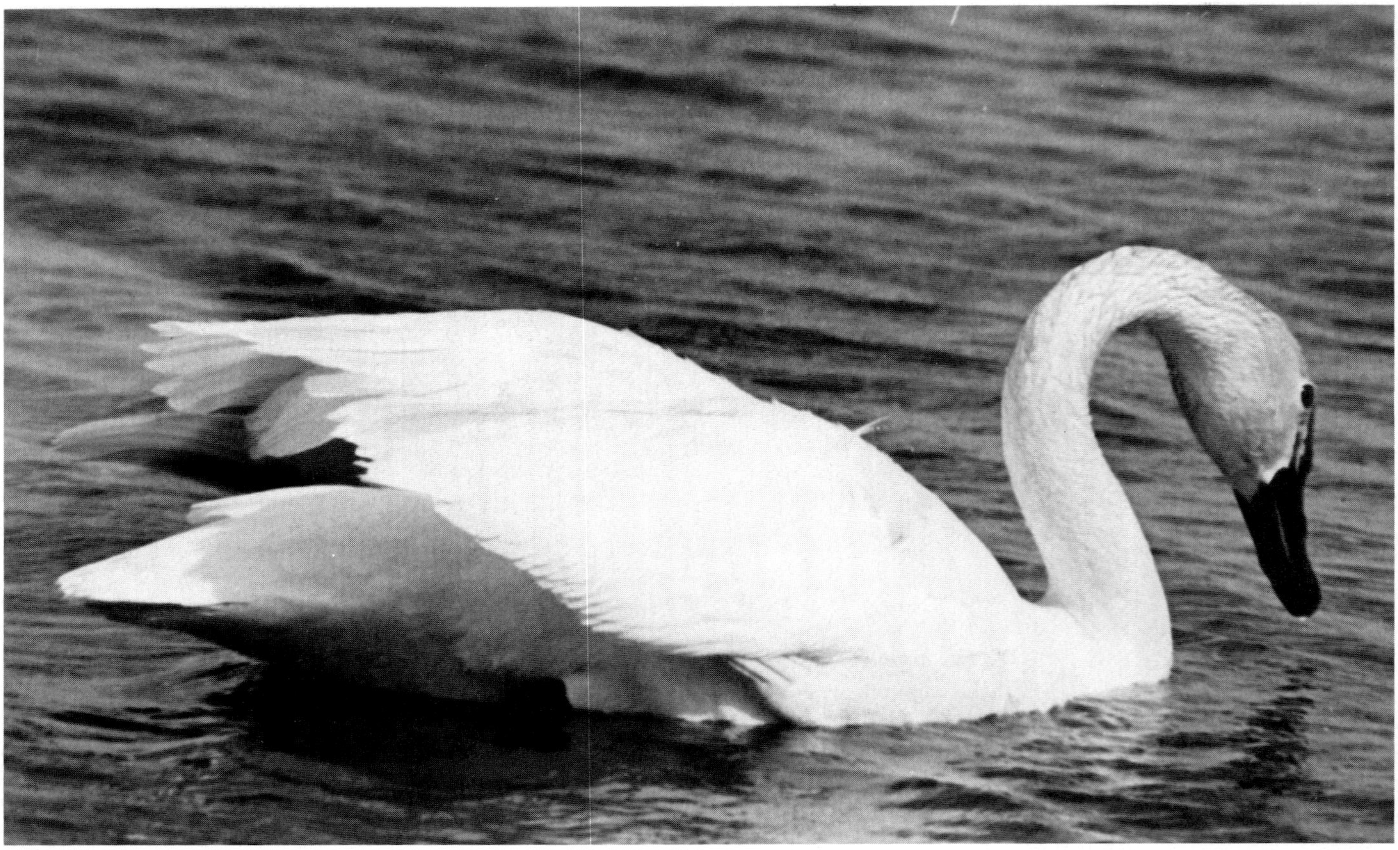

43-30

Whistling swan raises his wings and scapular, possibly to allow them to dry while he dabbles in the water.

43-31

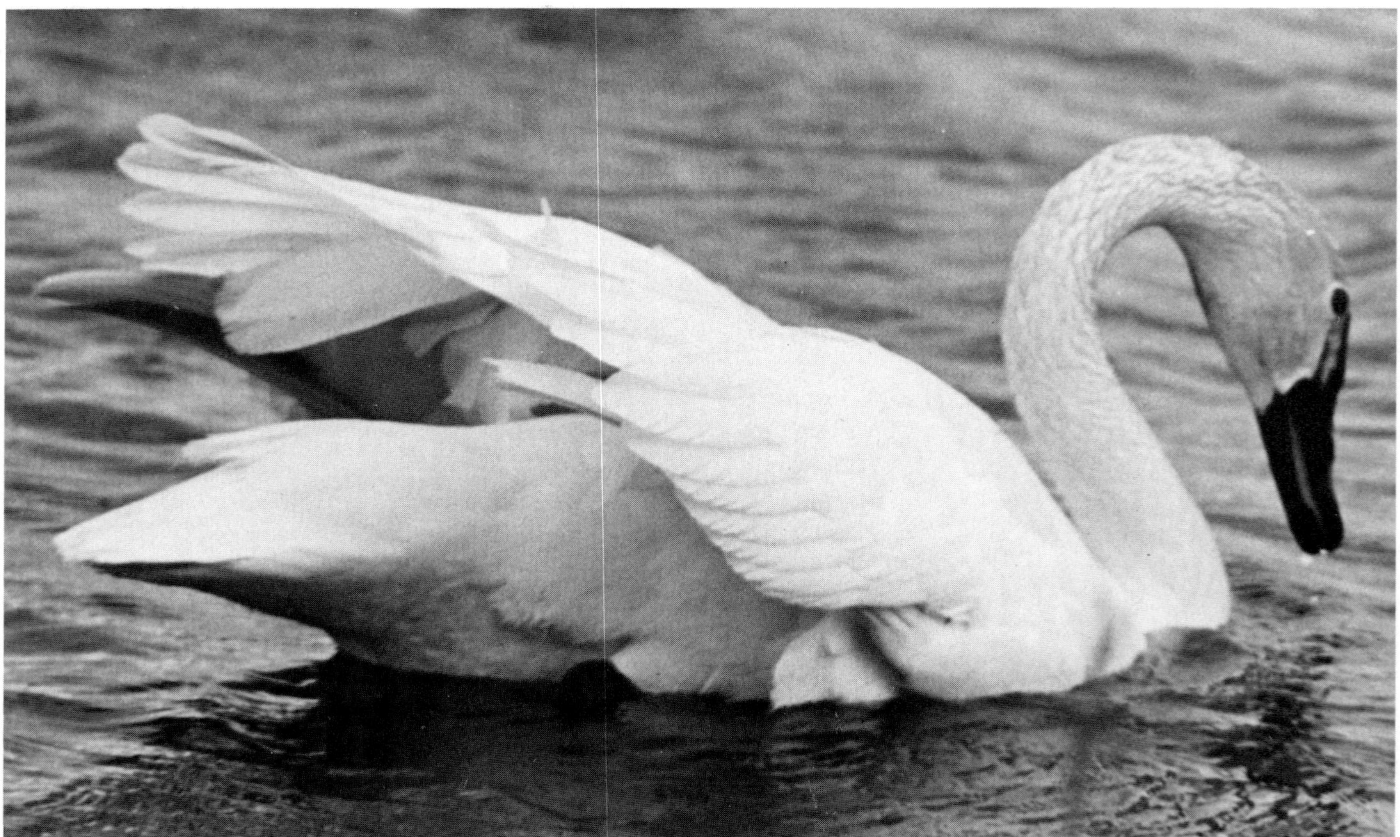

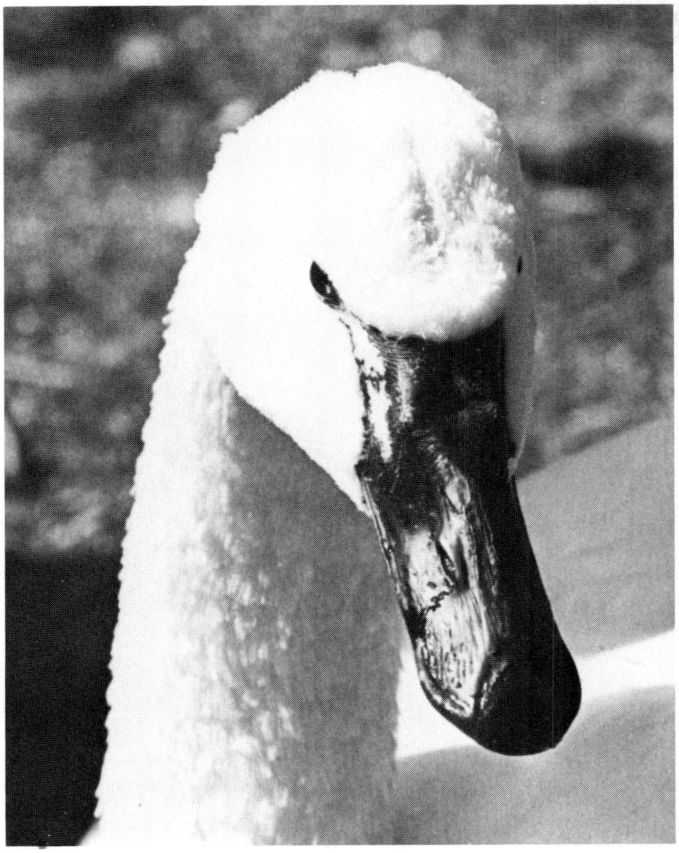

43-32

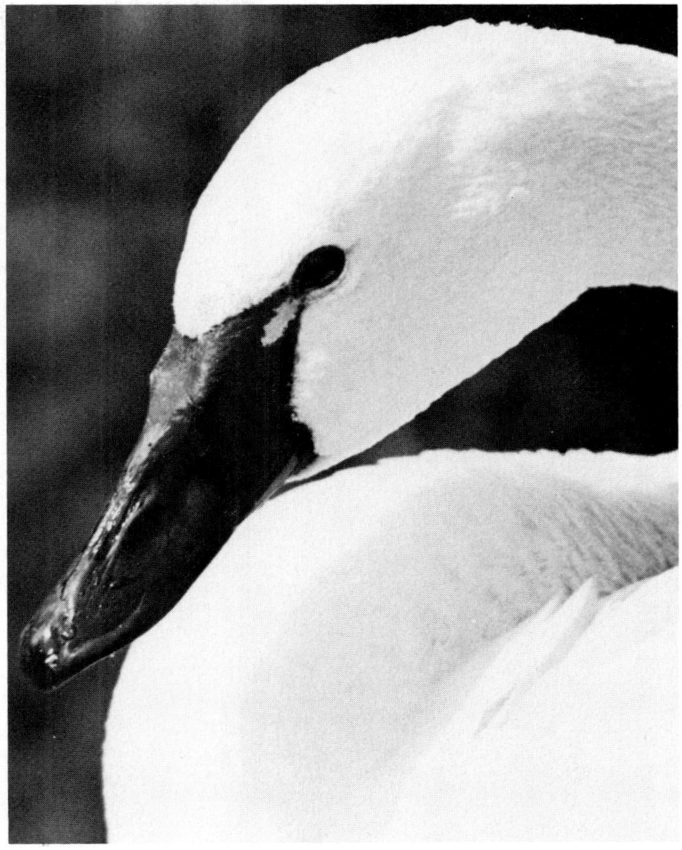

43-33

Three studies of the whistling swan's head and bill.

43-34

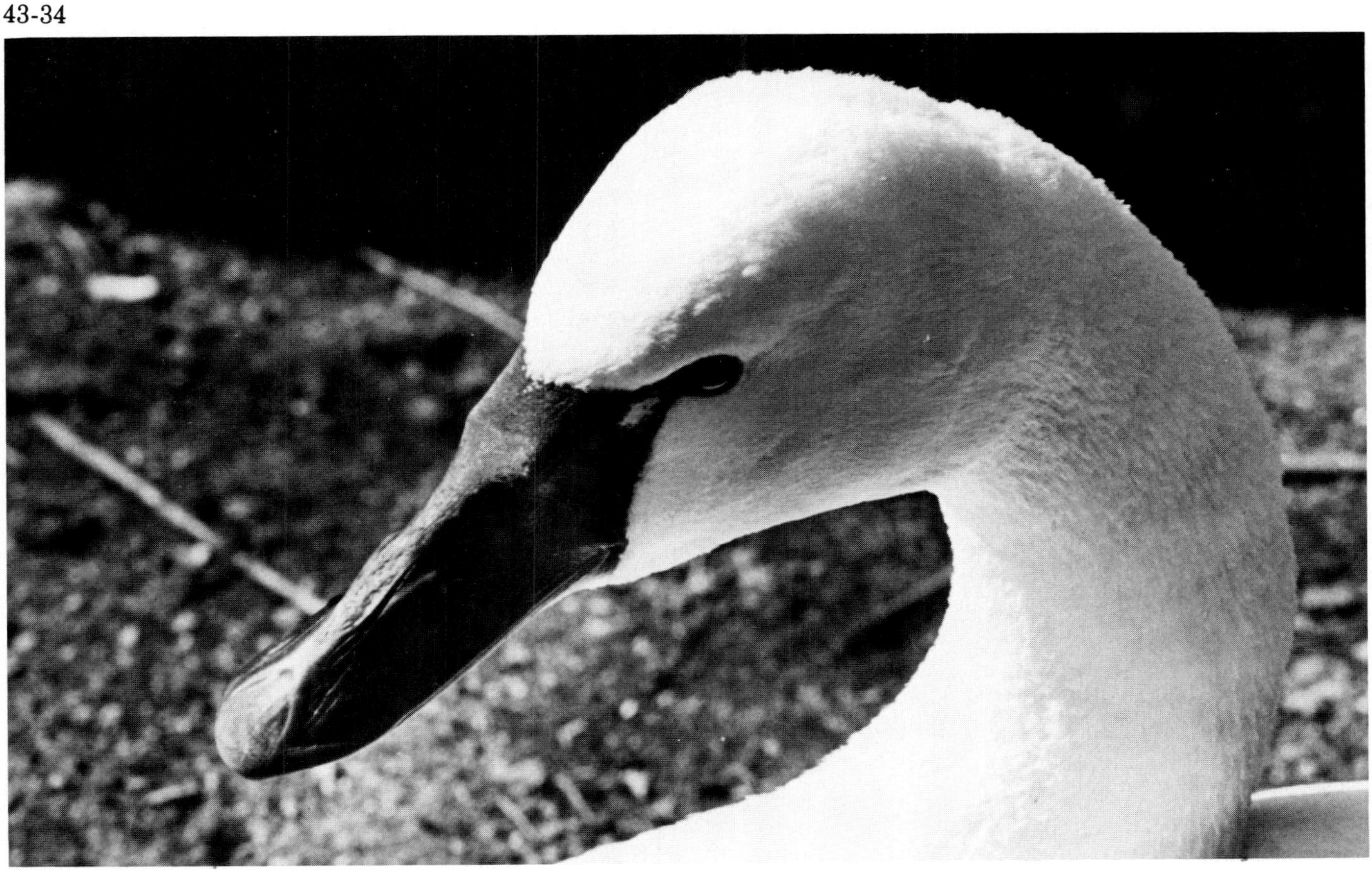

CHAPTER 44

Trumpeter Swan

Cygnus cygnus buccinator
(Color Photos-Page 168)

By 1900, trumpeter swans, the most majestic of our waterfowl and also the heaviest of all flying birds, were on the verge of extinction. During the eighteenth and nineteenth centuries, both the trumpeter and whistling swans were ruthlessly hunted. Their skins were used for powder puffs and the quills for pens. The Hudson's Bay Company reportedly sold over 100,000 swan skins to the London market between 1823 and 1880. Very probably a large percentage of these were trumpeter swan skins, inasmuch as this species nested in areas, both in the United States and Canada, where the fur trade flourished.

Trumpeter swans, in former years, bred throughout the northern, western, and central parts of North America, from Alaska and northern Canada as far south as Missouri. Many of them wintered in the central Atlantic States, along the Ohio and Mississippi River regions, in the Gulf States, and in northwestern Oregon. They now avoid the long, dangerous flights and migrate, or more correctly, move only far enough to find open water and food. Their formerly wide range has now been reduced to a few scattered colonies in southern Alaska, British Columbia, Alberta, Montana, Wyoming, and South Dakota.

Although swans have been protected since 1918 by the Migratory Bird Treaty Act with Great Britain (including Canada), the number of trumpeters inhabiting the United States in 1931 was believed to have been only thirty-five. In recent years, strong comebacks have been made by this species at the Red Rock Lakes National Wildlife Refuge in southwestern Montana and in the Yellowstone Park area. Unlike other waterfowl that, for the most part, are very gregarious, trumpeter swans are very antisocial during the breeding season. They apparently return to the same nest every year; when these sites have been selected on a small lake or slough, the breeding pair will not permit other swans to trespass. Nests on larger bodies of water are usually located ½ mile apart and territorial rights are rigidly enforced. Breeding trumpeters do not object to ducks and swamp birds nesting within a new feet of them, but will not permit the intrusion of other swans or geese. As a result of their large breeding area requirements, established colonies soon become saturated. Flocks of nonbreeding birds, many already mated, have difficulty not only finding nesting sites but also feeding areas. Although attempts have been made to relocate some of these nonbreeding pairs to other locations, these efforts have been only partially successful.

According to Delacour, "Trumpeter swans do very well in captivity. They soon become tame, prove completely hardy, easy to feed, and they breed readily." They do, however, retain much of their inability to get along with other large birds.

While the extinction of the trumpeter swan is no longer threatened, their distribution and numbers will very likely always remain limited.

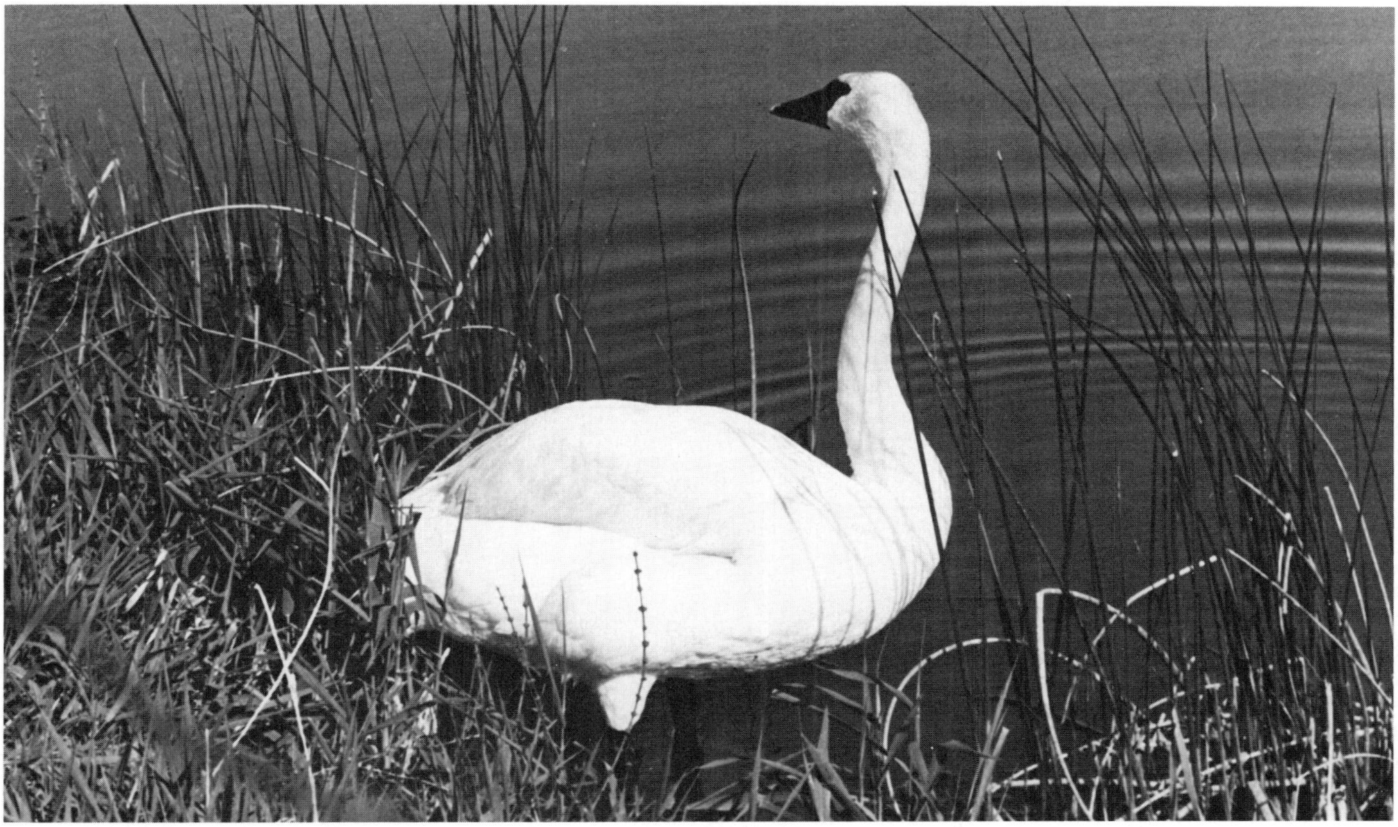

44-1 The majestic trumpeter swan, the heaviest of all flying birds. Almost extinct in the early 1930s, they have made a comeback but their number will always be limited.

44-2 Trumpeters sometimes attain weights of 35 pounds, an overall length of 72 inches, and a wing span of 98 inches.

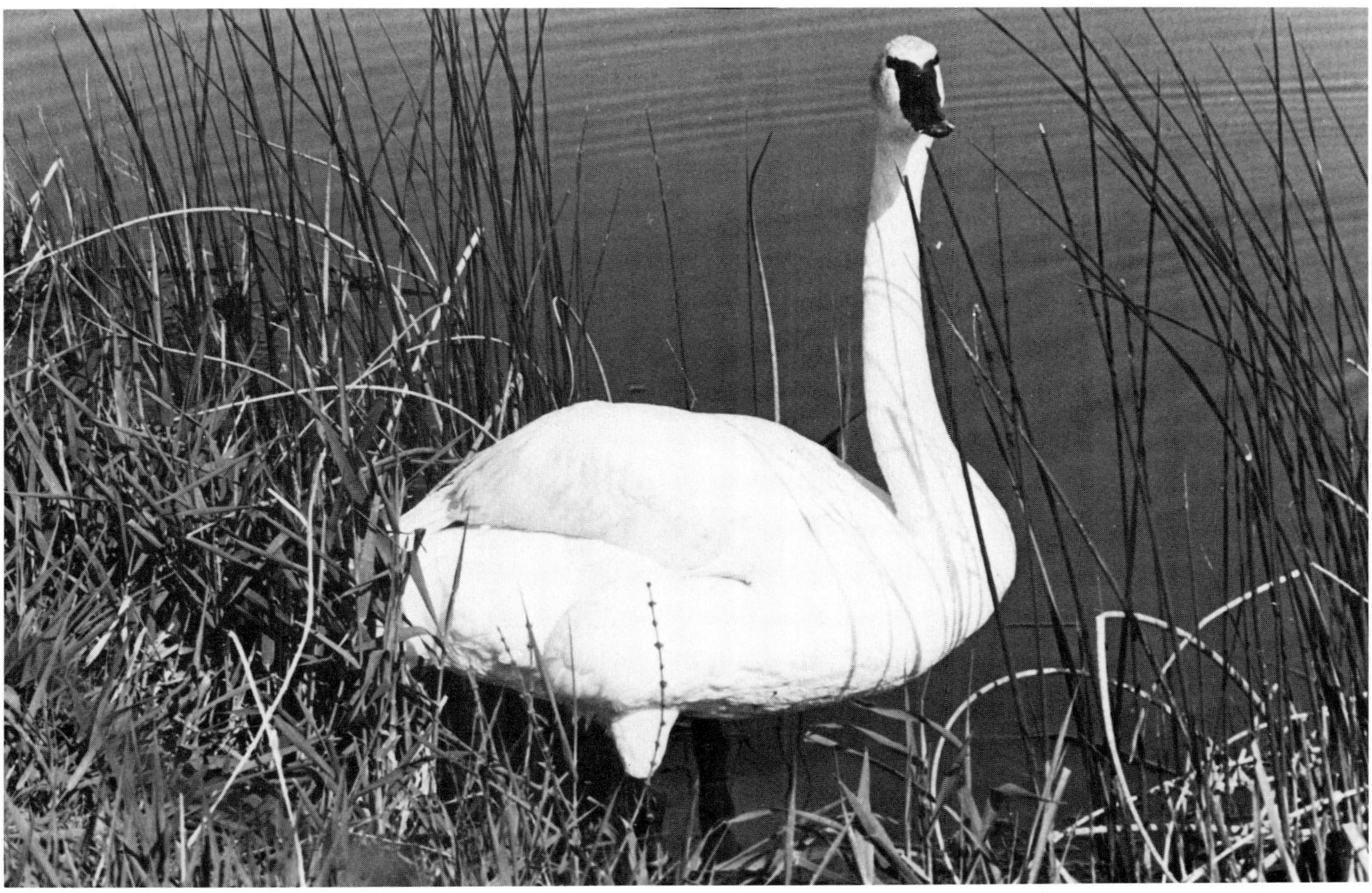

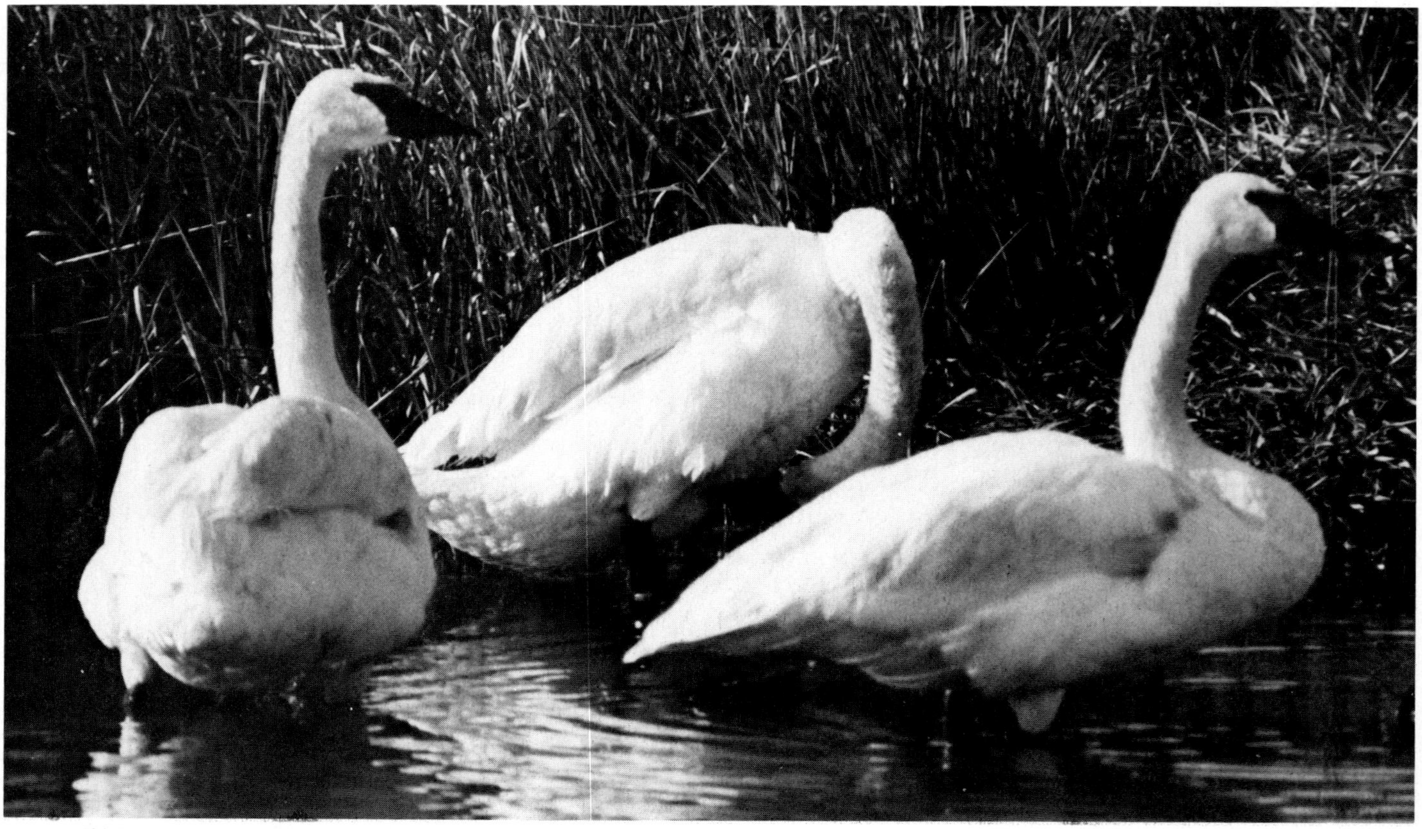

44-3 Three trumpeters relax in shallow waters.

44-4 Good front view of a trumpeter swan. Note large feet and powerful legs.

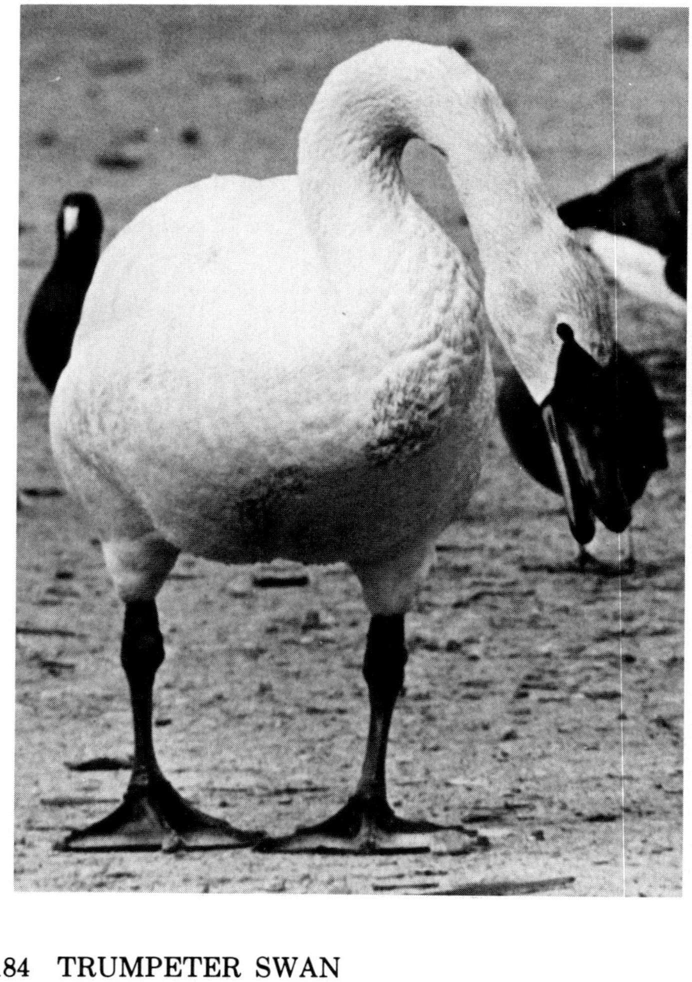

44-5 Trumpeter preens his feathers.

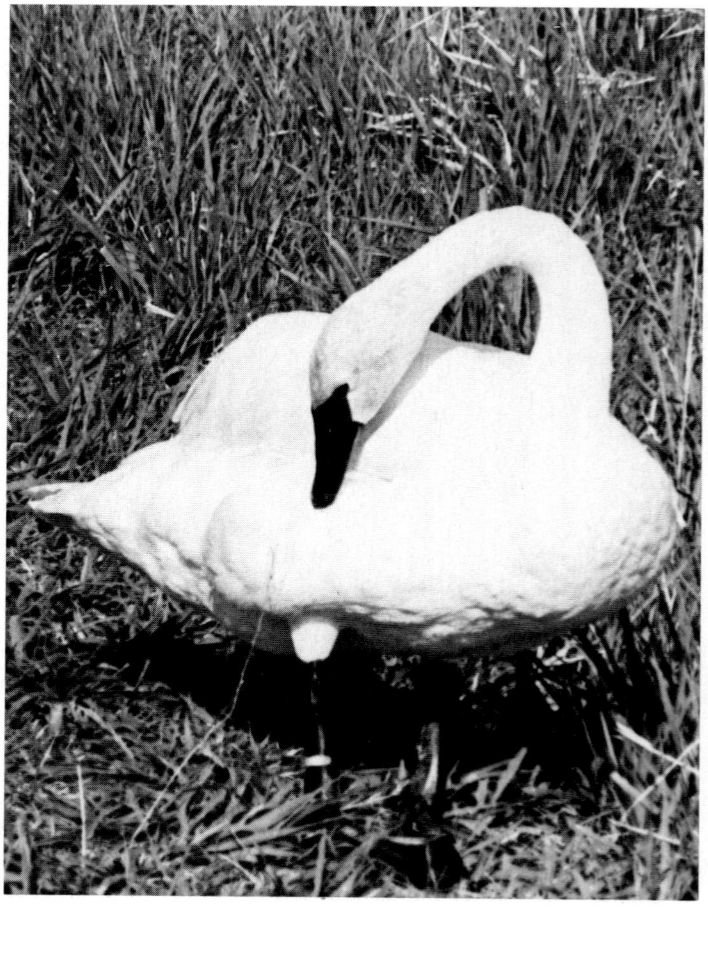

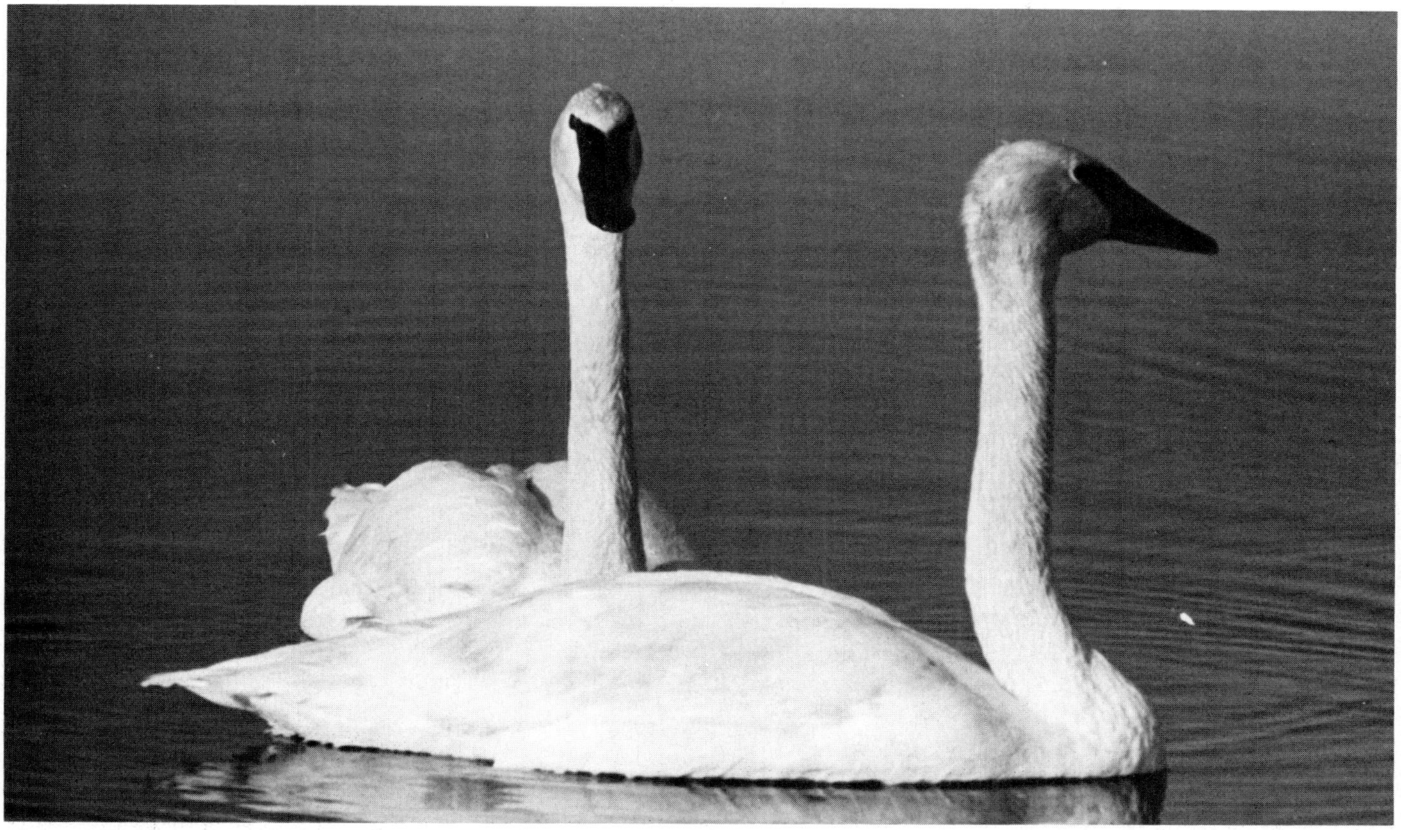

44-6 Mated pair of trumpeters. The male is called a "cob" and the female, a "pen". They normally hold their long necks erect.

44-7 Rear view of a trumpeter in an interesting pose.

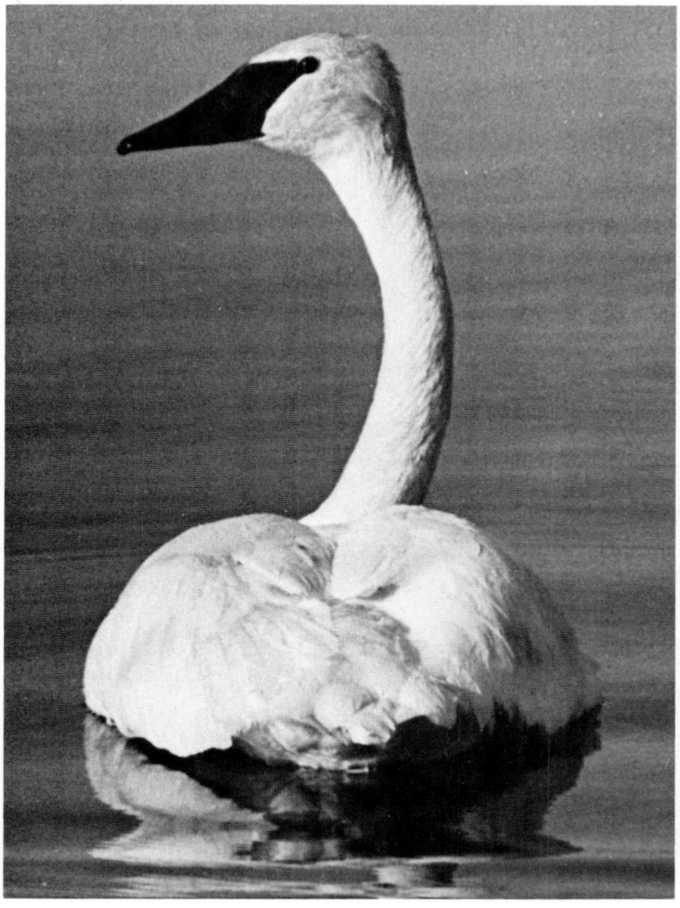

44-8 Trumpeter swims toward the camera.

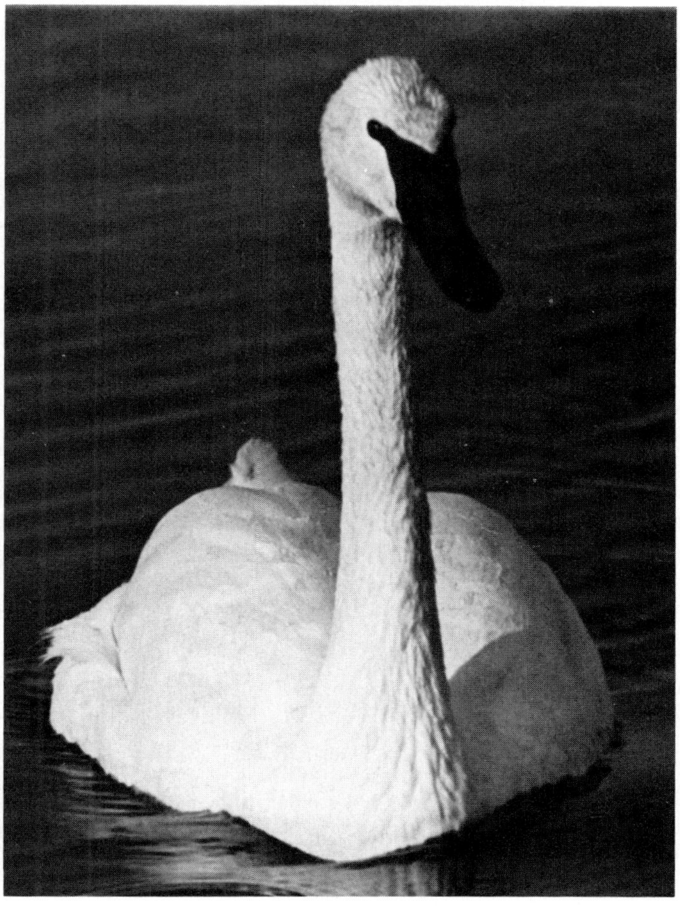

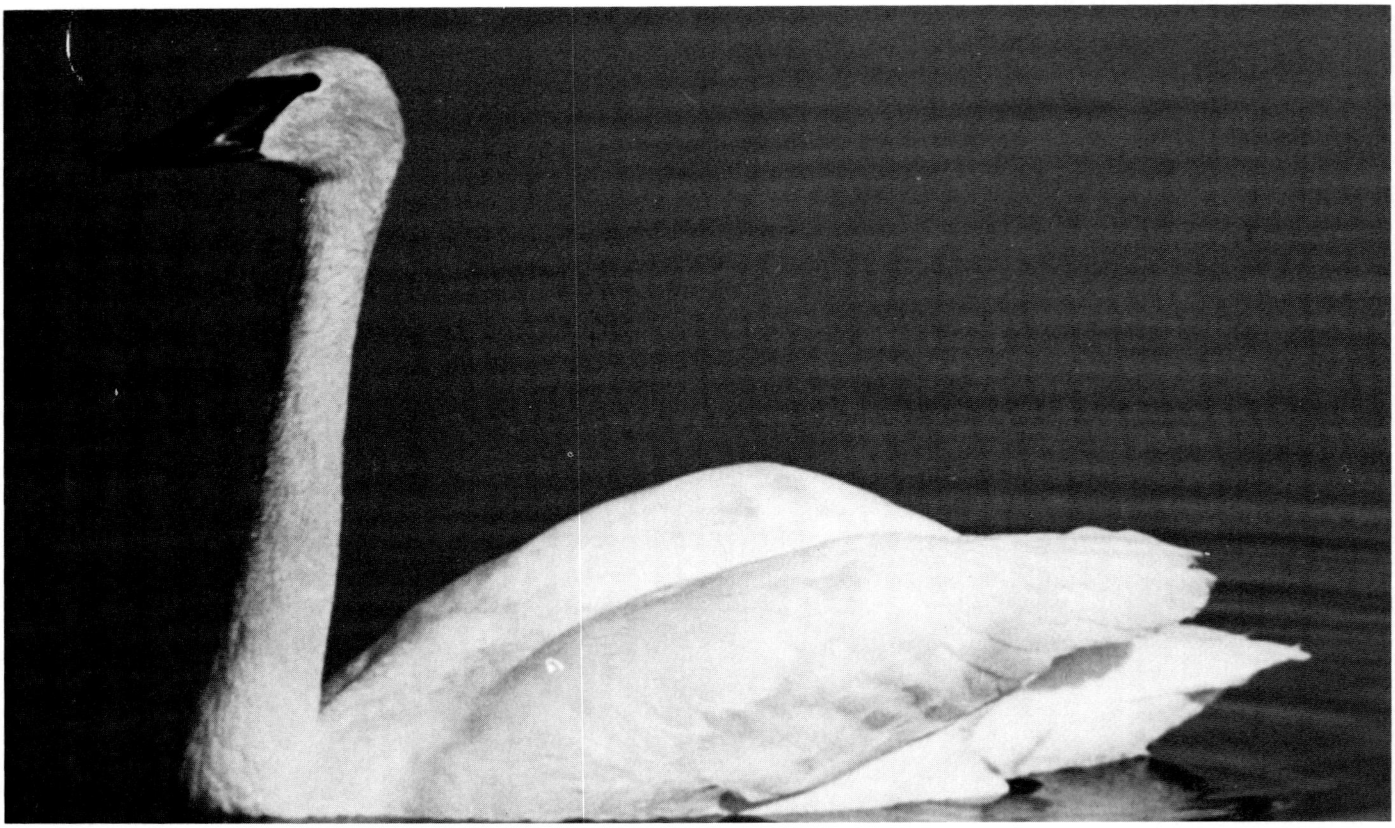

44-9 Profile study of the trumpeter in a typical pose.

44-10 More front and rear views of a swimming trumpeter. 44-11

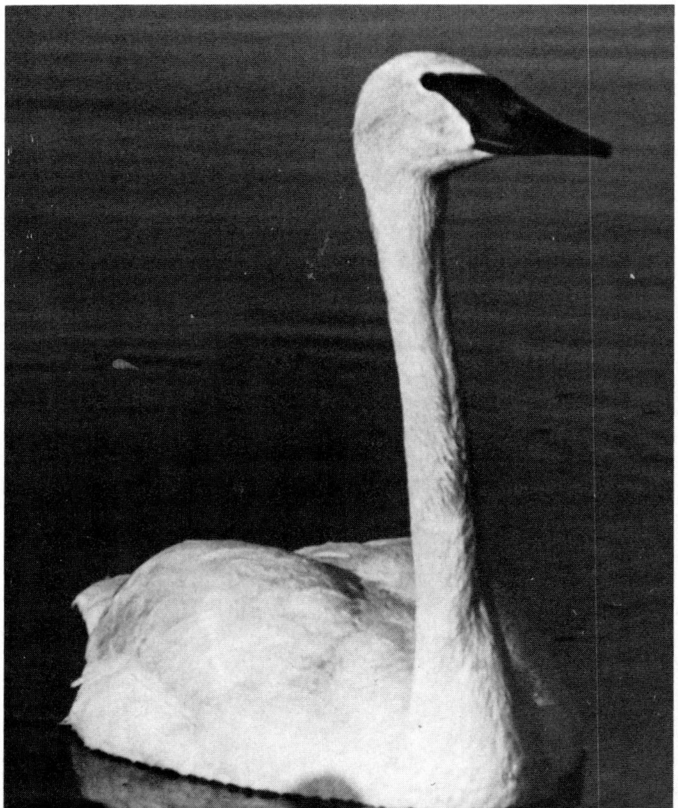

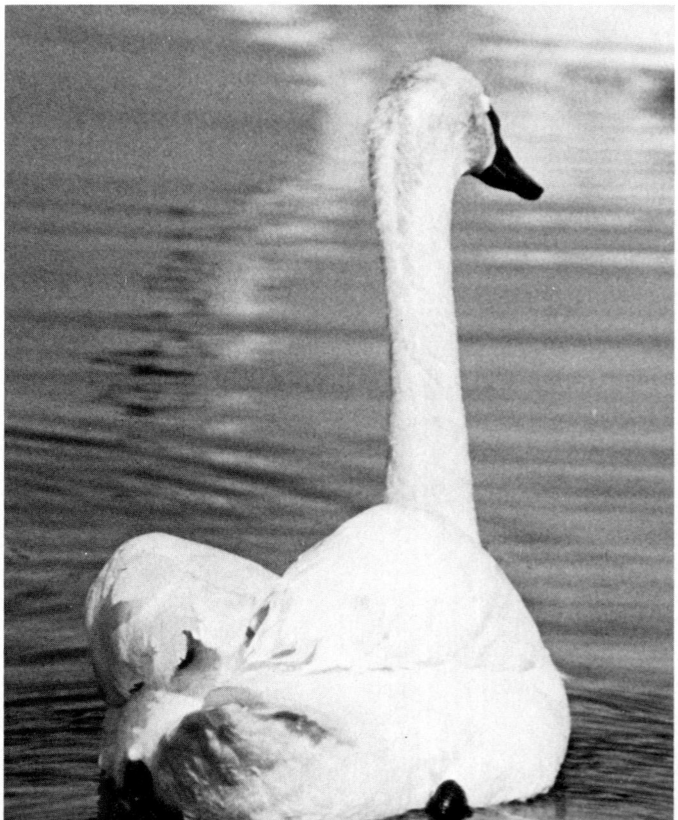

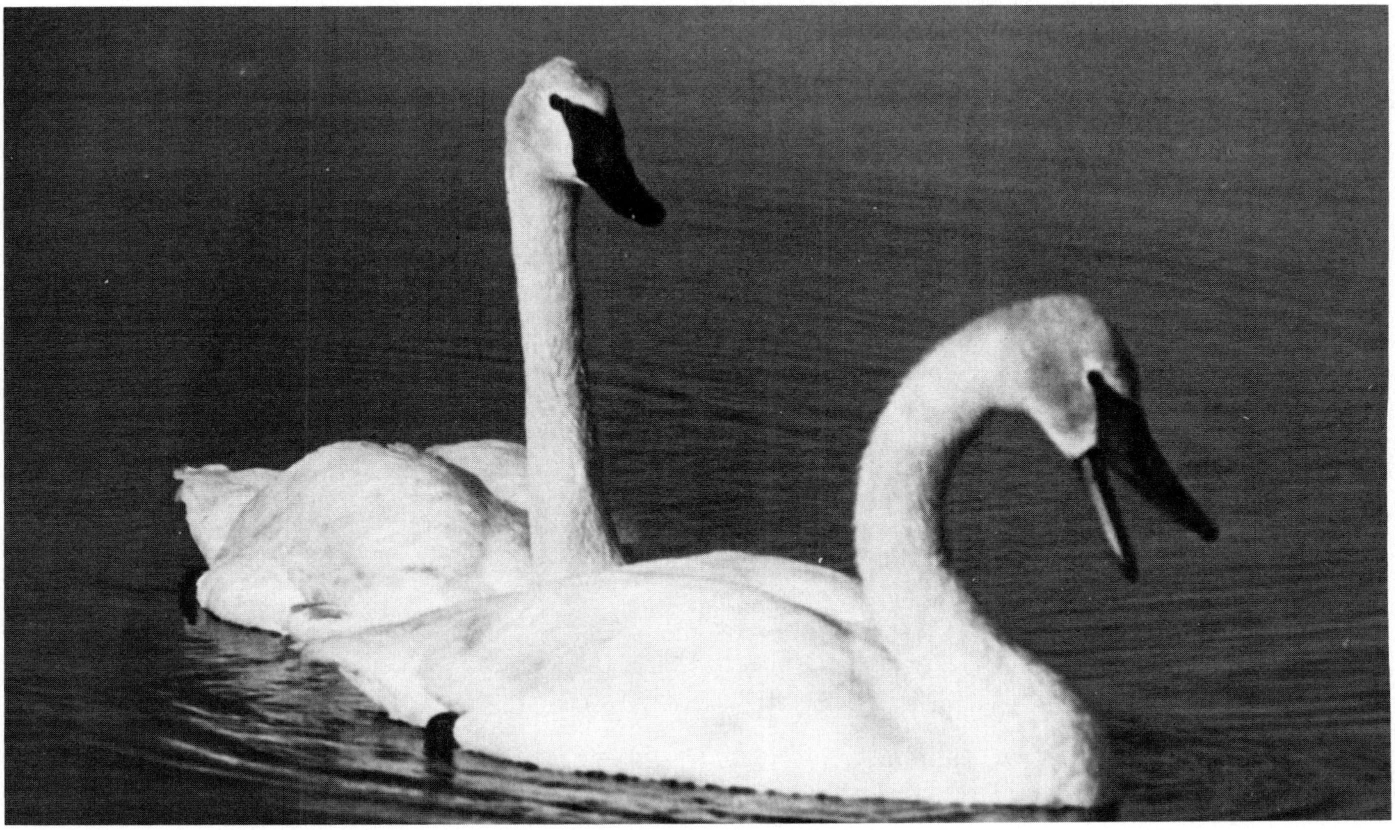

44-12 Pair of trumpeters. Note open mandibles on bird in foreground.

44-13 Two trumpeters in almost identical quizzical poses.

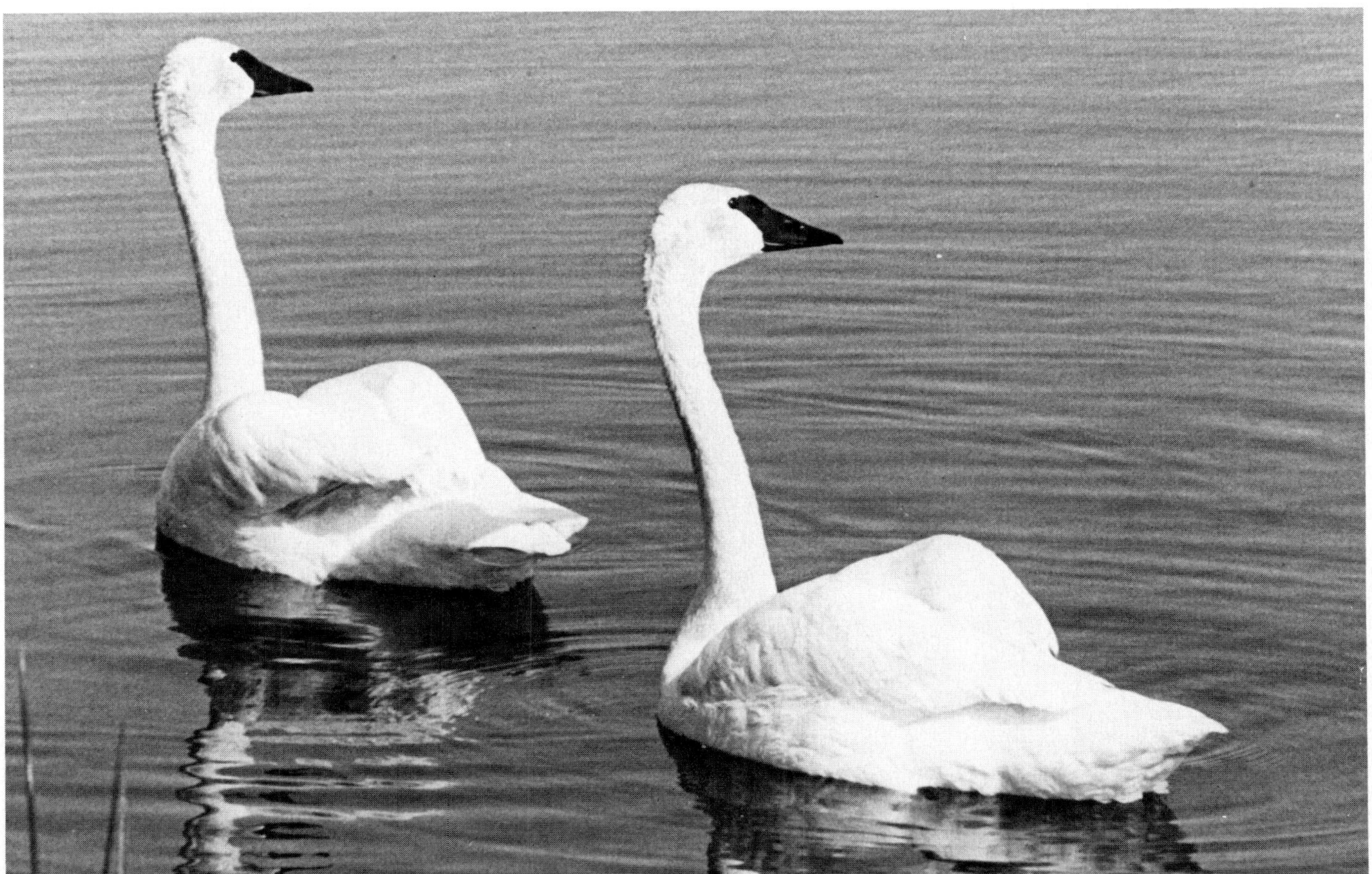

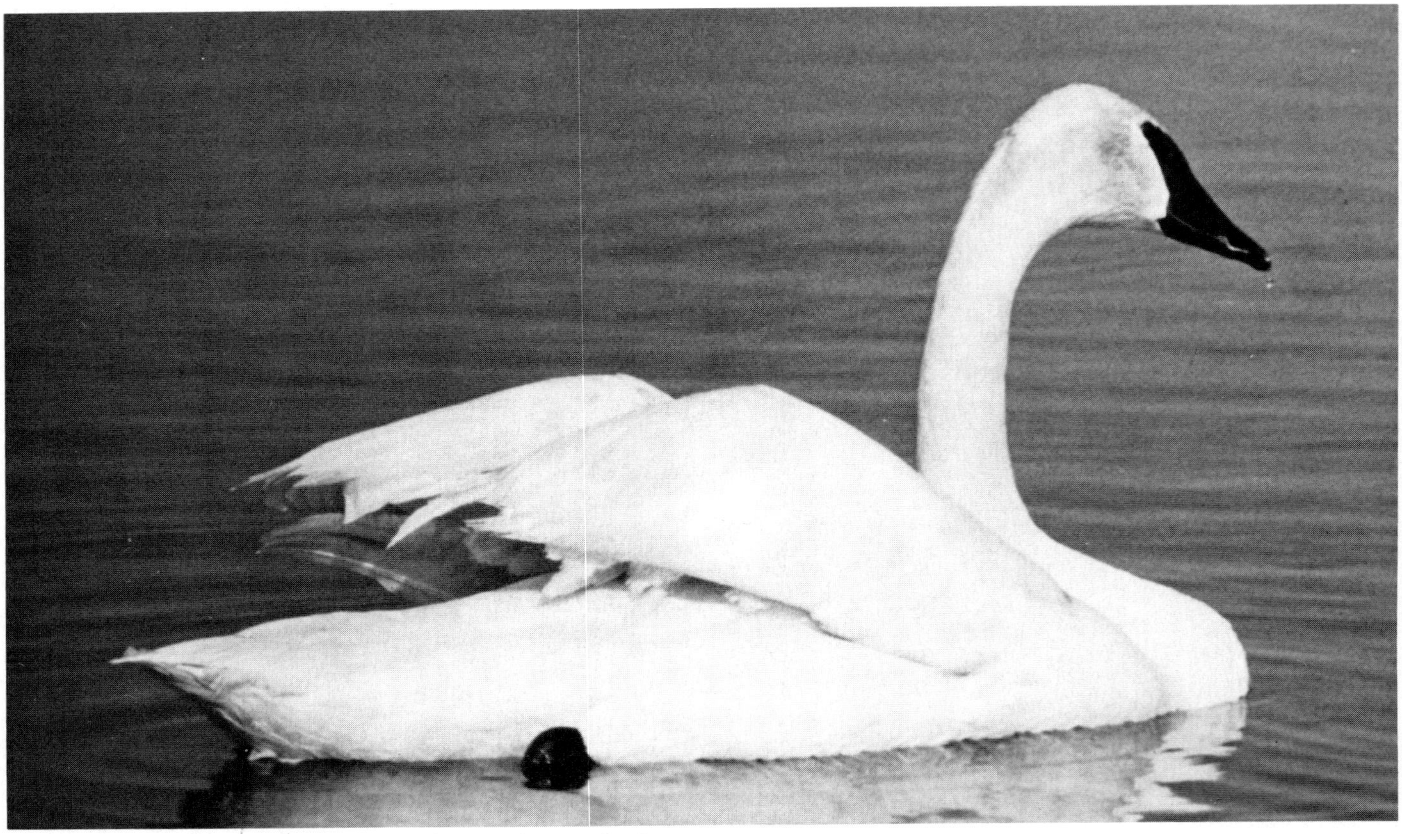

44-14 Trumpeter with wings and scapulars raised.

44-15 Mated pair of trumpeters. Bird on the right is in a pleasing pose.

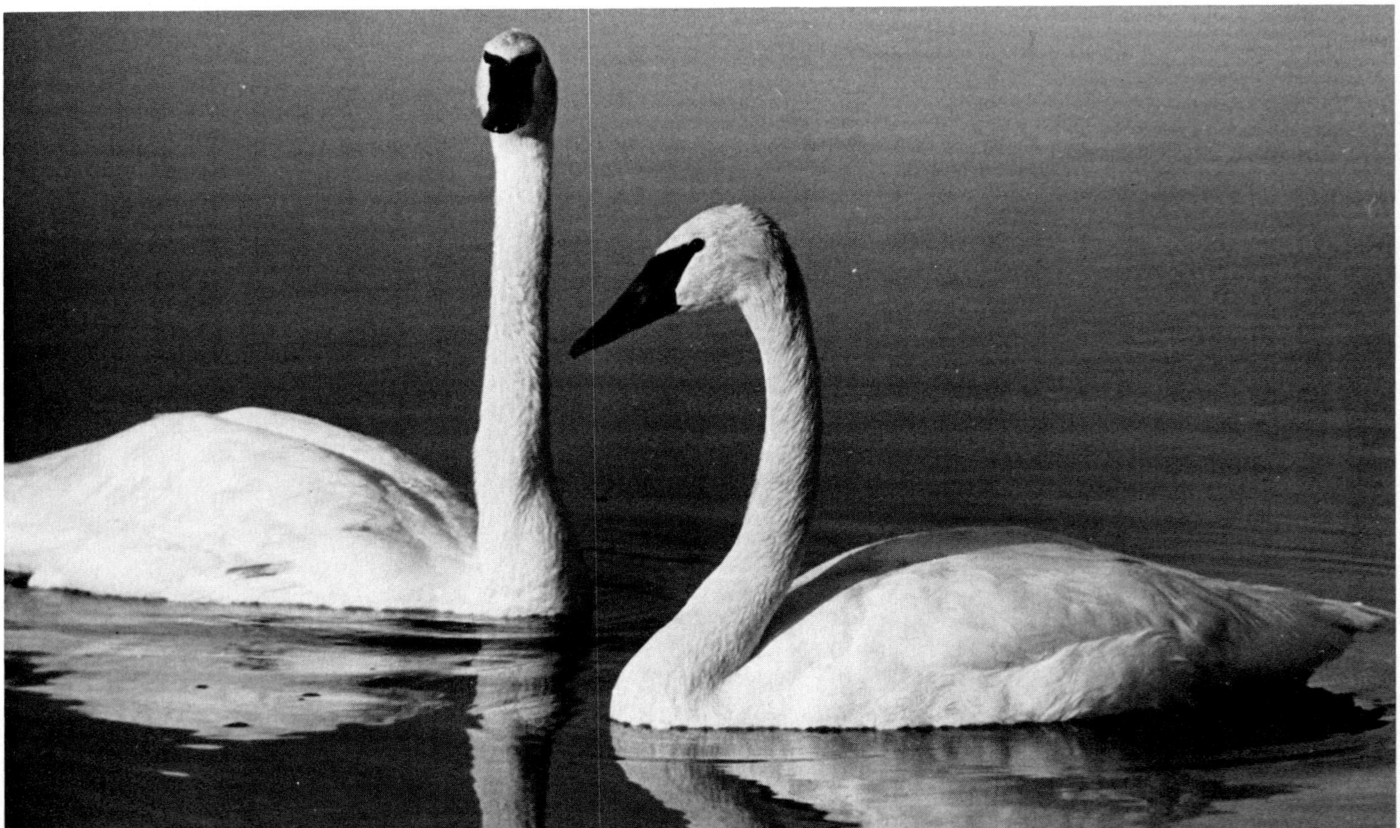

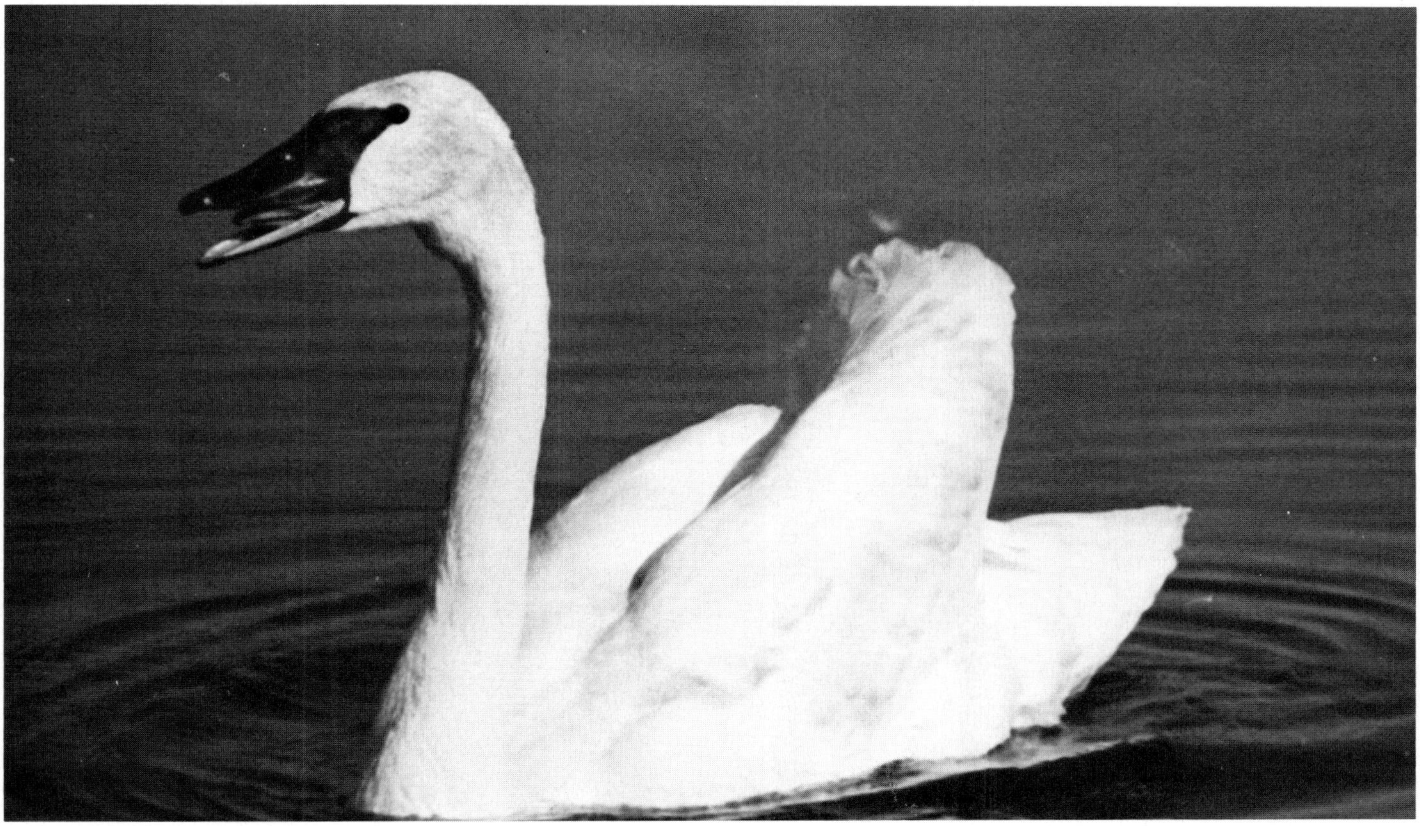

44-16 Trumpeter cob in a somewhat aggressive pose.

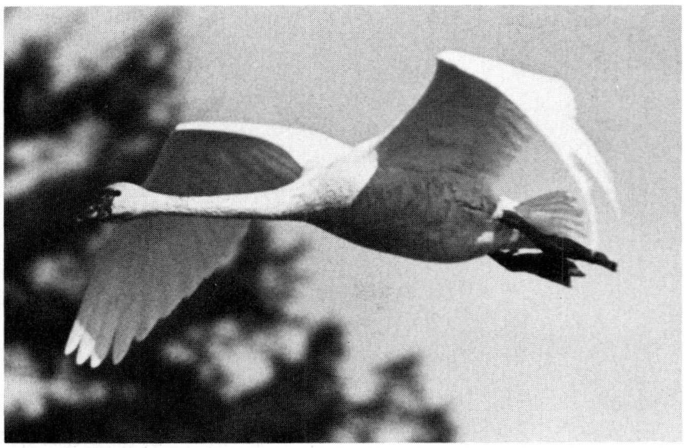

44-17

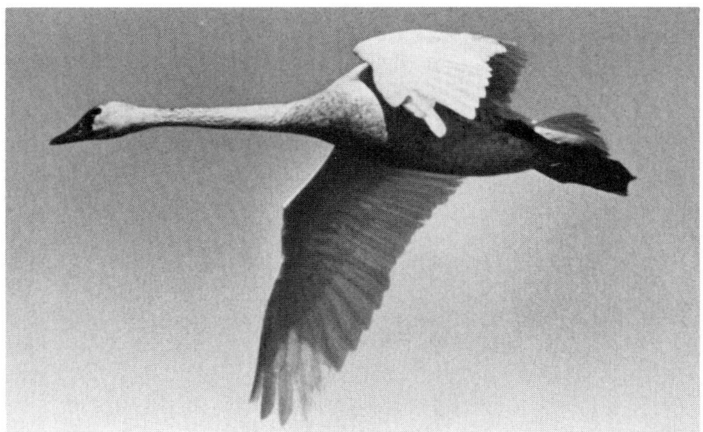

44-18

In flight, swans are grace personified.

44-19

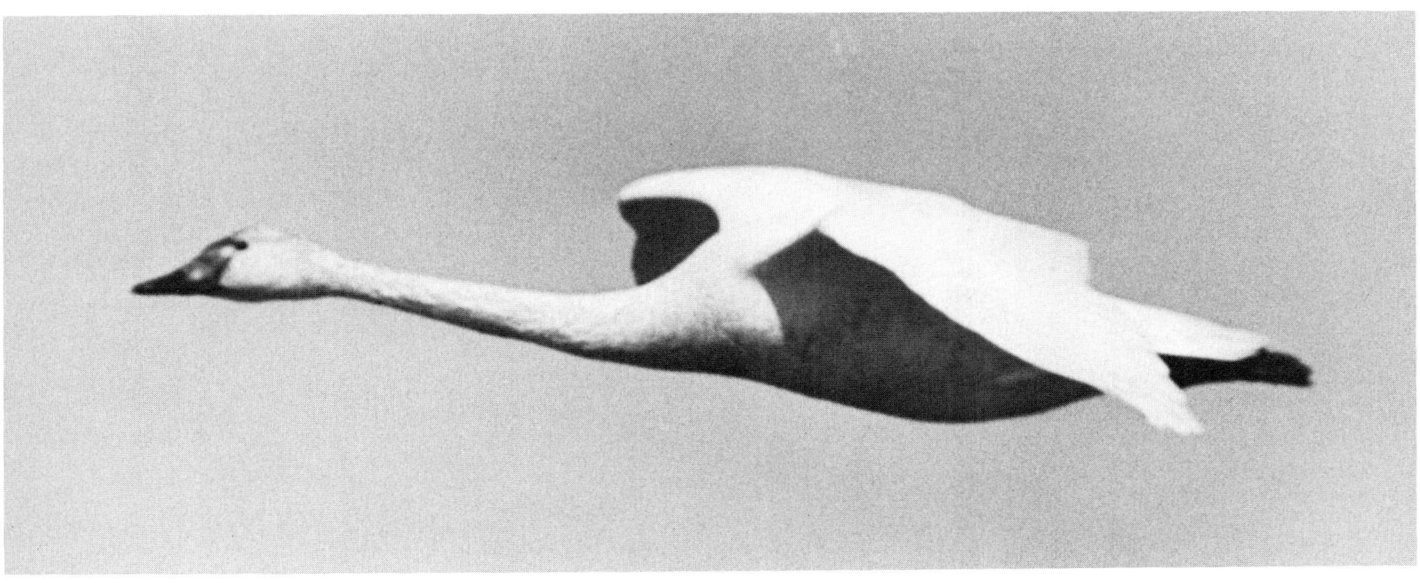

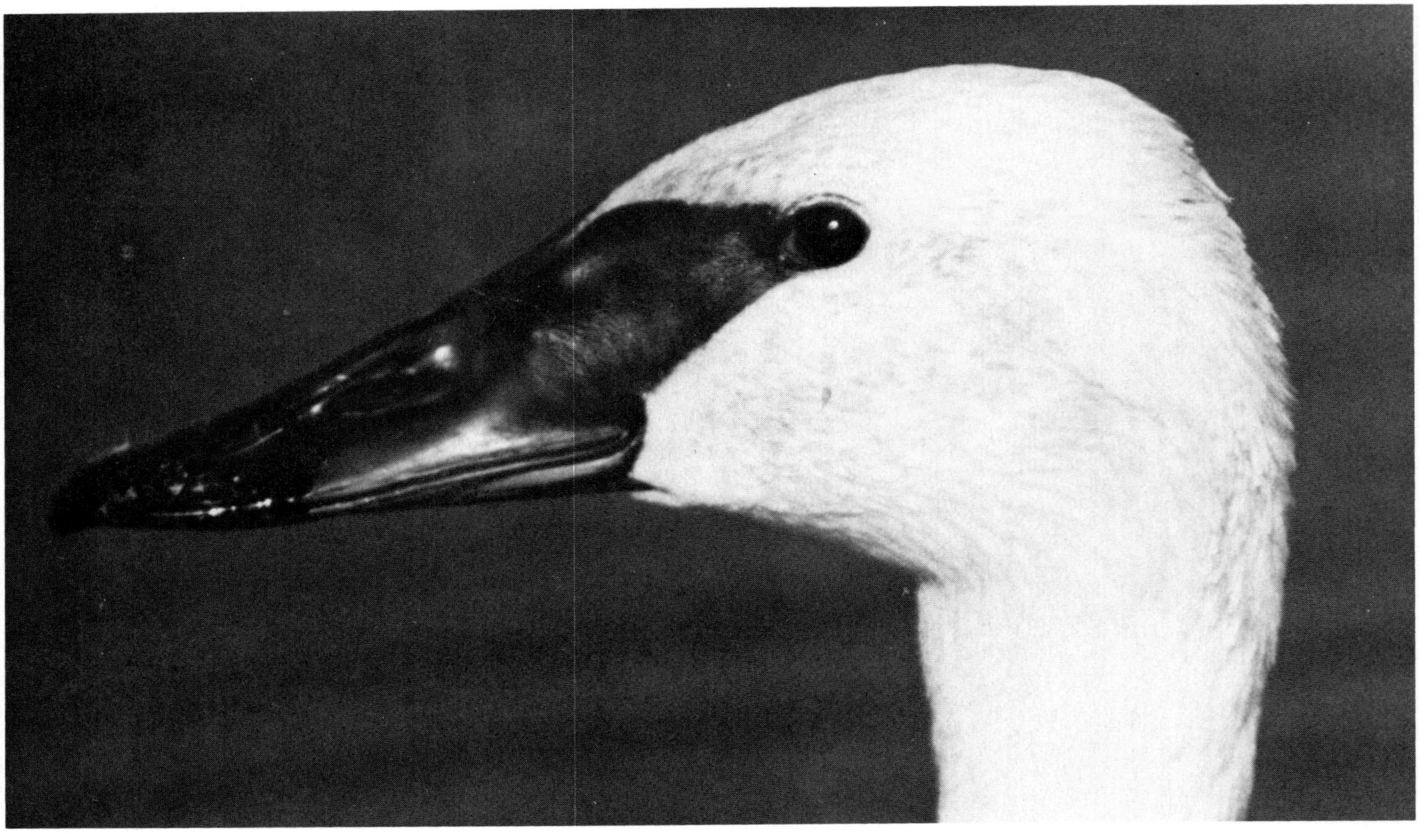

44-20

Profile, front, and rear views of the trumpeter's head and bill.

44-21

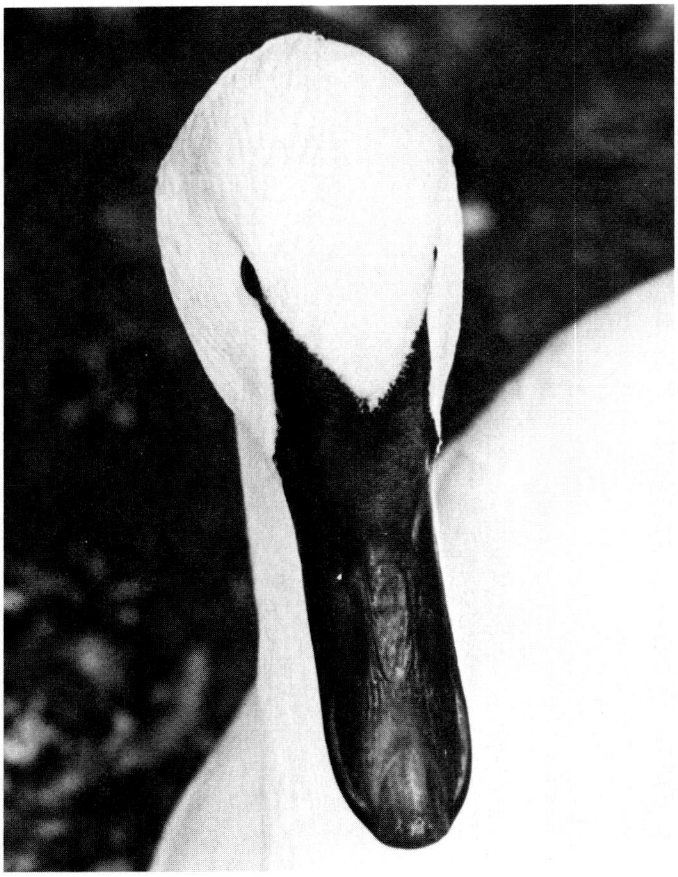

44-22

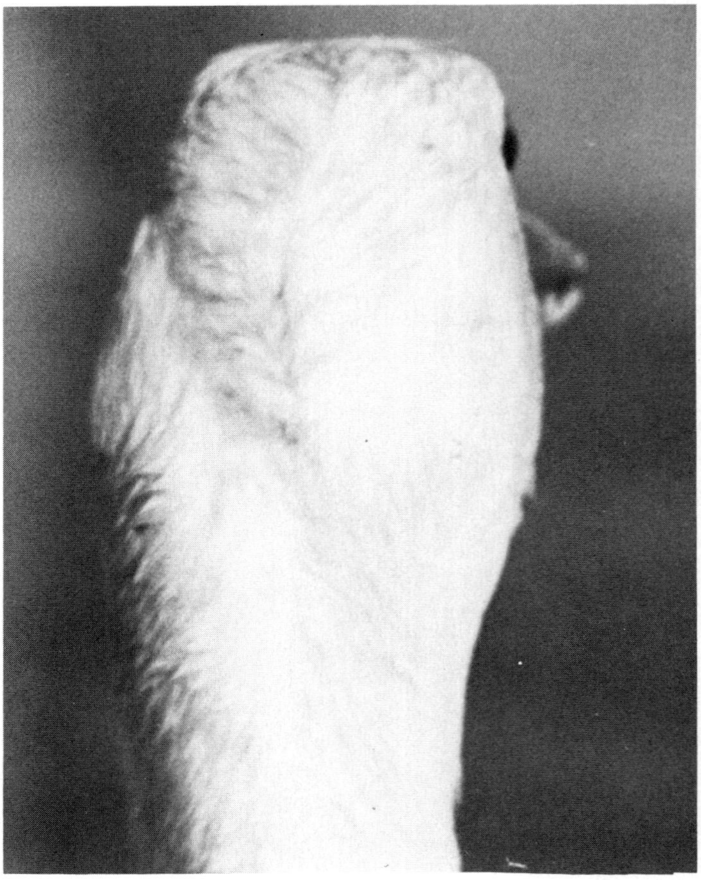

CHAPTER 45

Mute Swan

Cygnus olor
(Color Photos-Page 167)

In England during the 12th century, wild mute swans were captured, pinioned, and semi-domesticated. From the 13th to 18th centuries, all swans were the property of the Crown and private ownership was prohibited without a special grant which was given to some communities, corporations, and private individuals. The swans' welfare was strictly governed by laws, orders from the Crown, and by established old customs that were enforced through the King's Swan-Master and his aides. Along with this special grant, the Crown gave out a ''swan-mark'' which consisted of a letter or some markings usually made on the upper mandible of the bird for identification purposes. During the 18th century, this custom became less prevalent although the birds retained their royal status. The tradition is still being carried out to a limited degree and all of the swans on the Thames River are owned by the Crown and two corporations—the Dyers' and Vinters' Companies, who received their swan marks during the late 1400's. Each year, on Monday of the third week in July, young swans are caught and marked with the same mark of their parents and pinioned. This procedure is accompanied by a certain amount of ceremony headed by the Queen's Swan Keeper. Most other swans in England have reverted to the wild state and are generally distributed throughout the country.

Wild mute swans breed in the temperate portions of Europe, eastern Siberia, and western Asia. Semi-domesticated birds were introduced to this country, Australia, and New Zealand many years ago. Feral mute swans now breed through much of Long Island and along the entire shores of Rhode Island. Another population center is reported in upper Lake Michigan. Other small flocks are springing up in several states and Canadian provinces. The total feral mute swan population in this country may exceed 4000.

Mute swans are large birds, some approaching the size of trumpeter swans. They are actually not mute and are capable of making hissing noises and on occasions can produce a trumpet-like note. Like our other swans, they are graceful and powerful flyers, although they experience difficulty becoming airborne. In flight, their pinions make a musical whistling sound that can be heard for some distance. They are rather clumsy on land and walk with a characteristic waddle. Unlike our other swans, who hold their long necks quite upright, the neck of the mute swan is usually held in a graceful S-shape. When swimming, mute swans have a habit of extending a leg and foot up and over their body, giving the appearance that the leg is growing out of their back. They have a delightful habit, shared with a few other bird species, of carrying their young on their back while swimming and feeding. Mute swans, like other swans, are very aggressive and ill-tempered during the mating and nesting season and sometimes become downright ferocious and dangerous, especially for children.

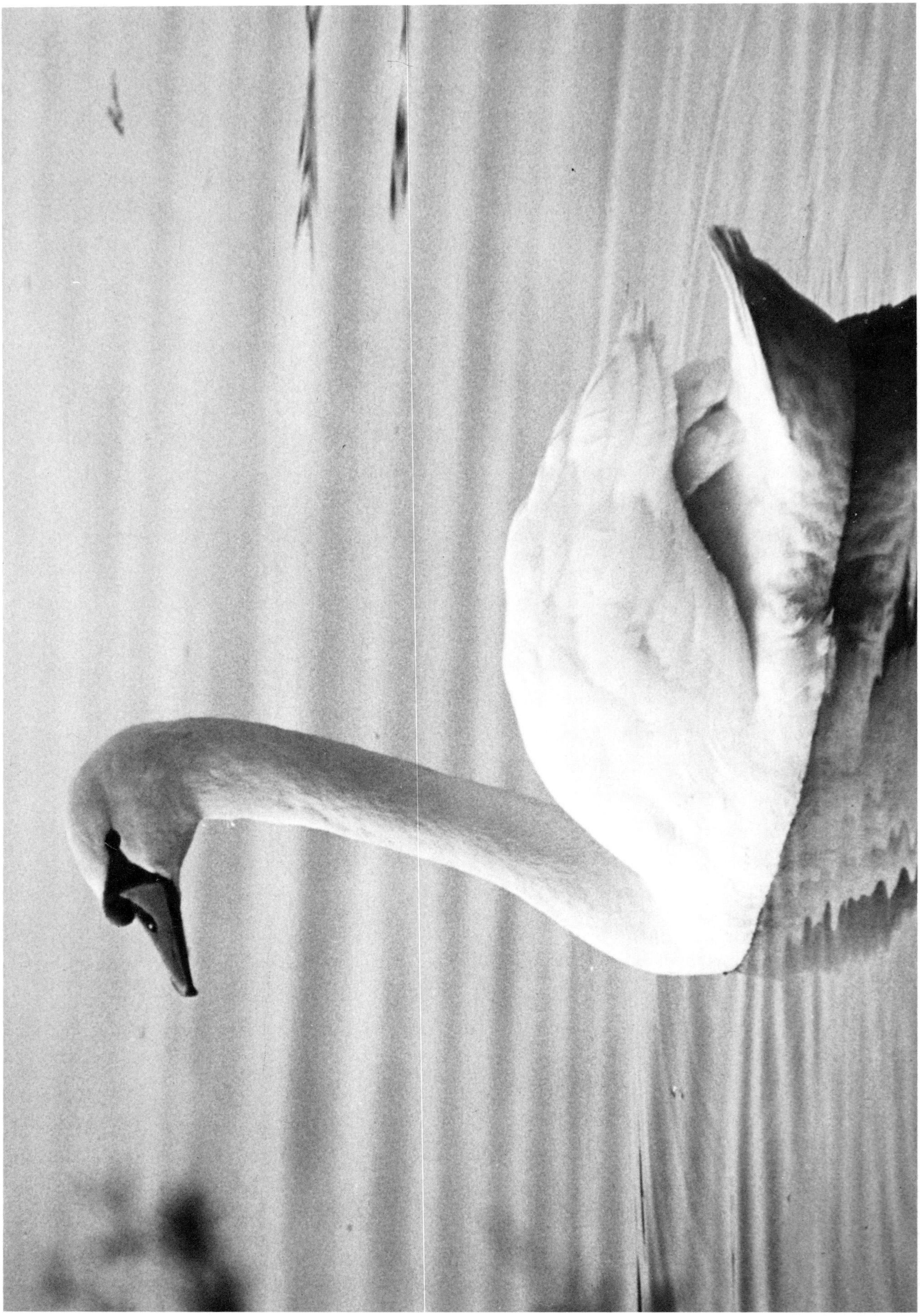

45-1 The graceful mute swan. They have retained royal status in England for centuries.

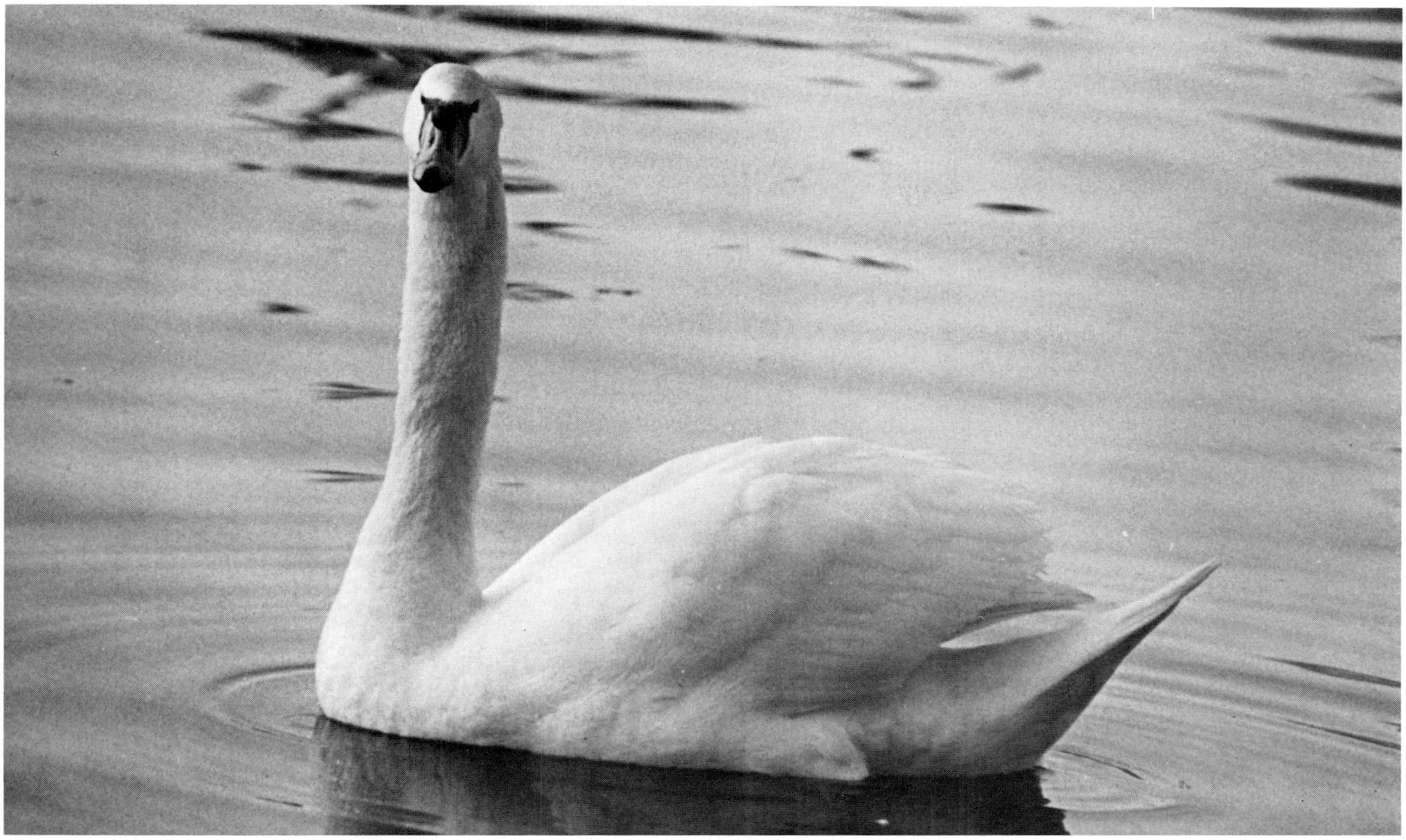

45-2 Profile of the mute swan. Note his long, heavy, and flexible neck. Swans have a far greater number of neck vertebrae than any other warm-blooded animal. All mammals have seven, including the giraffe—swans have either 24 or 25.

45-3 Pair of mute swans swim slowly by. They are powerful and fast swimmers when the need for speed arises.

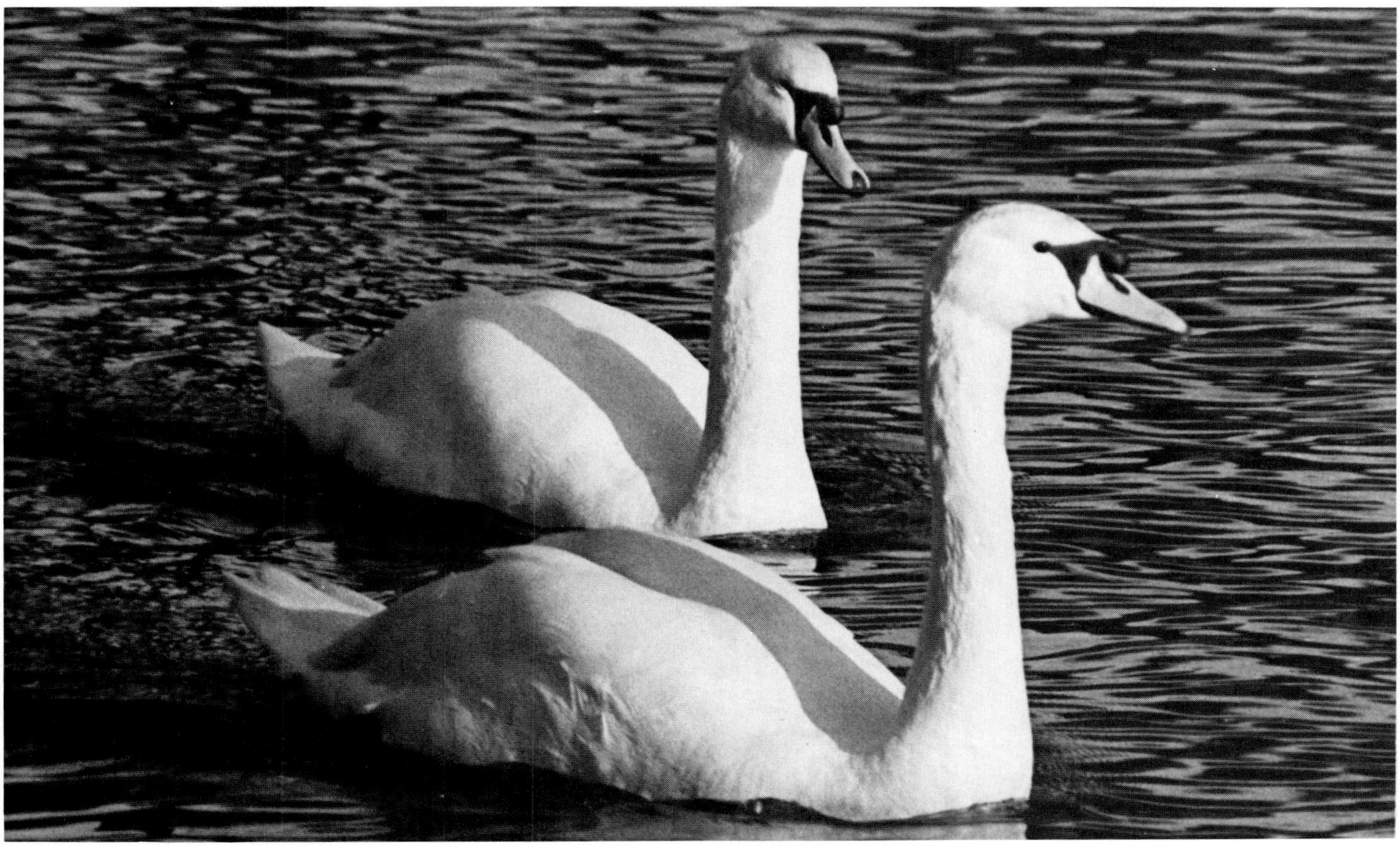

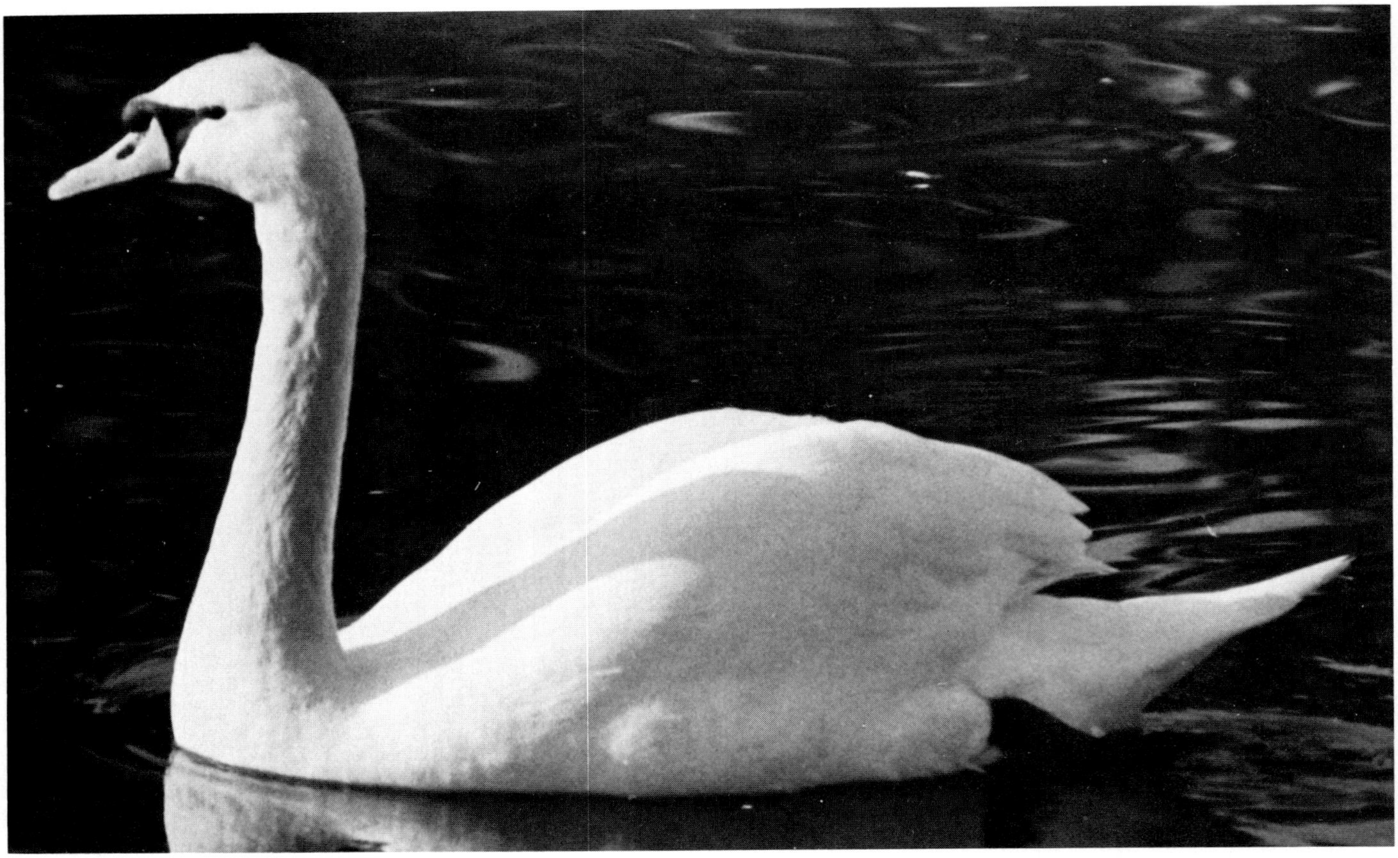

45-4 Good profile of the mute swan.

45-5 Front and rear views of the mute swan. Swan on the right has raised his wings—a typical posture for these birds. 45-6

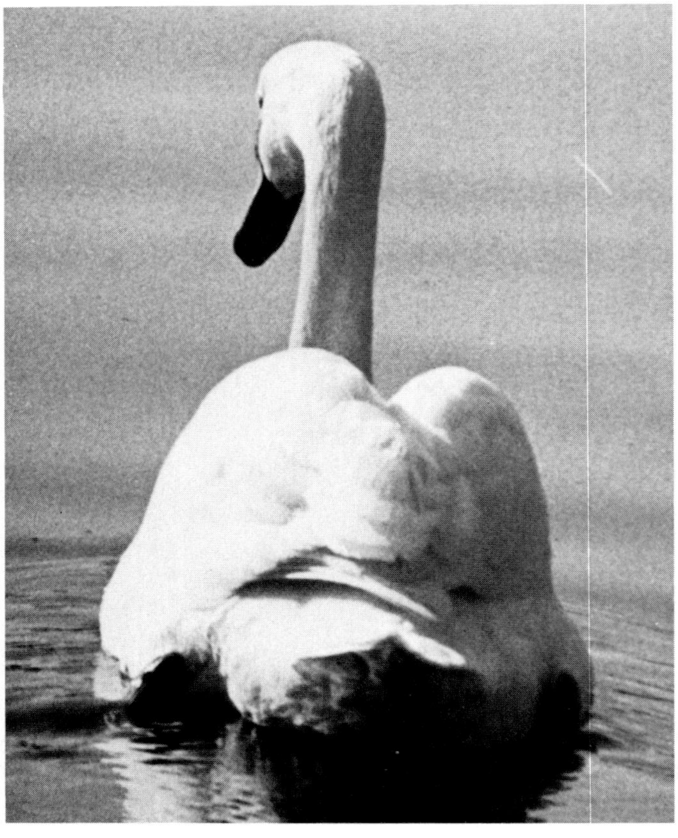

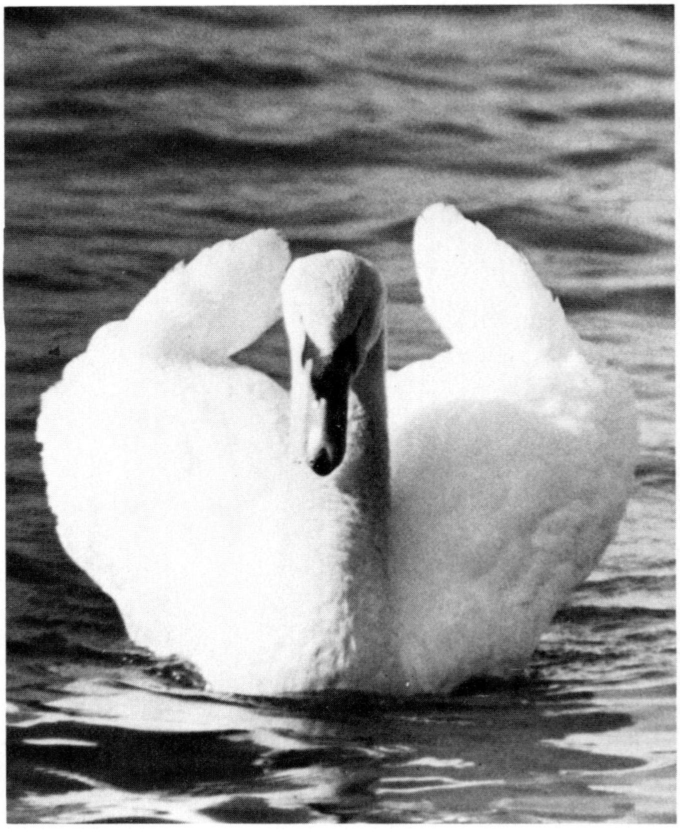

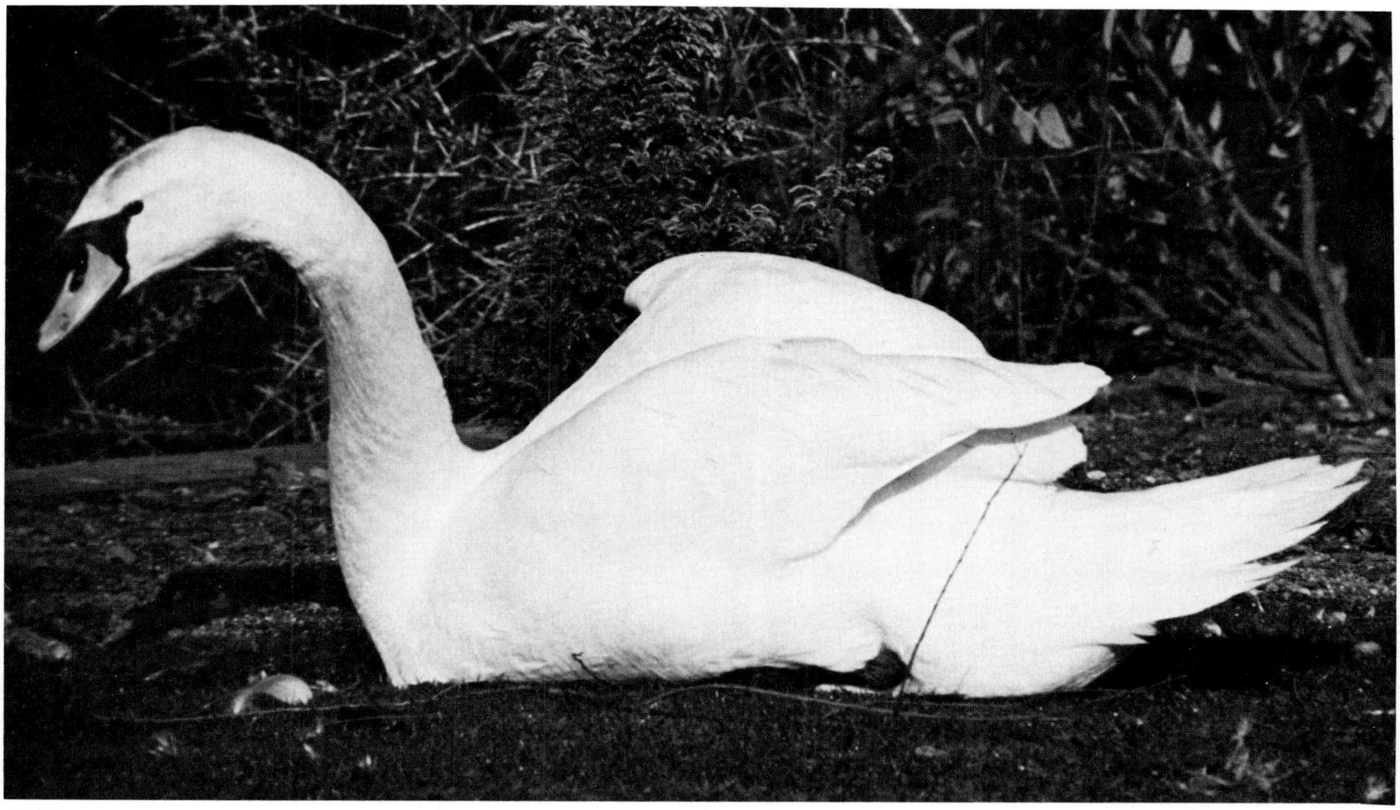

45-7

Mute swan relaxes on the grass. They are large birds, approaching the size and weight of trumpeter swans.

45-8

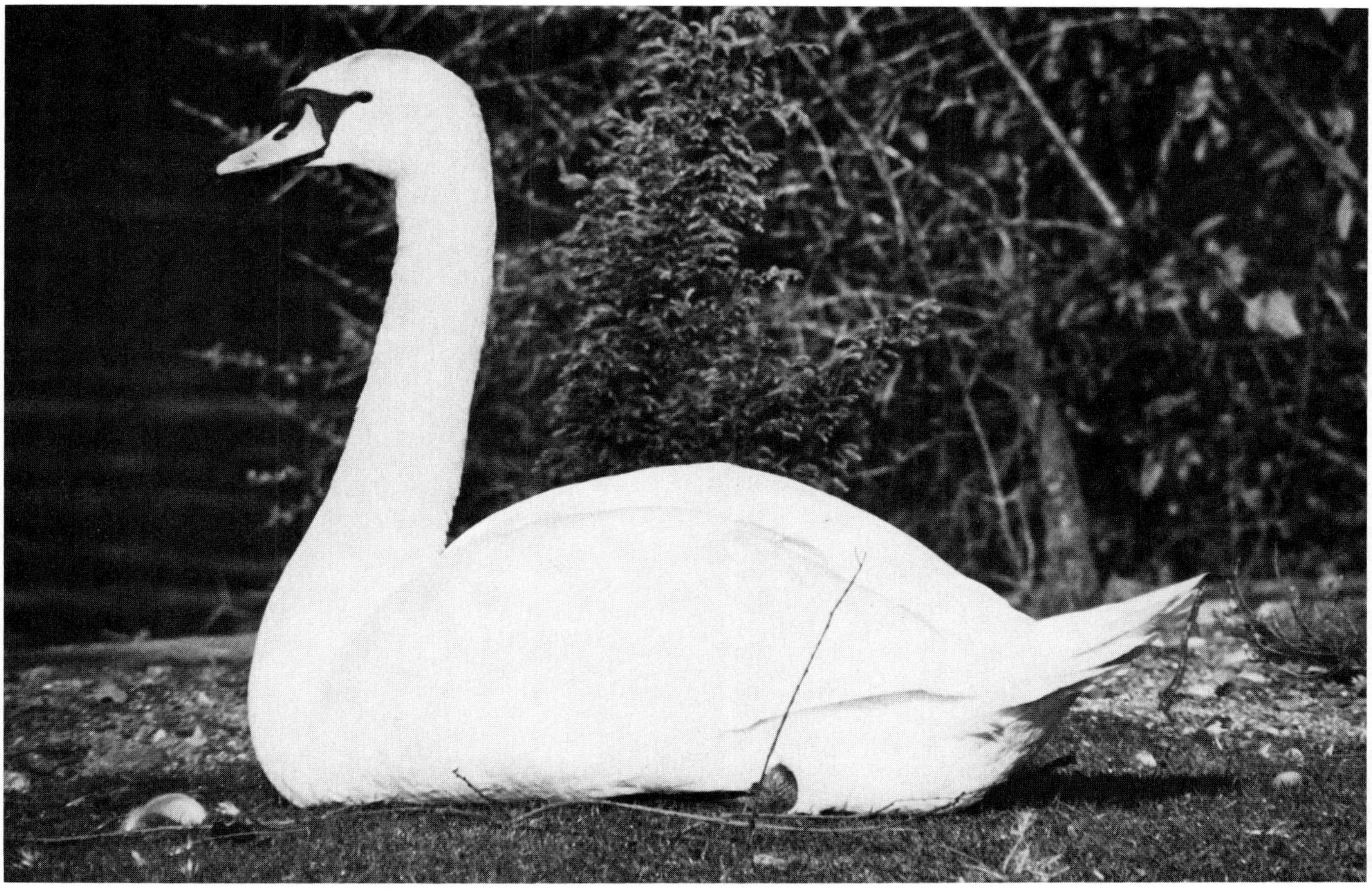

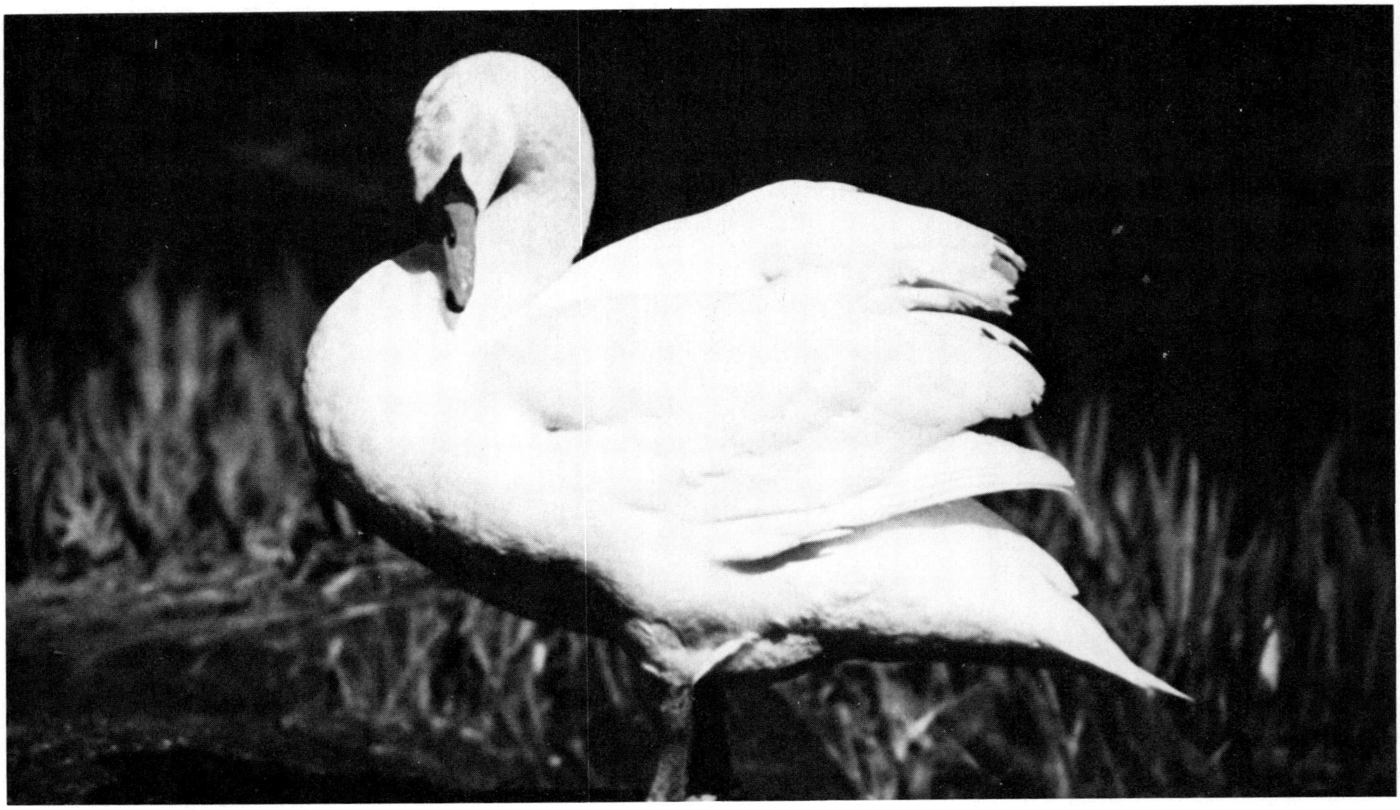

45-9 Mute swan preens his plumage. Nice pose.

45-10 Mute swan in another pleasing pose.

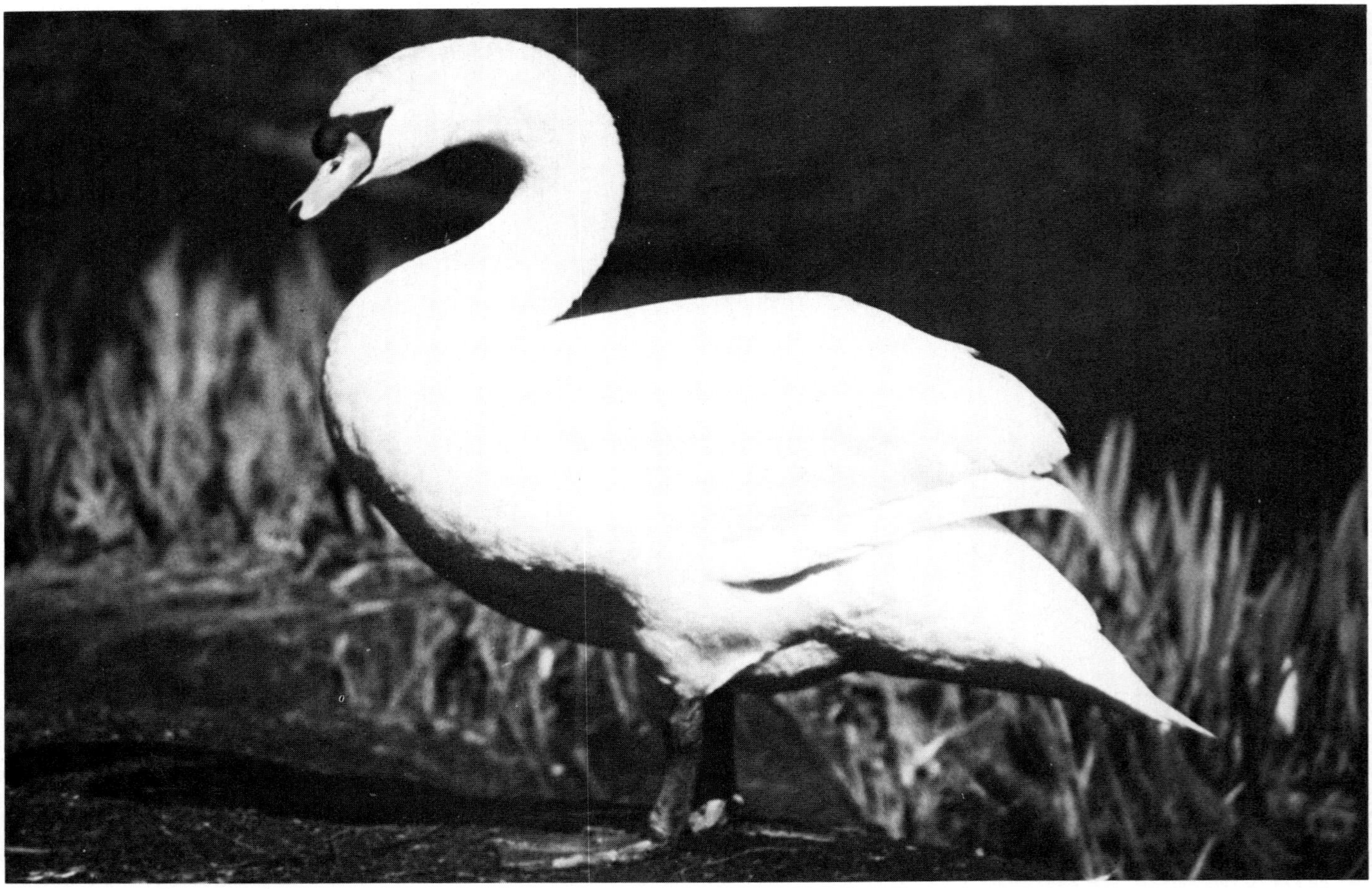

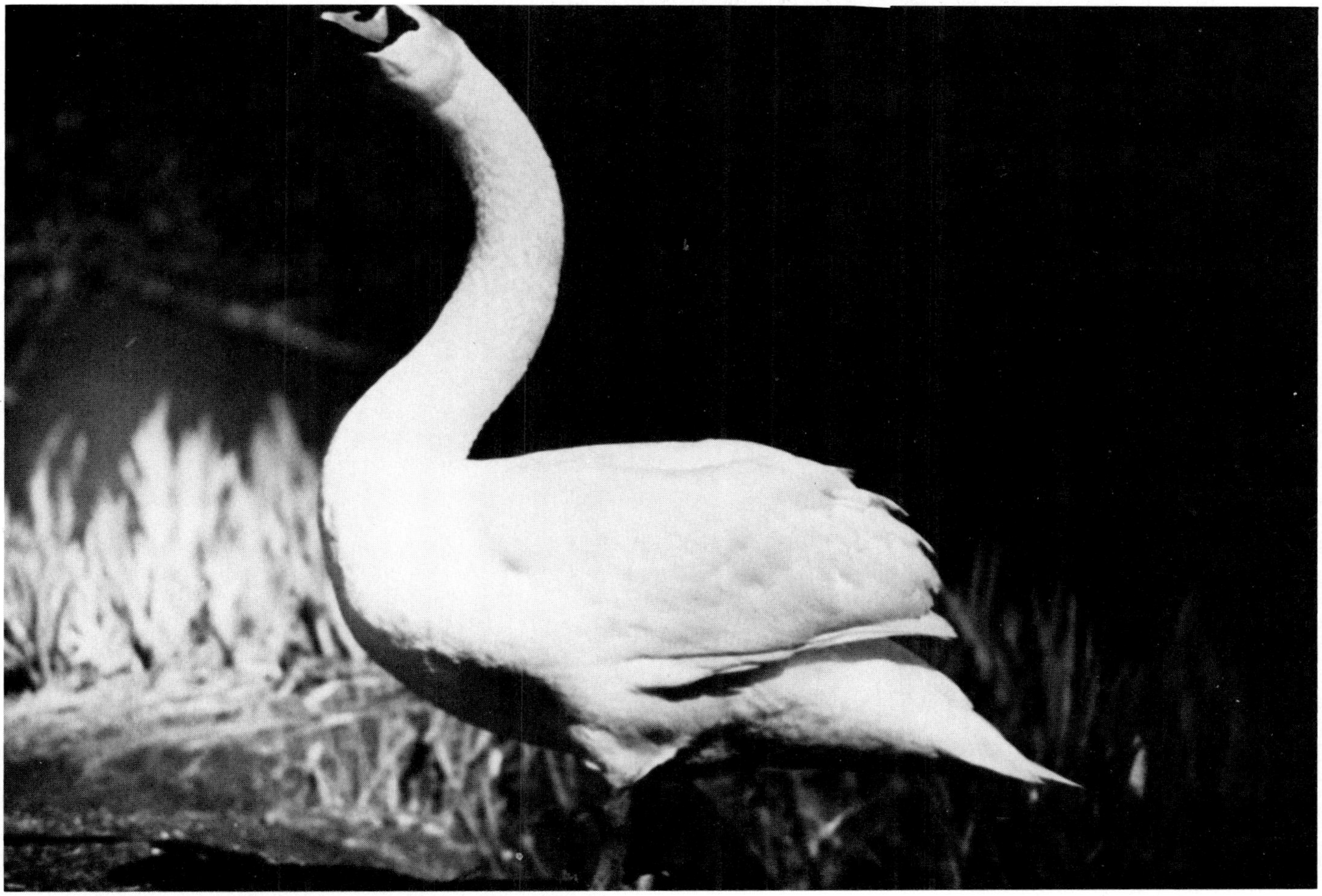

45-11 Mute swan displays his long and powerful neck.

45-12 Two studies of the mute swan's head and bill. 45-13

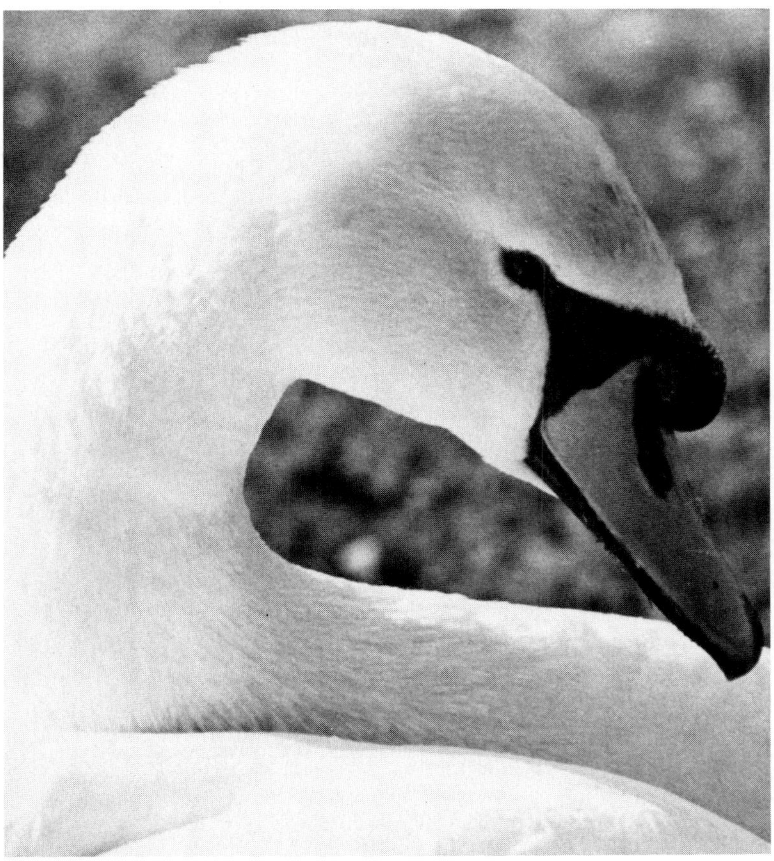

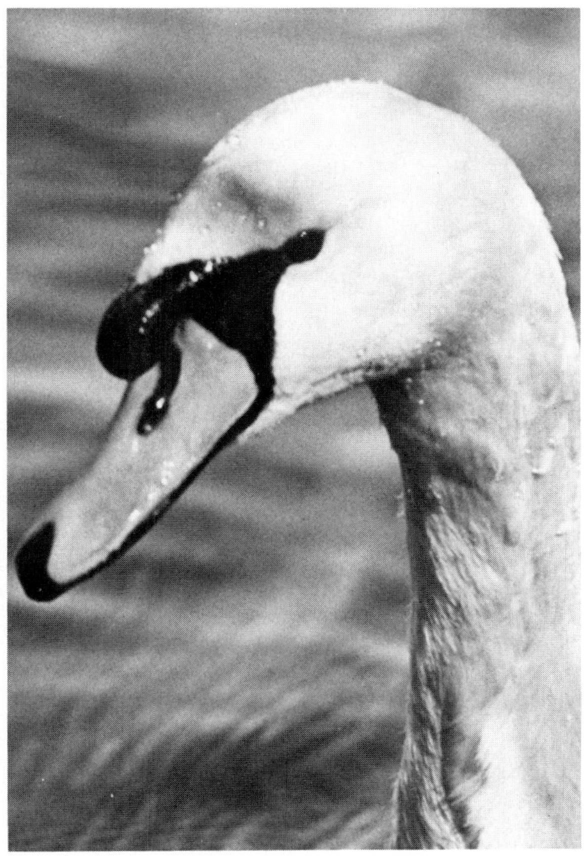

See Volume I

APPENDIX: Bibliography, Topography of Waterfowl, Skeletal Structure Of Wings and Legs

Game Bird Pictures

Allan, Arthur A. *Stalking Birds with a Color Camera.* National Geographic Society, (out of print).

——. "Duck Hunting with a Color Camera." *National Geographic,* October 1951.

Audubon Magazine. National Audubon Society, 950 Third Ave., New York, N.Y. 10022.

Bauer, Erwin A. *Duck Hunter's Bible* (paperback). Doubleday, n.d.

Butcher, Devereau. *Seeing America's Wildlife in Our National Refuges.* Devin-Adair, (out of print).

Clement, Roland C. *The Living World of Audubon.* Grosset and Dunlap, (out of print).

Hanson, Harold C. *The Giant Canada Goose.* Southern Illinois University Press, 1965.

Heintzelman, Donald S. *North American Ducks, Geese, and Swans.* Winchester Press, 1978.

——. *Handbook of Waterfowl Behavior.* Comstock Pub. Assoc. (Cornell University Press), 1965.

——. *North American Game Birds of Upland and Shoreline.* University of Nebraska Press, 1975.

——. *Waterfowl of North America.* Indiana University Press, 1975.

——. *Waterfowl: Their Biology and Natural History.* University of Nebraska Press, 1968.

Kortright, F.H. *The Ducks, Geese, and Swans of North America* (rev. ed.). Stackpole, 1975.

Lansdowne, James F. *Birds of the Eastern Forest.* 2 vols. Houghton Mifflin, 1968.

——. *Birds of the Northern Forest.* Houghton Mifflin, 1966.

Linduska, Joseph P., ed. *Waterfowl Tomorrow.* Washington, D.C.: U.S. Government Printing Office.

Line, Les, and Russell, Franklin. *The Audubon Society Book of Wild Birds.* Harry N. Abrams, 1976.

National Wildlife Magazine. 1412 Sixteenth St., NW, Washington, D.C. 20036.

Queeny, Edgar M. *Prairie Wings* (reprint of 1946 ed.). Schiffer, 1979.

Rand, Austin L. *American Water and Game Birds.* Dutton, (out of print).

Terres, John K. *The Audubon Society Encyclopedia of North American Birds.* Alfred A. Knopf, 1980.

Todd, Frank S. *Waterfowl: Ducks, Geese, and Swans of the World.* Harcourt Brace Jovanovich, 1979.

Van Wormer, Joe. *The World of the Canada Goose.* Lippincott, 1968.

Water, Prey, and Game Birds of North America. National Geographic Society, n.d.

Williams, Cecil S. *Honker.* D. Van Nostrand, (out of print).

Zim, Herbert, and Sprunt, Alexander. *Game Birds.* Western, 1961.

Bird Anatomy

Aymar, Gordon. *Bird Flight.* Dodd, Mead, (out of print).

Beebe, C. William. *The Bird.* Dover, (out of print).

Darling, Lois and Louis. *Bird.* Houghton Mifflin, (out of print).

Pettingill, Olin Sewall, Jr. *Ornithology in Laboratory and Field.* Burgess, 1970.

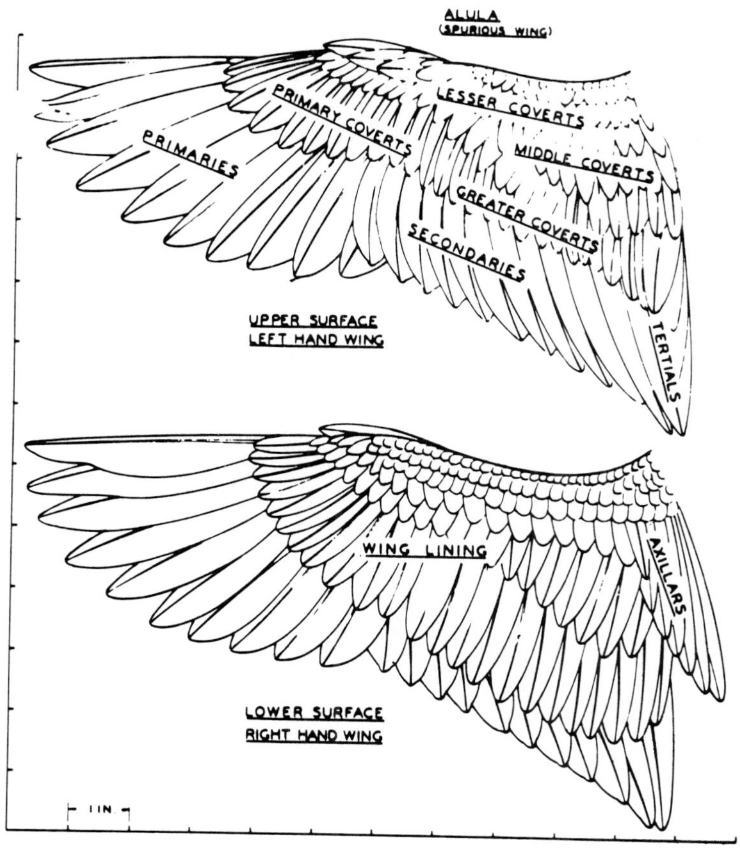

Wing of a cinnamon teal.

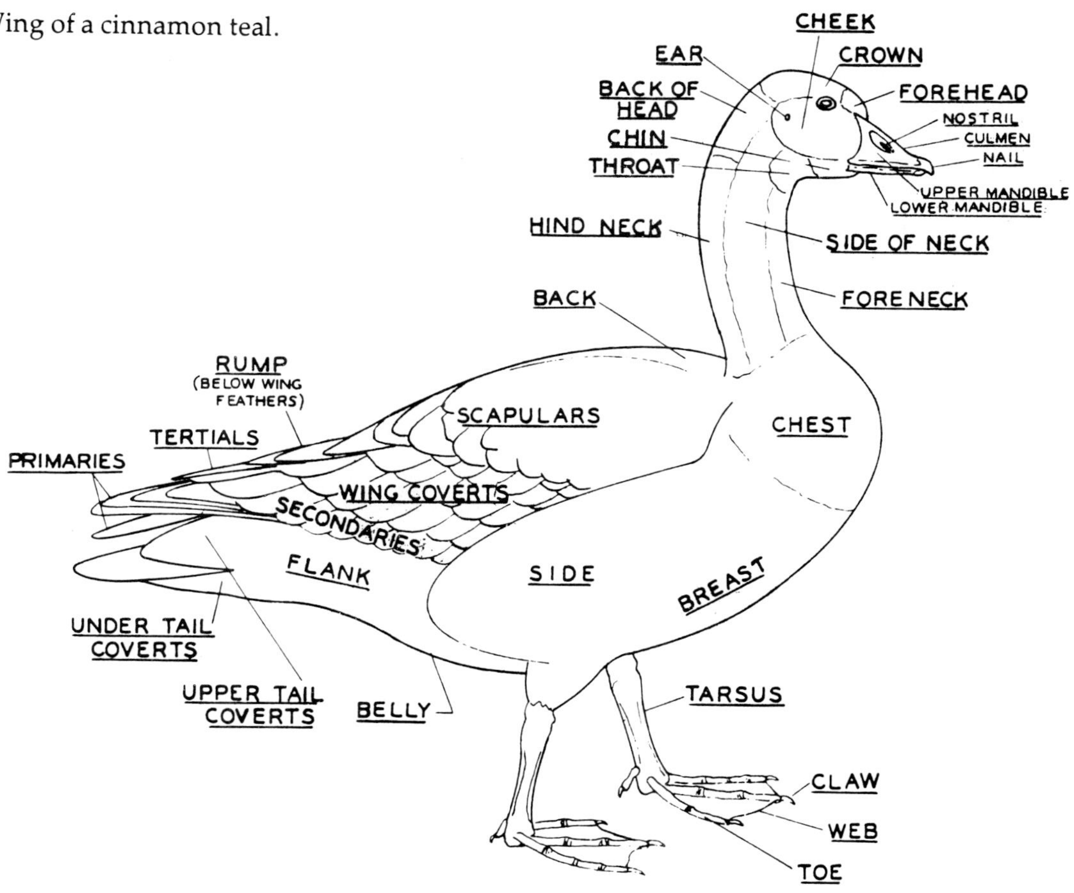

Topography of a goose.

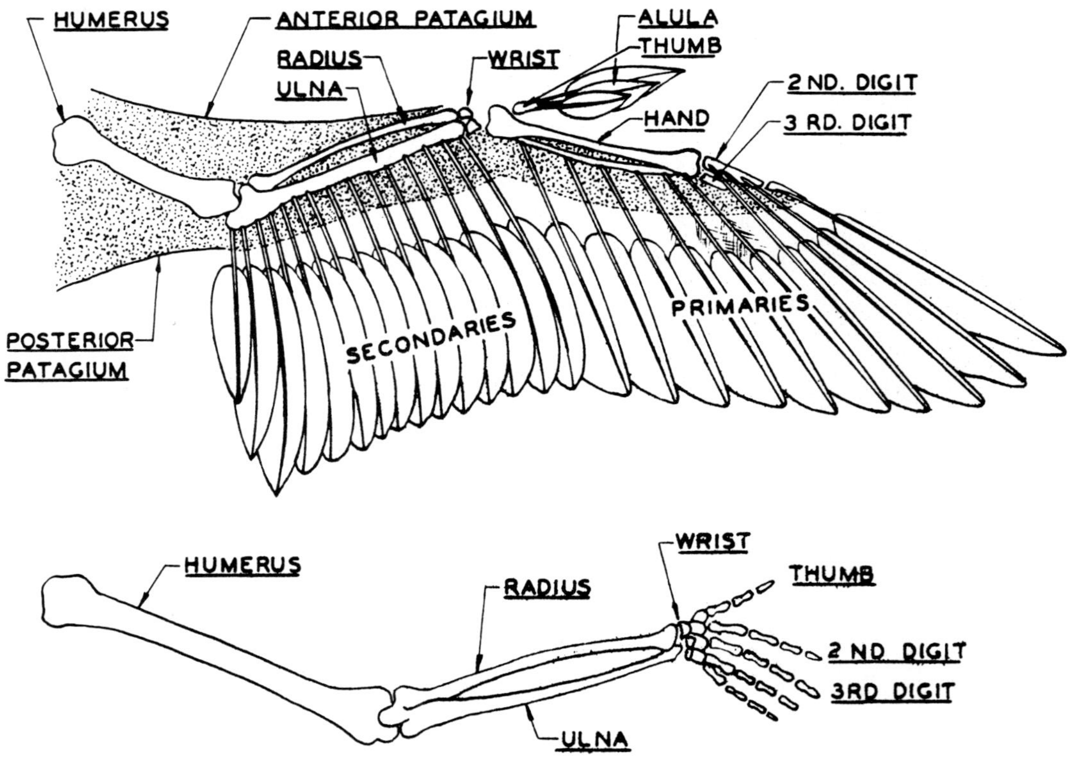

Comparison of a duck's wing with a man's arm.

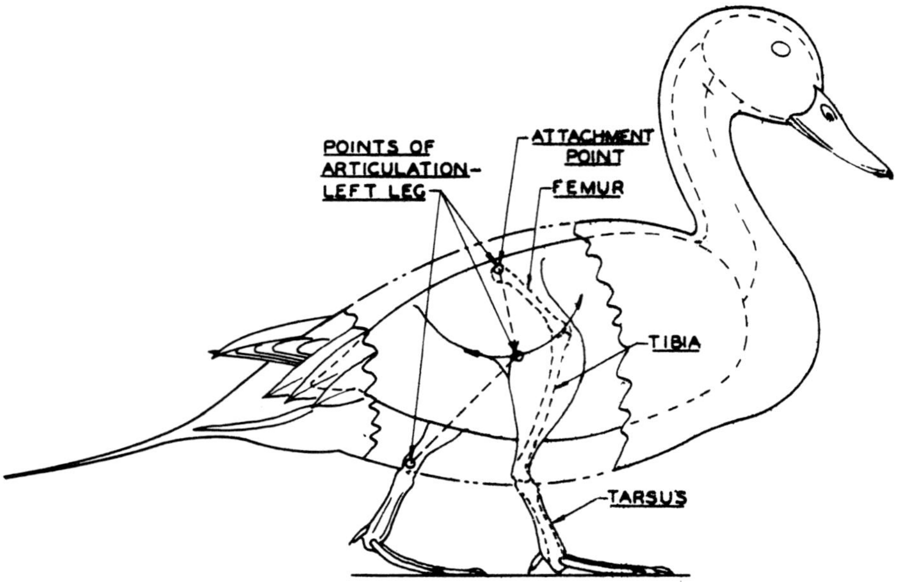

Leg movement and musculature of a pintail.

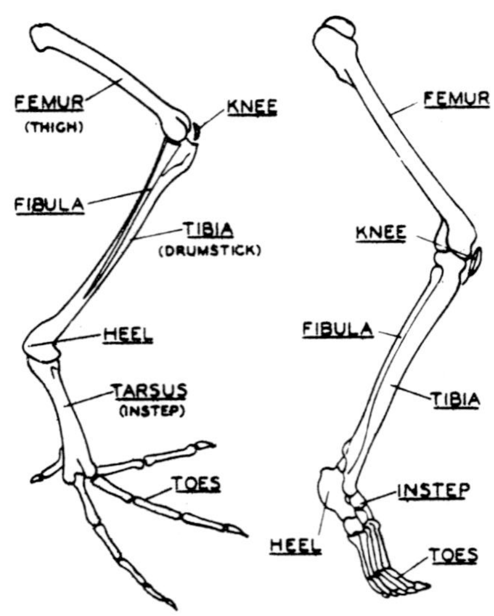

Comparason of a duck's leg with a man's leg.